The Struggle for Iraq

The
STRUGGLE
for IRAQ

A View from the Ground Up

THOMAS M. RENAHAN

Potomac Books
AN IMPRINT OF THE UNIVERSITY OF NEBRASKA PRESS

Library of Congress Cataloging-in-Publication Data
Names: Renahan, Thomas M. (Thomas Michael),
1941– author.
Title: The struggle for Iraq: a view from the ground up /
Thomas M. Renahan.
Description: Lincoln, Nebraska: Potomac Books, an
imprint of the University of Nebraska Press, 2017. |
Includes bibliographical references and index.
Identifiers: LCCN 2016056686
ISBN 9781612348827 (cloth: alk. paper)
ISBN 9781612349244 (epub)
ISBN 9781612349251 (mobi)
ISBN 9781612349268 (pdf)
Subjects: LCSH: Democracy—Iraq. | Political
corruption—Iraq. | Iraq—Politics and government—
2003– | Postwar reconstruction—Iraq. | Renahan,
Thomas M. (Thomas Michael), 1941–
Classification: LCC JQ1849.A91 R46 2017 |
DDC 320.9567—dc23
LC record available at https://lccn.loc.gov/2016056686

Set in Lyon Text by Rachel Gould.

To my Iraqi staff—in Amarah, Baghdad, Basra, Erbil, and Hilla—who took the risks to share the struggle for democracy in Iraq and made my service in their country an inspiring and life-changing experience

Contents

Maps

Abbreviations

AC	Anti-Corruption
ADF	America's Development Foundation (USAID contractor)
AID	United States Agency for International Development
CAG	Community Action Group
CDP	Civic Dialogue Program
COP	chief of party
COR	Council of Representatives (Iraqi parliament)
CPA	Coalition Provisional Authority
CPI	Commission on Public Integrity
CSO	civil society organization
CSRC	Civil Society Resource Center
DCOP	deputy chief of party
DDA	Democracy Dialogue Activity
DFID	Department for International Development (UK)
DG	director-general
GC	governorate coordinator
HR	Human Rights
IBTCI	International Business & Technical Consultants, Inc. (USAID contractor)
ICMA	International City/County Management Association
ICNL	International Center for Not-for-Profit Law
ICSP	Iraq Civil Society Program
IDP	internally displaced person
IG	inspector general
IGC	Iraqi Governing Council
INA	Iraqi National Alliance
INL	Bureau of International Narcotics and Law Enforcement Affairs (U.S. State Department)
IREX	International Research & Exchanges Board

ISCI	Islamic Supreme Council of Iraq (political party)
ISIS	Islamic State of Iraq and Syria
IZ	International Zone (Green Zone)
KDP	Kurdistan Democratic Party
KRG	Kurdistan Regional Government
LGP	Local Governance Program
M&E	Monitoring and Evaluation
MMA	Michael-Moran Associates
MOM	Ministry of Municipalities (Kurdistan)
NGO	nongovernmental organization
PC	Provincial Council
PKK	Kurdistan Workers Party (Turkey)
PMFS	Popular Mobilization Forces
PSA	public service announcement (TV/radio)
PSD	personal security detail and, by extension, an armed security person working in one
PUK	Patriotic Union of Kurdistan
RTI	RTI International (USAID contractor)
SCIRI	Supreme Council for the Islamic Revolution in Iraq
SIGIR	Special Inspector General for Iraqi Reconstruction
SIV	Special Immigrant Visa
TAL	Transitional Administrative Law
TI	Transparency International
TOT	Training of Trainers
UIA	United Iraqi Alliance (political coalition)
UNAMI	United Nations Assistance Mission for Iraq
UNESCO	United Nations Educational, Scientific and Cultural Organization
UNHCR	United Nations High Commissioner for Refugees
USAID	United States Agency for International Development
USRAP	United States Refugee Admissions Program

The Struggle for Iraq

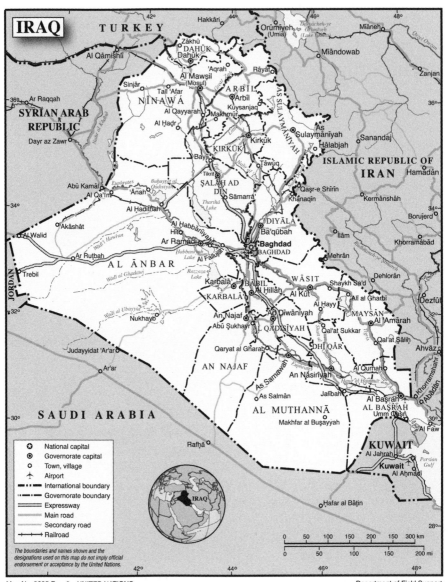

MAP 1. Iraq. Courtesy of the United Nations (map no. 3835, rev. 6).

Introduction

Iraq from the Ground Up

On December 18, 2011, the last American troops left Iraq, or so it seemed until 2014. That milestone event completed a difficult but successful military mission that had overcome enormous and daunting challenges. About 4,800 Coalition troops had been killed in the struggle for Iraq, almost 4,500 of them Americans. Great Britain's losses constituted most of the rest. Hundreds of thousands of Iraqis had died, most as innocent victims, a toll still rising every day.

Less noticed amid the understandable focus on military battles and casualties were the thousands of foreign civilians who joined the struggle for Iraq. I was one of those people. We started arriving soon after the Coalition invasion in 2003. I joined a small civilian army of American, British, and other expatriates deployed to help transition Iraq toward more democratic and more effective government, improve living standards, and rebuild much of its infrastructure.

As a political scientist and former city manager, the immediately critical democracy and governance work was where I thought I could help, but nothing in my education or career experience suggested that someday I would be working in Iraq. It was an adventure into the unknown and a dangerous one.

Eventually, I did three civilian tours in Iraq, one in each of its three major areas: southern Iraq, Central Iraq (Baghdad), and Kurdistan. People often ask me what it was like. This book is my answer. I was a small part of a nation's struggle to forge a new identity and a witness to history. My time in Iraq was often rewarding and even joyful, sometimes horrifying and sad, and ultimately unforgettable and life changing.

So much has been written and said about Iraq that one might assume we understand it clearly by now. In fact, there is still a lot we don't understand. Media reports, expert analysis, and political spin in Washington and London focused mainly on how military and political events in Iraq affected U.S. or British interests. This was understandable but left an incomplete and misleading picture. The impact of those events on Iraq itself was often ignored or treated as secondary. Many media and political explanations were contradicted by reality on the ground. Meanwhile, those civilian projects got little coverage despite their importance in the overall Iraq policy. The view from the ground up has been missing. My purpose is to provide some of that perspective.

What we learned on the ground in Iraq is not just a history lesson. The internal struggle for Iraq is as intense today as it has ever been, its stakes are just as high, and it will continue for years to come. When President George W. Bush declared victory in 2003, Iraqis knew their struggle was not really over. When President Barack Obama declared in 2011 that the American military mission in Iraq was over, Iraqis knew his message was not about them. Such grand pronouncements from Washington convey the unintended message that developments in Iraq are mostly about us.

The withdrawal of American troops did not mean that Iraq did not need the United States anymore or that our commitment to Iraq was over. Too much was at stake for both countries. Those who believed we had no continuing interests in Iraq or that the country would succeed on its own or that further armed conflict would not occur there made a serious misjudgment. This became obvious in mid-2014 when the Islamic State of Iraq and Syria (ISIS) invaded northern Iraq, supported by many of the same Iraqis the United States had defeated in 2003 and helped to defeat again several years later.

In December 2003 I arrived in Amarah, the capital of Maysan Province north of Basra, to join the Local Governance Program of the United States Agency for International Development (USAID or AID), the Department of State organization that initiates, funds, and manages projects in foreign countries. What timing! Three days later Saddam Hussein was captured.

Although public attention focused initially on the Coalition Provisional Authority, which led the government until mid-2004, most of America's civilian effort was led by USAID. Britain's Department for International Development (DFID) led the British effort. Many other civilian-type projects were carried out by military units or under their protection. USAID enlisted not only its own personnel but also international development companies and nonprofits. They in turn recruited thousands to carry out their projects and hired security companies that recruited thousands more to protect them. USAID itself called this civilian campaign "one of the largest efforts to provide foreign assistance by the U.S. government since the Marshall Plan."

I came with no political agenda about whether invading Iraq was the right decision. That decision was hotly debated and raised doubts that will never go away but had already been made by others. I was a civilian public servant who came to help. From that motive I became part of the struggle for Iraq. I could not have imagined how difficult that struggle would be or the extent to which Iraq would come to dominate my life.

I soon became the advisor to the new Maysan Provincial Council and soon after that launched a major democracy campaign. Our Amarah team was making great progress, and I had a job that hugged me back. Seemingly quiet Maysan, however, proved to be dangerous. The invasion that deposed the Baathists set off a major internal power struggle, exposing major fault lines in Iraqi society and cultural tendencies toward threats and violence. The issues dividing Iraqis made our work harder and more dangerous. It's not a good feeling when your success is interrupted by an insurrection. The southern Iraq experience is part 1 of the story.

The civilian focus of the book implies no disregard for the U.S. and British military, whose members performed heroically in Iraq and buried too many fallen heroes. The military story has been well told in countless books, articles, and media accounts, and many more will be added to chronicle the military struggle against ISIS. Much less has been reported about the thousands of dedicated public servants, from both government and contract organizations, who took personal risks and endured daily hardships to help Iraq. Many accomplished good things that never got reported. Many experienced heartbreaking tragedies and difficult crises. Not all of them returned home safely. This part of the Iraq story has seldom been told.

I have written this book to tell a small but meaningful part of that missing story. In doing so, I seek to represent, indirectly, a thousand other stories that deserve to be told.

My second tour of duty, described in part 2, was a memorable tenure in Baghdad, from late 2005 to the end of 2006, as the national Anti-Corruption manager for the Iraq Civil Society Program. This stint coincided with the worst of the sectarian violence that overwhelmed Baghdad and surrounding areas and made life there nearly unbearable for Iraqis. The view from our high-wall compound was often the smoke wafting up from deadly car bombs that sometimes shook the building. Still, my program had projects in all eighteen provinces, with innovative Iraqi civil society organizations that did great work. Time would show that the Iraqi public was more impressed with our anti-corruption campaign than were the corrupt. The timing of my Baghdad departure was as fortuitous as for my arrival. I left for the airport just minutes after Saddam was executed.

Working on the ground in Baghdad opened a window on the tribulations of the Iraqi people. When I arrived in Maysan, their big problems were the economy and massive unemployment. There were, however, underlying political tensions, rival militias, an emerging power struggle, and deadly incidents. Many Iraqis joined the Coalition-supported struggle to create a new and democratic Iraq, but others took up arms against it. Once the sectarian violence rolled over Baghdad, millions of Iraqis found themselves trapped. Those caught in the crossfire lived in fear and struggled to survive, and tens of thousands did not survive. I was responsible for a national Human Rights program too. It was not a good time for human rights in Iraq.

It is generally acknowledged that the Coalition's good intentions were undermined by a lack of knowledge and by political and strategic mistakes. My on-the-ground account puts more emphasis, however, on the terrible things Iraqis have done to each other. A balanced analysis is impossible without reference to Iraq's culture of violence, its religious extremism and intolerance, its gender inequality, its widespread lawlessness, and its pervasive corruption.

The better print and electronic media have covered Iraq almost continuously since 2003, understandably focusing mainly on military news and political debates in Washington and London. There was extensive reporting and analysis of the sectarian violence, but the full impact on Iraqis could not be grasped from those media accounts. They reported the mass casualty statistics from suicide bombs and other terrorist attacks but not the vast number killed one at a time by death squads and individual assassins, political and religious extremists, insurgents and militiamen, Iranian agents, and common criminals. The awful impact on the victims' survivors was part of the unreported story. While the West debated how to deal with terrorism, the true meaning of terrorism was experienced by the Iraqi people.

The appalling security conditions directly affected our Iraqi staff members, who had to get home safely and return to work the next morning. My view from the ground up covers a small but important part of this mostly missing story. Security conditions greatly improved starting in 2007, from the success of the "surge" strategy led by Gen. David Petraeus, but life for most Iraqis remained difficult and often dangerous, and the violence worsened again starting in 2013.

My first-person account is also the context for analyzing Iraq issues in nontechnical language. Readers will learn a lot from this book, but please have patience for the explanations, as international development involves inherent complexities. I learned many important lessons, summarized in multiple chapters, including one addressed to USAID issues. During all its years in Iraq, USAID has collected thousands of official reports. This is an unofficial report.

The lessons learned address what went wrong but also what went right. Much of the cynicism about Iraq is misplaced. For sure some ideas did not work out as intended, more because of uncontrollable factors than USAID or contractor mistakes, but some of those ideas left something to build on, and many would work in other countries too. One of my projects finally succeeded four years after I left Baghdad. Despite the violence, and conceding the setbacks, people like me and my civilian counterparts accomplished a lot that wasn't reported. Iraq's continuing troubles don't invalidate the contributions of those who went to help.

In late 2007 I went to Iraq a third time, as a consultant to the Ministry of Municipalities of the Kurdistan Regional Government, in Erbil, an agency with 30,000 employees in all corners of the region. I thus became one of the few expats with the distinction of having served in all three major areas of Iraq. I traveled over much of the region, made official visits to its largest cities and many smaller ones, and stayed throughout 2008. This is part 3 of my story.

The political viewpoints of Iraqis within the three major areas are as different as for people in three separate countries. The opportunity to compare them enabled me to relate developments in all three areas to the overall picture. That is one of my advantages in this book. The majority Shia, located mainly in southern Iraq, hated Saddam and hoped to inherit political power based on their numbers. The Sunni Arabs of Central Iraq, favored by Saddam, now faced an Iraq in which their traditional dominance was over. The Kurds, also Sunnis but not Arabs, looked forward to shaping their own future without deferring to Baghdad. The Baathist legacy hung over all of them but in sharply different ways.

My departure from Erbil was not the end of my story. I remained engaged with people and events in Iraq. My story brings events up to the present time. I have also described my efforts, with mixed results, to help Iraqis threatened because they worked for my projects or for other Coalition organizations to move to the United States or other countries for their own safety. I wish my government had done more to help such people, and some of those they failed died as a result.

In April 2014 Iraq held its national election in an atmosphere of crisis but with no inkling the situation would lead to disaster two months later, when ISIS seized Mosul and rampaged through much of Iraq. As events deteriorated, I was looking for a way to help. In mid-2015 I became coeditor of a new web-based newsletter based on Arabic-language sources, called *Daesh Daily*—*Daesh* being Iraqis' pejorative term for ISIS. It's a ground-up perspective that hopefully helps many government, military, think tank, media, and other practitioners. As Iraq's military fortunes improved, we chronicled and commented on its progress, made with enormous American help, but also its continuing internal problems. Iraq desperately needed meaningful reconciliation among its Shia, Sunni Arabs, and Kurds; a major reduction in political corruption; and a security climate in which people could finally feel safe. By 2016 it was making progress toward these goals, but its future was still uncertain.

Part 4 outlines a reconciliation strategy for solving these complex and difficult policy issues and especially the future relationship of Iraq and the Kurds. These issues are much debated in both Iraq and the United States, often with wrong answers. Reaching successful outcomes depends on better answers and on continued U.S. diplomatic engagement with Iraq.

In total contrast to all the Iraqi bad guys we often read about are the modern-thinking, often college-educated Iraqis who want to live in a meaningful democracy, who relate easily to people from different religious traditions and different parts of the country, and whose worldviews are not anti-Western, anti-Christian, or anti-American. Some of those Iraqis worked for me and the organizations I served, and many times that number have worked for similar organizations, for the U.S. or British government, or for Western or other foreign news organizations.

Sadly, many Iraqis who went to work for Coalition organizations later realized they had risked their lives for their patriotism and those good-paying jobs. They were *not* protected by security once they left work. Especially in Baghdad, they went home to often dangerous neighborhoods and returned the next morning, never knowing who might be following them or whether this day might be their last. No position was low enough to avoid being targeted for working for the foreigners or for an Iraqi government accused of cooperating with them. Many kept their jobs a secret, even from people they knew. They were subject to death threats, and some of the death threats were carried out. Many others heeded the warning and quit their jobs. Hundreds of thousands left the country if they could. Some did not leave soon enough. None of these scenarios are hypothetical. All of them happened on my watch.

Because of continuing security risks in Iraq, I faced difficult decisions on the use of Iraqi names in writing this book. Some Iraqis identified as working with "the foreigners" are still potential assassination targets. Yet writing about people's work and achievements by using a string of aliases is unsatisfactory. Forced to choose, I used real names for those who left Iraq or died or who live in Kurdistan, where security is much better, or who told me they don't feel threatened. I also used the real names of public officials and a few others already well-known and so not at risk of being exposed by appearing in the book. I used only first names for some staff. I avoided using any names for most of those appearing once or twice in the story, depriving them of a little recognition but preserving their anonymity. All other names I changed in the interests of caution.

My story is written primarily for the informed general public, to provide a perspective on Iraq that helps in understanding the country better. Both international development practitioners and academic experts should find new information and insights from reading it, as I did from writing it, comparing my experiences with theirs and learning lessons from both. Readers will hopefully include USAID and other government staff who have served in Iraq. Military readers will finally find out what some of those civilian types were actually doing.

I have been extremely careful to get facts right. Because I am not from Iraq, there are probably passages that reflect some personal misunderstanding or relied on information from some Iraqis that might be disputed by others. At times I had to sort out direct contradictions. I can only apologize for any errors. English spelling of names and places and of Arabic words in general is often arbitrary and unavoidably varies by author. I put most Arabic words in italics.

This book is intended as a politically independent and balanced account. Yes, I do mean that. Attacking others is not my purpose. Mistakes were made and have been noted, and some were more apparent to those of us on the ground. Readers with sharply defined ideological perspectives may be disappointed with this approach. Those still trying to understand Iraq may appreciate it. Much about Iraq is just hard to understand, and it will take years to sort it all out.

Iraq has been a great professional challenge to all of us who have gone there to help and also a great learning experience and personal adventure. For me being in Iraq was an intensely personal journey. I have not tried to hide the emotional highs and lows. Iraq provided some of the happiest moments of my life, thanks to all the shared experiences with expat and Iraqi colleagues, but some of what I observed and experienced was truly tragic.

Before going to Iraq, I had virtually no experience in coping with tragedies such as losing a friend to assassination or having a friend self-imprisoned at home under threat of assassination. As a lifelong civilian, I had never experienced the loss of buddies in warfare. I had no coping mechanisms for creating professional distance so as not to feel overwhelmed. I still don't, and the tragedies I experienced have changed me.

It will be apparent that I care deeply about the Iraqi people and came to feel I was a small part of their struggle. Serving in Iraq was a highly emotional experience that lives on. This is the world where I lived, and some of those who joined the struggle for the future of their country worked for me. They are among the people I care about most in this world. They are my friends and my heroes, and my spirit is with them.

For all of these reasons I came to think of myself as an American from Iraq. From that perspective I feel a personal loyalty to the people of Iraq in their ongoing struggle for security, stability, democracy, justice, and a better life.

I

Southern Iraq

MAP 2. South and South-Central Iraq. USAID's Local Governance
Program had a project team in all nine provinces and in the other
Iraq provinces.

An American Advisor in the New Iraq

Down by the River

Welcome to Iraq

It all started with a newspaper story. In mid-2003, shortly after the American-led overthrow of Saddam Hussein, a front-page *Washington Post* story announced a local governance assistance project for Iraq. The United States Agency for International Development (USAID) had awarded the contract to RTI International of North Carolina. I had extensive experience in local government. I applied without waiting for an announcement.

After several months' delay, I was hired by an RTI subcontractor, the International City/ County Management Association (ICMA), of which I was a longtime member. The delay gave me just enough time for a thyroid cancer operation that saved my life. At RTI's excellent three-day training program in North Carolina, the opening statement was "Never trust anyone in Iraq." I was assigned to Amarah, a southern Iraq city near Iran.

My decision to go to Iraq met two contrasting responses. One, from my pastor and others, was "What a great opportunity!" The other, often preceded by a puzzled expression, was some version of "You must be nuts!"

Although my education was internationally oriented, including a master's degree in Asian Studies, I had never worked abroad or served in the military or studied the Middle East or the Arabic language. None of that concerned me, as I was a political scientist with a PhD and had spent my career in government-related work, including city management and managing federal projects for contract firms. I had also served for years in civic and community organizations.

Going to Iraq reflected my career commitment to public service and my Christian social commitments. That's not usually a path to affluence, and USAID-approved salaries are based on recent earnings, presumably making me one of the lower-paid project staff despite my career experience. As money was never my goal in life, I had no issue with that. Moreover, we had a six-day week, to match the Iraq workweek (with Friday, the Muslim Sabbath, off), and were paid for the extra day. Like U.S. government personnel in Iraq, we got large add-ons for hardship pay and, ominously, danger pay. That didn't influence my decision to go but was one reason some were willing to work in Iraq. Countless others refused to go there at any price.

As for the risk, I considered several factors. I was long divorced, and my only child, Lisa, was an adult with her own family. The job came with substantial life insurance, which would pay my obligations if the worst happened to me. I was already sixty-two.

And so it was that on December 8, 2003, I landed in Kuwait, just south of southeastern Iraq. After a long transatlantic flight and a long connection from Europe, I arrived at RTI's Kuwait office a bit tired but eager to get started. The pleasant downtown and thriving modern commercial scene offered sharp contrasts to what awaited me on the other side of the border.

Two restful days later I was squeezed into a heavily loaded vehicle convoy. It rolled up the highway to the Iraqi border about sixty miles (one hundred kilometers) away, where we presented our U.S. passports at a dusty border post and were met on the Iraq side by an RTI security team for an escorted convoy to Basra, southern Iraq's major city and Iraq's second most important city. RTI's still-in-progress South Region offices there were co-located with its Basra provincial team behind extremely high walls and constant security.

Among others on board was Jabir Algarawi, an Iraqi American real estate agent from Arizona, returning to help his native country, where his family still lived. He had escaped Iraq in 1991 after joining the failed rebellion against Saddam, walking for days to reach the Saudi Arabia border. Jabir also had another unusual distinction: a significant acting role in a 1999 Gulf War–themed movie with George Clooney called *Three Kings*. Jabir became a good friend who helped offset my lack of familiarity with the natives.

The next day, after sleeping on the floor for lack of beds, Jabir and I took another convoy, headed for Amarah, the capital of May-san Governorate. As we drove through Basra, a fast-growing city of 1 million people by United Nations (UN) estimate and 1.5 million by British estimate, the bustling street scene seemed promising, despite decades of decline under Saddam, but was overwhelmed by poor and marginalized people. It is a Shia Muslim city but also has a Sunni Muslim minority (including some who had positions or elevated status under Saddam), and Christians (some prominent in business). Basra had been a city favored by foreigners—more cosmopolitan, diverse, and tolerant than other Iraqi cities—the kind of place where you could buy a drink.

Amarah is about two hours north of Basra, or an hour and a half at convoy speeds. Security people had figured out that a really fast-moving vehicle is harder for armed bad guys to hit. Other road hazards included the donkey carts, seemingly accorded the status of vehicles; overloaded pickup trucks; the fast-rising number of imported cars; and Iraqis' myriad carefree and unsafe driving practices (straddling lanes, to name one). There were apparently no rules of the road and no driving instructors either.

Pulling away from Basra toward the countryside, the view for mile after mile was a bleak arid landscape interrupted by settlements of crude homes. Green space gradually increased. Shepherds, including children, walked with small herds, and cattle grazed near the road. There were occasional agricultural plots. Maysan is mostly rural and agricultural, but its dominant economic sector is oil. About 70 percent of Iraq's oil came from southern Iraq. It was clear from my passing observation, however, that oil had not brought the region's people out of poverty.

As the convoy pulled into Amarah, we got the first glimpse of our new home city on the Tigris River.[1] It was densely settled, with mostly run-down brick buildings, people moving in all directions, and a lot of children, reflecting the typically large Iraqi families.

RTI was at the end of a dirt path, separated from the Tigris by a narrow road. Iraqi security guards admitted our convoy through a locked gate. We were eagerly welcomed into a moderately attractive five-building compound called "the villas." It had a high wall all around, though not nearly as high or reassuring as the one in Basra.

Just across the river was Amarah's main commercial area, where the Coalition Provisional Authority (CPA) and Maysan government had their offices. I would be spending a lot of time across the river.

From the moment we exited the vehicle, we saw a flurry of activity. RTI-Amarah, like RTI-Basra, was a work in progress. Only Building 1 by the main gate had been in use, and it was really cramped. Everyone was working, eating, socializing, and sleeping in one small house. Jabir and I became the first residents of Building 2 just down the walkway. The hardship-level bathroom featured yellow shower water—a mixed blessing from the Tigris.

My orientation to Iraqi customs began immediately. That very night gunfire broke out. Startled, I demanded to know "What is that?" Not to worry, I was told. "It's Thursday night—wedding night. People always fire their rifles into the air at weddings."

The Civilian Coalition in Maysan

Building 2 soon had more bedrooms, a kitchen and nice dining room served by a cook and kitchen crew, and a cleaning crew. We already had drivers, maintenance men, and enough security men to guard the entire perimeter 24/7. All made wages trivial by our standards but higher than most of Amarah and were happy to escape its pervasive unemployment.

The master of this emerging domain was Ahmed Al-Harazi, a Yemeni now from New York. He had arrived in August, with a water engineer and one security man. Al-Harazi had a master's degree from the University of Pennsylvania but also an intuitive skill at dealing with the natives in their own language. Despite his clashing cultural identities, "the Yemeni tribesman from New York City" smoothly bridged the differences.

Ahmed was supported by Yuen Huang, a Californian and former Peace Corps volunteer in Mongolia. His sharp management skills, some learned at the former Arthur Andersen consulting firm doomed by the Enron scandal, offset the lack of an operations officer. Engineer Nicholas Adrien, a Haitian from Miami, was coordinating engineering work for reconstruction projects projected to cost tens of millions of dollars. Amarah was a long-neglected mess.

We were officially the Local Governance Program (LGP), but our short-term focus was mainly on the provinces, called "governorates" (a really ugly word in English). Local government units in Iraq are districts (*qadha* in Arabic), divided into subdistricts (*nahiya*), but all were administrative units of the national government in the absurdly overcentralized Iraq system. Local councils were almost powerless and were not democratically elected and in some places were self-appointed or controlled by tribal sheikhs. It was an easy decision, as a former city manager, to favor local self-government. John Doane of the Basra team, another former Maryland city manager and a previous acquaintance, had already drafted a decentralization plan.

Maysan was in the British military zone and the regional coordinator a British diplomat, but the CPA-Maysan civilian staff was a mix of Brits and Yanks, while CPA-Basra reflected many nationalities. Other Coalition countries in the four-province South Region included Italy, responsible militarily for Dhi Qar Province, and The Netherlands, responsible for Muthanna, where Japan had a contingent of 600 military engineers. Japan also contributed major sums to reconstruction projects. Denmark had a large number of civilians in Basra making a major contribution. The United States had recruited many nations for the Coalition, in part to counter international criticism of the invasion, and seventeen had joined up, many in minor roles. RTI teams included many non-Americans, and our South Region coordinator was an Australian, Ross Worthington. On the ground there really *was* an international coalition in Iraq.

Maysan reflected the historical tendency of Iraq's population centers to develop along the rivers. Amarah's 337,000 people were 45 percent of Maysan's 741,000. Straight north along the Tigris were Kumait (39,000), Ali Al-Sharqi (18,000), and Ali Al-Gharbi (23,000). To the south were Majar Al-Kebir (80,000) and Qalat Salih (41,000), both with problem reputations, especially Majar, ungovernable even for Saddam. Others included Maymouna to the west and Al-Kahla to the south, plus about three hundred small villages.

CPA-Maysan held weekly NGO (nongovernmental organization) coordination meetings on Saturdays, and I attended my first one two days after I arrived. The NGOs included foreign NGOs with established reputations and Iraqi NGOs too new to have any reputation.

Foreign NGOs had an important role in the civilian coalition. Most prominent NGOs in Maysan were British. The Salvation Army (big in America but founded in England) was renovating schools and other facilities; Mine Tech was removing land mines and other unexploded munitions; Ockenden International was registering and helping thousands of returnees from Iran; the Mercy Corps (U.S.) was working on schools and health care facilities, as was the Czech group People in Need, which had selected Maysan as the province most in need.

There were about fifteen Iraqi NGOs, several represented at the meetings, showing that even in conservative Maysan people were trying to promote change and help others. Most were without resources, and some hoped to get a contract from the CPA or RTI, as a few did.

One idea I brought to Iraq was using television to convey democracy messages to the general public. One impressive and handsome young man at the first NGO meeting caught my attention as a possible spokesman. Haider Al-Maliki had cofounded one of the Iraqi NGOs, the Iraqi Society for Change, though he was only twenty-four. As the main English-Arabic interpreter for these meetings, he skillfully and effortlessly interpreted between people on opposite sides of the room from anywhere in the room.

The Bitter Legacy of Saddam

Sunday, December 14—just three days after my arrival. Suddenly, widespread gunfire broke out. I was again startled—but it was happy gunfire. People had just learned that Saddam had been captured! The celebratory firing went on for hours. It seemed to me that every household in Amarah owned a gun and an inexhaustible supply of ammo. Similar barrages erupted in Basra and other cities.

This was not just a spontaneous celebration, however. It was a deeply felt reaction to the misery Saddam had inflicted on his own people for over three decades. Understanding this emotional outpouring is a key to understanding the post-invasion struggle for Iraq. Saddam's bitter legacy is our first "story behind the story." Count all the dead people and their miserable survivors.

The story behind the story. First, there was the horrible impact of Saddam's *military adventures*. Just a year after seizing full power in 1979, he launched his war against the new Islamic regime in Iran. It lasted from 1980 to 1988, and its often ghastly violence killed at least several hundred thousand people, making it one of the deadliest wars in history, and produced enormous damage in both countries. Iraq has never fully recovered. Basra and Maysan Provinces were especially hard-hit, as most of the fighting within Iraq occurred there. Tens of thousands of families were shattered and often made destitute by losing their men in the war.

Thousands of Marsh Arabs, culturally distinct people inhabiting a large rural area between Amarah and Basra, fled into Iran, and some joined a military division there, the Badr Brigades, which fought on the Iranian side. At times during the war Saddam launched attacks against his own people. His worst was the 1988 Anfal genocide against the Kurds in the North, punishment for their support of Iran during much of the war. The Anfal campaign killed between 60,000 and 80,000 people, including more than 5,000 in the infamous March 1988 poison gas attack on Halabja, near the Iranian border, a city I would later visit. Over 100,000 Kurds fled to Iran and others to Turkey.

In August 1990, just two years after the Iran-Iraq War ended, Saddam's troops invaded Kuwait, quickly overran much of it, and captured Kuwait City. The U.S.-led coalition, organized by President George H. W. Bush, drove the Iraqis out in about three months and killed at least 20,000 to 25,000 Iraqis, including between 2,000 and 3,000 civilians.

Bush then urged Iraqis to overthrow Saddam but sent no help. The largely spontaneous March 1991 uprising at first succeeded throughout southern Iraq, then was crushed. Another 30,000 to 60,000 people were killed, maybe more; some were just massacred.[2] Tens of thousands escaped to Iran. Jabir Algarawi was one of 50,000 who escaped to Saudi Arabia. By 2003 Bush's mixed message was twelve years past, and its deadly consequences still reverberated in southern Iraq, where many Iraqis still called it a betrayal (and many still do).

Saddam's army retaliated especially against the Marsh Arabs, attacking the historic but ecologically fragile marsh areas with bombs, troops, and house burnings, and executing many. He then ordered the marshes drained, which turned one thousand square miles into desert; displaced about 200,000 people, close to 90 percent of the population; and destroyed a way of life built around fishing, farming, and livestock raising.[3]

A simultaneous uprising in the Kurdish north also had early success but was then overwhelmed. The *peshmerga* guerrillas and a high percentage of the population evacuated their cities and villages and fled into the mountains, where thousands died from impossible living conditions, and a half million fled into Iran and Turkey. The United States responded by imposing a no-fly zone, which grounded Saddam's helicopter gunships. The operation enabled the rebels to regain control of most of Iraqi Kurdistan and establish two autonomous governments, a historic development.[4]

Saddam's wars imposed a huge financial burden on the country. United Nations economic sanctions, imposed right after the Kuwait invasion, continued to the end of his regime in 2003. Until 1999 Iraq was prevented from selling much of its oil, which had generated well over 90 percent of its revenues. The sanctions had a deadly effect on Iraq's economy and health care system, adding greatly to people's misery, and led to the deaths of thousands more.

Second, there was the disastrous impact of *Baathist economic policies*. Throughout their thirty-five years in power, the Baathists spent government revenues disproportionately on Central Iraq, even though the oil revenue came from the South and North. While the Baghdad-area economy improved until the UN instituted sanctions, southern Iraq was deprived of infrastructure improvements and gradually deteriorated. People complained that Amarah had stood still for thirty-five years.

The UN sanctions forced huge cutbacks in government employment and salaries. Even university professors made only about $20 a month; schoolteachers made less than $10; most medical doctors made not much more; others did even worse. Many decided to make their living on the black market, and many government employees supplemented their incomes by soliciting bribes. (One of the CPA's first moves was a big increase in government salaries.) Countless families eked by only because the Baathists' recently established ration card system allowed households, regardless of income, to get highly subsidized food, fuel, and medical services. In intergenerational households many family members survived on the income of others.

The impact on public services was profound. Hospitals suffered chronic shortages of drugs, medicine, surgical equipment, and other basics—largely from inside theft, I later learned—resulting in many needless deaths. Infant mortality rose sharply; more women died in childbirth. School attendance plummeted: illiteracy rose above 50 percent. A huge number of people left Iraq, many of them educated professionals it most needed. Unemployment was so bad that even many college graduates had no work. When I got to Iraq, one U.S. dollar was worth 1,440 Iraqi dinars, so a 1,000-dinar bill was worth about 70 cents.

Third, there was the impact of *Baathist favoritism*. The regime helped those who declared loyalty to the party but ruined the lives of countless others. As almost all government employees worked for the central government, even typical professionals such as teachers and doctors often had to choose between career and principle. Those who stayed outside the party, often from principled opposition to its power, policies, or excesses, were often rejected for college or graduate school, blocked in their careers, or deprived of other recognition.

Those policies also reinforced long-standing sectarian discrimination. Even after the Sunni-led monarchy the British had installed in 1932 was overthrown in 1958, Sunni Arabs maintained their dominance. Saddam's power base was in Central Iraq, where his tribe lived. Sunni Arabs were favored, Shia Arabs marginalized.

Finally, there was Saddam's *state terrorism against the Shia*. Some of it was retaliation against opponents of his military adventures, some of it just political repression. We in the West often read about Saddam's ruthlessness. To actually live among the people of southern Iraq, however, is to understand its horrifying scale. It is often called "The Terror"; the victims are often called "martyrs." Southern Iraq had countless thousands of martyrs.

Saddam's consolidation of power included violent purges and widespread executions. As the opposition came mainly from Shia parties led by clergy, his repression had a strong sectarian impact. His executions of Islamic Dawa Party leaders and thousands of its members and those of other parties forced a huge number of people to flee to Iran.

According to the UN High Commissioner for Refugees, 202,000 Iraqi refugees were in Iran when the regime fell, two-thirds from southern Iraq, one-third Kurds. About 50,000 lived in the twenty-two camps in Iran's western provinces near Iraq. Most were now returning, including 80 percent of those in the camps. The return-ees were a focus of CPA and NGO support efforts, but most of the Marsh Arab area was no longer habitable, and housing elsewhere was hopelessly lacking.

Those forced into Iranian exile were in a way lucky. Saddam had multiple intelligence services to spy on the population (and each other) and report dissent. Many Baath members served as spies, and the party pressured citizens to inform on others, even encouraging children to inform on parents. Many of those identified and impris-oned were executed, often without their families' knowledge. After the 2003 invasion, numerous mass graves were revealed, mostly in southern Iraq, holding an uncountable number of bodies. This is how thousands of Shia households finally learned the fate of their lost family members.

All of this disastrous history explains why an overwhelming majority in Maysan, and southern Iraq in general, *hated* Saddam. Their hatred went far beyond opposition to his policies. It came from thirty-five years of real experience, real tragedies, and real sacrifices, measured in the toll of the dead and the destitute. The feeling was emotional, personal, and powerful.

Overwhelming Joy, Underwhelming Gratitude

A core assumption behind U.S. strategy was that Iraqis would wel-come the end of Saddam's regime. The accuracy of that assumption was well demonstrated by all the gunfire hailing his capture; this was equally true in the Kurdish north. Even in Central Iraq, Saddam was widely feared and hated. It seemed logical that Iraqis would be grate-ful for their liberation, support the Coalition, and embrace democ-racy. The Bush administration had a lot riding on this deduction. Alas, that's where its analysis went wrong.

There were many democracy supporters, even in the most conser-vative places. This support was strongest among educated profession-als, who saw democracy as a vehicle for societal improvement and personal advancement. Many appreciated our help and were ready to work with us. Their dreams collided, however, with the ambi-tions of political factions who saw the fall of Saddam as their chance to gain the political power over others that had always been denied them. Most had opposed the Baathists through violence, not by promoting democracy.

Opinion on Saddam was much more divided in the Baghdad area, where his legacy was seen as disastrous but less so than in other parts of the country. Many were overjoyed to be liberated. Many others resented the U.S. military for the deaths and destruction from the invasion and its failure to maintain order after destroying the government's authority. That resentment led to the nearly comprehensive looting and destruction of government buildings, even hospitals, schools, university buildings, and public works facilities, causing billions of dollars in losses. The hugely publicized looting of the National Museum was only the best known of these incidents. Rampant crime and failure to restore adequate electricity further undermined confidence in the United States.[5]

Many Sunnis realized their historical status as Iraq's dominant minority was probably over. Any elected government would likely be led by the Shia—about 60 percent of the population.

The presence and movements of U.S. troops in Central Iraq met with strong resentment. Disparate armed groups united against what was generally seen as a U.S. occupation. They included Baathists and other Saddam loyalists, extreme nationalists, Sunni and Shia militants, and early groups of foreign fighters. Many who hated Saddam decided they hated the Americans too. The U.S. takeover was seen variously as an offense to national pride, to Islam, to Arab culture, or to personal dignity. A growing number of police and other government employees were assassinated for perceived collaboration with the United States. It was the start of the insurgency in Central Iraq.[6] In our Shia-dominated British zone, the atmosphere was much calmer, but beneath the surface were developing problems we could not yet see.

With all these issues in play, it was soon apparent that the joy over Saddam's removal did not portend much gratitude toward the Coalition. Iraq's emerging forces had their own political agendas, and the Coalition would not be able to control them all. For the civilian Coalition this meant that our efforts to bring democracy to Iraq would meet strong opposition.

None of this analysis applied to the Kurds, whose gratitude was almost total and who became one of the most pro-American populations in the world.

Iraqis in Amarah celebrated Saddam's capture by shooting joyfully into the air. They did not wave American or British flags. There was overwhelming joy but underwhelming gratitude. The ensuing struggle for Iraq would reflect this tragic irony.

Getting Organized at High Speed

My work in Amarah was quickly defined by two unrelated events. One was the first meeting of the new Maysan Provincial Council (quickly dubbed the Maysan PC), set for Monday, four days after my arrival. I quickly found a role assisting our other Local Governance specialist, Peter Pollis, with the preparations.

When the historic day arrived, the members came with enthusiasm. There were greetings from CPA governorate coordinator Molly Phee and others, plus positive statements by PC members. They came forward one by one to take the oath of office with one hand on the Koran. There was a feeling of pride and optimism.

What I didn't know was that Peter was about to leave the project. He moved on to Baghdad to work for USAID. Having just arrived in town, I became the first advisor to the Maysan PC.

The second event was a team meeting called by Ahmed to discuss a new initiative from Dr. Peter Benedict, RTI's chief of party (project manager), for a democracy outreach program in all governorates. His carefully worded letter gave no program details, but I grasped the implication: a political campaign in which Democracy itself was the candidate. Four of us had a follow-up meeting, and I then drafted a "Democracy Plan."

RTI's program staff were organized around four specializations: Local Governance, Civil Society, Public Services, and Public Administration. With Pollis and another colleague leaving, we had a team of five but needed eight. RTI sent Dr. Frank Hersman from Baghdad as the new Civil Society specialist to work with Jabir. A longtime public administrator living in Austin, Texas, Frank was over seventy but in amazing physical shape. He also had a young Russian wife and two little girls, three reasons to keep working at his age.

On January 5 Tressan Sullivan, an experienced planner, transferred in from RTI-Kut (Wasit Province). A delightful Irishman from South Africa, he had just transplanted to Australia with his lawyer wife and five children. Tressan brought an idea he had pioneered in Kut: the Neighborhood Council Program. Two-member facilitator teams, one man and one woman, would visit local communities and hold a series of public meetings where people could set their own community priorities. We loved his idea, and everyone agreed to my suggestion to focus first on communities outside Amarah, to give our program geographic balance.

Unfortunately, we then lost our engineer, Nicholas Adrien, to illness. Ahmed promoted his Iraqi assistant.

To keep us safe, RTI hired a newly formed Rhode Island security firm called Custer Battles. For Amarah it hired two rugged cops from Perth in Western Australia, team coordinator Jim Gladstone and Mark Hutton, later joined by a towering American, Mark Hunter, and then Jock Taylor, a Scot by way of Australia. Security personnel in Iraq were known as PSDs, though the abbreviation stands for teams called Personal Security Details. Custer Battles would later run afoul of the U.S. government as a result of financial improprieties on other projects. (And yes, the irony of the company name, given the famed General Custer's last battle, did occur to me.)

Four PSDs, three gas-guzzling vehicles, and 24/7 coverage with security guards made security expensive and indirectly took money away from programs. PSDs were highly paid, with generous leave and frequent home visits. There was, however, a daunting downside. They earned this money at considerable risk to their lives.

We tried to get back to the compound well before dark and rarely drove anywhere at night. Amarah was not considered especially dangerous at this time, but there were bad incidents elsewhere in which expats were captured and often killed. The gruesome pattern of beheadings started around this time. These incidents got my attention.

The PSDs' shortest and usual route into town started with a right turn out of the compound and a left onto a narrow two-lane bridge across the Tigris. It's a nervous experience when a bridge rattles and moves up and down while you're on it. It was sort of a pontoon bridge, but the base was seemingly assembled from floating junkyard pieces. It also supported a steady flow of pedestrians on both sides. A major project was under way to build a dam and a new bridge.

To reach the CPA by the shortest route, our two-vehicle convoy then turned left on the median-divided main street and drove directly to the compound, called CIMIC (Civil-Military Cooperation) House to reflect its blending of roles. To avoid being predictable, the PSDs sometimes turned right after the bridge, then U-turned back. There was also a third and completely different route. Amarah was not beautiful by any route, reflecting its age and Saddam's neglect.

Most meetings were at the CPA compound, which was surrounded on two sides by the Tigris and a small tributary and on the land sides by a high concrete wall with gates. As office locations go, it was rather nice, having been the governor's residence before. I could look across the river and feel a connection with nature. Inside, its two stories were pleasantly cramped. Outside, projects were ongoing to expand the facilities. A small but nice cafeteria sat behind the main building, by the river.

Ahmed had hired about a dozen Iraqis to work at the CPA, on interpreting and translating, admin support, and other assignments. Most were young, but a few were established professionals. I soon latched onto Jawaad, a slender Marsh Arab in his midtwenties, a skilled interpreter and translator destined to become my go-to guy.

The makeup of the expat CPA staff reflected our location in the British zone. The first Governorate Coordinator (GC), appointed temporarily in September 2003, was Rory Stewart, a Scot from the British Foreign Office. Just thirty but brilliant, he quickly acquired a better understanding of Maysan's problems and personalities than its residents had.[7] By November CPA administrator L. Paul Bremer had appointed Molly Phee, an Arabic-speaking career Foreign Service Officer, as his Maysan GC. Stewart became her deputy. GCs in Basra and Dhi Qar were British, the Muthanna GC an American.

The British military has well-trained Civil Affairs teams with impressive capabilities. The Maysan team, reservists on six-month duty assignments, worked with a range of Iraq ministry directorates in Amarah. Maysan was fortunate to have such talented people.

I also had meetings in the governorate building just across and up the street, known affectionately as the Pink Palace for its color.

It was a large, relatively modern three-sided building overlooking a courtyard. I summoned my few words of Arabic to greet the guards and many others who acknowledged me as we entered and walked through the building. *A salaam aleikum* (Peace be with you), or to answer that greeting, *Wa aleikum a salaam* (And to you, peace). For any courtesies provided, *Shukran* (Thank you).

Communicating in Arabic-speaking Iraq proved to be manageable. I had frequent meetings but learned some basics on using interpreters. I spoke directly to the person I was addressing, even though he might not understand English, not to the interpreter—the instinctive tendency. When the other person spoke, I looked directly at him. The interpreter is the key participant—the one who knows what all the others are saying. Interpreting everything makes meetings too long, so I often let the Iraqis talk in Arabic without interruption, with Jawaad relaying key points to me in a low voice, and interjected when I had something to add. Jawaad was so good that I adjusted to speaking two or three sentences at a time, which helped give the conversation a better flow. When I needed another staff member for interpreting, Dr. Kifaya Hussein, an English professor, was excellent, and others helped too.

Iraqis address people by given name (first name) rather than family name. This is why Saddam Hussein was called Saddam and not Hussein. My doctorate was always honored, so I was Dr. Tom, which I quickly decided I liked. My older appearance helped, as age gets respect in Iraqi culture. Iraqis always seemed friendly and were happy to see this American who to them seemed important. Maybe I unconsciously played up to this perception, as my role *was* important.

The CPA leaders and Civil Affairs team lived mostly at the Abu Naji military post seven kilometers (four miles) away, surely one of the ugliest military installations on Earth. Molly Phee had to live there too, probably not one of her career highlights. Abu Naji was "home" for about a thousand British soldiers; units rotated in and out every six months. The enterprising Brits created an efficient operation at this forlorn outpost, making effective use of big tents.

Despite many features that would offend Martha Stewart, Abu Naji was pleasant enough to visit, as the Brits were happy to share their space, their Western mess hall food, their version of a PX, their

Sunday religious services, and their gym, and the dusty streets welcomed walkers and joggers. Abu Naji was also our backup location if we had to bail out of the villas in a hurry—which turned out to be good planning.

The Maysan Provincial Council

Members and Leaders

December 2003 was a blur. I arrived on the 11th, witnessed the wild celebration of Saddam's capture on the 14th, and spent the rest of the month supporting one of Iraq's fastest-moving political development projects—the Maysan Provincial Council.

The forty PC members had just been appointed. There was no realistic way to hold an election—besides, the CPA had ruled that out—but deciding whom to appoint was not easy. The two conflicting priorities were to represent Maysan political factions and interests relative to their estimated public support and, even more important, to create a democratically oriented PC that might move Maysan away from its reactionary tendencies.

The three major factions were those of Maysan's longtime anti-Saddam guerrilla leader Kareem Mahood, known to all as Abu Hatim; the Iran-linked Supreme Council for the Islamic Revolution in Iraq (SCIRI); and the Sadrist movement, now led primarily by Moqtada Al-Sadr, youngest son of a popular ayatollah who had been assassinated by Saddam. Appointments from these factions would include nondemocratic people. Appointments from more progressive elements would not reflect where power actually lay.

Not surprisingly, the number of claimants exceeded the forty available seats. Each brought an argument for why he or his tribe, religious group, or party should be represented. Some exaggerated; some lied, miscalculating that Molly and Rory wouldn't know any better; and a few tried to win by making threats, an unfortunate cultural habit, as I would soon learn.

In the end seven seats each went to leaders from the larger tribes, religious leaders, party representatives, and other local leaders. Six went to professional men, including Riyadh Mahood, engineer brother of Abu Hatim.[8] The remaining six reflected the Coalition priority on inclusiveness: three professional women and three from religious minorities (including Christians, of whom Amarah had few). Three women out of forty is not gender balance, but having any woman making government decisions was rare in Iraq.

Those selected appreciated the honor, except the Sadr organization representative, a cleric, who denounced the appointment process as illegitimate and declined his seat. His response seemed a minor annoyance but in retrospect was a bad omen.

The PC met in the Pink Palace, and its fledgling staff had offices there. A large council meeting room was set up on the second floor. Seats were arranged in a rectangle, with the chairman's position slightly elevated in front. Council members sat across from each other on both sides, like a mini House of Commons, or sat in the back facing forward. Their differing backgrounds showed in their clothes, ranging from tribal dress to suits and ties. Molly Phee led a CPA entourage, including British military officers, seated mostly in front behind the dais, reinforcing their importance in the new order.

Following that ceremonial first meeting on December 15, the December 20 second meeting was devoted to electing a governor. Molly asked my opinion on whether the election should be decided by plurality, in which the highest vote getter on the first ballot wins, or by majority, in which additional voting is held if no one gets 50 percent plus one. I advised strongly that the majority rule would more likely produce an outcome acceptable to most PC members. She accepted my advice.

That decision proved inconsequential. The election was set up in two stages, reducing the twelve candidates to six, then holding a runoff at a second meeting. There were, however, only two political heavyweights in the race. Riyadh Mahood was the candidate primarily of the PC's secular and progressive members. Kadhim Ibrahim Al-Jabiry was a local SCIRI representative and former Badr military commander, well liked and not an Islamic extremist. Still, one sensed Riyadh's outlook was closer to the CPA's. Later developments would suggest this might not have been true. The process looked routine, but the experience of electing someone through a process in which the outcome was not prearranged was novel to Iraqis.

For the second stage, on December 27, three court judges were recruited to administer the process, an idea well received. The members voted one at a time. Each was called by name, walked to the front, was handed a ballot, went to a table in the small back room to vote, then walked back in and dropped the ballot into a ballot box. I was struck by the feeling of pride and sense of importance they attached to this moment.

After the voting each ballot was read by one judge, and its vote was recorded on a blackboard by another. Riyadh stayed slightly ahead from the start. He was inaugurated the next day.

Someone had decided that if elected governors were PC members, they would retain their seats. That someone was not me. It was one of several decisions in which the CPA opted to emulate the British parliamentary system rather than the American separation of powers. We would have done better by giving governors a separate but equal role that might earn public respect for the position and create accountability to the public. I felt the same about the later decision to make Iraq a parliamentary system. My judgment about both levels of government was proven out by the near-constant state of crisis that followed and still continues.

In the week between ballots for governor, the council met December 22 to elect its chairman and deputy chairman. CPA-Maysan had decided to elect the chairman by plurality, perhaps to save time, and nobody asked my opinion. This decision proved to be a mistake.

Among the four candidates, the indomitable Sheikh Rahim Sagaati, a religious and community leader known for making verbal attacks and unreasonable demands on CPA leaders, had been jailed for ten years by Saddam and tortured. (The term *sheikh* is accorded to religious as well as tribal leaders.) The affable Sheikh Mohammed Al-Abadi was an independent cleric and community leader who enjoyed politics. Local party leader Hussein Chaloub (called Abu Muslim) was a highly distinguished Islamic scholar but politically progressive. Firebrand lawyer Ali Hmood was prone to bombastic statements at meetings that even in Arabic made me nervous. I later learned he was accused of sending armed men to shoot up Sheikh Rahim's house two or three days before the election, to intimidate him out of running.

The candidates, inexperienced with elections, didn't grasp the implications of the plurality rule. Rahim, Al-Abadi, and Abu Muslim, personally friendly and politically compatible, split most of the vote three ways, making Ali Hmood the chairman with much less than a majority. He worked hard to be a strong leader, but some never accepted his leadership.

Sheikh Al-Abadi was assuaged by getting elected the same day as deputy chairman. On January 5 Sheikh Rahim was elected deputy governor, a vaguely defined position the CPA decided must be filled by a PC member, further blurring the legislative-executive line.

Developing a Legislative Framework

At the second meeting, on December 20, the PC had also, at my suggestion, established a Rules and Procedures Committee. I reasoned that an early start on rules was important because legislatures need written procedures to transact business efficiently.

On December 29 seven of the PC's best members held their first meeting. The chairman was Abu Muslim. Others included Kadhim Ibrahim, the governor candidate; Sa'ad Geetan, Maysan leader of the moderate Islamic Dawa Party; Hassan Al-Timimi, an accountant, political activist, and leader of Maysan's new neighborhood councils, the *majlis al baladi*; and the engaging Rahman Kadhim, Maysan representative of the Communist Party.

Before leaving for Iraq, I had actually anticipated the need for a legislative rules document. I called my city hall in Greenbelt, Maryland, for a copy of its city council rules. Although Maysan was a much larger constituency, the PC was new and needed simple rules. Adapting Greenbelt's provisions, I created a clear and complete set of rules and procedures. Jawaad translated them into Arabic. The committee members, with surprisingly good organizational insights, adapted them to Maysan.

There was no discussion of parliamentary procedure, so I wondered what would happen when the inevitable moments of confusion or contention arose. It turned out that Iraqis have a few tricks of their own. At the first meeting a small argument roiled the meeting slightly. The clever Mohammed Al-Abadi suddenly interrupted loudly with a one-line Islamic prayer. Islamic protocol requires a particular response, which all the members immediately gave. This tactic of course interrupted the argument. When similar moments occurred in later meetings, Al-Abadi did the same thing. This ostensibly religious tactic amused the members and always restored order.

Creating a committee system was my other top priority. In good legislatures committees play a critical role in evaluating legislative proposals. This system keeps meetings of the full legislature to a manageable number, focused on legislation with a realistic chance of passing.

With only forty members, I was reluctant to give anyone more than two committees, which meant a maximum ten committees with eight people. Continuing the Rules Committee was a given. A Public Safety Committee was already in place, though not a legislative committee. Key industries, oil and agriculture, had to be covered as well as public services such as electricity, water, and sewer. Even combining related areas, I had too many committees, but Hassan Al-Timimi's plan put all the public services under one committee. Combining our formulas, we got a committee structure that lined up with all the ministry departments in Maysan.[9]

I created a form for all council members to designate their first, second, third, and fourth choices. I laid out a precise sequence of steps that honored individual preferences. Ali Hmood was too eager, however. He bypassed a PC discussion and vote on the plan, which would have brought buy-in from the members, whose attendance at meetings would be needed. He filled the committees himself, using the members' preferences but not following my system carefully, putting stronger members on three committees and lesser talents on only one.

Still, I looked forward eagerly to the committee meetings. I already had an agreement with the governor to link the committees to the corresponding ministry directorates. A directorate at the province level, typically headed by a director-general, was an office of the corresponding national ministry, but Bremer gave governors limited coordinating authority. My plan was to bring the committees into policy and budget issues early and initiate the legislative-executive coordination common in democratic countries. I congratulated myself on a great breakthrough.

It was soon clear, however, that signing up for a committee and actually attending its meetings were not connected in the minds of some PC members. When committees failed to call meetings, I persuaded Ali Hmood to have them set specific meeting days. I attended several meetings myself to help them get started, but typical committee meetings got maybe half the members, not enough to work effectively. As a result, the PC lost its opportunity to generate early results. The linkage to the ministries now seemed premature. The committee system suddenly looked like a longer-term project.

The next priority was a competent legislative staff. The PC had a secretariat, headed by an inexperienced but politically independent director, Abu Zainab. After a few meetings I passed along my council agenda duties to him, with suggestions he agreed to follow.

Pink Palace renovations produced a council office area often bustling with citizens, a scene I found encouraging. Once the leaders were elected and committee names known, Abu Zainab created offices for both, with public signs, two committees per room—a solid accomplishment.

He assigned staff members to take notes at each committee meeting, but few were college educated and able to provide the specialized expertise committees require. Much of the work was handling correspondence from the public, all of it recorded handwritten in a book; hardly anything was automated. The forty-person staff was excessive and confused. I made an issue of that, and Abu Zainab managed to drop half of them.

I gathered an RTI study team in late January 2004 to interview staff and develop recommendations. Some staff were still underutilized: one had work in the morning but not in the afternoon; one driver had no vehicle to drive. All did six-hour days and left by 2:00 p.m. Virtually everyone reported directly to Abu Zainab, who was overwhelmed. It was still a work in progress.

Sensitive Issues

In general the PC's meetings were conducted efficiently and with appropriate decorum and mutual respect, and its progress was encouraging, despite some dubious individual statements. It was especially encouraging that some members affiliated with Islamic parties were politically progressive by Iraqi standards. This revelation taught me not to equate *Islamic* and *conservative*, as many others still do.

As meetings went on, the CPA team continued to sit in the front and participate directly in discussions. This arrangement met increasing resistance, and I felt it was unwise. Meetings were held up to wait for "Ms. Molly" to come. Although I had deferred the agendas to Abu Zainab, Molly still wanted them submitted for her approval and deleted items she didn't like. Even the members friendliest with the CPA complained about the lack of freedom to manage their own meetings. Eventually, the council started holding separate meetings, one on Monday morning for members only and the other in the afternoon with the CPA.

An even larger issue was about getting paid. Many PC members lacked regular jobs, so the small salary (paid in all governorates) was important. Yet the powers in Baghdad seemed unable to generate the payments. As weeks went by, the complaints mounted along with growing disrespect for the CPA. Many members put less effort into the job. The PC did not get paid for the first time until March 26, three and a half months after the first meeting.

The central issue, however, was the lack of clarity on the PC's authority. Without knowing the scope of its role, many members felt powerless to do anything and got increasingly frustrated. Governor Riyadh's powers and duties were clearer but limited. He showed me a one-page summary that seemed reasonable, but CPA-Maysan had something less in mind.

The Elusive Search for Law and Order

The Public Safety Committee

Beneath the democratic process we were working to create, a subterranean power struggle was emerging among political factions supported by militias, including Abu Hatim's militiamen, SCIRI's Badr Corps, and the Sadr faction's newly created Mehdi Army. Each had reasons for disliking and distrusting one or both of the others. These militiamen numbered in the thousands.

On October 24, shortly before my arrival, the able but controversial police chief Abu Rashid was shot dead coming out of Friday prayers at the mosque. His assassination set off an argument over who had done the crime and who should succeed him. To control the police was to have enormous power, and bringing in a chief from an opposing faction was unacceptable to all factions. Abu Rashid was from Abu

Hatim's faction, so Abu Hatim had something to lose. Whoever was hired would also start with the uneasy awareness of what had happened to his predecessor.

On December 27, after the governor's election, the PC elected the fifteen-member Public Safety Committee, which was to be a governing board, not just advisory, starting with the appointment of a police chief. It included seven PC members and a mix of factional representatives and other citizens, the strategy being to create broad enough political support to avoid making the chief a factional figure. It was modeled after a successful local initiative in England, but the merging of executive, legislative, and citizen roles bothered me.

Governor Riyadh had assumed security was under his authority, which made CPA-Maysan nervous. They limited his role to chairing the meetings. This settled the immediate issue but created longer-term problems. Choosing from fifteen candidates, the committee, by process of elimination, named Ismael Fi'el, known as Abu Maythem. Arguably the most qualified, he was also a former commander in the Badr organization linked to Iran. This appointment created a kind of power balance in Maysan but antagonized the Mahoods.

The Mahoods persuaded the minister of interior in Baghdad to block the appointment and choose someone else, from Baghdad. He came to visit, saw what he was up against, and quickly left. Molly and Rory meanwhile sent letters to Baghdad supporting Abu Maythem. Bremer's office forced the minister to back down.[10] So, Maysan got a police chief scorned by both the governor and the Ministry of Interior. Its government now represented two major factions. The Sadrists remained excluded—by their choice and others' distrust.

Politics, Jobs, and Violence

January 9, 2004—just two weeks later. A major demonstration started at the Pink Palace. It resumed the next day. About 500 people gathered between the CPA and Pink Palace. Unrest over the massive unemployment had been exacerbated when Governor Riyadh grabbed control of a CPA-funded jobs program that had been controlled by the *majlis al baladi*, which helped instigate the demonstrations. Control of the program meant having the power to decide who got the jobs. The British troops showed restraint in general and let people demonstrate.[11]

We could hear the ruckus from across the river, especially the frequent explosions of improvised grenades. Our security at the villas was on high alert, and the PSDs had our vehicles positioned for a fast exit. We had all put together an emergency "grab bag," including toiletries and a change of clothes, to grab on the way out or leave in the vehicle.

Then came the gunshots. These did not sound to me like people shooting into the air. We headed for our vehicles, rolled out the back way, and sped off to Abu Naji.

Members of Riyadh's personal security team, lacking the British experience with crowd control, had shot into the crowd to stop a group of demonstrators surging toward his office. They hit twenty men, killing two, which only amplified the size and violence of the crowd. The Brits ordered the governor's men out and guarded his office themselves. One grenade-tossing rioter was shot dead by a British sniper. In all, five were killed.

After most of the crowd went home, others looted the governor's office anyway, along with Provincial Council and other offices, after the British commander declined to risk his soldiers to prevent it. He justified his decision as placing lives above property, but standing by while a mob ransacked the governorate building was to many council members, including Riyadh critics, a failure that undermined confidence in the British.[12]

After we returned, there were days when Jim Gladstone decided it was too dangerous across the river and put us in "lockdown." My already delayed meeting with the governor got delayed again. Thankfully, he decided that because he lived in our neighborhood, he could meet me at RTI. We discussed several subjects, but Riyadh made a point of telling me he was not the source of the employment dispute, as his opponents claimed, and was trying to be part of the solution.

Given all the problems the CPA would have with the governor, I always wondered why he seemed like such a solid, responsible leader when talking to me. Did I not see him often enough to get an accurate picture? Was he just being careful so as to make the right impression on me? Or did the CPA efforts to marginalize him drive him in the wrong direction?

After the riot things remained tense. Men now hung around every day just outside the gates. British soldiers patrolled the Pink Palace rooftops. I saw Ali Hmood besieged in his office by unemployed people he was trying to help. Council meetings were moved to the other side of the building because of the meeting room damage but also because the new room was less vulnerable to attacks from the outside. The new space couldn't be laid out the same way, and the positive group dynamic from the mini House of Commons layout was lost.

Insecurity and Hopeless Economics

One underlying cause of crime was massive unemployment. No one knew the unemployment rate in Maysan or Iraq as a whole, but my impression was that most working-age people in Maysan were unemployed. In March 2004 a new job center in Amarah soon registered 50,000 job seekers.

Part of the problem was the Baathists' socialist economy. Maysan's private enterprise was at shop level. Employment was heavily in government jobs and government-owned factories. Maysan had four such enterprises—a vegetable oil factory, plastics and paper factories, and a sugar mill. These establishments had produced a lot of low-quality products while the Baathists limited imports. Now competing imports poured over the border, as did a flood of used cars, such as those I saw on the road from Basra. Bremer and company were devising overly optimistic and arguably ill-timed plans to end counterproductive state subsidies and privatize much of the economy.

Maysan's government enterprises job base was largely destroyed by the massive looting after the invasion, leaving thousands jobless. The cost to rehab or replace those factories was prohibitive. To limit unrest, CPA-Maysan kept paying many displaced employees to do nothing.

Agriculture was Maysan's second most important economic sector after oil, with wheat the main crop, but it was little help to the jobless. Maysan and Basra Provinces were the most fertile, but the regime had made little investment there. Capt. Tommie Smith of the British Civil-Military Affairs team wrote a great but discouraging report for me on Maysan agriculture. Farming methods and conditions were antiquated. Most farming was subsistence. Livestock, mainly cows and sheep, were owned entirely by subsistence farmers, so there were few large herds. Tractors were old. Rural land ownership was based on tribal land rights, so sheikhs controlled the land, and the farmers were like rent-paying tenants.

As with manufacturing, agriculture was overly centralized and highly inefficient. The Ministry of Agriculture planned all crop production and issued permits to buy seed and fertilizers from a government-owned company at subsidized prices. Most crops were then purchased by the government. This system gave farmers security but left little incentive for them to improve production or farming methods or market their own crops.

Because the system provided security, Bremer's hope of privatizing agriculture met serious flak. The wheat and barley bought by the government provided the flour distributed to all Iraqi families through their ration cards as part of the monthly "food basket," which also included sugar, tea, and other essentials. In short the system helped everyone, not just the farmers. When I dared suggest one day to the PC's new Agriculture Committee that loosening some government controls might help, I got a determined counterargument from an old tribal sheikh who, I quickly realized, knew more about Maysan agriculture than I did.

The subsidies were a Baathist strategy to limit unrest by providing a safety net ensuring that all families got food. Electricity was also subsidized, though for most of the day there was none. Gas subsidies fueled a thriving black market in gas smuggled to neighboring countries and sold for a higher price. This created increasingly critical shortages and long lines at gas stations, the ultimate irony in an oil-producing country.

In the absence of civilian jobs, the militias were a major source of employment, including for the illiterate, reinforcing a serious public safety problem. One of the CPA's hardest tasks was getting some of these people off the streets.

In the midst of all this, a British Civil-Military Affairs team jobs project earned my admiration, especially given my long-ago experience managing a federally funded manpower program in Massachusetts. The project would hire 2,500 men for temporary work. To ensure fairness, men had to bring the family ration card to apply, ensuring only one person per family could be hired. Everyone applied in a one-day, open-air event at the Amarah stadium. I was told 11,000 people applied. Each was recorded in a computer database. The computer randomly selected the winning applicants. The work started within a few days. I thought this was an awesome accomplishment.

The Other End of the CPA Pipeline
Guidance from Above, Frustration from Below

Amarah is far from Baghdad—about a four-hour drive. Physical distance correlates with distance from decision makers' attention. The lower level of scrutiny let me do my own thing (and make an occasional mistake that would not be noticed). Any lost guidance was more than offset by the freedom to make local decisions based on local circumstances. Indeed, Bremer was later described as almost entirely Baghdad focused, and the British regional coordinator for the South later said that "Bremer appeared to regard all Iraq as a suburb of Baghdad."[13]

Still, my work with the Maysan PC made me attentive to *some* guidance from Mr. Bremer. Unknown to me, at the far end of the pipeline, his temporary kingdom had serious problems. Any number of mistakes had been made in critical policy areas, one being the counterproductive decision to disband the entire Iraqi Army, which added 350,000 people to the ranks of the unemployed, thousands of whom were angry enough to join the insurgency, though pensions were paid to almost all of them and some joined the new army.

The scene at CPA headquarters was chaotic.[14] Working there had its own hardships. Coalition staff needed secured housing, so even high-level appointees lived in small metal trailers in the Green Zone, described by one as "graceless tin cans," each divided into two halves and housing two people each. They were not cozy and were no real protection if a mortar round visited your trailer.[15] We had it better at the villas.

As terrorist incidents gathered momentum, CPA-Baghdad came under increasing pressure. Deadly attacks had occurred in August 2003 on the Jordanian embassy and the United Nations compound and in October on the Al-Rashid Hotel in the Green Zone, which housed much of the CPA expat staff, forcing them to move. On January 18, 2004, a suicide attack at the Green Zone employees' entrance killed thirty-six people, causing awful injuries to others. Iraqis working there now realized they were risking their lives to hold those jobs. Many quit. Some would pay the price for not quitting. In far-off Amarah the atrocity registered but seemed not to affect us.

The one problem at CPA-Baghdad that did affect me was the lack of clear guidance on the authority of provincial and local governments, which seriously impacted the PC. Bremer issued major decisions in a series of CPA Orders, many highly important and constructive, which had the force of law. He had issued preliminary guidance on provincial and local powers, but without his final guidance, there was no *official* guidance. I wanted to use the preliminary guidance, but Molly insisted I could not distribute or implement it, as it had no legal standing.

This left me in a ludicrous situation: I had CPA guidance that I was prohibited from using as guidance! I complained about it two or three times to Molly, who had a good if frustrating answer: CPA Orders had to come from Baghdad, and there was nothing she or I could do about it. She confided at one point that Bremer was just slow—and not only about provincial and local powers—and that it was as frustrating for her as it was for me.

The clock was ticking, however. Bremer and the Iraqi Governing Council (IGC) had already agreed on November 15 that sovereignty would return to the Iraqis on June 30, 2004. This meant the CPA had to finish its work within seven and a half months. The June deadline was good news in some ways, but the new democratic institutions needed time to develop, and PC members needed time to create a positive record before the first election. Bremer's delay on the final guidance was setting them up to fail.

The Meandering Road to Decentralization

Few disagreed that government in Iraq was overcentralized. This was much of USAID's rationale for setting up the Local Governance Program. The solution was devolution of central authority—giving provincial and local governments autonomy, including separate budgets, taxing authority, and in general a measure of self-government. Some in Baghdad wanted to defer that priority, however, and focus instead on decentralization—sharing functional control rather than constitutional powers.

I attended a decentralization conference in mid-February at the Convention Center in the Green Zone. This was my first (and as it turned out, my only) trip to Baghdad during my Amarah tenure. It became a travel adventure when one of our two convoy vehicles spun off the road into a ditch in Kut, capital of neighboring Wasit, in rainy weather. The accident caused a delay and an unplanned though pleasant overnight at RTI's South-Central Region headquarters in Hilla, south of Baghdad.

Governor Riyadh and key Maysan PC members attended. RTI prepared a strong presentation, combining federalism and decentralization. RTI's Peter Benedict was a conference leader, as was Nasreen Barwari, a Kurdish woman recently named to head the corrupt Ministry of Municipalities and Public Works. Barwari and others carefully skirted the devolution of powers issue and focused on decentralization. Some thought had clearly gone into this deft distinction, but I found it harder than they did to separate the issues.

So did Mowaffak Al-Rubaie, a British-trained medical doctor and Shiite moderate of considerable reputation, who argued eloquently that devolving power was necessary to overcome fears and achieve national unity. Kurds feared another Anfal massacre, southern Iraq feared more Sunni oppression, and Sunni Arabs feared the new Shia majority—and small minorities had their own fears.[16]

Driving back through Kut brought another misadventure, caused by gridlock at a critical bridge. Giving up for the day, we spent a pleasant overnight with RTI's Kut team, co-located with the CPA and a small garrison of Ukrainian soldiers in a row of former Baath buildings along the Tigris. It was a pleasant spot that might have been more picturesque if less dusty.

March 28, 2004—a follow-up South Region decentralization conference in Basra. The conference was not so consequential, but it did cause my worst personal crisis in southern Iraq. The focus was the men's room. I had to go, in the way that requires a sedentary posture. The villas had Western-style toilets, but the conference location had a traditional Iraqi community bathroom. There was no toilet to sit on, only square spaces side by side on the floor separated by ridges a few inches high to keep the urine and "deposits" inside. There was no privacy. There was no toilet paper or any other paper. Not only was the place scary, but I didn't know the "protocol" for using it and was not inclined to guess with so many guys standing around.

I left, but it was only late morning, and the conference would go until late afternoon. As my need grew, I went back a second time but still couldn't figure out the answer. I looked in vain for another bathroom. In desperation I put off a decision, hoping without much confidence to survive until after the conference. I managed to last the day but don't know how.

Some days later I asked Ahmed Al-Harazi, my cultural advisor on unfamiliar Arab habits, to explain. He said the key asset is water. You need to squat over the toilet without benefit of a seat (which seemed too athletic for a guy my age). Your left hand is the substitute for toilet paper. (I kid you not.) The water is there to wash it off. (Well, thanks for that.) This is why you shake hands with your right hand. I concluded that Iraq needed further modernization.

Living in Genteel Hardship

Back at the villas, we finished our expansion into Building 2, with its new kitchen and nice dining room. The big dining room table facilitated team interaction. Our chef was doing great. Three meals a day with no between-meal snacks helped me lose weight in Amarah.

Best of all, we had electricity, a scarce commodity in Amarah, thanks to a huge generator outside. When the electricity went off, it roared into action. It often kicked off, but Ahmed had Iraqis on duty for all but sleeping hours, just to walk over and crank it up again.

Our computers were wireless, but at first we could only access the internet from Building 1. RTI's regional IT manager and wizard, Andy Noser, came from Basra with his assistant and set up a network that linked the buildings, enabling internet access from our rooms. We all suddenly had a private office, the better to work all that late-night overtime.

Shortly afterward we expanded into the adjoining Building 3, adding more bedrooms and a laundry room. We later arranged for a washer and dryer and hired a man to do our laundry. This was the nicest building and had a pleasant sitting room, which facilitated a little RTI hospitality and gave me a place to meet with PC members and others.

USAID classified our positions as "hardship," as they certainly were.

The hardship, however, was not in the accommodations or the food, conceding the water was undrinkable and "unshowerable." (Bottled water is huge in Iraq.) Iraq had access to most modern conveniences but with exceptions. Napkins were unknown; our table had boxes of tissues. Paper towels were equally unknown. Toilet paper was a foreign idea for Western toilets.

The real hardship was lost freedom of movement. We couldn't go anywhere except on official business. It was thought too risky to wander around Amarah to shop, eat in a restaurant, or just meet ordinary people. It was, however, a genteel hardship. We never had to cook, wash dishes, clean, dump trash, or do yard work. We never had to drive; we had professional drivers and armed escorts. Every morning, early, women cheerfully washed the Building 2 floor *by hand*, with cloths. This left us with virtually no duties beyond our jobs but no place to go in our free time, though we did acquire TVs and a satellite service. It often came down to a simple truth: When your eight-hour day is over, it's more interesting to do more work than to do nothing.

That truth is part of the rationale for USAID's forty-eight-hour workweek. It would be unfair to pay people for only forty hours when the jobs demand so much time, but there is no reliable way to monitor overtime for contract workers overseas. As with all people working more than a forty-hour week—and those of us working far more than forty-eight—the extra time is a burden cheerfully accepted if you love the job.

In time I grew accustomed to the daily calls to prayer from the *muezzin* (criers) at the local mosques. Calls from the minarets are not announcements but prescribed prayers often chanted by men with impressive voices, albeit amplified electronically to extend their range. They would often broadcast simultaneously, producing a slightly dissonant chorus across the city.

Contributing to the positive atmosphere was the near-perfect weather. Southern Iraq in the winter is a warm-weather location anyway, but the winter of 2003–4 was particularly beautiful.

For unexplainable reasons time seemed to move extremely slowly in Amarah. It was amazing how much happened in such a short time. Each week brought significant, even historic developments. It seemed like I had been in Iraq far longer than I actually had. Events moved fast, but time stood still.

In January 2004 our low-visibility project suddenly ran into issues with RTI management. U.S. contracting law says federal staff may not supervise contractor staff. RTI felt our on-site CPA staff had become an extension of the CPA, an issue with other RTI teams too. There were also a few issues between the regional director and Ahmed. RTI named a new team leader, let Ahmed work directly with the CPA, and told the rest of us to work more autonomously.

The new team leader was Dr. (and Col.) Denny Lane, son of a well-known World War II British spy and an American heiress from St. Louis. Educated among Europe's elite, he chose the U.S. Army because it offered more varied career options than the British Army. He was thus a retired U.S. military officer with a slightly British accent. A fabulous résumé aside, Denny defied military stereotypes, being both unconventional and highly opinionated, and unlike Ahmed, he actually liked doing those annoying daily USAID reports. Most important to me, he continued Ahmed's policy of trusting us to manage our own programs and make our own decisions.

Denny pulled off an immediate coup by arranging for a full-time operations manager—Thierry Husson, a French former military ops guy he had met in Kosovo. RTI was moving our acting ops manager, Katie Donahue, to Baghdad. Thierry quickly set up a solid operation. Our staff at the CPA was gradually moved to offices at the villas. In February Thierry opened Building 4, adjoining Building 3, just in time for my next big project.

2

The Campaign for Democracy

The Democracy Team

The Campaign Manager

The Campaign for Democracy would become one of the most reward-ing experiences of my life. It would also encounter bad moments, dangerous situations, and tragic events.

We were soon working on parts of the twelve-stage plan I had writ-ten in December 2003. I developed a Democracy Survey, consisting of ten yes/no questions intended for Iraqis to self-evaluate how favor-able (or not) they were toward democracy. I also sent two Iraqi staff out to survey media outlets in Maysan and even Basra. This antici-pated a key element of my strategy—using mass media to reach the public directly, to get around possible interference by political fac-tions, religious extremists, and controlling husbands.

Then came big news from Baghdad that would give my plan a much bigger impact. RTI suddenly announced a major new democ-racy initiative. Word came from the CPA Office of Democracy and Governance with high priority and CPA administrator Paul Bremer's enthusiastic support.[1] I was astonished to read that this Democracy Dialogue Activity (DDA) envisioned thirty-five Iraqi staff in every Local Governance Program (LGP) city, regardless of the provincial population, mostly to conduct public forums on democracy. The CPA had big plans and developed specific themes defining key democ-racy concepts. RTI issued an imposing 167-page spiral-bound book of concepts and ideas.

The project overlapped with Jabir Algarawi's new initiative with women's groups, so we merged his NGO team into the project. That still left us needing about twenty-five new people. So, at the start of February 2004, we went into a hiring frenzy. We posted a notice in the city and had no shortage of eager applicants. We had a complete Democracy Team by March 1, including some of Maysan's most capable professionals. Three had doctorates; there were retired and current teachers, lawyers, a manager from the vegetable oil factory, journalists, a veteran artist, and a creative writer known for his lyrics to typically sad Iraqi songs.

The hiring process generated a few odd stories, including the disgruntled journalist. Many new journalists had joined the profession after Saddam fell, and hundreds of new daily and weekly papers were created. I knew Iraq couldn't support them all; one CPA-backed Amarah paper was already defunct. As most journalists had no experience as reporters in a democracy, however, RTI wanted to help train them.

On that mid-February day when I returned from the Baghdad conference, I had just stepped out of my vehicle when I encountered two young women from the RTI-Basra regional office, Nour Al-Khal and Robbie Harris, an Arabic-speaking American, who had come up to meet with local journalists about the training. They pleaded with me to introduce them, saying it would help them to be accepted. The meeting was starting in an hour. I knew nothing about the event but let them talk me into it. About fifty or sixty men crowded into the room on the second floor of an old, run-down building. I did my promised introduction.

There are risks in being a nice guy. The journalists had issues I wasn't aware of. To my dismay, they immediately turned on *me*. I suddenly felt like I'd been set up. A tall thirtyish journalist named Nazaar Abdul Wahid was particularly aggressive. He railed that RTI was training Basra journalists but had failed its promise to train Amarah journalists. The group's verbal assault continued at length. The women and I eventually talked our way out of the meeting and down the narrow stairway, but with considerable difficulty.

A few days later Nazaar showed up at the villas applying for a job on the Democracy Team. Startled by his about-face, I asked him for an explanation. He smiled broadly and told me he had meant nothing personal by his outburst. Jabir cited his good community connections and talked me into hiring him. Forgiveness is good, sometimes.

One day I encountered a wildly enthusiastic but inexperienced applicant I will call Bassam. I didn't need him, but he was persistent in a disarming way, and Jabir liked him, so I agreed to hire him. Bassam, ignoring my disrespect, overflowed with gratitude. From that moment on he clung to my every word and was one of the team members who liked me the most.

Just before March 1, Jabir and I moved to Thierry's new space in Building 4. Its large open room downstairs became the cramped but happy workplace for the Democracy Team, who named it Democracy House.

The team members came each day with motivation, anticipation, and even excitement. When I walked in at 8:00 a.m., I could count on a room full of smiling people, greeting me warmly and waiting on my word. Who wouldn't feel great about employees like that?

Admittedly, some of the happiness was about salaries. Ours had been $100–$200 a month, far below Baghdad level, but Ahmed Al-Harazi felt we should avoid disparities with local CPA and NGO salaries. DDA was a national program, however, and RTI decided the same positions should have the same pay. It fixed monthly salaries, most over $500, that were nothing by Western standards but princely sums in Amarah. Their decision forced us to raise the salaries of our other positions commensurately. There was even a small benefits package. But it all came with a huge caveat: this was a four-month project, scheduled to end June 30.

Work started at 8:00 a.m. and ended at 4:00 p.m., with a thirty-minute break for noon prayers and lunch. The team would let me delay lunch but not the prayers. A few talented people needed to start later but worked until 6:00 p.m. Saad, my interpreter, kept my communications flowing with his high-speed buzz saw delivery.

We organized the team into three-member presentation teams, including a leader for each. As with any political campaign, I wanted to reach the maximum number of people. The largest target audience was in the schools. In Iraq, however, school classes end in mid-April, after which the students enter a period of in-school study and exam taking going into early May. In Iraq's summer heat, with no air conditioning, schools can't go later. My goal was to visit every intermediate and secondary school in Maysan. From March 1 we would have six weeks to reach 25,000 students!

The team's teachers told me that access to the schools required the approval of the superintendent, Mr. Laith. I met with him to explain my plan; he agreed enthusiastically. Wanting to get all schools on board so everything would go smoothly, he called a general meeting of principals for March 4. The event became a bit of a confrontation.

Laith invited me to sit with him at the front and assured me everything would be fine. He explained to the principals the purpose of the meeting, and I made a brief presentation of our plan, including our democracy booklet. Several principals objected. Two demanded to review the booklet for approval before it was distributed. Laith stood his ground and made it clear *he* would decide whether to accept the booklet. An older woman principal, perhaps a religious extremist, attacked the whole idea and said she would refuse to let us in. Laith cut her off, saying, "*I* am the superintendent." He stated emphatically that the program would be coming to all schools and cooperation was required. In general, however, the principals seemed positive about the program.

Laith suggested we forget about visiting individual classrooms and do one presentation to each school. This greatly improved the odds of reaching 25,000 students. We quickly followed up to schedule all the schools before classes ended. I had educators on the team make the calls, to facilitate school cooperation, and designated one of our most organized team members to record each presentation on a master schedule, to avoid mass confusion.

One day we got a visit from a senior Iraqi staffer from Basra, helping to coordinate the DDA project. He arrived unannounced on a Provincial Council meeting day, but I invited him to ask team members anything he wished and promised to see him after the meeting. I was risking my reputation, as I didn't know what they would say. When I returned, he was still there, smiling. A bit nervously, I asked, "How are we doing?" His answer was startling: "Great. Everyone loves you."

Reconciling Islam and Democracy

Although 167 pages long, RTI's DDA resource book said nary a word about Islam. This omission reflected a belief based on past experience that getting into religion, especially in Iraq, risked unmanageable complications. In Maysan, however, whether democracy was compatible with Islam was *the* big issue.

The team members were almost all overtly religious Shia. For them the Islamic context was important. Kifaya Hussein made an explanation at one team meeting that I found convincing. If we avoid the subject, she said, the audience will sit politely through our presentation, but many will remember others telling them democracy is incompatible with Islam. So, they won't fully accept our words.

Therefore, we made the opposite judgment from RTI-Baghdad. We made Islam and Democracy our lead subject in the presentations. Everyone was enthusiastic. My sixteen-page, easy-to-read democracy booklet, called *You and Democracy*, made "Islam and Democracy" its first section. I used the disarming tactic of pointing out that the Koran, the Islamic bible, written in the seventh century, contained important principles of democracy, such as the four freedoms—personal freedom, intellectual freedom, political freedom, and economic freedom—which predated Western democracies by hundreds of years. So, democracy is not just a Western concept but is an important concept in Islam from long before Western countries adopted it. In short, the booklet appealed to people's Islamic pride.

I also included sections called "Concepts of Democracy," "Freedom and Individual Rights," and "Democracy Is About You." Writing up democracy principles sounds easy enough for a political scientist, but I had no textbooks in Iraq, and my professor days at Western Illinois University were long past, making this a memory test. In the end I was proud of the booklet. It had a colorful cover by our artist, with a nice photo of a mosque (reinforcing our strategy) plus our logo on the cover and a framed outline of Iraq on the back.

However, in accordance with the rule that no good deed goes unpunished, we hit two crises. The first came from the Arabic-fluent Molly Phee, who read a virtually final draft at our request. She accosted me one day at the CPA, objecting particularly to a sentence saying that Iran's theocratic system was an ideal version of democracy. This stunned me, as I had written exactly the opposite statement into the booklet. I immediately suspected that someone had sneaked in the offending revision. The problem was quickly fixed.

The second crisis occurred after twenty-five thousand copies had been printed in Baghdad. I arrived at Democracy House one morning to an open revolt. The booklet looked great, but some team members took offense at the term *secular constitution*, as a democratic alternative to *Islamic constitution*. One hostile comment followed another, supported by nodding of heads. It was an object lesson about the sensitivity of Shia on matters relating to faith. All the love I'd been feeling seemed to have suddenly disappeared.

It was my most discouraging day. Explaining carefully that *secular* did not mean "anti-Islamic" seemed to mollify no one. Reluctantly, I substituted *democratic constitution*, which I had earlier avoided as having a slight Western bias. At a long evening work session with Jawaad and our IT specialist, I revised the booklet, quickly printed again at project expense. (U.S. taxpayers reading this will do me a favor by not mentioning this little cost overrun to the others.)

Still, a serious problem remained. We had paid for twenty-five thousand booklets now stuffed in a hall closet. To avoid having the original version used against us, we had to get rid of them. When I asked Jabir for advice, however, he told me with a sly smile that he had already put them all in a huge barrel and started a bonfire.

The fire didn't quite end the booklet story, as Molly, unaware of my gallant efforts, complained to RTI headquarters about it. Her objection alerted RTI that in my rush to get it printed, I had not first cleared it with Baghdad as required. I assumed no one would care, until I got a personal visit from Chuck Costello, RTI's deputy chief of party, all the way from Baghdad. Chuck emphasized politely, but in a faintly intimidating way, that documents intended for the public *must* be cleared.

Once RTI read the booklet, however, they became enthusiastic. CPA-Baghdad apparently read it too. I got messages congratulating us for our great materials, also including the artist's five huge and beautiful posters, likewise belatedly approved. We expected to hang them all over Maysan. RTI now wanted to publish the booklet for all of its LGP teams.

Meanwhile, at the invitation of team leader Denny Lane, Molly showed up one day at Democracy House and met with the team. I felt nervous about her visit, with reason as it turned out, as she attacked the linkage of democracy to Islam and veered into other objections. She met vocal opposition, however, and two team members insisted it would actually be dangerous in Maysan to talk about democracy without addressing Islam. Molly seemed taken aback and dropped the issue.

Democracy and the Grand Ayatollah

Notwithstanding all this talk about Islam and democracy, I knew public opinion would in the end turn largely on the opinion of Grand Ayatollah Ali Sistani. He had a towering reputation as the preeminent Shia religious leader, reinforced by issuing fatwas on matters of faith (analogous to papal encyclicals). Sistani was an old man, living almost like a recluse in the Iraqi holy city of Najaf. His white beard and Islamic garb conveyed a really conservative image, and he was actually from Iran.

There was a general feeling, therefore, that Sistani would be a big obstacle. But buried in a few recent newspaper stories was a rumor that he actually disliked the Iranian system and wanted a real democracy for Iraq. I decided to bet on the rumor. Sistani soon vindicated my faith, making our campaign widely acceptable to the public. His later support for elections and democratic Islamic parties helped galvanize public opinion. He was too democratic for the CPA, insisting on direct elections and other changes to the CPA's plans for the transitional government.

The core DDA idea was to facilitate dialogues about democracy. It sounds simple, but it was a novel concept in Iraq. Facilitators were apparently expected to be neutral and not steer the discussion to predetermined conclusions, but I never got that part of the message. Our events had elements of dialogue, and the Democracy Survey elicited feedback from all participants, but our format was a civic education presentation with interaction. As we were hustling to reach all the schools before the school year ended and would be talking to large student audiences more than to small adult discussion groups, our approach made sense.

The CPA wanted us to address one subject in particular: the just-issued Transitional Administrative Law (TAL), written as a temporary constitution. I found the document impressive and deduced (correctly, as it turned out) that the CPA strategy was to write democratic provisions on controversial subjects into the TAL to set precedents for the constitution. When later disagreements arose on those subjects, the TAL could provide a basis for resolving them, making decisions in a democratic direction more likely.

However, TAL became a huge issue. Sistani and other Shia leaders did not want precedents set by nonelected people to be in the way once the constitution was being developed nor to have the TAL be the basis for governance in the meantime.

The TAL's many excellent provisions got lost in the debate over a few. Its authors received too little credit, for lack of U.S. media coverage and because Iraqi reactions focused on provisions that were unavoidably controversial. The key figures were the distinguished elder statesman Dr. Adnan Pachachi, chairman of the Iraqi Governing Council (IGC) drafting committee and the IGC's most progressive member; Feisal Istrabadi, an Iraqi American lawyer from Indiana; Salem Chalabi, another American-educated Iraqi lawyer (and nephew of the controversial IGC member Ahmed Chalabi, the subject of many media stories); and Dr. Larry Diamond, the CPA governance advisor from Stanford.[2] It was a heavyweight committee for sure, but its members were highly Westernized, its Iraqi members were exiles with no connection to Islamists, and they were all far more progressive than the average Iraqi or IGC member.

All the divisive issues of the nation had been loaded onto this law. Getting final agreement within the IGC required intense, exhaustive negotiations. The Kurds and most Sunni Arabs supported it, assuming it was a precedent for the constitution. Sistani opposed it for the same reason. In the end the Shia members signed the law on March 8, only to demand changes as soon as the signing ceremony was over. Sistani issued a religious decree attacking it, shifting a large bloc of public opinion against it and setting up a possible crisis once the constitution drafting started.[3]

This is where we came in. The CPA was concerned about the bad public reaction, and RTI was asked to address the Transitional Administrative Law in its DDA events and report back on what people were saying. I sensed this would not be easy in heavily Shia Maysan. However, we weren't being asked to sell the law, only to introduce it and let people state their own opinions. We put it on our presentation agenda but gave it a neutral explanation. For adult groups we passed out copies.

Larry Diamond later reported that in his own DDA appearances even well-educated people raised strenuous objections. Failure to consult with the public in advance was a big issue; so was the influence of the "occupation forces." The CPA launched a national media campaign for the TAL, but Sistani's organization had already issued its own publicity against it.[4]

The other major issue, even more controversial than the law, was how to choose the transitional government. June 30, 2004, was the date set for returning control to Iraqis. Direct elections before June 30 were impractical for many reasons. The CPA devised an intricate caucus system under which a National Assembly would be elected by provincial electors, who would first have to be somehow selected themselves. Even to me, a political scientist, this formula was complicated. Sistani insisted only direct elections were acceptable. Despite repeated entreaties, he remained intransigent, creating a political crisis for the Bush administration.

Finally, and with some desperation, the United States persuaded the UN to make its own recommendations, hoping that having the UN tell Sistani the same thing the CPA was saying would allow him to back down gracefully. The UN sent a seven-member fact-finding mission led by Ambassador Lakhdar Brahimi, an Algerian who had recently brokered difficult compromises that helped facilitate the post-Taliban government in Afghanistan.

The UN team arrived February 6, went into a whirlwind series of meetings, and issued its report February 23. Its in-depth analysis through a haze of diplomatic language concluded that direct elections before June 30 were impractical. It offered UN help in managing the later election process. Sistani finally acceded. The UN also concluded, however, that the CPA's caucus system was impractical. Brahimi's team took on itself the task of forming the government, in consultation with the CPA and IGC.

The Democracy Survey

Although I wrote the ten Democracy Survey questions early on and had them translated, every survey carries the risk that questions will be misunderstood. Applying a little political science, I decided to do what is called a pretest. We passed the survey out to Iraqi staff at RTI, then at CPA-Maysan, and I analyzed the results.

The results for one question, on women's rights, puzzled me. I expected it would closely divide the respondents, given Iraq's known gender inequality, but I was getting a heavy majority of pro-women's rights answers, even from illiterate men. My only hunch was that men thought women already had equal rights and so were just voting for the status quo. Rewording the question to state that women do not have equal rights and asking whether they should increased the no votes and confirmed my hunch.

I consulted several PC members about our democracy campaign and had each fill out the survey and then comment on the questions. One result was to revise the women's rights question again, to preface it by saying that "Islam stands for equality, but cultural traditions in Iraq have given men more rights than women." The change followed an explanation from a Dawa PC member who said that the inequality of women, widely believed (especially by men) to be based on the Koran, was in fact the result of cultural habits enforced by men over all the years.

The PC members surprised me at times. A few voted no on the seemingly simple question of whether any adult should be able to run for office, arguing that Iraq had already seen enough losers in public office. This turned out not to be an isolated opinion.

In the end we agreed on ten questions, each based on a principle of democracy.

DEMOCRACY SURVEY: YOUR PERSONAL OPINIONS ABOUT DEMOCRACY

Answer the ten questions below by circling YES or NO. Do not sign your name. Your answers will be analyzed later.

1. The priorities for Maysan should be set by people in Maysan rather than by the central government in Baghdad.

    YES   NO

2. I want political leaders to be elected by the people, and I will vote when the elections are held.

    YES   NO

3. Any adult citizen should have the right to be a candidate for elected positions.

YES   NO

4. People should have rights that cannot be taken away by their governments.

YES   NO

5. I should be allowed to express any opinion without fear.

YES   NO

6. Journalists should be able to write any honest story, even if it is embarrassing to the government.

YES   NO

7. Democracy is in harmony with Islam.

YES   NO

8. The constitution of Iraq should be consistent with Islamic principles.

YES   NO

9. Government laws should be separate from religious laws, even though they may reflect Islamic principles.

YES   NO

10. Islam stands for equality, but cultural traditions in Iraq have given men more rights than women. Should women be given rights equal to those of men?

YES   NO

Getting It All Together

Meanwhile, the Democracy Team finalized our presentation strategy. We would hang our big democracy posters on walls at each school, to reinforce our message after we left. We would do an introductory explanation, then hand out the Democracy Survey, to be filled out and then discussed and collected. We would discuss Islam and democracy, the most critical topic. We would explain the basic concepts of democracy. We would address the Transitional Administrative Law and citizen responsibilities in a democracy. We would give the participants time to dialogue and ask questions.

At the end the three-member team would hand every participant a "Democracy Kit" with a clear plastic cover that enclosed the democracy booklet and had either an art pencil set for girls or an accompanying "Democracy Yes" baseball-type hat for boys. Cultural norms wouldn't let girls wear the hats. Buying all these materials was a challenge because we needed so many. The plastic covers and art sets could be bought locally, however, and Sijad (not his real name), my go-to guy for admin tasks, was all over it.

I had a larger strategy behind the booklet. Although most participants would be students, the booklets would go home, where parents and other family members could also read them. This approach would extend the impact of the school presentations far beyond 25,000 people.

The Democracy Yes hats, translated to "Yes democracy" (*Na'am democratia*) in Arabic, would be worn by kids over a long period of time and were in effect a long-range advertising technique. My questions focused on the colors, which I finally resolved in favor of green lettering (the Islamic color) on a black hat. When they arrived, we handed some to Iraqi staff at the villas. The pleased reaction persuaded me we had a winner.

Much of the time leading up to the first presentations was spent assembling thousands of Democracy Kits. Team members sat for hours, day after day, putting the items into the clear bags, clamping them closed, putting them in boxes. It was boring and repetitive, but I could see they were highly motivated.

I was proud of all this preparation. We had a plan, a schedule, a strategy, handout materials already packaged, and everything ready to go.

The Media Team and the Voice of Haider

RTI-Baghdad gave us more DDA positions than we needed for presentations. I used eight on a media team. Apparently, I was the only DDA coordinator who did this. RTI's plan had not included media, as its core concept was face-to-face dialogues, but my core idea was still a political campaign. I felt the dialogues would mostly reach people already favorable to democracy, whereas a campaign tries to reach the maximum audience, including the marginally interested and the confused. My prototypical target was the illiterate rural housewife who wouldn't even know about the democracy dialogues, never mind attend one, but who had a TV set. A recent survey showed that the great majority of households now had TVs.

So, while most of the team prepared for presentations, the Media Team, headed by the determined and delightful Ta'meem, worked on media ideas. Her impressive group included three journalists, one writing part-time for *Azzaman*, the nationally famous Iraqi paper printed in London since the mid-1990s, plus the artist and writer.

The artist's five democracy posters featured patriotic messages and depictions of Iraq coming out of the darkness and into the light. I ordered two thousand of each from a print shop in Basra. We made a list of Maysan locations to put them up. He also developed a campaign logo for project materials, centered on an artistic version of the Iraqi flag. The writer wrote several poems on democracy for dramatic readings at the presentations.

The earlier media survey produced a contact list for print and electronic media in Maysan and Basra and a few in Baghdad. We would get our message into as many newspapers as possible and hopefully the U.S.-developed wide-area radio station, Radio Sawa, in southern Iraq.

Most important, we would produce TV and radio public service announcements (PSAs). I felt they could be our biggest achievement and was already working on PSA scripts. I thought we could get them not only onto southern Iraq TV and radio but maybe even the national Al-Iraqiya TV network. Al-Iraqiya was the Iraq satellite channel most people watched; its network included a locally owned Amarah station. Media outlets in the West play PSAs at no cost, which lacked precedent in Iraq. One Media Team member talked to someone at Al-Iraqiya about airing our PSAs, however, and got a favorable reaction.

I admitted to myself that the plan was really audacious for someone with no media experience, but I did know a lot about political campaigns and elections, and my success so far in Iraq gave me a lot of self-confidence. My talented Media Team members knew their way around. My plan had strong support from Michael Knowles, RTI's regional communications manager in Basra, a Conservative member of Parliament in Britain during the Maggie Thatcher days.

The plan assumed compelling scripts of about one minute. Jawaad would translate my words into Arabic. Our poet would make the Arabic version sing. The last line of each PSA would be our campaign slogan, "Democracy Yes!" (*Na'am democratia!*). Four or five citizens of all ages, previously filmed, would then repeat "Na'am democratia!" There would be music at the beginning and end. The artist created a studio backdrop in the colors of the Iraqi flag. The right spokesman would make it all soar.

Most people would have looked for an experienced announcer. I went with my hunch—the inexperienced but charismatic Haider Al-Maliki, who had impressed me at the NGO meetings. He was also Ta'meem's brother. Haider was only twenty-four but brilliant, a graduate of Baghdad University with a master's-level diploma in English. He was an NGO cofounder, a known democracy advocate, and worked for international NGOs. Thinking like a campaign manager, I reasoned he was also one of the best-looking young men in Iraq, and women are over half the population.

We found a fledgling but trained TV producer from Amarah and signed a contract with strict performance standards, including my bottom-line requirement for an Al-Iraqiya-level quality standard. In fact I had no idea of what that actually meant in technical terms. Our producer in turn hired an experienced crew in Basra and arranged a studio there.

I decided to start with five scripts, using several of RTI's DDA themes, and do more later if they went well. The first PSA, "Democracy Is About You!" emphasized citizen participation. The others were on "Freedom"; "Friendship, Peace and Reconciliation" (with neighboring countries and within Iraq); "Anti-Violence"; and "Women's Rights." Here and there I surprised even myself. Best line (about Saddam's victims): "We cannot bring back the victims of the terror, but we can build a new Iraq in their name." Best idea (about national unity): "We are one nation, one people, one Iraq." (That one seems overly optimistic in retrospect.) Favorite line (in the women's rights PSA): "Love *one* woman for the rest of your life." That last one was addressed to men but was intended for wives and unmarried sisters watching TV.

One day in March a security team drove me to RTI-Basra, and the next day Michael Knowles and his assistant Nour Al-Khal accompanied me to the studio, a pleasant place on a quiet street. Haider had belatedly told me he hated suits and didn't have a good one. I told him to buy a couple of different suits and ties and we would share the cost. I should have been more specific. Our Iraqi flag backdrop was red, green, and black. He showed up in a brown suit, though the second one, light green, was good. (Two years later in Baghdad I played the PSAs for an international media expert, who had two comments. One was to praise my excellent choice of a spokesman; the other was to ask why the hell he was in a brown suit.)

The studio was good, the camera crew excellent, and we were excited. The taping session was not without adventure. We stopped and started a lot, to fix places in the scripts or to allow me or the crew chief to talk to Haider. We did multiple takes to make each script just right.

Haider was not totally comfortable at first but was on a roll by the time we finished and wearing the light green suit. We all left happy. The Media Team identified technical corrections, such as refining the backdrop for better color contrast, changing the music, editing the *Na'am democratia* endorsements and reducing them to three per PSA to save time, and standardizing the length to one minute and thirty-five seconds, the better for working with Al-Iraqiya. However, the Media Team decided that Haider's orations were ready for prime time.

Hitting the Road to Success

RTI-Baghdad was not keeping up with its own timetable. Promised guidance, handout materials, and needed equipment such as loudspeakers and microphones weren't getting to us. We could buy locally available items on our own. That and the other admin tasks kept Sijad hustling. As for the rest, the furniture showed up; the rest came late or not at all.

Fortunately, I had a great ally in Deanne DeVries, the determined DDA coordinator at RTI-Basra. As issues arose, she took it upon herself to do battle with RTI-Baghdad and kept the project on track in both cities. However, the delays postponed the start of our presentations. At some point I couldn't wait any longer. I did a three-day training workshop in early March; everyone was in high spirits. On March 22, after a few more obstacles, my presentation teams roared out with enthusiasm.

By the end of March, nine days later, they had made presentations to about fifty groups, averaging over 250 per group and reaching about 12,500 people. The huge numbers reflected the high attendance at schools. Audiences at women's NGOs, hospitals, and factories were necessarily smaller. Scrambling to make up time, we were up to five or six presentations a day, with some teams doing one every working day and sometimes two. The Democracy Yes hats were going over big, with factory workers as well as schoolboys.

No one was stopping to celebrate, however. Classes would end in two weeks.

On the Front Lines in the Struggle for Democracy

The Democracy Team was not our only big project at LGP-Amarah. The Community Development Team of my colleague Tressan Sullivan had started, and CPA-Maysan had decided to fund it. By February he had assembled a forty-member staff, assigning thirty-four of them to two-person facilitator teams.

My earlier suggestion to start in rural areas had worked out. Indeed, the program was officially recast as a rural program in discussions with CPA-Maysan, mostly to avoid political complications from its pending effort to reform district and subdistrict councils. Tressan's plan started with 120 communities. It was unrealistic to go to every village; Maysan had about 300, some described as unsafe. It turned out some "relatively safe" ones weren't safe either.

For each place a facilitator team conducted a series of four public workshops. Residents were asked to identify the needs and priorities of the village; decide on a small project to deal with one priority, within a $5,000 budget; and elect a development committee to oversee it. The plan sounds straightforward, but letting citizens make their own decisions on community priorities was almost unheard of in Iraq. Including women in such decisions was even rarer, and in some traditional villages this required separate meetings. Most villages were too poor to launch projects on their own, so the $5,000 incentive was essential.

Villagers identified a range of needs illustrating the poverty of rural Maysan. Some wanted basic infrastructure such as roads, water, and electricity or generators for homes in villages without electricity. Others proposed basic services such as health clinics, schools, a kindergarten, recreation facilities, training for village health care workers, and a literacy program. Others favored agricultural projects.

Aside from the educated Iraqis we met each day, Maysan was a largely traditional society with reactionary tendencies. My Democracy Team facilitators were going to schools and other controlled settings, where they could feel relatively safe. Tressan's were going unprotected to places where law, human rights, and other modern governance principles meant little. They were mostly younger urban dwellers visiting mostly older, rural villagers, and they were on their own—truly on the front lines in the struggle for democracy. Local police did provide security in places, but not surprisingly, our daily project reports to RTI recorded some bad moments.

In one shocking incident near the end of the third workshop, the two facilitators witnessed a revenge killing. One, a medical doctor, was told he would be shot if he attempted to treat the victim, who died unattended. The facilitators left but did return later to hold the final meeting. In another incident Sadrists in Majar Al-Kebir accused the facilitators of being Israeli spies and RTI of being an Israeli organization and told one facilitator he would be killed if he ever returned.

In one village local authorities chose their own development committee instead of allowing an election. The male facilitator was manhandled and the woman facilitator threatened when they refused to accept this arrangement. In several villages men tried to exclude women from voting for the committee; in four reported cases they failed twice and succeeded twice. In another incident the local sheikh tried to pass off nine personal appointees as the elected committee. When the facilitators balked, he tried the same trick using fourteen of his extended family members. The facilitators again refused and then left.

In some cases the facilitators decided the village was just unsafe. At one, near Qalat Salih, the locals seemed almost primitive and culturally ignorant, and some were known looters. The facilitators' driver feared for his car. The facilitators witnessed an argument among women outside the school hosting the meeting, and some were armed! Many people demanded to be on the committee that would manage the $5,000. The facilitators sensed that public service was not their motive and just wanted to *escape* the place. Village leaders later came to the CPA to ask for the money and were told evasively that they had to wait until the next stage of the project. One facilitator told me later that if the project had continued, villagers would have killed each other for the $5,000.

Still, by the end of March, Tressan's teams had conducted 387 workshops in about 90 different communities, had done all 4 meetings in many places, and were still going strong. Average attendance was 60; women made up 39 percent of participants. There were 55 places where men and women attended together, 32 with separate meetings (the facilitators would split up), and 8 for men only. By the time the project ended, the team would work with over half of Maysan's 300 villages.

Between the CPA-funded Community Development Team and my USAID-funded Democracy Team, we were employing 76 Iraqis. Add the taxi drivers and independent drivers hired to take our facilitators to and from their presentations. There were 17 more program staff working for other colleagues. Overall, the RTI project in far-off, low-visibility Amarah had 177 Iraqi staff by March 2004, making it one of the largest in the entire LGP, with an impact across all parts of Maysan.

Equality, Justice, and Basic Services
The Struggle for Women's Rights

The gender discrimination observed by the Community Development Team reflected one major obstacle to a democratic society. Women's rights is *the* social issue in Iraq. Modeling part of the solution, we hired about as many women as men, including supervisors.

Our commitment to gender equality raised no issue with the men on the Democracy Team, PC members I worked with, or the governor. Their acceptance persuaded me that support for equality correlates with education level. However, my Democracy Survey results eventually showed that equal rights for women was supported by about 70 percent of *all* respondents, a highly revealing and encouraging result.

Actual practice lagged behind opinion, however. In his work with women's NGOs, Jabir encountered the sad consequences. Daughters were less likely to be enrolled in school or continue past primary school, so many women lacked literacy and work skills. Domestic abuse is a known problem, and women have almost no recourse. A divorced woman can be trapped all around: no husband to earn money; no hope for a new husband, as Iraqi men disdain marriage with divorced women; no job; and often illiterate, with no employment skills. Divorce customs are hopelessly discriminatory, though a Baathist law gave divorce rights to women who dared to go to court and use them. I learned, however, that while men are allowed up to four wives, only a few can afford more than one at a time.

Abuse of women now extended to the streets. With the Baathists gone, religious extremists harassed and intimidated women about their clothes. Many modern-oriented Amarah and Basra women, even Christians, adopted conservative Islamic dress to avoid these men.

A systemic obstacle for Jabir Algarawi and Frank Hersman in their civil society work was that southern Iraq had little precedent for women participating in government decisions or women's advocacy. Jabir was encouraging capacity building with several Maysan women's groups and trying to focus them on common goals. He found an overwhelming need for literacy classes and classes in sewing, a useful skill not dependent on literacy.

On February 18 I attended an important conference in Amarah on the "Role of Women in Iraqi Society." Our Dr. Kifaya had a prominent role, Molly Phee gave the keynote address in Arabic, and both Governor Riyadh and PC chairman Ali Hmood spoke. A presentation on important women in Islam began with the historical importance to Muslims of Mary, mother of Jesus. I learned later that this connection is well understood.

Frank followed up the Amarah conference with several others in different places. The events were not entirely without incident, with efforts made in two places to block them.

Our big idea for Maysan women was a women's center, to give them a place of their own and be an incubator for developing their capabilities. Jabir secured cooperation from a few women's NGOs, and I helped him develop a funding proposal.

Dr. Kifaya took the lead on the women's center. She had spent most of her career as a headmistress and supervisor in secondary schools, then earned a doctorate and became an English professor. Her daughter, Saba, a medical doctor, was also a key RTI staff member. Kifaya's own life reflected the inequality and unfairness of Iraq's male-dominated society. She was married, with two daughters in their early to midtwenties, and a seventeen-year-old son adopted because her husband wanted a male child. He reportedly found the adopted son too dark to look like a family member and wanted a natural son, so he divorced Kifaya and married another woman. Kifaya had a career to support her financially but was in the hopeless trap faced by virtually all divorced women in Iraq, as custom prevented her from dating or remarrying. This has no Islamic basis; in fact, the Prophet Mohammed married divorced and widowed women after his first wife died. Kifaya took a liking to me and conveyed this indirectly in various and occasionally humorous ways.

The women's center idea got strong support from Molly Phee and the governor too. CPA-Maysan set aside $50,000 to rehab a public building. The building, however, was occupied by two political organizations; even the governor couldn't get them out. Kifaya's next idea, a former Baath Party building, was occupied by squatters—homeless returnees from Iran. There was no way the redoubtable Kifaya or anyone else could get them out. So, our planning proceeded as if a building would be available, while the major obstacles to acquiring one remained unresolved.

In the Shadow of Hammurabi

Judges were an immediate focus of the British Civil-Military Affairs team. Many were Baathists who disappeared or were removed after Saddam fell. A gentlemanly English lawyer and Civil Affairs captain found himself in a position of power. By the time I met him, he had hired most of Maysan's new judges. Still, Maysan had a shortage of judges.

Every Maysan court building was looted after the invasion, as were courts in Basra, and most of the records were destroyed. Frank Hersman, who had an LLD along with his PhD, was deputized to help implement CPA-Maysan's project to build or rehab six courthouses and a prison. He soon had regrets about the assignment, however, due to complications from dealing with unethical contractors. The CPA also donated furniture, computers, and money for a law library.

At a Law Day dedication RTI gave the central court a bust of Hammurabi, king of ancient Mesopotamia, much of which is now Iraq. In the eighteenth century BC, Hammurabi produced a written Code of Laws and thereby became a founder, in a way, of the rule of law.

Beyond court buildings the rule of law was not well established in Maysan or any other province. Its key principle is that everyone accepts and abides by the same laws, enacted through constitutional and legal means, and there are no higher laws. We take this principle for granted in the West, but many Muslims affirm Islamic law as a higher authority and don't accept the separation of government and religion.

Being a judge carries personal risks anywhere, but I was astonished one day at a PC meeting to hear members discussing a threatening letter that a *lawyer* had sent to a judge to get a potentially dangerous client released. Apparently, it was not an isolated case. Security for each judge was increased, and a fence was erected around the Amarah Central Courthouse.

The Struggle for Water and Electricity

In the optimistic early days of the CPA, infrastructure projects for electricity, oil, and water were at the heart of the much-ballyhooed $18.4 billion voted by Congress to help rebuild Iraq. Our Iraqi engineers worked daily on project plans for Maysan, but less than $500,000 had been spent. This was the pattern throughout Iraq. These delays were a political issue in Washington, as the Bush administration was anxious to show progress in Iraq.

Part of the problem was the CPA's priority on infrastructure projects, which necessarily have long timelines, while giving little priority to smaller economic development projects that might create employment and produce visible results in a short time. USAID faced serious internal obstacles to getting adequate funding for its projects until the CPA left, by which time public antagonism toward the United States could not be reversed.[5]

Infrastructure improvements were certainly needed, however. Public utilities took a beating over all the years of Saddam's neglect. The regime failed to modernize plants, distribution networks, and such, which became less and less able to meet demand. The post-invasion looting made everything far worse. CPA and Iraqi engineers were left with a two-sided dilemma: The infrastructure needed immediate repairs to restore inadequate service levels, but much of it needed to be replaced altogether. Insurgents who attacked those trying to repair or build such facilities compounded the problem. These conditions help explain why reconstruction was crippled and vast sums of taxpayers' money eventually wasted.

Maysan had Electricity, Water, and Sewer directorates but lacked resources. About 40 percent of its system assets were lost to looting, but most of the losses were overcome by the Civil-Military Affairs team and CPA-Maysan. Nevertheless, the network was old. The capacity of Maysan's four power plants was well below current needs, demand was rising fast, electricity was more often off than on, and 40 percent of rural areas and 10 percent of urban areas had no electricity at all, in an area where summers soar well over 100 degrees F (38 degrees C).

Water treatment plants used surface water from the Tigris. The process did not mean clean water, as our morning showers reminded us. RTI engineers put the price tag for needed water projects at $110 million. Much of the funding would come from $82.8 million promised by Japan for southern Iraq. Indeed, Japan was a major financial donor in Iraq, though its contributions got little attention. International NGOs, including the International Medical Corps, a California organization with a British branch, and Relief International, another California group, completed many Maysan water projects. Despite these efforts, most rural residents remained unserved by water stations and were forced to rely on untreated, sometimes contaminated salty water from the marshes.

A literally festering problem was the sewage system. Only about 50,000 people in Amarah were served by closed sewers. Each house was supposed to have a septic tank, but there was no reliable collection service, so most people just discharged sewage into sewer system ditches. Most shops, offices, and industrial plants did the same.

In theory, elected district and subdistrict councils would have helped close the gap between existing and adequate public services. Empowered local governments could influence local decisions made by national ministries. Current local governments lacked budgetary authority to set local priorities and typically lacked adequate staff and equipment, even for basic services such as maintaining buildings, vehicles, and streets. Some of the limited money sent by Baghdad was diverted by corrupt officials and contractors.

The Reluctance to Let Go

Sovereignty was returning to the Iraqis June 30. Yet the CPA continued to control governance decisions rather than let Iraqis make some of their own decisions and learn from their experience and mistakes while the CPA was still around. The lack of final guidance on the powers of provincial and local governments left us with nothing to build on.

The LGP was not affected by the June 30 date. I emphasized to PC members that we were not part of the CPA, were not leaving with the CPA, and would continue to help them. I also noted at times that I was not required to agree with everything the CPA did. This always brought smiles to people's faces. At times I laughed along with their comments about the CPA. I did at times explain, however, that some things were beyond Ms. Molly's control.

Denny Lane repeatedly pointed out the ticking clock in his reports to RTI and repeatedly raised this concern with Molly. She finally told him matter-of-factly that there were things going on in the CPA that he was not privy to.

The CPA tendency to keep control affected Governor Riyadh especially. He lacked any meaningful budgetary authority or spending discretion and complained that numerous CPA projects had started with no Iraqi input. But CPA-Maysan saw him as power-hungry and a threat to their efforts to keep peace among Maysan's rival factions. Despite his professional demeanor, he was not a Western-style politician who reached out to political opponents.

The CPA and the governor were thus competing for control of Maysan. Rory Stewart later suggested that in retrospect it had been a "fundamental mistake" to "second-guess" the governor. Conceding his ethical flaws and authoritarian ways, "the bottom line was that he was the governor and he was going to run the province when we left."[6]

The net effect of Bremer's policy was contradictory: a fixed deadline for the CPA's exit but no aggressive implementation plan at governorate and local levels that would help Iraqis to be effective once on their own. The effect was to undermine all the governors, provincial councils, and local councils and limit their opportunity to accomplish things for the public.

Larry Diamond, the CPA governance advisor, later put some of the blame on Bremer himself. Bremer was necessarily isolated from the broad range of Iraqi opinion by the security-imposed obstacles to getting around freely; his seeming lack of complete trust and thus underutilization of the senior diplomats assigned to him; and his tendency to want total control, which inhibited interoffice integration and planning. Part of the problem came down to Bremer's reluctance to let go.[7] That reluctance and the slowness of a decision-making process centralized in one person led to resentment among the Iraqis we were counting on to lead their people once the CPA went home.

The Cause That "Refreshes"

Local councils had in some cases been selected hastily by U.S. and British military teams that preceded the CPA or were self-appointed, so few of them were accountable to the public. A lot of corruption was added to low professional competence. A few places had two rival councils. To create meaningful local governance, all these councils had to be replaced. As the term *replaced* was not politically correct, especially to the replaceables, CPA lingo was that the councils would be "refreshed." This proved to be an adventure.

One major CPA motive was to hold the caucuses intended to help select the transitional government. It was thought illogical to select a democratic government through unrepresentative councils. Lakhdar Brahimi and his UN team would later kill the caucus plan, but CPA-Maysan had already started its efforts to refresh the councils before sovereignty returned to the Iraqis. On February 3 they asked us for help—not exactly a welcome assignment.

The thankless task of heading the CPA-Maysan effort fell to Stephen Anderson, an earnest, likable State Department economic affairs specialist. Steve later became Molly's deputy, when Rory Stewart moved on to become deputy governorate coordinator for neighboring Dhi Qar, which had even bigger problems than Maysan.

Anderson decided to start with five of Maysan's six districts. A second round would cover the Amarah district and the province's eight subdistricts. The strategy was to select local electors who represented a cross-section; allocate a set number of seats to different types of groups; have candidates register via a petition signed by at least twenty-five residents; give each candidate a few minutes to address the electors at a public meeting; give each elector five votes; and declare the twenty candidates with the most votes elected. The elected council would then elect a chairman. The eventual formula, adjustable to local circumstances, was five seats each for the tribes and political parties; three each for clergy, educated people, and women; and one professional.

The hard part was step 1: Someone had to choose the electors, thus the need for organizing committees—people who knew the district but were politically independent. I got involved at Steve's request but had no answer, so I asked my friends on the PC's Rules and Administration Committee to help. They came up with a formula. In the end each organizing committee had five people—two PC members, one representative of the governor, and two "educated people."

Registering candidates by petition didn't work out. Candidates just stood before the group and gave their names and professions and usually little more. The electors wrote down three or four names and put them in a makeshift ballot box. Someone read the ballots, and the votes were recorded on a blackboard. In some places they had to let men and women be elected separately, which in effect limited elected women to the seats reserved for women.

Usually, a committee member advertised the meeting, and Steve showed up with an interpreter and military PSDs. Haider Al-Maliki was sometimes the interpreter and later helped advertise and conduct the elections. Steve attended the district and subdistrict election meetings himself until worsening security conditions made that too dangerous.

The response of those being "refreshed" was, shall we say, not uniformly cooperative. Constant diligence was needed to ensure that no one looked over the shoulders of the electors during the balloting to intimidate them. In Kumait the count was interrupted by an about-to-be losing candidate screaming that the about-to-be winner was a Baathist. A riot ensued, and Steve headed for the door with his PSDs. Kumait, after the ruckus, remained in the same hands.

In Ali Al-Sharqi, north of Amarah, one of Frank Hersman's women's conferences was mistaken by tribal leaders to be part of the council election effort. His staff arrived to find that the locals had removed all the furniture from the hall. The organizers had to reassure tribal leaders that the conference had nothing to do with that unpopular refreshment process.

The results were a mixed bag. The larger Maysan parties decided to take advantage of the political opportunity while there was still British military protection. In one small place south of Amarah, the British Army had to deploy to enforce the outcome. One apparent success was Ali Al-Gharbi in northern Maysan, where a democratic election produced good secular winners and people danced afterward. SCIRI and other Islamic parties dominated in Majar Al-Kebir, much to the frustration of rival power broker Abu Hatim. Results there and elsewhere reflected a Sadrist boycott, but rumor had it that some of those elected as "educated people" were Sadr friendly.

Qalat Salih was particularly difficult. Steve had to go back several times, with increasing numbers of bodyguards and bigger weapons, and a key religious sheikh was corrupt. In one small, very tribal sub-district, the organizing committee manipulated the election, and a corrupt leader took over. In Maymouna a sincere effort to redo the women's elections after allegations of bias made the situation worse.

As an incentive to be refreshed, CPA-Maysan had $1.5 million in project funds to divide about equally among districts and sub-districts that completed the process. Projects were submitted to Anderson and the PC for approval. Some were impressive, but the larger purpose was to give local councils some control over how their money would be spent. The intense efforts of some officials, including the governor, to funnel money through their own hands were a sad sign of control-oriented habits and the ingrained reluctance to trust others.

All this refreshment was supposed to be done by mid-March and the councils sworn in by mid-April. That timeline became impossible because of predictable opposition and unpredictable events. Steve would eventually finish the last one in June, just before the CPA left, leaving Amarah to the end. To do that he and others took serious personal risks. No one could predict the future of the new councils, as the CPA would be leaving just as some were getting started.

By mid-2004 Maysan's local councils would be to some extent renewed. To say they were "refreshed" might be an overstatement.

A Job That Hugs You Back (While Others Want You Dead)

Within a few months of my arrival, the work environment went through a dynamic change. The RTI compound had some of the world's happiest and most motivated employees. Dr. Tom was happy too—the happiest I ever felt on any job. I had never been so popular with those who worked for me. I found myself working fourteen to sixteen hours a day and still struggling to keep up with my own ambitious schedule and RTI's deadlines, but when you love your job, you tend not to count the hours. It was the job of a lifetime. After years of typical professional frustrations, I had a job that hugged me back.

This good feeling reflected comparable experience. I had spent several years in city management. As a municipal manager, you have a position of authority and the opportunity to do a lot of good, but it often comes with all the frustration and ingratitude you can handle, from both city council members and citizens self-appointed for the role.

Some of the good feeling from PC members and the Democracy Team undoubtedly came from my evident dedication to Iraq. PC members were looking for help and appreciated that we were helping them at some risk to our lives. In relating to the Democracy Team, it helped, too, that I was genuinely fond of my team members and cared about them. Somehow Iraqis sense this better than Americans and are more likely to respond in kind. Treating women as equals made a positive impression, as Iraqi supervisors often discriminate against women. Trusting Iraqis to make some of their own decisions won some appreciation, as they are accustomed to taking orders. The simple if novel lesson learned is that showing some love is a management method that works. (I wonder if they teach that in those prestigious MBA programs.)

If one is willing to take the risk and endure the hardship, the pay on a USAID contract is quite good. One could do it for the money and see it as just an interesting job, but I felt emotionally attached to the mission. With very few exceptions, our multinational team got along well and enjoyed each other's company, whether the conversation was over dinner or centered around the hookah, a Middle Eastern smoking stand featuring a long tube bringing aromatic smoke from an urn of water to the smoker—one of life's great satisfactions, according to my smoking colleagues. The group solidarity might seem like a small point, but the isolated living arrangements, the 24/7 security protection, and the awareness that some of the natives are hostile make intragroup relationships especially important. A lesson can be learned from that too.

I had for all my life been one of the world's most analytical and least emotional people. I could feel this changing. At some point I realized I might as well be an Iraqi because I cared about Iraq as much as the Iraqis did.

With so many employees and activities, the LGP was now well-known, in Amarah and around Maysan. That made many people happy, but our kind of progress threatened the political power aspirations of others. Moreover, democracy was not an immediate solution to every problem, especially the massive unemployment. Maysan was now boiling beneath the surface, making us increasingly cautious about our security.

No one thought our Iraqi staff and the other educated people we met were typical of the whole population, and no one was naive enough to think all the natives were friendly. So, despite all the good vibes, I never forgot those other Iraqis—the ones who would have been happy to see me dead. This job was about doing good without undoing yourself.

By April 1, 2004, RTI-Amarah had reached its high point. Our compound was fully in operation; our two big programs were on a roll all over Maysan; our women's rights and rule of law initiatives were moving forward; our Iraqi staff was at peak level; and Iraqi leaders were often coming to our door. In retrospect what we had accomplished was remarkable, and we were on the verge of major breakthroughs. USAID had extended RTI's contract for another year, through March 25, 2005. My contract was extended too. There was a good feeling all around. We thought it would all just get better.

Within one week the good days would be over.

3

Democracy and the Culture of Violence

Rumors, Lies, and Threats

First came the rumors. A prominent citizen told Denny Lane just after February 1 of rumors being spread in Amarah that RTI was an Israeli intelligence operation. Some cited the ongoing buildup of Hesco sandbags near our main entrance (like those at checkpoints all over Iraq) as evidence. There were two incidents of shots fired toward the compound from across the river. A cleric speaking at Friday prayers on February 6 objected to women working for RTI, which he accused of being a terrorist organization and a Zionist spy organization. Denny identified that rumormonger as a substitute cleric from Najaf. He wanted to invite him for a chat, but the cleric did not return to Amarah.

The unavoidable reality that we lived in a walled compound surrounded by guards, paid the locals high salaries, had large and imposing vehicles, and brought armed men wherever we went provided grist for the rumormongers. An RTI policy, presumably based on USAID policy, discouraged talking to the media, a counterproductive and risky policy in our situation.

In a society in which half the people are illiterate, rumors are an important and potentially destructive medium. Much of what people "know" comes from the rumors that circulate. Rumors can't usually be verified, and those who start them can't usually be identified. Some people take advantage of this by spreading rumors to advance political and personal agendas—thus, *the common use of rumors to spread lies*. This is neither innocent nor inconsequential.

The Zionist accusation against RTI was a variation on this tactic. Anti-Israel sentiment is high in Iraq, thanks to the constant anti-Israel propaganda in Arab countries and the lack of education that might give people a more balanced perspective. Such an accusation is therefore guaranteed to hit a responsive chord.

The anti-Jewish propaganda is a sad development of recent times. Iraq's cultural heritage includes Mesopotamian lands that were part of the "cradle of civilization," and it has historical connections to the Hebrew tradition back to Babylonian times. Places south of Baghdad witnessed some of the Bible's most important events. For a long time Iraq had a large, culturally important Jewish population, perhaps a few hundred thousand, most living in Baghdad. As late as 1948, despite persecution that caused thousands to leave, there were over 100,000. The creation of Israel in 1948 led to intense discrimination and persecution. With difficulty, almost all remaining Jews left. Decades of anti-Israel propaganda followed.

Then came the threats. Like spreading rumors, making threats is a common practice. Some are in writing, usually not signed. There is often a clear "or else" message: "Do X or we will kill you." Threats are a tactic for getting one's way by intimidating someone into doing or not doing something. Some threats are frivolous or empty and won't be carried out. But how do you know? Threats *are* sometimes carried out, so people take them seriously. In the West such threats will usually bring police to your door, but not in Iraq.

One day I was startled by a threat posted on four Amarah school buildings against a talented young woman on the Democracy Team I will call Jinan. There was nothing controversial about her or her work, so the threat was puzzling. The message insulted her and demanded she stop working for the foreigners or else. I assumed this was an isolated incident. I didn't know what to do about it.

Jawaad was attuned to the nuances of messages on the street. He advised that Jinan stay home while RTI continued to pay her. We would have to do this until she was no longer under threat. It was not clear to me how we would determine that. My instinct was to call the police and help them catch the SOB, but he might retaliate before the police could do that, assuming they even tried. The purpose of Jawaad's proposed countertactic was to persuade the threat maker he had won, leaving no reason to carry out his threat. At some point he might feel he had gained enough satisfaction to let Jinan off. Most threats are not permanent. I took Jawaad's advice. Jinan stayed home. It was a large and personally offensive step in my cultural education.

Then came the second threat, against Yousif Hannoon, a valued interpreter. I had assigned him to work with Denny, so this threat was not against the project. It was ominous, however, that the person writing the threat knew his full name and that the letter was delivered to his home. It seemed someone had inside information. The message was clear: We know where you are. Yousif quickly decided to take the threat seriously and go into hiding. He went to Syria, forced to live the miserable life of a refugee for several years.

Then came a highly threatening message directed at Dr. Kifaya, her daughter Dr. Saba, and Sijad. This one was probably not about my project either, as Saba didn't work on it, but it was certainly about RTI. Kifaya was accused of being a Coalition spy, violating the moral principles of Islam, and working with RTI, the Israeli organization. Sijad was accused of taking photos of Friday prayers at the Sadr office, which is permitted and common, but then turning them over to RTI. The nasty wording made this threat even more serious than the others. It was posted on a door at the hospital where Saba worked part-time. The message said to quit working for RTI or be killed. Kifaya was determined, however, not to let the threat stop her work. She reduced her schedule but went on, as did the other two.

With the advantage of having copies of three threat letters, we did a comparative analysis. Ominously, those accusing Yousif and then Kifaya, Saba, and Sijad were both probably produced at the Sadr office in Amarah. The first threat was later attributed unofficially to an in-law linked to the Mehdi Army, not the Sadr office. Jinan eventually went back to work but not at the RTI compound. Her presentation team picked her up at home.

These threats were not the end of the story.

The Culture of Violence

Resorting to threats is a common negotiating tactic in Iraq because resorting to violence is common. People are accustomed to either giving in to threats or settling their own scores. Going to the police is rarely an option, largely because they are believed from much evidence to be ineffective and are sometimes criminals themselves.

Crimes are often still dealt with under tribal law, especially in rural areas. Instead of going to the police, victims go to their tribal chief. This may spur negotiation between tribes under which the perpetrator's tribe punishes him, makes him pay compensation, or turns him over to the police. In murder cases he may have to pay "blood money" to the victim's family to avoid being murdered, and/or having relatives murdered, in retaliation. The classic retaliation for murder of a tribesman is to kill a member of the murderer's tribe, even though he is personally innocent. This is horrifying, admittedly, but often has more deterrence value than the police.

Living under tribal law did not mean all tribesmen were law-abiding. Many Marsh Arabs, including entire tribes, compensated for the loss of their livelihood by engaging in looting, petroleum smuggling, roadway banditry, kidnapping, and other illegal and often violent activities. Tribes feuded with each other in pursuit of illegal gain.[1]

I use the term *culture of violence* to conceptualize the interrelated elements of violence in Iraqi life. It is a subject worthy of a book by a learned sociologist, but the basic elements seem clear. There is a continuum of force that links intimidation tactics, such as men menacing women on the streets about their dress; threats of violence as described earlier; actual violence short of murder, for which victims can be oddly grateful, as many Iraqis justify killing others over very little; murder, for personal or criminal reasons or for political views or social behavior opposed by extremists; and counterviolence, including revenge murders.

Over time I heard different opinions about the criminal justice system. At the court level it needed help but had many good judges who would do the right thing. At the police level, however, the system failed abjectly. This situation is partly from history. The basic concept of a police officer serving the public interest above private interests is foreign.

I heard this story thirdhand, but it's more than plausible. A man was kidnapped by two men with a gun who were about to kill him. Acting heroically, he grabbed the gun, killed both criminals in self-defense, and escaped. Feeling greatly relieved, he went to a police station and reported the incident to a policeman. When he named the would-be murderers, the cop shouted at him that one of the men he had killed was the cop's cousin and shot him dead.

The British were working to train and upgrade the police. But the selection process, highly sensitive in the West, was extremely flawed, and Mehdi Army, Badr Corps and other militiamen, and corrupt former Saddam-era police increasingly infiltrated police departments. The Coalition was training too many of the wrong people.

One result was impunity for militiamen who committed even the worst crimes, including militia death squads that assassinated people under the deceptive cover of police uniforms and police cruisers. People saw that reporting a crime might bring retaliation and endanger *them*. Others considered militia members their real security. As a result, militias in southern Iraq (and elsewhere) gradually usurped the legitimate power of police departments, paralyzing the already weak relationship between police and public and making the lawlessness dangerously worse.

Saddam fueled the culture of violence by executing so many people and by wasting so many lives in the ghastly war with Iran and later conflicts. This led some opponents to use violence too, and some were religious leaders, giving a religious rationalization to killing others. Everyone has heard Islamic extremists' rationalization that their killing of others is justified because they are on a jihad against foreign infidels. They have twisted the Koran for that excuse, but it is widely accepted.

People usually don't intervene or report murders even when someone is killed right in front of them. Fear of the police is one reason, and the person reporting a murder is often the first person investigated. Fear of retaliation is another reason. Yet part of the explanation is that murders often come with rationalizations. I swear the following is true, even though it is admittedly bizarre. When someone was murdered in Amarah, a rationalization often hit the streets quickly and got around via the rumor mill: "So-and-so was killed because . . ." Logically, this rumor had to start with someone involved in the crime or who knew the murderer.

Within the culture of violence this tactic encourages people to weigh the rationalization against the crime, perhaps even to wait for the rationalization. Shrugging the murder off is easier than facing the horror of what was done to the victim. Sadly, a common rationalization is that so-and-so worked for the foreigners. To many Iraqis it was (and still is) a completely acceptable explanation. That's one reason so many Iraqis who worked for foreign organizations would end up dead.

Given the traumatizing societal impact of all the violence during Saddam's time and the fact that many literally got away with murder because there was no one to stop them, it follows that lack of trust is the great cultural divide among the Iraqi public. It poisons relationships between neighbors and within government agencies. At the national level Shia Arabs don't trust Sunni Arabs, and vice versa; the Kurds don't trust the rest of Iraq in general. *All of this helps explain the public acceptance of violence against groups and individuals they oppose.*

A related cultural tendency I cannot fully explain but often observed is that many Iraqis have an instinctive tendency toward controlling others. There is a fixation on who is in charge. It shows up in government offices and at home. Ideas such as delegation, democratic decision making, shared authority, and working together for common goals are foreign, despite instruction in the Koran to consult with others, even non-Muslims, to solve common problems. The *instinct to control* was well defined by esteemed imam Farqad Al-Qizwini in Hilla, South-Central Iraq, who told Iraqis, "We must get rid of the little Saddam in each of us."[2] This instinct to control was playing out in Maysan among Abu Hatim, Sadrists, and SCIRI—all with their own militias.

Rory Stewart reported numerous meetings in which Iraqis representing a party, tribe, or other organization, or themselves, bargained for power and resources in a totally selfish way. Some made threats to get what they wanted. Anything done or said favoring another group got responses trashing them through accusations or belittling remarks of one kind or another.[3]

Similarly, Mark Etherington, the British CPA governorate coordinator in Wasit, reported that as soon as he started his job, Iraqis showed up to see him—"tribal chiefs, heads of parties, trade union delegates, police officers, contractors." Many demanded power but could not say what they would do with it. "There was no all-embracing society in Wasit to speak of, but rather a series of camps and cliques—miniature societies—each with its own place. Most were quick to denounce the others, and compromise was rare." So, it was hard to learn the truth about anything, as the response was almost always self-serving, conflicted with other opinions, and depended on the loyalties of the person asked.[4]

Power and money are thus zero-sum games: One group's gain is another's equal loss. It's hard to build a democracy on attitudes like that.

Storm Clouds and Hazy Forecasts

On November 12, 2003, a suicide truck bomb had killed nineteen Italians and nine Iraqis at the Italian military police station in Nasariya, capital of Dhi Qar, south of Maysan. The police station was next to the RTI compound; RTI staff were injured by shattered glass and the building slightly damaged. It was an opening signal to RTI and the CPA that their facilities and employees were not all safe.

Security noticeably deteriorated by early 2004, marked by a series of kidnappings, beheadings, and other atrocities. Iraqis working with the Coalition in Basra were assassinated. On February 12, 2004, someone with a grenade and a knife tried to enter the same RTI-Nasariya compound. On February 22 an RTI convoy in northern Iraq was fired on, striking the vehicles but fortunately missing the passengers. The RTI-Mosul team in northern Iraq relocated after bad incidents threatened its compound. RTI-Ramadi in Anbar, west of Baghdad, was downsized as a result of major security problems.[5]

On March 9 Fern Holland, a successful and charismatic CPA human rights advisor from Oklahoma, was murdered near Hilla along with her Iraqi interpreter, Salwa Oumashi, and CPA colleague and retired U.S. Marine colonel Robert Zangas. Many RTI staff had worked with Fern. By all accounts she was awesome—incredibly effective, tirelessly dedicated, and an inspiration to Iraqis in women's rights and other human rights groups. This advocacy made enemies, and she and the others were shot dead in their car by men in police uniforms. Fern was only thirty-three.[6]

Increasingly, the major threat to the Coalition and its programs came from Moqtada Al-Sadr and his growing band of followers. The media coverage followed the military developments but mostly missed the larger story unfolding at ground level.

The story behind the story. Moqtada's father, Mohammed Mohammed Sadeq Al-Sadr, was controversial but was revered by many of the Shia faithful. He had made himself an alternative "object of emulation" (called a *marja*) to the grand ayatollahs of the Islamic studies seminary (*hawza*) in Najaf, where Sistani was the acknowledged leader. Al-Sadr directed his charismatic appeal at the illiterate, poor, and marginalized, gathering a corps of young clerics to make Friday prayers at the mosque an occasion for emotional political rhetoric before large crowds.

Al-Sadr the father managed to get along for a time with Saddam. But his moves antagonized the *hawza* leadership in Najaf—the real target of his movement—and he was opposed by SCIRI and other exile groups, in part over his perceived Saddam connection. However, having developed a very large following and having refused Saddam's demands to end the politically focused Friday services driving his popularity, his movement was targeted. He was assassinated in February 1999 on Saddam's orders, along with two of his four sons. A massive Shia protest in Baghdad was brutally suppressed, with 3,000 arrests and nearly 450 executions.[7]

Formal leadership of Al-Sadr's organization was assumed by his top assistant. Once Saddam fell, however, Moqtada quickly started his own organization and began a bid for power. Sadrist militants ran the Baathists out of the huge Saddam City slum in Baghdad—whose residents were overwhelmingly from rural tribal areas in southern Iraq—and renamed it Sadr City for Al-Sadr the father. His appeal to the poor had made him highly popular among its marginalized residents and had earned the deference of most tribal leaders and clergy there. That legacy gave Moqtada instant popularity and enabled him to assume a measure of control in a place where other Shia leaders and the CPA had little influence. Sadr City had 2 to 2.5 million people—almost half of Baghdad's population—crowded into a relatively small area.

Even more ominous was the simultaneous power play against the Shia establishment. In March 2003 Moqtada seized control of important Shia shrines in Najaf, including its holiest, the Imam Ali Mosque, a rich source of revenue from religious taxes.

That move was quickly followed on April 10 by the assassination of Imam Abdul Majid Al-Khoei at the Imam Ali Mosque by a Sadrist mob. Al-Khoei was only forty but was well-known and well regarded and had returned from exile in Britain just one week earlier. Moqtada was accused of ordering the murder. The charge hung over his head while the CPA weighed when or how to arrest him. Based on a U.S. investigation, Sadr had ordered Al-Khoei's assassination, refused to let him in when he somehow broke away from the mob beating and stabbing him and banged frantically at Sadr's office door, and ordered the men to kill him after he was helped across the street into a shop. Al-Khoei was dragged out and shot in the head.[8]

Moqtada was only thirty and made no pretense of being an emerging Islamic scholar. But he had not risen suddenly out of the desert. The apparent purpose behind his moves was to remove the Shia leadership in Najaf from their position of dominance in favor of a new power structure linked to his father's teachings.

By contrast, Al-Khoei's father, Abulqasim Al-Khoei, an Iranian like Sistani, was Iraq's leading grand ayatollah from 1971 to his death in 1992 at ninety-two. He mostly stayed out of politics and avoided challenging Saddam. He was succeeded by the scholarly Sistani, who had moved from Iran to Najaf in 1951 to study under Al-Khoei and became his most distinguished disciple. Sistani likewise avoided any overt political role and remained silent during the remaining years of Saddam's rule, seldom appearing in public. Sadr the father wanted to move the Shia in a much more political and nationalistic direction.

Al-Khoei the son was thus a presumed Sistani ally and had strong Western connections. He symbolized the compatibility of Islam and democracy. The British and Americans had counted on him to play an important role in the new Iraq. His death was a huge loss. The clear effect of this outrageous crime was to eliminate a pro-Sistani imam who was a potential rival of Moqtada.

Moqtada vigorously denied the murder charge, but the shocking move that followed reinforced the suspicions. Right after the assassination, armed Sadrists surrounded the homes of the three foreign-born grand ayatollahs, including Sistani, and ordered them to leave. It was the ultimate power play. Had it worked, the only cleric in position to inherit the leadership of the Shia in Iraq or designate a new grand *marja* would have been Moqtada Al-Sadr. The coup was stopped by the intervention of thousands of armed tribesmen.[9]

Moqtada's Mehdi Army was started in mid-2003 and cast as a religious movement. It was the latest example of Iraqi religious leaders endorsing violence to achieve political ends. It soon had several thousand members, weapons for all, and an array of rocket-propelled grenades (RPGs), mortars, and improvised explosive devices (IEDs).

The Mehdi Army owed its name and mystique to a Shia prophecy. *Mehdi* means "the promised one." The Mehdi is the twelfth imam, who will reappear as the redeemer of Islam and bring justice to the world. The connection to the Mehdi is not mentioned in the Koran. However, Moqtada exploited the prophecy to build up his leadership image; members were encouraged to call him "son of the Mehdi."

In October 2003 Moqtada tried to seize the central Karbala area that includes its two holiest shrines. He was foiled because the CPA learned of the plot; U.S. troops blocked the road from Baghdad to Karbala and intercepted 362 buses carrying about 10,000 Sadr militiamen. There were also significant power plays in Sadr City, Basra, and other cities.[10]

Some tribal and religious leaders in the South-Central Region saw Moqtada and his Mehdi Army as a serious threat. Many would have felt relieved to see him in jail, though they dared not say so publicly. As for the *hawza* leaders in Najaf and the southern Iraq religious establishment in general, it was known that privately they intensely disliked Moqtada Al-Sadr.

By March 2004, just as my Democracy Team presentations were about to launch, there was much talk in the United States and at the CPA about finally confronting Moqtada. Other considerations favored waiting and hoping for a better moment to move against him, as arresting him could provoke a major uprising.

A simultaneous concern was the crisis in Fallujah, a hostile anti-U.S. city of over 200,000 and historically a crossroads for cross-border trade and smuggling. The ugly March 31 incident in which four private Blackwater Agency security men were ambushed, murdered, dragged through the streets while people celebrated, and two of their bodies hung from a bridge, grabbed attention in the United States, including at the White House. The tough U.S. military response killed a lot of people but further galvanized anti-American opinion, and a wider revolt followed in Anbar. The president, who had famously declared victory in Iraq a year earlier, now faced a military crisis on two fronts.

Larry Diamond was in Hilla as security there deteriorated. On April

1 he returned to Baghdad and met Bremer that night, urging him to send in the marines. Bremer would not consider this. He refused even to send twenty marines and two Humvees to Nasariya to help Rory Stewart, who was facing repeated attacks.[11]

As Diamond feared, they were out of time. He was later critical of the CPA's refusal to confront Sadr, which only made him bolder. "Sadr kept pushing, and the United States kept waiting, warning, wavering, delaying, and debating."[12] This failure was about to have major consequences for our Local Governance Program in Amarah.

Getting Run Out of Town

The Sadrist Uprising

There had been demonstrations and people gathering outside the Pink Palace lately but no inkling of any major unrest. In faraway Baghdad, however, U.S. soldiers on Bremer's orders shut down the inflammatory Sadr newsletter on March 28, and on April 3 a senior Moqtada aide and twelve others were arrested for alleged roles in the Al-Khoei assassination.[13]

April 4, 2004. Amarah suddenly came under attack as part of a coordinated campaign by the Mehdi Army to seize power in southern Iraq. They overcame Coalition troops in some cities, seizing Kut from the Ukrainians; part of Nasariya and its CPA compound, before the Italians regained control; Najaf and Kufa from Spanish and Salvadoran troops; and part of Karbala. Sadrists then ambushed a U.S. patrol in Sadr City, killing eight soldiers. One was Casey Sheehan, whose mother, Cindy, became a nationally prominent antiwar activist in reaction to his death.[14] Bremer issued a tough statement but still made no move against Al-Sadr.

The Amarah uprising sent us scurrying back to Abu Naji for the second time in four months. This time it was more serious. I noticed the reluctance of Iraqi staff to come out to Abu Naji—for fear of being targeted if seen there.

Although it was a secret from me, Kifaya and others were organizing a celebration for my birthday on April 7. We got run out of town three days before the party.

Being at Abu Naji was more dangerous this time. The Mehdi Army was firing mortars at the base; I could hear them as they landed, though not close. I was told they had always been inaccurate and that their rounds allowed British gunners to zero in on their positions. Somehow the reassurances and being tired from a stressful day let me go to sleep. No mortars landed close by. It was, however, the first time in my life that people were actually trying to kill me. As I thought about it later, it did not seem like a casual matter.

Other expats also evacuated to Abu Naji, including a small team from Hart Security, out of London, responsible for protecting newly rebuilt power lines in Kut. Sadrists had attacked their house, just 500 meters (1,600 feet) from the CPA compound. One team member bled to death on the roof, where the group had fled. The Ukrainian troops ignored urgent CPA pleas to help them. The Hart team had to jump from the roof and commandeer a car to escape.[15] Now they looked dispirited, unable to do anything but wait and talk quietly among themselves. Maybe I should have said something in sympathy, but they seemed disengaged from everyone else, and I left them alone.

The Kut uprising also started on April 4, when 500 Sadrist protesters blocked the compound's two exits, trapping the RTI and CPA staffs. On April 5 no Iraqi security guards on the morning shift showed up. The police deserted their posts, as did the Iraqi Civil Defense Corps. The Ukrainian troops withdrew from the city, then refused to budge.[16]

On April 6, Sadrists occupied the roofs of houses overlooking the compound and started firing RPGs into it. All but two RTI guards on duty ran away; over two days seventy-eight of eighty guards failed to perform. The Iraqi Civil Defense Corps members again fled. The governorate coordinator's bodyguard team, PSDs, and even RTI civilians were forced into a desperate self-defense struggle aided greatly by the few Ukrainians accidentally trapped on the compound side of the river when the others took off.[17] Members of our Kut team later told me of their harrowing ordeal on the roof of a building, bullets whizzing past their heads and they returning fire.

The next morning the Ukrainians ignored an order from the U.S. commander in Baghdad to evacuate the civilians. Two U.S. Apache helicopters finally showed up to provide protection as the civilians escaped across the bridge to the Ukrainian base.[18] The recently renovated compound that provided room, board, and hospitality on our unscheduled one-night stop was totally looted and destroyed.

The near-disaster in Kut exposed the unreliability of some Coalition military partners. It was a good thing for us that Maysan was in the British zone.

Back in Amarah, the uprising showed that the Mehdi Army had significant support in Maysan. The British did not immediately counterattack, leaving a situation of instability. In fact, the unit at Abu Naji rotated out on April 18.[19] By contrast, the Sadrists were only a small minority in Basra, making that uprising an "abject failure."[20]

All of this happened just as my Campaign for Democracy was going into high gear. Our school schedule was already as tight as it could be if we were to finish by the end of classes in mid-April, and now we faced an indefinite delay. After all my work, I feared that much of my democracy program was about to be lost.

With no time to lose, I immediately started writing instructions to the Democracy Team. I mean that literally, as my laptop was unusable at no-tech Abu Naji. I wrote (actually printed) furiously for hours. First, I asked the team to make an emergency appeal on my behalf to Superintendent Laith to let us extend democracy presentations into the schools' study period, between mid-April and the end of the month. Assuming, hopefully, that he would agree but without knowing if he could, I revised team assignments to shift our entire short-term schedule to the schools, delaying all other presentations until after schools had closed. Maybe I was crazy to think we could still pull this off, but for Dr. Tom in Iraq, every big decision so far had worked. This one worked too. Laith came through again and agreed to my request.

On April 6, two days after the Sadrist uprising started, Bremer chose to release his final guidance on the authority of provincial and local governments. At that point there was nothing I could do about it.

A Slight Change of Plans

With its southern Iraq projects interrupted and no place for expats to work, RTI decided to let anyone who so desired go on R&R. Ahmed, Frank, and Yuen left for Dubai. But Denny, Jabir, Thierry, Tressan, and I made a calculated, if somewhat risky, decision to return to Amarah. There was no ongoing military action there, and we worried about the impact of our absence on our staff and programs. We made a big decision—to leave the next morning.

Early the next morning Denny got a message from RTI's top managers in North Carolina. They had made a *really* big decision. They ordered all southern Iraq staff out of Iraq. Everyone was ordered to go to Kuwait.

A nerve-racking incident ongoing in the South-Central Region helped drive the decision. An RTI expat had been kidnapped—a Palestinian Christian with an Israeli passport. Dr. Victoria Haynes, RTI's president, issued the get-out-of-Iraq order after the kidnapped expat was put on TV by his captors, in part to avoid further kidnappings. To its credit, RTI later got him released, at a time when other kidnapped expats were being killed.

And so it was that instead of returning to Amarah, we found ourselves in metal vests and helmets in the back of a military truck, jouncing mercilessly over rough terrain with no road or path to the Sparrowhawk military airstrip about 4 kilometers (2.5 miles) from Abu Naji, en route to Kuwait by way of Basra.

A C-130 Hercules transport plane finally arrived after a couple of restless hours. It has cargo space in the middle and back and a huge cargo door at the rear, lowered to serve as a ramp. Passengers sit around the perimeter, holding straps for balance. It was not exactly British Airways. Given the military crisis, the thought of getting shot down in this plane was certainly on my mind. It was a great relief when it landed. Then the pilot welcomed us—to Nasariya! The nastiest city in southern Iraq! No one had told us Basra was the second stop. Thankfully, we made it to Basra, where Thierry had arranged to convoy directly to Kuwait.

In Kuwait the larger story emerged. Other cities were more dangerous than Amarah. Nasariya's team had been forced out earlier—for the second time. Karbala and Najaf had been largely seized by the Mehdi Army. Members of the Kut team had fled for their lives. The Ramadi team was out of food and well into its emergency C-rations (issued to all teams), as food convoys could no longer safely go there. For a couple of teams even getting out was dangerous. One saw an RPG rattle off its windshield. RTI had probably made the right decision, avoiding further risks to its expats. Other USAID projects also removed their expats from Iraq, some to Amman, Jordan. However, hundreds of Iraqi staff were left behind, in harm's way.

Courage under Fire

As we gathered in Kuwait, the Coalition gradually regained control of Iraq. On April 16 the United States sent its own troops to retake Kut and other Wasit cities, inflicting serious casualties. Aided by local tribesmen, they took back Diwaniya and Karbala on May 5, then attacked in Kufa and Najaf after angry Najaf residents attacked the Mehdi Army. The militia took heavy losses in Najaf, and its remaining fighters retreated into the Imam Ali Mosque. A deal was then negotiated through Sistani for their withdrawal. The Coalition also asserted control in Sadr City.

For three days in mid-May, however, Rory Stewart's CPA-Nasariya compound endured a fierce mortar and RPG attack. The Italians did little to help, then took offense when he complained to Baghdad. They finally evacuated all his civilian expats but drove them through an ambush to do it. His bodyguard team saved the compound. The United States finally sent one helicopter gunship, which took out the mortars, and many Sadrist militiamen.[21]

In Maysan the newly arrived British troops faced frequent ambushes and IEDs. But good intelligence pinpointed the southwestern Amarah location of Mehdi Army leaders. On May 1 the Brits made numerous arrests there and captured a lot of arms and ammunition but had to shoot their way out, suffering numerous injuries. They fought a fierce daytime battle just to get needed ammo and supplies to CIMIC House; the gutsy Molly Phee was still there! On May 8, shortly after midnight, they sent a large armored contingent into Amarah, supported by a U.S. helicopter gunship, and gradually defeated the militia, suffering more injuries in the process. After storming the Sadr office before dawn and removing a huge cache of weapons and ammo, the British resumed control of the streets.[22]

On May 14 they fought off a series of Mehdi Army roadway ambushes north of Majar Al-Kebir. The outnumbered Brits outgunned them from their armored vehicles, killing about seventy.[23] A bizarre scene then unfolded that illustrates the destructiveness of rumors in Iraq. The Brits recovered twenty bodies and brought them to Abu

Naji, some in gruesome condition. The British commander arranged to hand them over to Majar's chief of police. A rumor was circulated at the handover, however, that the dead militiamen were not killed in action but had been captured and executed. By one account Governor Riyadh, Abu Hatim, and a third Mahood brother showed up, and Abu Hatim converted the rumor into an accusation that the men had been tortured and mutilated. When the chief disagreed, a brief argument was ended by one of the Mahoods shooting him in the head, killing him. A medical doctor was produced to give credence to the apparently false accusation.[24]

By another account the British used local intelligence on the planned ambush to set up a counter-ambush. Those killed were fellow tribesmen of Abu Hatim. After the rumor started, the British commander sent the bodies to the hospital morgue so as to get independent confirmation that the rumor was false. The Mahoods confronted the Badr-linked chief at the morgue, and Abu Hatim accused him of tipping off the British to the ambush, which suggests a different motive for the shooting. In the ensuing argument the chief was shot dead, reportedly by the governor![25]

Riyadh was soon indicted. The Badr-linked Maysan police chief, Abu Maythem, felt he could not arrest him, however, as he would be accused of political motives. The British also felt it politically unwise to arrest him. Molly talked the governor into stepping aside temporarily. Riyadh delegated some authority to Sheikh Rahim, the deputy governor, until the situation calmed down, but did not resign. When the CPA, through Molly, turned over authority to the Provincial Council shortly afterward, Riyadh simply resumed his position. I learned later that the Mahoods paid "blood money" to the chief's family. By different accounts the Mahoods got the Ministry of Interior to drop the charges and/or Riyadh got a pardon from a judge in Baghdad.[26] None of the brothers went to jail. The whole truth may never be known.

The Majar accusation against the British soldiers reached Great Britain and reverberated for years. There was a court hearing, and in late 2009 a public inquiry was announced by the Ministry of Defense that didn't begin until March 2013. In March 2014, ten years after the rumor started, the lawyers for the Iraqi families dropped their allegations for lack of evidence.

The Mehdi Army took several hundred casualties overall. It was eventually persuaded to give up, and its fighters were allowed to leave Najaf. Sadr was never arrested; the Mehdi Army was left intact.

Meanwhile on April 20, my Democracy Team, with Mr. Laith's approval, resumed its school presentations, which had been suspended since April 5. Kifaya's upbeat email assured me that "nothing is wrong, the situation is quiet, the villas are safe, all the staff are well." The team reached over 10,000 students over the next week—and this was almost two weeks before the British resumed control of Amarah. Some presentations were cited in a USAID weekly report. These accomplishments under such tense conditions made me proud of them—but also nervous.

After the clashes in May, the British CIMIC unit resumed its community projects. It created fourteen community centers around Amarah, each with a staff member, meeting rooms, TV, videos, and a library; offered self-improvement classes; helped start 109 new businesses through $500 incentive payments; and implemented a $7.5 million program to upgrade water and sewer services. These and other projects won citizen cooperation.[27]

Britain's Maysan military commander resumed his diplomatic offensive with political factions and other groups, including the Sadr office. He saw the Sadr political organization as separate from the Mehdi Army, with "many sane and reasonable members."[28] I understood this distinction at long distance but found it hard to discern the separation when the party office was also the weapons depot for the militia.

The result of the Sadrist uprising was a complete military victory for the Coalition, but for the civilian coalition it started a downward spiral in the South that would not soon be reversed.

Project Management from Long Distance
So Near and Yet So Far

Kuwait and Iraq are next-door neighbors. They have almost nothing in common.

Like Iraq, the much smaller Kuwait is an oil-producing state. However, it produces so much oil, and without the corruption afflicting

Iraq's oil business, that it can make every native-born Kuwaiti economically self-sufficient just from the revenues.

People with money to spend need stores and services on which to spend it. This drives a thriving commercial sector, which in turn needs workers—hence, all the non-natives who came to Kuwait to create businesses or to work jobs Kuwaitis don't need. The million or so native Kuwaitis are outnumbered by 2 to 2.5 million non-Kuwaitis ineligible for citizenship. Some come from Iran or from Egypt or other Arab states, but many are from India, Pakistan, Bangladesh, Sri Lanka and the Philippines, none Arabic speaking and all with English as at least a second language. Many native Kuwaitis have learned English, and at least in Kuwait City they often need it. So Kuwait seems like an English-speaking country in the heart of the Middle East.

Official census statistics say the vast majority of Kuwaitis are Muslims—70 percent Sunnis, 30 percent Shia. A large minority of the non-natives however, are not Muslims. The Filipinos are heavily Catholic, and the South Asians seem to include a disproportionate percentage of Christians. Kuwait is one example, and not the only one, of the great diversity among Middle East nations that we typically fail to see.

RTI now had almost its entire Iraq staff in Kuwait and had to house and feed them. That money was not in the contract, and the cost of living was far higher in Kuwait than in Iraq. After about four days each at the Sheraton and a new European hotel, we settled in at the six-story Salmiya Palace, less modern but with lots of Middle Eastern personality. The units were two stories, the bed, with a mirror directly above it, occupying the second level. (I know what you're thinking.)

The neighborhood was astonishing. For many blocks on both sides of the main street, it was a major commercial strip mixing Western and local businesses. Past Hugo Boss on the left and an Italian coffee shop on the right was a fast food heaven, with Hardee's, Kentucky Fried Chicken, Baskin-Robbins, Pizza Hut, and Subway, among others. We now had a daily expense allowance and ate on our own, except for the hotel's breakfast buffet. A range of sit-down restaurants within walking distance included a sushi bar, which was Ahmed's favorite, plus Chinese, French, Iranian, and other international cuisines. I discovered a locally owned sandwich shop just off the main drag and a café run by a young Indian Christian. For in-room munching, a modern food store co-located with a department store offered food choices comparable to supermarkets in the West.

Commerce was booming, much of it in large, multistory indoor malls full of upscale jewelry stores and other shops with mostly Western goods. Foreign investment is evident on every block. The rhythm of Kuwaiti commercial life is different, however. In mid to late afternoon, stores seemed almost deserted; many closed temporarily after 2:00. Adjusting to the heat, people prefer to shop at night. Stores deserted at 2:00 p.m. were bustling even at 9:00 p.m. or later.

As we adjusted to the neighborhood, we learned more about what it could do for us. I used the modern International Clinic a few blocks away for overdue cancer-related lab tests. A modern office supplies store was a needed convenience, ditto the money exchange in the same building. A brisk walk away, a Marks and Spencer (British) clothing store was a boon to the wardrobe, especially as most of mine was still in Amarah. More shops and restaurants were an easy bus ride away. Along the road to downtown and RTI's office, I saw many familiar American restaurants and other businesses. Best of all, we were free to roam without security.

All of this affirmed the power of private enterprise and international commerce to advance a nation's prosperity. The mirror opposite was just north across the border, where the Baathists' state-run socialist economy drew almost no foreign investment and impoverished almost everyone, despite all its oil wells.

Meanwhile, back in Amarah, Molly Phee advised us they had identified a building for the women's center—a former youth center needing serious rehab. CPA-Maysan offered $50,000 to help the project, added to the LGP's $90,000. Denny asked Kifaya to follow up with Molly.

A Management Dilemma in Three Parts

While the hotel was pleasant, RTI's situation was unpleasant. It faced three simultaneous management crises. First, the budget for Year 2 coming up was actually lower than for Year 1. USAID ruled out allocating additional funds to cover escalating security costs, now *one-third of the entire project cost!* The Kuwait stay, which had no time limit, was also on RTI's money, as was the cost of restoring buildings looted in our absence (though not in Amarah). So, the organization had to downsize, and word was out that cutback decisions were imminent. Having escaped Iraq under dangerous conditions, people now had to worry about being laid off.

Second, RTI had to downsize the project plans we had just completed to accommodate the reality of having fewer expats to carry them out. This would have to be done by people who didn't know if they would still be around to implement what they wrote.

Third, RTI had accumulated a serious level of bad feeling within the staff, partly from the unavoidable circumstances but also from a range of other issues. Previously, it could deal with each team separately, from a distance. Now it had to face the entire crowd in one place at one time. I sympathized with some of the grievances but also felt bad for RTI.

Making it all more difficult was the reality that no one knew when we would return to Iraq. Yuen had been the most pessimistic, predicting when we were still at Abu Naji that we would never be able to return.

Chuck Costello had just resigned as deputy chief of party (DCOP), and to its credit RTI replaced him with Lamar Cravens, the well-regarded Diwaniya team leader, a lawyer by training and one of the project's most articulate critics. In another smart decision Peter Benedict stayed in Baghdad for a time and let Cravens deal with everyone, leaving the unpopular status quo without a spokesman.

The result was disarmingly effective. Everyone not on R&R gathered on April 14 for the day 1 all-day mass meeting. Cravens let it all hang out, showing people he was on their side. He had a sure grasp of every issue, gave straight-up answers to every question, often answered critical comments by agreeing with them, and in general conveyed the message that RTI management was finally going to address people's concerns.

Cravens needed immediate help, however, to revise each team's project plan. He apologized that this had to be done in the face of impending cutbacks. Yuen, our main planner, was on R&R, so it was me or nobody. Who knew, anyway, what the real plan would be in a few months?

The real heartache was in the staff reductions. RTI decided it needed a stable, albeit reduced, staffing level that would continue for a year instead of counting on attrition to gradually bring the project within budget. This decision meant more layoffs now. The gravity of the situation was clear from the presence of numerous RTI home office officials. They could only express appreciation to those being laid off and regrets for the situation, but not doing that would have left people feeling worse.

RTI determined the number of program staff it could support in each city and delegated the cutback decisions to its team leaders. Denny called a very brief team meeting at the Salmiya Palace, expressed regrets and his appreciation for everyone's contribution, but said he could not drop his key program managers, Tressan and me. He and three others were not defined as program staff. So, Jabir and Frank lost the game of musical chairs.

Jabir first went back to the family home near Diwaniya to get his wife and child, who had flown over to visit, and say good-bye. Security had deteriorated so badly that he felt unsafe in his own village and had to abandon his plan to visit the Democracy Team in Amarah before leaving. The whole situation was discouraging. It would get worse.

Two weeks later, on April 27, RTI dropped the ax on more people, both operations and program staff, including some of its most established staff. Not to his surprise, Denny lost out, as did Thierry. Ahmed, saved by Peter Benedict's personal intercession, was again the team leader. RTI had now laid off one-third of the expat staff. They were cutting in Baghdad too.

At a "remobilization meeting" for remaining staff later the same day, RTI leaders were at pains to reassure and encourage people. They said the project still had bipartisan support in Congress, that it had exceeded everyone's expectations, that Bremer had expressed his admiration, and that USAID administrator Andrew Natsios had called LGP the best project in Iraq. Benedict said our field reports showed we were still succeeding despite not being there, an evaluation to which my Democracy Team was a major contributor.

Through all this stress RTI kept encouraging us to take our R&R, and many did. I had put it off for five months, as I felt it would hurt our progress in Amarah if I left, especially with our democracy campaign approaching peak activity. Now I couldn't be there anyway, but aside from knowing my continuing remote guidance was critical, I felt nervous about leaving, as many of those axed had been on R&R at the time. Maybe it was a coincidence, but the management analyst in me discerned that it was easier and cheaper to cut people already sitting at home. My initial contract period was up on May 31. I decided to wait until then and take no chances.

Lost in Translation

RTI was working against contradictions. It was planning for an early return but didn't know when or to where. Some RTI cities were still too dangerous. I was one of those whose return was the last step in the process. The target start date was June 1; I sensed it was written in pencil.

Meanwhile, discussions were under way about the Civic Dialogue Program (CDP) and its Democracy Dialogue Activity (DDA). The provincial coordinators and headquarters staff started meeting four days after we arrived in Kuwait. As discussions went on, I started to win a few policy arguments, like the need to incorporate media strategies.

Gurbux Singh, the dynamic new CDP manager from England, was working hard to get the DDA extended past June 30 to the elections in December. His able deputy and national DDA manager, Jared Hayes, also visited Kuwait. Planning for the extension was our main focus. The elections would be a perfect civic education opportunity. We had about 550 dedicated and trained Iraqis already working on DDA, and still succeeding in spite of everything.

Indeed, I was impressed with how much some other RTI teams were accomplishing under such duress. Minda Hedges's Basra team was doing events for more groups than Maysan even had; we reached more participants because we did the schools first. By the end of April DDA had reached 172,000 people across Iraq. Shortly after that, the total went over 500,000. Eventually, AID estimated on its website that the DDA had produced 22,000 dialogues with 790,000 participants (36 per event). It's not clear how AID got numbers so much higher than RTI's.

So, why was Singh still having a struggle to extend DDA? The inside scoop was that AID wanted to extend it but emphasized its "limited resources"; that is, it wanted RTI to extend without additional funds. As we had just cut expat staffing in half because of

AID decisions, this was unfair. Meanwhile, it was late May, and I had thirty-five Iraqis back in Amarah wondering if they had a job after June 30.

Nothing could change the bottom-line fact that just when the project was most needed, we were being forced to cut back. At the policy level, this made no sense. It was not the only time or the last time that decisions made in Washington would be lost in translation.

Letters of Sadness

Someone in Kuwait offered an amusing analysis that caught on, perhaps because it rang true. "One-third of RTI staff are still working hard; one-third are pretending to be working; and the other third are not even pretending." From day 1 at Abu Naji, I was in group 1. I still had thirty-five employees in Amarah. Telephone connections to Amarah being unreliable, I had to rely on daily emails to send my often detailed guidance to the team. Jawaad was monitoring the Provincial Council alone, as I had no way to keep up with it from Kuwait.

On April 23 I wrote a nine-page "Message of Thanks, Sadness, and Hope to the Democracy Team." I thanked them for continuing our work in spite of the instability in Maysan, explained our hasty exit from Iraq, and reported sadly on Jabir's departure and on the other staff reductions, which had left us with only four of our eight expats. I explained how to reorganize the presentation teams now that the school phase was over and reported the efforts to extend the DDA and their jobs past June 30. I also told them I would leave soon for two weeks of vacation and medical appointments in the States. Anticipating some anxiety on that, I said, "I have every intention of returning to Amarah to work with you. *I will not abandon you.*"

Four days later I learned I was being transferred to Kut. I was shocked. The decision wasn't adversarial toward me, but I thought it insensitive and unwise. Continuity had been compromised already by losing half our expat staff, and we had already put enormous stress on our Iraqi staff by leaving them during an armed uprising. The decision makers had failed to consider the likely damage to existing relationships or the difficulty of replacing them. Nothing else RTI ever did caused me so much unhappiness.

This news meant a second sad letter. I had added some optimism to the first letter; this one was just sad. I was almost in tears just to write it, as I knew it would cause discouragement. I told them in conclusion, "You may have lost me from your work, but you have made a friend who will always be loyal to you. I will never forget you." There was not much else I could say.

I received responses that were heartwarming but deeply sad. Jawaad said he had spent his "best moments of life" with me. Ta'meem responded to "the saddest message of my life" with a long and emotional message "to the Angel from America." Other team members were also devastated, she said, quoting a saying, "Brave is the person who sings while his eyes are filled with tears." She added that Dr. Tom had gained "full confidence from Iraqis, who only with difficulty put their confidence in people."

These words reminded me in the most personal way of why I loved my team in Amarah. Would anyone receiving such messages ever want to leave the people who sent them?

Despite all the heartache, however, the reassignment was so far meaningless. No one could go to Kut right now anyway. No one from the Kut team came to see me, and when I asked how I could help, they had no requests. RTI was obviously clueless about how much work I was doing. So, I kept working with my Democracy Team in Amarah. The team was still doing great things.

The Democracy Team: Against All Odds

One Awesome Success Story

In spite of all the turmoil, the Democracy Team continued its presentations. By the end of April, as our extended school presentations ended, they had reached over 28,000 people, one of the highest totals of all RTI offices, despite Maysan's relatively small population.

Team members showed courage in the face of Sadrist pressure. Shortly after the expats left, a team member suspected of Sadrist sympathies urged presentation teams not to go out, saying it was too dangerous. Others, however, including Kifaya, insisted on going out. Ta'meem offered to go with Kifaya, feeling that her courage should be supported. Kifaya was vocal in saying she was loyal to RTI and refused to be less effective in its absence than when it was there.

The team rolled into May with my revised organization and worked factories, hospitals, the court system, and ministry offices. For the month they reached about 2,000 adults. By the end of May they had reached a total of 30,000 people directly and thousands more at home through the hats and booklets. It was an amazing achievement, one that I will remember for the rest of my life.

In late May, Ta'meem told me in one message that the team was "still happy despite the fact that you are not with us, because you are in our hearts." The feeling was certainly mutual.

The Real Majority

At the end of May the team tallied up all the Democracy Survey results and sent them to me. The results reveal a lot about how Iraqis actually feel about democracy.

DEMOCRACY SURVEY: YOUR PERSONAL OPINIONS ABOUT DEMOCRACY

Answer the ten questions below by circling YES or NO. Do not sign your name. Your answers will be analyzed later.

1. I want political leaders to be elected by the people, and I will vote when the elections are held.

Adults:	YES	84 percent	NO	16 percent
Students:	YES	85 percent	NO	15 percent

2. Any adult citizen should have the right to be a candidate for elected positions.

Adults:	YES	76 percent	NO	24 percent
Students:	YES	75 percent	NO	25 percent

3. People should have rights that cannot be taken away by their governments.

Adults:	YES	94 percent	NO	6 percent
Students:	YES	82 percent	NO	18 percent

4. I should be allowed to express any opinion without fear.

Adults:	YES	99 percent	NO	1 percent
Students:	YES	87 percent	NO	13 percent

5. Journalists should be able to write any honest story, even if it is embarrassing to the government.

Adults:	YES	98 percent	NO	2 percent
Students:	YES	89 percent	NO	11 percent

6. The priorities for Maysan should be set by people in Maysan rather than by the central government in Baghdad.

Adults:	YES	80 percent	NO	20 percent
Students:	YES	70 percent	NO	30 percent

7. Democracy is in harmony with Islam.

Adults:	YES	92 percent	NO	8 percent
Students:	YES	78 percent	NO	22 percent

8. The constitution of Iraq should be consistent with Islamic principles.

Adults:	YES	98 percent	NO	2 percent
Students:	YES	87 percent	NO	13 percent

9. Government laws should be separate from religious laws, even though they may reflect Islamic principles.

Adults:	YES	41 percent	NO	59 percent
Students:	YES	60 percent	NO	40 percent

10. Islam stands for equality, but cultural traditions in Iraq have given men more rights than women. Should women be given rights equal to those of men?

Adults:	YES	73 percent	NO	27 percent
Students:	YES	67 percent	NO	33 percent

Several clarifications apply.

The YES (pro-democracy) answers for adults were consistently higher than for students. The likely explanation is that most adult programs were held before self-selecting, more-educated audiences, whereas the school programs reached a 100 percent cross-section of Maysan so got a higher percentage of conservative responses.

The one exception was question 9, on which students were much more willing to separate government from religion. I have no theory for this outcome.

Notice the fault line on questions 8 and 9. One can infer that about half the population preferred an Islamic state to a state that separates religion and government. Based on their other answers, however, the same people assume that such a state will be highly democratic.

The percentages on women's rights, question 10, are encouraging no matter how you look at them. One is left to contemplate why opinion and practice are so divergent. Or, if we had counted male and female responses separately, would we have explained some of this difference?

In general the Democracy Survey results showed that the real majority of Iraqis want to live in a democracy. While the results were being tallied, we were learning how easy it is for people using threats and violence to overrule the real majority.

Matters of Concern

As our absence dragged on, day-to-day decisions in Amarah were left to Iraqis with limited or no management experience. Staff whose job was to provide direct services to expats (e.g., food) were eventually terminated, creating unhappiness. Some staff who were happy to follow expat guidance were less willing to accept instructions from Iraqis. Personality conflicts developed. These stress factors added to the personal risks every employee was taking.

Each expat had named one person to a management team that served in our absence. One of the engineers was designated the team leader but got threatened and was a married man with a baby, so he quit. Ahmed then designated Dr. Saba, Kifaya's daughter, in whom he had always had confidence. She tried to be a strong leader, but issues arose, and she met opposition.

Saba and Kifaya were getting a security escort to and from work every day because of the earlier threat letter. Each morning three RTI guards came to their house to pick up Saba, and Kifaya went with her. This stress was added to all the other pressures.

All of this gave us reasons for concern as our pleasant but anxious exile in Kuwait neared the end of its second month.

4

Bottoming Out

Murder in Maysan

May 29, 2004, a routine Saturday morning at RTI-Kuwait. Suddenly a local staff member walks into the main office area and announces that someone at RTI-Amarah has just been killed! Totally stunned and horrified, I demanded to know who. He didn't have the name right, but it sounded like it could be Kifaya. Ahmed quickly grabbed a telephone to call Amarah. He confirmed the worst.

How are you supposed to react when a friend is murdered? When someone dies from cancer or a heart condition or old age, there is usually time to adjust mentally before the event. This was beyond anything I had experienced in a fairly long life. It was worse because I had worked closely with Kifaya, she had been very loyal, and I knew she was fond of me. I started thinking about how terrifying it must have been in her final moments but did not want to think about it. I went through the motions of working through the rest of the day, but I felt numb. When I finally got back to the hotel and walked through my door, I broke down in tears, then in prayers. Hardly anything in life had ever made me cry and never in this way. It was all too much.

Reflecting on it later, I realized in a personal way how soldiers feel when they lose a buddy. I felt an instant connection to those who live with this risk every day and endure terrible moments. I now understood at an emotional level why soldiers can feel haunted by traumatic events for the rest of their lives and why old soldiers can break into tears even decades later.

Ahmed wanted to go to Amarah for the funeral period, security risks be damned. A funeral period in Iraq follows the burial and includes individual visits to the decedent's home over three or more days to express condolences to the family and sometimes to offer money. Saba had always been Ahmed's special favorite and needed his support. I wished I could go with him but had no realistic way to delay my U.S.

trip, scheduled for the next day. Ahmed put in an urgent request. Not surprisingly, he was denied. It was just too dangerous to go.

For reasons unknown to me, Saba later decided to write a detailed account of Kifaya's assassination and its horrible aftermath. It came to me unsolicited by an indirect route and was also the basis for an account of her death in the *Winston-Salem Journal* in North Carolina.[1] Saba's account made me even more upset.

The murder itself was particularly horrible. Saba learned the details from a neighbor who was with Kifaya and from other eyewitnesses. There were three gunmen and a driver in a gray Peugeot with no license plate. They were waiting for her. She saw them as she started out of her house to get a taxi and felt suspicious, so she asked a woman neighbor to walk out with her. Two gunmen approached. They were clumsy and shot her several times, inflicting maximum pain and leaving gruesome wounds. As she pleaded that she needed to go to RTI, one said they were killing her so that she would never go there again. She died on the sidewalk.

Saba's uncle came to the villas as she was preparing to meet with Tressan's team. He took her with him but would not explain why— until they arrived at the hospital and she learned her mother was dead. She became distraught and passed out. They took her to her aunt's house, then her grandmother's, still unconscious. Meanwhile, three gunmen in a white car circled her house, asking neighbors where she was. Had she been brought home, she would likely have been killed.

On top of this threat, she had to bury her mother, and in the Muslim tradition this must be done within twenty-four hours. By that afternoon she was in Najaf. The body was first taken to the place for the Islamic "washing the dead" ritual, which includes scenting the body and a sheet (*kafan*) to cover it for burial. Saba then saw what the assassins had done to her mother. She again became distraught. Yet in spite of her trauma, she had to clean her mother's brutalized body for burial. Being in Najaf may have saved her life again. The same white car was seen driving around the neighborhood, its occupants refusing to answer neighbors who bravely tried to stop them to ask why they were there.

Saba returned home the next day, Sunday morning, to start the funeral period. Amid the condolences came the street rationalization for why Kifaya had been killed. She was, according to these planted rumors, a spy for a Jewish organization, worked with the foreigners and occupiers, and brought only disappointment and shame on herself, so she deserved what happened to her. Notice the personal shame accusation used to impugn the reputation of women seen as political opponents.

Kifaya's murder stunned the Democracy Team and everyone else at RTI-Maysan. It also frightened them—because their own vulnerability was now starkly clear. Many avoided going to the family home during the funeral period, from fear of being targeted themselves. Molly Phee, however, made a point of coming and offered strong emotional support. Molly was close to Kifaya, who had often been at the CPA in her efforts to help women. To some rumormongers, however, her visit confirmed that Kifaya and Saba were spies for the foreigners.

The rumors grew in intensity as it became increasingly clear that the perpetrators intended to kill Saba too. She had been denounced at the mosque, basically a call to kill her. The Sadr office offered a financial reward to anyone who killed her, which showed that the Sadrists were also behind Kifaya's murder. By day 3 of the funeral period, almost no one dared to visit, even relatives.

When Kifaya's adopted son, Firas, went to the court to file a complaint, one judge declared, "Your mother was guilty." The hospital director came to the home and fired Saba from her night shift job, mainly because the hospital had been told she was at the top of the assassination list and it could not protect her. He gave her some money out of kindness. Saba had worked for years to develop a medical career, so she took this especially hard. The constant insults and threats, the feeling of isolation from lack of support, and the sheer trauma of the whole experience finally overwhelmed Saba so greatly that, by her own account, she was on the verge of suicide.

Saba's father, Kifaya's former husband, offered verbal abuse instead of emotional support. He cursed her, accused her of being a spy, and told her she had brought shame to him and his family. When she asked his advice about an RTI offer to live in another place, he slapped her in the face, told her this would make her a "bitch," and told her she should stay home and die there. He changed his mind after the mutilated body of a murder victim was found just behind her fence, convincing him she would in fact be killed if she stayed.

People friendly to Saba urged her to leave Amarah to save her life. Ahmed and Tressan called almost every day. Saba survived but was totally traumatized, her entire world shattered. She had lost her mother, who had been her inspiration, in effect had lost her father from her life, was in immediate fear for her life, yet felt responsible for her younger sister and brother. She was in no mental condition to help anyone. Somehow a way was found to get her out of Iraq. She sneaked away from home one night, camouflaged in traditional clothes, and left at dawn. Saba's sister got married shortly after her mother's death, and a local job was arranged for her brother.

Saba's written account also contained statements I was forced to take personally. She said Kifaya had left home for RTI in order to help me. Saba had gone to RTI without Kifaya, accompanied by RTI guards as usual, as they had decided Kifaya was not going that day. An hour later, however, she decided to go in. According to Saba, Kifaya was trying to find a receipt I had urgently requested for a minor expenditure, to satisfy two RTI accountants dogging me in Kuwait. By this account my message was sent to the RTI-Amarah office, someone called Kifaya that morning, and so she changed her mind and left without the usual security escort.

I checked my own records and talked to Jawaad. The story about the receipt did not match up. I had earlier asked Kifaya for a receipt or statement to cover a $50 cash item, which she sent May 19, so I would not have needed more documentation on the 29th, when I was about to leave for the United States. I always communicated to the team through Jawaad or Ta'meem, and occasionally to Kifaya, never to the main office. It remains a mystery as to who might have called or why they called or if they called on that fateful morning.

Even before reading Saba's account, I thought a lot about who had killed Kifaya. All but one of the threats against my team members had come from the Sadr office. By continuing to work after being threatened, Kifaya had defied them. The crime occurred in broad daylight in her own neighborhood in front of a witness. Based on the vehement public denunciations and men openly driving by her house looking for her, something occurring shortly before the murder could be the explanation. I know from other experience, however, that the seemingly logical explanation for a crime is often wrong. I also know that I will never forget this unforgivable crime.

Kifaya's death sent shock waves through the RTI ranks, from Amarah to North Carolina. Among the expats in Kuwait, there was a sinking feeling that the Local Governance Program had just experienced a disaster. It was like listening to the air hissing out of a huge balloon. During the summer an RTI-Baghdad employee was shot dead as she left her house for work, and RTI also suffered a third fatality.

Denny Lane later compiled all his RTI reports into a single volume dedicated to Kifaya. His dedication said that "Dr. Kifaya, more than anyone else associated with LGP-Maysan, represented both the past and the future. And if a courageous intelligentsia is a *sine qua non* of the start of any meaningful political and social reform, Dr. Kifaya was everything that the name implies. . . . That she hoped for the betterment of conditions as they pertained to the role of the women of Iraq was widely known, and it is in this capacity that I shall always remember her. She died so that the women of Iraq might enjoy a fuller life."

Kifaya became an instant symbol of much that was wrong with Iraq: its culture of violence, its political and religious intolerance, its abuse of women in every aspect of their lives. She had overcome the odds faced by most Iraqi women—becoming a successful educator while raising three children, earning a doctorate, and touching many lives. For this she had been dumped by her husband, threatened for her advocacy of democracy and women's rights, and finally shot dead on the sidewalk when she was only fifty years old. Then she was trashed through the rumor mill. These were responses of pathetic men to a woman of strength who had stood up to them with determination, dignity, and courage.

No man making excuses for the treatment of women in Iraq deserves anything better than contempt.

Progress Undone

I flew home on May 30, the day after Kifaya died. It had been the longest six months of my life. Until she died, it was also the happiest and most rewarding six months of my life. As the plane headed west, I tried not to dwell on Kifaya, but my mind was troubled.

When I left, Gurbux Singh was still trying to get the Democracy Dialogue Activity (DDA) extended past June 30. The date for RTI teams to return to Iraq was still unknown. The "final" staff cutback had been made.

I had been home two days when I heard about yet another cutback. The list of the terminated included several DDA coordinators. The next day I learned from the International City/County Management Association (ICMA), my direct employer, that I was out too. I was not on RTI's announcement list because I was on leave. For six months I passed up R&R opportunities to stay with my job. Now, just as I was finally on leave, I was also unemployed. RTI never wrote to me and never thanked me for my service.

The decision, however, was not about me. RTI had reached another big decision. It decided *not* to return to its governorate offices in the South and South-Central Regions and to close them all. It would work from regional offices only, meaning Basra and Hilla. All that hopeful planning we did in Kuwait became meaningless. Those on-paper transfers to new teams were also meaningless; no one was going to Amarah or Kut. All the work to extend the DDA was for naught. RTI's decision was an admission that the previous status quo was irretrievable. It was also a clear sign that much of our progress would be lost. My work in Amarah was being abandoned. The Maysan Provincial Council was on its own. The Campaign for Democracy was over just when it was most needed. So was the joy from a job that hugged me back.

Two months earlier the Amarah team seemed to have everything going in its favor. Project officials had described us as the most successful team on the project. We had a very large staff, creative programs, funding support from CPA-Maysan, and an impact extending to almost all of Maysan. Now it was all gone. The same fate befell the eight other governorate-level programs in South and South-Central, each with its own accomplishments and plans. It was a decisive moment of the wrong kind.

I wrote my third sad letter to the Democracy Team, already stunned by the assassination of Kifaya. I was not coming back to Iraq after all.

The Amarah office was closing. They needed to find new jobs. I shared the good news that my cancer tests showed no new cancer. As the team was no longer meeting daily and some could not read English, I had to count on my message being passed on to everyone by those who could. Although I later returned to Iraq, leaving all my friends behind in Amarah was a moment of sadness I have never fully overcome.

Back in dispirited Amarah, Jawaad became the team leader after Saba fled, supervising over a hundred staff members. This completed a rapid and remarkable professional ascent in less than one year—if only the circumstances had been less tragic. Jawaad's primary duty was transitioning RTI-Amarah for closure and laying off employees. The Amarah compound gradually closed.

A few team members found a place with another international NGO in Amarah, but for most there was no position that could bring the joy and satisfaction, and the income, from working for RTI. There would be a new civil society contractor, but it would not start until later, would also operate only from regional hubs, and would hire only two of my staff to work in Amarah. I met them later when I joined that same project in Baghdad.

All the belongings of the Amarah expats were packed up and sent via Basra to Kuwait for shipment home. Jawaad helped pack my suitcase and two boxes. His efforts were undone, however, by a bizarre border incident with Kuwaiti customs officers, who found "contraband" in the vehicle (not in my stuff). They confiscated all fifty-five bags and boxes and arrested the truck driver. Then they removed the entire contents of every single one of the fifty-five bags and boxes and threw them into one huge pile. After that there was no way to tell who owned what, and much of it was just lost. Few of my possessions came back, though RTI paid for the loss, nor did my project papers (making it harder to write this book). Let's be thankful for computer files. I received little beyond the box of items I had left at RTI-Kuwait pending return from my "vacation."

In early August RTI eliminated the positions of Gurbux Singh and his deputy, Jared Hayes, closing the final door on the Civic Dialogue Program (CDP) and DDA. They were terminated after they went on leave, by then a well-refined technique. The remaining CDP details were left to my former Amarah teammate Katie Donahue, whose earlier move to Baghdad proved good for her job tenure. She later moved over to USAID and became a Baghdad veteran.

Larry Diamond, Condoleezza Rice's democracy expert, left Iraq voluntarily two days before we left involuntarily and did not return. He saw that the insecurity from the Sadrist insurrection and the upsurge in violence threatened both expats and the Iraqis helping us. Diamond described a breakthrough moment of recognition I related to only too well. "I was speaking to this women's group, and one woman got up and asked, 'If we do these things, who's going to protect us?' That was the moment when I said to myself, 'Oh my God, some of these women are going to be assassinated because they are here listening to me.' It just struck me between the eyes."[2]

Lessons Learned: The Final Balance Sheet
Evaluating the Campaign for Democracy

Diamond later wrote about the demise of RTI's democracy program as its expats were forced to leave Iraq and the risk faced by the Iraqi facilitators left behind. He cited the DDA's accomplishments but lamented that the strategy tended to reach the converted, primarily the educated urban elite, rather than a geographic and socioeconomic cross-section. "Nevertheless," he argued, "the political culture of the country had been so brutalized that we had to start somewhere, and the dialogues at least put some key democratic issues into circulation, by reaching a segment of opinion leaders."[3]

The audience factor was one point on which the Amarah team could be especially proud, however. Because I defined our program as a political campaign, we devised strategies to reach *all* segments of Maysan society. By going to all the intermediate and secondary students first and sending materials home, we reached a broad cross-section of the population. Some of our adult democracy presentations were in factories. Had we been able to hang all the posters and distribute all the bumper stickers, implement our community-based programs in tribal areas and urban neighborhoods, and especially implement our media strategy, our campaign could have reached the vast majority of Maysan citizens. Our TV and radio PSAs could have reached millions in the South and around the country. The Sadrist uprising preempted a nationwide barrage of uplifting "Democracy Yes" messages.

By focusing attention on the Transitional Administrative Law (TAL), which had already passed, the CPA generated a lot of dialogue, but Diamond admitted that public reactions were mostly negative. We chose to downplay the TAL, and here also our judgment proved right. In southern Iraq, with Sistani and other Shia leaders having attacked it, the issue would have dominated our events and produced no solutions. It's hard to exaggerate the power of Sistani's opinions. Whatever he says, a high percentage of people immediately support it.

The CPA was criticized for failing to trust Iraqis to make decisions. We empowered Iraqis. Many Democracy Team decisions were delegated or were made through discussion and consensus. Our facilitators had freedom to tailor democracy messages to their own perspectives and went out unsupervised, as did Tressan Sullivan's facilitators. This empowerment policy was one major reason why the DDA kept succeeding after I left. I did not forget this lesson, and when I returned to Iraq, I made it my policy to leave as many decisions as possible to Iraqis.

Another lesson to be learned is that sometimes the people at the other end of the pipeline have a better idea of how things should be done than the people in charge.

That applied to the Local Governance Program too. I was certain from the start that RTI's regional hub structure wouldn't work. Eliminating the provincial offices and their Iraqi staffs made it even less likely to work. The rush to close provincial offices presumably reflected the Kifaya disaster and a conclusion that closing them would lessen the risks to Iraqi staff. The two hub teams were deployed in June and lasted until December, when the money ran out. Ahmed Al-Harazi was later the South Region "coordinator" in Basra with almost no one to coordinate. I met him in Baghdad after I returned.

Still, USAID needed a local governance program, so after deciding not to renew RTI's contract for a third year, it finally gave the organization a new contract. LGP-2 started small but became another large project and did a lot of good work.

Evaluating the Project Results

After all that effort and USAID money, undercut by the Sadrist uprising and its aftermath, what did we have to show for our efforts?

The DDA program in Maysan was by any reasonable measure a great success. The courageous Democracy Team members made it work under high-stress conditions. Those thirty thousand presentations, the thirty thousand democracy booklets, and all the "Democracy Yes" hats must have had some lasting impact on public attitudes. Unfortunately, there is no way to measure their effect. Whatever our accomplishments, the lost opportunity for follow-up undermined them. In the difficult times that followed in Maysan, much of our message was surely lost. Any satisfaction about our success was further reduced by the martyr's death of Kifaya Hussein.

The DDA events were only part of our Campaign for Democracy. The end of LGP-Amarah meant that all the other campaign initiatives were also cut short.

We never got to put up most of the thousands of beautiful democracy posters, or to make and distribute the planned bumper stickers. Any overt democracy activity risked retaliation and possible assassinations.

None of the TV/radio PSAs were ever put on the air, partly because we weren't there and partly to avoid making Haider a target.

We couldn't publicize the results of our Democracy Survey, which would have encouraged people in their democratic views.

RTI's intended republication of my democracy booklet for the other DDA programs was overtaken by events.

Most important, we lost our opportunity to help the transition to elections. The Democracy Team needed another seven months to continue democracy education through the first election. The election results in Maysan would be disappointing and reflect our absence.

Tressan Sullivan's community development program generated a lot of local participation and projects and was a huge accomplishment. His vision for the program was realized in spite of the dangers and obstacles faced by his facilitators. As with the Campaign for Democracy, however, we had no chance to follow up or to extend the program to villages not yet reached.

At the end, that program generated both greed and intrigue. The CPA's Wyn Hornbuckle scheduled distribution of the $5,000 in project money to each of seventy-four communities for June 22 at 10:00

a.m. at the Pink Palace, but he had to stop after thirty-one because some villagers were just too unruly. He paid forty-one more the next day. The remaining two villages didn't come, but people from two villages that were not part of the program managed to infiltrate the proceedings and collect the money. There was no one to evaluate how honestly the money was spent or to track what happened to the local project committees once the CPA left. In Tressan's plan, establishing a precedent for public participation in priority setting was more important than the money. The undignified scramble at the Pink Palace suggested this distinction was not fully appreciated.

Our departure also pulled the plug on the women's groups and other civil society organizations that were starting to benefit from Jabir and Frank's capacity-building efforts and Kifaya's leadership. Our women's center project died with Kifaya, despite Molly Phee's support.

Our hopes of helping Amarah and the Marsh Arabs came to nothing, likewise our intended training program for municipal officials. Good engineering documents were developed for future reconstruction work but not implemented. The Amarah journalist training was never held.

The Maysan PC was certainly helped by my efforts and Jawaad's support to get organized quickly, though political and security problems undermined some of our progress. The rules and procedures recommended by the Rules Committee were at first not passed by the PC, but a version slightly revised by Abu Muslim and Hassan Al-Timimi was approved.

I had no chance to implement Paul Bremer's provincial and local government order, issued as I was leaving the country. He waited too long.

When the CPA left, we weren't around to help smooth the transition to self-government. Whether our presence would have tempered the power plays by the governor and others is unknowable, but my relationship with him was good, as was my reputation within the PC.

Left on their own, Maysan's leadership demonstrated a gift for corruption. The CPA left town before all the $1.5 million in incentive money for "refreshed" local councils had been allocated. Steve Anderson put the rest in the local bank and tried to protect the money by requiring withdrawals to be signed for by five responsible people, but he was not optimistic it would not be diverted by people wanting to spend it their way. In fact, after the CPA left, the PC members appointed new people to sign for those who refused, then diverted the money to their own projects.

LGP in general accomplished much, and more in Maysan than in most other provinces, but much of our progress was undone, as were our plans for the future. Our departure put Iraqis who had trusted and worked for us at risk. Kifaya's murder was the clearest evidence in that story but not the last chapter.

When Bremer closed shop on June 28, two days early, Molly did likewise, transferring authority to the PC without a formal ceremony. The British military company stayed on.

The turnover was followed by instability and heavy political maneuvering. I got conflicting reports. On June 2 the Sadr office contacted a PC member to say it wanted to regain its seat. A June 3 security report said, "Several PC members close to CPA have been threatened and grenades have been detonated in front of the house of at least one PC member. An ever-increasing number of CPA employees are also being threatened." By now the Mahoods were allied with the Sadrists and by one account Riyadh forced SCIRI-affiliated PC members and moderate clerics to give up their seats.[4]

According to local sources, a Sadrist demonstration was staged against the PC on July 18. The PC was then expanded from forty to fifty-five, to include educated people, representatives of professional associations, and other independents. One motive was to add people who were less lazy than some current members and not illiterate, like some tribal members. Three members of my Democracy Team were appointed, including Salim Abd Ul-Ridha, the lawyer, and Nazaar Abdul Wahid, the journalist. The PC leadership stayed the same.

Sadrist attacks against British troops continued and the British decided to stop defending CIMIC House, turning the compound over to the Maysan police.[5]

Evaluating the CPA from the Ground Up

Many books and articles have been written on the impact and legacy of the Coalition Provisional Authority. Most reflected the view from Baghdad or Washington DC. The view from the ground up got less attention.

In the end the CPA's role was as a bridge over troubled waters. Iraqis roiling the waters made that bridge shaky. The CPA's mistakes were well chronicled, but it deserved more credit for things done well and for things it tried but could not do because of the violence. Some province-level CPA offices, including Maysan, performed at a high level in spite of the problems in Baghdad and the flawed assumptions of Washington's planners.

While I felt mostly unaffected by the CPA's problems, others had to live with them. Hilary Synnott, an experienced British diplomat who was CPA regional coordinator for the South, later described the CPA as a "neocolonial organization" and a failure. Many of its ideas "starkly highlighted the disconnect between the Green Zone's theoreticians and those with experience on the ground." Its instructions and action plans "became increasingly divorced from reality" and often had to be set aside in favor of local solutions. Reconstruction needs in the South lacked CPA priority because of Bremer's heavy focus on Baghdad, an imbalance not shown by USAID or RTI. CPA-Baghdad pushed big projects that lacked adequate security and adequate time to complete before the CPA left, disdaining smaller, shorter projects that would have created jobs and accomplished something tangible. It often committed "disproportionate political effort and attention" toward "inappropriate political outcomes," privatization for one, while missing opportunities for practical achievements.[6]

Ali Allawi, a three-time Iraqi government minister, who wrote a wonderfully detailed history of the U.S. administration of Iraq, reached a similar conclusion:

> The terrible social legacy of the previous two decades was hardly recognized by American troops who entered Baghdad on 9 April, 2003. . . . The naïve, ideological or self-serving analysis of Iraq, conducted from the vantage points of Washington or London, bore little relationship to the facts on the ground. The CPA was handed this legacy to manage. It was not only hampered by its own weaknesses and shortcomings but was also bewildered by the total strangeness of the Iraqi social, political, institutional and economic landscape. . . .

The task of administering, let alone reforming, Iraq in the face of such hurdles, was well nigh impossible.[7]

In Synnott's view the sudden decision to close the CPA early, made at a hastily called top-level meeting in Washington, was an admission that the CPA could not in fact run the country and meant that the United States was settling for a faster exit with fewer accomplishments. This decision changed the whole direction of the CPA, from building on progress to winding down for a "dignified exit."[8] I wish someone had told me all this at the time.

A later evaluation of "hard lessons" by the U.S. government's Special Inspector General for Iraq Reconstruction (SIGIR) summarized the U.S. mistakes and ground-level conditions that left the CPA trying to "do the virtually impossible" and greatly inflated reconstruction costs. One was the failure to anticipate or prepare for "a 'post-conflict' environment torn by violence, looters, criminals, and a nascent insurgency; a government system in a state of complete collapse; and an economy that had slipped into idle and then switched off." A second factor was the grandiose nature of CPA reconstruction plans, which assumed post-conflict conditions and could not be carried out within the CPA's tenure anyway, especially after it was shortened. Third, de-Baathification removed many of the senior government managers who were needed to implement those plans, and disbanding the military had the same effect while also worsening the security and economic problems. The lack of an integrated strategy, lack of coordination across U.S. agencies, and inadequate consultation with Iraqis were also major factors.[9]

USAID's reputation fared much better. AID had a difficult relationship with Bremer, and State and AID did not concur with all of the CPA's rosy assumptions. LGP and other projects had a positive impact.

The most meaningful evaluation of our work would come from the elections and the performance of the Iraqi government established by the CPA and the United Nations, with our prior support. Evaluating from the ground up, however, some things clearly went wrong.

There was no way to create a truly democratic system without more time. Democracies don't just get set up. They have to develop, and people need time in office to do that. Larry Diamond later said:

"To be sure, elements of political pluralism emerged, as independent media outlets appeared and NGOs and parties formed. But in the quest to create a democratic, tolerant, and participatory culture, we had only halfheartedly broken the ice."[10]

The CPA moved too slowly in transferring its authority to Iraqis, at all levels. This undermined our efforts. The CPA decision to move up its departure made a difficult goal impossible and left less incentive for Iraqis to work through the new democratic institutions.

The failure to create effective provincial police departments free of militia infiltration was the Coalition's most consequential failure, conceding CPA-Maysan did better. Similarly, the Coalition and Iraqi government had yet to stand up army units willing and able to establish control in designated areas and confront the militias. The militias held much of the control the government lacked, executing and intimidating people inconvenient to their aims.

The decision to tolerate Moqtada Al-Sadr rather than arresting and prosecuting him allowed Sadr to expand the Mehdi Army and accelerate his efforts to seize power. This led directly to the disaster experienced by the LGP and other civilian projects, led to conditions under which countless Iraqis were assassinated, and undermined the legitimate, moderate Islamic leadership.

A critical citizen's lesson for every person reading this book is that we cannot control all the variables when working in foreign countries. Even our best plans and strategies can be undone by circumstances beyond our control.

The Struggle for Political Consensus

Showdown in Baghdad

The Sadrist uprising did not stop the transition to Iraqi control that the LGP helped to facilitate. Lakhdar Brahimi, the UN envoy, had arrived back in Iraq on April 4, 2004, just as the uprising started. His difficult task was to facilitate the structuring of the Interim Government and fill the top leadership and minister positions. Much was at stake.

For the United States, desperate for the political cover the UN could bring, Brahimi's arrival was welcome news. To many Iraqi Governing Council (IGC) members he was a threat. They wanted an expanded IGC that would extend their positions beyond June

30 and give them the power to appoint the ministers. The White House favored this, but Bremer, who had to work with them, was not enthusiastic. Public opinion and even IGC members faulted the council's performance.

Brahimi decided to replace the IGC altogether and appoint technocrats, not politicians. The government would have limited powers; it would have a consultative body but no legislature with power to pass laws. This placated Sistani and also created a weak government structure that would not threaten U.S. interests.

Brahimi returned again in early May. His efforts to choose the government of technocrats in consultation with the United States and IGC encountered intense political maneuvering from those consulted. For prime minister his first choice was a politically independent nuclear chemist close to Grand Ayatollah Sistani, Dr. Hussein Shahristani, who had been tortured and imprisoned for years by Saddam. Shahristani was vetoed by all IGC factions, forcing Brahimi to choose an IGC member. Neither of the two leading Shia parties, SCIRI and Dawa, would accept a prime minister from the other, and both the Sunni Arabs and the Kurds opposed naming someone from a Shia Islamic party. By process of elimination, this left Dr. Ayad Allawi, a secular Shiite and former Baathist official who in 1978 had survived an attack by an ax-wielding regime assassin in London. By happy coincidence he was also the Americans' highly preferred candidate, hardly surprising given his long-standing ties to U.S. and British intelligence. The IGC endorsed him unanimously, and Sistani accepted him. Everyone seemed happy except Brahimi.[11]

Allegations persisted, however, that the United States had manipulated the entire process.[12] Based on an inside account I heard, Dawa believed its leader, Ibrahim Al-Jaafari, would win. Bremer's announcement that Allawi won infuriated Dawa leaders, convinced that Bremer had manipulated the outcome. Bremer's own account described a decision-making process mostly within the IGC but conceded it was influenced by key U.S. officials, and discussions involved President Bush.[13]

For the less powerful president position, slated for a Sunni for political balance reasons, Brahimi and many others preferred the respected and distinguished Adnan Pachachi, who arguably had earned the job based on his work on the IGC and the TAL. Unknown to the State Department, however, a key National Security Council official, Robert Blackwill, opposed his appointment, and a cabal within the IGC stirred up late opposition, prompting Pachachi to decline it. Some IGC members considered him too emotional and too confrontational; the Kurds also opposed him. He was also eighty-four years old.[14] According to my Iraqi source, Dawa, feeling burned by the Allawi decision, opposed Pachachi because they saw him (inaccurately) as another U.S. candidate. At the last minute Brahimi had to select the other contender, Sheikh Ghazi Al-Yawer, a U.S.-educated engineer and IGC member from a major tribe in northern Iraq.

Dr. Al-Jaafari and Rowsch Shaways of the Kurdistan Democratic Party got the two vice president positions; SCIRI's Adel Abd Al-Mahdi was named finance minister; the Kurdish incumbent foreign minister Hoshyar Zebari was retained. Brahimi and his team appointed the remaining thirty-two cabinet members, including six women, but most were on a list prepared by Bremer and Blackwill, revised somewhat in consultation with Allawi. All but six were technocrats, however, including holdovers who had performed well.[15]

The new government was announced on June 1. Ministry authority was transitioned during June to the incoming Iraqi ministers. Bremer went out with a flurry of executive orders, some of major importance, not all destined to be followed. The violence worsened as insurgents increased their attacks on the Green Zone, targeted government officials, and unleashed a string of bombings intended to disrupt the transition.

The CPA turned over power on June 28, two days early, to reduce the risk of insurgent violence against the transition, and no public ceremony or celebration was held for what was arguably a major historical event. Bremer left in some haste for the airport and flew out of Iraq.

The Struggle to Maintain Order

The CPA had hardly left when, in July, the Sadrist uprising resumed in southern Iraq. In Maysan the Mehdi Army tried unsuccessfully to seize the Amarah police stations on August 6. Four days later the British again moved against Mehdi Army leaders in their home area, meeting heavy resistance, and the militiamen were defeated by British armored units supported by U.S. airstrikes, taking significant casualties. It was all over by August 26.[16]

The Mehdi Army in Basra was stronger and more organized this time, helped by fighters from other southern provinces, and seized parts of the city. The Brits left them in control for a few weeks, then cleaned up these pockets one at a time; they then raided the Basra Sadr office on September 17, removing a huge haul of weapons and ammo.[17]

As the current British unit rotated out, however, it had endured a lot. Three men had been killed, and fifty had been wounded, some of whom would never fully recover. They had endured hundreds of attacks. Their exploits and sacrifices got inconsistent coverage in the British press and sometimes anti-Coalition coverage from Al-Jazeera and similar sources.[18]

U.S. media again focused on Najaf, where the Mehdi Army trashed homes and businesses and attacked a police station. The militia fought street battles with U.S. Marines and Iraqi troops, then retreated to the vast Valley of Peace cemetery, the Arab world's largest, next to the Imam Ali Mosque complex. U.S. troops had to battle through the cemetery. An August 27 Sistani-brokered cease-fire restored order and let the militiamen surrender their weapons and go home.

The Mehdi Army took heavy casualties and alienated a lot of Iraqis, many of whom quietly approved of the Coalition crackdown. There was also political and public opinion against the crackdown, and efforts were made to persuade Moqtada to give up armed resistance and join the political process. After more fighting in Sadr City, with many Mehdi Army casualties, Sistani brokered another cease-fire in October, furthering his reputation as Iraq's most powerful man. That development had large political implications for the first Iraqi elections, just four months away.

Uncertain Futures
More Lies, Threats, and Violence in Amarah

Back in Maryland, the break from Iraq was at first pleasant, then unpleasant. From the start I was preparing to go back. I got messages almost daily from Democracy Team members, and I appreciated and returned each one. Unfortunately, the threats in Amarah did not stop.

June 22, 2004, less than one month after Kifaya's murder. Ta'meem suddenly received a nasty threat letter reflecting the antifemale out-look of religious extremists. It basically said, "You are a bitch, and so we will kill you." The word *bitch* is intended to be both insulting and humiliating. Extremist logic is that a woman working for a foreign organization is a woman of the lowest morals. The unstated implication is that if you worked with them, you slept with them. Ta'meem cried in response to this heartless insult. The message promised a "simple gift"—the bomb that would kill her. The letter also named her two brothers, Haider and Ali, the latter formerly on Tressan's team, making it even scarier. Ta'meem had to live inside and avoid going out.

A few days earlier a threat against two other team members had been posted on a wall at the Pink Palace. I worked on getting one out of Iraq to another Arab country, but complications arose; he decided to stay and was not threatened further. Another team member threatened by a tribal issue not specifically against him tried with my help to relocate to Hilla. The tribal issue was later defused, and he returned to Amarah. Although I was off the project, the unpaid job of trying to help threatened Democracy Team members took serious time. I finally compiled a "Threat Summary" that showed eleven had been threatened. Adding poor Kifaya, threats or hostile incidents had targeted over 30 percent of my staff!

I continued to follow up with threatened team members, with help on the ground from sources I won't reveal. The threats were similar and from the same copy machine. Ta'meem's family lived in a largely Sadrist neighborhood; people there were the likely source of her threat. We could not determine the risk to Haider and Ali but got the word in July that Ali was off the list. Haider was a larger worry, as he was well-known for his multiple democracy initiatives. He became concerned about his safety and more cautious about his movements.

Thousands of miles away the threat to Ta'meem dominated my life. I tried to find a way to get her to the United States but quickly encountered all the obstacles the United States places in the path of refugees who are not from favored countries. Every day we exchanged messages, and I called a few times, trying to give encouragement and lessen her feeling of isolation. Ta'meem was special, and I was in a constant emotional state over the thought that someone might kill her. That should have been unthinkable, but in Iraq nothing is unthinkable.

After four months of home isolation, Ta'meem ventured outside one day in October with her sister and then went alone to the market, right by her home. She soon saw someone whose surprised and disapproving reaction made her realize instantly that she had miscalculated and her threat period was not over. In November she took the risk of taking a job with another international NGO, but for some time it was a scary moment when she left home each day.

Sheikh Al-Abadi, deputy chairman of the PC, was a cheerful man, well liked and one of my favorite people. Not long after I returned home, two men waited for him in the dark outside his mosque in the market area, then shot him when he came out. Struck three times in his stomach, he managed, thankfully, to survive.[19]

Maysan's security kept deteriorating. The Brits remained under attack, especially from roadside bombs and from mortars aimed at Abu Naji. Tensions grew between the Sadrists and the Badr-led Maysan police. There were increasing reports of assassinations, some targeting interpreters and other current or former Coalition staff. Outright criminal acts, including kidnappings for ransom or execution, increased. Extremist violence against citizens and businesses rose (including liquor stores, legal but opposed by Shia extremists). It was a troubling irony that lawlessness in Iraq was increasingly being driven by people professing religious motives.

Glimmers of Hope

While I was still in Iraq, the internationally known Freedom House organization in Washington DC selected Haider Al-Maliki as one of its ten Iraq fellows in a nationwide competition. My reference letter on his behalf predicted he would be one of their "shining stars," and the Freedom House rep who interviewed him in Iraq reported that Haider had made an overwhelming impression.

However, Freedom House ran into State Department and other complications in bringing Iraqis to the United States that were not encountered with its fellows from other nations. Haider meanwhile got to the United States on a three-week State Department cultural exchange tour, just in time to observe the 2004 presidential election campaign from New York, Ohio (the pivotal state), and California. Haider loved San Francisco; one of his proud moments was having his photo taken near the Golden Gate Bridge. While he was in DC, we shared some time and he and a colleague visited me at home. After he left, we spent many hours on Yahoo chats, always a reminder of how amazing his written English was, even though he had never lived in an English-speaking country.

I kept following up with Freedom House, recognizing that its program could be a major boost to Haider's career. His soaring talent and enormous charisma made him a potential future leader of Iraq. His pro-American views made him an ideal Iraqi for the United States to encourage. However, Freedom House could not overcome the visa frustrations thrown up by State.

A week before Haider's visit, Jawaad arrived on a similar State Department tour. The group was in the United States through the election. After several days in Washington, they were taken to Boston; Portland, Maine; Dallas; Philadelphia; and New York. The DC days were a chance to get together and for him and a young colleague, Ahmed Hashim, to visit me at home. That visit had a sad aftermath, however. Ahmed, from the Council of Ministers media center in Baghdad, was assassinated soon after returning to his job.

In early May 2005 Ta'meem arrived in Canada on a cultural exchange program organized by Great Britain's Women's National Commission. I made my first trip to Canada to meet her and five impressive colleagues in Ottawa. It was heartwarming to see her after all her troubles. Once back in Amarah, she was expected to pass on her new knowledge through a training program for women—a gutsy decision for a woman recently threatened, in a city where democracy was losing ground to extremists hostile to women's rights.

Moving On

The Amarah expat team had moved on with their lives. Ahmed and Tressan got to the Basra regional hub in June. Tressan soon left, later taking positions in Kuwait and then spending years in Afghanistan. Thierry Husson soon resumed working in Iraq, in Basra, then Tikrit, and I met him in Baghdad before he was transferred to Amman, Jordan. Jabir Algarawi went back to selling Arizona real estate. He then joined a training project in Baghdad, but it had internal problems, and he soon returned to Arizona. (George Clooney hasn't called him yet about a return to the screen.) Frank Hersman continued intermittently in overseas jobs; I later met him briefly in Baghdad. Ahmed Al-Harazi was the ultimate survivor. He came near the start of the LGP and outlasted all of us who came after him.

Yuen Huang swore off returning to Iraq. He got married and joined the U.S. Foreign Service. Denny Lane returned to his beautiful family home in southern Switzerland and made side trips to his other homes, in the United States, Great Britain, and Thailand. He eventually settled for a while in DC and went to work for the State Department.

Many local governance initiatives we couldn't finish under LGP-1 were accomplished under LGP-2. There was later an LGP-3, and RTI continued playing a major role in Iraq. Sadly, our LGP-1 chief of party, Dr. Peter Benedict, died of cancer in May 2006 at sixty-seven. He had served over thirty years in international development, much of it with USAID.

As for me, three possible Iraq positions came and went. In the third case I was hired by a contractor of Britain's Department for International Development (DFID)—for a job in Amarah. The prospect seemed ideal—return to Amarah and my friends and work for the British, for a high salary. Staying safe, probably at ugly Abu Naji, loomed as a challenge. Still, I was one of the happiest guys in America—until my position got overruled by some DFID functionary in London. This was the first and only disappointment in my otherwise happy association with the British.

The Voice of the People

Electing the National Assembly

All of the CPA and USAID democracy and governance work had a logical connection to the elections that would later decide Iraq's political leadership. That's why the premature departure of province-level LGP teams and their democracy programs was so harmful. Seven months later the people to whom we had only introduced all those democracy principles went to the polls.

January 30, 2005, a historic day. Iraq came out to vote. At stake: 275 seats in a temporary National Assembly tasked with writing the constitution. Insurgents threatened to attack voters, but people proudly showed their purple finger, dipped in ink, to prove they had voted.

This was meant to ensure they would vote only once, but its more important effect was to give them a sense of pride. U.S. media commentators could hardly contain their enthusiasm.

The Shia parties ran a combined slate, the United Iraqi Alliance (UIA), using Sistani as their inspiration and symbol. Sistani brokered the coalition himself, and then made a major public effort with many other Shia clergy to get people to vote, framing it as a religious obligation. The Kurdish parties also ran as a slate, dominated by the two major parties. Prime Minister Allawi headed a secular list, attempting to bridge the sectarian divide. Unfortunately, Sunni Arab parties chose to boycott the election as a protest,[20] and no prominent Sunni party offered a list of candidates. This decision would prove both self-defeating to the Sunnis and damaging to the political process.

The UN decided against election districts, for lack of reliable census data, forcing all parties to run national candidate lists. The UN should have done better. It could have at least made each governorate an election district. Its system, which Sistani opposed, forced people to vote for the party, or more often a coalition of parties, rather than individuals. Voters rarely saw issues debated among candidates or parties or even learned much about them. This helped some scoundrels and was unfair to incumbents who had tried, despite great obstacles and personal security risks, to serve their people, including many I knew in Maysan. It also encouraged voting choices based on non-merit considerations, especially religion. The UN's decision devalued the election and undermined the impact of LGP and other democracy projects.

The CPA actually supported the UN's decision, implemented in a CPA Order. Some suspected its motives were less about unreliable census data than about limiting the ability of conservative Islamists to dominate the election.[21] This fear increased as the religiously defined UIA campaign gathered steam and the boycott sidelined most Sunni Arab voters.

Given little other information, voters followed preconceived instincts. Shia voted for Islam; Kurds for Kurdistan; secular Iraqis mostly for Allawi's list; and Sunni Arabs heeded their leaders and the pro-insurgency Association of Muslim Scholars, plus insurgents threatening death to anyone who voted, and boycotted the election.

There were forty-four deaths around polling stations. Despite enthusiasm in the United States about the turnout, the boycott limited actual turnout to 58 percent.

Seats that would have gone to Sunni Arab parties and Allawi's list went instead to the UIA and the Kurds. The UIA won 48.2 percent of the vote and 140 seats. The Kurdish alliance, supported also by Kurds outside Kurdistan, won 25.7 percent and 75 seats, with turnout in Kurdistan well over 80 percent. Allawi's Iraqi List won just 13.8 percent and 40 seats, reflecting the Sunni boycott and maybe some dissatisfaction with his tenure in office but especially the felt need to vote for Islam. Sunni parties competing despite the boycott fared badly. Interim president Ghazi Al-Yawer's party won just 5 seats. The party of the much-admired Adnan Pachachi was shut out, a sad outcome after all his contributions. About one hundred lists competed; only twelve won seats.

Dr. Ibrahim Al-Jaafari, leader of the moderate Islamic Dawa, eventually emerged as the prime minister. Jalal Talabani, cofounder and leader of the Patriotic Union of Kurdistan, was elected president, creating a huge irony. Just fourteen years earlier he was a guerrilla leader fighting Saddam's troops in Kurdistan and for anti-Saddam reasons was on the Iranian side in the Iran-Iraq War. Now he was succeeding him as president.

Electing the Provincial Councils

The National Assembly election got enormous Western media coverage. Hardly any media focused on the simultaneous elections for the 41-seat provincial councils, but they had enormous consequences. In southern Iraq the results clarified public opinion but were a big step backward.

At the provincial level parties and factions ran on their own, not on national slates. So Moqtada's faction, the other Sadrist faction, the Fadhila Islamic Party, SCIRI, two Dawa parties, and Allawi's Iraqi National Accord competed against each other and many smaller groups.

In Maysan a Sadrist-organized slate won, getting 15 seats. SCIRI, the two Dawa parties, Fadhila, and six smaller contenders also won seats. Only a few of our CPA-appointed PC members were elected.

The PC elected a moderate Sadrist from Majar Al-Kebir as governor. One of my Democracy Team members, who knew him, worked briefly in his office but found the new political environment intimidating. In Wasit a Sadrist-supported list won big.

Elsewhere, however, other major Shia parties prevailed. They split the vote in Dhi Qar and Muthanna, and a SCIRI governor was elected in both. In Basra Governorate a SCIRI-organized joint list with Islamic Dawa and smaller elements got 20 of the 41 seats, but Fadhila, which won 12, assembled a four-party coalition with a bare majority of 21 seats to elect Mohammed Al-Waeli as governor. Nothing but trouble followed, as he fended off SCIRI efforts to unseat him by dispensing heavy patronage funded by oil smuggling and other grand corruption.[22] His leadership contributed to a wave of assassinations, armed clashes, and other violence.

In South-Central Iraq SCIRI won outright majorities in Babil and Karbala and almost half the seats in Qadisiya and Najaf, winning the governor position in all four. It also won in Baghdad, where the self-defeating Sunni boycott handed the Shia near-total control of the city.

The National Democratic Institute (NDI) and International Republican Institute (IRI) had offered training for about four hundred political entities and candidates. NDI did campaign management seminars (e.g., planning, organization, managing volunteers, door-to-door campaigning, and posters). It produced a "Political Campaign Planning Manual" and other publications and printed seventy thousand posters per candidate. USAID funded a national voter education campaign, managed primarily by IRI and Iraqi NGOs. These little-publicized civilian projects contributed to the relatively successful election process.[23] Given some of the results, however, one might wonder whether the programs helped the right people.[24]

In general, the divided results in southern Iraq showed an encouraging level of political competition. However, the winning parties were backed by militias that were a law unto themselves. Their members committed assassinations, intimidated people and neighborhoods, violated human rights, and engaged in heavy corruption, with no fear of the police. The moderate, democratic PC members selected by the CPA were largely relegated to the sidelines. As Rory Stewart later explained it:

This is not the kind of state the coalition had hoped to create. During 14 months of direct rule . . . we tried to prevent it from emerging. We refused to allow Shari'a law to be "the source of legislation" in the constitution. We invested in religious minorities and women's centres; supported rural areas and tribal groups; funded NGOs and created "representative bodies" that were intended to reflect a vision of Iraq as a tolerant, modern society. We hoped that we had created the opportunity for civil society to flourish. This was a dream we shared with many Iraqis. We refused to deal with the Sadr militia and fought a long counter-insurgency campaign against them. Then we left, an election was held and the dream collapsed. . . . The rural sheikhs, the "liberal" middle classes and the religious minorities mostly vanished from the government.[25]

There is, however, a little political science on the optimistic side. Efforts toward democratic governance are an investment in the future and can be evaluated only over a period of years. Conceding the provincial election outcomes were disappointing, it was only the first of hopefully an indefinite number of elections. A central requirement for sustaining a democracy is the assurance of holding the *next* election. The fact that there was a fair election was significant and a huge Coalition accomplishment. Who won was less significant.

Given fair elections, voters will adjust their decisions over time based on perceptions of how well the government is performing. Provincial elections four years later in southern Iraq would produce much more encouraging results.

Ratifying the Constitution

The Transitional Administrative Law required a draft constitution by August 15, 2005, for a referendum October 15. The National Assembly appointed a fifty-five-member drafting committee, but the boycott left Sunni Arabs with only two members, so fifteen were added and ten more named as advisors. Two of the fifteen were assassinated within a month.

The draft was completed with difficulty and in haste due to the tight deadline, leaving myriad issues for unpredictable later decisions. TAL provisions controversial a few months earlier remained largely intact, validating the TAL drafting committee's strategy of setting democratic constitutional precedents in the law. The result was aided by a last-minute Kurdish-instigated TAL provision, supported by the Sunni Arabs, allowing any three or more provinces voting no by at least a two-thirds majority to veto the constitution. The Shia drafters felt compelled to accept other Kurdish-supported TAL provisions to avoid that veto.[26]

Among several significant changes, the constitution set a referendum on whether Kirkuk Province would join the Kurdistan Region, destined to remain a huge issue; reaffirmed that oil revenues from current fields will be allocated by governorate population but gave Iraq and Kurdistan joint responsibility for developing new fields, also destined to be a huge issue; and dropped the provision mandating use of sharia law for cases such as divorce and inheritance, letting families choose whether sharia or civil law will apply in their case, still leaving huge controversy with women's groups.

A few of these changes were unacceptable to Sunni Arab leaders, who campaigned for a no vote. They saw the provision on control of oil as a direct threat, as there is relatively little oil in Central Iraq, where they live.

October 15, 2005, referendum day. Voters divided along the same sectarian and ethnic lines as in the National Assembly election, except that Sunni Arabs voted no instead of staying home. The result was a polarized electorate in which the once dominant Sunni Arabs were outvoted. The constitution, endorsed by Sistani, passed by 94–98 percent in the Shia governorates and over 99 percent in the three Kurdish governorates! In religiously divided Baghdad 77.8 percent voted yes, reflecting support from moderate, secular Sunnis as well as Shia.

At the other extreme, just 3.4 percent of Anbar voters supported it. The rejectionists also made the threshold in Salah Al Din (only 18.25 percent in favor) but did not approach two-thirds in Ninewa, the only other province where a majority (55.1 percent) voted no. Diyala voted yes by a slight majority (51.3 percent). The large Kurdish minorities in the northern parts of Diyala and Ninewa affected the outcome. Overall the constitution won 78.6 percent approval, with a turnout of 63 percent. After all the struggles to build a democracy in Iraq, this was a huge step forward.

The U.S. ambassador to Iraq, Zalmay Khalilzad, wrote that the constitution "contains an enlightened synthesis of universal values and Iraqi traditions." It "requires that Islam be interpreted to be consistent with democracy and human rights."[27] In short it affirmed the compatibility of Islam and democracy—a historic development validating one of my key goals.

So, Iraq had established a democratic political system, at least on paper. It was a huge achievement, to which my civilian colleagues and I had made a major contribution. Everything considered, in October 2005, after over a year of living Iraq from America, things were again looking up. This was appreciated on a personal level because my return to Iraq was imminent.

II

Baghdad and Beyond

MAP 3. Central and western Iraq. The northern boundaries differ in places from the administrative boundaries of Iraq and the Kurdistan Regional Government.

5

"Welcome Back to Your Country"

Returning to a Different Place

October 10, 2005. The telephone call came from out of the blue. It was Michael Miller, founder and president of America's Development Foundation (ADF), a small nonprofit specializing in civil society work. I had tried unsuccessfully after RTI-Maysan folded to get back to southern Iraq on ADF's new contract.

It turned out I had not been forgotten. Miller needed an Anti-Corruption manager to run a nationwide program from Baghdad; he had promoted the current manager to deputy chief of party (DCOP). Managing a smaller Human Rights program was also part of the job. Miller remembered my résumé and wondered if I could do this job. He needed someone immediately. I could tell he was serious, and I was already psyched. Absolutely, I could do this job.

Miller negotiated a contract over the phone, and we both signed it quickly. I was hired—sight unseen—even though ADF's office was just twenty miles away, in northern Virginia. I had just solved one of his biggest problems. He sent a few documents to read and told me to show up two days before my flight for a brief orientation. Miller, a U.S. Navy man from Alabama and son of a Swiss immigrant father, had made the civil society field his career. ADF's project proposal was insightful, and it inspired a few ideas, one of them to aggregate civil society organizations (CSOs) into national networks, an idea I would soon pursue. I was on an overseas flight November 10, exactly one month after Miller's call.

The transatlantic flight showed me how tiring it is to fly such a long distance in coach. RTI had used first-class. Dead tired, I had to wait six hours in Vienna for Royal Jordanian's connecting flight to Amman. It had been dicey to reserve a seat, but a terrorist attack on Western hotels in Amman two days earlier triggered mass cancellations. At the airport I was greeted by an extremely tall travel agency representative, who drove me to a modest locally owned hotel downtown, far from the airport. I slept well but not for long; I was up at 3:30 a.m. for our return trip to the airport for an Iraqi Airways flight at 7:00 a.m.

Having entered Iraq in a vehicle convoy in 2003, this would be my first time by air. The airport was the adventure, however. It was overwhelmed with travelers, had no apparent signs telling me where to go or what to do, and relied on public address system announcements that were repeated in English but inaudible. The guards at the entrance to the check-in area would not let me in. I was surrounded by a restless and ever-growing crowd.

"Don't worry," said my travel agency friend. "Just stand right here." Taking my ticket and passport, he used his familiarity with the guards to get into the area and go through the line for me. Despite the chaotic scene, I could see him occasionally, as he towered over everyone else in the room. Eventually working his way to the front of the line, he waved at me to come with my two large suitcases. After all that, I was rewarded with a $145 excess baggage fee.

Once in the air, the sold-out Iraqi Airlines flight was good—a Boeing 737 with diligent on-board service. Most passengers were Iraqis seemingly from the business class, and several PSDs and other expats were returning from leave. The plane flew uneventfully over the Jordanian and Iraqi deserts and then a large lake west of Baghdad.

Having heard about the corkscrew landing technique for Baghdad International Airport, I expected an uneasy experience, but it wasn't bad. I learned later that the technique was designed to keep planes circling *within* the airport perimeter, making them less vulnerable to snipers and to insurgents with surface-to-air missiles. How comforting to know that. This requires more turns and sharper turns. Once on the ground, my U.S. passport and my still-valid 2003 Department of Defense (DOD) badge quickly got me through the security gate inside the entrance. I was back in Iraq.

Several minutes after finally getting all my stuff through the final baggage check, a few friendly South African PSDs in greenish uniforms showed up to welcome me. After meeting the rest of the three-vehicle convoy team in the airport garage, I was the lone passenger for a nervous trip down the most dangerous road in Baghdad.

The airport road was infamous for insurgent attacks, and traversing it took "either ten minutes or the rest of your life."[1] The roadway was good but beyond the airport property were deadly hazards. Large houses on both sides were separated from the road by a block-wide stretch of grass. The three months between April and June saw fourteen car bombs, forty-eight roadside bombs (more than one every other day), and eighty small-arms attacks (almost one a day), and sixteen people died. By the time I arrived, however, Col. Michael Harris of the Third Infantry had set up a system of barriers at the roadway entrances, guarded by Iraqi troops 24/7.[2]

Just outside the airport, the PSDs reloaded their weapons, and we headed down that airport road for what I assumed would be a high-speed dash. Instead, they weaved slowly, left and right, while the lead-vehicle PSDs carefully checked the near side of the road. I realized immediately that their focus was on possible roadside bombs. Sitting in the middle of the second vehicle, my protection was from the trained eyes of the PSDs in the lead vehicle and the well-armed PSDs in the trail vehicle watching for vehicles moving up on the convoy as well as "snakes in the grass."

Along the way I saw Colonel Harris's guarded roadway entrances, allowing no vehicles to enter until the convoy passed. Thankfully, there were no bombs or other incidents. The convoy then turned and proceeded through the city to the Karrada District south of central Baghdad. Passing through a commercial area, it turned into a narrow side street, past a row of shops, and was admitted through a security gate, then an inside gate, to a high-walled compound. I was home.

Wael's Palace

ADF's building had five floors, three for offices and two above them for housing the expats. As a nonsmoker, I got a room on the fifth floor and was happy to finally sit in it after a really tiring trip with little sleep. After moving in, I wandered down to the third and then second floors, getting introduced to seemingly everyone. The details are a blur. I slept well and rolled out with enthusiasm and no jet lag the next morning.

Wandering outside, I discovered I was living in a fortress. Extremely high walls had been erected to enclose one block of an existing side street that had buildings on both sides. A short street starting by the entrance gate created a crossing intersection with that street. The other end of the street overlooked a busy commercial strip. It was open but guarded by armed security, and concrete Jersey barriers arrayed on the street limited vehicles to slow S-turns. There were hotels and other big buildings but also several houses. Directly across from my office lived a three-generation Christian family.

Down the block one of the office-hotel buildings was the Marble Hotel, occupied by RTI. It had supported the Local Governance Program (LGP) earlier, but now its most visible activity was a health project. The compound's third foreign NGO, the National Democratic Institute, housed its staff in the Cedar Hotel across the street from ADF but worked in a separate building, diagonally across the intersection from the Cedar.

ADF's rented building was a once-decrepit former hotel renovated by Wael Lahham, its finance and administration director, aided by fellow Jordanian Ragheb Mohammed. It had been a major project but in the end was a triumph for Wael. Room accommodations were basic but pleasant, and the air conditioning worked. The fifth floor had a social room with a big-screen TV, a one-room gym, and a pool table in the open space between them. I had little time for TV and was never a pool shark but should have used the gym more often. An outside corner patio overlooking the city was a frequent evening gathering place. The fourth floor had a laundry room, a kitchen, and a plain but functional dining room.

The third floor was for the chief of party (COP), the evaluation and reports officers, and Wael's staff. The program staff, led by the DCOP, Dr. Craig Davis, occupied the second floor. The first floor was the Baghdad regional office, later expanded by renovating the basement level.

The extra hard mattress was my only big issue. Wael cheerfully explained that he bought hard mattresses for all the rooms because *he* had a bad back, leaving an obvious question unanswered.

Otherwise, we had some comforts of home. There was daily maid service, by two brothers. Our laundry could be left out for pickup. An oddity of the Palace was that the laundry room had two washers but no dryer. They hung the wet clothes on lines inside the laundry room and delivered them stiffly dried two days later. As we could have had a dryer, I asked Ragheb why not. He explained that he liked his clothes dried in the sun—apparently an irrefutable argument for reasons I couldn't discern. There was also a cultural issue over men washing women's clothes, which frustrated my one female colleague; after several tries she finally gave up. All in all, the genteel hardship I felt at the villas in Amarah was experienced again at Wael's Palace.

The expat team had hired a caterer but switched to a $15 per diem. That worked for me as I dislike interrupting my work to eat on a schedule. The Arab expats liked it because they enjoyed cooking for each other and anyone else who wanted to join them, as I occasionally did. I could not leave the compound, of course, for security reasons, but there was a nice enough restaurant in the Rimal Hotel diagonally across the intersection and a lunchroom-level but okay place in the Cedar Hotel across from the Rimal. With the compound's residents mainly from the West, the food was largely Western with some Middle Eastern touches. Both places were Christian owned and so more Western oriented.

The last point mattered because both were places where you could buy a drink. Although unfaithful to the Irish drinking tradition, I enjoy a beer now and then. For those more attuned to relaxing at watering holes, there was The Bunker, the Cedar's well-stocked basement-level bar. It would be excessive to call it my colleagues' favorite hangout, as it was the only hangout, but a good time was had by all, and it provided someplace to go for people who couldn't go anywhere. Alas for my Muslim colleagues, alcohol was *haram* (forbidden). Helped by neither the restaurant fare nor the bar, most seldom left Wael's Palace.

I found the Rimal, surrounded by blast walls inside and outside the compound, a comfortable and calming place. Its restaurant featured large windows covered with green decorative curtains, untrained but friendly service, and an evening piano man who had learned many American standards (even if some sounded culturally disconnected in his renditions). The printed English menu featured amusing misspellings that required deciphering exactly what the dish was; the Cedar's menu had its own spelling atrocities.

The Rimal also had other idiosyncrasies. Some days I heard a curious loud pounding noise from the kitchen. I eventually figured out that this occurred when I ordered steak. It turned out that to get a ten-der steak, they had to pound it into submission. So, Steak Versailles wasn't French cooking and you had to study the spelling to discern what they *were* cooking, but I ate well.

At the open end of the compound was the Sindbad Hotel, named for the famed Sinbad of Middle Eastern tales, a sailor from Basra. I would later rent its second-floor facilities occasionally for meetings and civil society organization training sessions, but had to take a few PSDs with me, as it fronted on the commercial strip and so was potentially vulnerable. It had little business otherwise—a sign of the bad times in Baghdad.

Renovation achievements aside, Wael's Palace acquired a reputation among the expats for its unwritten rules. This was not a problem because these were Wael's rules, and Wael knew all the rules by heart. It was easy to find out what the rules were: You wanted to do something a certain way and were told this was not in accordance with the rules. If the rule seemed illogical (as it often did), an explanation was always cheerfully provided. To avoid any impression that the rules were being made up on the spot, you were always told that this had *always* been the rule. If you did not like the rule (also a frequent occurrence), you did not need to spend any time debating it because it was not written down and so there was nothing to debate.

The ICSP Team
Joining the Cast of Characters

ADF was doing business as the Iraq Civil Society Program (ICSP) instead of using its own name, good thinking from a security perspective, given the anti-U.S. elements in Baghdad. It had six program sectors: Anti-Corruption, Human Rights, Women's Advocacy, Civic Education, Civil Society Capacity Building, and Independent Media. Each worked with Iraqi CSOs. This was a national project, reaching all eighteen provinces.

Many international development people have fascinating personal and career backgrounds. None at ICSP were more colorful than the civic education manager and civil society advisor, Jean-Sebastien Roy, who arrived just after me. A Haitian who lived many years in Canada, his creative advice reflected in-depth experience and a pas-

sionate belief in civil society. We talked a lot, or more precisely I lis-
tened a lot, as Jean-Sebastien liked to talk and always had interesting
things to say. In his checkered career he had once played in a big-time
musical band in Spain, an experience that helped shape his ebullient
personality and explained his vast collection of songs, many broad-
casted pleasingly from his office after business hours.

My predecessor, Craig Davis, originally from Indiana, now the
DCOP, was my supervisor. Some would feel pressured by that, but I
worked cheerfully in the next office and enjoyed the collaboration.
He helped in many ways without telling me how I had to do things.
Craig was both dynamic and charismatic, leading with his personality more than his authority. He was also our main link to USAID in
the Green Zone, a key role.

Chief of Party Dr. Issam Adawi (accent on the first syllable) was
an Egyptian. It is not unusual for COPs on USAID projects to be non-
Americans, and an Arab in Iraq has the obvious language advantage.
Issam had been in international development for years, most notably with Save the Children. More charming than dynamic and almost
unfailingly pleasant, he reflected the "easy rider" school of management. This left the program leadership with Craig and the management side with Wael.

Another Egyptian on the team was Dr. Youssria Ahmed, the Capacity Building manager and resident soccer fanatic. Educated as a medical doctor, she had spent many years in international development.
Capacity Building was largely a training support organization for the
other five sectors. ADF touted itself as a training organization, but
its training materials still needed a lot of work, and Youssria had no
staff to help with that.

ICSP's six sectors awarded competitive grants to CSOs, amounting
to millions of dollars. One of its lead characters was the new grants
coordinator, Kristin Joplin, who had development experience in three
countries. Kristin, in her mid-thirties, was a popular member of the
team, and not only because she was a woman, as she was otherwise
"one of the boys." A determined iconoclast from Oregon who liked
living outside the United States, she had served in the army, endured
a couple of life's bad bounces, and acquired a touch of cynicism to
match her sense of humor.

Arriving from Washington just after me was the intellectually talented Ethan Arnheim, hired to write our reports to USAID. Still in his twenties, he had several years of Middle East experience, including in Iraq. Writing reports sounds like a straightforward job but has pitfalls, due partly to their number and complexity (weekly, monthly, quarterly, special reports, etc.) and partly to the deft language required by diplomatic and CYA (cover your a—) considerations.

Proving again it's a small world after all, in January ADF hired as its Monitoring and Evaluation (M&E) director Dan Killian, who had helped me deploy to Amarah in 2003 while at the International City Management Association (ICMA). Originally from Illinois, he was a thoughtful analyst who fit the mold of M&E directors even at his young age and gradually upgraded our M&E function. Notwithstanding news reports of projects gone bad and taxpayers' money wasted, USAID does have a system for monitoring and evaluating projects, though I would develop some doubts about how well it works.

The Independent Media program, subcontracted to the International Research & Exchanges Board (IREX), had the critical mission to develop and support an independent media sector in Iraq. Its program manager, Joe Raffelberg, was an impressive, wonderfully engaging German media maven with a Catholic social perspective and a career's worth of experience in other countries. His expert German deputy and best buddy, the burly Matthias Wirzberger, had done similar projects in three countries.

The Anti-Corruption Team

Anti-Corruption (AC) was the largest ICSP program, successful thanks to Craig's leadership and gaining momentum. Still, there was much more to do to make it a program with national impact. To do that I had about four AC staff at each of the four regional offices and four more at headquarters.

My biggest asset was my Anti-Corruption coordinator, Dashti, a Kurd from Baghdad in his mid-thirties, who had worked for Craig at the Ministry of Labor and Social Affairs. Dashti had transparent organizational skills, a calm but gently forceful way with people, and a great sense of humor. Dashti had married a woman in her early twenties, whom he had hired at the ministry. I suggested that was a conflict of interest, but he said with a sly smile that there was no conflict because "I hired her, and *then* I married her."

I observed Dashti briefly to understand how he operated, noticing that much of his time was spent on the phone with the four regional coordinators and that he was very good at explaining what needed to be done and by when (often within the day). I resolved to apply my democratic management approach and let him handle day-to-day operations.

Dashti's assistant for most things was the handsome Ameer, who had started recently and was still learning but was a solid and dedicated worker in a constantly busy office. The delightful and charming Miami (Me-*ah*-me) Talib, whom I sometimes called Miss Florida, had the specialized task of writing pretests and posttests for CSO surveys.

For the smaller Human Rights (HR) program I had only one headquarters staff member: Usama, my national coordinator. We had just one or two HR staff in each regional office, struggling to make a difference in an area where Iraq needed a lot more help. Only twenty-five but brilliant, Usama had a solid grasp of Iraq's troubled human rights scene. He was well connected; his father was a just-elected parliament member, and his grandfather was once a high-ranking diplomat. As his name can also be spelled *Osama* in English, I advised him that it would remind people of that other Osama, so he should spell it with a *U* for the rest of his life.

Human Rights had no separate status officially, despite Iraq's critical need. It was defined as a "cross-cutting theme" incorporated in all the other sectors. The Anti-Corruption manager was given this nonsector to manage along with AC. The cross-cutting theme formula was not working out, and I quickly saw that any real HR progress would have to come from me.

Helping to keep this happy group together was my take-charge office assistant, Ghassak, a small but mighty Christian woman around thirty who worked from enthusiasm. While continuing to support Craig, she smoothly expanded her role to support me too. She seemingly could solve any problem and execute any plan, and her computer science degree helped overcome frequent laptop and system problems.

Our program implementation depended on the regional offices, called Civil Society Resource Centers (CSRCs). Aside from the co-located Baghdad Center, they were in Erbil, the Kurdish capital; Hilla in the South-Central Region; and Basra in the South. My regional staffs worked with a large and growing number of CSOs, generating projects and events in every province. Altogether, I had about thirty staff members. That wasn't enough to ensure democracy in Iraq, but hopefully it would be enough to make a difference.

The Basra connection gave me hope that I would see all my Amarah friends again. Amarah was unsafe, but maybe we could get together someday in Basra for one of the world's happiest reunions. I gradually got the word out to my Democracy Team members that I was back. One responded with one of the nicest messages I ever received: "Welcome back to your country."

A New Role for Haider

Baghdad's security risks drove ICSP's recruitment policy. In Amarah we posted job openings on the street. ICSP posted nothing and advertised nowhere. Any public recruitment could draw attention from the wrong people. Applicants could have links to the insurgency; any such person who got inside Wael's Palace could be a deadly threat. So, Iraqis were hired through existing staff who could vouch for them. I was encouraged to recommend Iraqis I knew, potentially an opening for some in Amarah, but Amarah was four hours away.

Jean-Sebastien soon needed a national coordinator for Civic Education, his top Iraqi position. The Amarah person at that talent level with interest in civic education was Haider Al-Maliki. I was anxious to get Haider out of Amarah, where he still felt nervous about his security. He typically stayed home during the day and ventured out at night. I recommended him, and Jean-Sebastien immediately wanted him. Haider quickly agreed and moved to Baghdad.

For some time after he arrived, Haider came by my office each morning to say hello. He was readily accepted by other staff and his great English skills soon got attention. His good looks and personal charm also got attention, though in Iraq women feel constrained in what they can say to men. Just after starting at ICSP, Haider drew interest from a Baghdad TV station seeking a host for a new weekly public affairs program but had no way to combine that with his ICSP job.

I saw a lot in Haider. With his high intelligence and master's-level education, energetic interest in the politics and future of Iraq, modern orientation, political skills, and charisma, he had much to offer as a future leader of Iraq. That made his career moves and personal decisions potentially important. Consciously, I became his mentor, out of friendship but also because of what he might contribute if his fast-moving career continued to ascend.

What separated Haider from others in southern Iraq were his progressive political outlook and his freedom from old social norms. His CSO, the Society for Change, reflected his outlook in its name. In total contrast to the nationalism and anti-Americanism in Iraq, he was strongly pro-Western. He once told me that "America *deserves* to be the leader of the free world." He was a committed internationalist who had loved his trips to the United States, Lebanon, and Cyprus. His lighthearted but insightful take on Islam's ban on alcohol was, "Give a Muslim two beers and you will learn his true personality." All of this made him less different, however, in Baghdad's more open social environment, and he fit in well with the mostly Sunni staff.

Occasionally, he confided in me about some personal matter, which led one day to a funny story reflecting his personal appeal and nontraditional outlook. Male staff didn't usually wear ties to work, but one day Haider had a meeting set for the afternoon and brought one in his pocket. As the meeting approached, he asked a female colleague to help put it on. As husbands and wives know, this requires standing very close to each other. As his friend finished with the tie, Haider said casually, "Do I get the kiss too?" He did.

Haider had for some time had occasional girlfriends, which would cause no comment in the West but was not typical in Iraq. There was the college girl he had dated, the girl he liked in Beirut, and now one in the United States who desperately wanted to be his girlfriend. He appreciated the attention but recognized he was not ready to make long-term commitments. By contrast, there was the young woman from northern Lebanon who met him in Cyprus and seemed to dislike him. He launched a charm offensive to change her opinion, and she became a good friend.

Aside from Haider, my hope of bringing Democracy Team members to Baghdad didn't work out in the end. I tried four or five times with different people. One Amarah team member already in Baghdad had a well-paying but risky field engineering oversight job with the Coalition. Two former team members were already with ICSP, as its Maysan governorate coordinators. ADF hired two for each governorate, most working from home for security reasons.

Creating a Civil Society
Civil Society and Democracy

The term *civil society* is unfamiliar to many in the West, yet the concept is in practice everywhere. Everyone who has joined a civic organization, coached a team of kids, joined a neighborhood project, or collected charitable donations understands it from experience. The civil society is in a way the sum total of civic participation.

In nondemocratic nations, however, the lack of a strong civil society is a defining flaw. No element of the citizenry acts as a check on government power. The flow of communication between government and citizens goes only one way. Volunteers are lacking; so are donations for needed projects. One major USAID goal in any country is to improve the capacity of the civil society sector. ADF held AID's primary civil society contract in Iraq.

The CSOs did not have to be created by us. Once Saddam fell, they sprang up on their own, pursuing countless missions, and numerous volunteers joined up. Haider's CSO was one among thousands. ICSP's mission was to encourage, train, fund, work with, and sustain them.

To accomplish those goals, AID needed a decentralized organization accessible to CSOs, thus the regional offices, about equal in size and importance. This structure faced growing security problems, however. The decline of Baghdad since my first Iraq tour was largely matched by the decline of Basra and later Hilla. Erbil, the Kurdish capital, was by contrast generally peaceful.

ICSP operated on a kind of matrix management system, in which general supervision came from the expat manager and Iraqi director in each CSRC, while program direction came from the expat managers and our Iraqi coordinators in Baghdad directly to our regional coordinators.

Supporting all this was the grant money. The project was set up to implement numerous short-term CSO projects—typically a few months long. Once the money was awarded, our regional staffs monitored all the projects and provided technical assistance.

I quickly saw a fundamental difference between all the civic endeavors that made me a civil society veteran in America and those of Iraq's fledgling CSO members. The vast majority of active citizens in the West are volunteers, though larger organizations have paid staff too. The voluntary approach works for us because most volunteers have jobs or other means of support. Iraq had massive unemployment, and many jobs paid barely enough to live on. CSOs had many dedicated people, but each grant served the not-so-incidental purpose of providing temporary employment with decent pay for a few people and part-time work for a few others.

Before this project was over, there would be, by one count, 1,964 CSOs registered with ICSP, about equally divided among the four regions, and hundreds of completed CSO projects.

Not Quite the BBC

An effective civil society includes media organizations independent of the government. On October 15, 2005, just before I arrived, Joe Raffelberg and his IREX team achieved a major milestone: official launch of the National Iraqi News Agency (NINA), just in time for the referendum on the constitution. NINA was started by a group of journalists led by a Saddam-era journalist returned from exile. It set up offices near the Palestine Hotel, a well-known home away from home for journalists where I had stayed on my Baghdad visit in 2004. Just nine days after NINA moved in, a triple bomb attack against the Palestine and nearby Sheraton badly damaged its offices, but thankfully, the last shift had left minutes earlier.

ADF called NINA the first independent commercial news source in Iraq, though it did have competition. In concept its role was comparable to Reuters at the international level—a commercial news agency that sells information to print and electronic media. The plan was to start as a free service, then transition to a paid subscription service. Widely used from the start, NINA became an official USAID "Success Story."

When Saddam went away, so did the official Iraq News Agency and the Ministry of Information. A profusion of new electronic media emerged, and a huge number of people bought televisions, needed for their new satellite dishes, previously prohibited. Iraqis were now much more likely to get their news from TV than from radio or newspapers.

Joe's team was also helping to transition the Iraqi Media Network (IMN) into a more independent organization. The CPA created IMN in 2003 to operate the newly created Al Iraqiya satellite TV network, radio network, *Al-Sabah* newspaper, and a magazine. *Al-Sabah* quickly achieved a large circulation. IMN was directed by Bremer's Order 66 to operate independently but soon faced criticism that it was a Coalition mouthpiece. ICSP was getting major support from Iraqis for Public Broadcasting, a CSO leading efforts to pass a law making IMN independent, akin to the British Broadcasting Corporation (BBC) and the Public Broadcasting System (PBS) in the United States. This would prove to be a struggle.

One of Al Iraqiya's key roles was to serve as an alternative news source to the frequently anti-Coalition, anti-Iraq coverage of the widely watched Arab satellite networks Al Jazeera and Al Arabiya, now available through those new satellite dishes. TV news organizations in other Arab states also reported from Baghdad. Al Iraqiya also competed with many new Iraqi stations. Its news and entertainment programs included *Good Morning Iraq*, started with ICSP technical assistance. Another ICSP success story was the thirty-two-part series developed for Al Iraqiya called *Our Constitution*, preceding the October constitutional referendum.

To counter biased outside coverage, the United States funded a new Middle East–oriented satellite channel called Al Hurra (The Free) in 2004, and then an Al Hurra Iraq directly targeting Iraqi viewers. As a creature of U.S. foreign policy, funded by U.S. money and telecasting from Springfield, Virginia, Al Hurra faced unavoidable criticism that its news was not independent, though it is under a self-managing nonprofit corporation. Al-Hurra did not compete well against other Middle East media, and some maligned it as a waste of money, but Al Hurra Iraq became one of Iraq's most-watched stations. Another U.S. initiative, Radio Sawa, on the air since 2002, offered a news and music format targeting younger viewers especially.

Shortly after I arrived, Joe found himself in Tikrit, Saddam's home city. He needed to go from the local U.S. military compound to a new satellite TV station downtown, set up by the military and being turned over to an independent board. Joe found he either had to go by military escort, compromising his image of journalistic independence, or go into town without protection. Most people would have taken the escort, but intrepid Joe ventured into a dangerous city with no security and lived to tell about it.

High Walls and High Anxiety

In Amarah the risk to our lives was a given, but no military action threatened us until the Sadrist uprising. In Baghdad the chances of being targeted, in person and especially in a vehicle, were much higher. No part of the city was safe; some parts were more unsafe than others. Karrada was at first one of the safer areas but was just waiting its turn. A series of four car bombs had killed seventeen people there a few months before I came.

Indeed, I arrived just as the danger to expat civilians was accelerating. U.S. civilian deaths alone had reached 147 by October 2005, 117 of them killed by insurgents. Those numbers were destined to rise sharply.[3]

Our security was entrusted to Reed Inc. of northern Virginia, founded in February 2003 by a South African immigrant and staunch Christian experienced in business and war zones. He started with a small logistics contract at IMN, which brought him to ADF's attention.

Reed's ICSP operation included three nine-member PSD teams— South Africans and a few others, primarily responsible for transportation security. It hired no Iraqis as PSDs at that time, reasoning that Iraqis could be readily targeted by insurgents or pressured to betray the company and its clients if family members were kidnapped or threatened. For the same reason Reed hired no Iraqi security guards. Working security for the foreigners was risky; an Iraqi with another NGO in the compound was later killed while I was there.

A lot of that PSD time was unused. While other expats worked all day, PSDs had little to do and no place to go until one of us had a meeting outside the compound. Down periods could last for days. They had high salaries and generous leave but lived an often tedious life.

Shortly after Christmas there was a serious blowup in Reed's PSD contingent. Company policy prohibited drinking alcohol within twelve hours before any road assignment; so no night drinking was permitted before early-morning deployments. The owner learned this policy was being violated and sent in a new PSD to check out the situation. This led to the sudden departure of several PSDs along with the genial, well-liked security manager. Hamish MacIntyre, another South African but more top-down, took over.

Reed's building security men were from Nepal: seventy-six in all. Nepalese have an honored place in British military history due to the exploits of the Gurkhas of Nepal. Our Nepalese were all mild-mannered, extremely polite men, mostly small in stature, but operated with quiet efficiency and had a tested ability to shoot straight.

The large numbers of security personnel illustrate one of USAID's major problems in Iraq. Our expat program staff was far outnumbered by the security personnel hired to protect us 24/7. About 25 percent of project costs went to security—comparable to other USAID projects.

Reed soon became a large and successful company. It later had 800 people in Iraq and even more in Afghanistan. This success came at a high price. A Reed PSD on another Iraq contract was killed and another badly injured when their vehicle was hit by a roadside bomb. By 2011 six Reed employees in Iraq had died, and seventeen were wounded.

Private security companies in Iraq were becoming a highly publicized issue, much of it focused on fatal incidents involving the controversial Blackwater firm. Far less publicized were ethical companies like Reed that had clean records and the professional organization and code of conduct established by Reed and other security firms working in Iraq.

One of Reed's South African PSDs came with an amazing personal story he told the expat team shortly after I arrived. Siegfried was a towering guy, perhaps six foot seven in U.S. measurement, and also a deeply Christian and exceedingly nice guy. He had been in Iraq before, in different places, working on water and other projects for a small foreign religious NGO, and spoke good Arabic.

The NGO job turned into a horrible ordeal. Its small staff lived in a house in Diwaniya, in South-Central Iraq. Four of their five security guards were killed after the Mehdi Army insurrection started, leaving the civilians helpless, with only one guard. Sadrist gunmen joined by two Muslim clerics came to the house, shot the guard dead, and barged in. Siegfried, the Swiss project director and his wife, and another staff member were kidnapped, thrown into their own vehicles, and driven through illegal Sadrist checkpoints to an unknown location.

The ordeal lasted seventy hours, with frequent and often brutal interrogations and the horror of knowing they were in danger of being killed like other kidnapped expats. They were set free only after an intense investigation of their records showed the Sadrists that the Iraqis with whom the NGO was working included relatives of Moqtada Al-Sadr! In spite of that ordeal, Siegfried stayed committed to Iraq and found his way back.

Our compound was not close to the Coalition-guarded Green Zone, famous from news reports. Karrada was in the Red Zone, basically the rest of Baghdad. These terms came from military lingo, but *Green* and *Red* acquired the connotations, respectively, of "safe" and "unsafe." More properly, the Green Zone, located along the Tigris River in the center of Baghdad, was officially called the International Zone, or IZ. Coalition-issued ID was required to get in. The IZ was four and a half square miles, however, and several thousand officials and other Iraqis lived there, some in homes abandoned by Baathists.

The CPA set up shop in the IZ, as did a growing number of government agencies and the new parliament, reflecting the security concerns. The U.S., British, and Australian embassies were located there. A resident U.S. military unit provided security, supported by personnel from small Coalition countries. It seemed that every building was surrounded by tall blast walls and high-profile security, allowing IZ employees to feel somewhat secure. The IZ military hospital also served Coalition civilians like us.

Living in the Red Zone meant there were no U.S. troops in the vicinity if someone decided to attack the compound. Such an attack was not implausible but would have been risky with so many armed men from the compound's three NGOs on duty. In general we felt secure in our version of a gated community, but our level of concern would gradually rise.

A war zone atmosphere was provided daily by the relentless overflights of U.S. military planes and helicopters, seemingly at all hours of the day and night. After midnight on a seemingly daily basis, I heard the low droning sound of large military transport planes.

The few Iraqi residents of the compound came and went without much notice. I felt sure they were happy to live behind the high walls, especially after other city neighborhoods became infiltrated by insurgents. Some other Iraqis were allowed to walk across the compound, through one gate and out the other.

Our Iraqi staff were safe behind the same walls during the day but had to get to and from work from other parts of Baghdad, where others might take a prying interest in their comings and goings. We were somewhat flexible about arrival times and knew people couldn't stay past the normal workday.

We also had a lot of smokers, in a country where official antismoking campaigns had been unknown. Wael's Palace was a smoke-free building, but a sociable group of puffers could always be found gathered just outside, including expat colleagues setting a bad example. My antismoking views were oft-repeated, but I soon realized that even Iraqis in their twenties were already hooked—a sobering reality about life and health in Iraq. When you know you could die on the way home, smoking a cigarette doesn't seem that dangerous.

High-Profile Transportation

The high walls were comforting, but most of us couldn't stay in our fortress all the time. We had meetings or other business in the Green Zone or elsewhere in Baghdad or had to get to or from the airport. These were the moments of risk. That risk was reinforced by news stories reporting the deaths of too many expat civilians in Iraq. Most occurred when they ventured out onto the roads. When I got to Baghdad in October 2005, the situation seemed less scary, and convoys through Baghdad streets usually proceeded uneventfully. Usually.

We all knew the drill. I requested my ride in advance. The security manager set a specific departure day and time, on a calendar. Demand was high, so trips were often combined. The PSD convoy gathered thirty minutes before departure, and the passenger vehicle parked outside the door. We made sure to bring our DOD badges or other authorization and signed out at the desk, recording our destination and estimated return time. We then walked out to the vehicle, a PSD helped us put on flak jackets, and we got in.

The PSD in charge of the crew sometimes issued simple instructions, perhaps adding an alert about recent bad incidents. With that the three vehicles sorted into the proper order, our passenger vehicle in the middle, the gate was opened, and we rolled through fast.

From there, different organizations used different approaches. The key difference was between "high profile" and "low profile." Each had advantages and disadvantages. Reed liked high profile. Its rationale was that stopping in traffic makes you a stationary target, and in congested Baghdad you were unlikely to reach your destination without stopping. The solution was to bust out of the roadway where you were about to be stuck. This might mean diverting to side streets, but sometimes it meant crossing the median and proceeding down the closest lane on the *other* side, in the face of oncoming traffic. On streets without medians any vehicle occupants coming the other way were seen as a potential threat, so the PSDs forced people to the side of the road by waving their weapons at them. A big sign in Arabic on the back of the trail vehicle warned drivers not to approach the convoy.

Baghdadis saw us coming and got out of the way—a learned response, as they saw many of these annoying foreign convoys. I wondered what people were thinking when treated this way; it could not have been positive. After all, they were just driving down their own streets, minding their own business. High profile is arrogant. That was a serious disadvantage in the Coalition's constant battle for Iraqi public opinion. High profile also had practical disadvantages. It brought attention to the convoy, increasing the risk of being targeted.

Going low profile means being less conspicuous, to avoid attention and avoid antagonizing the locals and triggering a violent response. PSDs don't stick their weapons out the window or wave people aside. Our neighbors, the National Democratic Institute, adopted this approach. They had nice solid vehicles, often Mercedes, and well-trained PSDs but preferred to blend in with the city traffic. Low profile accepts the risk of being stuck in traffic at times. Its downside is that if your convoy *is* targeted, you are more vulnerable and more likely to die.

It's easy to see both sides of this argument or to think of scenarios under which either would prove helpful or disastrous. I heard the same arguments on the RTI project. It's impossible to predict what evil people will do because we don't know which evil people will show up at a given time and place. Most of us in international development are instinctively sensitive to local populations. We were in Iraq to move attitudes in a positive direction and did not want to make people angry. But I also appreciated that high profile was intended to protect me from the real possibility of getting killed. It's not insensitive to feel that this trumps other considerations.

A later incident involving Reed PSDs illustrates the dilemma. A Reed convoy on the airport road encountered a driver ahead who kept slowing down and backing into the convoy's space—decidedly suspicious behavior. He persisted despite warning signals. Finally, the lead vehicle pulled up alongside the driver to emphasize the point. The guy was a *suicide bomber*. He detonated his bomb, blowing himself and his car up but fortunately just missing Reed's vehicle and PSDs.

From Karrada there are main roads going toward the Green Zone, but access was controlled by a U.S. security checkpoint on our side of the river. This typically meant a significant wait, and we had to exit the vehicles while they were searched, but at least we got the favored treatment of a separate line. Iraqis sat through indefinite delays in the usually stopped regular line, stretching for blocks in the right lane. Once past the checkpoint, our convoy proceeded across the Fourteenth of July Bridge. At the Green Zone there was another U.S. checkpoint, but no vehicle search, so we were waved through after showing our IDs to U.S. soldiers peering into the vehicle.

Once past that point, it was easy enough to negotiate the modern street system, despite being surrounded almost everywhere by enormous eighteen-foot-high concrete barriers, typically arrayed end to end and often with razor wire at the top. There were shelters along some streets where you could duck in if an incident occurred, and incidents did occur, especially mortar and rocket strikes. On one visit to the military hospital, I and others were told to wait inside, after a rocket landed noisily within the IZ, until cleared to leave some minutes later. Overall, however, I had the feeling of being in a safe place, as compared to the security risks taken to get there.

After our meetings we usually spent a little time at the PX. PSDs were always happy for this diversion. The always-busy PX store offered light food choices, including various munchies, plus magazines, electronics, music, and other useful stuff. It also had a barbershop and rudimentary fast food outlets. It was a pleasant surprise that I could get lunch from Burger King. The coffee shop was a PSD favorite; all seating was outdoors but with umbrellas to mitigate the heat. On Fridays, our day off, expats sometimes got together for a convoy to the PX. Whether I went or not, it was important psychologically to know that I could.

The PX was across a parking lot from the former Republican Palace serving as the U.S. Embassy, one of eighty-eight Saddam palaces. It had been Bremer's CPA headquarters and where the CPA Governance Office set the guidance for my Maysan democracy program. I had a few meetings in the palace, which had marble corridors and other nice features. One central space had been converted into a large cafeteria and tearoom, useful for holding meetings. While I was in Baghdad, construction began on a new and huge U.S. Embassy complex.

The Green Zone was no tourist destination but did have noteworthy features among its boulevards and dusty palm trees. Saddam's former military parade ground was a long and wide passage featuring arched gates soaring high above the ground at both ends, formed by huge sculptures of crossed swords held by forearms and hands. Built as a monument to Iraq's self-declared "victory" in the Iran-Iraq War (while the war was still on), it was also an intended monument to Saddam's military leadership. Maybe it was grand in Saddam's heyday, but it was now an abandoned curiosity. I also checked out the Liberty Pool, a popular expat gathering spot so nice that it had a huge fancy-shaped canopy above it to protect luxuriating swimmers from the baking Iraq heat.

(Not So) Beautiful Downtown Baghdad

Baghdad is a historic city, dating from the eighth century, but also modern and densely settled with a functional roadway network, multistory buildings, and a busy though faded commercial scene. It's the second most populous city in the Arab world after Cairo, with over 5 million people, and the Baghdad governorate in total has around 6 million, about 20 percent of Iraq's population. It occupies an ideal location on both sides of the Tigris.

Our drives through this famous city went through some nice-looking neighborhoods, including parts of Karrada, the IZ, and the deceptively attractive airport road. More common were scenes of a poor city in decline. Shops were typically drab and cramped for space, and merchandise was often placed outside during business hours. This seemed to show a remarkable confidence in such a poor city that people would not steal it. Karrada was once largely Christian, but its better days were in the past, and it was now mainly Shia. Still, its reputation as a shopping area attracted people from elsewhere in the city.

I was always fascinated by the many business signs in English, as if there were still foreigners in Baghdad who might want to eat or shop there. The ubiquitous trash suggested that trash removal was no one's job, but I often saw street sweepers cleaning dust and debris. Occasionally, I saw groups of goats munching lunch in the green space roadway medians, an incongruous urban scene.

At the occasional evening get-togethers on our fifth-floor patio, the distant view was faintly appealing. Looking more closely, however, many of those hotels and other big buildings were actually closed, a visible symbol of the hard times brought on by the Baathists, the invasion, and the insurgency. Another empty multistory building was just outside our back gate.

The economic struggles of Baghdad reflected wider problems. While Baghdad's economy faltered, oil and agricultural production, the pillars of the economy, were declining nationwide. The impact of lower oil production is better appreciated when you know that well over 90 percent of Iraq's budget is funded by oil revenues. That puts a lot of eggs in one basket.

What to do about Baghdad was a big question, but usable answers required more peaceful times. Baghdad's political structure had already been transformed by the RTI Local Governance Program. By mid-2003 the LGP-Baghdad team had created a system of district and neighborhood councils. Under the old system, Baghdad city, called Baghdad Amanat, was divided into 9 administrative districts (qadha). Within those 9 districts LGP identified 88 neighborhoods (nahiya), later increased to 94, and created advisory councils in each. Each district got an advisory council. Then a 37-member Baghdad City Council was created. This three-level structure brought a huge increase in citizen participation. The selection of council members, coming so early in the CPA period, resulted in some Baathists getting seats and some councils with limited legitimacy, so Baghdad, like Maysan, went through a "refreshment" process that was similarly necessary, helpful, and not uniformly appreciated.[4]

The city is the major part of the Baghdad governorate. Its suburban area had another 6 district councils, created from 20 neighborhood councils, rolling up to a 35-member Baghdad Regional Council. By early 2004 a 41-member Baghdad Provincial Council was created with combined authority for the entire governorate. It got direct elections in 2005, like the other PCs.

This enormous democracy project was a major LGP achievement. As violence overtook Baghdad, however, councils were increasingly forced behind closed doors or forced to disband altogether, and members were targeted and some killed over their public service. It was a consequential and tragic story.[5]

Coalition money was being poured into infrastructure projects, though some were undone or compromised by operations and maintenance problems once turned over to the Iraqis. Security problems stopped or delayed other projects, and some weren't even started. The priority on big-ticket projects over short-term job creation reflected the perceived importance of improving public services and not just providing employment.[6] Some large projects were moving forward, and CPA initiatives had improved the faltering health care system I encountered in southern Iraq. Civilian reconstruction projects, including short-term projects, were also a military priority, in the belief that community stabilization and economic development help to improve security.

A key point is that most U.S. reconstruction money was going to contractors and their expat staffs; only a small percentage was going to Iraqis themselves, a point glossed over by politicians but well understood by Iraqis. In contrast, ICSP, RTI, and other NGOs implemented no big-ticket projects, hired thousands of Iraqis, avoided long delays, spent money at local businesses, and probably got more appreciation.

Another major cause of public discontent was the failure to improve electricity and water services. These failures produced widespread unhappiness with the Americans and their perceived broken promises, though most of the problem was from the poor condition of the system, the post-invasion looting, and sabotage by insurgents. By the time I arrived, the daily output of Iraq's electrical system was below the prewar level and going down.

Indeed, a high percentage of Baghdad residents relied on either a home-sized generator they bought, if they could afford one, or privately operated generators connected to multiple homes and businesses by improvised overhead wires hung on utility poles. When the grid went down, generators (usually) went on. Selling generator time was a growth business despite the bad times. In all parts of the city the "generator man" was a critical figure, especially when the summer heat made air conditioning a necessity, at least for sleeping. That didn't make him popular, as the coverage and service could be less than promised, making the generator man, by one account, "the most vilified figure in Iraqi society after Saddam Hussein."[7] Those hurt most by the lack of electricity were those too poor to rent generator time.

The view of Iraq from Baghdad was different from my earlier view from the other end of the pipeline—and more ominous. Baghdad was nothing like Amarah, and Iraq was not the same country I had left in mid-2004. In the immediate aftermath of Saddam's exit stage right, the Baghdad economy had seemed okay. The insurgency then made street life risky and commerce a struggle. A lot had happened, much of it bad, and I was destined to be there as it got worse.

6

Islam and Democracy in the New Iraq

Signs on the Walls

Those rides I took through the streets of Baghdad told me a lot about the emerging politics of Iraq. My November 2005 arrival coincided with the campaign for the first Council of Representatives (COR). Election Day was December 15. It was the third election day of the year, after the January 30 election for the Transitional Government and provincial governments and the October 15 constitutional referendum. The new national government would replace the Transitional Government. I took a lot of interest in this election, as the results could affect our work at ICSP.

The profusion of political campaign signs was positive evidence of an emerging democracy. A typical campaign sign in Baghdad was a banner hung from a wall. Baghdad is full of walls, as brick walls along property lines are common. It also has many temporary barriers and other good sign locations. Many signs were attractively done, often with photos. Almost all of them featured one of the three-digit numbers assigned randomly to each party by the Independent Electoral Commission of Iraq. For some voters, numbers were easier to remember than party names.

I couldn't read the Arabic but paid attention to the numbers. The 555 of the United Iraqi Alliance (UIA) (۵۵۵ in Arabic) looked dominant. Other slates and parties reported in news accounts as major contenders, including the Iraqi National List of former prime minister Ayad Allawi, had nowhere near the street presence of the UIA.

At Wael's Palace interest in the election matched the palpable buzz on the streets. There, however, I saw a lot of hope and enthusiasm for Allawi, suggesting he had wide support among educated and professional people, Christians as well as Sunnis. Iraqi staff told me, for example, "My family is voting for Allawi" and "I think Allawi is going to win, and I hope so." Their loyalty was touching but didn't change my street-level evaluation.

Although Baghdad is the heart of Sunni Arab territory and was the center of Sunni political power, the city actually has a Shia majority. Sadr City alone has over 2 million people, and most other districts east of the Tigris, including Karrada, were mainly Shia. The UIA also had high-level coordination and countless campaign workers, whereas Sunni Arab parties mostly ran on their own or formed slates with small parties. In mostly Sunni western Baghdad the signs of the Iraqi Accord Front, led by the Iraqi Islamic Party, were prominent. Elsewhere it seemed at street level that the Sunni Arabs had been outorganized and outhustled. To a political scientist reading the signs on the walls, the election outcome seemed predictable.

The positive feeling surrounding the election reflected favorably the efforts of USAID and its contractors, as well as the CPA, to foster a meaningful democracy. It was a point of pride that we helped Iraqis reach the stage where they could elect their own government. This was an undeniable success story that helped offset some of the CPA's mistakes. Now leaders with competing sectarian and ethnic backgrounds would have to work together to make the new government effective. No one thought that would be easy, which was why we were still there.

Islam and Iraqi Politics

Shia and Sunnis

That political parties are defined in religious terms is a story in itself. That story is complicated but critical for understanding the politics of Iraq. The political alignments evident from the parties and slates competing, largely the same as for the first election in January, raised puzzling questions to people in the West. Why do Shia and Sunnis act like separate religions if they're all Muslims? Why are they in separate political parties?

The story behind the story. The religious division between the Shia and Sunni branches of Islam resulted from one long-ago historical event. The Prophet Mohammed was born in the sixth century and died in the seventh, in 632. He had no sons and designated no successor in writing, but Shia interpret something he said to be an endorsement of Ali, his son-in-law and fervent supporter—an interpretation disputed by Sunnis. Ali was then only twenty-five to thirty years old. The father of one of the Prophet's wives was named as the first caliph.

Twenty-four years later, in 656, Ali became the fourth caliph and moved the capital from Saudi Arabia to Kufa, Iraq, but internal conflict ensued, and he was assassinated by rivals in 661 at a mosque in Kufa. Ali's followers saw his son Hussein, the Prophet's grandson and an outspoken reformer, as next in the line of succession, but there was a power struggle, and in 680 Hussein was killed and beheaded during a battle near Karbala that also killed all seventy-two men in his contingent. The succession was thus taken from the Prophet's family. *This is the issue.*

Shia believe Hussein is buried in Karbala, the second most important religious city in Iraq after Najaf. They regard Najaf's Imam Ali Mosque, honoring his father, as the third holiest shrine in Islam, after the Kaaba in Mecca and Mohammed's burial place in Medina, Saudi Arabia. Much of the lingering emotion is because Hussein died in Iraq, and Shia Iraqis feel he belongs to them. The circumstances of his death, described by the Shia as a betrayal and murder, make the event more wrenching and emotionally overwhelming. Hussein became a martyr for all time. The animosity over his death has lasted through the centuries.

"So what?" you say. "This happened over 1,300 years ago. Can't they let it go?" In fact, no. To hear the devout speak, this long-ago moment in history is as unforgiven today as it was in 680. The event is endlessly reenacted and relived as if it happened yesterday.

Religious history became political history. These two major branches of Islam have never reunified. Their conflict in Iraq is part of a broader conflict affecting most of the Middle East. Worldwide, the Shia are vastly outnumbered, but in the Middle East they are outnumbered only about three to two. Over the centuries, however, political power in the Middle East has been held primarily by Sunnis, cause for a thousand-plus years of Shia resentment.

In Iraq, however, Sunni Arab dominance was *not* based on numbers; they are only about 20 percent of the population. Shia make up about 60 percent. The Sunni Kurds plus smaller numbers of Christians and other religious minorities total about 20 percent. But the Shia had never been in charge. The British left Iraq to a Sunni monarchy. After the Baathists took power, they suppressed the Shia, though also the Sunni Kurds. Over the years Sunni Arabs also developed feelings of cultural superiority toward the Shia that didn't end in 2003.

The post-Saddam political awakening in southern Iraq was thus a religious awakening too—an affirmation of Shia identity. Awareness of their numerical majority created hope among the Shia that they would finally gain political control.

Those sectarian differences don't mean most Shia and Sunnis hate each other, despite impressions created by news reports. The Kurds, who are Sunnis but not Arabs, have no stake in the sectarian conflict. Their shared anti-Saddam history puts them politically closer to the Shia than to their fellow Sunnis. Until the post-Saddam period it was safe for Sunnis to live in southern Iraq. Several million Sunni and Shia lived in close proximity in Baghdad and nearby areas, along with many Kurds. Parts of Baghdad were mixed Sunni-Shia areas, and Sunni-Shia intermarriage became more common.

I detected quickly that the religious orientation of ICSP staff was different from my Amarah team. Most Amarah staff were overtly religious Shia, but the mainly Sunni and Christian ICSP staff reflected a balance of religious and secular priorities in their daily lives. This isn't to say they were not religious; some were not, but others prayed in their offices. Their social orientation was less strict, however. Some women were less meticulous about Islamic clothing standards. They were less uptight in social situations; some initiated handshakes, for example. They were more receptive to parties and dancing. By contrast, as noted by the ever-perceptive Haider, from a Shia family, most Shia are totally serious and even grim about everything relating to their faith and, having no sense of humor about it, are readily sensitive to perceived slights.

The Shia and the Grand Ayatollah

Major events throughout Islamic history since the Prophet's death have been marked by political conflict. The anti-Baathist movements were mobilized primarily by religious leaders, who also organized armed militias. All five major Shia political parties emerging after the Baath fell came from party histories in which religion and politics were combined.

My Democracy Survey results in Maysan showed that the role of Islam in politics and government was the most divisive issue in post-Saddam Iraq. Provisions in the constitution that made Islam and democracy compatible pleased some while antagonizing others. The most influential man in Iraq held a distinctive position on this critical issue.

Despite his preeminent status and contrary to impressions from many news stories, Grand Ayatollah Ali Sistani had avoided public criticism of Saddam's regime and seemed apolitical until just after Saddam was deposed. With the Baathists gone, Sistani suddenly embraced political advocacy. In opposing CPA plans for forming the transitional government and for the Transitional Administrative Law, Sistani launched almost a PR campaign, using major media to spread his message. In so doing, he made himself a major political player.[1]

While his leadership role seemed to combine religion and politics, Sistani's specific actions were pro-democracy and nonsectarian.[2] As I learned while in Maysan, he did not favor the pro-Iran agendas of the Supreme Council for the Islamic Revolution in Iraq (SCIRI) and Iraqi Dawa Party, and he was no ally of Moqtada Al-Sadr, who had tried to overthrow him. He issued an early fatwa telling clerics to avoid seeking political office and to play only a general advisory role in politics. He was, however, a shrewd political strategist whose apparent purpose was to get the Shia political factions to work together so election results would reflect the Shia majority.

Sistani had played a huge election role so far. His call for all Iraqis to register, and to vote on January 30, had ensured a high Shia turnout. By letting the UIA invoke his name and use his photo, he tacitly endorsed its campaign, though he did not participate directly. In October his endorsement of the constitution helped ensure its passage with huge Shia majorities, though he disliked some provisions and remained silent until the last minute. He did all this without calling press conferences, doing media interviews, or even meeting with Coalition leaders. He was at once mysterious yet powerful, reclusive yet the nation's most prominent public figure.

As December 15 neared, Sistani avoided making any endorsement, but UIA leaders repeated his January injunction to vote and publicly claimed his support anyway. He said nothing publicly to suggest his previous implied support had been withdrawn.[3] There was speculation, however, that he was unhappy with the performance of the Transitional Government.

Sistani's leadership had greatly helped my democracy project in Maysan. By the time I arrived in Baghdad, his influence was that much greater. For those of us trying to help Iraq become a meaningful democracy, Sistani was a huge asset.

Sunni Arabs and the Politics of No

By contrast, the outnumbered Sunni Arabs had a lot of political power to lose in the new Iraq and needed to work together. They did the opposite. Their boycott of the January election served only to help the Shia and Kurds, though voting would have implied acceptance of democracy and the end of Sunni Arab dominance. In the October referendum their unsuccessful No campaign again set most Sunni Arabs against the rest of the country and the flow of events.

For December the major Sunni parties reacted to the UIA coalition by organizing *competing* coalitions. The Iraqi Accord Front was led by the moderate Iraqi Islamic Party, the largest Sunni party, which supported the constitution. The Iraqi National Dialogue Front was a secular but rejectionist coalition that led opposition to it. Many of those other signs on the walls, some with nice color photos of candidates, were hopeful messages from well-meaning but inexperienced gentlemen who had no chance of winning much of anything in this election.

One huge Sunni Arab disadvantage was the lack of a leadership figure comparable in stature to Sistani. Sunni clergy, moreover, had compromised their public reputation over the years by playing ball with Saddam. After Saddam fell, there was a backlash against the clergy. The leadership vacuum was increasingly filled by younger and more militant preachers spouting political extremism, exactly the opposite of Sistani's leadership.[4]

By reputation the strongest, most hardline Sunni Arab group was not a political party but the deceptively named Association of Muslim Scholars (AMS), founded just after the fall of Saddam. Its eager role as mouthpiece for the insurgency was neither Islamic nor scholarly and actually undermined Sunni interests. AMS had strongly supported the counterproductive boycott in January. It urged Sunnis to turn out for the constitutional referendum in October but to vote no as a rejection of the U.S. "occupation" and the Iraqi government accused of cooperating with it. AMS pronouncements got some popular support, but its leaders' statements were often criticized. The annoying tendency of Western media to treat the AMS as an official voice for all Sunni Arabs greatly inflated its real importance.[5] For December it didn't advocate a boycott but didn't participate either.

Iran and Iraqi Politics

The subject is religion and politics in Iraq—so what does Iran have to do with it? The answer is that the ideology and policies of the Iraqi political parties are based largely on their differing orientations toward Iran. It's a complicated but important story that helps counter the often misleading statements from the media and various "experts" that have persisted to this day.

The story behind the story. When Ayatollah Ruhollah Khomeini overthrew the Shah of Iran in 1979, Saddam took it as a direct threat to the secular Baathist regime. The Iran-Iraq War started in 1980. Khomeini's revolution was openly supported by Mohammed Baqir Al-Sadr,[6] leader of the Dawa (Islamic Call) Party in Iraq, founded in 1957 largely as an Islamic rival to the long-standing, secular Communist Party. The Baathists seized power in 1968 and declared Dawa illegal in 1970. Five of its leaders were executed in 1974 and many others jailed, forcing it to operate underground. For its part Dawa assassinated several Baath leaders and in 1980 tried to assassinate Foreign Minister Tariq Aziz. Saddam promptly tortured and killed Al-Sadr and his sister, arrested and executed tens of thousands of Dawa members, and issued a decree condemning *all* Dawa members and sympathizers to death.[7] Many remaining leaders and a huge number of members went into exile, mostly in Iran. In 1982 Dawa tried to kill Saddam himself in the Shia town of Dujail in Central Iraq. His retaliation against Dujail was in the end the specific charge (among the many) for which he would be executed.

Later, Dawa split into factions. Islamic Dawa shared the traditional democratic concept of governance represented by Sistani, and the elder Al-Khoei before him, which was inconsistent with the Rule of the Cleric enunciated by Khomeini, apparently with himself in mind.[8] Dawa distanced itself somewhat from Iran, established itself in Syria under the protection of the Shia-dominated Assad regime, and developed connections in the West, especially in London. A Dawa splinter group kept close ties to Iran, worked under Iranian leadership, and emerged after Saddam as the Al-Dawa Party Iraqi Organization, or Iraqi Dawa.

In Maysan, Islamic Dawa was a cooperative and productive party, whereas the misleadingly named Iraqi Dawa was considered so pro-Iran that CPA-Maysan excluded it from the Provincial Council altogether.[9]

Thousands of Shia from southern Iraq fought on Iran's side in the war. The Iran-supported Badr Brigade grew into the Badr Corps, a paramilitary force of several thousand, organized and trained in Iran. It operated there for twenty years. In 1982 the Supreme Council for the Islamic Revolution in Iraq, headed by an imam, Mohammed Baqir Al-Hakim, became its political arm. Al-Hakim supported Khomeini's revolution and envisioned a wider Shia nation in which southern Iraq would join as some kind of autonomous region. While some Shia supported this agenda, most stayed loyal to Iraq, supported their country in the war, and lost thousands of their men. They distrusted SCIRI's motives and opposed political collaboration with Iran.

After Saddam fell, the Badr Corps moved into Iraq, was renamed the Badr Organization, and operated as an open if shadowy entity, still with Iranian financial support. While SCIRI as a political party worked to overcome public suspicions about its Iran connections, Badr acquired a sinister reputation for collaborating with Iran and for assassinating former Baathists, often minor functionaries guilty of no crimes, as well as others inconvenient for Iran's interests.

With SCIRI now a major player in Iraqi politics, its original purpose was overtaken by events. Al-Hakim articulated a moderate, cooperative line toward the Coalition. He abandoned his idea of bringing southern Iraq under Iran's theocracy, which Islamic Dawa had abandoned years earlier. SCIRI could not afford a public perception that it was more loyal to Iran than Iraq.

On May 12, 2003, when Al-Hakim returned from his twenty-three-year exile in Iran, he was greeted by 10,000 people in Basra and by tens of thousands more in Najaf.[10] On August 29, 2003, however, he was assassinated (along with eighty to ninety others) by a car bomb detonated outside the Imam Ali mosque in Najaf by an Al-Qaeda in Iraq hit man. Al-Hakim's funeral procession in Najaf was attended by a half million people, reinforcing his enormous political importance.

The assassin was tried and executed. He had also confessed to participating in the attack on the Italian police in Nasiriya and assassinating an Iraqi Governing Council member. Al-Hakim's SCIRI mantle was inherited by his brother, Abd Al-Aziz Al-Hakim,[11] who became the most prominent UIA leader.

The fourth major Islamic party was Al-Ahrar, the Sadrist faction led by Moqtada Al-Sadr, continuing his father's activist and nationalist movement. The Sadrists owed nothing to Iran and made political capital out of that independence. Al-Sadr the father and Al-Hakim the father had strongly opposed each other, with Al-Sadr criticized for trying to create a rival organization separate from Sistani, instead of cooperating with Khomeini.[12] The differences were more complex, however. Al-Sadr the father supported Khomeini's concept of the "Rule of the Cleric" but wanted a separate theocratic government in Iraq under his own leadership.

Moqtada's emerging Mehdi Army became a competitor of the Badr Organization. The Badr militia was the most important at first, but the Mehdi Army soon became much larger. Other parties also had militias. In Maysan the secular militia leader Abu Hatim was militantly anti-Iran and anti-SCIRI. Collectively, the Shia militias were a huge and worsening problem, compounded by the Sunni militias fighting American troops. By the time I got to Baghdad, southern Iraq was under increasing militia control and Iraq's security was deteriorating.

A second, more moderate Sadrist faction became the Fadhila (Islamic Virtue) Party, founded in 1999 and led by Mohammed Ali Al-Yaqoubi, a student and deputy of Al-Sadr the father. Like the Moqtada faction, it was a nationalist party rather than pro-Iran. It had more support from the educated professional class, in contrast to Moqtada's constituency among the poor, but its support was likewise primarily in southern Iraq, especially the Basra governorate.

The orientation of these three political movements and five political parties was therefore in all cases Islamic but had major ideological and policy differences reflecting different orientations to Iran. Once the post-Saddam era began, the two Dawa parties, SCIRI, and the two Sadrist parties emerged as major competitors for power in the democratic Iraq our civilian coalition had worked so hard to create.

The UIA had now added the Moqtada faction, putting all five major Shia parties in the same coalition, along with pro-UIA independents. This reflected a judgment that having the Sadrists inside the tent was better than leaving them to be an unpredictable opposition. The erratic Moqtada had major popular support and could be a dangerous opponent. This decision would have many large consequences, some bad.

The People's Choice

Of the Council of Representatives' 275 seats, 230 were divided among the governorates based on the number of registered voters. This was a huge improvement over January, when voters were forced to choose among national candidate lists. Seats were now allocated under a proportional representation system—based primarily on the percentage of the governorate-level vote won by each party.

One effect of proportional representation is that small parties are represented in proportion to their popular support, whereas in a system of single-member constituencies—as in the United States and United Kingdom—the parties getting the most votes consistently win the seats, and small parties tend to get shut out because they can't win a plurality in any constituency. The reasoning behind the Iraq system, developed with heavy Coalition advice, ironically, was to be inclusive above all else so the great majority of voters would feel represented and accept election results peacefully. The downside of such a system, in Iraq as elsewhere, is that it produces weaker governments. The downside was destined to overwhelm the upside.

Proportional representation encouraged more people to run and more groups to form slates—great for participation but confusing to voters. By one account there were 7,655 candidates; 996 candidate lists; 307 political entities, including parties and individual candidates; and 19 coalitions. Baghdad alone had 2,161 candidates and

106 candidate lists competing for 59 seats.[13] No wonder there were so many campaign signs! So, it was a mess, but it sure was inclusive.

Yet because the focus was on the alliances and parties rather than individual candidates, voters had little chance to relate voting choices to issues in their areas. People were expected to vote for candidates they didn't know, who were perhaps not even from their area, and who did not debate or establish positions on public issues.

Voters anywhere always have some basis for their votes, however, or they wouldn't vote at all. The UIA again appealed successfully to voters' Islamic loyalties. The Sunni Arab vote also went largely to Islamic parties. Many who didn't want a sectarian government voted for Allawi's coalition, but they were outnumbered. So, the election rules and clever coalition building again turned an election into a referendum on Islam. Once again, Islam won.

The UIA won 128 of the 275 seats (down from 140 in January); the Kurdistan Coalition, led by its two dominant parties, won 53 (down from 75); and Allawi's National Iraqi List won 25 (down from 40). The lost seats went to the two main Sunni parties, who won 44 and 11, finally creating a meaningful Sunni bloc. Seven smaller parties won the rest, each with under 2 percent of the vote. The truly impressive turnout was almost 80 percent, a figure U.S. voters can only dream about.

Lost in the Islamic shuffle was Allawi's fifteen-party list. It incorporated the parties of former president Ghazi Al-Yawer and the distinguished Adnan Pachachi and the Communist Party. It was the one consequential list that bridged sectarian differences. It would have helped Allawi if the campaign were more about policy issues or his previous stewardship, instead of Islam.

In the South the UIA won 35 seats, compared to 4 for Allawi's coalition. In South-Central Iraq the UIA won by 35 seats to 5. The Iraqi Accord Front (Sunni) got 1 seat in each region.

The much more splintered vote in the Sunni-majority Central Iraq governorates gave the Iraqi Accord Front 34 of its 44 seats, 13 in Baghdad, and gave the Iraqi National Dialogue Front 8 of its 11. The UIA, however, won big in Baghdad, getting 34 seats and 59 percent of the vote, and it won 5 seats from three other Central Iraq governorates. Those signs on the walls were an accurate barometer. Baghdad was also where Allawi's list did best, winning 8 seats.

The Kurdistan alliance won big in the three Kurdish provinces and won 11 seats in adjoining Diyala, Kirkuk, and Ninewa.

Beyond the great turnout and the other statistics were the thousands of Iraqis feeling the joy and pride from having voted in a meaningful election. After all their troubles, the United States and United Kingdom could take a lot of credit for that. Creating a democratically elected Iraqi government was a huge success story for which those of us who went to help could feel some personal pride.

Yet many U.S. media commentators created misleading impressions. One was that Islamic parties are all right wing and pro-Iran. The election was seen as producing a pro-Iran government that favored an Iranian-style regime, a view that was simply uninformed. Moreover, from my on-the-ground perspective, some of those elected from Islamic parties were fairly progressive, such as the Dawa politicians I knew in Maysan. Others were primarily secular. Many had lived for years in the democratic West. The media's image of the UIA as a monolithic Islamist bloc just wasn't accurate.

The actions of Iran itself were another matter, especially the materials for explosively formed projectiles (EFPs) it sent to Iraq to make roadside bombs that killed American and British soldiers, often using a long-standing smuggling route through Amarah. It later made even more lethal EFPs in Iran itself and sent them into Iraq. The militantly anti-Coalition Sadrists, despite their supposed anti-Iran stance, were willing collaborators in this deadly game.

Overall the election results confirmed the transfer of political dominance from the Sunni Arabs to the Shia. The Sunni Kurds also gained influence. Shia parties won in ten of the eighteen governorates, the Sunni Arabs in four, and the Kurds in four. Various poll results showed that the once-dominant Sunni Arabs were now feeling much more negative, pessimistic, and disaffected toward their government than other citizens.

Christmas in Muslim Iraq

As the election campaign reached its final days, I was not even in Baghdad. For security reasons—specifically the conceivable risk of an attack on the compound around election time—ICSP management decided to move some of us to Erbil, the Kurdish capital. The logic was that if there was an attack, they would have only half the expats to move out, whereas moving everyone at once would take more vehicles than we had. I felt that an attack driving to or from the airport was a higher probability, but we flew to Erbil December 11, four days before the election, and returned December 18, three days after.

This trip turned into a pleasant week in the historic Erbil suburb of Ankawa, whose Christian roots go back to the missionary travels of the apostle Saint Thomas. Its ancestors were among the first Christian converts, in 33 AD. It has kept its Catholic identity through the centuries. We stayed comfortably in a large Christian-owned house where our (Muslim) Erbil regional manager lived.

The neighborhood had been turned into a compound, with security checkpoints at each entrance. USAID and several contractors had offices there, attracted by the relative safety of a Christian neighborhood. Hana's Restaurant was a modest spot but offered good food and a chance to meet other expats. We got out and walked the streets. It looked like the safest place in Iraq.

I also met with my Erbil Anti-Corruption and Human Rights teams, whose office was across the street from the house. Unfortunately, we had just had to replace the Anti-Corruption coordinator, leaving issues to discuss. I was learning that Anti-Corruption programs lacked political support from the Kurdish political leadership and at times encountered outright interference. The official line, sometimes stated in an intimidating way, was "There is no corruption in Kurdistan." This would not be my last trip to Erbil.

I returned to Baghdad for my second Christmas in Iraq in three years. Wanting to buy small gifts for my Baghdad staff but unable for security reasons to get out and shop, I let Ghassak help me. I was not sure that novelty coffee mugs, like one in the shape of Bugs Bunny's face, were a winning idea, but she assured me Iraqis would love them. My visit to the army PX the Friday before Christmas helped me get a few more things. So, I found myself wrapping Christmas presents after all. (I still can't do it well, but let's face it, it's just not a guy activity.) Ghassak thoughtfully bought me "To/From" cards to attach to the presents. I guess you can't find "Merry Christmas" cards in many Baghdad shops, but I had to explain that "I Love You" was not the appropriate substitute message, especially to men.

Ghassak organized a staff Christmas party for everyone, helped by Christian friends on the staff. Almost every Muslim came. A Muslim project official opened the party with a thoughtful statement about the importance of people from different cultural traditions working together. Iraq could have used more of that message. There was a gift exchange and somehow a second gift for everyone under ICSP's Christmas tree. Ghassak could organize anything.

Then came the sound of music and dancing. Almost everyone was in motion, mostly in circle dances. Then they played a Kurdish dance tune. Kurds sprang from their chairs. People I had thought were mild-mannered led the wildly enthusiastic circle. Watching the Kurds dance was perhaps the most joyful experience I ever had in Iraq. Someone told me that Iraqis like to celebrate but the security risks and hard times had limited their opportunities. Even weddings were scaled down, to lower the risk of being targeted by terrorists. So, a chance to let loose in a secure environment was cherished.

On Saturday and again Christmas morning, a Sunday, I noticed at the Rimal Hotel that the Christmas masses were being televised. As in America, the churches were crowded.

One night just before Christmas, I was in my office when I heard a child singing outside my window. "Jingle bells, jingle bells, jingle all the way." It took me a few seconds to realize I was hearing a Christmas carol in English. Looking out my window, I saw two small children and their parents entering their house across the street. It was another moment of inspiration from Christmas in Iraq.

The People's Government

Once the UIA won, its internal rivalries appeared. The big question was who would be prime minister. Both SCIRI and Islamic Dawa wanted it. Like Ayad Allawi, Dawa's transitional prime minister, Dr. Ibrahim Al-Jaafari, had lived many years in exile, mainly in London. His tenure had begun with great hope, but fate was unkind, and deteriorating security undermined him. Unlike Allawi, a reputed tough guy willing to confront people, Al-Jaafari failed to show strong crisis leadership and did not stand up to the Mehdi Army, which defined him to Sunni Arabs as a sectarian leader. He also antagonized the Kurds. U.S. officials lobbied against him, and Bush wanted him out.

I had noticed in preelection U.S. press coverage that Adel Abd Al-Madhi of SCIRI was paying an official visit to Washington to meet high officials and members of Congress. I read something into his trip, as he had a heavyweight inside reputation, and no other Iraqi leaders made similar visits. I suspected the deal was in to make Al-Madhi the new prime minister. His visit seemed like a kind of preparation tour.

Indeed, a deal probably was in, but it didn't hold up. Moqtada opposed Al-Madhi, and the large Sadrist bloc refused to vote for him. He lost by one vote. This appeared to save Al-Jaafari, but in a U.S.-brokered compromise, Al-Jaafari was forced to drop out in favor of his Islamic Dawa deputy, Nouri Al-Maliki.[14] The presidency stayed with Jalal Talabani, who had given the position a visible and active role in the government.

From there it was a major adventure: thirty-five days to release the results (January 20); two more months for the COR to officially convene (March 16); and another two months for Al-Maliki to present his minister nominees (May 20). With an absurd thirty-four ministries plus three ministers without portfolio, too much time was spent on too many politicians. In the end the Kurdish alliance, Iraqi Accord Front, and Allawi's coalition agreed to join the government. The ministers included eighteen Shia, eight Sunni Arabs, seven Kurds, and one Christian. The Ministry of State for Civil Society went to the Sadrists, a decision that would soon cause me a lot of anxiety.

All this bargaining in pursuit of the elusive unity government prized by U.S. strategists was also the starting point for politicizing the ministries, as the party controlling each ministry replaced incumbent technocrats with an excess number of party loyalists, most inexperienced and of lesser competence. Their loyalties were to themselves, their parties, and the parties' agendas, not to the prime minister, the government, or the people. Not much unity there. It was the start of a corrupt process that would get worse with each cabinet reshuffle.[15]

For many successful candidates, getting elected was easier than staying alive after getting elected. Being elected, and especially getting a cabinet or other high post, made you a potential target. Insurgents learned where you worked, where you lived, and how you moved from place to place. It was impractical to give everyone large security details, and some that were provided proved to be not large enough.

Many officials were assassinated along with their security men or escaped but with deaths to security men, family members, or others. One Sunni leader had been assassinated one day after appearing on TV to urge Sunnis to vote. Those living in the Baghdad area were at greatest risk. Some COR members decided to live largely outside Iraq. One potential cabinet minister I personally knew about gave up his seat and moved his family to Jordan. Getting members to attend sessions and meetings became an acknowledged problem.

December 2005 confirmed the pattern set in January 2005, but it was an election on the way to somewhere else. A more meaningful measure of public opinion had occurred in the provincial elections in January, in which the UIA's component parties competed with each other. Those provincial governments were not transitional and continued in office. My regional teams and their CSOs were already working with many of them. Yet at the national level the Islamic parties' marriage of convenience left unpredictable possibilities. Much had happened in the two and a half years since the Coalition invasion. The four years to the next national election were a long time, and much would happen by then to change the political equation in Iraq.

The Shia coalition won as the signs on the walls had foreshadowed. The new government reflected the downside of the Coalition's political legacy, however: an Iraqi government so inclusive it could neither govern effectively nor control its own corruption. That was not good news for me because I was ICSP's Anti-Corruption manager.

7

The Struggle to Reduce Corruption

No Small Problem

Defining Corruption in Iraq

While we awaited word on the makeup of the new government, my Anti-Corruption (AC) Team was gaining momentum. In the two months since my arrival in Baghdad, however, it had become clear that Iraq's corruption was far more advanced than the efforts to stop it.

One of many naive assumptions of Coalition policy makers was that Saddam's departure would lead to a less corrupt government. Reality was that while his regime was corrupt in ways benefiting Baath leaders and insiders, strict laws, the spy network, and the intimidation factor made it dangerous for others to take personal advantage. With Saddam gone, the lid was off. Countless government employees found ways to enhance their paltry salaries, and some got rich. Corruption was so bad when I arrived in November 2005 that Iraq was rated one of the world's most corrupt nations, tied for 137th out of 159, by Transparency International (TI), the world's leading anti-corruption authority. By 2006 Iraq was already the third most corrupt, beating out only Burma and Somalia.

Iraq's precipitous decline from its already lowly standing reflected astonishing corruption schemes that began after authority was transferred to Allawi's Interim Government. To quote one inside observer, "The Interim Government did not invent corruption, neither could its successor governments claim to have clean hands, but it did preside over a veritable avalanche of corrupt practices, some breathtaking in their range and size."[1] Several new ministers and other high officials, even well-regarded returnees from other countries, proved to be thieves on a grand scale. Many fled Iraq before they could be brought to justice. Most astonishing was a Ministry of Defense scheme that diverted almost $2 billion budgeted for military equipment to private accounts in foreign banks.[2]

An even bigger corruption racket was smuggling oil out of southern Iraq, begun as a scheme by Saddam to partly offset the UN's crippling post–Gulf War sanctions but now a lucrative opportunity to profit at the government's expense. Dubious socialist policy provided subsidies making fuel less than half the price of the same fuel in neighboring countries—a big incentive to steal imported fuel and smuggle it out of Iraq for resale. Those two factors, plus outrageous government mismanagement of fuel supplies, helped explain the incredibly long lines we saw at gas stations (extending many blocks). The lost revenue was in the billions of dollars. Iraq tripled the official price and lowered subsidies in December 2005 under pressure from the International Monetary Fund—a hugely important reform. Still, as of July 2006 the U.S. comptroller would estimate that 10 percent of Iraq's oil and 30 percent of imported fuels were being stolen.[3]

Iraq offered obvious rationalizations for the corrupt. One was massive poverty caused by massive unemployment. A second was the increasing lawlessness, which made criminal activity easy, profitable, and for most criminals risk free. The crime problem stemmed partly from the UN sanctions, which undermined the state-run economy and led to smuggling, extortion, and other criminal enterprises that continued after the invasion. A third rationalization was the awful government salaries, which bottomed out due to the UN sanctions, creating incentives for soliciting bribes. Salaries were raised significantly under the CPA but remained low. Finally, the vast amount of money spent by the Coalition, often with inadequate controls due to the desire for quick results, was itself an invitation to take corrupt advantage.[4]

Corrupt behavior is usually, though not always, criminal too, but anti-corruption programs focus mostly on "administrative corruption" by public employees, often in cahoots with fellow employees or people outside government. In socialist Iraq an inordinate percentage of the labor force was employed by the government. Administrative corruption might start with a bribe, either offered or solicited, to obtain what should be a free service or to get an unauthorized service.

The CPA governorate coordinator in Wasit described the corruption inherent in projects: "Iraqis regarded the embezzlement of government money not as theft but rather as a form of holy calling. Contractors would commonly form cabals before bidding and share any proceeds. One city's construction companies would attack other companies who won a contract on their turf. Work was often shoddy and materials inferior. An engineer sent to check a contractor's work might be bribed to keep silent; he in turn might bribe anyone else whose silence he required." In one case a school headmaster complained that his newly refurbished school had no interior doors, but it was proved that he had removed the new doors himself and sold them.[5]

Some corruption is not about money. Nepotism, basically hiring or promoting your relatives, is considered a family obligation by many Iraqis. It's one example of a conflict of interest, defined as using a public position for private benefit. Iraq had countless conflicts of interest, but many were hard to trace, even in the unlikely event someone wanted to try.

From the same motive, officials hire their friends and steer contracts to people they know. It's all about *wasta*, a well-understood but counterproductive Middle East custom of favoritism. A friendly interpretation is that personnel decisions based on personal relationships rather than professional qualifications tend to ensure workplace harmony and don't always reflect corrupt motives, conceding the bad organizational consequences. TI says culture is never the cause of corruption. That may be a matter of definition.

It troubled me that much of Iraq's corruption was about life and death. Some corrupt activities helped fund insurgent and militia groups, leading to the deaths of Coalition soldiers. Medicine and equipment stolen from hospital pharmacies caused the deaths of patients. Infiltration of police units by militiamen led to countless murders. Officials or police who stood up to the corrupt would be risking their lives, so it was safer to look the other way.

The View from the Green Zone

After transfer of authority to the new Iraqi government in June 2004, leadership of the U.S. reconstruction effort moved from the CPA to the U.S. Embassy, which created an Iraq Reconstruction Management Office (IRMO). Just before I arrived, the embassy restarted an interagency anti-corruption working group, including IRMO, USAID, and the Justice Department, to bring some coordination to the anti-corruption effort.

I cheerfully accepted an invitation to join the group, even though it meant more work and risking a weekly trip to and from the International Zone (IZ). I believe in interagency coordination, and in Iraq we needed more of it. It also seemed like an opening to participate at the policy-making level and maybe increase our impact. They handed me a policy paper then under discussion.

The document cited several factors behind Iraq's corruption: free market distortions, including massive subsidies such as the food rations and below-market oil prices; the state-dominated economy and opportunities for rip-offs by government employees; cultural tolerance; the undeveloped civic culture, including lack of political leadership and a weak, overregulated CSO community; and lack of government capacity, including lack of transparency, inability to run politically impartial investigations, ineffective judicial and administrative systems, and penalties too weak to deter the corrupt. In short the paper blamed a combination of inherited socialist policies and weak government for enabling "pervasive" corruption.

The document proposed market reforms to eliminate subsidies and dismantle state-owned enterprises; standardized and transparent budget and procurement procedures, plus active efforts to investigate and combat corruption; and public integrity measures such as adherence to the rule of law and ensuring that resources were not wasted on corruption. It also proposed programs to strengthen the police and judiciary and provide rule of law training. Media, NGOs, and the public needed to be active in anti-corruption, and we needed to assist anti-corruption agencies and CSOs. I was skeptical about attacking the entrenched socialist economy as part of an anti-corruption strategy, but the analysis was otherwise solid.

Then I was told the group was for U.S. government officials only. Their invitation to me was a mistake. I was out. As USAID knew ICSP was running an important anti-corruption program and could bring on-the-ground experience to the meetings, the restriction seemed illogical, but it was pointless to argue with the U.S. government. The task force never contacted me about anything, and I forgot about them. I did meet a few times with IRMO officials, who were helpful.

In retrospect this closed-door policy was consequential. There were times when the task force, with its organizational clout, could have helped me have a larger impact, and my ground-level observations could have helped them. A U.S. government audit report in July 2006 would say that anti-corruption programs in Iraq suffered from a lack of coordination. Well, no kidding.

The International Perspective and USAID

In general corruption is worst in the poorest countries. This makes it an international issue, because international development money comes largely from foreign and international donors. All that outside money creates big incentives to make personal or political use of it.

The World Bank, which provides grants and loans of tens of billions of dollars annually to nations in need, has given a lot of attention to corruption and has made anti-corruption a critical part of its development strategy. All development agencies recognize that corruption wastes development money. Even the Vatican has an official statement about this. The logic is that every donated dollar diverted by corruption reduces the money spent on development. Once a corrupt pattern is set, moreover, the financial loss continues indefinitely and may increase.

The United Nations has also joined the anti-corruption battle. In October 2003 the UN General Assembly passed the United Nations Convention against Corruption. It designated December 9 as International Anti-Corruption Day. And so, on December 9, 2005, the world celebrated this event (or at least the sliver of the world's population attentive to such things). It was an early chance to grab some public attention for our Anti-Corruption program. My staff arranged a special program at the Baghdad Convention Center and invited the media. We got an experienced CSO leader to organize it, arrange for top-level speakers, and issue invitations.

I had experience in putting on events. I kept asking how things were going and asked a lot of questions, getting repeated assurances: "The CSO is really good." "A lot of people will come." "Everything will work out great." Don't worry, be happy.

December 9 fell on Friday, the Muslim Sabbath, so people were available. It turned out, however, that Friday was not a good day and that all those assurances were not good for anything. The event started over an hour late. Only a small percentage of the CSO's 200 invitees came. Vague promises that Talabani or perhaps Al-Jaafari would come, or at least send a representative, proved empty. The previously invited media did not arrive until well into the program and only after our Independent Media sector's Iraqi coordinator made a phone call. As the whole purpose was to raise public awareness, the delays undermined the event.

Our program included several speeches—by my South-Central Region coordinator (to describe our program), a representative of the Commission on Public Integrity, representatives of the CSO, and a well-known attorney with a dramatic speaking style, who then launched a loud and distracting on-camera interview in the back of the hall. The show was stolen by a delightful children's performing group. I chalked this one up to experience and let the UN celebrate the 2006 International Anti-Corruption Day without me.

USAID, the agency responsible for spending U.S. development dollars wisely, took an early anti-corruption leadership role. Most of its projects have anti-corruption components. Its official manual, *USAID Anticorruption Strategy*, calls corruption "a major barrier to development."

One major USAID finding is its distinction between administrative corruption (low-level) and "grand corruption" (high-level), conceding that the former often derives from the latter. The grand corruption concept certainly applied to Iraq, but ICSP's entire AC program was focused on the low-level corruption more accessible to CSO efforts. Transitioning from that to deal also with grand corruption would have required new strategies, a bigger program, an arsenal of weapons, and a lot more money than I had.

Another important USAID distinction is that anti-corruption programs focus on either "prevention" or "enforcement." USAID's role was limited to prevention, so ICSP worked under the same limitation. It seemed to me, however, that a *comprehensive* anti-corruption program would *link* prevention and enforcement. Therefore, I did not like this limitation nor, as it turns out, did USAID. The *USAID Anticorruption Strategy* says, "Legislative prohibitions generally restrict

USAID's ability to engage with law enforcement agencies to bolster the criminal aspects of anticorruption enforcement." This restriction "prevents USAID from implementing comprehensive prevention strategies" because it is prohibited from incorporating police and prosecutorial agencies in its projects. In Iraq this was a counterproductive policy.

Another U.S. agency pushing anti-corruption is the Millennium Challenge Corporation (MCC), proposed by President Bush in 2002 and formally established in 2004 to help reduce poverty. "Control of corruption" is part of the requirement for good governance. Instead of penalizing countries with excessive corruption, MCC rewards countries that perform well, based on carefully developed guidelines. Those meeting the guidelines are eligible for the Millennium Challenge Grant program. This approach has been praised by Transparency International. Based on TI's country ratings, however, Iraq was unlikely to qualify as an MCC nation anytime soon.

Promoting Transparency and Accountability

The key words in the anti-corruption business are *transparency* and *accountability*. Transparency means, among other things, that citizen participation is encouraged, meetings are public and announced in advance, documents are made available to media and the public, and the media are independent and allowed to print stories critical of the government.

Accountability follows from transparency. It means the public knows enough to hold elected officials accountable; media attention exposes corrupt behavior; the government has one or more independent agencies to investigate corruption allegations; and corrupt officials can be identified and prosecuted, then punished through an honest judicial system. In democracies we take these things for granted. In a place like Iraq, creating conditions that ensure transparency and accountability is a tall order.

The Baathists fostered the idea that government jobs are a benefit for the jobholders; the Western concept of public jobs as an opportunity for public service was poorly understood. It was unusual for an Iraqi government employee to be fired. As the worst penalty was some kind of verbal reprimand, there was generally no real bottom line. A manager actually confronting a corrupt employee could be threatened or worse, reflecting the culture of violence.

It followed that any supervisory job was a patronage opportunity, often followed by movement of relatives and allies into the office and transfer of current staff elsewhere (though they would not be fired). Such exercise of a man's presumed obligations to his own circle was thought to enhance his own standing and possibly lead to reciprocal favors later. Failure to do so would bring loss of status and potentially a loss of opportunity. The result was a personalized hiring system that was thoroughly corrupt even when no one was doing anything illegal. Of course, a supervisor surrounded by cousins and cronies had less incentive to be accountable, making corruption in his office more likely.

Transparency International's official bible, by Jeremy Pope, is *Confronting Corruption: The Elements of a National Integrity System*, often just called the TI Source Book. A key finding is that corruption happens from a combination of opportunity and inclination. Iraq had plenty of both. Attacking corruption effectively requires political will, which means anti-corruption measures are not only formally established but also enforced by government, which is more likely if broad segments of public opinion help to keep government officials honest. Among the many "institutional pillars" of a national integrity system, along with government and the private sector, are an active civil society and independent media. This is where ICSP came in.

Over time I found TI simultaneously welcoming and frustrating. On the plus side it was happy to include ICSP in some of its events. Indeed, when I arrived, Dashti was away at a TI Middle East conference in Berlin. He had also attended TI meetings in Beirut, Amman, and Kuwait during the year. For the next conference, in Amman in March 2006, we created a good PowerPoint presentation that summarized our accomplishments. Dashti was a good spokesman, and TI officials were impressed at how much we were doing.

I had hopes of establishing a Transparency International chapter in Baghdad and maybe a second one in Erbil for the Kurds. TI made it difficult to form national chapters, however, and with Iraq they played hard to get. TI was hung up on the fact that ICSP was U.S.-funded; it wanted to deal only with Iraqis. This suggested some anti-

American bias and in any case showed a lack of enthusiasm about TI chapters in Iraq. Even if the right Iraqi partners could be found and trained and we did everything else right, it could still take five years to get TI's final approval, and there was no assurance of that. My time frame was necessarily a lot shorter.

Raising Public Awareness

The National Anti-Corruption Awareness Raising Campaign

When I started, virtually all ICSP Anti-Corruption efforts were focused on the National Anti-Corruption Awareness Raising Campaign. As a first reaction, "awareness raising" may seem unexciting. In the West people promoting or opposing various civic goals are ubiquitous. In a nondemocratic society, however, that kind of activism is largely unknown. To create a democratic society, citizens have to be engaged, not just the government.

The capacity of CSOs to fight corruption had to be developed, as almost all of them were new since 2003. They needed training on anti-corruption strategies and techniques, including specific techniques for detecting corruption in government agencies and for raising public awareness of corruption. Our campaign was being implemented through workshops conducted for CSO members by our regional Anti-Corruption staffs and by grants awarded to some CSOs for community projects.

The workshops were spreading anti-corruption awareness to increasing numbers of people, including many with local influence, and because most events were covered by local print and electronic media, the impact was extended to the general public. A large and increasing number of CSOs had signed up with us, and many of the CSO grant projects got public attention. Craig Davis had done great work to build all this up and create a strong organization at headquarters and the regional offices.

My arrival in Baghdad was closely followed on November 20 by British lawyer Fiona Darroch, the latest international consultant to develop and present a new training workshop. Hers was the "Review of Existing Iraqi Laws, Regulations, & Policies for Combating Corruption." After revisions by AC staff and translation into Arabic, it was sent to all four AC regional teams.

These international consultants brought good ideas on awareness raising and on possible grant projects. Regrettably, Fiona would be the last international consultant I saw. A workshop on designing AC media campaigns didn't happen because potential consultants couldn't come. The second appearance of a Danish expert, working on a double-length workshop, was lost because Baghdad's escalating violence persuaded him not to return. Based on the first presentation and other research, however, Mohammed Adil of my Baghdad team and two CSO members created a complete workshop on "Efficiency in Administration and Results-Driven Management: A Strategy to Eliminate Corruption in Public Office"—a major accomplishment.

Combining new and previous titles, we had materials for nine training modules. These were presentations with covers, not professional training packages. Still, we required our regional offices to use only our "standard" training materials. The workshops were designed to last two days, and it was a policy not to water them down to one day, though we made exceptions.

As reports kept coming in from all the workshops, I learned that Iraqis like to talk. Those attending spoke freely, showed an understanding of corruption, and generated many ideas. One frequent opinion was the importance of involving CSOs in monitoring government offices, an idea I was pursuing.

Gradually, I also learned an important lesson from all the successful workshops reported to me. In a nation where so much was controversial, anti-corruption events were generally not controversial. Provincial and local officials, even governors, often attended to show support. Even in the most conservative corners of Iraq, anti-corruption had a constituency. This reflected people's awareness of corruption from their own experience and the congruence of the message with their Islamic faith. The surprising exception was the more secular and supposedly more democratic Kurdistan, where anti-corruption activity was discouraged.

ADF had set a goal to reach one million people through the Awareness Raising Campaign. This was a daunting challenge given the small scale of our events, but I eventually found ways to meet this goal by expanding the number of events and using mass media.

Completing a workshop made CSOs eligible for competitive grants to do community projects, typically lasting two or three months. Our regional AC teams gave technical assistance (TA) to these CSOs for their proposals and additional TA if they were funded. The other ICSP sectors used the same approach.

This system produced a fascinating variety of projects. Frequent approaches included creating and displaying anti-corruption aware-ness posters, banners, and signs; writing booklets, brochures, flyers, and other anti-corruption material; developing TV and radio pro-grams and other media campaigns; conducting opinion surveys and citizen investigations; organizing workshops, forums, and confer-ences; presenting art and cartoon exhibitions; and putting on plays and mobile theater presentations.

We had a lot of grant money for Anti-Corruption CSOs, over $1 million at times, though the amount on paper was often subject to some budget complication. Every few months Kristin Joplin would announce a new round of grants for a major amount of money, allo-cated among all six program sectors, though AC received the most. As with all U.S. government grants, CSOs had to meet precise crite-ria, some of them mandatory, to avoid disqualification. We got many more proposals than we could fund.

Proposals are complicated, however, even for people familiar with them. Iraqi CSOs had no familiarity with the U.S. government pro-curement system, so they were learning on the fly. All the instruc-tions were in English. So, while the large number of proposals was encouraging, getting more proposals that were actually good was another matter. Some CSOs improved from experience, but many just did not seem to "get it" in spite of our support.

There was a sharp difference of expat opinion on why we got so many bad proposals. One side of the argument blamed inexperienced or "lousy" CSOs. I actually had many years of proposal experience with U.S. federal contractors. I blamed the proposal instructions. This did not endear me to Kristin, but at times I proposed clearer instructions in places where CSOs were misreading them or miss-ing the point. Kristin accepted well-considered changes and made revisions of her own. Over a period of months we finally got to a version we both liked and which worked better. I wish I could say it solved all the problems.

Over time I saw that the other big hurdle in grant proposals was the requirement that they be in English. Many CSOs had English-speaking members, some excellent. Writing in a foreign language, however, is much harder than speaking it. Getting a proposal into clearly understandable English was a challenge for most CSOs, and our short proposal deadlines often left too little time to get the translation right or maybe to find the right translator.

Although the rules said proposals must be submitted in English, most CSOs, understandably, wrote theirs in Arabic (or Kurdish), then translated them. Some submitted their Arabic version too. At times we found that something unclear in their official English version was completely clear in the Arabic. In short the translation was the problem, not the substance of the proposal.

Lesson learned. Proposals for AID funding should be accepted in Arabic (or other native language). This policy would get more and better proposals. Those with proposals good enough to consider further would be invited to translate them into English and be given a week or two to do it. The extra time would be more than repaid in better projects.

A little cultural sensitivity would have helped. We were in an Arabic-speaking country. Why must proposals from Iraqis to help Iraq be in a foreign language? Sure, having the initial proposals in Arabic would be inconvenient for some expats. The question is whether we trust local staff (and Arabic-speaking expats) to screen and evaluate proposals. People can be trained for that and learn from doing it. Final USAID approval would still be based on the later English version. To any who say this approach leaves too much room for bad evaluations, I say they could not be worse than some I experienced in my days working on federal projects in Washington DC.

Civil Society Success Stories, Part 1

It won't insult many readers to say that most of us have no clear idea of what happens on our taxpayer-funded projects in other nations. Whatever expert help we provide, the bottom line is that the projects have to work on the ground, which means host country nationals have to make that happen. Those projects rarely get coverage in our newspapers. The good news you missed from Iraq is that those awareness-raising grant projects did work, and many were inspiring in their creativity and their results.

A CSO in dangerous Anbar Province gave eight anti-corruption workshops with the cooperation and protection of tribal sheikhs. Security conditions there made projects difficult to impossible, so this one made a big impression on USAID and became one of its official "Success Stories." The well-attended workshops drew some of Anbar's most important people. A common workshop complaint was that corruption was funding some of Anbar's insurgent activity. A few events were followed by swift action. One group organized a follow-up committee that seized control of a corrupt gas station. Another removed a corrupt city manager. It bothered me that these actions were not done democratically, but Anbar was the "Wild West" of Iraq, and I had to concede that the actions were decisive.

The General Legal Center boldly put up fourteen large anti-corruption signs in front of ministry headquarters buildings in Baghdad. These solicited anonymous corruption complaints to their hotline. A lot of people called. The CSO's legal committee checked out the credibility of the complaints and then transferred them to Iraq's new anti-corruption agency.

A project in Hilla, south of Baghdad, by the Civilian Dialogue Organization produced newspaper inserts with specific corruption allegations. One of several results was a committee formed by the Babil Governorate Council to investigate corruption in contracts to pave village roads. A separate volunteer effort produced a string of charges against a local hospital, prompting an investigation.

The Iraqi Center for Combating Administrative Corruption, one of our top Baghdad CSOs, used a citizen survey in two areas of Baghdad to expose corruption in the "food basket" (free food) program run by the Ministry of Trade, then held a public forum to report the findings. This ministry was essential to Iraq's safety net but was widely known for its corruption.

The Organization for Defense of Children's Rights in the South exposed the theft of medicines and equipment from Basra General

Hospital and their diversion to the black market. This was one of our favorite projects. The CSO devised survey forms and interviewed patients and visitors; held meetings with hospital staff to help identify the sources of corruption and the medicine and equipment missing; then held a public meeting to reveal the findings, inviting the media. A hospital administrator who did not embrace the findings found himself fired. It was one small victory over the endemic corruption in Iraq's Ministry of Health.

The Islamic Independent Administrators CSO back in Maysan worked with the anti-corruption agency to set up committees to receive corruption complaints. One led to the firing of the prison director in Amarah for stealing money and other crimes. Another led to removal of an Agriculture Directorate manager over hoarding seeds and fertilizers for his personal use.

A CSO in Kut organized a weekly anti-corruption program on local TV. It exposed cases of corruption, and changes sometimes followed.

A CSO in Muthanna Province in the South converted citizen complaints into an artists' exhibition of photos and posters. The complaints were sent to the Health Directorate, which agreed to set up an investigative committee.

Anti-corruption mobile theaters were a technique I didn't think much of at first, but they became a great success in southern Iraq. An acting troupe traveled to several cities, drawing remarkably large audiences. An audience discussion followed each performance, underscoring points made in the drama.

Several of our best CSOs were in Kurdistan. A similar mobile theater project was done in far northern Iraq, in Dahuk, by The Voice of Older People. Its fifteen performances, mainly in smaller places that would not normally see such an event, drew 500 people. Its mini-dramas highlighted bribery, nepotism, and medical clinic corruption.

Another Kurdish CSO ran eight live radio programs on Radio Nawa in northern Iraq. The programs hosted academics, anti-corruption activists, and government officials to discuss the effects of corruption and how to combat it.

There were many more success stories. Not all projects had a big impact, but their collective influence on public awareness was significant, especially because of the media coverage. There was nothing inevitable about these success stories. They were a credit to my regional teams that provided the training and technical assistance. It wasn't just my opinion that Anti-Corruption had the strongest team at ICSP.

Even more than in Amarah, I relied on democratic management. I delegated day-to-day management to Dashti, often sought his opinion, and generally took his advice. Dashti, Ameer, and Miami, plus Usama doing Human Rights, worked as a team, with smiles and a sense of purpose. I held numerous staff meetings to resolve specific problems together, often including the talented Baghdad team to let them participate in wider decisions. This may all seem like a small point, but the failure of ICSP's higher-level management to adopt a policy of delegating and transitioning authority to Iraqis later became an issue to USAID.

Taking the Fight to the Enemy

One day I learned that my Baghdad team had started doing occasional workshops for government employees inside government offices, using CSO presenters rather than ICSP staff, which would have raised issues. The motive was to stretch our limited monthly workshop budget. Holding events at government offices meant not having to rent a hall or pay participants the usual transportation allowance. We could fund two workshops for the price of one.

Craig and I envisioned a larger breakthrough. Workshops targeted to government workers had a larger potential impact on corruption than those directed to CSOs or the general public. In highly centralized Iraq the national government had ministry offices in every provincial capital. We had an almost unlimited potential audience. It was like taking the fight to the enemy.

I quickly got the word out to the other regional teams. We encouraged CSOs to go out and arrange their own presentations. Some had qualified presenters and were happy to earn the fee we paid for their services. Within weeks we were doing workshops in government agencies in most of Iraq. By February they were a majority of our workshops. The total workshops sharply increased. Our USAID project monitor was very happy. Workshops in government offices became one of our most successful innovations.

"There Is No Corruption in Kurdistan"

The USAID *Anticorruption Strategy* manual says, "Public sector reforms in environments of low political will appear to have limited chances of success." This statement absolutely applied to the Kurdistan Regional Government (KRG). The Kurds have cultivated a reputation in the United States as a democratic, pro-American bastion compared to the rest of Iraq. The pro-American part is true and reflects appreciation for U.S. protection after the 1991 Gulf War under the northern Iraq no-fly zone imposed against Saddam. The Kurds achieved self-government under this protection, actually two separate governments, giving them a twelve-year head start on the rest of Iraq.

The democratic part of the Kurds' self-image was exaggerated, however, and political corruption was the main reason. The burden of this contradiction between public posture and ground-level reality was on my regional Anti-Corruption Team in Erbil, capital of the KRG.

The KRG includes three of Iraq's eighteen governorates: Erbil, Dahuk, and Suleimaniya. Real control was divided between two major political parties—the Kurdistan Democratic Party (KDP) for Dahuk and Erbil, the Patriotic Union of Kurdistan (PUK) for Suleimaniya. The KDP, headed by Masoud Barzani, president of the KRG, is the political preserve of the Barzani family; PUK leader Jalal Talabani was then the president of Iraq.

In reality the two parties operate on the Soviet communist model, both headed by a politburo. The PUK is still avowedly socialist, while the KDP has repositioned itself as center-left. As in the old USSR, the parties placed themselves above the government, with authority to appoint all high government officials and many others, take money from the government treasury, and avoid public accountability. Party appointees dominated the courts. Mass media were largely controlled at this time by the two parties, leaving little incentive for transparency.

Given this concentration of power, corruption started at the top. It was economic as well as political, with officials gaining private benefit from their positions and development projects going to business investors with high-level connections. Both Barzani and Talabani had taken huge financial advantage of their leadership roles.

The distinctive problem we faced in Kurdistan was that the two parties were known to threaten or act against people who suggested publicly that there was corruption in Kurdistan. Our KRG anti-corruption awareness campaign actually had less political "space" for its events than we had in Iraq's other three regions.

In one memorable incident preceding my tenure, the Erbil AC Team supported an anti-corruption theater performance by an acting troupe in Erbil. Government permission was obtained, but security personnel prevented them from doing the performance, and the director and cast were arrested and mistreated.

In March 2006, when Zhian Health Organization presented workshops for 129 government employees of Erbil Education Hospital, the hospital manager walked out, refusing to admit there could be corruption in his hospital.

Governor Tamar of Dahuk refused to let a CSO run its anti-corruption grant project in his governorate. The CSO had to move the project to Kirkuk. I met the governor a few years later in his office and considered asking him about this incident, but the conversation was already a bit testy, and I thought better of it.

These incidents illustrated the real standing of Kurdistan's CSOs and the real limitations on citizens exercising their constitutional rights. Those limitations affected my team in Erbil. It was important to be aggressive, but doing so involved risks. My new coordinator, Zito Siany, made a positive difference and in February made a noteworthy diplomatic opening with the speaker of the Kurdish parliament, who pledged his cooperation. Most of the KRG corruption problem was still there, however, when I arrived to work in Erbil two years later.

Turning Awareness into Action

We all come into new positions with insights from our past. I had learned not to overrate the impact of public exhortations. We were holding public events, inviting media, and creating a lot of public awareness. However, that USAID manual stated, not to my surprise, that "public awareness campaigns are ineffective when not linked to specific reforms." Equally, "reform efforts are only successful when they incorporate elements of public education and engagement." How could we link our public awareness campaign to actual changes?

Cue the ICSP civil society advisor Jean-Sebastien Roy. He could talk for hours about *advocacy* and wanted ICSP to do more of it. Instead of just raising awareness, we should go a step further and propose specific changes. Because advocacy has specific objectives, it is more focused than awareness raising, and you have to advocate *to* an official or organization (e.g., the governor or the legislature).

Craig Davis soon convened a high-energy meeting about *impact*. Discussion was on impact-oriented events and grants. How could we go beyond even advocacy by revising our workshops and other events so advocacy would result in positive *outcomes*? It was good to attend an awareness-raising event, even better to advocate for a specific change, but it would be really great to make the change happen. CSOs that had done this were our success stories.

My solution for Anti-Corruption was to revise our workshop format to add an advocacy section toward the end. That also required participants to develop a follow-up *action plan*. In some places, especially government offices, there could even be follow-up committees.

Eventually, with help from our M&E manager, Dan Killian, I settled on *corrective action* as the ideal outcome. A corrective action could be a changed decision by a manager; a changed or new policy; enactment of legislation; investigation, prosecution, and conviction; a measurable change in public opinion; a measurable change in behavior; or another measurable change. It was easier said than done, but you have to start with the concept.

Lesson learned. The important lesson learned is that a fully effective anti-corruption strategy involves a series of conceptual stages. Awareness Raising (stage 1) can have both a public awareness component and a government agency component. Awareness Raising leads to Advocacy (stage 2). Effective advocacy supported by an action plan can lead to positive Outcomes, ideally including Corrective Actions (stage 3). All three stages can be planned together, as an *integrated strategy*. I wish I had understood this before I started. If you work on anti-corruption programs, read this paragraph again.

8

Extending the Anti-Corruption Struggle to the National Level

The Commission on Public Integrity

Linking Prevention to Enforcement

To go beyond advocacy to achieving specific outcomes, we needed to connect Anti-Corruption to the enforcement side of the prevention-enforcement spectrum. To do that, I needed to work with Iraq's new Commission on Public Integrity (CPI). The Iraq Civil Society Program (ICSP) could not participate directly in enforcement actions because of the legal limitation placed on USAID, but I felt that we and our civil society organizations (CSOs) could play an important supporting role.

The CPI resulted from a Bremer initiative to the Iraqi Governing Council and an executive order (no. 55). It was one of the CPA's most important accomplishments. The CPI was set up as an independent commission to discourage political interference. It started work in July 2004 with a commissioner, appointed just as the CPA was leaving town, and a few American advisors. This was Iraq's primary anti-corruption enforcement agency, though some of its work was on the prevention side. It was empowered to receive complaints from citizens (including anonymous complaints), investigate corruption allegations, refer violations of law to the criminal courts, and propose legislation to strengthen ethical standards for government employees.

I can't recall how our first meeting developed in January 2006, but it was a fascinating conversation. The CPI representatives cited two noteworthy accomplishments: a public employee "Code of Conduct," which all government employees had to sign a pledge to follow; and an annual financial disclosure form required of all high officials up to and including the president and prime minister.

The CPI representatives explained that the agency had six general directorates, including one for nongovernmental organizations, where they worked. Its main job was to develop positive relationships with CSOs. Their explanation sounded, however, like its primary role was to investigate CSOs. They said they couldn't work with any CSOs that had not been cleared. They wanted me to provide a list of all of ICSP's CSOs so they could screen them for us.

Startled by their audacity and unwilling to just turn over our entire list of CSOs, I tried "noncooperative reassurance." I explained ICSP's civil society mission and how we support and use CSOs. I said we did our own screening. Then I changed the subject. I had to use the same tactic at a later meeting.

They agreed to a second meeting, and several more followed. These alternated between ICSP and CPI headquarters, recently moved to a low-rise building at the east end of the Green Zone. The CPI had staffed up to about 400 to 500 employees and would be over 1,000 by mid-2006. The director-general of the NGO directorate, Hasan Alsafi, soon left CPI to become the inspector general (IG) at another ministry, but gradually a trio of sharp young CPI staff, including a supervisor with a doctorate, began working with us on a continuing basis.

CPI soon invited me to speak at a meeting of some of their cleared CSOs to explain ICSP. The event led to a bizarre scenario. ICSP security regulations for vehicle convoys limited passengers to expats, so Dashti and Usama had to get there separately. At the Green Zone entrance, Iraqi security wanted documentation the guys didn't have and would not let them in. Sitting at the CPI as the meeting started, knowing they had left when I did, I got worried and called, only to learn they were stuck at the gate. As I needed Usama to interpret, I tore myself away from the event to try to talk them through the Green Zone security. My PSDs had left for the PX, however, as I had told them I would be at the CPI for two hours.

So, in my most surreal experience in Baghdad, I found myself in a private car with no security, driven by an unarmed CPI staff member, rushing back down the road to the same busy security gate I had entered shortly before. I wandered around the security station, with all its Hesco bags and wire and the big (and unguarded) machine gun emplacement, looking for someone to talk to. Finally, I found a young army corporal who knew not and cared not about my problem but was certain his instructions meant he could not let my staff members enter.

Rushing in frustration back to the CPI, I accepted an offer from its interpreter to help me and did my presentation. Unfortunately, several CSO reps had issues with ICSP that were not about the Anti-Corruption program but needed tactfully worded answers. The CPI's guy was helpful but no Usama, and I could tell that parts of my answers were getting lost. Otherwise, it was a fine event.

One CSO attendee, physically handicapped, led a CSO whose mission was to help the handicapped. Having tried and failed twice to get a grant from ICSP, he felt desperate for help and was a sympathetic figure. As I finally drove out of the Green Zone with my PSDs, maybe a mile from the CPI, I saw this poor man almost at the exit, walking on crutches. Seeing how far he had already walked in this way, I better appreciated how much he and probably many other CSO leaders were sacrificing to help other Iraqis.

As we neared the end of our third or fourth meeting at the CPI, I suddenly I got an urgent-sounding request: "Please wait after the meeting. The commissioner wants to see you." After a delay lasting most of an hour, we were ushered into the large office of Radhi Hamza Al-Radhi, along with our new friends from the NGO directorate. Al-Radhi, from Kut in Wasit Province, was a judge by profession, a 1979 graduate of the Judges Institute, and sixty years old, though he looked older. He was jailed and tortured by Baathists in 1969 while working as a job safety inspector, after declining repeated offers to join the party. He managed to become a judge anyway because the Judges Institute, founded in 1976 to train lawyers as judges, didn't require Baath membership for admission until 1978. Al-Radhi enrolled in 1977.

Pleasantries aside, Al-Radhi had a lot to say, some of it in his limited English, and the meeting went on for some time. His blunt comments reflected frustration with Iraq's government. He identified its two most corrupt departments as Interior and Defense, in that order. A few *hundred* Interior personnel were under investigation. He complained that Iraq lacked even basic law enforcement technology, such as fingerprinting. As a result, he said sarcastically, "We get information from people the old-fashioned way. We torture them." He showed disturbing photos of people tortured and in some cases maimed by police. It was an engaging, eye-opening meeting with one of Iraq's best agency heads, and I left thinking we now had the kind of relationship we needed with the CPI.

As this relationship developed, it became clearer that the CPI knew what it wanted to do but was limited in what it could do. It had to worry about the security of its personnel and could not risk releasing contact information on its field staff to the public, including us. Its presence was geographically limited. Al-Radhi started with the major cities—Mosul, Basra, and Hilla, in addition to Baghdad—and the CPI was now in some other governorates, with roughly ten staff in each office, I was told, but not in others. Some of its work was being undermined by high government officials. So, while it was officially an independent agency, its decisions were nevertheless constrained by the Iraqi government and bad security conditions.

The CPI could not set up in the Kurdish governorates at all without a vote by the parliament of the autonomous Kurdistan Regional Government (KRG). We tried, and Al-Radhi tried. At his January 2006 meeting with parliament Speaker Adnan Mufti, my North Region coordinator, Zito Siany, raised the issue. Mufti told him the politburos of the two major parties had discussed this and that even if they agreed to such an agency, it would not be linked to the CPI. Mufti added regretfully that it would be hard to recruit for such an agency. If people were hired by the Kurdistan Democratic Party and Patriotic Union of Kurdistan—like most KRG employees—corruption within their parties would be ignored. If independent people were appointed, they would be prevented from taking action against any official linked to either party. It was hard to argue with his analysis.

Al-Radhi went to Erbil personally and met with the Speaker. He was told the KRG would set up its own anti-corruption agency, reporting to the KRG parliament as the CPI reported to the national parliament, but would cooperate with the CPI. In fact, the KRG did nothing to create an anti-corruption agency. (All together now: "There is no corruption in Kurdistan.")

Most CPI corruption complaints came through its telephone hotline, which by now had handled a few thousand calls. These complaints generated the vast majority of its cases. All complaints were funneled through four complaint officers in Baghdad. CPI's General Directorate for Investigations had about thirty investigators by the end of 2005, eventually increased to about ninety.

I later proposed to CPI that it set up a complaint office in each provincial capital to work with CSOs. This had precedent in some provinces, including Maysan, where corruption had been exposed in four ministry directorates with CSO help. My idea was accepted, though the lack of CPI offices in some provinces limited its potential impact.

There were other complications too. The CPI was formalized in the constitution, but there was no implementation law under which it could share information with ICSP or CSOs. They proposed creating a joint committee with ICSP, to establish a legal basis for providing summary statistics on disposition of cases. CPI would separate the CSO complaints from all the others and track their progress, in effect giving CSO complaints separate priority. The joint committee mechanism would also keep the identities of complainants confidential to protect them from retaliation. The limitations concerned me, but their idea seemed like a huge step forward.

As a practical matter, the CPI doubted it could handle all the corruption complaints our CSOs might generate, making the committee a necessary filter. What I had in mind was that when information gathered via a survey, workshop discussion, or follow-up committee indicated corruption requiring investigation, CSOs would take their evidence to the appropriate ministry Inspector General's office or to the CPI. This approach would also give government employees who observed corrupt behavior an indirect way to report it (i.e., through CSOs) and limit the retaliation risk.

Creating a National Integrity System

The CPI was a key component of a four-component anti-corruption system. The new Inspector General system, modeled on the successful U.S. system, also started from a Bremer executive order (no. 57). The new Office of Inspectors General was appointing IGs to five-year terms in every ministry. The goal was a politically independent anti-corruption unit in each ministry, in principle a great idea. IG cases would be referred to the CPI for investigation and possible prosecution. By mid-2006 the IG system was still getting organized, but thirty-one IGs had reportedly been appointed, much of the organizational structure was in place, and a lot of cases had already been initiated.

Aiming high, I pursued a meeting with the Interior Department IG office, an admittedly daring effort to help Judge Radhi. Corruption at Interior had left a lot of people dead. We met at ICSP with an official from the Office of Inspectors General, representing Interior and speaking completely bilingual English. Logically, the next meeting should have been at Interior, but my normally gung ho staff wanted no part of any meeting at Interior. They insisted it was just dangerous to be seen there, as some of those guarding the place were spies for the insurgents. As it turned out, I never got a follow-up meeting, despite several calls. Developing relationships with all the IG offices was impossible, as there were so many, and I didn't have time. The IG system was destined to encounter major political obstacles and got only limited support from the U.S. government, which had created it.

The third component in Bremer's anti-corruption institution building was the long-standing Board of Supreme Audit (BSA), established in 1927. It had been Iraq's primary oversight agency and had gained a good reputation, but it had lost authority under Saddam. It was reinstated as an independent agency by another Bremer executive order (no. 77), with authority to do financial and performance audits and program evaluations and to establish and maintain audit and accounting standards. It was to audit each ministry annually and write a report to the minister with a copy to the CPI. CPI investigators read those reports to identify potential cases.

The fourth and highest component of the anti-corruption system was the Central Criminal Court of Iraq (CCCI), the primary investigative and trial court. It would have four investigative judges (equivalent to prosecutors in the United States) handling cases referred from the CPI. Actual prosecution was reserved to the CCCI.[1]

It all looked great on paper. It was easy to see these institutions as key components of the National Integrity System that TI envisions as a central national goal for anti-corruption.

From April 17 to May 7, 2006, the Office of the Special Inspector General for Iraq Reconstruction (SIGIR) and the State Department's Office of Inspector General conducted a joint anti-corruption survey.

Their separate reports, in July and August, included references to our Anti-Corruption program. Not surprisingly, they concurred that U.S. anti-corruption efforts had a long way to go and made numerous recommendations.[2]

The State Department study called these new Iraq institutions "fragile" and the working relationships among them weak. It noted that few corruption cases had actually gone to trial. It cited the need for public education and outreach and the importance of CSOs, government, and media in that effort. It urged action on the facility Commissioner Radhi needed in order to train CPI, IG, and other anti-corruption staff. A commitment to anti-corruption institutions from Prime Minister Al-Maliki was so far lacking, even though reducing corruption was one of his government's official goals. The IG team noted ominously that "those who do stick their heads out are exposed both physically and professionally in the fragile political and security environment of Iraq."[3]

The State Department report cited the benefits received by CSOs from ADF's training and technical assistance and how this helped them express their own views through different anti-corruption techniques. One recommendation was that the embassy's anti-corruption task force should provide "the opportunity for working group members *and associated contractors* to share what they learn of Iraqi views on corruption and the campaign to eliminate it."[4] Thanks for that, but the embassy task force still didn't invite me to join.

According to the State Department, "The CPI cases referred to the CCCI are numerous, but court prosecutions have been few. Links among the four government institutions are still tenuous." The CPI received about 2,600 cases and forwarded 450 for prosecution, but there had been only eighty arrests, resulting in only six adjudications. Various theories and excuses were offered. The Justice Department was working on it and was also training CPI staff, in Iraq and in the United States. Meanwhile, said SIGIR, that august embassy working group that rejected me had done little for either the IG offices or the BSA.[5]

In short Iraq got the structure of a National Integrity System. The remaining and enormous challenge was to implement this structure in a government with a well-earned reputation for corruption and for government employees using threats and violence to avoid accountability.

The National Anti-Corruption Legislative Coalition

As we expanded and upgraded our awareness-raising campaign, I returned to my idea of developing the collective capabilities of CSOs by grouping them into organizations that could engage with government at the national level. The Council of Representatives (COR) having been elected in December, it was time to start.

Jean-Sebastien came to me with a related idea, a National Legislative Observatory to monitor and interact with the COR on behalf of all ICSP program sectors. It would have a small staff to, for example, create brief profiles of each COR member, arrange meetings with leaders and committee chairs, facilitate access to COR documents, lobby members, and track legislation.

My equally ambitious goal was to establish a National Anti-Corruption Legislative Coalition to engage with the COR on behalf of anti-corruption legislation. Getting Jean-Sebastien's big idea implemented would help me too. So, I helped him draft what the U.S. government calls a "statement of work" to define the requirements. My experience writing such documents as a contractor for federal agencies came in handy. CSOs from all sectors were eligible, several applied, and the project was won by a Women's Advocacy CSO.

For the AC Coalition I envisioned an organization at two levels. First was the *network* of all interested anti-corruption CSOs in Iraq, linked by internet to each other and to a leadership group in Baghdad, but also lobbying COR members from their own governorates to build political support for anti-corruption laws. The second level was the *coalition*, a subset of the network that would engage actively with the COR in Baghdad on behalf of the whole network.

To build the most effective national organization, we needed as many Anti-Corruption CSOs as possible to join. Nationwide, ICSP had about 750 Anti-Corruption CSOs. Here was a test of our list because at any given time only a limited number were interacting with us continuously. This would be a volunteer organization that needed long-term commitments. To help ensure it would actually work, I required that each CSO agree in writing to meet specified obligations to the network, and I set additional obligations for the coalition. A CSO could be in the network without coming to Baghdad more than occasionally, but a coalition member had to pledge time to lobby COR members and help build up the organization.

To organize and coordinate all this, I needed a managing CSO that was really good. This was not just another grant project. My statement of work said the CSO had to organize and equip an office, hire a staff, develop a database, design a website, publish an internet newsletter, create a national organization from scratch, create effective relationships with the legislators, and coordinate all of these elements. That was a lot. In a move I knew was over-the-top unreasonable, I added a non-mandatory provision asking the CSO to provide a separate office, believing that a professional office at an actual address would provide great practical advantages and give the Coalition some identity and status. I admit I had no idea how it would do that.

My efforts paid off in three promising proposals. One that absolutely stood out came from the Al-Noor Universal Foundation, in Diyala. Al-Noor said all the right things and was an organization with assets and experience. My crazy idea to request an office actually worked. Al-Noor arranged use of a house on a secure street in central Baghdad, where it set up an office and provided furniture and equipment. It was large enough to support a small staff and host crowded meetings.

Al-Noor took on the most daunting CSO project yet devised at ICSP. It had to create and support a new organization that would then elect its own board of directors. That AC Coalition was to engage the COR on behalf of anti-corruption legislation, review proposed legislation relevant to anti-corruption and monitor its legislative progress, establish common legislative proposals within the coalition, and develop good relationships with COR members. In short it would do what legislative lobbying groups do in the United States.

The project started March 15, scheduled to end August 20. I envisioned the Coalition getting one or two grant extensions, however, and then earning international donor support to operate long term without ICSP. I asked the talented Mohammed Adil to monitor the project—and make sure it worked. Unlike other grant projects, where I stayed out of the details, I took a hands-on role in the startup, meeting with the project manager and staff, emphasizing the need to implement all project goals, and encouraging a fast start.

Al-Noor went to work on the network and the coalition, first defining the procedures and specific CSO obligations for joining each. Within a few months Al-Noor signed up more CSOs than we had on our entire AC list—about 800. Later sifting left a network of 720. Of those, 103 also joined the coalition, about 1 in 7. I was blown away by these results. Al-Noor also developed an internal structure with democratic procedures, including membership rules; created the website; started meeting with COR members; designed a neat logo with the colors of the Iraqi flag and an image of Hammurabi; started developing the database; and later provided a plan for sustainability after ICSP funding ended.

I intervened at times through Mohammed to keep everything on track. The dragging pace of the parliament in getting itself organized gave us more time to set up but increasingly impeded our progress. It also slowed the work of the National Legislative Observatory, undermining the intended coordination between the two organizations. Still, Al-Noor had already set up an entire national organization, and it was moving fast. My plan was obviously coming together, and I was confident we were on the verge of something great.

Nothing else I had accomplished in Iraq made me prouder than the National Anti-Corruption Legislative Coalition. It was taking advocacy to the highest level.

Drugs and Thugs

The Money and the Plan

Sometimes things happening in Congress affect ongoing projects. In January 2006 USAID extended ADF's contract through June 2007. However, the $15 million to fund the extension was in a supplemental budget bill held up in Congress. So, we had a contract for another year and a half but would run out of money between July and September. It's the kind of crisis average citizens don't hear about but which can be consequential to international development organizations and those they are trying to help.

Around March this crisis hit the fan in Washington DC. When it hit the Washington papers, ADF got favorable mention as one of the organizations whose work was important but at risk. Michael Miller at ADF was frantically working to move the legislation and issued a summary of ICSP accomplishments. One of my two Maryland senators, Barbara Mikulski, was on the Senate Appropriations Committee, so I sent her a letter. I also paid a Green Zone visit to my former Amarah colleague Katie Donahue, now with USAID. Katie told me crises like this are common. There were limits to how much money Congress would put up for Iraq, so new priorities sometimes upended current priorities. It was not unusual to have projects undone by some political maneuver in Washington, sometimes by people with little or no knowledge of its accomplishments. This was not a comforting message. Indeed, a rumor came to me, later confirmed, that First Lady Laura Bush was behind a project to build a children's hospital in Basra that would also compete for funding.

Thankfully, the crisis in Congress finally blew over. The inside story was that some Senate Democrats, afraid the Bush administration was trying to cut back on democracy programs, insisted on including the funding. The reputation of the anti-corruption program reportedly helped to save the project.

Shortly afterward, I heard secondhand that Secretary of State Condoleezza Rice was impressed with our anti-corruption program and wanted to provide additional funding, a story later confirmed. After almost having ICSP wiped out just weeks earlier, this was welcome news that acknowledged our good work. The question was how we would spend the money.

Craig Davis answered that question in a great proposal, funded in August for $2 million. The money came not from USAID but from State's Bureau for International Narcotics and Law Enforcement Affairs (INL), cleverly nicknamed "Drugs and Thugs." Fighting the drug trade was not part of my job, but Iraq had more than its share of thugs, many working for the government.

INL's mission includes reducing both the volume of incoming illegal drugs and the impact of international crime on the United States. INL was providing technical assistance, training, and mentoring for the Ministry of Interior and Iraqi Police, working with the U.S. military, and was training CPI personnel.

Despite the significant expansion of project activity promised in the proposal, there was no additional salary money, so I had to do it all with current staff. However, I now had $195,000 for training workshops, so the artificial limit on the number of workshops was gone. I also had $1 million in grant money for CSO projects.

By the time INL's money showed up, Craig Davis had left us, on June 1, for a position in Washington DC. We had a great going-away party in his honor, which he more than deserved. Unfortunately, his departure would prove to be a turning point of the wrong kind.

Craig's proposal was decidedly impact oriented. INL workshops would be for government officials; we would train 3,200 in one year. This left our regular budget to cover workshops for CSOs and the public. Despite the high target, I felt we would reach it if we could certify enough new trainers. The plan also called for 320 "CSO Actions," 160 "Advocacy Activities," and 100 "Public Education and Information Actions." That was a lot for one year, especially without new staff, but my AC teams had been great so far.

The promised 160 "changes or corrective actions" were another matter. Corrective actions are not easy, even in Western governments, because of any number of practical, political, bureaucratic, personality, and other obstacles. Corrective actions that were achieved might come after the grant project or event was over, so would require volunteer follow-up time.

I called Craig in Washington to ask why he was so optimistic. He expressed confidence that 160 could be done (notwithstanding the probability no one had ever done it before). I refined the concept to specify outcomes that could constitute corrective actions. I then devised a "Corrective Actions Checklist" for AC staff and trainees to make it more likely they would report them.

The proposal now needed an implementation plan. I converted Craig's five project categories into thirteen specific INL projects, several being especially important. To train at least 3,200 government staff in one year and do it right, we needed more professional trainers in all four regions, all using upgraded training materials. One solution was a multi-site Training of Trainers (TOT) project.

Another big priority was extending Al-Noor's contract to manage the National Anti-Corruption Legislative Coalition at least through year's end. The KRG badly needed its own Kurdistan Anti-Corruption Legislative Coalition to help counter the KRG's political corruption. The Enforcement Agencies Project would support the CPI and IGs at the enforcement end of the prevention-enforcement spectrum.

The premise of the Provincial and Local Government Support Project was that networks can be extended down as well as up. I wanted CSOs to form Community Action Committees and bring citizen volunteers to provincial and local council meetings. Weekly Anti-Corruption TV and radio programs would extend the message to the public. My Erbil team was already working with Radio Nawa, a government-owned station with a wide listening area.

Craig had proposed creating one or two Transparency International chapters in Iraq. I had no reason to think TI's reluctance would go away soon, but the money would enable CSOs to attend TI training and conferences. To move the dialogue forward, I proposed a TI conference in Iraq, perhaps in Suleimaniya, and asked the CPI to cosponsor it, getting a definite yes.

Training the Corruption Fighters

To make the INL plan work, we had to reach a lot more people. That meant training a lot of CSO members to present government workshops, but it also meant upgrading ICSP's training materials. We needed full training packages with trainee manuals—not just PowerPoint presentations—and separate trainer manuals that would help instructors present the materials. That would provide more consistency in what the trainees learned. This may seem esoteric, but most of the INL program depended on completing the training first.

ADF's training experts were in Cairo and not paid by ICSP, but Michael Miller found a way to fund their participation. The ADF-Egypt team, led by Tom McClure, was happy to help but needed clarity on exactly what I wanted. Providing it took days of painstaking work. I gathered complete copies of all presentations in one place and compared them—not easy, as they were all in Arabic. I recorded the purpose, desired learning outcomes, and specific topics for each, then sent it to Cairo. Having compared them all, I dropped two, reducing nine modules to seven, but requested an eighth, on Anti-Corruption Advocacy. Ultimately, I wanted a loosely definable curriculum—not just a set of training modules. I eventually sorted out which were more suitable for government staff and which for the public (CSOs and individuals): a "poor man's curriculum" in two tracks.

This project meant a major increase in Cairo's workload. The trainee guide for one module was estimated to need forty-five pages, the trainer guide sixty pages, and the PowerPoint slides sixty-five pages. Multiply by eight modules to get the total pages. In truth, however, the project was long overdue after all the unsubstantiated ICSP claims about how good the original materials were.

Taking the direct approach, I went to Cairo personally in mid-May to work with the training specialists in their offices, combining that with an Egypt vacation. Cairo is by far the largest and most bustling city in the Middle East (or in my observation, 18 million people, and they all have cars). The Cairo team got it all together and began sending materials far better than what we had. Gradually, I received the four training packages likely to be used most. These still needed our revisions, then Cairo's final edit.

By midsummer, however, I faced a crisis. Other program managers caught on to my Cairo connection and wanted help on their materials too. Some general training topics also needed improved materials. Then ADF headquarters decided it needed my new materials translated into English. I had made a deliberate decision not to spend precious time on this, as none of our trainees would be native English speakers. It all added up to an indefinite delay.

With my training modules success story interrupted, I made a fast but major decision. I issued the four modules to my four regional teams as is. I hoped ADF-Cairo would eventually finish final versions, but that would not be soon, and what they had finished was a huge upgrade. This proved to be a timely and wise decision. The rest of my Cairo project never happened.

On June 19 and 20, 2006, ICSP and USAID had held a Civil Society Strategic Planning Conference in Amman, Jordan. The location may seem odd for a conference on Iraq, but Baghdad was now unsafe. ICSP and USAID expats were joined by several of our leading CSO reps, along with officials of other U.S. agencies, USAID contractors, and NGOs.

The conference was intended to share experiences and future

coordination ideas. It created a well-timed opportunity to tell a lot of people the good things we were doing. In putting our progress and emerging plans together in one presentation, I saw more clearly how much the Anti-Corruption program had accomplished so far during my eight months in troubled Iraq.

9

The Struggle for Human Rights

Going Up in Smoke

My other ICSP job was to manage the Human Rights (HR) program. The need for it was reinforced daily by an overwhelming barrage of horrible and tragic events that exposed the culture of violence and the disastrous state of human rights in Iraq.

Even before all the violence happening around us, human rights in Iraq did not have a positive history. There were laws offering some protection, but they were not generally enforced. Those mass graves with tens of thousands of Saddam's victims, along with countless thousands of other abuses, told the real story of human rights up to 2003.

The human rights provisions in the new constitution, based on universal human rights standards, were a source of hope. ICSP had done a lot to promote public dialogue about the constitution. In addition to its national TV talk show on *Our Constitution*, its three-day national conference in July 2005 generated many specific recommendations, including human rights provisions, and fifteen were included in some form.

The real problem was not passing the constitution but implementing it. So far, that was not going well, and human rights were about to hit an all-time low, right before our eyes.

The first wave was the car bombs—for a time almost a daily event. At first they were most often vehicles placed on the side of the road when no one was looking, often overnight, then detonated the next day to kill people driving or walking by. In 2005 there was a huge increase in car bombs, set off in every part of the city.

Even explosions at some distance could be heard, and some were close enough to shake Wael's Palace. The smoke was often visible outside our windows, usually a mix of black (from burning vehicle fuel) and grayish white, rising slowly toward the sky. A few went off close to the compound, immediately obvious from the louder noise, the bigger concussive effect, and the smoke in the immediate area. Especially startling was the car bomb just outside the compound, at the end of the block.

In general our Iraqi staff reacted rather stoically. The close-in bombs generated audible gasps or murmurs, but that was all. It was as if there was nothing more to say. Another noisy blast, more dead people— what else is new? As in the rest of Baghdad, the reaction was one of resignation, such incidents having continued past the point where people had any emotional energy left to react to them.

My own immediate reaction to each blast was always to register that people had just been killed and curse the perpetrators. Each incident added to the parade of wasted lives and devastated survivors, as more and more families lost loved ones in this senseless violence.

As months passed, suicide car bombers driving into crowded areas, even suicide bombers on foot, became more common. Their bombs were more deadly than the roadside bombs, especially when detonated next to market areas, which attract large numbers of people. Their purpose was to kill a lot of people indiscriminately. Life in Baghdad became more and more frightening.

The people of Baghdad proved resilient, however. They gradually got used to this. Death by violence was still horrible but now somehow routine. People were fatalistic, accepting that this day could be their last—a kind of coping mechanism. They spent much less time outside.

Knowing their government was mostly powerless to stop the carnage stirred anger but also a sullen resignation. When things got really tense, the government closed the streets for a day to moving traffic, which let people go out and do their shopping. Friday was the likeliest day, as people didn't have to drive to work. Still, the local economy was being devastated.

In the Iraqi "tradition" of using rumors to tell lies, the rumor mill was activated after many incidents to claim the Americans had done it. Even the many not taking the rumor seriously saw that the Coalition invasion had led to conditions that made their lives miserable. Surveys showed that people felt worse off than under Saddam, which was obviously true in Baghdad and arguably true in many other places. The Iraqi people, who had hoped for a better life, now worried about just staying alive.

In the early morning of February 22, 2006, three months into my tenure and only two months after the election, the revered Al-Askari Shrine in Samarra, about sixty miles (one hundred kilometers) north of Baghdad, was bombed and largely destroyed. Its golden exterior was blown completely off. One of the holiest of Shia shrines, built in 944, it had great symbolic significance. The perpetrators were a small Al-Qaeda in Iraq group, mostly foreigners, wearing Iraqi military uniforms. Their intent was to enrage Shia into attacking Sunnis, setting off sectarian violence.

Thousands of demonstrators gathered near the shrine, as Grand Ayatollah Sistani and other Shia leaders urged restraint. To many Shia, however, it was us versus them. If Sunnis are killing us, we have to kill them. By one estimate over 1,300 people, mostly Sunnis, were murdered in the next four days in Baghdad and surrounding provinces, most by death squads organized by the Mehdi Army.[1]

Incidents of Sunnis killed were regularly followed by counter-incidents of Shia killed, in a mindless but seemingly endless tit-for-tat. Many Sunni mosques were attacked, then mosques of both sects, even in cities far from Baghdad. The insurgents were Sunnis but had little connection to Sunni political parties. Many were Baathists displaced by the new regime and its Shia-led de-Baathification policy, or military officers displaced when the army was disbanded. Some were foreigners fighting with Iraqis as part of Al-Qaeda in Iraq, including the acknowledged leader, the Jordanian Abu Musab Al-Zarqawi.

As the violence became totally indiscriminate, people were attacked or kidnapped on the street—or dragged from their cars, homes, or businesses, identified as being from the opposite sect, and killed—in response to some incident in which the victim had no role. There were almost daily news reports about groups of bodies being found, often beheaded or otherwise mutilated. Torturing people before killing them was common. A favorite tactic was drilling a hole in the victim's head so as to kill with maximum cruelty. I learned of one Shia fanatic in Sadr City, originally from Amarah, like many there, who led a group retaliating for alleged "Sunni" crimes by capturing arbitrarily selected Sunnis and executing them in cruel ways. Thousands died from all this personalized violence. A religious motive would be hard to find.

Baghdad was particularly vulnerable to sectarian violence, as its 5.5 million people, and another half million in the Baghdad Governorate but outside the city, had major populations of both sects. The city's nine districts were mostly one or the other, with majority Shia districts east of the Tigris, including Sadr City and Karrada, and majority Sunni districts west of the river. However, Adhamiya on the east was mostly Sunni and Kadhimiya on the west mostly Shia, and they were connected by a bridge, making easy targets of people on both sides.

Baghdad had many mixed neighborhoods and many households in which Sunni and Shia had intermarried, a recently common practice that was now risky. Mixed neighborhoods became especially dangerous, as roaming groups of Shia militiamen targeted Sunni residents and forced people to either leave their homes or die and often moved other Shia into those homes. The Mehdi Army assumed effective control in some places. Similarly, Al-Qaeda and other Sunni insurgents threatened Shia residents to force them to leave, and also Christians and even Kurds. They assumed a measure of control in some western Baghdad neighborhoods and in Adhamiya. Some neighborhoods organized their own armed security and barricaded themselves or hired men to provide security. Thousands who were minorities in mixed neighborhoods moved to places where their sect was the majority. Thousands were left homeless. Thousands fled the country. Many who did not move ended up dead. This was sectarian cleansing in Baghdad.

There were constant reports of murders by "death squads." Armed groups invaded not only neighborhoods but also shops, offices, university campuses, and other places to kidnap and kill. Many government officials were targeted, usually by attacks on their security convoys or near their homes. Increasingly, officials slept in their offices to avoid the risk of going home. Many lower-level government employees were also victims. Others were often too scared to go to work or unable to reach their offices safely.

Hundreds of professors were killed; others were threatened on their violence-plagued campuses, causing many of them to flee Iraq. Even judges were targeted, and insurgents in Baghdad even attacked courthouses. Police and police recruits, likewise soldiers and army recruits, were frequent targets of insurgents, the perverted logic being

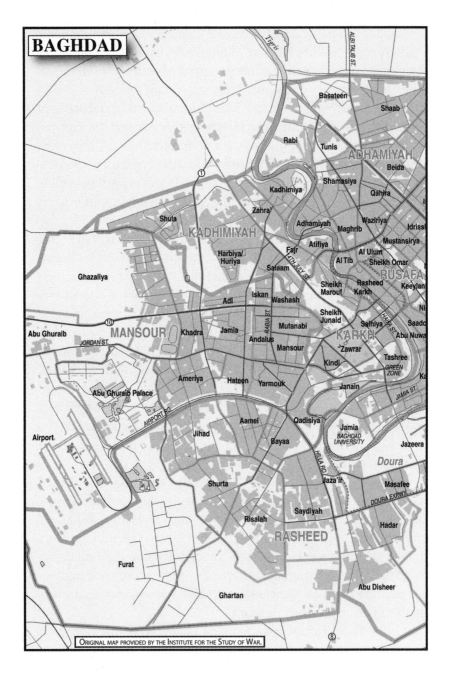

MAP 4. Baghdad. The Baghdad governorate also includes districts outside the city. Courtesy of the Institute for the Study of War.

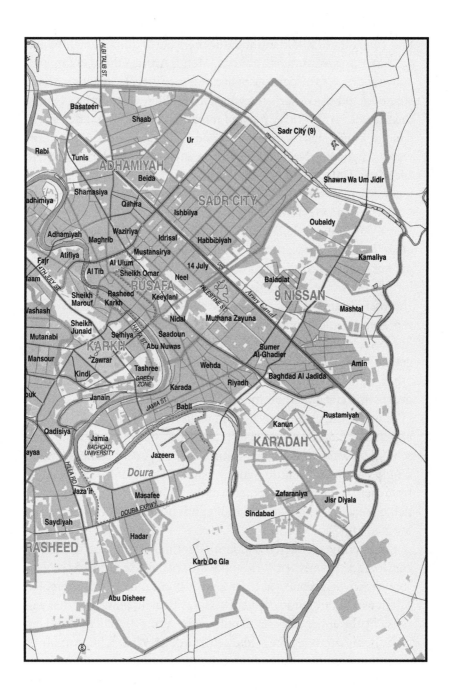

that killing them would intimidate others out of doing their jobs and weaken the government's control. Mehdi Army units also targeted police at times, to discourage police presence in their "territory." Each side targeted the other's mosques, and killing worshippers exiting the mosque after Friday prayers remained a familiar tactic. Attendance dropped sharply at mosques and at churches too. Islamic clergy were sometimes assassination targets, making other clerics afraid to speak out. Unfortunately, some clerics were part of the problem, aiding militiamen who were threatening, displacing, and killing people.

With all the Western media focus on "sectarian violence," it was easy to see the problem as a conflict between religious, albeit misguided, people. The killers did identify with different sects, but that did *not* make it a conflict among religious people. In fact, most Muslim terrorists are not religious zealots, as many believe. Research shows they tend to lack knowledge of Islam even while claiming to represent it, and people become terrorists from a mix of motives.[2] I have observed often that truly religious Muslims of different sects get along fine. By contrast, a lot of nonreligious people were killing others while claiming to defend Islam. The result was thousands of deaths and atrocities committed in the name of Allah.

Some of the violence was just outright criminal activity with no pretense of moral or political justification. Kidnappings became common, mostly for ransom, the victims often business owners or their family members, including many women. Some of the crime came from increasingly rogue elements of the Mehdi Army, which in Baghdad especially operated like independent criminal gangs beyond Moqtada Al-Sadr's control.

Other crimes reflected Saddam's decision, as the Coalition invasion loomed in early 2003, to empty the prisons. He decreed amnesty for virtually everyone—at least tens of thousands of prisoners. His intent was to buy some popularity at a critical moment, but that was offset by the anger of all the families whose imprisoned men did not come home—proving they were actually dead. While a large minority of released inmates were political prisoners or otherwise wrongly held, the rest were real criminals.[3] The effect on public safety was surely enormous.

As the realization of total lawlessness descended on the population, a climate of fear gripped Baghdad. Residents resorted to desperate tactics to lessen the chance of being the next victim. People avoided going out; many became increasingly housebound. Those who had to venture out minimized movement outside their immediate neighborhood, often because they didn't know whose police or militia checkpoints they might encounter.

Those with jobs avoided telling others where they worked or lied when asked. It was not safe to say you worked for a foreign organization like ICSP. Some names are readily identifiable as Shia names or Sunni names, so many Sunnis got ID cards with assumed Shia names, or vice versa, an alias that might save them if stopped at an illegal checkpoint or grabbed on the street or out of their cars for imminent execution. Some saved their lives with this tactic.

Islamic doctrine says Christians and Jews are also people of God so must be treated respectfully. Jihadist insurgents twist the doctrine to define them as "infidels." Christian communities in Iraq have a long history and tradition, mostly in northern Iraq, and predate the Arab Muslims by hundreds of years. Christians were generally treated tolerably under Saddam, and many enjoyed success in business or other fields. A notable example familiar in the West was Tariq Aziz, the foreign minister and deputy prime minister for many years until Saddam's fall (who was then arrested, prosecuted, convicted, and sentenced to death, then died in prison).

The Christian population in Iraq, overwhelmingly Catholic, had been gradually leaving for about twenty-five years, mainly for the West, and by the time Saddam fell, it was maybe half of the 1.4 million recorded by Iraq's last full census in 1987. After Saddam was deposed, life got worse for most Christians and later much worse. It became risky to attend church in Baghdad. Many churches were bombed, some abandoned. The general deterioration of life, and now the increasing incidents of Christians targeted in their homes, businesses, and churches by Muslim extremists and outright criminals, caused a large percentage of remaining Christians and other religious minorities to flee. Like other escaping Iraqis, most went to Syria, some to Jordan, but many moved north to traditional Christian communities in northern Ninewa and Iraqi Kurdistan.

A community of 34,000 Palestinian refugees, Sunnis but living in eastern Baghdad, was particularly vulnerable and lost people to death squads. Mehdi Army members forced some from their apartments and put Shia in. I heard a dramatic story about how some were saved after a large armed group showed up in a Palestinian neighborhood intending the worst. One local Palestinian called someone he knew at the UN Aid Mission to Iraq, who called an Italian military officer he knew in the Green Zone, who called a U.S. officer. The American troops arrived just in time. In general, however, the Palestinians' security kept deteriorating, and by late 2006 a majority would leave Iraq. Other isolated groups, including gay men, were also easy targets.

According to the UN's Iraq *Human Rights Report* for May and June 2006, 6,826 civilians were killed in just the first half of 2006 and another 13,256 wounded.[4] The pace of civilian casualties was increasing. The exodus of Iraqis from their country was increasing. The term *humanitarian crisis* was often heard. We were living in the Baghdad killing field.

All things considered, I had come to Iraq at a bad time for human rights.

Human Rights and the Culture of Violence

The United Nations had established its UN Assistance Mission for Iraq (UNAMI) on August 14, 2003. One key mandate was to "promote the protection of human rights, national reconciliation, and judicial and legal reform in order to strengthen the rule of law in Iraq." Just five days later, a suicide truck bomb attack on the UN offices at the Canal Hotel in Baghdad killed Dr. Sérgio de Mello, the secretary-general's special representative in Iraq, and twenty-one others. De Mello, from Brazil, had been the UN High Commissioner for Human Rights and was one of its most important officials. The UN quickly withdrew most of its remaining staff to Jordan, Cyprus, and Kuwait but moved some back to Iraq starting in mid-2004.

UNAMI's Human Rights Office aimed to "develop a more robust human rights strategy," working especially with the ministries of Justice and Human Rights. UNAMI described terrorism as "a serious violation of human rights." In 2004 it was already citing the failure to protect individual rights; targeting of civilians by insurgents and militias and targeting of police, government officials, foreign diplomats, and human rights advocates; abuse of prisoners and detainees, including systematic use of torture by police and the Ministry of Interior; extrajudicial killings; and inadequate judicial procedures. It was an overwhelming list.

The worst aspect of the human rights crisis was that so many whose rights were denied ended up dead. The antigovernment insurgents threatened death to anyone who worked with the foreigners. This made *every* Iraqi employee at ICSP a potential target. Indeed, a truly sad aspect of the uncontrolled violence was that the people trying hardest to make a positive difference were among those most likely to be victims, including some of our CSO members. People took a chance to even come to the ICSP compound or attend a public event. It became harder to hold events in and near Baghdad. The number of active CSOs declined.

Insurgent rhetoric justified the killing as part of a jihad, thus arguably sanctioned by the Koran. "Jihad" is an Islamic concept with variable meanings that translates in this context as a holy war against infidels. Few Iraqis were fooled by the twisted rhetoric, but the killing continued, further intimidating those who survived. In June 2006 the U.S. military finally caught up with Zarqawi in Diyala and killed him, but the violence kept rising.

This horror played out every day in the American press, but the horror on the streets could not be adequately understood from the daily drumbeat of casualty statistics.

Among those most at risk were members of the new councils set up earlier by the RTI Local Governance Program in Baghdad. The system had 127 councils, at four levels, and well over a thousand people were serving on them. As insurgent violence spread and government officials became soft targets, those council members were left exposed. Being on a council meant that your name was known and that you lived in a defined area where they could find you.

The first deputy governor of Baghdad was assassinated in November 2004, the governor two months later. Many councils were forced to work behind closed doors, away from public attention, which of course defeated one purpose of having them; some just stopped functioning; and some decided to save themselves by disbanding altogether. Many council members went into hiding. The same thing happened in many other places.[5] In August 2005 the Badr militia deposed Baghdad's mayor by force. By mid-2006 over fifty Baghdad officials had been killed.[6]

In Anbar, where Al-Qaeda in Iraq was strongest and pitched battles had destroyed much of Fallujah and Ramadi, the provincial and city governments were frontline targets. By summer 2006 the governor had survived twenty-nine attempts on his life. His predecessor had been kidnapped and assassinated, the deputy governor also killed, and the governor's personal secretary beheaded. Anbar's provincial and local governments existed on paper, but most ceased to function. It was amazing to realize that a few years earlier RTI had an LGP office in Ramadi promoting democracy and local governance in Anbar. In Anbar, however, the tide turned earlier than in Baghdad. By late 2006 Anbar armed groups that had fought the Americans would fall out with Al-Qaeda in Iraq and gradually go over to the U.S. side.

A large part of the human rights crisis was the Ministry of Interior, responsible for all the nation's police. Under the Transitional Government installed in April 2005, Interior was led by a SCIRI/Badr official, who promptly replaced a great number of Sunnis with Shia, mostly from the Badr Organization and Mehdi Army. The Baghdad police became dominated by those militias. There followed a growing number of executions of Sunnis in the Baghdad area, carried out largely by Shia death squads from the ministry. All of this showed Sunni Arabs that the nation's police ministry had joined the Shia side of a deadly sectarian conflict.

One Interior Department horror story showed up in a later Corporate Confidential report that came into my possession. Interior had charged fifty-seven of its own employees, some high-level, with abusing prisoners. Militiamen within the Iraqi Police set up a secret prison in eastern Baghdad, with over 1,400 mostly Sunni prisoners. When the site was exposed, in May 2006, many had signs of physical and psychological abuse. There had been a similar discovery earlier. The more independent minister named in June 2006 fired 3,000 employees!

Treatment of prisoners was a major issue addressed by my ICSP

Human Rights program. The victims included people legitimately arrested and people totally innocent. The court system was overwhelmed by cases, due to all the arrests by U.S. and Iraqi troops, and there was a huge backlog of detainees stuck in prison, some not guilty.

Prisons were in horrible condition but also feared. To be arrested in Baghdad was often to be in imminent danger of being tortured and/or murdered. Torture was frequently used to force confessions. When someone was arrested, his family was put in a desperate situation of not knowing where he was, not being able to communicate with him or do anything about his imprisonment, often until it was too late. Many were cut off from their families because there was no system in place to notify families.[7] Prisoners were held for months without trial or even without charges, and there was no reliable legal mechanism to get them out, even with a lawyer.

As my months in Iraq went by, I heard the term *rule of law* more often. Sometimes it was used as an adjective, as in *rule-of-law agencies*, which to a political scientist sounded like a new buzzword for the criminal justice system. USAID was right to focus on it, however, as the rule of law was certainly lacking. INL was one of several U.S. agencies trying to help.

A military reserves legal specialist and fellow Greenbelt, Maryland, resident, Lt. Col. Michael Noyes, did a 2006 tour of duty in Iraq and later joined me in a local presentation. He defined *rule of law* as "all the things we take for granted: (1) police who are equipped and trained; (2) a fair, efficient court system; (3) nondiscrimination in enforcement; (4) reasonably safe streets; (5) a legal and regulatory system providing predictability for business; and (6) government programs and services administered in a legal and transparent manner."

Iraq's civil law system (unlike the common law system in the United States and United Kingdom) includes an investigative judge who takes testimony and evidence and, if merited, refers the case for trial. A prosecutor reviews the file and sets a trial or may return it to the investigative judge for further analysis. The trial is held before a three-judge panel with no jury. The defendant is entitled to a lawyer, though many must rely on overloaded public defenders. The trial is usually brief, and if convicted, the person is sentenced quickly. A dismissal or acquittal should lead to quick release, but sometimes that didn't happen. The court system was under great stress. In general there was much room for improvement in the criminal justice system.

Human Rights from a Small Platform

A Question of Priorities

Given the horrible abuses going on every day, you might assume human rights were a major USAID priority. In fact, someone decided well before I arrived that ICSP's Human Rights sector would be dropped. There would still be an HR program with a small staff and CSO grant money but not a separate sector as there was for Anti-Corruption (AC), Civic Education, and Women's Advocacy. It was ironic that while women's rights are logically part of human rights, USAID gave higher priority to women's rights in particular than to human rights in general.

The deft alternative formula was to define human rights as a "cross-cutting theme" for all the other sectors. Each would devote some attention to human rights as it related to its own sector, by including human rights segments in its events. Someone had to manage the rest, so the AC manager was designated as HR manager also. That was fine with me, as I saw the need and wanted the responsibility.

I soon found the cross-cutting formula both disingenuous and ineffective. We did include Human Rights segments in Anti-Corruption events, but they didn't always fit, and I could tell there was little HR activity in other sectors. Our few Human Rights staff in regional offices were classified under Anti-Corruption, causing confusion and practical problems. When I complained, I was told this was no problem because HR was a cross-cutting theme. I soon hated this term and avoided using it in reports or pretending there were meaningful HR activities beyond what my small but dedicated staff was doing. In principle, however, anything Women's Advocacy achieved also advanced human rights.

There were no separate Human Rights training modules, so one of my priorities was to create one. The idea was actually opposed by project management and ADF, as it was not in the current plan. However, my Baghdad region HR specialist continued working on one with my encouragement, while we held HR workshops unofficially and reported on them. Eventually, the mayhem in Iraq forced USAID to give human rights more attention, so I finally won the argument. We produced an official "Advocacy for Human Rights" workshop, which also let me expand the HR workshop schedule to government offices, as we had done for AC.

The larger problem was that sending CSOs out to fight for human rights was only part of the solution. Human rights must be supported not only by government and civil society but also by citizens, reflected in how they treat each other. At the moment that was not going well.

Sistani repeatedly denounced the violence. The mayhem in the streets showed that too many Shia were beyond even his influence. Responding to widespread public disillusionment, he issued a statement conveying his frustration with the performance of the Iraqi governments he had helped to elect.[8]

Civil Society Success Stories, Part 2

Despite the limited scope of our Human Rights program, many CSOs were doing noteworthy projects and creating their own success stories.

Many workshops by CSOs provided a basic understanding of human rights, an unfamiliar concept in Iraq. For example, Haider's CSO, the Iraqi Society for Change, presented human rights workshops in Maysan using university law instructors.

A few noteworthy projects used mass media to spread the message. The Harikar CSO up north in Dahuk broadcast forty fifteen-minute radio episodes on two popular radio stations and ten twenty-minute telecasts on two TV stations, reaching audiences all over the province.

The Tribes and Sheikhs Assembly and the League of Human Rights Defense in Wasit collaborated to visit detention facilities, with court approval. This uncovered the sad situation of Afghan families who had traveled to Iraq on a religious pilgrimage only to be jailed as suspected terrorists. The team's report to the Ministry of Human Rights led to their release. Those two CSOs and other CSOs then formed a committee of volunteer lawyers, which secured release of prisoners previously unable to get a lawyer; got suspended cases brought to trial; and freed prisoners detained only on suspicion and without judicial warrants.

In Diwaniya, capital of Qadisiya, the Iraqi Humanitarian League for Human Rights visited the local jail to assess conditions and treatment of prisoners. This led to formation of a legal defense team that urged the investigative judge to get cases to trial faster and a medical team to do physical checkups and necessary treatment.

A CSO in Babil Province south of Baghdad visited a local police detention facility to document conditions. It sent a list of deficiencies to the Ministry of Health and police directorate, citing conditions such as overcrowded cells, lack of hot water, poor medical care, inadequate lighting, and unhealthy food. Both agencies responded with quick corrective action.

Protecting prisoners' rights was a sensitive issue. Their rights had no priority under Saddam, and old habits carried over. Getting police and prison staff to accept responsibility for upholding human rights was critical; otherwise, those rights were only on paper. Officials in several places saw this need and cooperated with our efforts to make HR presentations to police and prison staffs.

In Mosul a CSO conducted an HR training workshop at the Mosul Police Academy for police and Ministry of Interior personnel. One result was a police department committee to investigate allegations of excessive force and other violations against citizens. I recall a similar project in Basra.

Going into police stations and jails seemed to cross that official (if misguided) line between prevention and enforcement cited by USAID, and I did a double take reading the first report, but this kind of advocacy was critical, and I decided not to ask for USAID guidance. So, maybe I cheated a little for a good cause.

To these noteworthy projects could be added many others by which dedicated Human Rights CSOs, under the worst of conditions, made a direct helpful impact on people's lives.

The Ministry of Human Rights

While Anti-Corruption needed a national network from which to build a coalition, there were a lot of human rights groups, many already networked. Human rights has many subfields (e.g., women, children, disabled people, minorities, and prisoners), and different organizations advocated for different constituencies. The larger need was an umbrella organization to network them into a national human rights alliance that could speak with a louder voice to governments and the public.

The path to networking success seemed to go through the Ministry of Human Rights (MOHR), created in 2004 under the CPA with offices around the country. MOHR was a small ministry, with limited clout, headed by a Christian woman, a former parliament member. Its role was defined as protecting the rights of women and children as well as minorities. It had authority to monitor prison conditions and police detention facilities and to investigate human rights abuses under Saddam.

We arranged a meeting with a young MOHR department head responsible for NGO relations, hoping to leverage our efforts by working with the ministry. At the meeting I learned that MOHR hoped to become an independent commission, analogous to the Commission on Public Integrity (CPI). Its mission would be defined by "The Paris Principles" (officially the "Principles Relating to the Status and Functions of National Institutions for the Promotion and Protection of Human Rights"), endorsed by the UN Commission on Human Rights in 1992 and the UN General Assembly in 1993. Doing that would mean Iraq had adopted the same human rights principles as the most advanced and progressive nations.

A constitutional provision for an independent National Human Rights Commission enabled such an independent commission. In July 2006 the parliament established a Human Rights Committee to draft that legislation and other human rights laws. Like many other matters before the parliament, it would prove more controversial and time-consuming than expected.

What to Do About the Violence?

As the violence increased, I convened a team meeting to discuss what, if anything, we could do about it from our small platform. Dashti argued that broadcast messages and the usual workshops would not make enough difference. Any antiviolence campaign had to extend beyond provincial capitals to smaller cities and rural areas. The team decision was to build an Antiviolence Outreach Initiative through community forums.

The large number of forums required meant we needed many trained facilitators quickly. I outlined a TOT program similar to the basic training I had developed for Anti-Corruption. The local forums would start once our first trainee group finished TOT. Each forum would set up follow-up action committees. The forums would roll up to well-publicized regional conferences in all four ICSP regions. They would generate conference action reports and select delegates to a national conference promoted by heavy media coverage. The national conference would generate a conference action report to the Council of Representatives and prime minister. There could be follow-up advocacy through TV and radio spots.

In addition, we would expand "Advocacy for Human Rights" workshops into more government offices; expand our relationship with MOHR; and perhaps generate a school curriculum project to train teachers. But the most important audiences would be police departments, recognizing that the enforcers were often the abusers. I wanted to expand the number of human rights officers in police departments; so far there were only a few. This would link prevention to enforcement, as I was trying to do for Anti-Corruption.

All of this would take a lot of work, especially with so few staff in HR. Staff in other sectors could be called on to help, however—what a great "cross-cutting" activity. Even to me it seemed like more than we could expect to accomplish, but the status of human rights in Iraq was desperate. In concept at least, we had a plan. The implementation would be another matter.

Iraqi Women in a Male-Dominated Society

Women's Rights and Islamic Law

I did not have time to help Women's Advocacy, but that was not for lack of interest. I had realized in Amarah that women's rights were *the* defining human rights issue in Iraq—aside from people killing each other—and I was a strong women's rights advocate. After what happened to Kifaya, could I be anything less?

In January 2006 I introduced Zainab Salman, my intended Human Rights coordinator for the Baghdad regional office, to Craig Davis. I had met her in Ottawa the previous April when she came with Ta'meem and the British Women's Commission group. Craig was highly impressed but said someone with her talent was needed even more in Women's Advocacy. She became its headquarters coordinator, working with its four regional teams covering all Iraqi provinces. So, I helped Women's Advocacy anyway.

Zainab had been the Women's Program director on RTI's local councils project in Baghdad, organizing and supporting women's committees and training women council members in all parts of the city. Her computer science degree and career success had overcome a childhood polio condition that forced her to walk with a heavy brace. The indomitable Zainab lifted that extra weight up and down ICSP stairs without complaint. It was great having another friend on board, and she and Haider also became good friends.

Zainab proved to be an important asset to ICSP. In addition to improving the coordination of Women's Advocacy teams in the four regions and at headquarters, she launched several important initiatives, including an email network linking all women's CSOs and a training project for women parliament members.

Helping women in parliament mattered, as 31 percent of the initial members—87 of 275—were women, exceeding the constitutional requirement of 25 percent. Much was made of this breakthrough, achieved by a well-organized, diverse women's coalition. While it played well in U.S. media, however, it did not affect the inequalities women face every day. Nor did it create a progressive women's bloc in the parliament, as most women elected were Islamic conservatives.

The constitution contradicted itself on women's rights. Article 39 says: "Iraqis are free in their commitment to their personal status according to their religions, sects, beliefs, or choices. This shall be regulated by law." This handoff to religion is interpreted to mean such decisions will be based on sharia (Islamic) law, instead of the 1959 Code of Personal Status. The old law was still there for those wanting to use it but only until parliament passed a new law. Women's rights activists argued that Article 39 contradicts Article 14, which says "Iraqis are equal before the law without discrimination based on gender, race, ethnicity, nationality, origin, color, religion, sect, belief or opinion, or economic or social status." The contradiction seems obvious.

Women's rights activists saw Article 39 as a step backward from the Transitional Administrative Law, which it was. When the Iraqi

Governing Council voted in December 2003 to apply sharia to family law matters, Paul Bremer vetoed it after vehement protests by women's groups. Article 39 had been the most hotly debated provision in the drafting of the constitution. Including it was a concession to Shia factions (but also a lot of public opinion) and was made only as a political necessity to reach overall agreement.

ICSP's Women's Advocacy CSOs were now among those arguing that the constitution as applied to women was a step backward from the 1959 law. This was the biggest issue discussed in their forums. The 1959 law deferred in many places to sharia but established a minimum marriage age of eighteen (with exceptions down to fifteen); said no one could be forced to marry without his or her consent; put restrictions on polygamy; gave divorce rights to women while prohibiting arbitrary divorce; and gave women equal rights to inherit property.

In practice, however, women's rights under the 1959 law are undermined by old cultural habits and women's lack of awareness of the law. The law tends not to be applied, especially in rural and tribal areas, so many marriages and divorces are in effect still under sharia and not registered in court. There is fairly widespread polygamy, despite the law, so many second marriages are also not registered. Wives thus lack the protection of the law, during their marriages and in case of divorce, which often leaves their children unprotected too. Still, many women demanded that the constitution be revised and the old law reaffirmed.

The story behind the story. Sharia is the body of Islamic law whose development began with religious scholars shortly after the Prophet's death. It consists of interpretations of the Koran and of recorded teachings and practices of the Prophet called the Sunna. The most commonly used provisions address family law subjects, including marriage, inheritance, and divorce. These are the focus of family law in most Muslim countries. Initially, difficult questions were referred to legal scholars for independent nonbinding opinions, but in the eleventh century the then-dominant traditionalist scholars created a body of formalized rules that "have remained largely frozen for almost a millennium."[9] In recent years modern-oriented scholars and women's rights advocates have increasingly challenged some of these old interpretations.

About women as about many things, the Prophet Mohammed was ahead of his time. It has been argued that women's status under Islam as defined by the Koran was higher than in the Christian world at that time. Muslims believe the Koran is Allah's words, as Mohammed himself is believed to have been illiterate, thus unable to record them without divine help. Islamic lawgivers over the centuries, all men, turned his words into a rigid set of rules that could not keep pace with the times. (To be fair, some Christians have similar criticisms of their religion.)

Reformers argue that the equality Mohammed intended was undermined by selective and incorrect interpretations that became the basis of Islamic teachings, reinforced by tribal practices. Wearing a hijab, for example, developed from custom and tradition, not the Koran. The rule limiting a daughter's inheritance to half of her brother's was arguably based largely on the tradition that only men are responsible for providing for the family, a responsibility now more often shared. (Arguably still applicable, however, is that men must pay a dowry to marry, so need a larger inheritance.)[10] The problem is not Islam itself but how people are taught to interpret it—or choose to interpret it. Women are basically told (by men) that this is Allah's will. How does one oppose that? Those teachings and practices are now being disputed, and the clerical establishment is divided. The competing arguments have huge political implications.

Traditional Muslim scholars generally argue that men and women *are* equal under Islam. They cite specific passages. The Koran describes husbands and wives as a team, with neither subservient to the other, and extols the role and special importance of women. The woman has her own identity. Moreover, "as daughters, women have a right to just and equitable treatment from their parents"; "a woman has the right to accept or reject marriage proposals, and her consent is prerequisite to the validity of the marriage contract"; and "women are entitled to freedom of expression just as men are."[11] In practice, however, women too often don't have these rights. For example, fathers typically still control daughters' marriage decisions.

Having equal rights does not mean having the same rights. Men and women have different rights under Islam, but traditional scholars say these add up to "overall equality": "The rights and responsibilities of women are equal to those of men, just not necessarily identical."[12] In short traditional Muslim scholars define equality in terms of overall equality. Western scholars and many reformist Muslim scholars define equality as having the same rights.

In at least one respect, however, Islam *is* the source of inequality. Husbands can divorce their wives almost at will. Women don't have the same right; they must be faithful and obedient. It's easier for Sunnis; they can just tell the wife she is divorced. Shia men typically have to confer with their cleric and both families, but still control the decision. Women have more rights if the divorce is adjudicated in court, though men are still favored. This divorce disparity has huge consequences. Men can readily marry another woman within the rules, yet it is socially unthinkable to most men to marry a divorced woman. Divorced women are on their own for the rest of their lives. Widows don't fare well either. Not much equality there. This disparity is one big reason why women's CSOs don't want sharia applied to family law.

Beyond the Rule of Law

While people debated the legal issue, gender equality at street level was losing ground. Women always had more freedom in Baghdad than in southern Iraq. Until recent years Baghdad women could go out with their heads uncovered. In general women were arguably freer under Saddam. However, the harassment and intimidation by Islamic extremists on the streets of Amarah and Basra that forced even Christian women to wear hijabs became common in Baghdad too, even among university women. Women could come to Zainab's workshops and forums and denounce Article 39, but they had to be careful about what they were wearing going to and from the event.

It was not a safe time to be a Women's Advocacy CSO either. Extremists of both sects actively intimidated women. Some women prominent due to professional status or education were targeted and killed by militiamen or barely escaped. This was common in Baghdad, areas south of Baghdad, and Mosul. Others lived under threat. An increasing number were raped, some of them also murdered. A great many female university students dropped out.

One infamous 2005 incident in Basra had already defined much of what was wrong. Armed Sadrist militiamen invaded a large picnic organized by Basra University engineering students at a local park. The militiamen reacted against a minority of women not wearing hijabs; the music, dancing, and singing; and socializing between men and women. One female student was attacked with clubs and her clothes ripped off to shame her, which was videotaped by the perpetrators. Two male students coming to her rescue were shot. The girl later committed suicide out of humiliation. Many students were beaten viciously, especially women, and fifteen were injured. The militiamen carried ten students away to the Sadr office. The attack was in full view of numerous policemen, who did nothing.

The students protested angrily in the following days, which won public support but no action against the perpetrators. A local Sadrist leader, reflecting the cluelessness of many Islamic extremists, stated that the militiamen "had the right to intervene." The newly elected governor and Provincial Council chose political expediency over justice and finessed the issue, leaving the transparently criminal behavior unpunished.[13]

Some of the worst abuses are perpetrated by family members. One is the persistence of so-called honor killings, supposedly justified when someone's "immoral" behavior is felt to have brought shame on the family. To a civilized person, there is no such thing as an honor killing—neither sharia nor tribal law justifies it—but it's a well-known concept in Iraq and still applied by some who place "honor" above life. Many of these crimes occur in rural and tribal Kurdistan.

There is a huge gender discrimination factor, as it seems only the behavior of women brings "dishonor" on the family. The woman may be blamed even if she is the victim, and that includes being raped. Even disclosing a sexual assault may be seen as shameful. The punishment for being raped, as for alleged adultery, is sometimes to be stoned to death. Many women caught in this terrible trap have committed suicide. Some are forced to do so; others are put under enormous family pressure to kill themselves so as to relieve the family's shame.

The typical victim is a young woman. The typical murderer is her father, often aided by other men in the family. The perpetrators typically get away with it, often by hiding the real cause of death. A common evasion is attributing the death to accidental burns. Of course, when women are persuaded to kill themselves, their deaths can be correctly, if disingenuously, defined as suicides. In most cases it's obvious to authorities that they are neither accidents nor suicides. Often the police look the other way or decline to arrest the murderers. Several hundred women had been victims of honor killings in the past several years, and the statistics were not improving.

The horrifying extremes to which men will go to defend their "honor" are also reflected in other ways. Consider one truly sad example. Two British soldiers in Basra had a nice personal chat with a twelve-year-old girl, the substance of which could have raised no issue. Her father was angry, however, and beat her badly. The soldiers, seeing her bruises, accosted the man and beat him up in response. As British author Richard Holmes reported, "The man, feeling that he had been humiliated and emasculated, decided to rectify the situation by slitting his own daughter's throat. This apparently restored his honor."[14]

Short of murder but still a gruesome practice is genital mutilation of young girls, essentially partial removal of external female genitalia. Iraq is one of many Asian and African countries where this practice is common. Within Iraq it occurs most frequently in Kurdistan, in rural areas with low education levels. It has remained a frequent practice in some villages even though it has been widely denounced, including by the United Nations.

Beyond the transparently horrible things done to females are routine practices that are just unfair. As children, many girls are under stricter controls than their brothers. They are more likely to be kept out of school or removed from school, limiting their opportunities in life. A high percentage are told whom they should marry, sometimes first cousins, or are forced to marry very young, before their education is complete, or have their own choices vetoed by their fathers. These inequalities are from tribal customs, not sharia law. Once married, they are expected to bear many children, for whose care they are then primarily responsible. Many have to endure bad marriages and often domestic violence and may still end up divorced, disadvantaged by their discontinued education, and with little hope for the future. The many sons growing up with dominant or abusive fathers tend to follow the example and continue the cycle.

An Alternate Strategy for Women's Rights

In early 2006 I accidentally encountered an article by Dr. Isobel Coleman of the Council on Foreign Relations. She proposed a new strategy for women's rights in the Middle East. I never saw the women's rights issue the same way again.

Coleman observed that other Middle East countries live under sharia law, more strictly so than in Iraq. It could be a futile strategy for Iraq's reformers to try to replace sharia with secular law. She proposed instead that they adopt the strategy of reformers in other countries to "promote women's rights within an *Islamic* framework." According to Coleman, "This approach seems more likely to succeed, since it fights theology with theology—a natural strategy in countries with conservative populations and where religious authority is hard to challenge."[15]

The public argument over women and the constitution reinforced my earlier observation in Amarah that in the end the future of Iraq would be determined through a debate between Muslims and Muslims over the true meaning of the Koran. Some of that debate could be played out in courts. Coleman showed that while the constitution's provision on gender equality was unequivocal, the correct application of sharia law would most often be *debatable*. The women's rights side could bring to court its own experts on a range of sharia-related issues. To make that work, they would need a more aggressive strategy, supported by good lawyers.

THE VOICE OF HAIDER (from his women's rights public service announcement)

Love your daughter as much as your son. Give her the same opportunities as your son. When school begins again in the fall, make sure *all* of your children go. And keep your family together. Love *one* woman for the rest of your life.

10

The Struggle to Protect Civil Society Organizations

The National Conference of Civil Society Lawyers

Civil society organizations (CSOs) were often mistreated by government officials and usually could not do anything about it. CSO leaders were often targeted, and some were killed. My proposed answer was another national network: a National Organization of Civil Society Lawyers. I defined it as a Human Rights project but intended it as a service to all sectors of the Iraq Civil Society Program (ICSP) and all types of CSOs.

Almost all members would be lawyers, working in all provinces and also forming a national network coordinated from a Baghdad office. When a CSO ran into trouble, it could access a network lawyer, hopefully to resolve its issue but if necessary to represent it in court.

The organization would also take on constitutional rights cases. The classic example was the women's rights conflict between the nondiscrimination provision in Article 14 and the sharia law provision in Article 39. I believed precedents set by decisions in such cases could be critical. This kind of legal advocacy is an industry in the United States but is not well established in Iraq.

I developed a preliminary plan but left decisions to a National Conference of Civil Society Lawyers. I felt this would elicit the critical legal information and nuances only people familiar with the Iraq system could provide. We solicited for a CSO to organize and manage the conference under a special grant, won by the Hammurabi Humanitarian Association, an appropriate name for linking law and human rights. I made Omar, my Hilla coordinator and a lawyer, the conference director.

Before the conference I devised a three-page "Participant Survey," sent to conference registrants and other lawyers to collect contact information, professional and educational background, and CSO information and to ask how they could help and what kinds of cases they would take. We couldn't afford to invite all interested lawyers, but the survey could help expand the initial membership beyond conference participants and facilitate an automated database and a nationwide case referral system.

The audacity of this idea was not lost on me. I, a nonlawyer, was proposing in effect to create a pro bono legal service for CSOs throughout Iraq.

I was confident, however, that I could specify most questions the conference needed to answer. I divided them into five discussion group tasks. Group 1 would define the organization's mission and scope. It should represent CSOs to government at all levels, at no cost; represent CSOs in court, at no cost; and represent individuals in human rights, women's rights, and freedom of the press cases. Lawyers would be committing time to free public service—a well-developed concept in the American legal profession but not in Iraq.

Group 2 would define the membership requirements. By what criteria would lawyers be admitted? Would they join as individuals, law firms, or both? How would members be recruited and approved? Should members pay dues and, if so, how much? Group 3 would set the organizational requirements. Should there be a national office? What officer and staff positions would be needed? How would cases be identified, evaluated, and referred to lawyers? How would the organization be sustained financially after ICSP?

Group 4 would handle external relations and communications. How would the organization communicate with government, other lawyers' groups, and international organizations? How would professional standards be maintained and enforced? Group 5 would address interactions with government on security. How would the organization work with IG offices and the CPI? How could it handle cases of abuse by police? What should a CSO lawyer do if threatened?

As the saying goes, "Talk is cheap," so I wanted some idea of how CSOs would actually handle the cases, many of them complex and some even dangerous. I created seven brief real-world scenarios, based on actual or typical government abuses, and asked if they would take the case and what legal strategy they would use. The answers weren't so easy. For example:

Situation: It is well known that the police department in Basra has been infiltrated by militia members. One consequence is that innocent people have been murdered by men in police uniforms and/or vehicles.

Problem: If IC SP informed you that a CSO leader had been murdered in this way and asked you to represent the CSO, what would you do?

So it was that on April 18 and 19, 2006, I found myself at the Babylon Hotel near (but not quite in) the Green Zone, surrounded by all-day protection from several PSDs dressed in casual duds to cover their weapons and avoid looking obvious.

People were slow to arrive, so we started very late. One hundred or so delegates came, however, from all governorates, including independent lawyers, judges, and government officials. There was intense interest and strong participation.

Omar did the opening remarks, defining the conference objectives. I had arranged with Hammurabi to find a prestigious lawyer to be the keynote speaker, to provide critical information on the legal system. His speech was excellent. In general, however, I limited speeches. This had to be a working conference.

The five breakout groups took on the organization and policy questions, each reporting its conclusions to the conference. Five of my seven scenarios were discussed in separate breakout meetings. The lawyers affirmed that no one is above the rule of law. They seemed confident they would stand up for their clients even on cases with potential personal security risks, which addressed one of my unspoken concerns.

I gave a short prepared speech on the afternoon of day 2, with Usama interpreting, mainly to identify myself, as I had purposely stayed behind the scenes, letting Iraqis run the conference. I explained that IC SP was there to help Iraq but, appealing to Iraqi pride, also cited Hammurabi's historic role in setting standards of law and justice for the world.

The delegates then voted to establish the national organization, and they outlined a formula for donating pro bono time. Meetings at the end elected a Follow-Up Committee, Bylaws Committee, and Nominating Committee. Major satellite channels interviewed organizers and many participants, who gave the conference and ICSP a positive evaluation.

This still left a lot of work. Task 1 was learning how the court system works and how lawyers interact with it. In Iraq one can be a lawyer with just a bachelor's degree, but most CSO cases would need experienced lawyers. A lawyer on my Baghdad Center team explained that lawyers are classified into three levels. Those at Level C can handle any case within their specialty (i.e., criminal or civil). Level B lawyers qualify for lower-court civil cases below a set value threshold (about $3,500 then). Level A lawyers do only simple civil cases such as divorce and marriage for the first two years, after which they qualify at Level B. You have to work with a senior lawyer for at least ten years to qualify to work on your own. So, our referral system needed to engage senior lawyers, which still left roles for others.

From that information we outlined a courthouse-level referral system. Each provincial capital has a court compound (two in Baghdad), focused around the appeals court. That was nineteen courts to cover. The Iraqi Bar Society paid about $100 a month to have a contracted lawyer on call at each courthouse. We could do the same for the same price. CSO leaders needing help could call a central phone number.

We also set up the database, using the Participant Survey data. We needed to hire a managing CSO to set up the field-based case referral system; implement the conference recommendations; set up the internal governance; and elect officers. To make it all sustainable after ICSP left Iraq, we needed linkages to an international NGO, or perhaps UNAMI, and a sustainability plan.

Everything considered, I was doing great with this project. Other urgent developments and crises caused delays, however, despite all my overtime. A few months went by. Then other developments threatened the entire plan.

The Struggle for a CSO Enabling Law

First There Was the Plan

This was my biggest battle in Iraq—but it started as Jean-Sebastien Roy's biggest battle. The focus was Civic Education's proposal for a national CSO enabling law, which would protect CSOs by defining their rights as volunteer organizations and establishing democratic government policies toward them. The emphasis was on ensuring there was only minimum regulation; otherwise, Iraq would defeat the purpose of an independent civil society. Other Middle East countries had failed at this, or never tried. Much was at stake.

Allowing nongovernmental groups to operate independently was an idea without history in Iraq. Even professional associations had been extensions of the Baathist government. The instinct to control others was deeply ingrained and did not go away with the Baathists. Many believed that CSOs must be controlled too.

The parliament had factions whose dedication to democracy was suspect, starting with the large Sadrist bloc. The Sadrist-led Ministry of State for Civil Society had already drafted a heavy-handed, control-oriented proposed law that worried and antagonized many in the civil society sector. Jean-Sebastien wanted a law on the Western model. He was charging uphill.

His strategy was grassroots all the way to the top. Assuming no help from parliament members still groping to find their own way, he unleashed his regional Civic Education teams to create CSO legislative committees and develop a public dialogue on what the law should include, so as to create public momentum. Well-attended forums in each region generated ideas and positions, which were sent on to ICSP to be reconciled with input from the other regions. The ministry draft was always attacked in these forums.

Jean-Sebastien's process would roll up to a national conference at which CSO reps from all over Iraq would produce a consensus final proposal, with ICSP technical guidance, and present it to the parliament and prime minister as a proposal from the Iraqi public. It was an awesome strategy. It ran into a few complications.

The regional input went to a follow-up committee of CSO leaders, including lawyers and retired Judge Salah Al-Awsi, to create a common draft. The CPI supported this campaign, and two of our CPI friends joined the committee. Haider coordinated for Civic Education.

However, such a law was unprecedented in Iraq; the regional drafts were not quite professional level; and many provisions needed precise wording, always an invitation to debate small points. Judge Salah and the lawyers supported the purpose but wanted a law consistent in form with legislative precedent; but some precedents were very old, and Jean-Sebastien and I saw the need for new ones. I wanted the law's purpose explained at the beginning, for example—obvious to most, but Iraqi precedent was to put it at the very end.

Jean-Sebastien believed some provisions were absolutely essential. Most important, CSOs should not be required to register with the government or be beholden in any way to the government. That point *had* to be included. For CSOs interested in government grants or contracts, minimal registration and monitoring were sufficient to protect the public interest. The lawyers fully agreed with his purpose but argued that because this freedom could be understood from the constitution, there was no need to mention it.

Jean-Sebastien gave me his draft, reflecting all the input to date. It still needed work. My years in city management and other roles gave me a lot of practice and confidence in writing legalese, so I volunteered to be his legislative draftsman.

One challenge was how CSOs would be registered. It sounds like an administrative problem, but to me it was a life-or-death issue. CSOs would have to provide organizational information to meet registration criteria—fine in principle, but what information? Some information could get into the wrong hands, such as militias and insurgent spy networks, and be used to *target* CSOs and CSO leaders.

The transparent motive of the ministry's Sadrist leaders was to control CSOs. Sadrists in Amarah had shown me that spying on others was a priority activity of the Sadr office; they had even gathered information on my Democracy Team members. One team member, Dr. Kifaya, was already dead. So were a few CSO leaders. I was in no mood for blithe reassurances. I wanted a registration process requiring only minimal information and no detailed individual information such as membership lists.

The security risk also motivated our provision to abolish the small Ministry of State for Civil Society and replace it with something else. This made ICSP's campaign inherently confrontational. In our favor was the widespread CSO hostility toward the ministry and the widespread concern about the harm it could cause. My draft proposed a new agency whose mission was to protect, defend, and coordinate with CSOs without supervising them; to limit the information it could demand from them; and to prevent political interference.

Finally, I completed a draft law, conferring often with Jean-Sebastien. On some points his vision and his committee's preferences differed, but he stuck with his democratic process, letting them set out their own opinions and not pressuring them to ratify his. Where we could, we acceded to the Iraqis' way of organizing and wording things. On certain points, however, he felt unable to compromise because the issue was just too important.

Jean-Sebastien now convened a new committee with Iraqi legal minds, including a few from his working committee, to refine the draft—the last big step before the national conference. He might logically have injected himself into the debate by chairing this committee, but I persuaded him to let me do it. I reasoned that his passionate style, the stubbornness and legalistic bent of some members, and the need for constant translation would make it too difficult and time-consuming to reach agreement.

I set up my relationship with them by saying I was there to coordinate, not to impose a personal agenda. We would base discussion on my draft, already reflecting the working committee input and approved by Jean-Sebastien, but committee members could propose changes in any provision. I did have one bottom-line rule: I would control the document, and there would be only one document. *I* would incorporate their changes, arrange translations (by Usama, also my interpreter), and produce the final version. As it turned out, if I had not set this rule, the committee members would have trampled me under to do it their way.

ADF arranged for expert help from the International Center for Not-for-Profit Law (ICNL), in Washington DC. ICNL's comments on the ministry's proposed law were expert and highly critical, supported our views on the provisions needed, and cited "international best practices." The committee members, despite their over-devotion to old legal precedent, did want a law conforming to best practices. I made numerous revisions based on ICNL's comments.

Many provisions were readily accepted, including important innovations. The group dug in its heels, however, on some points. One was Jean-Sebastien's core provision that CSOs must have freedom to operate without having to register. The Iraqi lawyers were just adamant that this provision was unnecessary, and anything unnecessary must be excluded. Other provisions met the same objection. A lawyer and soon-to-be judge from Hilla was especially stubborn. I made adjustments for their explanations of how legislation was drafted in Iraq, reasoning that a draft law in a familiar format would get more acceptance, but it was hard to do on some points. The committee did not settle every issue, but we did produce a tentative draft law for the national conference.

Then the National Conference Got Hijacked

Crazy things can happen on international development projects. The next step was the three-day national conference Jean-Sebastien had set up for May 6–8, at the Babylon Hotel. Suddenly his plans were threatened by an unexpected development and a mysterious decision by project management. On May 4 came this memo from our chief of party.

> Dear Jean and Tom;
>
> I hope you are doing well. I discussed today your request to participate in the NGO conference. I am afraid we decided to make this event as a low-profile one, which means we will not go to the event with armored vehicles and PSDs. Also, we are taking certain security measures for attending such events by the International staff after we received two kidnapping threats, one of them was for Jean-Sebastien by name. We have been requested by the American Embassy to be careful and don't expose our international staff to any sort of risk, especially Jean.
>
> Therefore, I am sorry to tell you that I can not approve your participation in the NGO conference, for your safety and for the program sake. We can discuss the methods that keep both of you informed about the progress of the conference activities.
>
> Regards,
>
> Issam

Certainly, a threat had to be taken seriously. It's hard to argue with such decisions, as there is no way to prove them necessary or unnecessary. The rest of what Issam did was the real issue.

Without talking to Jean-Sebastien, Issam turned the entire conference over to the manager of the Baghdad regional center, who had been uninvolved in the project. He was also an expat, a Jordanian, which seemed to defy the expat security logic in the memo. The regional manager assigned conference roles to some of his staff, who also had no prior involvement, and left Jean-Sebastien's staff out. The regional Civic Education team was told to create its own conference plan and devise the agenda, and no one felt it necessary to confer with the actual leader of the project. Issam never explained this bizarre decision.

Maneuvering fast to stave off disaster, Jean-Sebastien and I each assigned two of our top Iraqi staff—newly arrived Usama and Mohammed, Haider and his colleague Israa Ali—to attend the conference as our unofficial representatives. The bottom line was to keep focus on the draft document and get as much agreement as possible on what it should say. As we had no control over the conference sessions, this had to be done outside the agenda at odd hours.

The Civil Society ministry, its proposed law already widely rejected within ICSP, was invited to speak at the opening session. Moreover, the regional manager and his Iraqi assistant met with ministry officials in advance and gave them a copy of my draft, which showed them that ICSP was proposing to abolish their ministry. An arrogant ministry official told the delegates no bill would ever be passed without ministry cooperation, creating uncertainty among the delegates.

The remaining details of the formal agenda were a blur, as I was too busy coordinating with Usama about the informal conference going on outside the agenda. After the official conference sessions adjourned on the first two days and the conference staff went home, Usama and Mohammed sat down with CSO delegates (including those on Jean-Sebastien's committee), starting at 7:30 p.m., and worked late into the night. They called it the Legal Kitchen. This produced good changes that did not threaten the direction of our draft and kept the project on track.

The formal conference then approved a draft with those changes on day 3. It left some gaps to fill and delegated completion of the final draft to a committee—those who had helped produce the pre-conference draft plus a couple of new members named by the conference.

So, we survived the hijacked conference. The regional manager never did report back to Jean-Sebastien, still seething about the takeover. As for me, I never brought up the subject with the regional manager, and we developed a good working relationship. I didn't bring it up with Issam either. Sometimes it's better not to say what you're thinking.

Then Things Got Really Confusing

Unfortunately, Jean-Sebastien could only commit seven months to the project and returned home to the Dominican Republic in June with his pet project still up in the air. I became the new front man for his enabling law project. Soon afterward the new deputy chief of party (DCOP), herself a lawyer, arrived on the scene.

Usama and I updated the pre-conference draft to reflect the conference draft, but some proposed provisions just wouldn't work and needed committee revisions. A few holdover committee members then made an intense effort to get more control of the document and to revisit all the wording issues they had reluctantly settled with me earlier. They meant well, but their scheming threatened the entire project.

I felt trapped by competing priorities. One was to keep this as a CSO initiative, to uphold Jean-Sebastien's democratic process. Realistically, however, we needed a draft law that would satisfy USAID and others in the U.S. government. I did not forget that we were not the only ones working on this idea. UNAMI had its own enabling law project, potentially a big complication if we had to compete with the UN for the parliament's attention. Another U.S. contractor had produced an earlier draft, another Iraqi group was working on one, and others were also involved.

As this had become a time-consuming project for the holdover committee members, they also wanted a significant daily "consultant" fee. They had succeeded with a similar demand earlier. The project management agreed to pay them but was angry about doing it. The DCOP decreed that by accepting money, the members had agreed to become ICSP employees so were no longer independent actors who could dictate terms. She seized control of the process, bringing in a young bilingual Iraqi judge to chair the meetings and make final wording decisions. She created a no-compromise three-day completion schedule.

Despite the three-day time limit, the members battled stubbornly over old details and did not even finish the first section (of many) on day 1. After day 2 they were even farther behind. ICSP then subdivided the group on day 3, assigning different sections to each subgroup, to get through all the remaining sections. This move finally forced the members to stop scheming over every provision. The judge would submit the final document to ICSP, not to the committee.

So, Jean-Sebastien's grassroots process didn't quite hold up to the end. I was hopeful, however, that the final result would reflect his vision and our efforts. As for me, I had given a lot of time to something I didn't have to take on but felt it was vital to civil society in Iraq. No one on the outside would ever understand what it took me to get the project this far.

Much later, Kurdish lawyer Hoshyar Malo, from Kurdish Human Rights Watch, published a detailed comparison of the Ministry of Civil Society draft and the version I drafted for ICSP. He described the differences as "a comparison of two very different views of civil society." Not surprisingly, he found our ICSP version a "superior law," primarily because it gave "more space and freedom to civil society." He called it "the best one among the many civil society law drafts that have been submitted to the Council of Representatives."[1]

As of late 2006, there was relief and reason for optimism. This assumed the parliament would take up the legislation. Instead, a long delay occurred, as the parliament was completely backed up, not to say messed up, and even legislation of this importance was not near the top of its priority list. In the political confusion of newly democratic Iraq, the battle for a CSO enabling law was destined to go on and on and on.

The Nagging Issue of Sustainability

Sustaining Civil Society Organizations

As ICSP built up Iraq's civil society sector, it was also required by USAID to plan for the day when we would leave. This meant leaving behind both sustainable CSOs and a sustainable successor to ICSP.

Youssria and a committee were developing an Organizational Assessment Tool (OAT) to evaluate CSOs' capabilities through answers to a series of questions, generating a score. By then shoring up areas where capabilities were lacking, CSOs could raise their scores in later assessments. ICSP's reports had been touting the OAT as if it were done. Once Youssria shared it, I realized it was just too long for these small community groups, most with no full-time employees and no office. There were four sections—Internal Governance, Advocacy, General Management, and Financial Management—with twenty-three subsections. By actual count there were 213 questions! They could have better used it on General Motors.

My other big issue was the mix of the questions—heavy on internal process, light on measuring effectiveness. It was more about compliance than capacity. Youssria agreed but couldn't stop the momentum to issue it prematurely. Her regional staffs started meeting with CSOs and of course got bogged down by the 213 questions. The scores showed that most CSOs still needed a lot of improvement. No surprise there. Comparing the results showed that ICSP's assessments were highly inconsistent. No surprise there either.

Still, the OAT was a step in the right direction. It encouraged CSOs of all sizes to create democratic organizations and procedures. They were then more likely to pursue a wider range of activities than just applying for ICSP grants. By encouraging capacity building now, the OAT potentially contributed to sustainability later.

Transitioning to What?

For me a necessary part of any sustainability strategy was placing more responsibility on Iraqi staff so as to create a transition to Iraqi management. I advised Issam in June that sustainability should begin with us. We could give Iraqis primary responsibility for some functions, such as evaluating initial grant proposals, and transition to an organization that could stand on its own once ICSP left. I also suggested filling newly vacant expat positions with Iraqis.

One idea would have been training our own program coordinators to succeed us. A similar transition was available at the four regional centers, where Iraqi center managers already shared management responsibility with expat regional managers. ICSP was not ready for such changes, partly because it was afraid to risk the project on less-experienced people and, to be honest, because not all expats shared my enthusiasm for democratic management. The instincts are to cling to expat control, live for today, and hope tomorrow works out.

USAID, however, wanted a sustainability plan. Jean-Sebastien was working on it, as were the four Civil Society Resource Centers (CSRCS). USAID assigned a young woman, Melinda Witter, to support this effort, and she was hounding Jean-Sebastien for help. He envisioned the successor organization as one CSO with four regional offices, rather than four separate regional organizations, as USAID assumed. It would be more decentralized than ICSP but retain some central support and coordination. His was the right idea. The four CSRCs were instructed to write sustainability plans, and their Iraqi center directors formed a coordinating committee.

To me money was the key. Without ICSP or equivalent USAID support, Iraqi management could not sustain much of anything without some combination of new revenue and reduced costs. The new organization would have far fewer employees, so it could not retain most current staff. Business development and marketing would be added costs. Moreover, the new entity would not inherit the high walls and highly trained security.

The Baghdad CSRC had organized an Advisory Committee composed of several CSO leaders with impressive experience, even international experience. I attended three or four of its meetings to help it get established. It soon suffered a tragedy, when one member, a young lawyer, was assassinated in his neighborhood. A friend who was with him, an ICSP employee, barely avoided death. There was a moment of silence at the next meeting, and people went on with the same feeling of resignation forced on too many in Baghdad. Another Advisory Committee member would be killed later in the year.

Jean-Sebastien did keep communicating with Melinda Witter after he left, but as her report neared completion, AID-Baghdad assigned it to someone else, then issued her incomplete report. The regional committees kept on, but there was still no ICSP transition plan.

Adding to the "small world" stories of life in Iraq, I would meet Melinda in 2008, not in Baghdad but in Suleimaniya, in Kurdistan, when we were both on new projects.

Those Damn Reports

For development firms, one prerequisite for sustainability after the contract ends is to keep the current contract going. So, it's critical to keep USAID happy. That makes the report system important. In my previous federal contract experience, I had found progress reports not especially burdensome. But ICSP reports reinforced the lesson learned from the RTI project that reports can be time-consuming and subject to complications.

Every program sector had to generate weekly reports. Ours started with the regional teams; were sent to my headquarters team; then to me; then successively to Ethan Arnheim, the reports manager; the DCOP; AID-Baghdad; and unknown-to-us offices in Washington. On the last report week of each month, we did a monthly report instead. All this added up to a lot of work.

I never resented the time required. I was happy to relate what my regional teams were accomplishing; they made us look good. However, the weekly drumbeat of stories on successful ICSP events could not have added much to AID's analysis. Monthly reports would have served its real purposes. Indeed, most federal contractors report monthly. That means less time on reports, more time pursuing project outcomes, and more efficient use of taxpayers' money.

Reports to USAID are unavoidably linked to internal considerations, of both the contractor and the government. All federal contracts can be terminated "for the convenience of the government," so contractors must be ever alert for anything that might please or displease AID. Moreover, some information was of interest to people in the White House and Congress. As Iraq was a huge political issue, the Bush administration liked good-news items that helped put a positive spin on what was happening there. So, those damn reports potentially served the business or political purposes of a lot of people.

Because weekly and monthly input reports were done by Iraqi staff, I had to be the final English-language editor. It was an unavoidable task, but I did lose my patience with fixing the same misspelled words week after week. So, I finally issued "Dr. Tom's Spelling List," with the instruction that mistakes were not permitted in any word on the list. This made my point and was accepted with the intended amusement.

11

The Personal Meaning of Terrorism

Disaster by the Numbers

Media in the United States and Great Britain provided detailed counts of Coalition soldiers killed and civilian expats killed in the struggle for Iraq. There will never be agreement on the number of Iraqis killed, but no one doubts that it is tragically high. Official U.S. and Iraqi estimates were generally lower than independent estimates. Most startling was the 2006 number from a statistical survey by the Johns Hopkins School of Public Health: 654,965, vastly higher than all other estimates. Although criticized—by George Bush and Tony Blair, among others—it was based on a carefully developed methodology, its interviews were conducted by Iraqi physicians, and its sample had about 12,000 people in fifty locations.[1] Whatever the "correct" number—which of course continues to rise—ground-level impressions from surveys and individual accounts suggest that the human toll of the struggle for Iraq has been *much* higher than official estimates.

One U.S. military estimate was immediately relevant to my work. In 2006, as I was trying to support human rights, over 2,100 civilians were being killed every *month*.[2]

One problem for researchers was that the deaths had multiple sources. People were killed by Coalition troops, Iraqi troops, Sunni insurgents, Shia militiamen, Iranian agents, common criminals, and the failures of the overburdened medical system. A huge number were targeted as individuals and just murdered—one-at-a-time statistics that don't show up in official casualty counts yet add up to an unknown but shocking total. Morgues can count the bodies they receive, hospitals can count the patients who don't survive, and bombs exploded to kill people result in fairly accurate counts. It is much harder to count all the victims whose bodies are dumped by the side of the road or discarded in some other thoughtless way.

To all the deceased, add all those who suffered permanent injuries; all the widows and orphans; and those displaced from homes and neighborhoods, many permanently, including those who fled the country. A large number were kidnapped for ransom, and many families had to raise far more money than they had to get them back, sometimes losing their loved ones and the money too. The toll of the struggle was felt by most Baghdad-area families and countless families in other areas. There is no adequate measure for the pain, the grief, the sense of loss, the frustration, and the hopelessness felt by all of them. The full scale of the disaster has no recent parallels in Western countries. Some statistics one *could* readily believe came from opinion surveys showing that most Baghdad residents felt life was worse than under Saddam. It wasn't just former Saddam loyalists saying that.

In 2005, 30 percent of "terrorist attacks" worldwide occurred in Iraq, an estimated 3,468. In 2006 it was 45 percent and 6,630, a 91 percent increase, and 65 percent of the worldwide terrorism fatalities were in Iraq. The number "killed, injured or kidnapped" rose from 20,685 to 38,713.[3] For an on-the-ground perspective, divide the terrorist attacks by 365 days. That comes to 9.5 attacks per day in 2005 and 18.2 in 2006, a major percentage of them in the Baghdad area, where my colleagues and I were trying to promote democracy and good government.

Based on varying estimates, the overall number of those who left Iraq during the violence would reach about 1.5 million by late 2006, rising fast toward 2 million, including a major percentage of Iraq's small Christian minority. Most went to Syria or Jordan, others to Egypt or Lebanon. Many were valued professionals, including physicians and other health care workers, professors and teachers, artists, and others whose education and skills were most needed in Iraq. Some returned later, often because their money ran out, and the Syrian civil war later compelled many to return, but many others did not. It was the start of a new Iraqi diaspora.

Add to that about 1.5 million internally displaced persons (IDPs) who had moved within Iraq, a number destined to go much higher later. Many moved in with family or friends or became squatters in public buildings.[4] Many went to live with relatives in safer places, often their original home communities in northern or southern Iraq; some escaped to Iraqi Kurdistan, even some with no Kurdish roots; and a smaller number had to live in tents in makeshift camps.

Taking émigrés and IDPs together, the violence caused around 3 million people to flee by the end of 2006. That number was still going up. The total Iraq population then was about 27 million, so *over 10 percent of the population had left!*[5] The exodus was especially dramatic in Baghdad, as a major percentage of those leaving were from that area. Measured in that context, it appears that a truly incredible percentage of the Baghdad area population fled.

Disaster on the Streets

Almost every day the news we all read from Iraq focused on military clashes and casualties and increasingly on the latest civilian body count. Those statistics could not convey the full impact on the Iraqi people. In those awful times everyone in Baghdad knew he or she was living close to death. Age had nothing to do with it. Iraqis woke up each day knowing it could be their last. Even if they survived, they had to worry about their family members, their friends, their neighbors. Too often, someone in their life died. The scale of the tragedy and the immediacy of its impact blasted normal human coping mechanisms.

In a sadly ironic way, people learned to cope by discounting the impact of the tragedies. Death increasingly lost its ability to shock people. In most places reactions to someone's death vary largely with the person's age; the older the person, the less devastating and less surprising the news. In Baghdad no death was entirely surprising or unexpected.

Anthony Shadid, then of the *Washington Post*, observed that the overwhelming violence of a place like Iraq can become dangerously meaningless. He observed something in early 2005 that I observed later as the death toll mounted: the resilience of the Iraqi people, which he considered their defining trait. As Shadid defined it, "Resilience can mean many things—fatalism, endurance, persistent hope and an ability to make the unusual normal."[6] I define it as the ability to endure tragedy and misfortune without giving in.

The lack of surprise at the latest murder could not overcome all the trauma, however. Families and neighborhoods lost one person, then another. The struggle for survival was reflected in the limited time people spent outside but also in their efforts to keep some grip on their emotions. Psychological problems now affected many children, thousands of them orphaned by the violence, some of whom saw their parents murdered in front of them. Countless children and adults had posttraumatic stress disorder.

Despite a huge increase in Iraq's health budget, the medical system was overwhelmed and deteriorating, still beset by shortages of medicine and vital equipment, with thousands of doctors leaving Iraq, many after being threatened or having colleagues killed. Many wounded victims died because most hospitals lacked adequate emergency departments staffed by trained personnel. Baghdad's morgues were overmatched.

University professors and administrators were frequent assassination victims from the start of the Coalition government. Most high-level academics had been Baathists, not necessarily by choice, and many lost their positions to the de-Baathification policy, but some were assassinated anyway, as were many other academics. Almost 40 percent of surviving professors left the country. Iraq's once prestigious university system declined precipitously.[7] There was a huge drop-off in university enrollment. School attendance also dropped sharply because parents were afraid to let their children leave home. Most of those kept at home were girls. In Damascus, Syria, schools were overwhelmed by all the Iraqi children.

While our own security in the Red Zone was so far reassuring, other NGOs felt compelled to leave Iraq or move operations to relatively safe Erbil. Other NGO projects were already being managed from Amman, Jordan. Withdrawal of these helping organizations reduced the collective impact of USAID and other programs. As time went on, the only relatively safe way to operate in some provinces was under the protection of military-secured Provincial Reconstruction Teams (PRTs). The risk of going to the Green Zone increased, putting even greater risk on Iraqis who continued working there, a risk sometimes fatal. I heard from Amarah about employees of the British at Camp Abu Naji who were murdered as collaborators.

As 2006 went on, sectarian cleansing by Sunni and Shia extremists continued apace, turning a large percentage of Baghdad's many mixed neighborhoods into segregated sectarian enclaves largely controlled by either Sunni insurgents or Mehdi Army militiamen or guarded by armed neighborhood groups. Roadside and vehicle bombs kept going up in smoke. At stake was nothing less than military control of Baghdad. U.S. and Iraqi troops were trying, but the Americans soldiers were too few and the Iraqis too often ineffective. Attacks against both increased dramatically.

These tragedies were not just observed at a distance. Some affected ICSP employees, including my own team.

An aunt of Mohammed Adil worked in the Green Zone but quit after being threatened. Soon after, however, she was with her ten-year-old son in a crowded Baghdad market area when a car pulled up. She was dragged into the car, right in front of the people in the market, leaving her horrified son outside. They shot her dead in the car and dumped her body on the street.

Mohammed had a cousin selling generator service in the Dora area, one of the most violent. It was a service much needed, as electricity service hours in Baghdad were dropping. An armed Sunni extremist approached him, saying loudly that the Prophet Mohammed could not cool off on a hot day because there was no electricity in that time so people should not pretend to be better than the Prophet. *Bang!* Others selling generator service met the same fate.

Lack of electricity also explains why people sell ice on the streets—the only way to cool water when there is no electricity. Some of them heard similar extremist logic about the Prophet not being able to drink cold water on hot days, just before they were shot dead.

One day a poor street vendor was selling ice cream in Dora after Sunni extremists told him to stop. A man with a gun approached him to demand an explanation, then killed him.

Usama had a young cousin who got on Bus 5 in Adhamiya. As the bus proceeded on its route, someone from outside shot at the bus driver. He missed the driver but killed the child.

The General Legal Center was a great CSO led by an appealing young husband and wife team. This was the CSO that erected those anti-corruption signs with a hotline number in front of ministry buildings. I met them at several of our events, and they were really nice, smart, and committed people. One day, coming out of his house, the husband was shot dead. His wife left the country. They would not be the only victims among ICSP's CSO leaders.

Some barbers were killed merely for trimming men's beards. This practice goes against an old Islamic tradition but is now broadly accepted—except by some Sunni extremists. Other barbershops then posted notices saying, "Sorry, we don't trim beards anymore. Do it yourself at home."

Despite the extremist religious rhetoric of the perpetrators, neither Shia nor Sunni street assassins represented any significant public opinion or any real Islamic principles. Many of the too few who got arrested admitted they did it for the money. Who paid them was the seldom-answered question, though Baathists were sometimes the unspoken answer.

The level of depravity in Baghdad's countless incidents of violence was shocking to civilized people. In one reported incident Sunni militants in western Baghdad approached a couple and their baby and shot both the husband and the baby in the head, leaving the wife alive and totally traumatized. The man's "offense" was that he had married a Shia woman.[8] In another incident assassins invaded the funeral procession in Baghdad for a young man who was murdered— and killed his two brothers.

In one cruel incident a man was not only murdered and beheaded, but a dog head was sewn onto his body in place of his head. In another a man was beheaded and his head put into his stomach, which was then sewed up again. Other murder stories had atrocities similar and even worse. I choose not to repeat one true story because it's so gross that readers might just drop the book and run for the toilet.

The Fear of Going Home

After Kifaya's assassination, I was highly sensitive to the risks Iraqi staff were taking to help their country. ICSP was, relatively speaking, a bastion of security and peace of mind for employees, protected by its high walls and tight security. The big difference was that at the end of the expats' working day, we were still protected by the high walls and tight security. The Iraqis had to go home, then return safely the next morning.

Their general cheerfulness belied the stress many felt about their neighborhoods and their daily commute. Less apparent was an Iraqi tendency not to trouble expats with bad news. Some had troubling stories I learned about only after leaving Baghdad.

Iraq now had many extremists prepared to kill anyone considered a collaborator. Not just Iraqis working in the Green Zone or for the military but anyone working for any U.S. organization could be targeted, as many were. Many quit their jobs; some fled Iraq to save themselves and their families. Even at ICSP there was a steady trickle of departures.

On April 11 Ghassak arrived in the office and told me she had to quit, immediately. She had hidden her workplace from others, but now someone she knew who was not friendly had noticed her in the compound. I was really fond of Ghassak, and I was stunned. No words could overcome the overwhelming sadness in the room. There was no way to replace her talents, and we never did, but losing her enthusiasm and smiling face hurt just as much. After a while she took a job in the Green Zone but soon immigrated through Turkey to the United States.

A woman working in the Baghdad regional center also left. Her son had been riding in a car with another boy when they encountered kidnappers. The criminals captured the other boy; her son somehow eluded them but learned they knew who he was and intended to get him later. The mother was distraught. The whole family moved to Kurdistan, where she was hired by our Erbil office. The other kid's parents reportedly paid a ransom to get him back.

Dashti was my next and biggest loss. His family was Kurdish, from Dahuk, but long settled in Baghdad. Their neighborhood had become too dangerous. He looked over his shoulder when traveling to and from work. He returned home by different routes each day to avoid scrutiny, while his family worried he might not get there. He was unhappy about leaving but had a wife and baby. On August 15 the whole family, including his parents, moved to Erbil. I would meet him there later. If Dashti would leave, there was no assurance about anyone else.

I promoted Mohammed N., another Craig Davis disciple, to be Dashti's replacement. One day Mohammed was standing by his outside door at home, watching his brother and other boys playing soccer just down the street. A car with four men passed by the boys to the end of the street, then turned around. On its way back it stopped beside a teenager, no more than fifteen years old. One of the men leaned halfway outside his car window, then shot the boy three times, killing him. The other children ran in fear. Mohammed ran to his room for his AK-47, opposed by the fearful screams of his family, but the assassins drove off by the time he got outside, leaving the boy lying on the street and his family shouting and wailing.

An impressive Iraqi staff member from one of the management offices also resigned in midyear and left the country. He went first to Egypt and eventually to Sweden. Later the Baghdad Center director suddenly told me she was leaving with her family for Egypt. They later got to the United States.

Ameer's neighborhood in the Kadhimiya District was next to a U.S. military camp but fell under the control of Shia extremists. They targeted government employees and Iraqi staff of U.S. military and civilian organizations, which put Ameer's life at risk. A cousin in a high government post had already fled the country after multiple threats and an attack on his convoy that killed two of his guards.

In March 2006 Ameer and his parents finally left their home, forced to live in another neighborhood. Eight months later Shia militiamen invaded their house, stole a computer, and searched it. They then accused the family of being spies and told them never to come back. They settled a Shia family displaced from a Sunni district in the house, with "authorization" from a Shia mosque. All of this caused his father great stress, and he was soon hospitalized, then died after the medical system failed him. Ameer did not return to his old house, but even his temporary neighborhood had Mehdi Army members actively looking for government officials and staff of U.S. organizations to assassinate.

Most of Usama's family had already moved to Syria. He had his wife live with her family, later with his. He took a taxi home most days but didn't go directly to his house in western Baghdad. He got off in different places each day, short of where he lived, then walked home. This strategy avoided creating a pattern that would raise curiosity about where he was coming from.

It seemed nobody's neighborhood was safe. My former Amarah

team member working for the Coalition project office in Baghdad was sitting in her home one night when a stray bullet from a shootout struck her sister, who fortunately survived.

In October, Firas, my Baghdad coordinator, had a frightening encounter with Sadr thugs. One of his brother's friends came to visit, and Firas, reflecting traditional Iraqi hospitality, later offered him a ride home. The friend lived in the Habibiya neighborhood, close to Sadr City. As Firas reached the road junction dividing his neighborhood from Habibiya, four cars approached on his side of the road, each with four or five armed men. They blocked traffic, commandeered the intersection, and ordered him to move. He objected that there was no room to move, then tried to maneuver away, but his side mirror accidentally touched one gunman.

Then it all became truly scary. Men pounded on his car and ordered him to stop. The thug he had lightly touched yelled, "Why did you hit me?" He then smashed Firas on his eyeglasses with his pistol handle, breaking the glasses and causing severe facial bleeding. Momentarily unconscious, Firas opened his eyes to see his T-shirt full of blood. He gunned the car out of there for a short distance, then couldn't drive. His younger brother, also in the car and a beginner driver, drove him home. His mother saw him and fainted. He needed surgery that night to repair his face. The incident led him to leave Iraq in 2007, though he later returned.

One day I needed something from a store, and Miami offered to go get it. Even this simple errand made me nervous, and when she failed to return after a long delay, I got more nervous. I could not reach her cell phone. Eventually, she arrived, saying she was caught in traffic caused by a road incident, but it showed that even simple errands now brought anxiety.

Going home was a risk-filled time for Iraqis working for the Coalition. Like Usama, many went by different routes and/or on different schedules, and some used different cars, but there was no way to avoid being seen leaving the Green Zone or other work location, and you could be followed. Numerous Green Zone employees of the embassy and other offices were killed on their return from work, including women. Word of these deadly incidents got around.

One of the most horrifying was the later kidnapping and murder of a Christian husband and wife working as high-level translators for the embassy. Hazim and Emel were accomplished in their careers and had been married almost forty years. They developed an elaborate system of alternate routes to the Green Zone, typically driving part of the way and then taking a taxi. The perpetrators, from Al-Qaeda in Iraq, were so cruel that they first let Emel go, then demanded she personally deliver a ransom to release her husband or he would be killed. When she brought it, they took the money and killed both of them anyway.[9]

Quitting was not an easy decision, however. Green Zone jobs paid very well, partly to compensate for the risk. Jobs with U.S. contractors also paid much better and were otherwise more rewarding than almost any job in the private economy or the low-paying government. Many who feared for their lives had families to support and felt they had no choice.

As security conditions worsened, I got more concerned about our Iraqi staff. Taking a brief survey of several, I found they all lived rather far from the compound. With demand for rental housing in the immediate area presumably minimal, I thought about getting some staff to live within close walking distance. There was a vacant tall building just beyond the gate by the Rimal. In early June I brought my concern to Issam. For coordinators, especially any at known risk, could we consider housing them with us? Should we try to identify available housing close to the compound? He was definite that housing senior Iraqi staff with the expats was out of the question and otherwise seemed disinterested. I felt we could have tried harder. Eventually, Usama and several other staff arranged to live in that vacant building outside the gate. It had no electricity, but the commute was a lot safer.

Waiting to Be Assassinated

While the media focused almost entirely on Baghdad, the violence and displacement also affected many other cities. Those with large populations of both Sunni and Shia were affected most, especially several cities in Diyala and Salahuddin in Central Iraq, in northern Babil Province just south of Baghdad, and Mosul in Ninewa, with its large Kurdish and Christian minorities.[10]

Life deteriorated in Basra and Maysan too. My Basra team faced a threatening environment but continued on as if unaffected. Team members often traveled to Amarah and other cities. U.S. media covered the mass mayhem in Baghdad as if it were the only story and mostly missed the increasing violence in the South, covered better by British media.

The assassination tide was rising in the South when I returned to Iraq in late 2005 and rose faster in 2006. Political parties were now defined by their militias. People outside those parties with moderate, nonviolent outlooks were marginalized, including intellectuals and other educated people. It was dangerous to express any public opinion in such an intimidating environment.[11] In short, the people silenced included those the public most needed to hear. Even from Baghdad, I could see that the impact of RTI's Local Governance Program had been undermined by people with guns.

The crisis was worst in Basra, dominated by Shia militias since the 2005 provincial elections. It was increasingly under siege from anti-Coalition violence, internal political violence, criminal violence, and personal violence. Much of this came from rogue elements of the Mehdi Army who were increasingly beyond Moqtada's control, in Baghdad as well as Basra. In some places, however, the Badr militia was the one most associated with assassinations. Other militias as well as rogue police also murdered many people, as did Iranian agents.

Dashti, son of a retired military officer, had told me about the mysterious string of assassinations of former military pilots in southern Iraq. Three years later U.S. intelligence reports revealed that Iran had circulated a list of 600 Iraqi officers targeted for assassination because of their role in the Iran-Iraq War.[12] The Iranians and their Iraqi friends were still settling scores after all these years.

The Baath Party had eight membership levels. Once Saddam fell, those at the higher levels lost their jobs along with their eligibility for new jobs, elected office, and other positions due to the CPA's de-Baathification order. Although the order did not remove lower-level Baathists, the fall of the regime left all Baathists exposed to the revenge of people who had suffered from the party's rule. The most hated Baathists were often the low-level members, Shia as well as Sunni, whose role as regime informants had often led to executions of their neighbors. In general anti-Baathist violence was not sectarian.

In the first few years after the 2003 invasion, individual Baathists were not frequent targets in southern Iraq, but this changed. According to a later Corporate Confidential report I received, over 1,500 Baathists were killed in southern Iraq in 2006 alone.

Sunnis were a small but important minority in Basra, and not just because some were high-level Baathists. Some became victims of anti-Baathist assassinations, but a much larger number were forced out of Basra by sectarian violence or just left. Many Christians, their job and business opportunities reduced in the new political order and their churches closed, also left.

The constant competition to control the multibillion-dollar oil smuggling business left many rich and many dead. Tribal chiefs caught up in the corrupt competition for resources with political parties or who opposed the emerging Islamist order were among the assassination victims. Anyone who opposed a militia party was a potential target. Others died in turf wars between militias or between militias and tribes.

Amid all the internal violence in the corrupt pursuit of power and profits, the political parties were essentially unable to govern.[13] Indeed, the focal point for the smuggling-related violence was the grand corruption of Governor Al-Waeli, whose Fadhila party in Basra was perceptively described as a "criminal activity" not essentially different from the bands of displaced Marsh Arab tribesmen competing with it.[14]

In the midst of this mayhem my Basra team was working with CSOs to fight corruption in southern Iraq. Anyone working for a Coalition organization was a potential target. One day I learned that a grants officer at ICSP-Basra had just had his life threatened in a note left at his home. I got Issam's approval to transfer him to my Baghdad regional team.

Although the Coalition could not admit it, it was losing control of Basra. The United States had to concentrate on Baghdad, leaving the Brits to cover the South with too few troops. Their keep-the-lid-on approach maintained a tenuous military control but increasingly left militias and thugs in control at street level. Many of the deaths were individual murders, few of which can be stopped by armies, necessarily focused on overall security. The lack of a reliable police department to fill this gap left civilians at greater risk and weakened the British hold on the city and surrounding area.

The Brits' Royal Military Police had made great efforts to develop and train a reliable police force, aided by Denmark, but their failure to control who got hired created a mess. Members of the Mehdi Army and also the Badr militia and Fadhila loyalists infiltrated police departments in Basra and the other southern provinces in large numbers. Many assassinations followed, often by militiamen in their police uniforms. The Basra chief of police, an Allawi appointee independent of the dominant factions, admitted he trusted no more than 25 percent of the officers and that half the force was primarily loyal to militias. Not surprisingly, his brave efforts to attack corruption in police services created heavy militia and political hostility.[15]

In Baghdad, in Basra, and elsewhere in the South, Shia militiamen often enforced religious extremism at the point of a gun. Lacking any formal authority, they imposed their own authority, intimidating and often eliminating the politically and socially inconvenient. It is ironic at the least that behavior obviously criminal in most of the world could be rationalized by religious arguments, but except for the zealots, Muslims did not take these arguments seriously.

It turned out later that Hilla was not safe either. I made an early decision that it was too risky for a Western civilian to go there. Its province, Babil, had major populations of both sects and saw major sectarian violence. I had gone by convoy from Hilla to Baghdad during my Amarah tenure with little fear. Now I couldn't travel that road safely either. An Iraqi employee could blend in with other travelers, but an expat would be a sitting duck at any illegal checkpoint.

By mid-2006 even my Hilla team members felt nervous about driving to Baghdad, which they had always done confidently. Hilla was less than two hours away. My Hilla Anti-Corruption coordinator, Omar, would in later positions receive four threats and gain the dubious distinction of having been threatened by members of both Al-Qaeda in Iraq and the Mehdi Army.

My Kurdish Erbil team did not face the same security threats but was also responsible for Ninewa, which included the huge and dangerous city of Mosul. Because of bad security conditions there, we had fewer projects and CSOs in Ninewa, and it would later get much worse.

In the Baghdad region, despite an excellent team, we felt some loss of momentum. While my Basra and Hilla teams kept progressing, despite increasingly tense conditions, and the Erbil team felt safe, the Baghdad team saw the impact of the violence. Even some of our best CSOs stopped calling, and some CSO leaders left Iraq.

Back in Maysan, election of a Sadrist governor in 2005 had produced a more peaceful political climate. The assassinations continued, however, some committed by death squads from Basra, including cops. Some kidnapped for ransom; others killed people for nothing. I learned of a series of murders of women in Amarah. The street rumor circulated that they were prostitutes, probably unproven but suggesting the killers were Shia extremists.

On the street Badr control of the Maysan police had brought an unsteady power balance, broken by clashes in August 2005. In October 2006, however, two months after the British handed over military control of Maysan to the Iraqi Army and abandoned Camp Abu Naji, Amarah blew up. A roadside bomb assassinated the head of intelligence for the Maysan police. His family kidnapped the teenage brother of the Mehdi Army commander in Amarah, to force the Mehdi Army to hand over the killers. When it didn't, the young hostage was beheaded. Sadrist militiamen then blew up three police stations, killed ten policemen while losing some of their own men, and seized control of the city. The Iraqi Army only belatedly restored order. The police chief, Abu Maythem, was replaced, and an uneasy calm gradually returned. Three chiefs would follow peacefully over the next few years, for brief terms, after which Abu Maythem returned in 2010. By then the power and popularity of the Mehdi Army in Maysan had declined.

While Iraqis working for civilian Coalition projects took personal risks to hold their jobs, those working for the military Coalition took even greater risks. Most of those in civilian jobs worked in one place, often a building that offered some protection. Military interpreters had to accompany troops operating outside the base. One RTI-Amarah staff member was later an interpreter for the Brits in Basra. He found it frightening and feared constantly for his life, while colleagues occasionally lost theirs. Even working within a base was unsafe if assassins found out about you, because you had to go home.

At one point during the war, about 40 percent of contractors' Iraqi staff who got killed were interpreters. Eventually, many U.S. and British interpreters were housed on the military bases for their safety. As for our former Amarah staff member, he could not take the pressure after a while and left, but the Brits later repaid his service, helping him get into Great Britain.

Working as an interpreter for journalists was also unsafe, and there were awful incidents. The kidnapping of *Christian Science Monitor* reporter Jill Carroll on January 7, 2006, made national headlines, as did her release eighty-two days later. But the interpreter she had brought into harm's way, Allan Enwiya, a thirty-two-year-old Christian with a wife and two small kids, had been shot dead at the scene. The kidnappers pointedly spared the driver and killed the interpreter.[16]

By 2006 Western reporters saw it was just too dangerous to travel around Baghdad. Media outlets were forced to rely on Iraqis for on-the-scene stories. I later met one who had worked for the *New York Times*. Hired as an interpreter, he was soon going out with news crews to do on-the-street interviews, always looking over his shoulder. He lived under heavy security at the *Times*' compound, separated from his wife and two small kids, until they left for the United States.

One day at ICSP, I met Saddam's former English-Arabic interpreter, a polite and friendly older gentleman. His risks were apparently over.

Life and Anxiety in the Red Zone

The Comfort of Friends

While working in Amarah, I went several times to Basra, occasionally to places with little or no security. Now, as personal "intelligence sources" in the South updated me on developments, I completely changed my evaluation of Basra. Issam and other Arab expats occasionally went there, but I now considered Basra unsafe. Throughout my ICSP tenure I never traveled there. This was a huge personal disappointment, as I had returned to Iraq in the hope of seeing my Democracy Team again, which seemed unlikely in Amarah but possible in Basra.

However, some Amarah friends came to see me. One day shortly after I arrived, Ahmed Al-Harazi visited the compound on RTI business. A few Democracy Team members living in Baghdad made multiple visits. Another visited his son at the university and took an extra day to drop in on me. Several actually rode all the way from Amarah and back—a four-hour drive or taxi ride each way. One was also Haider's longtime friend and came for a few days to visit him. It was a special occasion to see Jawaad, who came with another former team member.

Memorable was the visit of Hassan on April 10, a holiday. He drove four hours to see me and four hours back. Remember that birthday party the team intended for April 7, 2004, canceled by the Sadrist uprising? Hassan had bought me a nice tan shirt, made in Milan. He held that shirt for two years until he could give it to me for my 2006 birthday, special delivery.

Hunkering Down

From June 9 to July 9, 2006, much of the world was glued to the World Cup tournament in Germany. The world's love affair with the soccer version of football doesn't usually include the United States, but I was living not only with Americans but with serious aficionados from Egypt and Jordan, even though neither had teams in the tournament. Youssria took the initiative to buy satellite coverage. We had it all on wide-screen TV.

We also had some pleasant evenings on the fifth-floor corner patio, for cooking out, socializing, and gazing at the drab Baghdad skyline. The city seemed so peaceful at those times.

One peaceful evening in my office was dramatically interrupted by gunshots going off all around. I had no idea what was happening. After a few minutes I felt spooked about sitting next to my office window with bullets flying about, so I escaped into the hallway. Ten more minutes went by as the shooting went on unabated; then it finally stopped. The next morning I learned it was all in celebration of the Iraq national soccer team's victory over Syria. Neither of those teams was in the World Cup either, but Iraq's team was obviously a unifying symbol.

While I was in Baghdad, I was never threatened directly. A memo I received in early August 2006 did get my attention, however.

Subject: Shitty US democracy
 It happened that I attended a lecture to you talking about your country democracy. You cheated my mind for some time. I forgot that

you built your democracy on the bodies of Red Indians and backs of the Black people. Moreover, your country helped Israel rape the land of Palastine [*sic*]. Do not cheat other people. US is going to vanish, so does Israel.

Let me tell you that Hezbollah, Hamas and Moqtada will put the end to your country arrogance. . . . Bush is going to fall. . . . Another 11 Sept will happen. Very soon.

I had given no lectures and was unsure what the hell the guy was talking about, but this message reminded me I was not universally loved.

As the violence increased, there were signs our security margin had decreased. Later in August I was startled by a memo from Hamish MacIntyre, the Reed security manager, advising us of "an active sniper in the general vicinity of the compound." He asked us to avoid standing on the patios outside our rooms; to close the curtains at night before turning the lights on; not to "dawdle" in the open areas of the compound when going to or from the Rimal or Cedar hotels; and if there was an attack, to stay away from the windows to avoid flying glass. Such a reassuring message.

Emergency procedures for surviving an attack were discussed in an all-staff meeting. A key step would be moving everyone to the basement, for greater safety and easier communications. There we would hear the decision to stay or evacuate. Whoa! So there could be an attack so severe that it might be less dangerous to make a run for it under fire than to stay in the building! To me this scenario was not hypothetical. It recalled the nervous Amarah evacuation back in April 2004, when we actually did make a run for it—and never came back.

The new DCOP later issued an edict that we could no longer organize trips to the Green Zone PX, one of the few pleasures of our cloistered life. Project management decided the risks had increased to a level at which such personal trips were too dangerous. From now on PX trips had to be combined with trips on project business, which was the usual practice but did not help those whose work required no meetings in the Green Zone or allow any enjoyment on Fridays, our only day off. This edict landed with a thud. The feeling of disappointment was followed by the realization that life at ICSP now *was* more dangerous, whatever one thought of the decision.

One day in the late spring of 2006, Haider told me he had to get out of Baghdad and had decided to leave ICSP. He loved the job but now considered Baghdad unsafe. Like the other Iraqi staff, he had to get home after work and back the next morning. Returning to unsafe Amarah was not an option. He decided he had to leave Iraq for a while.

The precipitating event was a summer program in Caux, Switzerland, up on a mountain close to France, organized annually by the Initiatives of Change in Washington. The organization's mission is conflict resolution. As an inheritor of the old Moral Rearmament movement, it emphasizes the personal moral and spiritual dimensions of peaceful change in world affairs. Peace begins with you. Haider and I had talked about the program, and he applied and was accepted, but I advised him they needed students who could pay and Caux would cost more than he could afford. I suggested he ask them about scholarships for poorer students, believing a participant from Iraq would be appealing to them. After a while they found a benefactor among their members who paid for his scholarship.

The Caux program lasts a month. Under one of Wael's unwritten rules, you couldn't get that much unpaid leave. Wael's policy was that you resign, then if you want to come back, you reapply. You might get rehired—and Jean-Sebastien would have waited for Haider—but there was no guarantee. Both Jean-Sebastien and Issam believed he was coming back.

Unknown to them, the situation was more complicated. Haider's interest in Caux was inspired by a similar program in Cyprus a summer earlier. He had recently communicated his personal safety concerns to the director of the Cyprus program, who told Haider that once the Switzerland program ended, he would get him into the United States through his government connections.

I was immediately skeptical. It was hard to get into the United States. Many Iraqis had tried and failed. I knew of no reason why this individual, primarily a journalist, could beat the system when others could not. I told Haider not to be optimistic. Haider decided to trust the assurances. He accepted the Caux scholarship and resigned.

After his last day of work, on Thursday June 15, we went out one more time to the Rimal for a happy farewell dinner. There were many things to talk about and too little time, but he was engaging, as usual, and feeling positive about the next step in his life. He would go back to Amarah for four or five days to collect what he needed and say good-bye to his family, then stop in Beirut to spend a little time with his Lebanese girlfriend, then fly to Switzerland. The rest of the plan was unclear even to him.

Around 9:30 p.m. he had to leave, as it was getting late to be out in Baghdad. We walked toward the doorway in the main gate, from which he could take a taxi home. The realization then suddenly hit me that I had no idea when or where I would see him again. As we got to the gate, I reached out and gave him a little hug and said, "You will always be my little brother, and I will care about what happens to you no matter where you go." A bit startled, he smiled, thanked me, and walked through the gate.

12

The Day the Music Died

The Worst Day of My Life

Sunday June 25, 2006. Around 9:00 a.m. I walked downstairs to my office. Turning the corner from the stairway, I noticed Usama talking quietly to Salah from the Civic Education team but thought nothing of it. A few minutes later, however, Usama came into my office looking somber. "I have bad news for you, and I don't know how to start. Haider Al-Maliki was killed yesterday in Maysan."

I experienced a terrible sinking feeling. The horror overwhelmed me. I sat motionless, just staring at Usama, unable to speak a word. After many seconds passed, he said, "Sorry I was the one to carry this bad news to you." Not knowing what else to say—as there was nothing else to say—he turned and walked slowly out of my office.

The rest of the day is a blur in my memory. I told my staff what happened and talked to Issam. I retreated to my room to be alone with my thoughts. I was too traumatized to cry. After a while I wandered back to my office, but it was hard to think about work. I started receiving condolence visits from both expat and Iraqi staff who knew Haider was my close friend.

Back in Amarah the family was devastated. His mother, the family member who most strongly supported his democracy work and political outlook, was distraught. In a family with six smart children, Haider was the acknowledged star. They had killed the golden child.

The news reached me quickly because a former Civic Education staff member from Amarah had called Salah that morning to tell him. Jawaad had actually called me from Amarah within an hour of the murder, but I had lost my cell phone at the USAID conference in Amman, and he couldn't reach me. He sent a dramatic email message the next day. "Subject: We have lost Haider Abdul Hussein; Tami's brother has been assassinated????!!!!" Around 7:25 p.m. on Saturday, Jawaad was walking to the market area with friends and reached a traffic light by Al-Zahrawi Hospital. Another friend came up and told him Haider had been killed there at 7:00 p.m. In disbelief he called one of Haider's friends, a former Democracy Team member, and confirmed the worst.

The burial ground in Najaf is a long drive from Amarah, and even leaving home to drive there was a risk. There are no undertakers to help families with arrangements, only cemetery employees. The body has to be washed, then placed in a shroud, difficult enough when death is from normal causes but excruciating when the body is full of bullet holes and badly damaged. Ta'meem decided to be brave and help prepare the body, which meant seeing it as it was. When Jawaad went to the home a few days later during the funeral period, he was politely turned away because Ta'meem was still crying uncontrollably.

Haider's death left me with many self-imposed obligations. Some people needed to know, and would not unless I told them. Initiatives of Change was expecting Haider to arrive shortly in Switzerland. I twice called their DC number and twice got their recording. Feeling frustrated the second time at being trapped by the damn outgoing message for something so important, I announced Haider's death in a voice mail message. To an organization so devoted to peace and reconciliation, the assassination of one of their Caux Scholars was particularly cruel news.

Jean-Sebastien, by now Haider's good friend and one of his biggest fans, had just left the project. The news left him devastated. He said he had learned a lot about Iraq from his conversations with Haider, the Iraqi patriot, whose dedication to Iraq had made a big impression. In tribute he observed that "he suffered because of the great pains that Iraq and Iraqi people are going through now. He wanted this suffering to stop. He believed in the future of Iraq and her people."

Craig had left ICSP just a few weeks earlier. He was horrified. It turned out he also had lost friends in Iraq and felt the same devastation. It took time to learn how to "process the pain." His empathy meant a lot. I was not good at processing pain. Yet I never thought about giving up on Iraq and going home. The struggle was too important, and it was Haider's struggle too.

I also sent messages to Molly Phee, by now at the State Department's UN mission in New York, and to Rory Stewart. Molly then informed others who knew Haider from the CPA days. It was a painful message, as he was greatly liked and admired by Brits and Americans who had worked with him. Everyone saw his enormous talent, making his death a major tragedy as well as a personal loss.

The immediate concern was the safety of Haider's sister Ta'meem and the family. Molly called two leaders in Amarah with whom she had been friendly to ask their help on the ground. She sent messages to Britain's Department for International Development (DFID) in Basra, the British military commander in Maysan, and the U.S. Embassy.

Rory had known Haider well. He put the tragedy in political perspective:

> This is the most terrible news, a great loss not only to Haider's friends but to Amara. In a province dominated by all the contorted complexity of new politicians, old grievances, cracking social structures and reactionary ideologies, Haider, who was literate, polite, patient, tolerant of mistakes, trusting, optimistic, represented a compassionate, gentler faith in a more humane and settled Iraq. Haider talked about the dangers of his work. . . . But he continued to engage. . . . He did so with enthusiasm, not cynicism, not pompously but very seriously because he recognized he had a duty to remain and engage. He trusted the good intentions of the Coalition. . . . He believed genuinely in human rights. For that idealism, energy, intelligence and courage he has been killed. I liked him as a friend, admired him as an activist and we will all mourn him. Many people in Iraq are called martyrs, but Haider, without seeking it, actually was one.

Rory's book about his time in Maysan, *The Prince of the Marshes*, published when Haider was still alive, told some of his story, though using another name to avoid identifying him directly, which now seemed sadly ironic. It was unusual for a student from Amarah to be accepted at prestigious Baghdad University. Haider was a good student and even won the university's chess championship. Rory's most compelling observation was that Haider, at his young age, was an ideal partner for those trying to help Iraq because of his progressive, democratic outlook. Unfortunately, he was untypical of Maysan's main political actors—too young to have a leadership role and not supported by any militia.

Especially poignant was my correspondence with Charlotte Morris, a young but valued member of the British military's Civil Affairs team in Maysan. Charlie circled back to Basra after her military tour, then returned to London. She came up often in my conversations with Haider, as she was one of his favorite people and one of his admirers. She said, "Haider was one of my closest Iraqi friends, and we all admired his bravery, commitment and dedication. He was always so positive that things would get better and despite knowing the risks kept searching for ways to make a difference."

One other person needed to know, but I couldn't help. That was Haider's girlfriend in Beirut, whom he had intended to see on his way to Switzerland. Right after he died, Miami shared some photos he had given her of him and this young woman, but none had her name or address. I will never know whether she knew he was coming, or found out what happened to him, or was left wondering in disappointment why he never returned.

Molly and I immediately saw the risk to Ta'meem and her brother Ali, Haider's only brother, as they had also worked for the RTI project. We had to get them out of Amarah. In the immediate aftermath of Haider's murder, they were mocked and threatened by Sadrist neighbors, who declared themselves happy about what happened to him. The street rumor reaching the family through another Sadrist neighbor said Haider had returned to Amarah from London with a lot of money, creating the lie that he was a British collaborator. For Ta'meem, who lived indoors for months during her threat period, grief combined with another period of fear and isolation.

Molly immediately started working on this within the State Department. However, it was hard to get anyone out of Iraq at this time, even if you worked for State. There was a furious round of correspondence among numerous Haider friends in the States and in Britain in pursuit of a solution. It was amazing how many Western friends Haider had. This was the start of a dogged long-term struggle that consumed much of my evening time and extended well past my tenure in Baghdad. I pursued it with no reluctance, however. Getting his brother and sister out of Iraq was something I owed to Haider.

Inevitably, there were various and conflicting versions of what happened that day and various theories and speculations about who committed the crime. The explanation closest to fact is probably this. Haider left his house for the market, intending to update the software on his satellite receiver. He took a taxi from the main street crossing his neighborhood. Given the short time between then and the fatal shooting, he was probably watched by the killers once he left home and then followed, which suggests they were waiting for him to leave his house. The taxi stopped for a red light by the Al-Zahrawi Hospital. Four armed masked men wearing black got out of a Japanese-made car. They shot Haider many times through the body, and one bullet injured the driver. It was assassination by death squad. The car was described as a late-model white car similar to a "death car" associated with other assassinations.

The usual suspects in southern Iraq assassinations were the Sadr militia, the Badr militia, and Iranian agents. Haider was critical of all of them but was careful not to be publicly outspoken. Several factors point to Sadrists as the assassins. Haider's family lived in an increasingly Sadrist neighborhood. The earlier threat against Ta'meem (also mentioning Haider and Ali) almost certainly came from Sadrists in the neighborhood. It's a logical assumption that only someone in the neighborhood would know Haider was in Amarah. The quick reaction when he left home indicates that one or more spies was nearby who could identify him, and the four gunmen must have been in the immediate area to move so quickly. The street rumor linking him to the British came from Sadrist sources. The assassins' use of masks suggests they were from Amarah or a nearby area (perhaps Majar Al-Kebir), so potentially recognizable in Amarah.

Analysis of other assassinations occurring at that time also suggests this was likely a Sadrist hit. Badr and Iranian intelligence were more likely to target ex-Baathists and sometimes Sunnis. Moreover, the Supreme Council for the Islamic Revolution in Iraq, of which Badr was the military arm, had been cooperative with the Coalition in Maysan and on good behavior. Maysan's violence had come mainly from the Mehdi Army and smaller Sadrist elements.

The similarity of the death car story to assassinations in Basra was suspicious, but there were many such reports, and the cars were not consistently described. There was allegedly a death squad whose members had been arrested three times but then released by Governor Al-Waeli of Basra. After the third time, so the story goes, they moved their operation to Maysan. The story is plausible, but there is no proven connection to Haider's case. Notwithstanding all this logical analysis, I know that criminal investigations are subject to surprises and that probabilities don't always become facts.

Haider was a well-known democracy activist in Maysan, known to have worked for foreign NGOs and to have cooperated with the CPA. He was doing a lot of public service, had known political opinions, and was fairly well-known in Amarah. The shift of political and military control to the Sadrists and the fact that Haider's worldview ran counter to the extremists increased his risk, though the same was true of people not targeted. Still, this does not explain why they killed him at that time, when he was not even living in Amarah. His sad end validated the fears he had expressed to me about the risks of staying in Amarah, which we thought were solved by his moving to Baghdad. Obviously, returning to Amarah even for a short visit was a fatal decision, but he had visited home earlier without incident. Some questions will never be answered.

Jawaad was concerned about others who had worked for RTI or other foreign organizations. He called numerous people to tell them to be careful and stay home. His concerns were underlined by an explosion set off at the front gate of the home of a former Democracy Team member, a close Haider friend, injuring his sister. In fact, Haider's assassination was one of several within a few days, including even that of a tribal sheikh. You can imagine my contempt for a clueless article appearing shortly afterward in the *New York Times*, cheerfully explaining how violence had been reduced recently in Amarah.

Haider's death had a huge impact at ICSP. Issam issued a heartfelt announcement to the staff, saying Haider was "brilliant," "elegant," a "hard worker," and "enthusiastic" and that "he loved his people and loved his country a lot." Issam initiated a collection for the family that was well supported. His message and a montage of Haider photos were posted on the second-floor bulletin board. One young woman wrote an emotional note that said, "You will be in my heart forever." I noticed, however, that some were trying to hold it all in. Not all succeeded. In the wake of tragedies some people cry openly, while others cry inside.

Issam invited the family to ICSP to receive the gift. Ali and a cousin drove to ICSP to visit and receive the money, and an informal meeting was arranged with all the staff. It was an emotional event. I had met Ali before but hardly recognized him with the enormous pain ravaging his face. I could only hug him and say how sorry I was. Miami, a Haider friend who had been holding her emotions in, cried from beginning to end.

Haider's office partner, Isra'a Ali, tearfully confided to me some days later that she was struggling emotionally to deal with his death. They were about the same age, had gotten along really well, and she loved working with him. Now she came in each morning to see his empty chair. It was hard to accept that he wasn't there anymore.

Zainab Salman, a friend of Ta'meem from their days in the British Women's Commission program, became a close friend of Haider. They had shared some deep personal conversations. She could not control her tears. This was the second such disaster in her life, making it especially traumatizing. She would suffer a third one soon after, along with a serious threat against her own life, and finally fled Iraq in despair.

Aside from my grief, I was also angry. I was unwilling to just let this be another of the thousands of unsolved murder cases. Molly reacted the same way and called the "appropriate authority" in Maysan. She was promised that the case would be investigated. I learned that at least one witness was interviewed.

My own unproven assets were three Maysan lawyers identified through the database of my Conference of CSO Lawyers. Remembering the lawyers' promises to represent CSO clients even in tense situations, I tried through Usama to have these three do that. After all, Haider was a CSO cofounder. I sent a detailed request, asking them to talk to Haider's family, the Iraqi Society for Change, the chief of police, and the governor, urging a complete investigation leading to arrests and prosecution. Indeed, the family was angry because they had heard that one or more policemen was close to the scene and did nothing. I told the family to expect a visit from the lawyers. Beyond a nonverified claim from one that they had talked to the chief, however, the response was no action and several unanswered phone messages. This added to my frustration. People perhaps talk more bravely when the risk is hypothetical.

If anything came of this "investigation," I am not aware of it. In the wake of the Haider assassination, I heard that Kifaya's killers had been caught and were about to go on trial, apparently a false rumor. In 2009 it was reported that a man in Basra was executed for participating in *1,300 murders*. Identifying all those victims could help close a lot of cases.

Haider's death highlighted one of the bitter lessons I learned in Iraq. Contrary to conventional wisdom, no matter how bad things are, they can always get worse.

As I adjusted mentally to losing Haider, I thought a lot about why I felt so devastated. One reason was the loss of his incredible talent and promise. Another was that he died because he cared about his country and made himself part of the struggle to change it. His death also symbolized much of what was wrong in Iraq. I had supported him whenever possible, believing he was potentially a future leader of Iraq. Sadly, his story is not unusual. There have been many young people with great promise for the future who became martyrs instead.

All that could not fully explain, however, the personal devastation I was feeling. Haider and I became well acquainted in Amarah but, except for the public service announcements, had not worked together. After he came to Baghdad, I was his mentor in some things and his biggest career supporter, but he also brought some happiness to my demanding but often boring life in the compound. He had become much more important to me than I realized. In sorting through my feelings, I realized in tragic retrospect how much I had loved him as a friend.

The personal effect of Haider's death was profound. When they killed my little brother, part of me died too. I would not be the same again. June 25, 2006, was the day the music died.

Grief and Inspiration on a Distant Mountain

It was merely coincidental that I had previously scheduled a brief vacation in southern Switzerland, accepting the invitation of Denny Lane, my former Amarah team leader. His family home was in Morcote, a charming Italian town overlooking beautiful Lake Lugano. Haider's visit to Caux, on the eastern, French side of Switzerland, would have overlapped with my vacation. I certainly needed the vacation. On

Friday, July 14, I arrived in Milan via Istanbul and rode with Denny to the fabulous family home on a Swiss hillside. His father, a famed World War II British spy, had retired to Switzerland with his American heiress wife and become a renowned gardener. Morcote was the most picturesque vacation spot I had ever visited.

My first priority, however, was keeping my promise to Initiatives of Change to send photos and info about Haider, to be shared with the other Caux Scholars. With so much to do, this became a last-minute project, aided by Dan Killian's photo collage, with quotes from me and Jean-Sebastien and that emotional tribute from the young woman at ICSP. I also had a touching photo sent by Charlie Morris from London, showing Haider at his most handsome, sitting with some children. Looking at it while realizing this beautiful young man was dead made people cry.

On July 15 I took the boat tour of Lake Lugano. As the small craft glided from dock to dock around the lake, amid the mountains and picturesque villages, I was awed by the idyllic scenery. Then I suddenly remembered that this was the day Haider was to arrive in Caux and see some of Switzerland's wonders for himself. The contrast between my joyful experience and that sad irony filled me with emotion.

That night I sent Kathy Aquilina, the conference director, that fabulous Charlie Morris photo and Dan Killian's photo montage. They were compiling a binder of information to share with the other participants. They laminated Charlie's photo for the cover and inserted Haider's impressive application for the Caux program, along with Jean-Sebastien's tribute, which I had sent earlier. They were planning a memorial ceremony.

Kathy had invited me to come to Caux and somehow represent Haider, but my R&R time was only one week, and I had a critical meeting in Baghdad the next weekend for the Enabling Law project, part of Haider's legacy. My immediate concern was to write a "Mournful Tribute" for the event binder, describing Haider's achievements and personal qualities—the words to go with the photos. I emailed it to Kathy, thinking I had met my self-imposed obligation.

That done, however, I thought harder about how much it might mean to Initiatives of Change if I could somehow get there. Denny's sister showed me the official Swiss train schedule. I had one chance.

If I left early the next morning, stayed in Caux only for that day and overnight, and returned directly to Milan instead of going back through Lugano, I could get to the airport on time. This assumed the trains all ran on time, a naive assumption in many places, but this was the homeland of legendary Swiss efficiency.

And so it was that in the early hours of Monday, July 17, I left on a train through the Swiss Alps and the Central Valley, one of the most memorable travel experiences of my life. It was like Lake Lugano all over again, however. It was breathtaking, but I was not the one who was supposed to be there. Exhilaration and sadness are an uneasy mix.

The train rolled past one awesome vista after another, often crossing mountain gorges on elevated tracks wide enough only for the train and stirring my moderate fear of heights as I looked down at terrain a long vertical distance away. Arriving after several hours at Montreux, on the east end of Lake Geneva, I changed to a short mountain train going up to Caux, which seemed to move almost vertically. I arrived around lunchtime to a warm greeting and a fifth-floor room with a view at Mountain House, overlooking the mountains and lake in one of the most beautiful places on Earth.

July 17, 2006. It was Monday of week 1 at Caux; everything was in full swing. I was startled to learn the memorial ceremony would be at 10:30 p.m., after all other activities ended. My impression was that this would be a brief, informal ceremony. There was time to take a walk with Kathy along tree-lined paths around the property, chat with several of the scholars in a group, including Arabs and American Jews, and enjoy dinner.

The twenty Caux Scholars were only one part of a larger group of mostly middle-aged and older adults attending different programs. Everyone was invited to the ceremony, but with the program at the end of a long day and evening, I adjusted mentally to the expectation that only some of the Caux Scholars and a few others would be there.

Then I met the two young interns who had taken responsibility for organizing the program—a Muslim man from India and a Christian woman from Malta. I quickly realized that to them this was an important and meaningful event. They had assembled their binder of photos and documents with the laminated Haider photo on the front. Everyone had been told about Haider and encouraged to see the book before the event. It had a big emotional impact I had under-estimated. Haider's memorial ceremony turned out to be one of the most inspiring experiences of my life.

The two organizers placed the binder with the photos and docu-ments, an enlarged photo of Haider, and a lighted candle on a table at the front of the room.

Sixty people came, from a wide range of countries.

The Muslim intern, Altaf Mohammed Abed, asked the partici-pants to remove their shoes and sit on the floor, in the Indian tradi-tion, leaving a few chairs in front for older people, like me.

Everyone felt so sad, and many cried during the ceremony, even though they had never met Haider. I felt overwhelmed by all the emo-tion in the room, especially from young people. They related to Haider as if they knew him; he was one of them even though he was missing.

After Kathy introduced the program, Altaf offered a brief eulogy. He compared Haider's death to watching the tide go out while know-ing it also comes back in, sometimes higher than when it left. Haider could be even more important in death than he was in life. A young woman from Palestine read three verses from the Koran, in Arabic and English, through her tears.

I spoke to the group about Haider's great talents and promise and what a beautiful person he was to so many—and the incredible per-sonal loss and sadness from losing him. I told them not to be dis-couraged but to feel his inspiration, as they are young and have time to experience and influence a better world. An Initiatives of Change member to whom I had related the story of my last moments with Haider encouraged me to tell that story, and so I did.

Six young women each read a portion of Haider's long applica-tion letter to Caux, written in perfect English entirely by him. Sev-eral people spoke in different ways to express the sadness of his loss and to praise his accomplishments in a short life.

One man, perhaps a minister, read a perfect prayer that I later learned was the Prayer of Saint Francis. "Lord make me an instru-ment of thy peace. Where there is hatred . . . let me sow love. Where there is injury . . . pardon. Where there is doubt . . . faith. Where there is despair . . . hope. Where there is darkness . . . light. Where there is sadness . . . joy. O, divine Master, grant that I may not so much seek to be consoled . . . as to console; to be understood . . . as to understand; to be loved . . . as to love. For it is in giving that we receive, it is in pardoning that we are pardoned, it is in dying . . . that we are born to eternal life." After many centuries this is still an indelible message about public service.

The ceremony went on for over an hour, remaining emotional to the end—and not one person left early.

Several people spoke to me afterward about Haider and how touched they were by his life and how appreciative they were that I had come on his behalf. Many signed a book to express their condolences. I felt so grateful to everyone, for Haider and myself. I realized that it should have been unthinkable not to come to Caux.

Returning to my room on the top floor, I walked out on the balcony, still feeling the emotions of the moment. I found myself talking to Haider as if he were listening. "I wish you were here in this place instead of me. This is *your* place and *your* mountain, and this was *your* day. You would love these people. I wish you could have seen what these loving strangers have just done in your memory."

I will never forget this ceremony. The people in Caux had somehow discovered what many in Iraq and other countries discovered before them. There was much to love and admire about Haider Al-Maliki.

I wrote a detailed account of the ceremony and sent it to Ta'meem to read to the family. I confided to her that "even writing this story has brought me to tears." It brought Haider's family to tears also. What affected them most was the great irony that Haider, who died brutally and without recognition in his own country, had been embraced and honored by people in a distant country who did not even know him.

I was still feeling the inspiration as my train arrived the next day at the enormous Central Station in Milan, on my way back to Iraq.

Back in Baghdad, I resumed the difficult, time-consuming mission of getting Haider's endangered sister and brother out of Amarah. Getting them into the United States became a long-term, nerve-racking project. Several of Haider's friends joined the effort, and Molly Phee's initiative within the State Department eventually paid off, after a long delay. Getting them safely from their house to the Basra airport caused me great anxiety, and then they were stuck in Jordan for months. It was October 2007 before Ta'meem and Ali finally arrived in the United States. Five years later I was a happy witness to their swearing-in as American citizens.

Early in 2007 I attended a general meeting of Initiatives of Change in northern Virginia. Among some of the nicest people I ever met was Marvin Pace, the surprisingly young man who offered to donate the money for Haider's Caux scholarship.

Ever since Haider died, few days have passed when I do not think of him. The overall effect is schizophrenic in a way that others touched by tragedy will recognize. There is the enormous grief that becomes more manageable over time but never goes away and occasionally reaches back to seize one's emotions. There is also the enormous inspiration from his life, which somehow demands to live on and extend his impact. The sadness will never go away, but Haider Al-Maliki will be an inspiration for as long as I live.

AN OLD MAN'S LAMENT

Some of life's lessons are learned too late. I wish I were young enough to have a little boy and call him Haider and raise him to be like the Haider I knew and to live from his inspiration; a boy who would grow up to be great in the pursuit of the world's knowledge and learn fluent Arabic as the inspirational Haider learned fluent English; a young man dedicated to public service and peace and perhaps to the people of Iraq; one who would inspire others to follow his example and his leadership; and who would live joyously with freedom to control his own life and to make his own decisions on great questions.

If you can feel this inspiration and are blessed to have a talented child, whether Muslim or Christian, you can pursue this dream in my place.

13

Sinking Your Own Ship

The Fragility of Progress

Under New Management

Everything considered, our progress so far had been remarkable. Unfortunately, I was about to learn a bitter lesson about progress. Success on international development projects depends on how well they are managed by USAID and its contractors' corporate management, but at ground level it depends especially on people in project leadership roles. Much of ICSP had revolved around Craig Davis and Jean-Sebastien Roy, now gone, and I felt increasingly concerned. Subsequent events would show my concern to be well founded.

After Craig left, in June 2006, we worked without a deputy chief of party (DCOP) for many weeks. The new appointee made a dazzling first impression and brought a lot of energy, creating an early feeling of optimism. Expat staff meetings were held to discuss "the way forward." It was soon clear, however, that the input was not part of a democratic management process. The new top-down leadership style caused increasing unease. Program managers could no longer make their own decisions. It became difficult even to get timely decisions on things we had previously decided ourselves. It became clearer, too, that Issam, who proposed this appointment, had been sidelined by his new deputy. She stated repeatedly, moreover, that her decisions would not defer even to corporate management in the United States.

One aspect of the new leadership style especially bothered me. The new leader was one of those who believe the history of the organization starts with them. They have no interest in anything, or anyone, that came before. They start with a negative view of the organization, as a failure to be saved by their personal leadership. I could have done my own critique of ICSP, but it had accomplished a lot. I later learned the project was in no known trouble with USAID at the time, had received consistently favorable USAID evaluations, and so did not need to be "saved."

The frustrating implication of such egocentric management is that nothing you have accomplished matters. The future has just restarted. The success of my work for ICSP had always been acknowledged, but that was now irrelevant. Although I quickly diagnosed the syndrome, it was nothing I had experienced before, nor could I do anything about it. Some of my most important initiatives were soon to be undermined or lost. On June 30, 2006, ADF had extended my contract to the end of the project. On September 30 I sadly emailed my daughter that I was thinking about leaving but would try to endure for the rest of the year.

The Cross-Cutting Road to Nowhere

The new anti-corruption money from State's Bureau of International Narcotics and Law Enforcement (INL) added to my workload, which led the DCOP to relieve me of my other responsibility: Human Rights (HR). This decision involved no criticism of me but did reflect a determination that INL had to succeed in order to justify a project extension when the current contract period expired on June 30. My instructions were to put full-time attention on Anti-Corruption, but especially INL. As INL's money was separate, its project might continue even if USAID funding ended, whereas new accomplishments in HR and other sectors might not help ADF in the end.

The only alternative for HR, in theory, was to combine it with Women's Advocacy, a logical combination I had often contemplated. Alas, the incoming Women's Rights manager, Corey Levine from Canada, told me bluntly that she did not have time to manage Human Rights too. My only remaining fallback idea was to set Usama up to manage it and support him with advice when needed. However, the DCOP diverted him to a temporary but months-long assignment in her office. With no other HR staff at headquarters and having been ordered not to keep working on it, headquarters management of HR was suspended indefinitely.

Before going home for vacation in September, I provided a requested transition plan for managing Human Rights. I summarized my initiatives to build up the program, outlined current priorities, and explained that an HR sector separate from AC would need additional headquarters staffing. All of that was ignored. While I was gone, much of what I had built up was abandoned as if it had not existed, as were our new HR program priorities, including the antiviolence program. The expansion of HR staffing to two per region, which I had arranged with difficulty and Issam's help, was reversed.

The four HR regional coordinators continued to help CSOs. ADF continued to report its HR "progress" to USAID but finessed the unacknowledged downgrading of the program by changing its monthly report heading to "Cross-Cutting Human Rights Support." We were back to pretending.

None of these changes were ever explained to me. Apparently, because I wasn't in charge of Human Rights anymore, I didn't need to know. It would be several months before Usama was released from the DCOP office to help Corey manage what was left of Human Rights.

I considered the national CSO lawyers network an HR project, and the organization was unlikely to move forward without me. I proposed moving it to Anti-Corruption so I could keep it going. The "bottom-line" answer was that project continuation depended on INL and was too important to be spending time on anything else. This decision effectively killed one of my best and most important initiatives in Iraq.

Also blocked were my efforts to extend the Al-Noor Universal Foundation's contract to manage the National Anti-Corruption Legislative Coalition. Al-Noor kept working on it, spending its own money, and made a long-term commitment to anti-corruption and the AC Coalition, but the enormous momentum we had built up was lost. That story was not over, however.

As for the great idea to convert the Ministry of Human Rights to an independent commission based on the Paris Principles, it was an early victim of Iraq's absurdly bloated system of ministries. The political priority was to distribute as many portfolios as possible so as to placate the parties in the government coalition. An independent commission would mean one less minister. Applying international best practices was a lower priority. But that story was not over either.

The ADF-IREX partnership on the Independent Media sector had worked well, but in late 2006 it encountered an internal crisis that seemed to be neither organization's fault. Like Anti-Corruption, the project was getting new money but from the State Department's Bureau of Democracy, Human Rights, and Labor, not USAID. The two organizations, though both part of State, could not agree on what type of procurement should apply (contract, grant, or cooperative agreement). ADF worked under a contract. State would not accept that. This left the new project money with IREX and outside ADF's contract. Matthias Wirzberger and the two Iraqi media professionals left, taking the major components of the Independent Media project with them.

On October 11 Issam issued a cheerful memo putting a positive spin on this really negative development while failing to explain the decision or its real impact. He didn't even mention AID or State. It was a "mutual agreement" between ICSP and IREX and "in the best interests of both organizations." He said ICSP would implement the project that had been implemented by IREX. It seemed to everyone else that most of the headquarters-level project had just gone out the door with the IREX team.

Two efforts to hire a new media director failed. The regional Independent Media teams had to continue on their own, holding training workshops and forums and giving technical assistance to media outlets and college journalism programs.

Last Desperate Measures

As 2006 neared its end, along with my time in Baghdad, I felt renewed enthusiasm about the Anti-Corruption program, including the INL portion we officially launched in October. I lacked enthusiasm for leaving it to expats having no prior commitment to it, but I had confidence my staff could make at least some of it work. My last two months were a scramble to outline the thirteen INL tasks for them and launch the training program on which much of the INL plan depended.

To cover the planned 160 or more government workshops, we needed a corps of CSO-based trainers who could apply our new, more professional materials. That required a Training of Trainers program, called TOT in the training biz. Forced to become an instant training manager despite my inexperience, I managed to write a surprisingly good training outline.

In October, Youssria left. Another Egyptian, Hani Riad, moving over from RTI, added good ideas for my plan. It included three full days on a generic TOT workshop, then two on the new Anti-Corruption training modules—truly minimal. The arithmetic was 2 workshops per region times 20 trainees per session—a total of 160. I accelerated the schedule to finish by mid-January.

TOT training was generic, entrusted mostly to two senior trainers in the Baghdad Center recommended by Youssria; they eventually covered trainees in three of the four regions. To cover the new AC modules, however, I had to devise that training myself. I added our new workshop requirements, including corrective actions, even creating a handout "Corrective Actions Checklist."

The critical first Baghdad session, held November 11–15, went well. The first sessions in Hilla, Basra, and Erbil quickly followed. For reasons unexplained, Erbil's unpredictable expat regional manager, having approved the event, suddenly demanded after two days that the training be stopped. My AC coordinator there stood up to him and refused.

In the end my training program would upgrade the knowledge and skills of a lot of CSO trainers. The number of government workshops would rise sharply after I left. That training also served longer-term sustainability by developing a corps of trained and experienced instructors in many parts of Iraq whose impact could extend beyond ICSP.

On October 31 AID had issued me an authorization to use the Military Air Service to travel within Iraq. I could take a military helicopter to and from Hilla, to which it was now unsafe to drive. I had no plan to use it before I left, but it was yet another sign of the deteriorating security.

On November 21–22 the second ICSP/USAID Civil Society Conference was held, again in Amman, with 109 participants. This one had more high-level Iraqi officials. Coordination among USAID, Iraqi government, CSOs, and international organizations was again the theme, though the previous conference had not generated the coordination it could have, nor would this one.

The minister of state for civil society made a surprisingly concil-
iatory speech, however, declaring in an apparent about-face that his
ministry was now receptive to a CSO enabling law based on international standards. I took that as a personal victory.

Baghdad Exits

Farewell to Baghdad—and Saddam

Time had not moved as slowly in Baghdad as in Amarah. So much
had happened, however, that my fourteen months there seemed
much longer. Before leaving, I sent a farewell message of thanks
to all my staff members. As I did for my Amarah team, I shared my
contact info and offered help on their next CV and a place to stay
if they visited the Washington area. That last offer has since been
accepted often.

With all the time spent on the training project and other last-minute
tasks, like packing my bags, I failed to notice that Saddam's "departure" was also imminent. His execution had to be carried out within
thirty days of the appeals court rejection of his appeal. The thirty
days were almost up.

On December 30, 2006, I rose at a much-too-early hour to leave
for the airport. Kristin Joplin, leaving on R&R, was on the same ride.
As I got into the vehicle at 6:30 a.m., she casually asked, "Did you
hear they just executed Saddam about twenty-five minutes ago?" To
which my reaction was, "Oh no!" What awful timing for a trip to the
airport! Fortunately, it was the first day of the Eid Al-Adha holiday,
so the streets were quiet, and no one showed up to exact revenge.

The execution site was kept secret for obvious reasons. The day
before, one of the appeals court judges who upheld Saddam's sentence told NBC News, seemingly off the record, that it would be the
Baghdad International Airport. Saddam had been held at a U.S. base
next to the airport, making that location plausible, but NBC suspected
this was disinformation. Other rumored locations were the smaller
Al-Muthanna Airport and the Green Zone. Amid the speculation,
Prime Minister Al-Maliki and U.S. officials met to plan the final details.
The actual site turned out to be an old military intelligence facility in
the Kadhimiya District, where many of Saddam's victims had been
hanged—an appropriately ironic location. The United States helicop-

tered Saddam to the site and turned him over to the Iraqis. Al-Maliki signed the execution order and left the room.

The government announced that Saddam was executed just after 6:00 a.m. It failed to control the execution properly, causing international criticism, even from the White House, about the undignified, disrespectful way it was carried out. Witnesses and guards taunted Saddam, and one witness, an Al-Maliki staff member, recorded the moment of execution on her cell phone, then transmitted it, magnifying the issue. By one account Saddam was the only Sunni at a Shia-managed execution. The government thus turned a national unity opportunity into a sectarian event.[1]

As our convoy headed for the airport, a remarkable post-execution story was unfolding. *The following is inside information from an eyewitness and never before published.*

After Saddam was hanged, he was placed in a white shroud (similar to a body bag). He was put on a wheeled stretcher, placed in an ambulance, and driven to the prime minister's compound in the Green Zone, a considerable distance away. He was then taken out of the ambulance and wheeled into the compound. About twenty or thirty Shia from Al-Maliki's inner circle were gathered there, along with a larger number of staff members. Although it was still early morning, there was a strange energy in the air.

There commenced a kind of morbid celebration. The shroud was opened to reveal Saddam's head. People started circling the body, dancing and chanting in a spontaneous demonstration. These were Shia chants, shouted without joy or laughter. Some of the words were mocking in tone, hard to translate but roughly meaning, "Look at us now, and look at him now." The group seemed more excited than happy. This odd ritual apparently went on for some time. Saddam was then put back in the ambulance.

Most Muslims would have found such behavior shocking. Even Saddam, after all, deserved the normal respect traditionally accorded the deceased. This ritual was hatred extended beyond death. Had it been reported then, it would have added to all the criticism of the execution. This impromptu event was less about sectarian loyalty, however, than about a moment of quiet revenge for all the horrors Saddam inflicted on countless Shia families, probably including those of most of the people chanting. It was a symbolic moment in time when they could feel that the Shia had finally won their long struggle against Saddam.

I was unaware of this drama until much later. I was en route home from the second stage of my adventure in Iraq. Saddam's execution, one of the most important events in Iraq's history, produced a remarkable personal coincidence. I arrived in Amarah three days before Saddam was captured. I left Baghdad on the day he was executed. A lot had happened in that time, and the man crossing the Atlantic back to America was not quite the same person who first left for Iraq in 2003.

Back in Iraq a Shia joke making the rounds reflected Saddam's evil reputation. Its premise was that hell has many levels. Saddam was sent to level 12. Unsure of the directions, he managed to find level 1, then asked someone how to reach level 12. The man exclaimed in surprise to learn there were so many levels and could only direct him to level 2. The man he saw there was even more surprised, saying he knew of nobody who ever went below level 2. Saddam kept descending, finding no one at all on the next three levels, and at level 6 finally met the man who killed Hussein, the Prophet's grandson, in 680—the most hated man in the history of Shia Islam. He was the only occupant of level 6, even after 1,326 years! Saddam had six more levels to go. Even in hell, he was in a class by himself.

No Exit from Tragedy

I had been home just seventeen days when disaster struck back at the Karrada compound. On January 17, 2007, a National Democratic Institute (NDI) convoy leaving a meeting in western Baghdad was ambushed by a large group of Sunni gunmen. A recently hired staff member, Andrea Parhamovich of Perry, Ohio, only twenty-eight, was killed along with three PSDs.

Andi had left the compound for a training session with members of the Iraqi Islamic Party, the largest Sunni party. She was just doing her job, working with politicians to strengthen their role in the democratic process. In so doing, she became one of the countless martyrs in the struggle for Iraq. What happened to her could have happened to me or to any other expat traveling from one place to another in Baghdad.

NDI's chairman, former secretary of state Madeleine Albright, wrote words of tribute that also apply to many others who have died in the struggle: "There is no more sacred roll of honor than those who have given their last full measure in support of freedom. Yesterday, in Iraq, Andrea Parhamovich and our security personnel were enshrined on that list. They did not see themselves as heroes, only as people doing a job on behalf of a cause they believed in."

NDI established a fellowship program in Andi's honor.[2] It left Karrada, however, moving some of its work to Erbil, the rest to Amman.

I knew about the Parhamovich disaster from the news. However, no Western media reported the disaster in the ICSP Anti-Corruption program one day earlier. We had held only occasional events in Mosul because of the safety risks, but ICSP workshops there had rarely faced overt opposition. One of the CSO workshop presenters certified through my TOT workshop in Erbil was Majeed Shekho, from the Yazidi religious minority. He went from Erbil to Mosul with a facilitator and driver to do a one-day workshop on January 15. The next day he was kidnapped and then shot dead. They killed his colleagues too.

Feeling concerned about not hearing from him, his longtime girlfriend and head of the CSO had called his cell phone. One of the men holding him answered. She asked where he was, and the man said, "He is right here, and we are about to kill him." As she pleaded with them, she heard shots, presumably the shots that killed Majeed.

ICSP management made the tragedy worse by seeming to ignore it. The regional manager made no response to it. A condolence letter requested from headquarters by the Erbil AC coordinator was sent belatedly and only after some pressure. They apparently didn't even notify Michael Miller. When the CSO submitted its reimbursement request for workshop expenses, Finance and Administration at first refused to pay on the grounds that they had sent no receipts. Shekho's girlfriend, daughter of the KRG minister of health, was left embittered with ICSP. In 2010 she was elected to the Iraqi parliament and became a prominent voice for the Yazidis. By the time I met her, several years after the tragedy, there was not much I could say.

Conflicting Agendas

Both the DCOP and my Anti-Corruption manager successor came from NDI, which worked the political and legislative side of USAID strategy. Her strategy was to create a "big splash" that would raise ICSP's public profile. My successor, an Iraqi with an American passport, lacked Anti-Corruption experience but had political connections.

Unfortunately, his tenure started with a big ethical issue over grants. Almost fifty Anti-Corruption CSOs had applied in the last grant round of 2006. Our Request for Applications (RFA) document had received a lot of changes, to make the rules clearer and lower the number of CSOs disqualified for failing to meet mandatory requirements, basically compliance errors made from inexperience.

So, I was surprised, during that second Amman conference in November, to learn that about 75 percent of AC grant applicants had been disqualified. It seemed unlikely so many could fail, especially after all the RFA changes, so I was suspicious. However, I got trapped in Amman when the Baghdad airport closed temporarily (an occupational hazard) so did not return to Baghdad until after my vacation in Thailand, leaving too little time to deal with this before I left.

There was not enough time to start over; AC had hundreds of thousands of grant dollars that had to be spent. The obvious solution was to reissue the RFA to those who wrote otherwise good proposals, explaining how to fix the errors and resubmit. This is not what happened.

After I left, the whole grant cycle was canceled and reannounced. Most of the money was awarded by the new management to CSOs from NDI who had no prior connection to ICSP or anti-corruption projects. Only a small number of grants went to our own CSOs.

Despite the deference usually given to expat decisions, this one provoked a fight from Mohammed and other Anti-Corruption staff and was opposed by Kristin too. Their resistance brought procedural compromises (such as requiring registration with ICSP), but the proposals by NDI civil society organizations were funded by management fiat, and an AC staff member was told to help improve some of them to make them reviewable—help not given to our own CSOs. This is how ICSP abandoned some of its most productive CSOs. I could not believe they actually did this.

I was not home long before the complaints started from Iraqi friends back at ICSP about the new management. New work procedures made it harder for them to do their jobs. There was less room for creative thinking, so they adjusted to just following orders. Democratic management got lost. Much of the enjoyment went out of their work.

The workload increased greatly, at headquarters and regional offices, as the new leadership pushed to get ICSP's numbers up. They set quotas for workshops, forums, and even the routine technical assistance meetings with CSOs, which I had never even thought about counting. All those new grants added to the workload.

Expat regional managers were now encouraged to exert program authority, upsetting Michael Miller's delicate balance between program management (HQ managers' authority) and administration (regional managers' authority). The balance had been maintained during my tenure, with occasional arguments. Now one regional manager ordered headquarters program managers not to talk to his staff without his permission. He and another regional manager demanded to pre-review all correspondence to HQ program offices. In Basra the Iraqi center director, upset because AC got more grants than the other sectors, set up a separate committee to supervise the INL grants, causing delays.

In Erbil internal problems worsened after the Jordanian regional manager encountered accusations of favoritism toward Arab staff from the majority Kurds. His female Kurdish deputy had ongoing issues with him and a few with headquarters. She left in early December and talked to AID-Erbil before she left. A major issue developed over a new group life insurance policy after staff quickly determined it covered no plausible deadly eventuality.

Having gotten wind of the discontent, the project officer from AID-Baghdad, its Erbil director, and the Kurdish project monitor met with Abdulla Barzangy, the AC coordinator and now acting center director. Several weeks later, in February, the AID-Erbil officials met with the staff, with the regional manager present. Numerous issues were raised about the management. Headquarters got the message from someone and reassigned the regional manager to Baghdad, transferring to Erbil the more ingratiating Basra manager, an Indonesian from Egypt. By then many staff had resigned, and the operation had declined.

The new ICSP leadership did generate impressive numbers. ICSP apparently implemented most of my INL projects but with their modifications. Some AC activities exceeded plan targets, though inside sources have expressed skepticism about some of ICSP's reported numbers. It did not pursue the 160 corrective actions, however.

My TOT workshops paid off, and more were added. All those new trainers generated a huge increase in workshops at government offices. In the end ICSP reported 787, almost five times more than the planned 160, and an estimated 15,740 government trainees, almost five times the planned 3,200. Under the Provincial and Local Government Support Project, forums for Provincial Council (PC) and other government staff addressing public access to budget and other public information got an estimated 3,015 participants.

The AC teams in Basra and Hilla linked up with CPI offices there and included them in training programs. At times the outreach extended to Supreme Board of Audit and Inspector General staff. However, the critical enforcement cooperation I outlined between CSOs and the CPI was not followed up.

A national corruption survey conducted by 19 CSOs among 7,200 respondents established that 44 percent found public services worse than the year before; only 14 percent found them better. There were 509 one-day forums for government employees attended by about 12,400 people, including PC and local council members. In thirteen provinces they held follow-up "town hall meetings" (a term that makes no sense in Arabic). These were intended to create five-member elected advisory councils in all eighteen provinces to engage in anti-corruption advocacy to the parliament. This seemed to duplicate the mission of the National Anti-Corruption Legislative Coalition I had already established.

Al-Noor and one of the CSOs from NDI eventually got large grants to analyze all those citizen surveys and do advocacy training workshops. Al-Noor involved CSOs from the AC Coalition in part of its work. Coalition members continued on their own to brief parliament members about the organization.

The project to produce weekly anti-corruption TV and radio programs, based on contradictory data, generated about two to three hundred individual shows, 80 percent on radio. ICSP estimated these reached 3 million people, a wildly optimistic guess based on applying percentages of governorate populations. Adding that to the previous guesstimate of 1 million reached by our AC teams would make ICSP's total AC audience at least 4 million. No political science department will ever validate this method of estimating.

I had envisioned the proposed Kurdistan Anti-Corruption Legislative Coalition to be like the national coalition. However, the project was handed to a women's rights CSO with no ICSP experience. The well-connected project manager worked for one of the major political parties and even drove a government car. As KRG corruption is centered in those parties, the Erbil AC Team saw an obvious conflict of interest. No legislative coalition was established, but ICSP headquarters reported the project completed as planned anyway. This outcome was unfortunate at a personal level, as the AC coalition I envisioned could have helped me when I went to work in the KRG later in 2007.

The Lost Struggle for Sustainability

Expert Opinions

U.S. government contracts have inherent uncertainties. Most are for multiyear periods, typically a base period and one or more option periods. ICSP had a seventeen-month base period (through December 2005), plus two government option periods of eighteen months. The first was exercised by USAID, extending the contract to June 30, 2007. The question in early 2007 was whether it would exercise the second option.

ICSP was the primary civil society contract, and developing a stronger civil society was a high priority. That ADF had accomplished a lot should have been well accepted. That it might have accomplished more in some areas would have to be conceded. Logically, USAID needed this project.

Between March 5 and April 18, as ICSP's fate hung in the balance, USAID conducted a project evaluation, contracted to International Business & Technical Consultants, Inc. (IBTCI). USAID guidelines for the study severely limited its scope. As IBTCI explained, "The evaluation focuses on the management of the program, the model developed by ADF, the quality and impact of training provided and on the effectiveness and sustainability of the four Regional Civil Society Resource Centers [CSRCs]."[3] The narrow focus meant that the six programs that were the core components of ICSP were not directly studied. In fact, the Anti-Corruption program was specifically excluded by USAID, as was the Independent Media program. Unavoidably, these decisions led to some conclusions that were not well informed, though others were remarkably good.

IBTCI found that Iraqi CSOs had made a noticeable impact. ADF could take some credit for that. CSOs were adjudged too reliant on foreign money, however, and becoming more so.

IBTCI found USAID's oversight excessive and a burden on ADF. However, ADF's management was too top-down; ADF headquarters exercised too much control over the project management; program managers (like me) had too much control over programs, instead of delegating to the CSRCs (a finding from which I dissent); and the four expat regional managers, intended as mentors to Iraqi center directors, became line managers instead (generally true).[4]

The relationship between headquarters and regional offices was carefully considered by Michael Miller when he set it up. The CSRCs managed personnel and day-to-day operations, but the technical direction of each program sector came from headquarters program managers directly to our regional teams. This meant all regional offices worked from common strategies and procedures under experienced guidance. With the program sectors excluded from its study, IBTCI never got the full explanation of how the system worked.

On the plus side, IBTCI found that ADF had made a difference in stimulating a civil society sector. Some CSOs were effective—a conclusion necessarily lacking analysis, as all CSOs were coordinated through the program sectors. ADF's model for training and technical assistance had been effective. It had been good in meeting contract obligations. Its Iraqi and expat staffs were capable. The CSRCs had potential if sustained and empowered, and the analysts insisted the centers could manage themselves.[5]

On the minus side, the projects, targets, and timelines were too ambitious, and using a contract instead of a cooperative agreement had been a mistake—criticisms directed mainly at USAID. Curiously, the analysts said CSOs were doing more advocacy activities now but this was not attributable to ICSP.[6] In fact, most ICSP program sectors were heavily into advocacy, but IBTCI analysts didn't study them, so how would they know?

IBTCI found that the failure to create momentum toward a sustainable post-ICSP organization was a "serious project failure." It concluded that if the project closed on June 30, the CSRCs would collapse.[7] This failure occurred "because the objectives set forth in the contract were impossibly ambitious and . . . because sustainability planning was not immediately initiated."[8] It recommended that the CSRCs evolve into four autonomous entities and that headquarters be reduced to a support office that seeks donors for them,[9] a structure both unrealistic and impractical given conditions in Iraq.

IBTCI related the sustainability failure to the alleged failure to delegate more authority to the regions. It said CSRCs lacked authority to implement locally viable sustainability plans. In fact, sustainability efforts were mostly a headquarters priority when Jean-Sebastien Roy was there, but most of the later planning was at the regional level, including a collective arrangement involving the four Iraqi center directors. Lack of authority was not the real problem. Those responsible, at both levels, just failed to produce an executable plan.

IBTCI found that "none of the four CSRCs have developed a long range plan, a transition plan, or an exit plan." Their halfhearted efforts to create advisory boards had not produced effective organizations, though the Baghdad board I briefly helped got some credit. The CSRCs had not moved to create regional revenue sources, such as outside donations, business revenue, or fees from CSOs.[10]

IBTCI criticized the failure to hire Iraqis for top positions. This could be excused at the start of the project but not after it had been in operation since 2004.[11] This finding lined up exactly with my own views previously expressed to Issam.

In its "primary recommendations" the analysts proposed that ICSP focus on fewer CSOs and offer more tailored training and technical assistance. Having excluded the program sectors from the report, IBTCI missed the fact that Anti-Corruption, Human Rights, and Civic Education had networked many of these CSOs into national or regional coalitions in which even those less active had a role not dependent on grant money. It also glossed over the fact that the project's primary sustainability goal was to create a stronger civil society *sector*. The study conceded that this had been accomplished well. By contrast, sustainability for the CSRCs in violent Iraq was necessarily a longer-term goal that needed more time.

Finally, the study addressed the critical question of whether and under what arrangements ICSP should continue after June 30, offering four "Alternative Future Strategies":

1. *Terminate the program.* The study clearly opposed this strategy. "The consultants found that the program is [as] highly relevant today as it was when it was first implemented since it meets the needs of Iraqis working for their communities through CSOs."

2. *Continue to operate the same way under the sustained organization,* under a new name. This could be a transitional arrangement toward a sustainable replacement organization.

3. *Shift from generic capacity building for CSOs to focused support on a few CSOs.* ICSP had trained almost 2,000 CSOs, but most were not interacting with government, so it was argued that the program should focus on those that were. This was a flawed argument, as already explained.

4. *Shift primary emphasis to establishing strong regional offices* that would become independent after the transition period. This approach would be the most consistent with the original project plan.[12]

IBTCI's conclusions favored a combination of strategies 3 and 4. Society-wide CSO capacity building versus focused support for a small number of CSOs was, however, a false choice; ICSP needed to do both. Shifting control entirely to independent regional entities would not have worked, as outside coordination and outside income would still have been needed.

A fifth and better strategy would have been to (1) improve the still-variable effectiveness of the program sectors, focusing especially on expanding regional and national networks and government linkages that would give CSOs more collective impact, while (2) simultaneously transitioning ICSP to Iraqi management (not regional expat management). This approach would have provided a transition period for creating viable regional entities within a decentralized but coordinated structure, consistent with Jean-Sebastien's original concept. Implementation of that strategy would have required changes in ICSP's project management.

In the end the evaluation report only partially overcame the skewed USAID guidance under which it was written. It exposed questionable management decisions and made many good points. Having ignored most of what ICSP actually did, however, the analysts unavoidably underestimated its current and potential impact and could not offer a path forward for the program sectors that defined ICSP. It thus underestimated program accomplishments while playing up management issues more likely to justify negative conclusions. Even so, it proposed that the project continue.

Michael Miller later learned that USAID instructions also included not talking to him or anyone at ADF in the United States as part of the study and not allowing ADF to review the report before publication, leaving it no chance to refute inaccurate or objectionable statements.

Final Judgments

Craig Davis had been ICSP's liaison to AID-Baghdad. He was highly responsive to their numerous information requests, and his relationship with AID was extremely good. The funding of his INL proposal showed that our Anti-Corruption program was well regarded. The new State Department money for the Independent Media program, though most of it left ICSP, was another endorsement. AID evaluation reports were consistently positive.

After Craig left, his successor assumed this liaison role. In early 2007 Nicole Tresch, AID's project officer, left. Tresch had strongly supported the project, but the positive evaluations were at some point replaced by negative ones. Michael Miller later complained to me that decisions after she left were biased judgments by people with little knowledge of the project.

AID's intentions regarding the project extension were unknown at that point, but Miller was confident because of all the favorable evaluations, because the project was still needed, and because Congress had appropriated the money, even mentioning ADF by name.

The situation was compromised, however, by internal problems. The turmoil in Erbil was one, but as time ran down, the problems extended to higher levels. The new DCOP had created a string of issues and some hard feelings. Several expat team members complained to ADF about her management style, following earlier indications of discontent that reached Michael Miller. The DCOP decided to make an issue over the heretofore autonomous and sometimes frustrating management of Finance and Administration. She apparently also hoped to take over the chief of party position officially.

In late April 2007 USAID announced that the second option would not be exercised. ADF requested a no-cost extension so as to use unspent money already allocated, but AID refused. It did not solicit proposals for a new contract either.

AID explained its decision as a change in strategy, putting the money in something other than civil society. Given the recent developments, however, the official explanation was possibly a bit too convenient. It's also true that ICSP had some problems in its early days (before my tenure) and that Michael Miller had critics at AID. Sometime later ADF lost a possible contract in Haiti after someone at AID trashed ICSP, lending credence to Miller's accusation of bias.

Just before the project died, the DCOP who had said she was there to save it made her exit. She left in mid-April, citing personal security reasons but just after learning from higher management that she would not be appointed chief of party.

Understandably, the USAID decision caused disappointment and frustration. One of my former Iraqi staff complained bitterly that the new leadership "destroyed what we built two years ago." The mood at Wael's Palace became increasingly depressed.

The decision also caused important initiatives to be lost. Many projects were cut short because ICSP management decided it needed time to close out grants and finish paperwork. In April a new CSO was selected for the National Legislative Observatory (NLO), just as ICSP was about to end. If only they had continued the NLO we established a year earlier. The NLO might have helped the Human Rights CSO that was awarded a futile last-minute grant to lobby for HR legislation in the parliament. Civic Education's initiative for a national dialogue on reconciliation, mirroring our earlier antiviolence plan for Human Rights, also began too late and died with the project.

It was unfortunate and consequential that the new regime failed to develop these and other initiatives around arrangements we had already built up, instead of letting them lapse and then trying to reinvent them in its own image. The National Anti-Corruption Legislative Coalition and the National Organization of CSO Lawyers were major examples. Sustaining those initiatives would have at least extended ICSP's impact and left an enduring legacy. Happily, the Independent Media Project that left with IREX lived on for a while as a separate project.

To the very end Women's Advocacy placed its highest priority on amending Article 39 of the constitution, to overcome its concessions to sharia law. On April 26 the team met with American, British, European Union, and UNAMI representatives to solicit international support. This effort was another casualty of the project shutdown. So were the public awareness efforts of the Erbil Women's Advocacy team to combat female genital mutilation through a CSO grant.

In my opinion, knowing the project but also how federal contracting works, USAID should have either extended ADF or rebid the project. The requested no-cost extension would have bought time for a proper procurement process. Abandoning all the CSOs who worked with ICSP to make a difference in the new Iraq was both insensitive and counterproductive—one of those Washington decisions that make no sense on the ground. In 2012 USAID in effect belatedly reversed itself by establishing another contracted civil society project.

One of my former AC coordinators told me four years later that CSO people still talk about the Iraq Civil Society Program. It changed their perspectives on their country and made a real difference. Many ICSP staff continued to have successful careers, helped by the skills and abilities they acquired from working in the program.

In the aftermath Wael's Palace was rented to Management Systems International (MSI), a USAID training contractor destined to play a major role in Iraq. AID required ADF to remove all equipment and furniture that Wael brought in at such great expense just a few years earlier—everything valued at $500 or more—including huge generators that had to be lifted off the roof and hauled to Basra. These items were given to other AID-funded NGOs, but of course MSI then had to replace all that stuff at U.S. government expense. Your tax dollars at work.

Several of my former staff went to work for MSI, so ended up working in the same building. Still, Wael's Palace was not quite the same without Wael.

No Heirs to the Kingdom

When ICSP died, the goal of creating a successor Iraqi entity also died. In retrospect this goal faced major practical obstacles, starting with the violence. Generating enough revenue to break even would have been difficult at best. Still, the goal was attainable.

A meeting of the expat regional managers in June 2006 replaced the four independent entities concept with the Iraqi Civil Society Institute (ICSI), a single organization with four decentralized branches. The plan assumed a nine-month transition period through June 2007. ICSI registered with the government in March 2007, as the Center for Development of Civil Society in Iraq (CDCSI). But ADF did not develop an exit strategy or a transition plan keyed to the June 30, 2007, end date.[13]

With the pressure on, there was a flurry of activity. Each CSRC elected directors, from which a national board of directors was formed. While ADF's program manager, Karen Diop, was at ICSP in early 2007, a work plan was hastily put together. Michael Miller came to Baghdad, in part to put the final touches on the transition plan. CSO membership forms were distributed to the staff. In Baghdad, however, the realization seeped through that the transition to CDCSI would eliminate most of their jobs.

ICSP rented and set up a CDCSI office and provided some furniture and office supplies. It was no Wael's Palace—just an apartment in that building outside the compound where Usama and others took up residence earlier. A flurry of ICSI activity preceded issuance of IBTCI's report, but its central executive committee did not hold its first meeting until April 18, setting out objectives for the next three months. This all came too late.

In fairness, organizational sustainability needed more time. In equal fairness ICSP's management had wasted time by failing to transition to the new organization with a sense of urgency. ADF could have retained some technical direction over its programs and helped sustain ICSI, by subcontracting them to ICSI (or by awarding grants) under strict performance standards. Each CSRC could also have developed business with other USAID contractors and international NGOs in areas where it had specialized expertise. None of this happened, and ADF's whole regional edifice died with the project, as IBTCI had predicted.

The impending end of ICSP did not eliminate the risks to its employees. Its four outreach coordinators in Anbar and Diyala all resigned due to threats. As the project ended, two men came to the home of a key Basra staff member and announced to him and his wife that they were there to kill him. Somehow he was able to run out of the house, past other homes, and escape. The would-be assassins kidnapped another family member, whose freedom had to be negotiated, presumably by ransom. Iraq at ground level was still a place where no one was safe.

Lessons Learned: The Almost Final Balance Sheet

ADF's Final Report

On September 1, 2007, ADF submitted its *Final Report*. It had done a lot with the nearly $61 million from U.S. taxpayers. Its self-assigned list of accomplishments cited "a stronger, more visible role for civil society in Iraq; increased capacity of Iraqi CSOs; formation of CSO networks, coalitions, and other forms of cooperation; critical civil society involvement in core national politics and practices; expanded civil society involvement in local decision making; development of independent media; expanded civil society action for conflict mitigation and reconciliation; increased capacity of civil society to advocate for citizen interests; expanded technical resources for the ongoing development of Iraqi civil society."[14] I can verify all those claims.

ADF's statistics for each program sector were impressive. Aggregating its numbers, there were about 91,500 participants in ICSP events, 30,000 of them at Anti-Corruption events, some counted more than once to be sure. There were 2,247 workshops, 1,037 (46 percent) by AC, reflecting all the workshops at government offices. For the Independent Media sector, ADF claimed it had trained more than 8,000 media professionals, and "the total number of participants in the workshops and training courses represented 50 percent of the active journalists in Iraq."[15]

Despite the problems getting its grant money out, ICSP disbursed over $4.8 million in 538 small grants. The figures reflect the higher priority on Anti-Corruption grants (195) but also the short-changing of Human Rights (36).[16]

The Organizational Assessment Tool (OAT) was applied to over 1,000 CSOs, and about 25 percent were retested after going through capacity-building activities. Instead of eliminating unnecessary questions, however, ICSP actually increased the questions from 213 to 300. The average score for those retested rose from 100 to 148.[17] Even that was under 50 percent, but because many questions were unnecessary, percentages were largely meaningless. Still, the OAT did provide some objective data for evaluation and reporting.

As for the failure to transition the four CSRCs to sustainable organizations, ADF cited the worse-than-anticipated security conditions and the impossibility of outside donor support under those conditions. Beyond those justifications, it blamed USAID. It claimed it was making good progress on sustainability, including registration of ICSI, when the contract was terminated. Had ICSP/ICSI been extended, sustainability could have been achieved within the eighteen-month extension period.[18]

Moreover, even though ICSP's structure did not survive, many ICSP-trained CSOs and individuals became resources for training others. Many ICSP staff moved on to positions in other international development organizations.[19]

Lessons Learned, or Not

ADF's report summarized key lessons learned in Iraq. CSOs are generally receptive to working together on common efforts. Government officials are generally receptive to CSO initiatives. CSOs eagerly accept expert help. My observations emphatically confirm all three lessons.

Among other lessons are these. In times of conflict it is still possible and highly important to strengthen CSOs and the CSO sector. CSOs are valuable for their ability to operate in places too dangerous for expats. High levels of project activity can be maintained despite bad security, as ICSP did. I can confirm those three lessons too, but some host-country employees and CSO members may die in service to your mission.

ADF suggested that projects in conflict areas like Iraq rely more on the company's home office for support and it is more engaged in the project. This was true for RTI, but I found ADF headquarters to be, alternately, very helpful or uninformed.

It may be a measure of ADF headquarters' distance from events that in claiming credit for forming networks and coalitions it cited groups with 28, 17, and 5 CSOs, without mentioning the National Anti-Corruption Legislative Coalition, which had 720. If its project management had not lost the national CSO lawyers' organization, ADF could have claimed a big-number success there too. In general ADF underreported its accomplishments in Anti-Corruption, Women's Advocacy, and Human Rights. Its many recognized Anti-Corruption accomplishments were only mentioned and not highlighted.

ADF also commented that recruiting and retaining staff is a difficult challenge in conflict zones. While this is true, and for Iraqi staff too, I personally found my expat colleagues to be almost uniformly capable people dedicated to their work. Expats did leave at times but typically for compelling personal reasons, not because of the danger.

ADF's *Final Report* is a good example of evaluating more from process goals than progress goals. We can, for example, schedule more events or meetings to meet targets (a process goal). We can also encourage more people to attend (another process goal). The more important question is what those events or meetings accomplished. Did they generate a measurable or noticeable impact (a progress goal)? It's easy to criticize ADF on this point, but the larger problem was with the flaws in USAID's project evaluation system.

ADF's *Final Report* is all about compliance, and its evidence is largely about numbers. Collectively, those numbers are impressive. However, the more important question is about impact, about outcomes. What do those numbers prove? It's a safe bet that neither ADF nor AID could come up with a convincing answer.

The same questions apply to all international development projects. How many corrective actions were achieved? How many lives were affected? How much of the project's progress can be sustained, realistically, after it ends? In cases like ICSP, what future positive outcomes were lost because AID terminated the project?

The bottom line for ICSP is that it accomplished a lot yet was undermined in the end, by its own project management but also by USAID's management. This was ADF's project to manage, but it was implementing AID's project under AID supervision. Both did well for most of the project but not so well in the final months. In the end, they combined to sink their own ship.

14

The Instinct to Control

The Culture of Violence and the CPI
Politics and Criminal Corruption

I wish ICSP had done more after I left to support the Commission on Public Integrity (CPI). It got back to me that my departure caused disappointment there. As it turned out, however, the CPI had bigger problems.

The constitution made the CPI an independent agency, but Commissioner Radhi Hamza Al-Radhi met increasing political opposition—led by Prime Minister Nouri Al-Maliki. CPI efforts to investigate corruption were frustrated in many ministries; most of its recommended prosecutions were blocked; and its investigators and other staff were left exposed to the threats, intimidation, and murders that define Iraq's culture of violence.

The threats started in midsummer 2006 during major investigations of the Defense and Interior ministries. Several months later Al-Radhi was warned by a friend at Defense that he was now on its "cleansing list," which identified targets for assassination. One morning a sniper's bullet landed near him as he stood outside his office. In late June 2007 a truck-launched missile just missed his house. He started sleeping in the Green Zone and other safe places, aided by his witness protection staff; other CPI staff often slept in their offices. Just after he came to the United States with a training group on August 24, another missile just missed his house but hit a neighbor's house.

Al-Radhi finally announced his resignation on September 6, while still in the United States. Al-Maliki gloated that he had fled the country. On October 3 Al-Radhi applied for asylum. Instantaneously, he went from a high position of great importance to being a lowly immigrant, trying to survive in a new country with his limited English—"a feather in the wind," in his words. I was happy to meet him in America but most unhappy about what had happened to him.

Even more horrifying was his later testimony to a House of Representatives committee and then to a Senate committee that thirty-one CPI staff and twelve family members had been assassinated, most shot to death at close range and some tortured. He provided gruesome details on individual cases.[1] The victims included investigators but also security men and drivers, some killed by bullets aimed at others. Assassins unable to catch the CPI's chief of security killed his father instead, hanging his body on a butcher hook.

Al-Radhi described the corruption as rampant. He blamed it primarily on Al-Maliki, who never accepted the CPI's independent status. From 3,000 cases brought to court in Al-Radhi's tenure, only 241 defendants were convicted. The vast majority of cases were undone by three Al-Maliki decisions.

First, the prime minister revived a 1971 law requiring permission from the minister of the relevant agency before taking a corruption case to court. This enabled ministers to block investigations in their ministries and protect subordinates from prosecution. Al-Maliki simply ignored the inconvenient fact that the old law was inconsistent with the CPI's constitutional powers. This decision blocked hundreds of CPI prosecutions.

Second, Al-Maliki followed up with a formal notice to Al-Radhi on April 1, 2007, that formal charges against any current or former minister, Council of Ministers staff, or Presidential Office staff now required approval of the prime minister. So, he could protect all the ministers he chose to protect, and they could in turn protect their cronies.

Finally, Al-Maliki made a decision that protected a lot of corrupt officials retroactively. He took advantage of a 2008 proposal by Sunni parties for a general amnesty covering a wide range of accused people by including officials convicted in 2,772 pre-2007 corruption cases. This move wiped out 90 percent of the CPI's 3,000 cases! Another 498 were released in 2009, despite having collectively stolen almost $200 million.[2]

Al-Maliki's interference focused almost entirely on Shia-led ministries, giving his obstructionism a sectarian pattern. Sunni Arab politicians complained increasingly about the pattern of targeting their alleged misdeeds while giving Shia politicians a free ride.

The CPI by now had about 1,300 employees, three times more than when I first went there. Its investigators, however, could not even gain entry to some ministries, and thanks to Al-Maliki's decrees, ministry officials could now refuse information requests with impunity. Even worse, it became dangerous to investigate corruption in some ministries. At Interior, employer of the nation's police, any investigator naming names risked his life. Al-Radhi alleged that some ministries were controlled by "criminal gangs." Sunni and Shia militias controlled parts of the government's oil business; it was too dangerous for the CPI to investigate that. According to Al-Radhi, "This has resulted in the Ministry of Oil effectively financing terrorism through these militias."[3] That was a direct threat to Coalition soldiers.

In March 2008 Al-Radhi testified to Congress that CPI had uncovered a total loss to corruption of about $18 *billion*. Some cases more than met USAID's definition of "grand corruption." The ministry causing the largest number of cases was Defense. In one outrageous case a huge amount of money was sent out of Iraq to pay for vital military equipment, but no equipment was received, and the money vanished. There were grand corruption cases in several other ministries too. A Ministry of Oil official responsible for protecting the oil pipelines stole millions and fled Iraq. He was sentenced in absentia to fifteen years. A big contributing factor was that Iraq still paid its obligations in cash, leaving fewer financial records and making it easier to steal.

Al-Maliki and parliamentary allies deflected criticism by blaming Al-Radhi. After Al-Radhi's October 2007 testimony to Congress, Al-Maliki threatened him with prosecution, even making charges of theft over documents Al-Radhi had taken with him to the United States. The chairman of the Integrity Committee in the Council of Representatives (COR), from Al-Maliki's coalition, unleashed a string of financial and administrative corruption charges against Al-Radhi.

In Al-Maliki's defense the security of the country was hanging in the balance, and sectarian violence was rampant. There were parties and factions threatening to defect from his cabinet. Arguably, he had to tolerate some corrupt politicians to stay in office. Pursuing corruption charges against ministers and other high officials arguably destabilized the government at the worst of times. Moreover, the CPI was doing a lot of investigations, so Al-Radhi was making a lot of enemies. It didn't help that he avoided press conferences and interviews, which might have given him a stronger public profile and more political clout.

Even conceding those points, however, the extent of Al-Maliki's corruption tolerance was breathtaking. In a U.S. government report in mid-2008, an embassy official conceded that not a single major Iraqi official had been taken to court since Al-Radhi left.[4]

Whose Side Are We On?

You might assume U.S. officials defended the CPI. In fact, Al-Radhi felt that some of the U.S. "experts" assigned to each ministry were part of the problem. Some did not support, or even opposed, the CPI investigations. The State Department was asked to stop releasing CPI reports criticizing the ministries.

State chose not to support Al-Radhi publicly, apparently deciding it was more important to avoid antagonizing Al-Maliki. Secretary of State Condoleezza Rice ordered her staff not to publicly discuss Iraq's corruption. After Al-Radhi moved to the United States, no one from the Bush administration talked to him. The Special Inspector General for Iraq Reconstruction, Stuart Bowen, who had worked with Al-Radhi, said his departure from CPI was a big loss, which was my opinion also.

Two former leaders of the Baghdad embassy's Office of Accountability and Transparency, one a former judge, later told U.S. senators that Al-Maliki's office deliberately derailed or prevented investigations at ministries controlled by Shia parties. High officials who *were* prosecuted were men with little clout. The officials charged that the administration had blocked release of their report.

The White House, like State, was highly sensitive to negative press as it waited anxiously for the military "surge" to salvage its Iraq policy. The new Democratic leaders of Congress, elevated to majority status by the 2006 congressional elections, were intent on early withdrawal. State avoided congressional questions about corruption and withheld documents requested by Congress. The Office of Accountability and Transparency, set up as the focus of U.S. anti-corruption strategy, was soon eliminated, in December 2007.[5]

A Justice Department "Fact Sheet" in February 2008 claimed its CPI trainees were responsible for 6,190 public corruption cases to date and that 2,371 cases had been referred to the Central Criminal

Court.[6] At face value the data seemed to show that CPI was again making progress. In fact, the 6,190 "cases" were just the number of calls to the CPI Hotline, going back several years to when it started. About half the cases arose during Al-Radhi's tenure and included the 2,772 eliminated by the general amnesty, plus the other cases blocked by Al-Maliki. After CPI endured all that political interference, suffered all those staff fatalities, and saw its commissioner threatened out of the country, this passed for public information in Washington.

As for the COR Integrity Committee, the same officials alleged its sole purpose was to be a forum for corruption complaints against Commissioner Radhi that were apparently false. Its chairman, Sabah Al-Saadi, insisted there were serious corruption issues at the CPI.

Meanwhile, the CPI was renamed the Iraq Commission of Integrity (COI), a change with no real significance. It expanded past 2,000 employees and opened new offices, but its personnel and investigative resources were inadequate for a country of Iraq's size, and it could not control its own budget or complete proper investigations. A sign of how things really were was the decision by the Bureau of International Narcotics and Law Enforcement Affairs (INL) to scale back training programs for the CPI, largely in response to "the CPI's diminishing effectiveness as a law enforcement institution."[7]

Al-Radhi's deputy was named acting commissioner but was quickly fired, and efforts were made to marginalize other CPI officials associated with Al-Radhi. Judge Rahim Al-Okaili, another former Al-Radhi deputy, was appointed in January 2008. He gained wider political support, including from Chairman Al-Saadi, and COI's cases and convictions increased greatly but with little effect on the political elite. He also fired some CPI employees over minor corruption issues. He faced ongoing political interference and heavy pressure, however, and in September 2011, after the government blocked prosecution of a major corruption case, he publicly resigned in protest—a truly rare event in Iraq. Al-Maliki appointed his own "interim" commissioner, ignoring a just-passed law requiring appointment by parliament.

As for that financial disclosure law the CPI staff proudly told me about in 2005, it became a dead letter. Over the next three years virtually none of the applicable officials complied, including Al-Maliki, Talabani, the COR Speaker, and virtually every minister and COR member.[8]

What about that American model inspector general system, with IGs in all the ministries? It was their job to initiate investigations and refer cases to the CPI. An absolute requirement for an effective IG system is the independence of the IGs, but Al-Maliki turned about half these positions into political appointments and replaced many Bremer appointees. The Defense ministry IG, a woman, was assassinated. They made it seem like she was killed accidentally by a bodyguard. The Housing and Reconstruction IG was replaced, filed a lawsuit, complained to the court, and was assassinated. The Education IG was killed with his son near Hilla while driving to Karbala. Staff members of other IGs also got killed.

Other IGs were forced out by imposing the retirement age, sixty-three, even though this can be extended twice for two-year terms. That former CPI department head who met with us at ICSP and who became the Ministry of Sports and Youth IG was one of the victims. The SCIRI-appointed minister didn't want him.

In the end, half of the IGs just refused to cooperate with the CPI. Their loyalty was to their parties. For example, the Ministry of Health IG, from Dawa, would not refer cases to the CPI. Yet ICSP Anti-Corruption grantees had repeatedly shown that this ministry was highly corrupt. As with the CPI, IG offices were left understaffed.

Moreover, IGs and their staffs faced the same personal risks as the CPI if they named names or moved against anybody. To their credit, some IGs did pursue corruption cases within their ministries, despite the intimidating environment.

The IG system would work in Iraq given the necessary political support, but it needs IGs with authority and political independence. The emerging consensus was that the IG system had been ineffective. There were proposals, both well intentioned and self-serving, to abolish it.

The Board of Supreme Audit (BSA) faced the same interference and the same risks as the COI and IG offices. People went to great lengths to avoid being exposed by the BSA. Many BSA officials were assassinated, including its Bremer-appointed director, as were at least twenty more BSA officials between 2007 and 2009.

The interference experienced by all three institutions also undermined coordination among them, further diminishing their impact. For example, as the CPI lacked authority to initiate investigations and had to wait on the IGs, the emasculation of the IG system hurt the CPI too.[9]

The Central Criminal Court of Iraq (CCCI) proved unable or unwilling to keep up with all the CPI's cases, even before Al-Maliki started blocking them,[10] though it seemingly did better later. CCCI judges also showed they could be pressured into protecting the corrupt for ulterior reasons, such as by dismissing cases of probably guilty defendants or issuing overly lenient sentences for major crimes. Their fears about personal security contributed heavily to this troubling pattern.[11]

So, while Iraq's U.S.-designed national integrity system was still functioning, its four major components still faced an uphill climb.

The Anti-Corruption Coalition in the Wilderness

Although ICSP failed in mid-2006 to extend the Al-Noor Universal Foundation's contract for the National Anti-Corruption Legislative Coalition, Al-Noor and much of the organization, now called the National Legislative Coalition to Fight Corruption in Iraq, continued on without money. Many in the inner coalition kept working, but the bad security made it risky to move around and caused anxiety over the linkage to a U.S. organization. Many became inactive, and Al-Noor lost contact with others. By 2011 the national network had 206 CSOs versus 720 initially and 36 coalition members versus the original 103—still large numbers, however. The decline also reflected a broader trend: CSOs going inactive because ICSP ended and other funding sources dried up.

Another obstacle for the AC Coalition was the government's unwillingness to register *coalitions* of CSOs. This obstacle limited its opportunity for public impact, though Al-Noor was registered and acted on its behalf. Al-Noor itself became an increasingly engaged, effective, and government-recognized anti-corruption advocate.

In March 2008 Iraq became a signatory to the United Nations Convention against Corruption (UNCAC). An Al-Noor representative to an earlier UNCAC conference in Amman wrote letters to Al-Maliki and the CPI urging the government to sign. CPI endorsed the proposal. Membership comes with obligations, such as aligning laws and institutions with UNCAC requirements and establishing a national anti-corruption strategy.

Ten CSOs in my AC Coalition, including Al-Noor, then convened meetings at their own expense, concluding with a workshop at the Al-Rashid Hotel in April 2008, to develop that national strategy. Al-Noor used its relationship with the COR Integrity Committee to arrange follow-up meetings with committee leaders, then submitted a national strategy document that was approved by the Council of Ministers with limited revisions.

The year 2009 was then declared the "Year of Anti-Corruption," and Iraq issued a "National Strategy to Combat Corruption." This PR offensive did not produce demonstrations of the political will so far lacking, however.

The anti-corruption public awareness ICSP helped to generate came to the fore as the March 2010 national election approached. Amid a rising tide of media stories, public anger, and parliament frustration, Al-Maliki suddenly took the lead in denouncing corruption. A wave of arrests hit multiple ministries, apparently authorized by Al-Maliki. The most publicized scandal caused the resignation of the minister of trade and later his arrest at the airport after his flight to Dubai was ordered back to Baghdad.

Alas, once the election was over, the scandal was quickly finessed. The minister knew too much. Many Al-Maliki advisors had sent foreign contractors they knew to the ministry with requests to give them contracts, which would generate commissions for the referring officials. Such payments are bribes under Iraqi law. The minister threatened to expose everything. So, big pressure was put on the judiciary to set him free, and in April 2010 it did, releasing him on bail and allowing him to leave the country. He was then charged and convicted in absentia in 2012 and sentenced (meaninglessly) to seven years in jail.

At times officials avoided jail in more traditional ways. In August 2006, while I was still in Baghdad, they arrested the minister of electricity for corruption. In October he was sentenced to two years in jail. In December he escaped.[12]

In early 2010 Iraq launched its so-called first Anti-Corruption Strategy, working with the UN. Al-Noor was appointed to lead implementation of the civil society portion. It was a comprehensive strategy with two hundred action items, but like many Iraq strategies, it looked better on paper than in practice. Court convictions in 2010 for corruption quadrupled from 2009, but the virtual immunity of high-level officials continued. Al-Maliki soon closed all criminal cases against officials accused of creating fraudulent documents, including bogus college graduation certificates, absolutely illegal but used by thousands—including ministers—to get government jobs for which they lacked the required college degree.

In February 2010 Iraq joined the Extractive Industries Transparency Initiative (EITI), an anti-corruption international agreement started in 2002 by British prime minister Tony Blair. The government has to publish all oil export revenue; foreign oil companies in Iraq have to publish what they paid the government; and all figures get published in an EITI report. Al-Noor was one of three CSOs appointed to the twenty-member Board of Stakeholders responsible for overseeing the process. Iraq published its first report in December 2011, completed its required final validation report in August 2012, and thereby achieved "Compliant" status in December 2012—a major accomplishment.

Meanwhile, a new law (described later) allowed my National Legislative Coalition to register under its own name in 2011 and to resume normal activities, which should further its participation in the legislative process. I continue to check occasionally on how it's doing. Hopefully, it will eventually have some of the impact I envisioned when I started it in 2006.

The Anti-Corruption Bottom Line

There was an *extremely* ominous development in January 2011 that got almost no Western media attention despite its huge implications. Al-Maliki persuaded the Federal Supreme Court that the COI, BSA, and other independent agencies belonged under the Council of Ministers, in effect the prime minister, instead of the COR, as the constitution provides. The other agencies even included the Independent High Electoral Commission, and Al-Maliki later added the Central Bank.

Many COR members attacked this move as another Al-Maliki power grab. The Court reasoned that having independent agencies reporting to the COR was in effect leaving them unsupervised, as it was not set up to supervise executive agencies.[13] The decision blunted the clear intent of the constitution and facilitated further political interference, despite the Court's statement that its ruling did not permit such interference. The decision was one of several that set off alarm bells.

We who live in Western democracies can take almost for granted that government officials carry out their responsibilities without fear. Officials in Iraq's anti-corruption agencies, court system, and ministries can't safely make that assumption. The pressure on judges was reinforced by the unprecedented threats and violence against them, due to their positions or to actual or pending decisions. About thirty judges and other judicial staff had been killed, a number destined to rise. This intimidated other judges out of handling cases involving senior government officials.[14] A former Iraqi judge estimated that nine of every ten common court system decisions are shaped by extrajudicial considerations, as are four to seven of every ten decisions in the CCCI courts. Most common court judges have to live at home, and even the CCCI judges, living in protected housing, aren't entirely safe all the time. Making the right decision is a priority; staying alive may seem like a higher priority.[15]

Iraq's political elite has corrupted the political process for its own benefit. Elected officials and political appointees have used their positions to enrich themselves and their parties. COR members gave themselves a $10,000 monthly salary, with huge expense accounts and generous benefits, despite the appalling attendance records of many. On September 1, 2013, protests erupted around the country against their monthly pension benefits of thousands of dollars—for life—even for those leaving after one term.[16]

Indeed, much of Iraq's political conflict, including its sectarian conflict, is a competition for resources. Once the CPA returned governance to the Iraqis, grand corruption schemes quickly followed. The permanent government then brought in a horde of party hacks and militiamen to share the largess. The more ministries there are, the more money there is for parties and party members appointed to high and other ministry positions. Meanwhile, the corruption cripples government's ability to provide even basic services.

What difference have all those women elected to parliament under the 25 percent quota made in fighting corruption? Not much, based on a 2011 Al-Noor survey; two-thirds of respondents rated the women's collective performance as poor.

I established the AC Legislative Coalition to interact with COR committees working on anti-corruption legislation. Reality is that the committee system underperformed, and any legislation of consequence took seemingly forever—if it passed at all. Even minor legislation was hard to pass. As the government's survival is politically paramount, and all parties of any size are in the government, effective oversight of ministries is discouraged. Any investigation risks accusations of sectarian motives.[17]

CSOs all over Iraq, many trained by ICSP, continued to try, but faced some of the same threats and violence as honest public officials. They and other critics have endured anonymous threats, phony arrests, violence by police and pro-regime thugs, and even assassinations.

Overall, the anti-corruption struggle has had many successes but is far from a success story. Government corruption sparked growing public anger, including occasional but major public demonstrations. In the wake of Egypt's massive Arab Spring protests, Al-Maliki pledged in February 2011 that he would not seek reelection as prime minister after the 2014 elections and proposed that prime ministers be limited to two terms, but he changed his mind once the pressure was off. In August 2013 the Federal Supreme Court ruled a newly passed term limits law affecting the prime minister, president, and COR Speaker positions to be unconstitutional.

Yet there are principled, courageous parliament members who have at times made a difference. One of their success stories was the April 2011 decision, finally and over government objections, to repeal that old law the government had used to block prosecutions of high-level officials.[18] It was said, however, that "the fact that the government resisted repealing what was universally regarded as an invitation to steal is a clear indication of its priorities."[19] A serious government reform effort, with heavy CSO support and street demonstrations, would come only after Al-Maliki left office.

Lesson learned. Numerous research findings have been published in recent years on the still evolving field of Anti-Corruption. Translating them into effective policies is an ongoing process pursuing an elusive goal. That process needs to incorporate evidence and practical lessons from ground-level experience.

My ground-level Iraq experience persuades me that *political will* is not just essential but also the anti-corruption bottom line. It is critical at all levels of government but especially at the top. Awareness that one's actions violate the constitution, law, government policy, or moral principles, or even make voters angry, does not force a corrupt person to change his or her behavior. In street language, the bottom line is: "Who's going to stop me?" In Iraq the answer too often is: "No one." All the well-intentioned efforts of U.S. and later UN officials, and of ICSP and thousands of CSOs, won't matter much in the end unless that defiance is overcome. The *USAID Anticorruption Strategy* manual should be revised to give more emphasis to this bottom line and explain how to overcome it. Solutions won't be easy.

One analyst commenting on Iraq's corruption noted that "most anti-corruption campaigns fail," not only because they are difficult but also because they target only low-level corruption. Even if such campaigns succeed, their momentum does not carry over to the grand corruption that has much greater impact on how citizens perceive corruption in their countries.[20] Grand corruption usually implicates people in leadership positions—the same people whose political will is needed to fight it.

As for Iraq's standing on Transparency International's (TI) Corruption Perceptions Index, it's not much improved. Iraq was second from the bottom in 2007 and third from the bottom in 2008, out of 180 countries, ahead of only Burma and Somalia. In 2009 it moved up smartly to a tie for fifth from the bottom, edging ahead of Afghanistan and tying Sudan, then slid back one place in 2010. The 2011 rating was more hopeful, as Iraq tied for 8th from the bottom, but it failed to move up in 2012 and slid down two places to 6th from the bottom in 2013 and 2014 (170th out of 175). It would return to 8th from the bottom in 2015. By now Iraq should be doing a lot better.

In fairness the TI index is based on perceptions, and a lot of progress could have been missed, but probably not. ICSP and others have helped create widespread public awareness and antagonism about corruption. That doesn't *prevent* it, however. Awareness and advocacy lead to prevention when politicians fear public exposure and especially when they fear prosecution.

USAID, INL, and other U.S. agencies generated visible progress on the awareness side of anti-corruption strategy but could have done much better on the enforcement side. That in turn underscores the finding in the USAID *Anticorruption Strategy* that an effective anti-corruption strategy has to combine public awareness and enforcement and that one without the other is ineffective.

The Culture of Violence and Independent Journalism

The Dangerous Life of Journalists

May 30, 2007, another sad day in my Iraq experience. The journalist Nazaar Abdul Wahid, former member of my Maysan Democracy Team and later a Provincial Council member, was shot dead in Amarah. He was only thirty-three and left a wife and children. Nazaar was a really nice guy, much liked by his RTI colleagues and dedicated to his profession. I was told he was shot multiple times, right in front of others, as he was about to enter a hotel for a journalism workshop. How sadly ironic, as I first met him at that journalists' meeting in downtown Amarah where he demanded that RTI start teaching its journalism workshops.

Nazaar had become a prominent journalist. He was working for Iraq's largest newspaper, *Al-Sabah Al-Jadeed*, and for the Aswat Al-Iraq news service. His death was widely reported in Iraq and by several international journalism organizations and websites.

Nazaar became the third member of my Democracy Team to be assassinated. Another Democracy Team journalist, Abdul-Hussein Sabith, who wrote for *Azzaman* and other papers, died early from medical causes. Another team member, the young, talented Dr. Salim Abd Ul-Ridha, died in a car accident. At least two others left the country. Others at risk stayed because they could not leave or by brave choice. I never imagined in 2004 that so many Democracy Team members would encounter personal tragedies and crises.

The sadness of Nazaar's senseless death, following those of Kifaya and Haider, forced on me the realization that on any given day someone else among my former Iraqi colleagues might be the next martyr in the struggle for Iraq.

Nazaar's death was a scene in a larger tragedy. Iraq's violence had made journalists' lives increasingly dangerous. Death threats were common; some were carried out. The danger was mainly from insurgents and militiamen targeting journalists because they were journalists or from being caught in a cross fire, but some of the danger was from government officials and police exposed by media stories.

Atwar Bahjat, a well-known journalist and sometimes poet from Samarra, was much liked and admired by other journalists in Baghdad. An attractive woman, just twenty-nine and planning to be married, she was with Al Jazeera when it was banned by the Iraqi government after telecasting a story considered insulting to Grand Ayatollah Sistani. So, she left Al Jazeera and joined Al Arabiya.

The bombing of Samarra's historic Shia mosque occurred just three weeks later, in February 2006. Defying advice it was too dangerous to go there, Atwar returned to her city to cover the story, interviewing eyewitnesses and residents. The next day she and her crew were kidnapped, and she and two of the other three were shot dead; the third somehow escaped. The tragic irony was that Atwar, daughter of a mixed Shia-Sunni marriage, had changed jobs to avoid Shia thugs and was then killed by Sunni thugs. Three brothers arrested in 2009 confessed to the crime.

Atwar's story was likewise one among many. One Iraqi *New York Times* reporter lost so many people from his life that, as he later blogged, he now had "no living friends in Iraq."

Iraqi journalists working with U.S. media were even more endangered. They faced a constant risk of death and lived under constant stress. It became dangerous to travel to story locations. Many left Iraq or quit their jobs. Many others couldn't leave or just refused to quit despite the risks. Salih Saif Aldin, a courageous Iraqi reporter for the *Washington Post*, made enemies but pressed on until October 2007, when he died covering a street battle.

The *New York Times* maintained a large news bureau in Baghdad. Like ICSP, it spent much of its budget on expat-managed security and housed its staff in a high-walled compound shared with other major media. Even some Iraqi staff were housed there, but any sent out on a story went with only a driver and no armed security, to avoid attracting attention. Any reporter identified on the street could be in immediate danger. A *Times* staff member in Baghdad was murdered, as was another in Basra.

In just under four years 170 journalists and other media staff were killed, mostly Iraqis but also foreign journalists. There were 68 killed in 2006 alone, 44 percent of the world total of 155.[21] Between 2003 and 2008 more journalists died in Iraq than in any other country. Very few of those murders led to a conviction.[22]

In July 2008 Nazaar Abdul Wahid was one of ten slain reporters and broadcasters honored by a memorial set up in Washington DC by the Broadcasting Board of Governors, the federal agency supervising government-supported international broadcasting organizations.

Backsliding on Independent Media

Deteriorating security was a major reason that development of independent media regressed—but not the only reason. The 2006-7 *Media Sustainability Index—Middle East and North Africa*, published by IREX, lowered Iraq's overall rating from 1.16 in 2005 to 0.91 on a scale of 0 to 4. It rose to 1.60 in 2008 and 1.87 in 2009 as security improved. The separately calculated KRG ratings were higher at first (1.48 in 2005, 1.45 in 2006-7, 1.80 in 2008) but actually lower than Iraq by 2009 (1.81). Ironically, one of the Iraq panel members for a previous *Media Sustainability Index* was Nazaar Abdul Wahid.

The instinct to control had frustrated efforts to make government media independent. The top priority of ICSP's Independent Media project and its IREX spinoff was to make the Iraqi Media Network (IMN) independent. The Iraqis for Public Broadcasting CSO, created by prominent media and civil society figures, drafted a proposed media law with ICSP help. The momentum toward an Iraqi version of the BBC or America's PBS ran into political headwinds, however, as the government sought to use Al Iraqiya and *Al-Sabah* to get its own messages out. The goal of an independent IMN languished.

The constitution "guaranteed" freedom of the press, but no law was passed to enforce it, and old law and CPA orders were still used, unconstitutionally, to control it. Government control actually increased under both the Iraqi and Kurdish governments. Self-serving interpretations of media laws were used to punish media for many stories criticizing government officials. Stories exposing corruption can be dangerous to reporters and newspapers. Direct threats and targeted assassinations have become part of the media's working environment, and some live under constant threat. Many print and electronic journalists have shown great courage, but many media outlets have suppressed their own stories to avoid the possible consequences of running them.

A common tactic has been to sue media organizations over offending stories, sometimes producing dubious decisions against them and at the least making it costly to run stories critical of the government. An editor I know at an independent, well-regarded Kurdistan paper reported in 2010 that there were twenty lawsuits pending against his paper. In 2009 Freedom House's annual press freedom index categorized Iraq's media as "not free."[23] That's pathetic in a country claiming to be a democracy.

Admittedly, some media outlets lacked the journalistic standards RTI and ICSP tried to instill, often printing stories that were biased, irresponsible, or just false, giving government officials an excuse. Political parties, plus ethnic and sectarian organizations, gained a major share of the media business, making the coverage more partisan. In Kurdistan the two dominant parties controlled the consequential media, including the major TV stations. Then three independent newspapers and other new media arose to challenge their dominance and their political corruption but endured frequent harassment and occasional assassinations often attributed to elements of the two major parties.

According to ADF, the National Iraqi News Agency (NINA), jump-started by ICSP in October 2005, was the first independent commercial news organization in Iraq and in the Arab world. This may be a matter of definition. Aswat Al-Iraq (Voices of Iraq), founded as a news cooperative rather than a commercial enterprise, started in November 2004 with support from the United Nations Development Program (UNDP) and the Reuters Foundation, among others. In 2005, however, it moved to Cairo and didn't return until 2007, to Erbil.

On May 1, 2006, NINA started converting from a free service to a subscriber-only service, with some trepidation. How many people getting the free service would pay a fee for it? By the end of 2006, sustainability was still a struggle and remained so. NINA's State Department subsidy eventually stopped around the same time Aswat Al-Iraq moved to become subscriber financed. NINA was then eclipsed by Aswat Al-Iraq and its ownership taken over by the government-linked Iraqi Journalists Syndicate, eliminating its independent status and its IREX support.[24]

Over time the IREX project got less State Department money, and the bad security made it hard to hold public training sessions or hire foreign trainers. Matthias Wirzberger returned to Germany at the end of 2007, but IREX continued to train and support Iraqi journalists and also helped advocates for a KRG media law, though the resulting law was less than ideal.

Other foreign media organizations also helped. The independent Al-Mirbad radio station in Basra, serving southern Iraq, was established by the BBC World Trust with major support from Britain's Department for International Development (DFID).[25] There are other success stories too. Certainly, foreign assistance helped the media to raise their standards and make a major contribution to the struggle for a democratic Iraq.

Conceding all the progress, however, the U.S. and British governments spent hundreds of millions of dollars to create an independent media sector in Iraq. By now it's clear that this is at best a long-term project.

The CSO Enabling Law: A Civil Society Success Story

On July 6, 2006, just two weeks after Haider's death, gunmen assassinated Judge Salah Al-Awsi, our committee chairman for the CSO Enabling Law project, as he left his house in western Baghdad with his son, who was badly wounded. Judge Salah was the leader of a judges' CSO, a member of our Baghdad Center advisory committee (and the second killed), and arguably our most valuable volunteer.

The struggle for a CSO enabling law continued long after me and ICSP. A March 2007 government draft law deservedly failed to pass. The United Nations Office for Project Services (UNOPS) and the NGO Coordination Committee in Iraq (NCCI), a large coalition of Iraqi and international NGOs, organized a "Roundtable" meeting with Iraq leaders in March 2008 that produced agreement. The Council of Ministers then broke its agreement by proposing a more restrictive law. Over a year later, in April 2009, at the Woodrow Wilson Center in Washington, Iraq's minister of human rights told me the government was still trying to pass a CSO enabling law.

ICSP's former legal advisors, the International Center for Not-for-Profit Law (ICNL), working for the State Department, issued comments identifying major defects in the new draft. The government was still trying to control CSOs, now called NGOs (nongovernmental organizations). ICNL was still arguing Jean-Sebastien Roy's central point, that NGOs are entitled to freedom of association without government approval or control. It cited the Universal Declaration of Human Rights in 1948; the International Covenant on Civil and Political Rights, signed by Iraq in 1976; and the Arab Charter on Human Rights, in effect since March 2008. ICNL's analysis was again mostly an argument for adopting international best practices.

Meanwhile, the maligned Ministry of State for Civil Society was still there but had been sidelined. An independent though understaffed NGOs Department reporting to the secretary-general of the Council of Ministers now handled registrations.

One set of issues was about restrictions on foreign participation, which endangered NGOs reliant on foreign support. Other issues were about registration, as the law gave no criteria for denial and registration certificates were good for only two years, raising prospects for endless reregistrations conducive to official harassment. Anyone active in an NGO found to violate the law or whose registration was denied would be jailed. This violated the Iraqi constitution and international law by penalizing unregistered NGO activity, exactly what Jean-Sebastien had feared. Other provisions were equally objectionable. The whole purpose of an NGO sector gets lost in such control-oriented thinking.

UNOPS quickly organized another Roundtable in May 2009. USAID weighed in with a statement that the law as written would hinder its work in Iraq.

January 25, 2010. A Law on Nongovernmental Organizations finally passed, almost four years after our ICSP project started! By this time almost everyone still involved had probably forgotten about ICSP's draft law. Still, I recognized many provisions and took pride in our contribution.

Dropping penalties for unregistered NGO activity indirectly eliminated the requirement that all NGOs register. Those seeking potential benefits of government recognition must register and provide organizational info but, for Iraqi NGOs, not including individual names and contact data other than founders and current leaders. I feel personal satisfaction about that, as it was my biggest issue when others were not focused on it. Foreign NGOs must register, however, and identify both Iraqi and expat staff, posing a serious security concern. "The Department may not disclose information to entities other than the concerned governmental bodies," but the strict enforcement procedures needed weren't specified.

The NGOs Department must approve registration applications within thirty days or explain its denial in writing. Existing NGOs had to reregister but would stay registered indefinitely. NGOs may establish branches, inside and outside Iraq, without prior approval. They can't be dissolved, nor have their bank accounts frozen, without a court order. They can merge and organize networks. The law dropped previously proposed bans on affiliation with foreign NGOs and accepting foreign funds without permission, but it limited foreign members to 25 percent.

On balance, however, Iraq now had a meaningful legal framework that NGOs and the government could work with. Kareem Elbayar, ICNL's legal advisor for the Middle East, pointed out that despite its remaining flaws, it was still better than most such laws in the Middle East–North Africa region. This great achievement followed a major struggle in which a large coalition of CSOs, UNOPS, ICNL, and determined parliament members led by Ala Talabani, chair of the Civil Society Organizations Committee (and niece of Iraq's president), finally wore down the government's instinct to control. The persistent UNOPS program manager for Civil Society, Adam Styp-Rekowski, earned praise from others involved.

The law authorized the Council of Ministers' secretary-general to issue implementation "instructions." It was agreed that passage of the law left a need for them, so it (and all NGO registrations) remained on hold several more months until they were worked out.

The NGOs Department isn't the independent agency that ICSP's CSOs wanted, but its authority is limited, and due process is required.

Its decisions can be appealed to the secretary-general and his to the court of appeals. The unpopular Ministry of State for Civil Society is not even mentioned. It became a ministry with no governmental purpose and was eliminated soon after. (Can you see me smiling?)

A positive change of personal interest was that the new law allowed coalitions, including my Legislative Coalition to Fight Corruption in Iraq, to register. A group of AC Coalition members met on February 15, 2011, and decided to register and resume formal operations.

The KRG already had an NGO enabling law, passed in January 2001, but it did not deter abuses against NGOs who dared to suggest there was corruption in Kurdistan. ICSP-affiliated Kurdish NGOs continued work on a new KRG law even as negotiations on the Iraq law dragged on. UNOPS and ICNL helped in the KRG too. Agreement was reached in September 2010, and a bill passed the Kurdish parliament in April 2011, its provisions largely paralleling Iraq's law. By then some ICSP and other CSO reps had been working on the KRG law for five years.

Democracy and the Instinct to Control

The enabling laws were a success story for Iraqi CSOs. They created a broad and expanding coalition, engaged government with determination for five years, and stayed the course until they won. On few other legislative priorities have Iraqi citizen activists sustained that level of performance or had that much impact. This success reinforced my belief in the importance of developing CSO networks and coalitions.

Success was achieved because CSOs, UNOPS, ICNL, the European Union, reform-minded parliament members, and others eventually cornered the politicians into doing the right thing. That it took so much time and so much lobbying to pass a law so obviously needed was a sad commentary on Iraq's elected leaders.

The same pattern played out on the issue of creating an independent High Commission for Human Rights based on the Paris Principles. This was a major priority of CSOs, the Ministry of Human Rights, and the UN, among others. In November 2008 the parliament finally passed the law. Alas, passage far preceded implementation, for political reasons. The Committee of Experts responsible for nominating the commissioners was not fully selected until June

2011, and the commissioners were not approved by the parliament until April 2012—four and a half years after the law passed.

The same instinct to control affected government dealings with anti-corruption agencies and independent media. In those two areas, CSOs and their allies have been less successful when measured by policy outcomes, but they have helped reduce public tolerance for corruption, and the media environment is better for their efforts, despite the setbacks. Many courageous Iraqis are prepared to stay engaged in these struggles, and they deserve continuing international support.

Developments in the three major policy areas described in this chapter highlight the efforts of Iraqi officials at all levels to control others. This instinct to control runs directly contrary to the principle that government employees exist to serve the public interest. Those who challenge this instinct to control often become victims of Iraq's culture of violence.

In the end, the Iraqi government we worked so painstakingly to set up as a functioning democracy became the major obstacle to our most important goals for Iraq and the biggest challenge to the civilian coalition sent there to help. Constitutions and laws can be written based on international best practices and enlightened Western ideas but have to be implemented within the political environments of specific countries. Sometimes, as in Iraq, those ideas encounter organizational and individual behavior that is counterproductive or even destructive.

Whatever the Coalition's failures, so often played up in media and political discourse, the core problems within Iraq's fractured society proved more consequential. This is why media stories analyzing Iraq developments primarily in terms of short-term U.S. and Western interests may miss the point and are often less helpful than the view from the ground up.

15

USAID and Lessons Learned in Iraq

USAID and Its Critics

The United States Agency for International Development was founded during the Kennedy administration in 1961 as the primary U.S. foreign aid agency. It became the lead American agency for international development projects around the world. My two tours of Iraq were a window on how its projects work at ground level.

USAID has accomplished a lot over the years. It has, nevertheless, always had its critics, though some of the flak reflects ideological opposition to foreign aid. That opposition has diminished over time as public awareness of America's global interests has grown, but many Americans still oppose sending money to foreigners when we have so many needs here at home. Others are influenced by critics who argue that a high percentage of foreign assistance is ineffective or just wasted and often goes to nations with corrupt and inept governments. Many conservatives in Congress want to vote USAID out of existence or eliminate much of its funding.

A friendly but tough critique by Thomas Carothers for the Carnegie Endowment for International Peace says that one of USAID's "institutional deficiencies" is "punishing bureaucratization that chokes off innovation and flexibility." He describes the basic USAID operating procedures as "a study in dysfunctional bureaucratization." Among his comments I relate to from experience are the tendencies toward "shifting priorities," often imposed from outside USAID; programs that "do not adapt to rapidly changing circumstances"; "programs that produce 'good numbers' but have little real impact"; or that "end just as important relationships have been solidified and crucial local knowledge gained"; and the importance of "reducing the chronically burdensome reporting requirements that soak up so much of program implementers' time."[1] Amen to all of that.

Another of Carothers's issues is that the required Performance

Management Plans (PMPs) that define the data requirements for evaluating each project are too rigid and "compound the headaches of implementation." They focus on readily quantifiable outputs rather than outcomes. USAID is compelled in this direction by congressional legislation intended to compel accountability for results. The net result is reliance on "simplistic, mechanistic indicators encouraging program implementation that is driven by the imperative of 'meeting the numbers' rather than doing what is necessary to produce meaningful results."[2] Amen again.

A less friendly critic has been William Easterly, a New York University faculty member and former World Bank economist. The heart of Easterly's critique is the belief that foreign aid work is dominated by planners whose top-down antipoverty efforts do little to reduce poverty despite all the goodwill behind them. Effective change is more likely to come from people on the ground searching for solutions to specific problems.

The international development profession is thus divided between "planners" and "searchers." Planners (including USAID, the World Bank, and other development agencies) produce unrealistic plans based on long-distance knowledge and good intentions. Searchers figure out what is actually possible on the ground and make something positive happen, even if it's not exactly what the planners had in mind.[3]

Easterly's views have been criticized by some as excessive, but the distinction between planners and searchers matches my own observations. Whatever the merits of the plans, about which I'm less negative than Easterly, most plans need to be adapted by innovative people working at ground level. Some of what I and others managed to accomplish was as searchers who figured out how to expand the impact of the project. My former Amarah team leader Denny Lane has his own take on this: "Expats in the international development world are divided between lunatics and bureaucrats. Unfortunately, the bureaucrats are winning."

No grand plan will work exactly as intended because no plan can anticipate all contingencies. Plans implemented in conflict-ridden countries such as Iraq are even more unpredictable. At the same time opportunities may develop at ground level to accomplish objectives not in the plan but consistent with its purposes. It follows that contractor personnel and USAID field staff need the flexibility to be searchers.

Some of USAID's problems are inflicted by others, however. Its bureaucratic rigidity stems partly from questionable congressional decisions and the constant political imperative of holding down the noise level on Capitol Hill. There have been unwise but sometimes successful demands to clamp more controls on AID. The inflexibility imposed on contractor personnel in the field also affects AID's own staff.

USAID was downsized over many years to a personnel level less than half of what it had been over thirty years earlier. The Bush administration was strongly criticized for downgrading and marginalizing AID following an expansion of Democracy and Governance work in the Clinton administration. It lost its autonomous status in 2006 and blurred into the State Department bureaucracy, a change former AID directors have said did not work.

The Obama administration came in with plans to reevaluate and revitalize AID as part of a broader foreign policy reorientation. Obama rhetorically upgraded Development to a "third pillar" of national security policy, joining Defense and Diplomacy. Under new administrator Dr. Rajiv Shah, AID initiated a major internal reform program, called USAID Forward. It moved to substantially increase its staffing and budget and made major policy and organizational changes, even as it faced continued Republican skepticism.

Most of AID's changes are at the policy level, but they affect the project level too. With that in mind, I have some nonpartisan suggestions from ground level.

Friendly Suggestions from Ground Level

Working on two USAID projects and interacting with other projects did not make me an expert on AID, but some of my Iraq observations reinforce critiques from people who *are* experts. Here are some specific changes that would make a positive difference.

1. Greater Flexibility and Adaptability

An inherent problem in USAID's system is its inflexibility. Planning documents such as PMPs and related Results Frameworks, devised when the project starts, must then be implemented under real-world conditions not conforming to all their assumptions. That doesn't mean the plan is bad but, rather, that there is no way to ensure predictable results on most international development projects. Conditions in some countries, especially those plagued by violence, may change greatly as the project proceeds. For example, the consultants' evaluation report on ICSP recommended that "USAID modify its Results Framework to better accommodate a civil society program."[4] Too bad someone didn't think of that before.

Flexibility means a willingness to adapt to changing ground-level circumstances. That would sometimes mean changes in the plan. Unfortunately, the more likely field response is to make project activities conform to the original plan, or at least seem to conform, even though some of the plan is overtaken by events. This preserves the plan from midstream changes that might complicate project evaluation but risks reducing the project's impact. AID should be more proactive in working with contractors to revise plans when conditions change on the ground.

2. Evaluating Projects Based on Outcomes

A lot of statistics are thrown around on USAID projects and are usually impressive, at least superficially. Those statistics most often measure outputs. How many training workshops did we conduct? How many people attended? How many grants did we issue?

Contractors succeed by producing numbers to meet AID's planned targets. This often means an excessive devotion to numbers by both the contractor and AID. A project should be evaluated based on progress relative to its mission and goals, not statistical compliance. AID's system needs to answer the "So what" question. Having produced all those outputs, what did we accomplish? What were the outcomes? While *outputs* are usually best explained in numbers, *outcomes* may be nonquantitative but are more important. This distinction is becoming more clearly understood.

Criteria that can be met with numbers are helpful to contractors but, I suspect, much less helpful to AID. They support self-justification more than objective evaluation. In fact, Dr. Shah quickly saw that AID spent far too much time evaluating and reporting on process indicators. It needed a new evaluation system more oriented to outcomes.

One complicating factor I discovered in Baghdad is that outcomes often depend on people outside the project. The parliament has to pass a law. A ministry has to change a policy. We have some control over project outputs but can seldom control government outcomes. However, focusing attention on the desired outcomes at the beginning, though more challenging, would give us a better chance of succeeding at the end.

We should also admit that we don't control all the variables when working in other countries, so some goals just can't be met. It might be politically incorrect to say that, but it would show some integrity. Be willing to say publicly that a facility could not be built as planned because insurgents repeatedly attacked the project site or threatened or kidnapped the personnel or that a local governance project was delayed because the government failed to cooperate as promised. Neither contractors nor AID should accept blame for uncontrollable events.

3. A Revised System for Monitoring and Evaluating Projects

USAID says it wants to improve its capacity as a learning organization. This goal is important, as Iraq's lessons have been learned too slowly. A similar criticism was made of the British government.[5] To be a learning organization, AID needs a more meaningful, more flexible evaluation system from which to learn, which it is working on.

The evaluation of a project can't be much better than the criteria devised for the purpose. AID has a daunting formula. Try to follow this. Projects in Iraq (and other countries) become components of a comprehensive and hierarchical Results Framework—a kind of grand plan as viewed by AID's higher management. For example, RTI's responsibility under the initial Local Governance Program was Strategic Objective (SO) 4.1: Efficient, Transparent, and Accountable Sub-National Government That Consolidates Iraq's Transition to Democracy. It sounds wonderfully optimistic. Within that Strategic Objective we were responsible for achieving four Intermediate Results (IRs), each further divided into four Sub-IRs, each with its own number (4.1.1.1–4.1.4.4). So our work had to be explained, and evaluated, in relation to twenty-one "boxes" (one SO, four IRs, and sixteen Sub-IRs). Other contractors were responsible for the other

Strategic Objectives (4.2, 4.3, and 4.4), all of them together adding up to the grand plan as seen from a wall chart in somebody's Washington office.

Much can be said about this type of system, good and bad. It's a kind of road map for contractors' project planning and evaluation. It's the basis (and quite often the outline) of their project reports. For AID it's an accountability mechanism intended to ensure that contractors perform the work their contract requires.

This system, with all its criteria, seems daunting, but appearances are deceiving. When a system is built on general goal statements like this, almost any activity can be plugged into it somewhere and recorded as a success. I soon observed, however, that actual progress is not well captured by this system. Important accomplishments can be understated; lack of progress can be papered over. Some IRs were vague or otherwise nonspecific or had multiple criteria. If you met two of the criteria last month but missed two others, did you succeed or fail?

That PMP completed before the project should have a large impact on project management, but its purpose gets blurred at ground level. Compliance falls mainly on Monitoring and Evaluation (M&E) staff and the reports manager, not program staff. The PMP becomes primarily a way to structure contractor reports to AID. Program managers produce input for the reports, but most don't have to work with the PMP on an ongoing basis. So, it has less effect on how the project is run, the main purpose, than on how project news is reported, a secondary purpose.

M&E professionals will be horrified at what I just said—but perhaps not surprised. One of their core principles is that they are not just recording results but also maintaining a feedback loop that improves project outcomes. For AID under its revised evaluation policy, there should also be a higher-level feedback loop that tells AID what works or doesn't.

Establishing the Millennium Challenge Corporation to promote democracy and governance in developing nations was one of the Bush administration's best and most successful initiatives. As MCC's mission overlaps with AID's Democracy and Governance mission, AID could construct its M&E system more in line with MCC goals.

This initiative might provide more outcomes-oriented evaluation criteria and further the ever-elusive but important goal of expanding interagency cooperation. Indeed, AID recently decided as part of its reform program to defer to the goals in MCC's compacts with partner countries when AID is working in the same countries.

4. A Less Burdensome Reporting System

One way to improve the evaluation system is to require fewer reports. USAID should build its reporting system around monthly reports or even quarterly reports and forgo the weekly reports (as with ICSP) and even daily reports (as with LGP at first) required on some projects. This change would give contractor staff more time for program priorities. I can cite my own experience. Over many years working for federal contractors on domestic projects, I wrote countless project reports but never more frequently than once a month.

To put it bluntly, a high percentage of reports to AID are a waste of time for both the contractors and AID. The more reports the contractor has to write, and AID has to read, the less opportunity there is to see and evaluate the big picture.

AID should also favor shorter reports. This recommendation is less because some of our news items aren't worth reporting than because I doubt the reports are read all that carefully anyway. Can't someone just be honest and admit this? Having fewer reports would leave a lot of good work without detailed explanation, but charts and other graphics could cover successful ongoing activities that change little from month to month. Quarterly reports could then be used to report progress against specific objectives stated in the previous quarterly report and to set specific objectives for the new quarter, injecting a measure of accountability.

The truth is that reports fill an endless contractor need for self-justification. Bad news is hard to find in most reports. An otherwise favorable USAID inspector general evaluation of RTI's Local Governance Program in 2007 noted that RTI "reported only on successful achievements rather than progress achieved toward specific targets."[6] I think most of us who provided input for RTI's reports thought that was what we were supposed to do.

Most of the fault lies not with the contractors but with AID and

Congress. When projects can be axed at any time, even for insufficient reasons, companies will adopt a defensive posture in their reporting. All accomplishments will get reported. Any unavoidable negative news will be reported with appropriate "spin." AID needs to change the dynamics surrounding its reporting system so as to get more meaningful reports that also facilitate objective evaluation and constructive feedback to the contractor.

5. More Reliable Contracts

Numerous projects have been victimized by shifting priorities in Washington. Some USAID "decisions" are dictated by political decisions higher up. I remember visiting its business development contractor in Baghdad to discuss possible cooperation, only to learn the project was in danger of being terminated. Dedicated people risking their lives to help in Iraq often found their projects discontinued or downsized. How deflating is that? You think you're doing something important for your country, and are risking your life to do it, and then you find out that your government actually doesn't give a shit.

Even with all the money spent on Iraq, Democracy and Governance and other technical assistance programs got only a tiny percentage of it. When new priorities and ideas arose for civilian projects, it was sometimes difficult to get Congress to put up new money, which forced the elimination or downsizing of existing projects in order to fund new projects. The future contributions of the project are then lost, and termination also wipes out much of the progress already made. This wastes taxpayers' money. At ground level such decisions make little sense.

When a project starts, AID should make a commitment and see it through, not just sit back and pass judgment. Projects need time to get traction and establish momentum. Even if a project has problems, supporting the contractor through the problems, even giving the project to someone else if necessary, is better than just dropping it and losing the investment already made. To get more value from its projects, AID needs at times to show more patience and perhaps get the White House and Congress to do the same.

One major recent USAID initiative was to contract more of its work to host-country governments and other organizations and rely less on U.S. organizations. AID's goal was to award 30 percent of its mission funds to host-country institutions by 2015. This responded to the criticism, well understood in host countries, that AID money goes mostly to salaries, transportation, security, and other expat costs, not to host-country beneficiaries. The overall 30 percent goal was not quite met, but the new direction was clearly established.

One big argument for the revised policy is cost. Putting an expat in the field is many times more expensive than hiring a local for the same position, especially with expat security costs included. In a related change, many contractor-managed Iraq projects now hire Iraqis for supervisory and other higher-level positions, and the need for less-expensive security has increased reliance on local hires.

Not surprisingly, international development companies, destined to lose money under this policy, raised issues with it. The goal of giving host countries more "ownership" of development programs is accepted. How to implement that policy without compromising aid effectiveness is the question. One obvious risk is the inexperience of local organizations with U.S. government projects. Another is the difficulty in ensuring that host country partners are not direct or indirect extensions of the political elite (a serious risk in Iraq). A related risk is that the mostly merit-based hiring of U.S. contractors will be replaced by corrupt local hiring practices that favor relatives and friends over professional competence. Conceding the risks, however, this is an important and needed change. Many of the Iraqis we trained can meet this challenge.

Learning the Lessons of Iraq

1. More Focus on Sustainability and Meaningful Transitions

It follows from the "more reliable contracts" suggestion that projects should be evaluated in part based on outcomes related to sustainability. *Sustainability* has become a buzzword, subject to a range of meanings. USAID is working out its own definition, from a Washington perspective. In my ground-level definition, sustainability of development projects is the relative capacity of a project to endure after our role ends—in terms of management and technical capacity as well as funding. A sustainability strategy should increase the capacity of the host-nation government, business, and/or civil society organization to manage and fund the project on its own. Just turning it over to the locals is not a sustainability strategy; it's a bailout strategy.

We all want development projects to have immediate impact, but the larger impact should be longer term. Therefore, an adequate transition period with specific sustainability goals should be part of the original plan, but with flexibility, so they can be finalized during the project based on an on-the-ground assessment. AID should be more open to transition funding for organizations managing the sustained project. This approach would be consistent with its new localization policy. When the transition phase runs out, it hopefully leaves a self-sustaining, effective organization that can continue the project indefinitely or bring it to a successful conclusion. Terminating projects before the transition takes place eliminates the possibility of a sustained project altogether.

I hear someone saying that this "sustained project" phase would require more money for some projects. I concede that, but lower labor costs from transitioning to local staff would offset much or all of that cost. AID now says its global development policy works from a more long-term orientation. If it's serious about that, it should be more willing to walk the talk.

2. A Clearer Strategy for Civil Society Projects

Sustainability is as important for civil society projects as for government capacity-building projects. USAID decisions in Iraq have not always reflected that priority. The IBTCI evaluation report on ICSP postulated a kind of philosophical issue reflected in all civil society projects: "On the one hand, there is an argument that civil society has an inherent value and that a legitimate USAID objective is to establish and nurture the civil society sector for its own sake. The alternative view is that civil society only has value to the extent that the activities of NGOs or CSOs accomplish desirable results. The first perspective constitutes the philosophy that provided the basis for the original contract with ADF. The second perspective constitutes the philosophy that tends to emerge over time as USAID searches for concrete outcomes and results."[7]

The either/or analysis is wrong. The civil society sector gets its value from what it contributes, not from its mere existence. It has *both* inherent value from its collective contributions to a democratic system *and* practical value from the public service work of individual CSOs and CSO coalitions. USAID planning for civil society projects should reflect this dual perspective in writing.

Building the capacity of the civil society sector is the first priority. The method used by ADF works, has also been used by others, and is a worthwhile model. Grants to CSOs yield practical results and also increase their capacity. A simplified version of ADF's Organizational Assessment Tool could evaluate individual CSOs that benefit from the capacity building. Most important, AID strategy should prioritize the creation of CSO networks and coalitions, so as to make CSOs collectively more effective.

AID strategy should also prioritize transitioning CSOs to volunteer organizations. This links directly to sustainability.

The bottom line for AID civil society strategy is that projects in any country should (1) continue to support the entire CSO sector; (2) network large numbers of CSOs for impact at all government levels, mainly as volunteer organizations; and (3) use high-performing CSOs to implement grants and sustain projects after the expats leave, perhaps with AID transition funding. AID could also help productive CSOs get funding from other donors. This conclusion gains urgency from reports that most of our CSOs in Iraq became inactive after ICSP ended. Dropping ICSP and de-emphasizing civil society work caused much of the problem.

AID-funded Community Action Groups and other groups have done good work, as have national organizations established by Iraqis. The Community Action Groups I later met in Kurdistan generated many valuable small projects, working with local governments. Unfortunately, AID abandoned the Kurdish Community Action Groups in 2009—not a positive example of a sustainability strategy.

I believe a lot of Iraqi CSOs and CSO members are still ready to make a difference. The dogged multiyear campaign for the CSO enabling law was a great example of their potential. I feel cautiously optimistic about Iraq's civil society, but AID can do more to support it.

3. Empowering the Lawyers

The U.S. Constitution is iconic, but much of its international stature is owed to decisions by federal courts, especially the Supreme Court.

The Court's definitive interpretations of the Constitution become "the law of the land," setting precedents for later court decisions.

We arranged for Iraq to have a Supreme Court too, but its impact on constitutional law will be disappointing compared to the U.S. Supreme Court unless its potential role in interpreting the constitution is strengthened. This applies to a range of potential constitutional issues, like the women's rights conflict over Article 14 and Article 39 and the 1959 Code of Personal Status.

Iraq has a civil law legal system, not a common law system like the United States and United Kingdom. For complex reasons better understood by lawyers, the principle that court decisions establish legal precedents for later decisions does not apply to the same extent. Moreover, there are unsurprising reports that women are failing to understand and use their new constitutional rights and still endure discrimination and inequality based on old law and sharia law.

This is why my proposed National Organization of CSO Lawyers was important and is still a good idea. There should also be other organizations prepared to go to court and stand up for the full meaning of the Iraq constitution. This role should include filing what lawyers call "friend of the court briefs," by which third parties, with the court's permission, can express legal opinions on civil cases before the court as to the legal rationale by which a case should be decided. To make this system work, the Iraqi organizations would need experienced lawyers, and they as well as judges would benefit from USAID or other training.

4. A Revised Anti-Corruption Strategy

Directly or indirectly, most of USAID's projects must deal with corruption. The USAID *Anticorruption Strategy* manual concedes the agency is still learning how to do that. It says anti-corruption is a relatively new field that has yet to show it can "achieve tangible impacts." Given the limited results on the enforcement side of its anti-corruption and rule-of-law projects in Iraq, its modesty is justified. I feel the same about my own efforts.

Anti-Corruption CSOs and the National Legislative Coalition to Fight Corruption in Iraq merit a continuing role in that revised strategy. The USAID manual recognizes civil society as a potential resource but needs a separate section on how to empower and work with CSOs to fight corruption. Topics should include how to create CSO networks and coalitions for greater impact, including at the national level; how they can interact with enforcement agencies and the judicial system, consistent with U.S. law and personal safety; how to help CSOs coordinate with or create independent media to increase the impact of their advocacy; and how to create an enabling environment for CSOs through constitutional, legislative, and administrative provisions.

5. Better Interagency Coordination

My own limited observations aside, the inadequacy of interagency coordination was a recurring theme of Stuart Bowen, Special Inspector General for Iraq Reconstruction (SIGIR). The enormous waste of taxpayers' money he documented reflects uncontrollable factors but also avoidable management deficiencies. Coordination between USAID and both State and Defense was poor. Or to quote State's Peter Van Buren, "We did not play well together." At ground level a few thousand projects were ongoing at different times but with no integrated tracking system.[8]

Bowen attributes the myriad Iraq reconstruction management problems to the lack of any agency with coordinating responsibility for reconstruction in conflict-ridden countries like Iraq. He proposed to Congress that they establish one. Whether or not they do that, there is a clear need for a coordinating structure reporting directly to the president that can be implemented at the start of our involvement in such countries. This structure should enforce coordination among State, Defense, USAID, and other agencies; coordination of criminal justice and anti-corruption programs; integration of key contract managers with government field units sharing the same mission; and coordination among USAID and other contractors, among other possibilities.

Some Personal Lessons to Share

Paving the Road to Hell

The old saying "The road to hell is paved with good intentions" certainly applies to the United States in Iraq. The SIGIR office's "progress" reports demonstrated the huge gap between good intentions and actual results. Many projects were finished successfully; many others, especially infrastructure projects, became impossible to finish because of bad security conditions. Corruption by Iraqis (and a few Americans) was a major problem.

That rumor I heard in 2006 about building a Basra children's hospital supported by Laura Bush turned out to be true, but it was almost another casualty of the bad security. It was started and half-completed by Bechtel Corporation, the huge U.S. engineering and construction firm, but was later transferred to the Army Corps of Engineers due to security problems. After multiple delays, and with additional funds from international sources, the 101-bed hospital finally opened in October 2010, well after Mrs. Bush was back in Texas.

Projects undertaken in war zones have inherently unpredictable outcomes. That doesn't make failure inevitable, but even with great intentions and great talent, actual accomplishments often fall short of what the original plan envisioned. One vital intangible asset of dedicated people working in fragile foreign nations is their willingness to keep trying in the face of obstacles and setbacks.

Some expats acquired a different perspective. Individual experiences vary widely, and different people bring different outlooks. One example is Peter Van Buren, a U.S. Foreign Service officer whose Iraq assignment left him negative and cynical about the experience, which he described as a series of mostly ill-conceived, ineffective projects.[9]

It's clear from my story that some of my important innovations were later undone or compromised, due to bad security, unavoidable circumstances, or dubious project management decisions. Nevertheless, I described these ideas in earlier chapters, in the hope that others can make them work, in Iraq or elsewhere. Many other international development professionals have offered compelling ideas that just lacked the necessary time or support when they initiated them.

In Praise of Democratic Management

Some of my insights from Iraq are about project leadership. USAID contract firms could make a big contribution to improving project leadership at the field level. Many would say they already follow the principles below; some could say so honestly. Many who have served on AID projects, in multiple organizations, would say differently.

First, commit to a *written democratic management policy* and hire project leaders who believe in it. Communicate the policy to managers at all levels of the project, to other expats, and to local hires. Hire project leaders who are good with other people and show respect to their staff, including local staff. At all costs, avoid hiring top-down managers who rely heavily on giving orders or on bureaucratic-minded rules to enforce their will. Dedicated professionals holding at-will jobs on foreign projects far from company headquarters usually have no practical recourse against such people.

Second, make it a priority to *minimize stress* on expat and local staff. In a place like Iraq there is already enough stress. Make a corporate commitment to keep overseas staff informed of developments affecting the project and give them a headquarters contact number they are welcome to call. Staff working abroad in strange places already feel somewhat isolated and may feel alienated if they hear through the grapevine what they should have heard from the company. Occasional group get-togethers also help ease the stress.

Third, hire project and program managers willing to give local staff a role in making decisions. This means *delegating some decision-making authority*, holding meetings to get input on needed decisions, and seeking group consensus. Part of capacity building is raising people's confidence that they can be effective managers. My principles of democratic management include: (1) better a mentor than a boss; (2) better to delegate than to control; (3) better our decisions than my decisions; and (4) better to earn respect than demand compliance. Applying these principles generated positive reactions, improved leadership capabilities, and furthered people's careers, so I feel deeply about this.

Insights for International Development Counterparts

Some lessons learned about international development directly affect the people who work in this field or aspire to it. I wish someone had imparted some of the following wisdom before I started.

With reports of your work sifted through so many levels of company and government managers, its impact will seldom be fully appreciated by higher-ups, no matter how well (or badly) you do your job. If you crave recognition, you are in the wrong business.

As for appreciation from the natives, remember that in violent places like Iraq, some of the people you are trying to help would rather kill you.

Speaking for myself and many others, when people are killing each other every day all around you, the politically correct term *post-conflict country* is "bull."

Relationships with colleagues are extremely important when you live and work in a confined space. You are in this together. It's like being the visiting team in a hostile arena in which some of the fans have guns.

Internal project management is absolutely critical to your work, and having the right (or wrong) people in leadership positions can make (or break) the project.

A good international development project should be increasingly effective over time. You have to keep learning and adjusting so as to keep the momentum going. If you feel at any time that you now have everything figured out, it's time to go home.

Believe in your own creativity, even if your colleagues think you are slightly crazy or way too idealistic. Remember the famous lyrics from *Man of La Mancha*: "And the world will be better for this / That one man, scorned and covered with scars / Still strove with his last ounce of courage / To reach the unreachable stars." To maintain perspective, remember that the hero of that story was certifiably "nuts."

It helps if you can keep your perspective in the face of the inevitable unexpected obstacles. The frustrations experienced with USAID projects and Iraq did not make me a cynic about either.

No matter how good your work or your project, your success is not assured. You don't control enough variables to ensure the outcomes.

Don't expect to have job security in international development work. Some achieve this; most don't. Projects come and go; so do talented and dedicated people like you.

Don't forget whose country it is. Our host-country employees own it. We are visitors with good intentions.

The heroes of any good project in Iraq or other dangerous countries are not the expats, whatever our accomplishments, but the local staff who risk their lives to come to work every day and go home at night and who have to survive in the country after we're gone. This point is especially poignant if one or more of your staff members die in support of your project.

The Unpredictable Future of USAID

Honesty requires the concession that some development initiatives in Iraq didn't work. A substantial percentage of the tens of billions expended there did not buy the intended outcomes. Even official sources concede that much of the money was wasted—$8 billion, according to the Special Inspector General for Iraq Reconstruction—and many more billions could have been spent more effectively. To quote the Special IG, "Some of these initiatives succeeded but . . . many did not."[10]

I sympathize with taxpayers who are aware of this and don't like it. But let's face up to the realities on the ground. Iraq's security was inadequate to poor, became nearly hopeless, improved somewhat, and in 2014 dissolved when faced by the ISIS challenge. USAID can't just make progress happen. Our military can't do that either.

Most of the money wasted was on physical infrastructure projects. Typical Democracy and Governance projects, including civil society projects, cost very little in relation to the overall Iraq budget and did not have to build structures that could be attacked by insurgents or mismanaged by the Iraqi or U.S. government. Governance programs can't be fully evaluated in dollars. The Iraq IG conceded that "it was hard to measure the impact of programs that sought to instill an understanding of, and allegiance to, the principles of participatory democracy."[11]

Sometimes, however, even those projects can be undone altogether or seriously undermined. Here is my partial list of the ways this can happen.

One category of explanations is *bad security*, including ongoing violence and threats in the project area; getting run out of town by an armed uprising; and assassinations of project staff and other personal tragedies. I experienced all of those.

Other bad scenarios reflect *host-country failures*, including endemic corruption that impedes project effectiveness; politicians blocking progress for self-serving reasons; lack of political will; plus incompetence and bad supervisory practices. I saw all of these, in Baghdad and/or later in Erbil.

Some projects are undermined by *internal problems*, including corporate-level mistakes or communications problems as well as field-level leadership failures. I saw those happen too, and heard about others.

Finally, there are *U.S. government decisions*, including AID dropping the projects; competing priorities set at higher government levels; project funding that runs out; and failure of Congress to appropriate money needed to continue. I observed all of those too.

Others who served on Iraq projects could add to this list. A lot can go wrong in international development work.

To put these issues in perspective, however, USAID has managed a lot of successful projects in spite of bad security; my Maysan Democracy Team succeeded in spite of the Sadrist uprising; anti-corruption advocates had success in many places in spite of government corruption; the enabling law project eventually won in spite of heavy political opposition; many projects have had excellent leadership in spite of difficult and dangerous conditions; and countless Iraqi staff and many expats did things that were truly brave.

One of the enduring myths among American citizens is that their government spends a large percentage of its budget on foreign countries. It follows to many that we should stop doing that, or do a lot less of it, and spend the money to help people here at home. The belief in this myth crosses party and ideological lines. A related popular myth is that the United States is doing this largely on its own and that other countries don't help much. Beyond emergency humanitarian aid, therefore, foreign assistance is hard to sell to voters.

Effective policies can't be built on myths (conceding that political campaigns sometimes can). Reality is that we *don't* spend that much of our money on foreign assistance—less than 1 percent actually. Reality is that other advanced countries *do* make important contributions, as do the World Bank, International Monetary Fund, UN agencies, the European Union, and other international organizations, and that the United States is part of a much larger effort to make the world safer and more livable.

Moreover, because we live in an increasingly interconnected global community in which no country is entirely irrelevant to our national interest, the purposes of our foreign assistance are not just altruistic. USAID projects support military strategy in conflict countries, such as Iraq, by helping to stabilize communities and develop the capacity for democratic governance and economic development. In many other countries they generate hope and progress and thereby help avoid armed conflict.

Unfortunately, some members of Congress have their own political issues with USAID and its mission. This threatens the consistency of effort needed for effective international development programs because AID budgets and staffing can rise and fall depending on which party controls the presidency and/or the Congress. Reality is that aid serves public purposes that are compatible with both conservative and liberal perspectives. Reality is that an untold number of people are alive today, or live in more tolerable conditions, because of our help.

I mention all this because AID does not control its own destiny. As it is not a separate agency, it cannot control its own budget, nor can it speak to the public with its own voice. Because its direct benefits go outside the country, it has no large or otherwise well-entrenched U.S. constituency to support its work, making it an easy political target. It has only limited ability to influence what Congress does to it. Presidents may advance its mission or undermine it.

Whatever its faults, USAID has done a lot of good. Its ongoing reform program is well considered and should result in better, more cost-effective projects. My own suggestions from ground level are compatible with most changes being implemented. However, the continuing absence of bipartisan consensus on foreign assistance and USAID is worrisome. AID needs a better and more trusting relationship with Congress to be fully effective in promoting American interests around the world.

III

Kurdistan from the Inside

MAP 5. Iraqi Kurdistan. The highlighted area includes the three Kurdish governorates plus adjoining Kurdish areas in northern Ninewa and northern Diyala administered by the Kurdistan Regional Government since 1991. The boundaries between Iraqi Kurdistan and northern Iraq are imprecise and subject to conflicting interpretations.

16

The Kurds—Red, White, and Blue and Shades of Gray

Life in a Different World

When I arrived home from Baghdad as 2006 ended, the struggle for Iraq was not going well, militarily or in American public opinion. The Democrats had just gained a majority in Congress and were demanding an end to the war. New Senate majority leader Harry Reid declared the war lost. President George W. Bush, in surely his most important decision as president, confounded his critics by instead *adding* over 20,000 troops and more civilians.

While Gen. David Petraeus and his team restored a semblance of order through this "surge" strategy, aided by U.S.-funded tribal militias, I found a perfectly timed opportunity to return. On July 30, 2007, an international development website advertised for seven senior advisors for one-year contracts with the Ministry of Municipalities (MOM) in the Kurdistan Regional Government (KRG). The mission was to support institutional reform at the ministry. I was a former city manager with Iraq experience. I was immediately confident I was going back.

The recruiting source was a Maryland consulting group led by consulting engineer Richard Michael of Michael-Moran Associates (MMA), working with Dr. Carole O'Leary, an American University program director and Middle East specialist with connections to the White House and top Kurdish leaders. The interviews and ministry delays took a few months, but in early December 2007 I landed in Erbil.

Going to Kurdistan gave me an unusual distinction among Iraq's international development veterans. I became one of the very few to serve in all three major areas of the country.

As the Christmas holidays approached, I also realized this would be my fourth Christmas in the last five spent in Iraq and my second in Erbil.

MMA's preliminary on-site evaluation, led by Lebanese specialist Faris Sayegh, documented the "functional gap" between ministry practices and international best practices in several areas. The gaps were so wide that even the preliminary evaluation needed 204 pages. The ministry lacked policies in general; patronage hiring and promotions prevented effective human resources policies; employees lacked needed capabilities and training; salaries were extremely low; and hardly anything was automated.

The minister, Nazaneen Muhammad Wusu, a well-qualified engineer but new at managing such a large agency, had no leadership team behind her. There was no deputy minister, and the seven directors general were political appointees of others, not beholden to the minister. She lacked confidence in some, and she complained to me that they had neither a planning perspective nor management ability. MOM's internal communications were hopelessly slow.

The plan called for seven advisors, one for each general directorate. The reality would be no more than four at any one time. I was the second to arrive. As the designated Local Government specialist, I became the advisor to the Directorate of Municipalities, which had 18,000 of the ministry's 30,000 employees. It was officially responsible for coordinating with all the municipalities, where most of its employees were, but its staff emphasized to me that it was mostly powerless. Its crumbling office building across the street would have been condemned in any city I ever managed.

The driving distance from Baghdad straight north to Erbil is about 220 miles (350 kilometers), the same as from Washington DC to New York. Erbil, however, is a different world in the same country.

One dramatic difference between Arab Iraqis and Kurds is their opinion of the United States. While most Arabs who cheered the fall of Saddam showed little or no gratitude to the United States, the Kurds were overwhelmingly grateful.

Indeed, the Kurds' history with America goes much further back; Kurdish leaders have been U.S.-oriented for a long time. They had felt grateful before but had also endured betrayals by U.S. policy makers. After 2003, however, the unforgivable was forgiven. The Kurds' loyalties are "red, white, & blue."

This has led to some happy myths in America about the Kurds. The biggest is that they run a model democracy, in contrast to the much-disparaged Government of Iraq. In fact, the KRG reflected some of the same dysfunctions as the Baghdad government, and the self-serving dominance of the rival Kurdistan Democratic Party (KDP) and Patriotic Union of Kurdistan (PUK) allowed for only limited democratic development. One constant issue, the issue that brought me to Erbil before, was the KRG's endemic corruption.

In total contrast to the stagnant Iraqi cities, Erbil was booming. The influx of new residents was reflected in several major housing developments, a lot of huge construction cranes, and soaring rents and prices. Erbil's population was pushing 1 million. This influx largely reflected the wave of rural villagers seeking a better life. Others moving in included Arab professionals escaping Iraq's violence with their families. The many new multistory buildings included a major high-rise development near the Erbil International Airport; the cramped little airport was about to get a major expansion. Part of historic Christian Ankawa was a construction zone. New malls and many other new businesses sprang up around the city, appealing especially to the growing middle class. A new retail complex opened just up the street from the ministry.

A lot of people wanted in on the boom times, and the rapid commercial development reflected serious investment money—much of it from outside Iraq, especially neighboring Turkey. Many of those new business facades fronted Turkish-owned businesses, many owned by Kurdish Turks, selling many Turkish products. Erbil's new construction was controlled heavily by Turkish companies, importing a lot of Turkish cement and other materials.

Dashti, my former ICSP Anti-Corruption coordinator, was the deputy manager of a new Turkish-owned shopping center I would visit often. It was great to see Dashti again, though he worked such long hours he was hard to reach. I had been a stranger in Baghdad, but in Erbil I had former staff to welcome and help me. There would be other personal reunions, including a few ex-ICSP staff visiting from Baghdad and even Jawaad from Amarah.

MMA was facilitating this project but not managing it. The project was arranged through Prime Minister Nechirvan Barzani, but his office didn't supervise it. The ministry didn't supervise it either. My first-arriving colleague, Dr. Ed Crane, was designated as the minister's advisor but not as project manager.

Ed was an engaging colleague who had been the mayor of Geneva, Illinois, in the 1980s, then transitioned into a long international career, partly from his public service commitments as a Lutheran layman. Ed was trying to figure out how the ministry worked but encountering too many unanswered questions—and an ominous problem: a minister always too busy to talk and answer his questions, though her office was just down the hall. He routed numerous meeting and information requests through a designated assistant, getting little response.

Ann Mirani, assigned to the project by the prime minister, gradually assumed a critical role as unofficial facilitator and team advisor. Ann was a dynamic Canadian woman long married to a Kurdish businessman. They had moved back to Kurdistan in the early 1990s, initially to his rural village, where, according to Ann, the natives didn't know what to make of that independent-minded crazy woman Omar had married. Ann knew Nazaneen and lived in her neighborhood, but even she would find it hard to focus the minister's attention on the project.

In February MMA hired Rob Katzensohn, a consultant from Colorado but living in the Netherlands, as advisor to the Directorate of Urban Planning. He provided expert technology skills and a steady stream of comical observations. In June, Delair Kittani, a solid accounting specialist from Ontario, Canada, arrived to help upgrade the finance function. Dr. Loay Froukh, a civil engineer and water specialist from Jordan with experience in several countries, arrived as advisor to the Directorate of Water and Sewage, located behind the ministry's main building. Loay was in my RTI training group in North Carolina five years earlier, showing again that international development can be a small world after all.

My minister-designated English-speaking ministry liaison at the Directorate of Municipalities was Luqman Goran, a military veteran originally from Baghdad.

Although the minister and Luqman spoke good English, as did some other staff, I needed an interpreter and translator to communicate with the others. MMA's talented interpreter, Wirya Hadad, was leaving for a bigger job. I hired Amanj Hassen, a recent college graduate and a similarly charming personality. He and Luqman were destined to be my companions on some fascinating adventures.

MMA's other MOM project was developing a Government Information Systems (GIS) capability. Its lead consultant was Wine Langeraar, a veteran Dutchman from Indonesia and one of international development's most delightful personalities. He was getting little help, however, at the ministry's fledgling GIS office, whose previous department head had resigned over the lack of ministry support.

Our Erbil home was the Hawler Plaza, *Hawler* (pronounced "howlare") being another name for Erbil. It was a modern, modestly impressive edifice with a good, if predictable, restaurant and good room service. It housed numerous foreign guests on business and government assignments. After a while I managed to buy satellite TV service from a local entrepreneur, the better to get the BBC News and Premier League games from Great Britain.

The ministry building, about a mile up the same busy commercial strip, wouldn't win any architectural awards but was a pleasant enough spot with a landscaped front yard. It was just past the locally prestigious "Sheraton" hotel, which was not a Sheraton at all but was a go-to place for dinner, socializing, and business meetings. The Chwar Chra Hotel, a little closer to the ministry, had hosted a major prewar conference of Iraqi leaders and U.S. officials but was by comparison a modest spot, despite its shiny, ornate restaurant decor.

Our rides from the ministry back to the hotel passed by an odd water feature on one corner from which streams of water were shooting at each other from three large balls. Ed quickly dubbed it "The Pissing Contest."

Two Erbil features especially caught my attention—one good, one bad. The short drive to the ministry went under one of its beautiful overpasses. In the United States few overpasses are aesthetic assets. In Erbil they are painted, typically in two nicely contrasting colors even on the underside, down to the street below—and the colors differ from one overpass to the next, creating variety.

However, the city had installed a local version of speed bumps along major roads, which seemed to invite rear-end collisions as drivers hit the brakes, especially as the bumps were less visible at night. Somehow the natives had adjusted to this.

Erbil's drivers were a story unto themselves, many with driving habits that get ticketed in America. One tactic observable at stoplight intersections was the late-arriving driver pulling up in the far right lane on a three- or four-lane road, then cutting in, maybe even cutting off two or three lanes of drivers to make a left turn. Somehow this road trick was considered normal. So was straddling the white lines. I was reminded of the bad driving habits I saw in southern Iraq. Unlike my other home cities in Iraq, I was free to drive in Erbil, but I didn't dare.

Kurds are predominantly Muslim but far less strict in their observance than most other Iraqis. Most are Sunnis, but about 10 percent are Shia, mostly Fayli Kurds living along the Iran border across from other Faylis. They were persecuted cruelly and deported by the thousands under Saddam during the Iran-Iraq War. A small but prominent Christian minority, concentrated in Dahuk and western Erbil Provinces and across the border in northern Ninewa, has a long history in Iraq that predates the Muslims. Most are ethnic Assyrians, predominantly Chaldean Catholics loyal to Rome, the largest concentration being those religious heirs of Saint Thomas the Apostle living in Ankawa. Many other Catholic Assyrians are in the Assyrian Church of the East; other Christians are in small Assyrian or Syrian denominations. The likewise important Yazidi minority is prominent in Dahuk and northwestern Ninewa. Their old monotheistic faith is a unique synthesis of different religious traditions.

The overall impression on the street, particularly in Erbil, is of a modern-oriented, secular population. Western clothes predominate. Few women wear Islamic dress. The traditional male outfit, seen mostly on older men, is described as "baggy trousers gathered at the waist with a wide cummerbund."[1] It has sentimental appeal in Kurdistan, but I suspect it will never be a style statement anywhere else.

An early subject of team discussion was security. We didn't have any. The hotel had external security. The ministry had only light security. At first it sent an unarmed driver to pick us up each morning, but I often walked back to the hotel without concern. Much later the team was assigned a car to share, though Amanj picked me up most mornings and often drove me home.

So, we were amazed to see U.S. organizations applying Baghdad security rules to Erbil at Baghdad-level costs. Some lived behind heavy perimeter security in Ankawa, near ICSP's former Erbil office. If we traveled there, we drove ourselves, but when someone from the U.S. complex there traveled to the ministry, regulations required the usual personal security detail convoy, and armed PSDs then positioned themselves inside and outside the ministry. This is how I ran into Mark Hutton, a PSD from my Amarah days, still doing his thing and making big bucks in Iraq.

The excessive security didn't bother me. An earlier official visit by a USAID team to a Suleimaniya university campus was ruined, however, by the goon squad behavior of its high-profile PSD team, later exposed in a book by an eyewitness.[2]

Kurdistan did have occasional bad incidents. A truck bomb outside the Interior ministry seven months earlier caused many deaths and injuries. Dangerous Mosul was just fifty miles (eighty kilometers) down a dangerous road that had seen more than a few fatalities. The Ansar Al-Islam (Partisans of Islam) terrorists still operated from a Suleimaniya mountain area near Iran. No one would forget its two suicide bombings on February 1, 2004, which killed 105 people at official KDP and PUK receptions on the Eid Al-Adha holiday, including KDP deputy prime minister Sami Abd Al-Rahman and his son.[3] Ann often mentioned Sami fondly. Ansar members had also assassinated parliament speaker Franso Hariri in February 2001. The large stadium directly across from Hawler Plaza had been renamed for him. Security was a big concern to the minister; she had been targeted before. To her, even walking out of the building was a potential risk.

As days went by, however, we felt safe in our daily routines and gradually stopped worrying about our security. Foreign expats in Erbil had not been targeted by terrorists. I took many exercise walks within a one-mile radius of the hotel, went shopping occasionally, and frequented neighborhood stores for my munchies and soda. Erbil became my new and welcoming hometown.

Dueling Organization Charts

Someone decided we would have the title "Subject Matter Expert." It seemed pretentious, as there was much I did not know about the KRG. Carole O'Leary assured me, however, that if I could sort out how its confusing government structure actually works, I would be among the few and would deserve the title.

The Ministry of Municipalities mission mirrored that of the Iraq Ministry of Municipalities and Public Works. Unlike the rest of Iraq, however, the KRG actually has municipalities—about 175 at that moment, from major cities to little towns. They go back to 2000 in Suleimaniya Province and 2001 in Dahuk and Erbil. Even more amazing, their governments were elected—both council members and the municipal presidents, essentially the city managers.

The government structure is two systems in one. Picture two organization charts side by side. The Government of Iraq structure still applies. Each province has an elected provincial council and a governor appointed at least nominally by the council. The local level includes district (*qada*) managers chosen by the governor, called "mayors," and often subdistrict (*nahiya*) managers. To expats, having mayors who were neither elected nor municipal officials was inherently confusing.

Beside the Iraq structure, insert the KRG structure: a president, a Kurdistan National Assembly, a prime minister, too many ministries (but fewer than Baghdad), and at the bottom of the totem pole all those municipalities reporting to the minister. Rural villages, mostly outside the municipal structure, are under the district mayors and subdistrict managers.

This dual structure puts two local government authorities in the same space. Not surprisingly, it has built-in conflicts. RTI's regional manager gave Ed and me an LGP document describing its two sides as "disconnected."

Unfortunately, the real power was not in any of the boxes on that dual organization chart but with the KDP and PUK. You might be surprised to learn that these two major parties have organizations modeled after the Communist Party of the Soviet Union, each headed by a politburo. It's a dubious heritage for a supposedly democratic government—especially as the USSR has been dead for years.

In the first provincial elections in January 2005, the KDP and PUK ensured total party control of the Kurdistan National Assembly by agreeing to run as one slate and divide the seats between them. "It was as if the Democratic and Republican parties agreed to run on a single ticket and divide Congress on the basis of some deal they had struck between themselves."[4]

The parties also positioned themselves above the government and controlled all high appointments—including the prime minister; all cabinet ministers, deputy ministers, directors general, and advisors; and even governors and parliamentary candidates—plus judges and other court officials, university presidents and other high academic officers. Their reach extended even to most lower-level jobs in the ministries. Professional advancement typically required membership in the KDP or PUK. The two party leaders made most top-level decisions.

Those leaders, Masoud Barzani and Jalal Talabani, had dominant roles. One was president of the KRG and the other president of Iraq, but in Kurdistan their party leader roles were more important. Talabani had been PUK's secretary-general since cofounding it in 1975; Barzani had led KDP since 1979. Other family members held major government or party offices. As the politburos are composed largely of former *peshmerga* freedom fighters, the parties cultivate patriotic self-images that tap into people's Kurdish patriotism. Both have extremely large memberships.

There is a Council of Ministers, but it seemed more like a control mechanism for the two parties than a forum for cabinet coordination. The Council of Ministers, in turn, exercised powers that should belong to the parliament. The net result was a government weak in all three branches and at all levels. One implication for Municipalities was that even if the minister felt an important management decision was needed, she might lack the authority to implement it.

The two parties' control of the political system has been leveraged to control much of the economy too. Each commands a large stake in the business sectors of their respective territories. Talabani and Barzani controlled business empires, were millionaires countless times over, and had family members with paramount roles in important commercial sectors. High-level "opportunities" were embraced by party members and others able to get in on the action. To do business in the KRG, one typically needed good connections at the top, and the implication left by conversations about the hush-hush process was that in most cases joint ventures, silent partnerships, or other financial considerations were extracted as part of the deal.[5]

Such a concentration of power lends itself to abuses. My previous Erbil role as the national Anti-Corruption manager was highly relevant experience. The good news on the anti-corruption front was that public antagonism was rising, widening the gap between party self-images and public perceptions.

As I ascended the learning curve, I saw the bigger picture beyond the dueling organization charts. Despite its democratic self-portrait, political power in the KRG is highly *centralized*, its political and governmental institutions are collectively too *hierarchical* to be called democratic, it is highly *personalized* at the top, and it is *corrupted* by both power motives and financial motives. It was also divisively *regionalized*, with one-party KDP control in Erbil and Dahuk and PUK control in Suleimaniya, making it even less democratic. It was conflict ridden in multiple ways.

This confusing and frustrating political system reflected a lot of Kurdish history, much of it still driving current events.

The Burden of History

Bad History

Erbil has been inhabited for about eight thousand years; UNESCO calls it the longest-inhabited place on Earth. A lot of history radiates from its historic citadel, commanding a high point above the traditional-looking and sprawling Erbil Bazaar, where I found you can buy almost anything if you know where to look. The Kurds have a long history for a people who have never been a country. Much of their recent history has been defined by armed struggle—in which the United States has played a recurring role.

The story behind the story. For many years that struggle revolved around Mulla Mustafa Barzani. His campaign for Kurdish statehood started in 1931 and became a lifetime commitment. He often

attacked Iraqi troops, had ever-shifting alliances with different countries, and in 1946 founded the KDP. Soon afterward he escaped to
an eleven-year exile in the USSR that ended in 1961. In later years
he developed ties to the United States that produced encouraging
high points and disastrous low points. When he died in the United
States in 1979, he had not achieved his dream but had become a
Kurdish hero. This legacy helps explain why his picture still hangs in
public buildings in Erbil and why Masoud, one of his sons, became
the first elected president of the KRG and his nephew Nechirvan
Barzani its prime minister.

The young Jalal Talabani, from a high-status family, was a Barzani
supporter, but ideological and policy differences caused tensions
between the tribally oriented Mulla Mustafa and leftist-intellectual
politburo members like Talabani and well-known author and poet
Ibrahim Ahmed, the KDP's secretary-general. In 1964 Barzani created
his own politburo and sent a military force that drove Ahmed's faction
and a few thousand supporters to the Iranian border and then into
a temporary alliance with the government in Baghdad. The Ahmed
group rejoined the KDP later, but the coalition remained unsteady.

Barzani's years in the USSR didn't make him a socialist; in fact he
was anticommunist, despite politically expedient public statements.[6]
Talabani was and is a socialist and married Ibrahim Ahmed's daughter, Hero. This ideological divide spawned a fierce regional rivalry
that has never been overcome. Dahuk and most of Erbil became the
political preserve of the Barzani family and the KDP. Suleimaniya,
plus Talabani's Koya home area in southeastern Erbil next to Suleimaniya, became PUK country.

After 1970 Mulla Mustafa was collaborating with the Shah of Iran
and the Nixon White House against Saddam when the Shah cut a
deal with Saddam and abandoned the Kurds, as did Nixon's national
security advisor, Henry Kissinger. Barzani never quite trusted the
Shah, but he had trusted the Americans. This betrayal left the Kurds
at Saddam's mercy. Barzani and tens of thousands of Kurds fled,
into Iran ironically, as Saddam's army razed over a thousand villages, including Barzani's home village of Barzan, and in 1975 captured and removed thousands of men. The United States refused
even humanitarian assistance to those it had sold out. It was Mulla

Mustafa's final defeat. He soon moved to the United States for cancer treatment and died there four years later.[7]

Talabani and his intellectual colleagues founded the PUK in 1975 after Mulla Mustafa left. Barzani's sons, Masoud and Idris, took over the KDP, but Idris died in 1987 at only forty-two years old. Nechirvan is his son.

Ayatollah Khomeini's 1979 revolution removed the Shah and led quickly to the Iran-Iraq War. Relations between the new-leadership KDP and the new PUK got worse, however. In 1978 two PUK military commanders were ambushed and captured while traveling to Turkey, then executed on orders from the KDP commander, Sami Abd Al-Rahman, the same Sami later killed in the 2004 Erbil bombing. The impact on KDP-PUK relations lasted many years.[8]

Thousands of the Barzani men seized in 1975 were later moved from southern Iraq back north to a camp in Qushtapa, in Erbil Province but outside of Kurdish control. When the KDP helped Iran seize an Iraqi border town in 1983, Saddam retaliated by seizing 8,000 Barzani men from Qushtapa. They were put on parade through Baghdad, then disappeared into mass graves that went undiscovered until after Saddam's fall, when some were found in far southern Iraq and some in the Anbar desert. The apparently clueless U.S. government, afraid Iran might actually win the war, started supporting Saddam just as he began using chemical weapons.[9]

So that is how, starting about 1986, the mutually antagonistic KDP and PUK fought together on the Iranian side while the United States was on Saddam's side. Saddam's retaliatory Anfal campaign began in 1987, near the end of the war, and continued briefly after the war. Even after the chemical attack on Halabja that killed 5,000 people, the United States was still blocking UN Security Council action against Saddam's use of chemical weapons.

Meanwhile, at least 60,000 to 80,000 Kurds died (and Kurds estimate more than twice that many), and 3,737 villages were destroyed and their people displaced.[10] Or it was 4,049, as stated in another account, leaving only 673 villages still standing in all of Iraqi Kurdistan and leaving 1.5 million people displaced or resettled from destroyed villages[11]—over one-third of the entire population of the Kurdish provinces. Saddam achieved his purpose, to gain a military advantage by breaking the Kurdish resistance. As in many earlier struggles, the Kurds ended up on the losing side.

In 1991 the first President Bush encouraged Iraqis to revolt against Saddam after the Gulf War but left them to fight their own battles. The Kurdish revolt started in Rania, in Suleimaniya, and spread rapidly to the three provincial capitals. The Iraqi Army counterattack sent a million people fleeing into Iran and another 250,000 or more to the mountainous Turkish border, where the Turks refused to let them in, though some managed to climb around the Turkish troops. Over 2,000 died, mostly children, unable to survive in plastic tents in the freezing mountain weather. The humanitarian disaster, news reports, and a few American officials courageous enough to oppose Washington's continuing indifference finally moved the U.S. government to do something. It sent military units into northern Dahuk from Turkey to spearhead a short-term mission with Britain and France to feed and support the huge number of Kurds returning to their cities and villages.[12]

The no-fly zone established by the United States, United Kingdom, and France in 1991 was intended to protect the Kurds from Saddam. In October 1991 he surprisingly withdrew the Iraqi government from the Kurdish provinces, a tactic that failed. These two historic events allowed the Kurds to establish de facto self-government and salvaged America's damaged reputation among the Kurds.

Even with this exhilarating reversal of fortune, however, the KDP and PUK still could not get along. There was a successful election for a Kurdish parliament, but the old animosities continued, including a bitter personal rivalry between Masoud Barzani and Talabani.

Interparty relations went out of control in May 1994, when a civil war started that lasted four years! *Peshmerga* militia units and others caught on the wrong side of the dividing line made desperate and sometimes unsuccessful efforts to escape back to their side. Minister Nazaneen—the daughter of a KDP *peshmerga* official—was threatened with rape just a few weeks after giving birth. I was told she had to jump over a wall, take refuge with friendly PUK families, and walk for miles with her baby to reach safety. Hero Talabani, a parliament member, made a desperate escape from Erbil. Tens of thousands were expelled from both territories. There were reports of secret prisons, torture, and executions.

At the ministry people still talked about the bizarre December 1994 PUK siege at the Sheraton against KDP fighters holed up inside, which left bullet holes in the building. In 1995 the elected parliament gave up and went home. The PUK gained the military advantage through help from Iran. Once in Erbil, it wouldn't leave. In August 1996 Barzani did the unthinkable, calling in the dreaded Saddam. His 30,000 to 40,000 troops supported by a few hundred tanks captured or killed several hundred PUK fighters, and en route to Erbil they also killed many of Ahmed Chalabi's small force of Iraqi National Congress soldiers camped in Qushtapa. Barzani's decision had in effect sold them out. The army dispatched the PUK from Erbil, and a KDP follow-up attack on retreating PUK fighters captured Koya and Suleimaniya, sending Talabani and the PUK scurrying toward the Iran border. A PUK counterattack recovered its original territory.[13] I know this account sounds complicated, but the full story is more complicated.

Take Tennessee, for example. A lot of U.S. officials working in Erbil had to bail out fast to avoid Saddam's troops and hightailed it to Turkey. About 7,000 Kurds fleeing toward the Turkish border were rescued, and the U.S. Air Force airlifted about 2,000 of them—to Guam! Most ended up in the continental United States, especially in the already-established Kurdish enclave in Nashville, Tennessee. This helps explain why "Little Kurdistan" in Nashville had more Kurds than any other city or state in America.[14]

In 1997 the PUK set up its own government to rival the KDP's in Erbil. The United States finally brokered a peace agreement in September 1998, but hard feelings remained. As many as 5,000 people had been killed, some after being captured, including an uncounted number who disappeared, many never found and so presumed dead. This absurdist drama was just nine years in the past when I arrived in Erbil.

The 2003 Coalition invasion came through southern Iraq, but the Kurds played an important role that went largely unreported. Ansar Al-Islam's base in the Suly mountains had become an Al-Qaeda outpost for Kurdish jihadists back from Afghanistan and for Al-Qaeda operatives and other militants driven out by the post-9/11 U.S. invasion there. The infamous Jordanian Abu Musab Al-Zarqawi, soon to lead the Sunni insurgency in Central Iraq, was one.[15] In U.S. and British political debates over whether the invasion was justified, antiwar voices argued that Iraq had no connection to Al-Qaeda or 9/11. In fact, the Saddam regime had supported Al-Qaeda leaders at times, and Saddam at least knew of Al-Qaeda's presence in Suly.

The United States knew about the jihadists from the PUK. Ansar had attacked PUK positions around Halabja and massacred some PUK men before being defeated in a PUK counterattack that killed a major Bin Laden operative. Ansar nearly assassinated Barham Salih, a key PUK leader well regarded in the United States, killing five of his bodyguards, and later did assassinate a PUK founding member and several others in a carefully planned setup. It was mortaring PUK outposts from its mountain refuge next to Iran. When the war started, the United States quickly targeted Ansar's base with missiles and bombs, and U.S. Special Forces on the ground helped eager PUK *peshmerga* retake the area. Many of the jihadists killed and captured were foreign fighters.[16]

Ansar still perpetrated the 2004 Erbil bombing and other deadly incidents in Kurdistan and elsewhere in Iraq. In 2007, as the U.S. surge battled the rampant violence in Central Iraq, hundreds of foreign fighters smuggled themselves into Iraq through Ninewa and Kurdistan.

Kumbaya

The history of civil war and dual governments notwithstanding, I arrived in Erbil to a lot of talk about reunification. The two parties had been transitioning toward a unified government, and as of 2006, it was officially declared unified, though *unified* was neither entirely accurate nor synonymous with *coordinated*. Nechirvan Barzani, an experienced leader himself at only forty-one, was the prime minister. Supposedly it would be the PUK's turn to lead the next government.

Rhetoric exceeded reality, however. The two finance ministries were not even unified on paper, though the parties were supposedly working on it. Too many party secrets would have to be shared. No similar effort was under way with the two *peshmerga* militias or the two security agencies (*asayesh*), showing the limits of mutual trust. These were party militias accountable to neither the government nor the public, so their thugs could abuse political opponents and other citizens with impunity, as they sometimes did. A "unified" *peshmerga* ministry would not happen until 2009, a unified force not until 2011, and neither change ensured that loyalties in the ranks would shift from the parties to the ministry. Events in 2014 would eventually overcome some of that problem.

As I settled into the KRG, however, new winds were blowing. A split in the PUK produced the breakaway Gorran (Change) movement, led by Nawshirwan Mustafa, a PUK cofounder and Talabani's longtime deputy. Corruption was his issue. His Wusha media company and two prominent independent newspapers, *Hawlati* and *Awene*, were bringing a lot of long-absent transparency to government issues. Gorran's core supporters included a lot of younger voters. Islamic parties were also gaining support. The KDP and PUK had reformers too.

Just a Few Internal Problems

Detailed study would soon reveal most of the ministry's management problems, but some were self-evident. One big problem was external. The ministry could not make its own decisions on larger issues. The Council of Ministers, the two finance ministries, and especially the controlling ways of the KDP and PUK limited its range of decision making and imposed higher directives that were often more harmful than helpful.

The second was the isolation of the minister, constantly stuck in her office. Tuesdays were allocated entirely to seeing visitors, including ministry officials trying to get or influence some decision, or perhaps to avoid making the decision themselves, and people referred by the prime minister who therefore could not be refused. Although the municipal councils could have been a source of political support, she did not visit them, for security and other reasons.[17]

The lack of inter-Ministry coordination was a third problem. One impetus for our project was a recent cholera outbreak in Suleimaniya Province during which the minister of health publicly blamed the Ministry of Municipalities. Minister Nazaneen, busy trying to deal with the problem, made no public response. So, improving the public relations function was a priority. Working with the head of the PR office, I developed a Media and Public Relations Strategy that would empower the director, expand his responsibilities and staff, and extend his operation to field offices; do a daily review of ministry-related media stories and brief the minister; increase press releases and public appearances and create public service announcements; and establish a field-based comment and complaint system linked to headquarters. The unavoidable weak point of my otherwise excellent proposed policy was that it required a little of the minister's daily time.

Many of MOM's core problems were about human resources policies, or more exactly, the lack thereof. Having relatives on the inside was key to getting a ministry job; so were KDP connections. One of the ruling parties' strategies for keeping public support was handing out government jobs to college grads who needed salaries. The salary was the focus, not the public service opportunity. By one calculation 76 percent of the entire working population was employed by government,[18] turning government employment into a vast jobs program for constituents.

The Council of Ministers sent lists to MOM telling it whom to hire. This interference left it with far more people than it could use or properly supervise but too few of the specialized personnel it really needed. Most ministry managers had no authority to hire on their own, and hardly anyone got fired. As people owed their jobs to the party, not the ministry, loyalties were external. The parties often controlled promotions too, favoring the party connected over those who had earned the promotions.

These dysfunctional policies left little incentive to be a dedicated public servant. Few employees worked full days. Even so, managers within the Directorate of Municipalities told me most employee work hours were wasted anyway for lack of work, and decisions were now made almost entirely at headquarters. Some field personnel got salaries without coming to work. The salaries, tied to the Government of Iraq pay scale, were so low that many employees could not live on them at Kurdistan's higher living costs.

Training was an obvious human resources priority, and MOM had a capable training director. Many managers treated training opportunities as a perk, however, repeatedly selecting their friends and favored employees, then objected when the director asserted final control over selection of trainees, a principle I supported.

USAID's training project, contracted to MSI back in Wael's Palace, did training in the KRG, but it was generic. An Arab American professor I met at the Ministry of Planning explained MSI's impressive five-course standard curriculum. I sensed, however, from my observations in all three major areas of Iraq, that some of the dysfunction in Iraq ministries is beyond Western experience and would be missed by standard training packages. The bigger challenge was to train people out of the bad habits that define Iraqi and Kurdish workplaces.

The instinct to control mattered in the KRG too. It showed in the reluctance of managers to work with others on an equal basis, which also meant reluctance to work across directorate lines to solve shared problems. This was a huge and constant problem.

The automation revolution had not quite arrived at MOM, especially in field offices, though some individuals had excellent computer skills. Most ministry staff lacked access to a computer. Indeed, lack of automation capabilities affected all KRG ministries. A whole information management system needed to be built. Even then, until the KRG had reliable electricity to power the computers, any automation benefit would be limited.

As time went on, the team's attention increasingly focused on Finance and Administration. Many MOM transactions went through this office, putting it at the heart of the administrative dysfunction.

Lack of access to the minister was a continuing frustration. Although we regularly talked to people all over headquarters, a working relationship with the minister would have facilitated a lot of progress. It proved difficult to get one-on-one meetings and impossible to get a group meeting. This problem would persist for the entire project.

After a few months Ed Crane's position as advisor to the minister was dropped, the explanation being that it wasn't helping her. Well, no kidding, if you're ignoring the person trying to help. Ed quickly landed a supervisory position with RTI in Ninewa. I made it my policy thereafter to request the minister's time only when I needed a time-sensitive decision or her personal intervention. I made meeting and other requests directly to her receptionist, bypassing the designated liaison, who I sensed was part of the problem. My occasional meetings were helpful, and the minister was impressive.

17

A Ministry from the Ground Up

Dr. Tom's Road Trip

After a month and a half of generating more questions than answers, I realized the only way to a real understanding of Kurdistan's Ministry of Municipalities was to start at ground level, with the municipalities. That idea launched "Dr. Tom's Road Trip," a series of site visits to all parts of Iraqi Kurdistan to meet with municipal presidents and councils, groups of employees, other officials, and citizen groups. Minister Nazaneen thought it was a great idea, made a few suggestions on places to visit, and promised to back me up with the field offices.

I included the biggest cities but otherwise chose places with a diversity of population sizes, locations, and local character. I developed a long set of survey questions. Luqman handled the advance work. I would bring only Luqman, Amanj, and a ministry driver and no security.

I knew even before starting out that these places lacked delegated authority and local autonomy. However, the municipalities of Kurdistan turned out to be one of the pleasant surprises of my time in Iraq.

This happy road trip would have a few misadventures that exposed ministry flaws. One office not on board was the motor pool, part of Finance and Administration. We needed a car that was clean and worked properly, exactly what a motor pool should provide. Alas, I learned that the vehicle operation was not run like a motor pool and that the minister's support was not always enough. Cars were daily perks, some with drivers, for favored staff. Using one for actual ministry business was almost a new concept. Taking one beyond the local area was a rare event.

Fortunately, I started with places close to Erbil, making the vehicle problem more tolerable at first. But the dirty, cramped car they provided seemed to undermine my image as the minister's representative to municipal governments.

January 23, 2008. Khabat (pop. 15,000) is a river city a half-hour west of Erbil, close to Ninewa, but with no main road.[1] It had a solid manager but too few employees (in a ministry overstaffed), an inadequate budget from the ministry, inadequate water and sewer service, and no indoor recreation facility for kids. It did have an excellent USAID-funded Community Action Group (CAG), doing impressive projects, helped by the Washington-based ACDI/VOCA organization. The manager was an active member, and most members had college degrees.

January 27. Qushtapa (pop. 10,000) is a half-hour south of Erbil. The council chairman, a teacher, began with the story of those 8,000 Barzani men seized by Saddam in 1983 and later executed. The disaster still reverberated twenty-five years later. Qushtapa's CAG had conducted an assessment highlighting current problems, including poor street conditions, a lack of parks, the overcrowded hospital, and teacher shortages.

Our Qushtapa visit also highlighted an amazing story that would be repeated in most other cities. The council was elected in 2001. No elections had been held as scheduled in 2005, or any time since, yet every council member was still serving.

January 28. Bastora (pop. maybe 3,000, too small for official statistics), a short uphill drive heading northeast, was chosen at the minister's suggestion to represent small municipalities. It reflected the same lack of resources as larger places but worse. Driving through town on a rainy afternoon, we saw primary school kids walking home on unpaved muddy streets. Building paved streets in Bastora wouldn't have cost much, but the ministry didn't have the money. That story would be repeated almost everywhere.

January 30. Shaqlawa (pop. 20,000), farther northeast from Bastora, is a vacation area, thanks to its relatively cool summers. The drive there was pleasant, the location picturesque, and the tourist-oriented shops included a large candy store offering a wide selection of wonderful stuff. As a municipality, however, it was failing. The manager didn't call council meetings anymore, and the councilmen agreed with him that meetings would be a waste of time as they had no real authority and no money. The municipal building was a dump, and the manager hadn't even provided enough desks and chairs for the number of employees.

After four day trips in eight days, I got off the road for a week to study the big city.

February 3–6. Erbil (pop. 900,000, growing fast) was one of six self-managed cities, a status the three provincial capitals acquired by law. The council meeting I attended left a solid impression, and sixteen of the seventeen members had college degrees. All that commercial investment in Erbil gave the city a huge advantage over every other city in Iraq. However, MOM's money problems drew an admission from the city manager that the city was as responsive to the governor as to the ministry, as he provided project money and MOM didn't. This scenario would arise in other cities too.

February 7. Erbil #6 (pop. 45,000) is a newer area of Erbil, not part of the central municipality—one of six such cities (numbered 1–6). Its manager, Anwar Rashid, had automated the city operations, making it truly distinctive in a virtually nonautomated ministry. He demonstrated the entire networked system, the computer room, his automated document tracking system, and his small information technology support unit. Replicating his model in other cities seemed like a great idea. His progressive, self-assured management was also impressive, as was the new municipal building. It was our most impressive site visit to date, and we made a return visit later.

February 10. Degala (pop. maybe 3,000) is another small town, located conveniently on the road west to Koya. Luqman had scored a vehicle upgrade—to a pickup truck! It had more legroom but more mechanical problems. Degala was a wide spot in the road that needed more people and some economic development but was too far from Erbil or Koya to benefit much from either.

February 10–11. Koya (pop. 60,000) is a university city at the southeast corner of Erbil Province next to Suleimaniya. One difference from the other Erbil cities stared at me as I entered its new city hall. Instead of Barzani photos hanging from the wall, I was greeted by the smiling face of Mam Jalal. Koya was in Talabani's home area. I had just hit PUK territory. The same smiling face appeared at every municipal building I visited in Suly.

Koya had a fast-moving, impressive operation headed by an upbeat, hard-charging manager and had impressive and helpful staff. It had an effective CAG too, which met with me in an old downtown building, across from a couple of liquor stores.

The manager was kind enough to offer the city's modern guesthouse for our first overnight on the road. Unfortunately, his hospitality triggered the one personal crisis I had managed to avoid so far: It had only Turkish toilets. They were newer and nicer than those in Basra but to me were almost as frightening, and this time I had no polite way to escape. Sparing my readers an embarrassing explanation, let's just say it did not go particularly well and leave it at that.

February 13. Akre (pop. 66,000) is a historic mountain city in Iraq's far north and one of the six self-managed KRG cities. This was our first visit in Dahuk, but Akre was well east of other Dahuk cities, closer to Erbil. Its impressive manager, commuting all the way from Erbil, was implementing creative ideas. The council members elected in 2001 were still serving. The district mayor, a former engineering school dean, was a skillful interagency coordinator adept at planning and implementing building projects helpful to the city. It had a CAG too.

Akre had both a modern outlook and a historic Old Town. From an observation point high above the city, I looked across to a beautiful vista on the steep opposite hillside, where Muslim, Christian, and Jewish communities once lived harmoniously in close proximity. City leaders were proud of that tradition and regretted the loss of their Jewish population. Akre had heritage tourism potential but needed a plan for exploiting it. It was an agricultural center but lacked a direct highway to Erbil that would get its crops to market while still fresh. Despite the scary downward views from its twisting mountain roads, Akre became one of my favorite cities.

February 17–18. Soran (pop. 100,000, growing fast) is in the mountains far northwest of the capital. Ed Crane joined in to help me before leaving MOM, but we had anxieties over the mountain roads, winter weather, and the latest dubious chariot from the motor pool.

Soran is another self-managed city, supposedly. The hospitable manager was a former KDP official still learning on the job, dealing with population growth spurred by returnees from Iran. The city hall was too small. The biggest problem, however, was an interfering and obnoxious district mayor who had everyone frustrated. The guy told me proudly that the city was under his authority (notwithstanding its self-managed status) and that the municipal president worked for him. He put himself in charge of all city projects, borrowing engineers from multiple ministries, which cut city engineers out of the project bonuses by which they normally supplemented their meager incomes. My in-depth meeting with the engineers also highlighted a broader issue—the uncertain relationship between the KRG engineering profession and the ministry.

Soran had arranged our overnight at the mountain resort in nearby Rawandoz, but as our first day ended, a major snowstorm hit. Facing a winding uphill drive, the ministry's malfunctioning car was a total risk. We got to Rawandoz by the kindness of a local staffer, who drove us up the mountain roads through the driving snow and picked us up the next day. The large resort looked modern and impressive, but the almost complete absence of guests signaled that it was a warm-weather business.

Rawandoz was an opening on another emerging KRG (and Iraq) trend—importing cheap foreign labor, maybe too cheap. Two employees greeted us at our guesthouse, one a young Bangladeshi wearing a T-shirt in the middle of a blizzard.

February 18. Mergasor (pop. 2,000) is a rural but progressive town way up north in Barzani country, where the snow resumed as we met with the council. The president, an articulate English-speaking teacher, and all the council members were from the Barzani tribe. Ann Mirani had told me about the accomplishments of the previous Mergasor District mayor in rebuilding the entire community, destroyed by Saddam in 1988, with new roads, schools, water and electricity, a hospital, and several hundred houses. Within Mergasor the municipality, the result is a picturesque but modern rural town. Mergasor was also the center of a multiyear ministry water project. Water was in short supply almost everywhere we went.

Mergasor completed my site visits in Erbil, and I had collected a lot of information from my survey and from my observations and meeting notes. The picture was getting clearer as I met with the minister for answers to some questions. The next step: a one-week tour of cities in Dahuk. That pushed the vehicle issue to crisis status. Luqman fared better this time with the motor pool, but we would have to stop

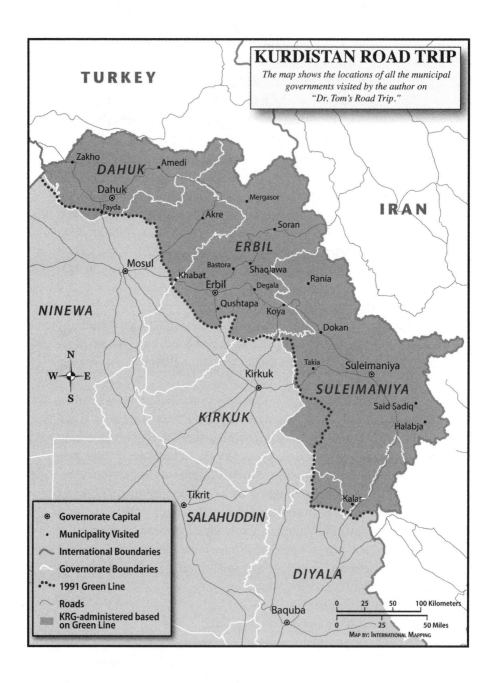

MAP 6. Kurdistan road trip.

a few times so Amanj could get out and push the dangling left head-light back into place.

February 24. First stop: Amedi (pop. 6,000), a small historic city perched on a mountain plateau ten miles or so from the Turkish bor-der. Originating as an Assyrian city around 3000 BC, it has a well-educated population and a sizable Christian minority. It once had a sizable Jewish minority too. It is fully built out, however, and the dis-trict mayor was blocking its expansion to the area below the plateau.

Amedi's leaders were more negative toward the ministry than any others we talked to. They felt that by giving them neither author-ity nor money nor planning assistance, it was setting them up to fail with their constituents. They were trying hard, however, holding two meetings a week and keeping daily office hours, in a municipal build-ing now way too small. My meeting with the impressive, planning-oriented Amedi CAG added to my positive evaluation.

February 25–26. Zakho (pop. 157,000, growing fast), at the KRG's far northwestern corner, is its fourth largest city. With Akre and Soran it was one of the three self-managed cities that were not also provin-cial capitals. Its commercial life as a fast-growing trading center and sometime smuggling hub reflected its role as the KRG's main gate-way to and from Turkey, just across the bridge. Like Amedi, Zakho had an Assyrian Christian tradition and community going back to ancient times, and it had a significant Jewish minority prior to per-secutions in the 1890s.

A highly educated council had stayed intact since 2001, except for one who was elected to higher office. The city manager was an impres-sive returnee from Sweden whose ideas were particularly helpful. The engaging chief engineer was a take-charge Muslim woman with low tolerance for nonsense. Zakho had one of MOM's few new city halls.

We arrived at a dramatic moment. Turkey had just sent troops across the border to pursue guerrillas of the Kurdistan Workers Party (PKK), from Kurdish southeastern Turkey, fighting for independence and the elusive ideal of a Kurdish state encompassing Kurdish areas of Turkey, Iraq, Iran, and Syria. The PKK operated from the *Iraq* side of the border, making occasional deadly raids into Turkey that prompted deadly Turkish counterattacks. The United States had cap-tured PKK leader Abdullah Ocalan in Kenya in 1999 and turned him over to the Turks. Now he was in jail there, but the PKK was still fighting. Many guests in our hotel lobby were glued to the heavy TV news coverage from Turkish stations. A Turkish tank sat on a prominent corner nearby—an oddly placed message from Ankara.

February 27–28. Dahuk (pop. 320,000, growing fast) is the provincial capital and thus another self-managed city. It was seeing a big population influx and strong commercial growth but retained the visual appeal of the surrounding mountains. We had a slightly unsettling meeting with Dahuk's governor, Tamar Ramazan, who seemed to think the Provincial Council worked for him, but we also met with his impressive English-speaking development director, who was funding well-planned projects proposed by municipalities.

Dahuk invited us to ask our questions at a formal city council meeting, and we were greeted by perhaps the most impressive council in the KRG. It had one of the highest percentages of college-educated members and had ensured diversity by including three women, a Christian, and a Yazidi. The manager was impressive too. As the meeting started, I was suddenly staring at a camera—Dahuk had a media department. It also had a parks department, an innovation adopted by only a few cities. No wonder it was the municipality in which the minister had the most confidence.

February 29. Fayda (pop. 15,000) is a Dahuk border city just across from Tel Keif, one of three largely Christian districts that constitute the Nineveh Plain area of Ninewa Province.[2] Were it not for the peculiarities of the Iraq-KRG border, it would be in Tel Keif's Fayda subdistrict on the Ninewa side. Stopping in Fayda on a Friday made it a six-day week in Dahuk, but the city was on our way back to Erbil. There were no government officials to meet, but local CAG members provided lots of information. Kurds and Arabs both had historical roots in Fayda, on both sides of the border. We were assured they got along great and that even most Arabs in the border area would prefer being in the KRG.

Being in Fayda and looking across into Ninewa was a window on an important oddity in the relationship of Iraq and the Kurds. The southern boundaries of the three Kurdish provinces actually don't define the boundary between Iraqi Kurdistan and the rest of Iraq. That boundary was defined in a de facto way by the Iraqi Army in

1991 and became known as the Green Line. Pieces of Kurdistan are south of the Green Line under direct Iraqi control, but parts of Iraq (mostly Kurdish) are north of the Green Line and managed by the KRG as part of Kurdistan. This includes the Akre area, where I visited before, still shown on maps as part of Ninewa but effectively part of Dahuk. It also includes parts of northern Diyala that are effectively part of Suleimaniya. However, this Green Line has never been definitively demarcated, and so the precise boundary is undetermined to this day. (See map 6.) This added to the confusion as the Kurds started maneuvering to permanently acquire parts of Iraq for the KRG, and not just Kurdish areas, raising Iraqi hostility and creating the "disputed territories" issue that now undermines all relationships between the government of Iraq and the KRG.

As we traveled back after dark, one person was unhappy—our driver—who complained with surprising bluntness for a Kurd speaking to an American that this road was dangerous, especially at night! In my enthusiasm about stopping in Fayda, I had neglected to realize that we would be just north of dangerous Mosul. Suddenly it didn't bother me that he was driving a bit too fast.

We took a week off after Dahuk, but the big challenge ahead—two weeks in Suleimaniya, largest of the three provinces—required serious planning. It had to be done in one trip, and Suly was too far and too big for a one-week trip. It was also more sensitive politically, being outside the KDP orbit, and the recent unification of municipalities ministries still left some uncertainty about the ministry's authority there, though the minister assured me there were only slight differences. Needing to understand the political context, which might not emerge fully from official meetings, I requested meetings with non-ministry sources too. For that I had a friend in Suly—Nasreen Rahim, a member of that British Women's Commission group I had met in Ottawa a few years earlier.

The drive west to Suly passed beautiful landscapes trying to burst out in spring green, but Suly also had some scary mountain roads. Fortunately, we finally had a decent car. At Luqman's insistence we had also left the ministry's driver at MOM and left the driving to Luqman, who kept calling himself the "rally driver." Despite my visions of careening around the mountains with the Kurdish Mario Andretti, Luqman proved to be a safe and happy driver. Indeed, through all our travels he, Amanj, and I were cheerful companions enjoying a fun and challenging experience. And why not? We were visiting many important places and people, talking with employees who cared about public service, and receiving great hospitality almost everywhere, sometimes including meals at the best restaurants in town. The minister was already anxious for my report, saying she wanted to move early on changes.

March 9. First stop: Rania (pop. 80,000 and growing), a northern Suleimaniya city surrounded by mountains, which launched the 1991 Kurdish revolution against Saddam. Now it faced uncontrolled growth, and half its population lacked basic services. MOM had managed to give it a new city hall, but no one put the cost of furniture in the budget, so it looked great on the outside but had old furniture and lots of empty room space on the inside.

All the council members, elected in 2000, as elsewhere in Suly, were still in office (except the president), even though Suly didn't pay the small stipend to council members that was paid in Erbil and Dahuk. The able current president was under siege, with the district mayor and PUK working to get rid of him. He was hanging in with some confidence, however, as he perceived that the public supported him and disliked the interfering mayor. It was a sign that public opinion mattered in some places.

Rania's leaders were the first of many in Suly to complain about having to work under two competing municipal directorate offices in Suly city and the still separate PUK Ministry of Finance. These issues and the stipend discrepancy showed that MOM was still not quite unified.

March 10. Next stop: Dokan (pop. 8,000), an attractive resort town at the south end of Lake Dokan, Iraqi Kurdistan's largest lake. Manmade Lake Dokan, built in the 1950s, is a favorite spot of the PUK leadership. That was an issue, however, to the Dokan council members, who complained bitterly about political favoritism toward PUK officials in land distribution on the lakeshore, where Talabani was among the homeowners.

Meanwhile, 80 percent of the residents lacked sewer service, and clean water was lacking in general. Water quality was a problem throughout Suly. Lack of basic services frustrated local leaders' hopes of developing a lake-oriented tourist economy. Downtown Dokan had an attractive, walkable retail area and a lively street scene, and the city manager was impressive.

March 12–13. Suleimaniya, the capital city (pop. 700,000, growing fast), provided a reminder as we arrived that Kurdistan was not entirely safe. A suicide bomber tried to drive into a hotel property. The security guard who bravely stopped him lost his life.

Because of the minister's concern about securing cooperation for all our visits, someone was supposed to call each city in advance to announce our arrival. This did not always happen, and Suly in particular seemed unprepared. No council members were there to meet us, and the president treated me like a CIA agent, so concerned about saying the wrong thing that he conferred with two aides on virtually every question before answering.

However, my nongovernment interviews filled in a lot of information. Nasreen arranged a meeting at the independent weekly newspaper, *Awene* (The Mirror), started in 2006, to meet Schwan Mohammed, the chief editor. He was joined by the founder, Asos Hardi, son of a prominent poet. It took courage for *Awene* to defend its political independence, given the KRG's lawsuit strategy targeting stories and opinion pieces that officials disliked.

Nasreen also arranged a meeting at the Women's Media and Education Center, where she was a member and the mother of prominent PUK leader Barham Salih was the grande dame. Once introduced, she proceeded to challenge my knowledge of Kurdistan and tried to put me on the defensive. It was a Kurdish version of "Who the hell are you?" She then launched into an almost-poetic soliloquy on Kurdistan and its beautiful mountains.

The most bizarre scene was at the Directorate of Municipalities for Suleimaniya. An effective MOM coordinating office headed by an interim director was trying, despite inadequate staffing, to help cities. However, there was a "director general" presiding over a separate office who was completely unnecessary to the operation, had no budget, and borrowed staff from the other office, mostly to keep up appearances. When I met him, he was in constant motion, demonstrating his presumed importance. Mostly, he signed documents, one after the other, about five hundred a day by his estimate. He had developed a signature technique that took only two seconds. The technique was impressive, but the signatures were unnecessary. Everyone in the other office complained to us that his role was meaningless and frustrating and caused delays in their work.

Another bizarre Suly story: As a capital city, Suleimaniya was self-managed, but while Erbil and Dahuk reported to MOM's director general for Erbil and Dahuk, Suly city had never reported to either of the municipalities directorates in Suly, a situation ministry headquarters had missed. As it didn't report to anyone else either, it was an anomaly—a truly independent city in a top-down political system.

The Advisor Team's former interpreter, Wirya Hadad, had told me enthusiastically back in Erbil that the most important person to talk to in Wirya's home province of Suly was Nawshirwan Mustafa, cofounder and longtime deputy leader of the PUK but now founder and leader of the breakaway Gorran (Change List), campaigning against the political corruption. Nasreen arranged a meeting at his house. To avoid making any waves in Erbil, I said nothing about it before I left, told only my two road colleagues about it later, and took only Nasreen to the meeting. Yet I learned more about Kurdish politics from the impressive, straight-talking (and English-speaking) Nawshirwan than from anyone else in the KRG.

I promised to keep meeting secrets confidential, but one was confirmed in print by the independent *Hawlati* newspaper several months later, when a just-resigned PUK politburo member disclosed that the KDP and PUK were each taking $35 million *per month* from the KRG budget, a fact they had always conspired to withhold from the Kurdish parliament and the public. By my arithmetic that's $420 million per year each. Meanwhile, most Kurds still lacked water.

The Ordeal of Halabja

March 16. Halabja (pop. 53,000) is a city of sadness still recovering from tragedy. It was the twentieth anniversary of Saddam's chemical attack on March 16, 1988, which killed over 5,000 people in Halabja. I planned my Suly schedule around this date and was then invited to the official ceremony, held in a very large, crowded hall, and was seated with the official visitors. After the ceremony we visited the solemn cemetery that buried the victims, sharing the moment with relatives visiting grave markers to honor their loved ones.

On our way out of the city, we stopped at the Monument of Halabja Martyrs, built over a three-year period as the focal point of the Halabja remembrance and opened in 2003 to much fanfare. It is imposingly tall, curving inward and upward from its wide base to a sculpture of clasped hands forming the top, and has photos, artifacts, and the 5,000 victims' names in its museum. Few of the day's tourists visited the memorial, however, as it had been largely ruined in a violent demonstration two years earlier, on the 2006 anniversary.

A small group of demonstrators gathered that day in 2006 to protest the city's lack of progress since the chemical attack, blaming it on the KRG's corruption. Some turned the protest into a riot by trashing the inside of the memorial and setting it on fire. Police firing on protesters killed a teenage demonstrator and wounded several others, causing a much bigger riot involving a few thousand people. The Kurdish and international press covering the event multiplied the impact, despite the political leadership's desperate efforts to minimize it.

Walking toward the memorial, I was surprised to hear a few workers hammering on the inside—working even on the anniversary. The structure seemed stable, but after two years the restoration still needed more time.

In the same location, closer to the road, is a pedestal sculpture depicting a tragic and iconic photo seen around the world—a father covering his little son with his body, trying in vain to shield him from the chemical attack.

Unfortunately, in all the excitement of the anniversary, our meeting with the president and council didn't happen. There would, however, be a remarkable follow-up to that.

March 17. Said Sadiq (pop. 60,000), up the road from Halabja, has a narrative all its own. It was unusual among Kurdish cities in not being politically dominated by one party. In the last KRG election, the PUK and Kurdistan Islamic Union (KIU) had won about an equal number of votes. All council members elected in 2000 were still in office, but the president had been replaced in an illegitimate PUK coup. The municipal building was now too small for the growing city.

March 18. Takia (pop. 17,000) is a small city next to Chamchamal on the way to Kirkuk and was one of the few municipalities with a woman manager. Unfortunately, an interfering and apparently male chauvinist mayor had made her job so miserable that she was seeking a transfer to another position. The council members elected in 2000 were all still in office. Takia lacked adequate water service, sewer service, and electricity, just like other cities, and needed schools and a hospital. Its offices occupied an ugly building it didn't even own. A productive CAG trying to help had facilitated well-attended community meetings.

My in-depth meeting with Takia's water engineers revealed a lot about how water service is managed in the KRG. How to move toward a fee-based service that would generate revenue for extending water service to more neighborhoods was my main topic. Whether to let municipalities directly manage Water and Sewer, as Suly cities were doing at the moment, was a decision with so many angles the engineers couldn't agree on the answer.

March 19. Kalar (pop. 130,000, growing fast) is the KRG's southernmost big city and its fifth largest. We circled mountains on two-lane roads to reach the safety of the earth below, sharing the roads with heavily loaded, slow-moving trucks and fuel tankers. A tunnel through the mountains was still under construction. Continuing south past Lake Darbandikhan and Darbandikhan city, we reached distant Kalar, located past the mountains in a flat area known for exceedingly hot temperatures. Here we were near the Diyala border, and the northern Diyala area controlled by the KRG, and just 120 miles (200 kilometers) from Baghdad.

We met with the entire council in one of our best meetings. They had many good questions and a positive interest, as they rarely saw ministry visitors, and the president was impressive. The subminimal pay for low-level jobs made it hard to hire and retain workers and cleaners, drivers, and park employees, and like many cities it had a shortage of vehicles. Kalar was better off in some ways, however; it had a fairly new municipal building, and most city residents had sewer service. Not surprisingly, their three-hour distance from Suly city made coordination difficult, but being too far away to control from Suly or Erbil limited outside interference.

Indeed, Kalar was a leading example of the need to let large cities manage their own affairs. The ministry's bureaucratic process was just too convoluted to be effective there, and the president and council had proved they could make their own decisions. Kalar far exceeded the legally prescribed 75,000 population for a self-managed city and had 420 employees. That bizarre director general of Suly municipalities had never mentioned this possibility to Kalar. He had also vetoed a self-management request from Halabja after the minister agreed to it. I eventually identified several other cities that should be self-managed, based on a minimum population of 50,000 and meeting critical quality of governance criteria.

As we drove the long road back to Suly, Luqman got a call from the minister. Her request to take the time to visit Kalar had paid off. They loved us in Kalar and called her.

We had similarly positive reactions in most cities we visited. This was perhaps an endorsement of my efforts but certainly reflected an appreciation that someone from Erbil had cared enough to come and talk with them and learn their problems and opinions. In a ministry so disconnected, geographically and organizationally, that simple gesture had an impact.

Kalar was supposed to be the last meeting, but to my surprise, Halabja's president and council, unavailable on March 16, called Luqman to set a lunch meeting for March 20, just before our departure for Erbil, at a prestige hotel up the street from ours. The entire council came with the manager, on a holiday, driving fifty miles (eighty kilometers) each way. They turned out to be one of the most impressive councils we met.

Halabja is just seven miles from the Iran border, and Islamic political orientations are strongest in that area. Most members were affiliated with one of two Islamic parties, yet this council had one of the highest percentages of college graduates and was pursuing progressive changes in Halabja. These attributes defied common media stereotypes but reminded me of what I had learned in Amarah, that many Islamist officeholders are not reactionary conservatives.

The oldest councilman, a tribal leader, apologized for having no formal education, yet he was highly articulate. Like the others, he defied the usual stereotypes. As the meeting ended, he grasped my fingers in the traditional Arab hand-holding gesture as we walked outside.

In Halabja the Anfal chemical attack was not just bad history. Beyond the 5,000 people killed that day, many others had died since from the medical consequences. Its people still suffered from unusually high levels of cancer and birth defects. Continuing environmental impacts caused breathing problems and throat conditions that had affected 2,200 people. The city had 87,000 people in 1988 but now only had 53,000. A general air of discouragement still pervaded the city, as did unhappiness with the KRG for not doing enough. Minister Nazaneen had tried to help, especially by trying to fund a water system, but Halabja still needed help for its unique public health and reconstruction problems. The ministry, however, had little money to help any city. The Ministry of Health also lacked resources. Still, I wanted Municipalities to take the lead in developing a special program to help Halabja.

Our long return trip coincided with the first day of the Nawroz holiday, originated by Iranians to mark the start of spring but adopted by Kurds as their major holiday. A common act of celebration is lighting a fire, and the boredom of our return trip was relieved by fires in several places along the roadway.

In the end we visited twenty-two municipalities—from the far northwest to the far southeast. We got a great reception almost everywhere. We held eighty-four meetings, many of them in-depth interviews, producing a surprisingly large volume of information and ideas. Simultaneous with my city meetings, Luqman casually dropped in at their Administration offices to pick up off-the-record information, often including a discrepancy between the number of employees working and the larger number on the payroll. We went through our thirteen pages of survey questions in each city, and I later tallied the results for my report.

Survey answers showed differences of perspective among the three provinces, but the answers in Suly to one simple question really got my attention: their general opinion of the KRG. In Erbil and Dahuk, the question got consistently positive answers, even from those critical of government performance. Suly officials gave the KRG a much lower rating. Beyond unifying its ministries, the KRG still faced the much harder job of unifying the Kurds.

Most important, I had connected the dots of a fragmented ministry. What I learned from the municipal and province-level offices showed me I could connect those dots to headquarters too, enabling a reorganization proposal that integrated all levels. This insight was beyond anything I had considered before starting out, and it faced big political hurdles, but at least I was getting the right answers.

18

Reforming a Ministry—Starting Low, Aiming High

A Ministry of Frustrated Hopes

The Structure of Dysfunction

Back in Erbil, I extended my interviews to headquarters staff, finding many of them as frustrated as the field staff. Even senior-level officials had trouble getting time with the minister. Directors general (DGs) had weak organizational connections to their field staffs, by their own admission. Headquarters understandings of field operations were surprisingly inaccurate.

The end result of all those meetings and all those notes was a very long report with about three hundred recommendations and an alternative organization chart for the ministry. An explanation of all the issues and recommendations in that report would require its own book. Here is an integrated summary you should read slowly.

1. *The ministry operated at six hierarchical levels.* Level 1 consisted of people outside the ministry making ministry decisions, such as KDP and PUK officials, the Council of Ministers, the two Finance ministries, interfering mayors and governors, and well-connected people arranging favors to which they were not entitled. That pushed the minister down to Level 2.

Those party-appointed directors general who didn't work much with the minister were a separate Level 3, along with the office directors.

The overlapping and competing province-level directorates—five for three provinces—were Levels 4 and 5. That left the municipalities on the bottom level looking up.

The answers seemed clear to me, but the solutions required major changes. To eliminate Level 1, the KRG must sideline party interference and allow the prime minister to be fully in charge and accountable to the parliament, with all ministers reporting only to the prime minister. That wasn't happening soon.

Based on my analysis, MOM needed three deputy ministers—responsible, respectively, for Management, Municipal Services, and Planning and Engineering—political appointees but working closely with the minister and with each other as a meaningful leadership team.

The six politically appointed DGs could be replaced by ten non-political "directors" appointed or promoted by the minister, each reporting to one of the deputy ministers. This arrangement would shift day-to-day management to civil service professionals selected on merit. At the provincial level I proposed to replace both the Erbil/Dahuk and Suly Directorates of Municipalities with a new Directorate of Municipal Services, redefined as a support organization with three province-level support offices.

The Level 1 problem was mostly beyond MOM's control, but the other changes would merge Levels 2 and 3 and eliminate Level 4, producing a four-level ministry that might actually work.

2. *There was a lack of authority at all levels.* Although the ministry organization was entirely hierarchical, that meant little because MOM did not empower people at any level. It needed to delegate authority at all the revised levels.

As demonstrated in Baghdad, delegation is something Iraq's managers do poorly. Top-down is long-ingrained, reflecting the instinct to control. Employees defer decisions to higher-ups for fear of offending them; they in turn defer them further up for the same reason. Cities couldn't even repair vehicles without higher-level approval. Because of MOM's many layers and communications loops, even simple decisions took a long time. The weekly parade of visitors to see Minister Nazaneen included many who were wasting her time to get decisions they or someone below them could have made. Empowerment would require serious reeducation and, in the minister's opinion, stronger managers.

3. *There was a general lack of supervision.* The ministry organization was so fragmented and its supervisory arrangements so weak that no one could make his or her authority consistently effective, including the minister. Most offices reported directly or indirectly to one director general, but I found that most DGs spent little time on oversight and seldom visited field offices. MOM's province-level offices for each directorate were typically in separate places, which discour-

aged horizontal coordination, duplicating the pattern at headquarters. So, there was a management disconnect at all levels, vertically and horizontally.

The supervision solution was to have less of it, by empowering people from the ground up. This meant giving municipalities more autonomy and increasing the number of self-managed cities, which I called "home rule cities," by lowering the population requirement to 50,000. Getting home rule cities off the workload of the province-level support offices would leave more time to help the smaller municipalities.

Personnel from all general directorates in each provincial capital could be consolidated in one place, ensuring daily on-site supervision and facilitating program direction from each headquarters directorate to its provincial teams. The ministry could then shift headquarters priorities to planning, policy development, major projects, technical direction, and evaluation.

Making those changes would eliminate the disconnects within the ministry organization.

4. *The work was undermined by bad work habits.* Those habits hurt productivity and were unfair to staff trying to make a difference. Until MOM solved the organizational and management problems, however, it wasn't quite fair to blame the employees, conceding that many did not present an image of Kurds as hardworking people. That excuse did not apply to the ghost workers receiving ministry salaries without coming to work. Those who went to work were often in overstaffed offices and/or had little work to do. Lack of work and ghost workers were problems across most of Iraq's ministries.

The central problem identified by our consultant team was the lack of meaningful human resources policies. Also lacking was a separate human resources directorate to manage those policies and deal with personnel issues. The low salaries were a big problem. Training needed higher priority and extension to the provincial and municipal levels.

Another productivity issue was MOM's time-wasting communications and approval loops. Every city we visited complained about this problem. Most frustrating were the absurdly excessive signature requirements up the chain of command. Signatures were required for even the lowest-level decisions. In Suleimaniya having to loop requests through the Suly Ministry of Finance and the DG for Suly

Municipalities wasted more time. A ministry-wide automated message system could eliminate much of this problem.

Staff at all levels told me there was a desperate need for change and that meaningful change was held hostage by people in higher authority. Too many staff had given up in discouragement.

Shared Problems, Shared Frustrations

While each of those twenty-two municipalities I visited had its own local problems, most shared the same problems, the following most of all.

The poverty of municipal governments. Lack of resources was the municipalities' dominant problem. They received inadequate financial support from the ministry and were prohibited from raising their own revenue. So they were typically unable to provide adequate basic services, buy enough vehicles, finance needed projects, or even pay low-level employees a living wage. While I was in a meeting in Said Sadiq, one of its street cleaners, an older man, waited for me in the hallway, then pleaded with me to do something to raise cleaners' salaries.

The lack of water. The water supply system was rudimentary and didn't provide much water. Sewer service was inadequate. Electricity, not a MOM responsibility, was in short supply. Rural villages were even less likely to have basic services. Although MOM's Directorate of Water and Sewer had province-level and some big-city offices, I discovered that its ground-level impact was limited and largely missing. Cities were doing most of its work, and those in Suly handled all water and sewer service. So who should control water and sewer in municipalities? The cities didn't have enough money to provide for everyone, but if they hadn't taken on this role, many more people would be going without. The minister, however, had committed to separating Water and Sewer from the municipalities, contrary field office opinions notwithstanding.

I suggested the ministry set consistent fees for water service and use the revenue to increase hours of service and expand its network to more people. Municipalities, however, were not allowed to keep fee revenue they raised due to a mysterious procedure that supposedly required sending their money through the Finance ministry to Baghdad. They also lacked borrowing authority to finance improvements. Creating a rate-driven system and putting fee revenue into a development fund could have generated a lot of money to expand water service.

The "black hole" of planning. Local governments did own land and did have a land-use planning function, producing so-called master plans for headquarters approval. I made the startling discovery on my road trip, however, that there was essentially no general or long-range urban planning. Aside from land-use planning, there was project planning, considered an engineering function. The main functions we in the West associate with planning offices, such as community planning, transportation planning, and economic development, did not exist. MOM had virtually no planners as we understand the word. Thus did I discover the KRG's black hole of planning.

A Few Basic Requirements

The lack of automation. In a dysfunctional bureaucracy great ideas don't always win. Lack of automation was a glaring weakness at all levels, yet Anwar Rashid in Erbil #6 had effectively automated his entire operation. Rob Katzensohn and I proposed enthusiastically to the minister to move him to headquarters to lead a task force that would automate headquarters operations and train city managers and staffs to automate theirs. Putting more computers in field offices would enable document transmission by internet, eliminating a lot of excessive signatures. The idea looked like a great breakthrough. To our amazement, however, Nazaneen vetoed it, saying Anwar was too friendly with the governor of Erbil, seen as a political opponent.

Financial management issues. One area in which automation was most needed was Finance and Administration. Delair Kittani was trying to make this happen. He wasn't attempting anything complex, just a basic system. The response from the DG for Finance and Administration was friendly but stubbornly resistant.

Direct deposit was another priority. Having it might have helped us too, as MOM had trouble processing our compensation, despite all our pleas. (Thankfully, they were paying the hotel bill.)

Indeed, after several months I had yet to get paid. This set up my most bizarre experience in Kurdistan. The KRG was still paying in cash. No direct deposit, no checks either. At some point the ministry's cash caught up with its contract, and they paid me the entire amount owed. I got a big bag with about $50,000 in cash. It was like I had just robbed the bank. My colleagues found the whole scene hilarious.

This created a small problem. My bank was several blocks down the main road, through a commercial area. I had no security guards and no weapon. That was a lot of money to just carry down the street looking like a bagman. Then, to send that much money to my U.S. bank, I had to provide signed legal assurance that I was not in violation of the federal money laundering act.

Space management issues. The minister did approve Rob Katzensohn's plan to streamline the intake and processing of applications and other documents at ministry headquarters, which had been a bureaucratic nightmare. He set up an access control system with a control point at the front gate and a reception desk in the lobby to handle incoming documents. A document flow process was set up to handle and track them.

The minister also accepted his plan to renovate one area on the upper floor to house the entire Urban Planning directorate and the GIS unit. He financed this from $400,000 in grants provided by the U.S. Provincial Reconstruction Team in Erbil. Ministry workspaces typically featured overly large executive offices that fed the ego of high officials while leaving their staffs in cramped spaces. Rob divided the renovated space more democratically, giving each staff member individual space and a usable desk.

Win Some, Lose Some

Opportunities Lost

Writing a report with three hundred recommendations was of course time-consuming, but I gave the minister completed sections as I went along, and Amanj was translating it. Translation being inherently complex, I persuaded a ministry engineer who had worked for several years in Harrisburg, Pennsylvania, to review each part of the translation; he made only minor changes. Even so, the Kurdish version was never quite satisfactory, and the minister often found the English version clearer. This highlighted an observed problem in Kurdistan, where language education produces many who can speak good English but not understand and write it at a professional level. You might say my report was "lost in translation." The minister's larger problem, however, was finding the time to read such a long document. In May I sent a memo identifying nine recommendations she could implement immediately but got no response. She was reading some of it, however, as she quickly removed the unofficial DG in Suly doing the five hundred daily signatures.

Around October 1 I provided a summary version of the completed report in English and later in Kurdish; even that was forty-seven pages. The minister was upbeat about some recommendations, however, and as I left for a vacation in Ireland, she was talking early implementation. She agreed to several parts of the reorganization, some based solely on my color-coded reorganization chart, showing all organizational units at municipal, provincial, and headquarters levels with their revised names and in their precise horizontal and vertical interrelationships. She agreed to my proposed Directorate of Municipal Assistance as the headquarters coordinating office to support municipalities through its province-level offices.

On many other points, however, she was still unclear. She also continued with previously devised organizational changes inconsistent with report recommendations, including the organizational structure of the province-level municipal directorates and separation of Water and Sewer from the municipalities. Ann Mirani tried repeatedly but unsuccessfully to schedule a PowerPoint presentation I had completed with Rob's help, to give her a clearer picture.

After my positive meeting with the minister in early November, she was again not communicating. None of us could get a meeting. All the recommendations she agreed to were still just on paper until she issued her decisions, which would require implementation documents. Frustrated by her silence, and with my one-year contract ending in early December, I started writing implementation documents cosigned by Luqman for her signature, one every day at one point. In early December I finally got an admission that the minister was not ready to move forward right now; maybe later. In late December I went home.

The report was arguably a major achievement. It was clear only in retrospect that even this change-oriented minister was not prepared to undertake such a major transformation of the ministry, especially changes needing higher-level approvals. The sheer size of the effort worked against her self-imposed tight schedule and her instinctive aversion to political risks.

My greatest regret was that my site visits had created hope around the ministry that positive changes would result from their cooperation and investment of time—hopes not to be realized. As I was the minister's representative, they had placed faith in me, which made it personal. The ministry staff I met almost unanimously favored major changes within the ministry. Many of our recommendations came from them. They deserved better support from their minister.

Discovering the Bottom Line of Kurdish "Democracy"

My most important recommendation was to hold new municipal elections in 2009, as required by KRG Law 6. This issue became a microcosm of the KRG's political corruption. It had not held the legally required new elections in 2005. No one was talking about the legally required 2009 election either, but most elected city officials wanted one so as to end their open-ended terms.

Unknown to me, Luqman, and apparently all those city officials was a Council of Ministers proposal to the KRG parliament that the elected councils be replaced by appointed ones, which the minister had opposed. She was amazed and agitated that no one had told me this, but the reality was that this power play was so outrageous that it was safer politically to keep it a secret from those potentially affected. So far, however, the parliament had not voted on it.

I went personally to the parliament to talk with the Legal Affairs committee chairman. He expressed support for an election but also called the minister, who got annoyed with me for initiating the meeting. The minister insisted she could not even go to the parliament about this matter and could not call an election unless the KDP and PUK wanted one, *even though the law required her to do so!* That said a lot about "democracy" in the KRG.

I then learned the parliament would not agree to appointed councils. So, on November 16 I drafted a letter for her signature to the prime minister, asking his approval for an election on June 4, 2009. That move got the expected nonresponse.

Just before leaving Erbil, I requested an explanation from the one person who would tell me the real story. Nawshirwan Mustafa told me matter-of-factly that the committee chairman's supportive comments were meaningless and that there was no chance of holding a municipal election in 2009, as the KDP and PUK were trying to kill the independently elected councils, which they don't control, by blocking implementation of the law. Later history would record no municipal elections in 2013 either. Once again, all together now, "There is no corruption in Kurdistan!"

In February 2008 the Iraqi parliament had passed a "Law of Governorates Not Organized into a Region," commonly called the "Provincial Powers Law," which established an elected local government level while excluding the KRG, which already had municipalities. How sad that the government of Iraq voted for elected local governments while the KRG was avoiding them. In fact, the KRG had not held provincial elections either since 2005—and would not hold the next ones until 2014, by which time provincial powers in the KRG had also been increased.

Unfortunately, the 2008 Iraq law prompted USAID to pull out of the KRG and withdraw its support from the Community Action Groups there. When Ann and I met with USAID's man in Erbil on October 29 and politely complained, we were advised coldly that they had to focus on supporting the new local governments elsewhere. I suspect that the KRG's failure to set municipal elections for 2009 made USAID's decision too easy. Perhaps the larger mistake was USAID's failure from the beginning to focus RTI's *Local* Governance Program more on the Kurdish municipalities that were Iraq's only elected local governments and a potential model for the rest. Instead, a leading Kurdistan expert later complained that "aside from a few water and sanitation projects, the democracy mission had no important investments or results to show in the Kurdish north."[1]

A Few Modest Victories

The consulting terms of Rob and Delair started after me and so extended past my tenure. They eventually won a few battles.

The space reallocation enabled Rob to create a digitized mapping system for Urban Planning that allowed large maps to be printed multiple times—an important breakthrough, as they were required of all business permit applicants. An office cabal at Urban Planning had supplemented their salaries under the old system, however, by charging huge fees for lower-quality single copies and pocketing the money. Rob's later departure left the new map production system controlled by the same people.

As for Wine Langeraar's separate GIS project, intended to expand the mapping capacity of Urban Planning and the entire ministry, he developed a methodology for village boundary mapping and other innovations, but the capacity of the GIS team never matched its friendliness.

Delair finally won his battle to bring some automation to the Finance function. He got the ministry to install basic software for accounting and personnel. Another major accomplishment was his system for automating the payroll process, implemented at province-level offices in Erbil. That success enabled another big change: paying by direct deposit. His pilot project partially automated the accounting system of the large Erbil city water directorate. Perhaps his biggest achievement, however, was getting the heretofore resistant Finance and Administration DG to buy in on these changes.

As Rob and Delair's terms ended, however, the project faded out with far less reform than would have occurred with proper ministry support. Most needed changes were still on paper waiting for action. The MMA partners, who had sold the project to the prime minister, thought my report was great yet could not show him the results they intended. To quote one colleague's parting evaluation, "It was less of a mess but still a mess."

The Winds of Change

Soon after we left, Kurdish politics blew up. In the 2009 Kurdish parliament elections, the anti-corruption Gorran party beat the PUK in Suleimaniya, though it had less impact elsewhere, and won 25 seats in the 111-seat parliament. Gorran insiders told me their actual results would have been even better except for vote rigging by the KDP-PUK alliance. The results stunned the major parties and forced the PUK into a closer alliance with the rival KDP.

When the new government was set up in late 2009, with the PUK's Barham Salih as prime minister, there was a new KDP minister of municipalities, now expanded to be the Ministry of Municipalities and

Tourism, but no consulting team to help implement all the changes needed, despite his initial expression of interest to MMA.

The following minister, Dilshad Shahab, appointed in 2012, seemed more in sync with my report recommendations made a few years earlier. He stated a new ministry policy to delegate authority to lower levels, transferring some of his to the headquarters DGs and province-level directors and some of theirs to lower levels. He announced that promotions would be based solely on qualifications and performance. He said providing drinking water was MOM's top priority. MOM still couldn't afford to install sewage systems but was trying to start. Contracted street cleaning, started in Erbil city when I was there, had been adopted by Dahuk and Suleimaniya.[2]

Under the minister's decentralization policy, local water and sewer decisions were delegated to the municipalities. He made good on his promise to give water projects higher priority. That Mergasor area project was completed, also those for the Shaqlawa area and Dahuk city. An Amedi area project was well under way, and projects were ongoing or anticipated in six cities.[3] There were other big projects too.

The Model Ministry

Conceding that the Ministry of Municipalities had some unusual problems, the dysfunctions encountered by the consulting team were also a window on most other KRG ministries and the national ministries in Baghdad. We had seen Iraq's ministry management problems from the inside. The view was not encouraging.

There was no real chance of a ministry reform program covering all KRG ministries. The party-dominated power structure precluded that. The chances were even less in Baghdad, where ministries were increasingly partisan and corrupt. Still, a successful reform program at one KRG ministry could set a powerful example and create momentum toward a broader reform of Kurdish ministries. This idea inspired my concept of the "Model Ministry."

The Ministry of Municipalities, while failing to implement comprehensive reforms, did inadvertently provide a wealth of information to help define the concept, mostly through a profusion of management practices that were far from international best practices.

From an international development perspective, the Model Ministry concept is potentially important, so lessons learned from ministry projects potentially matter. Third World countries are full of dysfunctional ministries; moving them toward a meaningful level of effectiveness should be a major priority. Different ministries in Erbil or Baghdad or other foreign capitals would produce a somewhat different list of requirements. My list of best practices follows. I encourage my international development counterparts and other governance experts to add to this list.

Nonpartisan Governance

The ministry is strictly nonpartisan in hiring and promotion and makes no hires or promotions based on political connections, excepting only leadership positions legally designated for political appointments.

All hiring and promotion decisions are based on merit as defined by previous job performance and position requirements, are sensitive to gender equality, and are made through a fair process under written rules.

Hiring decisions are made by the ministry and never by people outside the ministry. Hiring is based on actual staffing needs, and there is no excess hiring.

The ministry sets and enforces high performance and ethical standards for employees. All employees are expected to put service to the public ahead of personal, family, religious, tribal, or political considerations and to treat all citizens equally and with respect. Any corrupt activity is strictly prohibited and subject to involuntary termination and possible prosecution.

The ministry supports and encourages its personnel, provides meaningful work within a supportive and secure workplace, advocates for adequate compensation at all pay levels, and maintains a fair process for adjudicating personnel grievances.

Ministry decisions and actions are not politically motivated, treat all people and all geographic areas equally, and reflect sensitivity to minorities and those most disadvantaged.

Democratic Management

The ministry defines its mission from the ground up, putting citizens first.

The ministry empowers employees and delegates decision-making authority at all levels.

Supervisory practices follow a democratic management policy at all levels, and noncompliance by supervisors is a basis for demotion and/or disciplinary action.

There is priority attention to training at all levels—for improved staff and management performance, improved ministry work routines and communications, and employee development.

Organizational Effectiveness

The ministry has an effective leadership team, effective horizontal coordination among directors and offices, and effective day-to-day management by civil servants selected on merit.

The ministry has an organizational structure consistent throughout the ministry.

Ministry operations are streamlined for maximum efficiency; continuously improved through evaluation and feedback, management training, and automation; and consistently conform to international best practices.

The ministry constantly seeks resources adequate to its mission, controls its own budget process and other ongoing financial management decisions consistent with broader government policy, and maintains transparency to the public.

The ministry has an internal office with delegated authority and capabilities to investigate illegal and unethical behavior by its employees, contractors, and clients.

External Leadership

The minister and other top officials are strong but democratic leaders, are future oriented and planning oriented, and represent the ministry effectively within the government and to the media and public.

The minister and other top officials coordinate effectively with other ministries and government offices but stand up to political interference from outside the ministry.

The ministry welcomes interaction with civil society organizations that support its mission.

The ministry welcomes media coverage, has an effective media liaison office to get the ministry's story out and help ensure fair coverage, but respects the freedom of the press.

IV

America and the Future of Iraq

19

Picking Up the Pieces in a Shattered Country

Iraqi Voters and the Struggle for Democracy

In international development work you don't control enough variables to guarantee success. Being on the scene and part of the action does give you the chance to make a difference, however, even if you can't immediately create the Model Ministry. After spending so much time in Iraq, it was only natural to ask what I and the other democracy and governance specialists had accomplished there.

One answer was that Iraq was now a democracy, thanks largely to our help—but a democracy performing badly. It was doing better in more peaceful Kurdistan, but even there it still needed reform at all levels. Iraq was therefore a democracy with an uncertain future. Events soon highlighted the uncertainty.

First the good news. Some of our democracy programs have been directed at voters, because elections are critical. While media and expert attention focused on the failures of Iraq's politicians, Iraq's abused voters repeatedly provided reasons for cautious optimism. Voters have been the good news in Iraq.

If you're skeptical, consider a few invidious comparisons. Turnout for Iraq's national parliamentary elections was virtually 80 percent in 2005 and just over 60 percent in 2010 and 2014. Turnouts for most U.S. congressional elections don't even approach Iraq's turnouts, though turnouts in presidential election years come closer.

For Iraq's provincial elections the turnout was over 55 percent in 2005 (despite the Sunni boycott) and slightly over 50 percent in 2009 and 2013, the latter turnouts depressed because of voters still displaced from their homes by the sectarian violence. Most American states don't compare well. Still, the falloff in turnout also reflected voter frustration with government performance.

Iraq's voters have also pushed back against officials who are involved in corruption or refuse to confront it. The Gorran opposition movement in the KRG, for example, has grown since 2009 primarily because voters, especially in Suleimaniya, support its anti-corruption platform. When Iraq's parliament decided in 2009 for partial open-ballot elections, which gave voters a choice among individual candidates and not just party lists, the parties scurried after independents and other new candidates, to limit the anticipated anti-incumbent backlash.

With several elections now completed, all generally fair and well managed, the Independent High Electoral Commission and the electoral process in general have also earned positive evaluations from citizens and international observers, despite some issues. This success can't be taken for granted. It takes courage to be an election worker when extremists are using violence to disrupt the election and have killed some of your coworkers.

So the contributions of Iraq's voters deserve more attention, to add balance to the unrelieved, though often deserved, negative media coverage of the Iraqi government and constant assertions from some quarters that the 2003 Coalition intervention was a failure. Time will tell whether it ultimately succeeded or failed, but the positive developments should be part of the evaluation.

The bad news has come after the elections. The institutions of government have not only failed to approach the standards of the Model Ministry but have performed poorly, mainly because of the politicians and political cronies running too many of them. Each ministry became a fiefdom of its minister's party, and loyalty was to the party, not to the prime minister or the public. The ministers did not work together and did little to bridge sectarian and ethnic differences. Part of our civilian coalition in Iraq was still working in ministries and other agencies, but the positive changes they facilitated were obscured by the institutional corruption.

We can blame countless Iraqis for this situation, but let's reserve some blame for American constitution strategists who prized inclusiveness above all else. Giving all those parties a share in the government came at a high cost. Spreading the political "spoils" over forty ministries, give or take a few, was a huge multiplier of mismanagement and corruption. So the government lacked any real accountability to anyone. According to Iraqi American political scientist Adeed

Dawisha, our misplaced enthusiasm for governments of national unity led to governments of national disunity.[1]

In general, then, it's a good news–bad news situation. Here is a fast summary of the good news produced by voters.

January 2009. Many changes were in motion between the two 2005 elections and the pivotal 2009 provincial elections. Nouri Al-Maliki's 2008 decision to send the Iraqi Army to Basra to take control from the Mehdi Army and other militias (with difficulty and with U.S. and British help), then to Sadr City and Amarah, got little Western media coverage but had a huge political impact.

These moves were popular in southern Iraq, and in 2009 voters there turned away from the Sadrists, the Islamic Supreme Council of Iraq (ISCI), and Islam-based voting in general to support a new State of Law coalition started by Al-Maliki that included his Islamic Dawa Party and other groups. State of Law finished first in nine provinces, including Baghdad.

Security was only one issue, however. Voters disappointed with those they had elected in 2005 were looking for change by 2009. This especially hurt ISCI, which won big in 2005 and dominated many provinces. So did the switch to the partial open-ballot system (except in the KRG). There were now far fewer seats because a new representation formula replaced the forty-one-members-per-PC formula with smaller PCs whose sizes also varied by governorate population. Most incumbents did not run again, and only a small percentage got reelected.[2] Voters punished the Fadhila party, which had led Basra so disastrously, reducing it to minor-party status.

There were 14,431 candidates, however, representing 401 political entities, running for 440 seats in 14 provinces (excluding KRG's three and Kirkuk),[3] about 33 candidates per seat. That's a lot of participation. About 28 percent of the candidates were women. Sunni Arabs, most of whom had boycotted in January 2005, showed up in 2009. Many new parties and candidates joined the election process, some running only in their own province.

The separate July 2009 KRG election produced the political revolt in Suleimaniya, noted earlier, with Gorran winning 24 percent of the overall vote and creating the first meaningful opposition ever in the Kurdish parliament.

So the 2009 provincial elections were a watershed event. Voters evaluated incumbents' job performance and wanted changes. Parties were forced to acknowledge they are accountable to voters. As in 2005, provincial elections got far less Western news coverage than they deserved.

March 2010. The rearranging of political lines carried over to the 2010 national election. The United Iraqi Alliance (UIA) that dominated in 2005 had broken up. Its inspiration, Grand Ayatollah Sistani, refused to support any political faction or have his picture used.[4] The Sadrist and Fadhila parties defected from Al-Maliki and the UIA, joined by the new party of former Dawa prime minister Ibrahim Al-Jaafari. In August 2009 Abd Al-Aziz Al-Hakim, widely respected leader of ISCI and also a key UIA coalition leader, died at only fifty-nine. The partial open-list system again limited parties' control of the election.

Several high-level court decisions were needed even to hold the election. The biggest issue was the decision by a Shia-dominated commission led by Ahmed Chalabi (yes, that guy) to throw out 511 candidates in advance based on alleged Baathist sins and then another 52 named to take their places. Despite the political uproar, only a small number got reinstated.[5] This raised a divisive and unnecessary sectarian issue.

In the end, however, the Sunnis pulled the big surprise. The mostly Sunni Iraqiya coalition—formed around past prime minister Ayad Allawi, a secular Shi'i, and supported financially by the Sunni-led governments in Turkey and Qatar, narrowly won more seats than the Al-Maliki coalition, by 91 to 89, with 70 seats going to the remnants of the UIA coalition, now called the Iraqi National Alliance (INA), and 43 to the Kurds. The vote showed that Sunni Arabs could still have a major political impact if they worked together.

The overall national results also reflected voters' frustration with corruption, and they again showed voters outperforming politicians. Again, there was high candidate participation: over 6,000 candidates and about 20 candidates per seat.

For those of us who had promoted democracy in Iraq, the election results looked like a huge breakthrough. Allawi had accomplished something as surprising as it was significant—a sectarian political balance in national politics. *The 2010 election results were the high point in Iraq's political development.* It didn't last.

It had occurred to me often that Al-Maliki and Allawi were not far apart ideologically. They now controlled a majority of seats between them and could have formed an effective inter-sectarian government. It was observed later that "the people had done their part. All that was left to secure a national revival was for the majority to do theirs."[6]

Instead, the instinct to control prevailed. Both sides insisted on forming the government, and a nine-month stalemate followed. A debatable court decision allowed Al-Maliki the first chance to form the government, even though Allawi's bloc finished first. Iranian pressure eventually moved Moqtada Al-Sadr to support Al-Maliki in exchange for several ministries and pro-Iran considerations, giving him just enough support to keep his position.[7] Unfortunately, he mostly reneged on his reluctant agreement with Allawi that had ended the stalemate, and he broke his promises to the Kurds.

The Iraqiya coalition did not hold together in the parliament, one reason being that Allawi was seldom there to lead it. His success was therefore fleeting and the new political balance temporary. Al-Maliki's political "victory" and its frustrating aftermath for Sunni Arabs and Kurds reinforced his perceived sectarian bias and started a downhill slide toward disaster.

April and June 2013. The 2013 provincial elections backdrop was the outbreak of protests in early 2011 inspired by the Arab Spring revolts in Tunisia and Egypt. Antigovernment protests were unknown in Saddam's day, so these made leaders nervous. Al-Maliki responded at first with concessions. On February 4, as the protests gathered momentum, he announced he would henceforth return half his salary to the Treasury. On February 5 he announced he wouldn't seek a third term and would propose a constitutional amendment to limit prime ministers to two terms. On February 25, however, thousands of protestors hit the streets in several cities for a "Day of Rage," and twenty-three people were killed.

The protest wave hit Suly too, led by Gorran, and became violent after protesters were attacked, with 3 killed and 121 wounded, causing further demonstrations. Regime thugs then attacked media outlets.[8] Gorran called for disbanding the government, replacing it with nonpolitical technocrats, presumed to be less corrupt (a pet Nawshirwan idea he had told me in person).

The campaign showed again that running for office can be dangerous in Iraq. Sixteen Sunni candidates were assassinated before the election was even held.[9] Al-Maliki's State of Law coalition, expanded from 2009, won the most seats in six of the nine South and South-Central provinces and in Baghdad, winning both Basra and Baghdad by wide margins. Overall, however, it lost seats from 2009, and ISCI and the Sadrists regained some of theirs. Back in my former home province of Maysan, State of Law was edged out by a Sadrist comeback.

Allawi's Iraqiya coalition reflected its post-2010 decline, winning only a minor share of the vote. In the Anbar, Diyala, and Ninewa elections, delayed until June for security reasons, newer Sunni groups grabbed a large share of the seats. In Najaf and Diyala, local lists won the most seats. Even nationwide, a significant percentage of electees were politically unaffiliated. The results were so inclusive that every PC now had between six and fourteen political entities.

So no party won an absolute majority in any province, forcing coalitions in every province in order to elect a governor. Despite winning the most seats, State of Law lost leadership control in Baghdad, Basra, and other provinces to postelection alliances between ISCI and the Sadrists—politically unthinkable a few years earlier.

This is the point where voters lose control. This quadrennial horse-trading over governorships, in the face of clearly expressed voter preferences, reinforces my observation in Maysan that governors should be directly elected by voters, with term limits. That would make one incumbent personally accountable, reduce political fragmentation in the governorates, and probably increase voter support for democracy.

Stronger governors are needed also because of parliament's June 2013 vote to amend the Provincial Powers Law to mandate devolving specific government functions to the governorates, giving them more control of their own budgets and putting ministries' provincial directorates under the provincial governments as of 2015. Its provisions, if implemented as written—never to be assumed in Iraq—would implement most of the federal system envisioned by the constitution. It was a belated triumph for the proposal by John Doane of RTI's Basra team, going back to 2003, to devolve central government powers to the provinces and local governments.

September 2013. Kurdish elections are less complicated than elsewhere in Iraq but have become no less intense. The KDP scored a solid victory, while Gorran decisively beat the PUK in Suly and finished second in Erbil, though its total vote rose only slightly from 2009. Gorran thus displaced the PUK as the second strongest party—a historic development. Two Islamic parties also gained. One key to the KDP's success is its continued dominance in Dahuk, where it got 70 percent of the vote.

I immediately saw an opening for a broader government coalition that would add Gorran and the two Islamic parties and finally break the corrupt two-party stranglehold on the KRG. I sent my recommendation to certain individuals in Suly. Nechirvan Barzani, again the KDP's prime minister designate, was pursuing that idea and seemed to have the five parties on board, but it took seven months to get final agreement and establish the government.

April 2014. The deflating events after 2010's national election left much uncertainty as the 2014 election loomed. The stakes were huge for Iraq, yet no governing coalition was apparent. Al-Maliki's coalition had seen major defections, but no alternative leader was clearly visible, and he had changed his mind about seeking a third term. His opponents in parliament passed a term-limits law to prevent that, but he got it overturned by the Federal Supreme Court.

Iraq also needed a new president. Jalal Talabani, who had succeeded in the role, had announced in 2009 he would not seek reelection. In December 2012, at seventy-nine, he was incapacitated by a major stroke for the rest of his term, remaining hospitalized in Germany into 2014.

The election results were a clear victory for Al-Maliki. His Rule of Law coalition finished first in ten of the eighteen provinces and earned 92 seats, a number increased by pledges of support from smaller entities. By contrast, ISCI and the Sadrists each won only about one-third as many seats. Even collectively, the Sunni Arab vote was less than for the Allawi coalition four years earlier, and Allawi's new list won just 21 seats.[10]

Participation was again off the charts: 277 political entities and 9,031 candidates (including 2,607 women) for the 328 seats—27.5 candidates per seat. This led to fragmented results, however, with votes widely scattered among often small parties, especially Sunni parties.

The great irony was that Al-Maliki's victory did not guarantee a third term. Knowledgeable Kurds told me the Kurdish parties were unalterably opposed to him because he had lied to them in 2010. He had made a second dishonest deal with Allawi, and Sunni Arabs in general were antagonistic toward him. Some Shia parties were also strongly opposed. Even a friend of mine in Amarah who worked for Al-Maliki told me he had become too dictatorial. Although he had been a tough and often effective leader in tough times, Iraq desperately needed a fresh political start.

As the 2014 election ended, there were three critical requirements for overcoming Iraq's political divide. None were easy, and all three were about to become much harder.

Issue 1: Reconciliation

Shia and Sunni

Reconciliation is an important Christian concept and part of a democratic political culture. It is an elusive concept in Iraq, however, despite injunctions in the Koran. Efforts toward reconciliation clash with the instinct to control and with a "winner-take-all" mentality. One damaging consequence is an unwillingness to compromise, resulting in an inability to negotiate. Political crises linger for months or years or indefinitely.

Much of the Shia-Sunni impasse was really between Islamists and Baathists. De-Baathification removed some bad people from public life, but it also ruined the lives of thousands who had done little or no harm to others. The parliament replaced the policy in 2008 with the Justice and Accountability Act, but it had a similar albeit softened sectarian bias. It was used, for example, to bar those 511 Sunni candidates from the ballot in 2010 and to reinstate former Shia army officers but not Sunnis.[11] The Shia just wouldn't let the past go. The hostile reactions did cause revisions in the law in 2013.

Meanwhile, an antiterrorism law was interpreted loosely to justify mass arrests of Sunnis and to target Sunni leaders. The highest-profile example was Tariq Al-Hashimi, one of Iraq's vice presidents. Prosecuting Al-Hashimi brought the Shia-Sunni political relationship to a new low. He was charged with terrorist crimes in December 2011 that included numerous murders, using personal bodyguards as a hit squad, and arranging bomb attacks. He was implicated by his own bodyguards, then convicted in absentia and sentenced to death multiple times, after escaping to the protection of the Kurds and later the Turks to avoid arrest. In the context of prior similar incidents, however, it was easy for Sunnis to believe criminal allegations against Sunni leaders are politically motivated, leaving no need to weigh whether they are justified in particular cases.

At the citizen level, use of the Interior ministry and justice system for sectarian purposes persuaded Sunnis they were being targeted by the government, as some were. Instead of feeling protected from crime, they felt threatened by those paid to protect them.

Al-Maliki made many decisions that were arguably necessary but left him open to the "dictator" accusations. Instead of adjusting to people's feelings, he placated his political base and overplayed his hand, further polarizing Iraqis and weakening the government.

Less media attention was given to the continuing intransigence of many Sunnis who were hostile to the Shia-majority government from the start and to the U.S. government that helped establish it. Many thousands of innocent people have died from this intransigence and its consequences.

On both sides of the sectarian divide there is indifference to wrongdoing by people on one's own side—and to the death, pain, and suffering inflicted on their victims. Right versus wrong got replaced by we versus they.

Yet millions of Iraqis share a common and democratic vision of a unified Iraq that transcends sectarian lines. Many in the government, including Talabani and many parliament members, and most Islamic clergy, have tried to bridge differences. So I have never believed that reconciliation is impossible in Iraq, conceding that it is harder than in other countries. If Iraq is to succeed as a democracy, this is one part of the struggle that has to be won.

The Vanishing Christians

It seemed too late by 2014 for reconciliation with the Christians. Caught in the crossfire of the Sunni-Shia violence, targeted by extremists and criminals, a major percentage of them had already fled Iraq, along with Muslims driven out by the same violence.

Here is a sad and stunning fact: Most Christians who lived in Iraq when the Coalition invasion occurred in 2003 are no longer there. Conflicting population estimates leave modal figures of 1 million in 2003 and 400,000 ten years later. The number was destined to go much lower. A significant percentage of those still there, moreover, have been displaced within Iraq.

Christians have endured repeated and increasing violence since shortly after Saddam fell. By 2013 over sixty churches and other religious buildings had been bombed or otherwise attacked since 2003, mostly in Baghdad and Mosul. Over 800 Christians had been killed.[12] On October 31, 2010, Al-Qaeda-affiliated terrorists invaded a Sunday evening Catholic Mass in Karrada, killed fifty-two parishioners and two priests, and wounded most of the other worshippers. Three bomb attacks in other Christian neighborhoods in Baghdad killed thirty-seven on Christmas Day 2013. About 80 percent of Christian churches active in 2003 are now closed and some abandoned, and it's believed dangerous to hold services in many others. Active parishes typically have low attendance because of migration but also the fear of being in church. Ordinary Christians have often been targeted and shot dead in their homes or stores or elsewhere, even children. Even Kurdistan has occasional anti-Christian incidents, as in December 2011, when Muslim mobs in Dahuk, incited by Friday sermons at Zakho mosques, burned down Christian and Yazidi businesses in several cities and towns, and also churches, offices, and homes.

Part of the problem is that Christians are too few to protect themselves. They have no militia; no tribes protect them. They needed government to protect them. As it failed to do that, Christians fled in droves.

Even Christians in the KRG were leaving, mostly for Europe. About a half million Iraqi Christians live in Western Europe, especially in Germany and Sweden. In other words, there are now more Iraqi Christians outside Iraq than inside. The extent of the exodus was documented by the recent Iraqi Kurdistan Christianity Project, in which Rich Michael of MMA partnered with professors at the Catholic University law school in Washington DC to study the KRG's Christian communities.[13] Assyrian spokesmen variably estimated a remaining Assyrian population in Iraq of 500,000 or so and declining, with about 200,000 in northern Ninewa; there are also non-Assyrian Christians. Catholic U's detailed study, however, using parish records and other local sources, estimated the Christian population in northern Iraq to be substantially lower. That finding also indicates indirectly that the overall Iraq total is lower than public estimates. All such estimates would soon be overtaken by tragic events.

One focal point is the northeastern corner of Ninewa, including Mosul and the largely Christian Nineveh Plain, an area of major tensions among Sunni Arabs, Kurds, and Christians. In January 2014 the Iraq Council of Ministers proposed a new province in the Nineveh Plain, a concession to the Christians. It also proposed new provinces in the largely Turkmen districts of Tooz in northern Salahuddin and Tal Afar in northern Ninewa, plus the Halabja area in Suly and the Fallujah area in Anbar. The Nineveh Plain province faced potential complications, including the discovery of oil and Kurds' hopes of adding the area to Kurdistan. Keeping the Nineveh Plain, Tal Afar, and Tooz out of the KRG was one motive for the initiative.

For many Christians, of course, the initiative came too late; they had already left. A separate province, moreover, could still face anti-Christian violence from Mosul next door. After all, Christians have been leaving Iraq for personal safety, not political recognition. Most Iraqi Christians don't live in the Nineveh Plain anyway. Still, the mere idea of a self-managing Christian-majority enclave in a Muslim country is mind-blowing.

This raises a broader issue about the treatment of Christians in the Middle East that Muslims should find embarrassing. The Prophet Mohammed was very clear that Christians should be treated as brothers and allowed to worship in their own way. Christians felt relatively secure under Saddam's dictatorship but have been victimized under the supposedly democratic Islamic regime that followed. The Coptic Christians in Egypt were protected under Hosni Mubarak but targeted during the supposedly democratic Islamic regime that followed. Christians were secure in Baathist Syria until antiregime Islamic extremists started terrorizing their villages. Christians have risked and too often lost their lives to practice their faith in some Muslim countries.

This leaves an obvious question for U.S. policy makers and anyone espousing democracy for the Middle East—especially because people in the Middle East were the original adherents of the Christian faith.

Issue 2: Corruption

Whatever the outcome of future elections, no prime minister can solve the corruption problem without facing down a lot of corrupt people. This would take political will that had so far been lacking.

Early 2011 did bring a moment of vindication for me and my former ICSP Anti-Corruption Team in Erbil. When Iraq's protest movement reached Suly in late January, Gorran's proposal to replace the KRG government with a government of technocrats was rejected by all other parties, but their joint statement, to our amazement, finally conceded that *there is corruption in Kurdistan!*

In April 2011, with protests continuing in Suly, the KRG parliament created an independent Integrity Commission, reporting to the parliament, five years after my Erbil Anti-Corruption coordinator and Commissioner Al-Radhi both tried unsuccessfully to move the parliament Speaker in that direction. At the same time an Executive Office of Good Governance and Transparency was created under the prime minister. Alas, it took two years to appoint a director for the Integrity Commission.

Media trying to be part of the anti-corruption solution are still vulnerable to retaliation. In 2009 Asos Hardi, the *Awene* founder and editor-in-chief I knew from Suly, received a major award from the World Association of Newspapers, even as *Awene* faced more fines for stories disliked by the political elite, despite the IREX-promoted Kurdistan Press Law passed in September 2008. On August 29, 2011, his head was smashed by an assailant's pistol outside his office. The ensuing legal maneuvers were a window on justice in the KRG. The attackers were caught, and Hardi accused a high PUK official with having arranged the crime. One attacker was convicted in 2013 and sentenced to eight years; two were PUK *peshmerga* who could not be tried without Ministry of Peshmerga permission (still awaited as of 2016); and the accused PUK official and his bodyguard got off on grounds of "insufficient evidence."

Just days after the Hardi incident, Hadi Al-Madhi, a crusading anti-corruption journalist and Baghdad talk show host was assassinated in his own house in Karrada. He had helped lead weekly protests against government corruption and gathered a wide following. Making his death even sadder, Al-Madhi had returned to Iraq in 2007 after eighteen years abroad.

In December 2013 Kawa Garmiany, Asos Hardi's *Awene* reporter in Kalar, was shot dead in front of his own house. His family reportedly then sued a PUK leader. These are not isolated incidents. It's still dangerous to be a journalist in "democratic" Iraq.

Iraq proves conclusively that corruption in high places can withstand negative public opinion. Awareness raising is important, but it's not decisive. The ultimate question in Iraq is whether the voters and civil society organizations can compel governments to act democratically before politicians suck the system dry and persuade most Iraqis to give up on them.

Corruption is central to all of Iraq's problems. It undermines democracy, human rights, and public services. One positive trend I noticed was that people increasingly connected the corruption to the lack of electricity and water, the bad economy and unemployment, and the continuing poverty of ordinary people. They increasingly understood that corruption's consequences affect them. In late 2015 there would be a remarkable breakthrough in this story.

Issue 3: Law and Order

Both the reconciliation problem and the corruption problem fed into the law and order problem. The lack of reconciliation undermined stability. The corruption undermined government operations, including defense and security.

The sectarian bias of the Interior ministry was still an issue; government policies were still seen as sectarian by Sunnis. A Sunni protest movement starting in late 2012, spurred by the arrest of Sunni leaders, led to a series of bad incidents, the worst being a military raid on a sit-in protest in Hawija, in Kirkuk, where fifty people were killed, setting off a wave of violence.

The continuing criminal lawlessness added to the misery. Iraq's law enforcement capabilities were improving but still a work in progress. The recent upgrade of the Iraqi National Police, renamed the Iraqi Federal Police (IFP), seemed like a success story.[14] Still, while better law enforcement depended on police leadership and training, it also depended on making political decisions without sectarian motives.

The sheer scale of the continuing civilian devastation was revealed by a British research report in September 2011. Over 12,000 Iraqi civilians had died since the 2003 invasion from suicide bomb attacks alone.[15] The number was still rising. That month Iraq's lawlessness was illustrated by a mass grave found in Dujail in Salahuddin containing forty bodies—all Baghdad taxi drivers killed for their cars over the past two years by a criminal gang. Another thirty-five cabbies were missing in Babil Province.[16]

Security deteriorated further in 2013 and early 2014, returning Iraq to U.S. headlines for the wrong reasons. A wave of killings targeted soldiers, police, and other government personnel, plus Shia civilians. Violent incidents were staged, including attacks on Shia mosques, intended to set off Shia retaliation. Car bombs and suicide bombs in high-traffic areas again became daily occurrences, mostly but not only in Baghdad; two were in the KRG. Over 8,800 Iraqi civilians and soldiers died in this violence in 2013 alone. It would get worse in 2014.

The attacks against Shia generated occasional retaliation by Shia militias, though not the Mehdi Army, its demobilization announced by Al-Sadr in 2008. As the threat increased, so did the size of the militias and their collaboration with government security forces.

The proposed agreement to keep some U.S. troops in Iraq after 2011 was intended to deter further internal security threats but also to retain U.S. influence on military decisions. The Iraqis played politics with it, led by Al-Sadr and supported by Shia leaders heeding Iran's opposition. Obama declined to take a strong stand in favor, so the United States withdrew altogether, as previously agreed during the Bush administration, but by doing so it abandoned much of its leverage with decision makers in Iraq, reducing its political influence and its critical honest broker role between contending factions. So the withdrawal decision accommodated political considerations in both governments, but it angered U.S. diplomats and military commanders on the ground and caused unease in both countries. Many Iraqis felt the United States had abandoned them. The decision soon proved disastrous for both sides.

The Syria civil war made everything worse. Thousands of jihadists from other nations poured into Syria, seizing control of the anti-Assad rebellion and terrorizing communities. Many from the Islamic State of Iraq and Syria (ISIS) organization crossed into Iraq and renewed Al-Qaeda in Iraq's assault on the government and on Sahwa tribal fighters in Anbar—and were behind many deadly attacks in Baghdad's Shia neighborhoods.

In January 2014 ISIS took control of part of Fallujah in Anbar, just forty miles from Baghdad, and challenged the government's control of Ramadi, the capital. The Iraqi Army was so widely rejected in Anbar that it could not operate effectively there. Its initial efforts to halt the ISIS tide left hundreds of soldiers dead; many others deserted. It took major casualties in Anbar later in the year also. Meanwhile, over 200,000 Syrian Kurds escaped ISIS by fleeing into Iraqi Kurdistan,[17] adding to all the internally displaced persons who had moved there earlier.

The overlap between the internal political conflict and the jihadist invasion was worrisome. Many Sunnis already opposed the Shia-led government, and some felt marginalized and frustrated. Decisions by the prime minister deepened their hostility. They saw an armed struggle against a government they hated. In a we-versus-they culture, it's too easy for some people to side with violent extremists fighting a common enemy.

The Disaster of 2014 from the Ground Up

It's not a good experience to be watching TV news about Iraq and suddenly realize all your hard work is being threatened. Many other veterans of the civilian coalition in Iraq had the same reaction to the ISIS disaster of 2014. Many military veterans voiced anger that their sacrifices and especially the ultimate sacrifice by so many fellow soldiers could be rendered meaningless.

My oft-stated theme is that Iraq cannot be adequately understood from media accounts and policy debates and requires a view from the ground up. The military campaign by ISIS, which Iraqis call *Daesh* (pronounced "Dahsh")—a non-Islamic, uncomplimentary Arabic word—reinforced that theme. It got enormous media coverage and heavy debate, but information from people and places actually impacted challenged the prevailing narrative. The coverage caught up only gradually and only partially to what really happened.

On June 3, 2014, after the national election, I convened several visiting and resident Iraqis and Kurds to exchange ideas on Iraq issues, including a visiting official of the Gorran party, a former member of my Erbil Anti-Corruption Team, a former Baghdad journalist, a research consultant from Karbala, and a Kurdish American State Department employee from Kirkuk.

On June 6, ISIS launched a dramatic surprise attack on Mosul, Iraq's second largest city, at over 1.7 million people, and seized control. A half million of those people, including virtually all of the largely Kurdish and Christian populations and smaller minorities living east of the Tigris, fled into Kurdistan, as did the governor and other high officials. Almost all the Shia also fled.

On June 18 I hosted another former member of my Erbil team and two visiting scholars from Salahaddin University in Erbil. In the two weeks since the first meeting, the stunning events in Iraq had made many of the earlier discussion topics moot.

On the ground the Mosul news made little sense, as the ISIS force was small and outnumbered many times over by Iraqi Army troops in the area. Yet this huge city fell almost immediately, as Iraqi soldiers fled en masse before any shots were fired. ISIS immediately rolled on through Ninewa to the southeast, capturing Tikrit and other cities as well as parts of Kirkuk Province, and seemed to be marching on Baghdad. The Iraqi Army that had supposedly become a more effective fighting force through expensive U.S. training and equipment mostly abandoned its positions, and much of the equipment, and failed to fight at all. Making everything worse, the Kurds coldly took advantage of the army's withdrawal from Kirkuk to seize control of the city, making it clear that it considered Kurdish control permanent.

Based on ground-level reports, however, this was not primarily an invasion of foreign jihadists, as the media led us to believe. It was no coincidence that ISIS first targeted Mosul, bastion of the Baathists and Iraq's officer corps, or that its second major target was Tikrit, Saddam's home city. The army disappearing act in Mosul was reported to me as having started with top officers who abandoned their posts before the attack even started and told the soldiers to give up their weapons and flee, leaving no one to defend the city. How ISIS made that happen was the missing link in the story, and a parliamentary investigation and the removal of Ninewa's governor followed, but the circumstances were suspicious. Indeed, ISIS had begun seizing control of Mosul from the inside months earlier, and the city was already largely out of government control.[18]

In Tikrit one ISIS leader was a nephew of Saddam; one of my Iraqi friends who knew him personally recognized him from a photo. Media did report the prominent role of the Naqshbandi Army, a militant group centered around Saddam-era military officers and Baathist officials, which had also played a role in Mosul. On July 9, 2014, a British newspaper, the *Telegraph*, confirmed our suspicions, reporting that the two top ISIS officials under its leader, Awwad Al-Baghdadi, himself an Iraqi and the former Al-Qaeda in Iraq deputy and successor to Al-Zarqawi, were both former Saddam military officers, as were other top ISIS officials whose names and photos appeared in the story.[19]

In reality this existential crisis for Iraq had three sources primarily. First, the military campaign was spearheaded by several thousand foreign ISIS fighters but in collaboration with a larger number of Sunni Iraqis, including local residents attacking or threatening their own neighbors. Second, much of the top leadership came from Baathists, including former Saddam military officers and internal security operatives, aided by Sunni resistance groups. Their efforts to overthrow the government went back to 2003. Third, a significant minority of Sunni Arabs hostile to the government persuaded themselves that ISIS was on their side.

As the smoke cleared from this "foreign invasion," therefore, it became clearer it was also an internal revolt by the same Sunni elements that had always opposed the elected government and that much of this so-called invasion was actually an inside job. ISIS in Iraq consisted mostly of Iraqis. Evidence from a growing number of firsthand accounts has since reinforced my ground-up explanation and exposed one of the leading myths about the ISIS takeover.

Refugees from one place after another told one of my associates when interviewed that the attack on them and their property came from people in or near their neighborhood. This pattern started in Mosul, where ISIS supporters threatened soldiers with death if they stayed, and many Christians and others who fled had been threatened by pro-ISIS Arab tribesmen from the surrounding area.

After seizing Tikrit, ISIS fighters and Baathists arranged the massacre of 1,700 unarmed mostly Shia air force cadets from the training facility at U.S.-built Camp Speicher in Tikrit. Baathists told them ISIS was coming and they should leave or else. When they left, they were rounded up, paraded past local villagers—many of whom cheered— then were lined up and killed by men sent to ISIS by several area Sunni tribes. Tikrit was a case study in Sunni Arab resentment; the area's villagers felt proud and high status in Saddam's day but were now poor.

On June 16, one week after Mosul fell, ISIS seized Tal Afar, west of Mosul, a mostly Turkmen area of 200,000. Its Shia Turkmen were quickly victims of sectarian cleansing, many executed and most others forced to flee, mainly to Karbala or other Shia locations in southern Iraq. ISIS also attacked four Shia Turkmen villages in Kirkuk, murdering scores of civilians and causing many others to flee into Kirkuk city.

The Obama administration reacted quickly to these developments, promised help, and sent small contingents of military advisors and intelligence experts, their number soon increased, but rejected sending ground troops. Sistani issued a call to arms, bringing out thousands of brave Shia, many untrained but at least willing to fight in the Popular Mobilization Forces. Shia militias mobilized, including those with links to Iran. The security situation around Baghdad gradually stabilized.

However, ISIS then rampaged through the Sinjar area in far western Ninewa, home to Iraq's heaviest concentration of Yazidis, killing all the men who resisted and committing mass executions. Men were separated from their wives and children, transported or marched away, and massacred by the hundreds. Mass abductions of several thousand women and children followed.[20] Tens of thousands fled up a mountain, but many men were killed, and the others were trapped on the mountain with no safe exit; several hundred died.[21] The untold part of the story is that ISIS had paid tribal leaders in surrounding Sunni Arab villages to have their men attack the mostly Kurdish-speaking Yazidis.

ISIS also overran the largely Christian Nineveh Plain bordering Mosul to the east, driving virtually all the Christians into a simultaneous mad dash across the border into Kurdistan. ISIS then seized the strategic Mosul Dam and, in a stunning development, launched a military assault toward Erbil!

These events forced Obama to authorize airstrikes, to halt the advance and help thousands of Yazidis still trapped on the mountain to escape into Kurdistan. The airstrikes helped the Kurds to recover some lost ground and helped Iraqi and Kurdish military units to recover the dam and some of the area around it. A small number of Christians, from that district just across the border from Fayda, went home, but most others could not. The inrush of Christians, Yazidis, and other minorities added to all the Syrians already in Kurdistan, creating a massive refugee crisis.

The prominent role of local Sunnis in this supposedly "foreign invasion" continued even as media accounts continued to miss the real explanation.

The takeover of the predominantly Christian city of Tel Keif in the Nineveh Plain, just northeast of Mosul, was carried out by a small group of its Arab residents, after which a small group of Daesh fighters arrived to seize control of the local church.[22] The Shabaks, a small Kurdish and mostly Shia splinter group with a distinct language, living mainly in four Sinjar villages along with the Yazidis, were also attacked by nearby Arab villagers and forced to flee. The very small Kurdish Kakai minority, comparable in faith to the Yazidis and living near the KRG border east of Mosul, escaped the Daesh assault, but half their villages were destroyed.

Another case of Sunni Arabs attacking neighbors came in Salahuddin near the Kurdistan border, where Daesh paid a tribal chief $7,000 to have his men attack the neighboring Turkmen town. Two tribesmen who were captured confessed to the plot, which apparently failed.

Peshmerga who helped oust Daesh from the mixed Kurdish-Arab border cities of Makhmur and Gwer, southwest of Erbil, accused Arabs from surrounding villages of helping Daesh against them. The Kurds retaliated by refusing to allow Arab residents of either city who left during the fighting to return, an order that excluded the innocent along with the collaborators.[23]

The small, rural Shia Turkmen city of Amerli, in the Tooz District of eastern Salahuddin, is surrounded by Sunni Arab villages. Its desperate residents were under siege for almost three months by villagers and Daesh fighters, with no access to food, water, or electricity, but they refused to surrender. Amerli was saved from disaster by *peshmerga* and Shia militiamen aided by U.S. airstrikes. The Shia militiamen quickly retaliated against the surrounding villages, burning or otherwise destroying a few thousand homes.

The key point is that most of these attacks reflected the sectarian motives of local Sunnis. Most victims were from religious minorities, lacking their own militias and relying on Iraqi and Kurdish soldiers who in most places could not protect them. In northern Ninewa they included the Shia, a minority in that area. The Daesh attacks in northern Ninewa thus produced a highly sectarian result. Virtually all the non-Sunnis fled (joined by many Sunnis in Salahuddin and elsewhere threatened by the takeover). The great ethnic and religious diversity of northern Ninewa virtually disappeared.[24]

ISIS itself is ideologically more sectarian than any other group in Iraq. It executed Shia, including Turkmen, but also some Sunnis, even imams, who resisted their barbaric version of Islam, which claims to be a restoration of Islam's seventh-century origins and justifies beheadings and other atrocities as consistent with its theology.[25] ISIS actually follows an extreme version of the already extreme Wahhabist ideology originated in and still promoted by Saudi Arabia, so it is hostile to Shia, Christians, and other non-Muslims, but it considers the Saudis as enemies too. ISIS literally blew up both Shia and Sunni mosques.

In August 2014 the U.S. political tide shifted. Kurdish Americans organized demonstrations at the White House. A growing number of op-ed articles, even from liberal columnists, insisted something more must be done to stop the ISIS scourge. ISIS kept expanding in Syria at the expense of the U.S.-supported Free Syrian Army and the Syrian government, but its gruesome beheadings of previously captured American journalists James Foley and Steven Sotloff crystallized a growing public revulsion set off by the stomach-turning media coverage. Opinion shifted sharply toward doing something about ISIS and against Obama's foreign policy.

These developments gave Obama the political space to adopt an openly confrontational stance toward ISIS. In a September 10 address to the nation, he pledged to defeat ISIS, albeit gradually, and committed to a much broader campaign of airstrikes in support of future Iraqi and Kurdish ground operations and in Syria.

U.S. diplomatic pressure brought military cooperation from several Arab governments and NATO partners, at least for airstrikes. Turkey's implicit cooperation with ISIS, based on shared opposition to Syria's Assad regime, was ended, though the cross-border flow of jihadists could not be fully stopped, nor could purchases of stolen ISIS oil and gas. The United States thus started reversing the military momentum, as Obama continued to stress that defeating ISIS would not require U.S. combat troops and numerous military experts and Iraqis on the ground said it would.

Beyond the military crisis was a humanitarian crisis that was getting worse. ISIS was overrunning largely Kurdish areas in northeastern Syria as the airstrikes started, and upwards of 200,000 people had fled across the Turkish border, adding to the many already there. By mid-2015 the UN High Commissioner for Refugees estimated that Turkey had almost 2 million Syrian refugees, Lebanon 1.1 million, Jordan 600,000 (plus 2 million others, mostly Iraqis), plus the 200,000 in Iraqi Kurdistan, and the huge number of Syrians displaced within Syria. All these numbers were altered in 2015 by a massive wave of Syrian refugees and IDPs into Europe.

Based on KRG statistics, there were also 50,000 Iraqi IDPs in Erbil Province, 50,000 more in Suly, and 650,000–700,000 in Dahuk, mostly Christians, Yazidis, and other minorities.[26] People were living not only in official camps but in churches, schools (some closed to accommodate IDPs), and unfinished buildings. Many Erbil IDPs were outside the capital, in Qushtapa and near Khabat, and others spread out to Shaqlawa, Soran, and Koya, all cities I had visited earlier. It all amounted to a huge increase in the Kurdistan population. To their great credit, the Kurds willingly accepted this overwhelming challenge.

20

Winning the Endgame in Iraq

A Perilous Transition

The major loss of Iraqi territory to ISIS was directly enabled by the failure of Shia, Sunni Arab, and Kurdish political leaders to overcome their issues with each other. Whether they could finally achieve meaningful reconciliation in Iraq's no-compromise political culture, even when facing such a dire crisis, was a jackpot question with uncertain answers.

The prevailing media and political narrative said the crisis was all Al-Maliki's fault—that the support for ISIS among so many Sunni Arabs was because of him. This is what we all read. It was a simple, single-factor analysis. Like most such analyses about Iraq, it was mostly wrong.

Baathist and Sunni hostility to a government they no longer controlled went back to 2003, before Al-Maliki had even thought about being prime minister. It included the post-invasion violence against U.S. troops and the constant campaign to overthrow the new Iraqi government, which never really stopped; the self-defeating boycott of the initial election in January 2005; and the campaign against the constitution in October 2005. The three provinces voting against the constitution were later the same provinces mostly captured by ISIS—Anbar (97 percent opposed), Salahuddin (82 percent), and Ninewa (55 percent, its no percentage lower due to its Kurdish, Christian, and other minority voters). Who is fool enough to believe that's just a coincidence?

Many of the same people supported, or even joined, the sectarian violence set off by Al-Qaeda in Iraq in 2006, which caused a huge civilian death toll and was defeated only by an enormous and sacrificial U.S. military effort. ISIS was the successor to Al-Qaeda in Iraq, inheriting many of its leaders, fighters, and local operatives.

In summary, most of the oft-lamented marginalization of Sunnis stems from their own decisions.

Still, Al-Maliki made major contributions to the disaster. The army's collapse happened largely because, having appointed himself minister of defense, he assumed direct command of the military and replaced experienced Sunni commanders with less experienced officers loyal to him so as to strengthen his personal control. While his purpose may not have been sectarian (e.g., his appointees included ex-Baathists), it seemed sectarian. He did the same thing with the Iraqi National Intelligence Service, replacing its Sunni director (a former general) and most of its Sunni agents with Shia.[1] His army troops repeatedly abused Sunni civilians and communities, unnecessarily increasing antigovernment hostility. The army was also systemically corrupt in ways that undermined military readiness.[2]

Al-Maliki pursued a similar strategy within civilian ministries. He was constrained, however, in making appointments at many of them, including Defense, because of all the political deals needed to form and maintain the government. That excuse did not justify his moves to control the parliament, control even independent agencies, and compromise the independence of the judiciary. His generally dour personality and political paranoia tendencies magnified the impact.

So, creating a more democratic, more effective government required a new prime minister with a broader vision and a more inclusive message. Despite Al-Maliki's insistence that his decisive election victory legally entitled him to another term, his own party heeded the message from Sistani, parliament members of many other parties, and President Obama, who made Al-Maliki's removal a condition for desperately needed U.S. help. His party proposed the deputy parliament speaker, Dr. Haider Al-Abadi, also from Islamic Dawa but from a completely different background, including his British doctorate, longtime residence in Great Britain before 2003, and Westernized outlook. This followed the Council of Representatives election of a new speaker, Dr. Salim Al-Jubouri from Diyala, and a new Kurdish president, senior PUK leader Fuad Masoom.

Al-Abadi began making major changes and moved military coordination back to the Defense ministry, and his leadership style won friends among Sunni elected leaders of provinces where Daesh held territory. The situation stabilized and gradually improved.

I was sure most Sunnis did not support ISIS, though few living in ISIS-controlled areas dared to say that publicly. The few who did were executed publicly. Most of Iraq's Sunni Arabs had little in common with ISIS. The vast majority were not religious fanatics or willing to live under medieval Islamic codes, nor were they likely to accept ISIS's cruel tactics. A high percentage were largely or entirely secular, especially in Baghdad.

Initially, however, Sunnis had little incentive to rise up. The disaster fell mainly on Christians, Yazidis, Shia Turkmen, and other religious minorities in the North who could not defend themselves. ISIS tactics included mass executions; public individual executions, including beheadings and other gruesome atrocities, even crucifixions; and chopping off limbs for stealing. After killing so many Yazidi men, ISIS sold Yazidi women into slavery or forced them to marry ISIS fighters, and many others endured rape or other sexual abuse. Indeed, cruelty toward females is a defining ISIS characteristic.

Virtually all the Christians were able to flee, but they had to leave everything behind. ISIS took possession of their businesses, farms, and many of their homes, then looted them for items of value. ISIS supporters among their neighbors stole their possessions and often sold them. Those trapped in ISIS territory faced immediate execution if they refused to convert to Islam or pay a special tax. It was yet another milestone, possibly the final and decisive milestone, in the failure of Iraq to protect its Christians and other minorities. As one Muslim Iraqi told me, "If you have no protection, you don't live in a real country."

ISIS also worked systematically in northern Ninewa to destroy the religious presence of others, a grotesque application of its ideology. It blew up Shia and Sunni mosques; destroyed graveyards and cemeteries; destroyed historic Christian landmarks and Yazidi and Kakai temples and shrines; and destroyed or removed all religious symbols from churches, converting many to their own use. ISIS also looted and destroyed pre-Christian Assyrian archaeological sites and other historically important places. It was an all-out assault on Iraq's cultural heritage.[3]

Despite its atrocities and abuses, however, ISIS kept gaining recruits, money, and weapons, and its horrifying cruelty discouraged opposition. It was well financed—from captured oil wells, sale of looted artifacts, sale of the property of people who fled, special taxes, extortion from businessmen, extortion from government employees for shares of their salaries,[4] kidnapping ransoms, and bank robberies. Iraq alleged to the United Nations that ISIS even harvested and sold human organs from the bodies of people it executed.

In December 2014 I helped write the consultants' report on an Iraq public opinion survey by the Iraqi Research Foundation for Analysis and Development (IRFAD). One astonishing finding was that despite the horrors being inflicted on all the religious minorities and others in ISIS-controlled areas, Sunni Arabs still complained more about the government than about ISIS.

Another important IRFAD finding was that pro-government Shia militias were still a huge sectarian issue. With the army's collapse, there were soon far more militiamen than army soldiers. They were militarily necessary but politically divisive—hated and feared from their murderous role in Sunni neighborhoods during the sectarian violence. Some called them "Iranian" militias, a pejorative term reflecting Sunni Iraqis' long-standing dislike of Iran. Iran's ongoing military support—including weapons, surveillance, intelligence, and tactical military advisors—added credibility to this characterization.

It followed that the government needed to keep Shia militias out of Sunni areas whenever possible. However, Obama's decision not to send ground troops, and the slow pace of providing weapons and other military support, forced Iraq to depend on the militias. To his credit, however, Al-Abadi put all militias within a government-coordinated structure, the Popular Mobilization Forces (PMFs), including the many who responded to Sistani's call and the mainly Sunni pro-government tribal forces.

One practice with military rationale but sectarian impact was refusing in some places to let Sunnis displaced by the fighting return home after it ended, a practice of the army, Shia militias, and *peshmerga*. This practice brought heavy criticism, amplified by Western media, but showed an awareness that many of those displaced were core Daesh supporters whose return could again undermine government authority. Most, however, were innocent people. Here also, Al-Abadi reined in the militias, and displaced residents were encouraged to return.

Reforming the military was essential to the war effort. Al-Abadi replaced many senior officers but could not immediately solve other problems. He revealed on November 30, 2014, that the army had been paying salaries for at least 50,000 nonexistent "ghost soldiers," much of the money collected by corrupt officers. It turned out later that over 70 percent of the "soldiers" who had failed to defend Mosul were either ghost soldiers or were not reporting for duty so were not even there.[5] A later corruption issue was the highly excessive number of personal bodyguards provided to politicians and others, diverted from military and police units. Some people had bought their officer ranks, and being an officer created opportunities for corruption. Upper ranks were vastly overstaffed. At all levels most personnel were motivated by the salary, not patriotism. Organization and discipline were lacking in general. The net result was an army that was both expensive and dysfunctional.

Defeating ISIS in Iraq
Daesh Daily

In early 2015 I took on another Iraq assignment, as coeditor of IRFAD's fledgling *Daesh Daily*, a five-days-a-week newsletter summarizing the latest reports from Arabic-language media—government media, independent media, even Daesh media. Shortly afterward, we started adding *"Daesh Daily* comments" to some news items to clarify them and offer informed opinions. The email circulation grew to over a thousand professionals working on Iraq—not only in military and civilian agencies but also think tanks, academia, media, and elsewhere—and many readers further distribute it to others in their organizations.[6] There are a lot of us working on Iraq if you think about it.

Daesh Daily has been a window on ground-level developments important to this book and has provided an opportunity to see where developments are leading before they reach the mass media, if they do. The general impression in early 2015 from mainstream media and political commentary was that the situation in Iraq was basically unchanged. Our daily reports from Iraq indicated, however, that while the situation was still perilous, Daesh was gradually losing. Later events would show that the ground-level view was more accurate.

Information coming to *Daesh Daily* also provided daily examples of one of the most amazing and alarming things about Daesh: its relentless media propaganda.

The story behind the story. Much of what Daesh does makes no logical sense in the West. Its logic, however, is different. Daesh isn't trying to maximize its popularity; it's trying to gain new recruits. Its appeal is to the small minority who are young, impressionistic, naive, drawn to violence, and looking for adventure or fulfillment through some cause.

Daesh propaganda is a book-length subject best left for others. Briefly, however, its unique ideology has produced many ironies and contradictions. For one example, Daesh is highly Islamic and claims to be the defender of Sunnis, but it actually despises the religious orientation of almost all other Muslims, plus all non-Muslims.

In its propaganda Daesh is always victorious, even when it loses. It never admits defeat and produces videos even from lost battles, or borrowed from different battles, to create the impression it won. A suicide bomber who blows himself up (or much more often, who gets blown up first) is hailed as a success, even when his attack fails. His death is the evidence. Virtually all other fighters always return safely. The enemy always suffers many deaths. Daesh's response to defeats is also military. Defeat in one place is followed by a counterattack, or an attack somewhere else, even in other countries, carried out in a way that attracts maximum media and public attention and so distracts attention from the previous defeat.

Daesh has a large, sophisticated media operation with many online and social media supporters. The online and social media efforts of governments and many others to counter Daesh's messaging are also large, and IRFAD has had a small role in that too.

From our *Daesh Daily* perspective we see the ugly side of Daesh in news reports, including its own: the cruel executions, often of innocent people who have done it no harm; the constant targeting of helpless civilians; the exaggerations and made-up stories; and manipulation of its own ideology, often to justify killing people they just don't like. Daesh *likes* killing people.

Daesh's impact has spread well beyond Iraq, the stakes are huge, and we in the West *do* have reasons to worry. Daesh has backed up its threats by downing a Russian airliner over Egypt; launching major attacks on civilians in Paris and Nice, France; staging several bomb attacks in Turkey, including one in a major Istanbul tourist area I had visited twice, and another in Brussels, Belgium, among others;

and its propaganda has inspired mass murder attacks in San Bernardino, California, and Orlando, Florida, and smaller but deadly attacks in other countries. It was expanding territorially, with large military operations ongoing in Egypt, Libya (especially), Yemen, and Afghanistan. It seems illogical, militarily, to attack multiple world powers almost simultaneously, but doing so serves Daesh's ultimate purpose: to unite all Muslims behind its caliphate, the only Muslim organization truly standing up to the West, preparing for the final, apocalyptic battle between Muslim and Christian armies envisioned in a seventh-century Islamic prophecy—in Dabiq, Syria.

In analyzing all the Daesh ideological concepts, the one that increasingly seemed most important was Daesh's concept of territory. They insist that they are running a real caliphate, where people are protected and happy, that will keep expanding because it is brave and always victorious over its enemies. The best answer to Daesh's propaganda, therefore, is to take its territory away. As Iraq gradually did this, it effectively countered Daesh's core message.

A Shifting but Uncertain Tide

My hope from the beginning was that living for a while under the regime many Sunnis supported against their own government would bring a dose of reality. Gradually, this is what happened, though many were slow learners. Daesh rule became increasingly unpopular. Meanwhile, Baghdad's military direction improved greatly from Al-Abadi's aggressive and nonsectarian leadership.

By early 2015 the cracks in Daesh's foundation started to show. Internal issues arose, partly from battle defeats and growing casualties, partly from internal dissension. Daesh frequently executed its own members, mostly for disobeying orders or leaving the battlefield, and recruitment within Iraq met increasing reluctance.[7] A much-publicized battle lost, with over 1,000 fighters killed, was in Kobane, Syria, though most of the city was destroyed. A less-publicized but bigger loss was strategically located Jurf Al-Sakhar in western Babil Province, forty miles southwest of Baghdad, bordering Anbar and Karbala, recaptured by the army and thousands of militiamen. Jalawla and Sadiya in northern Diyala were recaptured by *peshmerga*. The Kurds also regained ground north and west of Mosul.

At the end of March 2015 combined army and militia forces recaptured Tikrit and surrounding villages, after defusing a huge number of improvised explosive devices (IEDs) set to slow their offensive—which became a standard Daesh tactic. It was a major victory, enabled by Coalition airstrikes. Using Coalition airpower to clear the way for advancing ground troops became a standard Iraqi tactic. This seemed to be the point at which the United States became Iraq's primary military ally, despite having few troops on the ground, and Iran's role was reduced.

Unfortunately, the Tikrit victory was followed in May by an embarrassing defeat, when Daesh captured Ramadi, the Anbar capital. This galvanized Iraq's political class, and Anbar's leaders joined a determined government campaign to regain control of their province. Tribal fighters gradually joined the government coalition, a brave decision, as many tribal leaders and fighters formerly from the Awakening movement had been assassinated over the past several years by ISIS and before that by Al-Qaeda in Iraq.

Meanwhile, Iraq's combined army and Iraqi Federal Police (IFP) combat units, along with militia forces, backed by Coalition and Iraqi airpower, gradually recovered most of Salahuddin, including the critical oil refinery city of Baiji in October, after more than a year of fighting that largely ruined the huge refinery. Baiji is also strategically located on the road to Mosul. In November the *peshmerga* scored another major victory against Daesh by suddenly recapturing most of Sinjar Province, in northwestern Ninewa.

In July 2015 Turkey finally ended its tolerance for ISIS activities in and through Turkey, let the United States use its Incirlik Air Base for bombing runs into Syria, and took an active role against Daesh as part of an internal security campaign also targeting Kurdish separatists. Flying from Incirlik, just two hundred miles from the Syrian border, made bombing runs far shorter, more frequent, and more effective. In other ways, however, Turkey's participation would be so self-serving that it would do more harm than good.

The airstrikes, as recorded in *Daesh Daily* reports, imposed a large toll almost every day, even though the U.S. military chose initially not to publicize these successes. For that reason and because the American public had been told so often that the U.S. military role in Iraq was limited, the huge and central role of the Coalition airstrikes and U.S. military leadership in the anti-Daesh struggle has never been understood in the United States.

By mid-2015, however, the United States estimated that the Coalition had killed 10,000 Daesh fighters in Iraq and Syria during the nine months of the bombing campaign to date, including a growing number of its leaders. The relentless daily airstrikes continued on, wiping out one Daesh-occupied building after another and devastating its leadership ranks, often with strikes targeted on leaders. The airstrikes also increasingly limited its movement from place to place, as any convoy or large vehicle could be bombed, as many were. Daesh's "caliph," Awwad Baghdadi, mysteriously disappeared from public view.

Daesh's military tactics became surprisingly one-dimensional. Almost every attack was led by vehicle-borne IEDs carried in cars, trucks, fuel tankers, and construction equipment, driven by an apparently limitless number of mostly foreign suicide bombers. Indeed, the availability of so many people willing to kill themselves was to me the biggest surprise in this conflict. One deadly suicide bomber incident in 2015 targeted Baghdad's Babylon Hotel, which had hosted my ICSP national lawyers' conference. Daesh succeeded at this tactic for a time, but the United States (and Russia) provided battlefield missiles that could take out these bomb-rigged vehicles from a longer distance. The failure rate on such attacks sharply increased, and gradually they almost disappeared from our *Daesh Daily* reports, except for attacks on civilian gatherings. As Daesh's recruitment dropped, the supply of volunteer suicide bombers also dropped, and it was forced to rely on Iraqi fighters—and by late 2016 even on kids.

As its military fortunes declined, however, Daesh continued its daily assassination campaign in Baghdad, using IEDs, vehicle-borne IEDs, and sometimes small-arms attacks, mostly targeting government employees and other defenseless civilians.

During the summer of 2015, Iraq's forces, led by its elite Counter Terrorism Service (CTS) troops, and supported by daily airstrikes by the U.S.-led Coalition and both the Iraq Air Force and Iraq Army Air helicopters, gradually displaced Daesh from areas around Ramadi in often heavy fighting. Ramadi city then fell easily in January 2016, though much of it had been destroyed.

Iraq then moved west along the Euphrates, along which most Anbar cities are located, to recapture Hit and Kubaisa, then Baghdadi, in Hit District west of Ramadi, then neighboring Haditha, close to the Al-Asad Iraqi base where U.S. troops are stationed. From Hit they made a sudden move across the desert to capture Rutba, in Anbar's far southwest, capital of the vast desert province of the same name, and moved quickly to secure other locations in western Anbar, leaving Daesh in control of only the far northwest along the river, including the cities of Anah and Rawa (Anah District) and Al-Qa'im, the last being a district capital and Daesh headquarters city close to the Syrian border, its strategic importance repeatedly demonstrated by all the Coalition and Iraqi airstrikes landing on Daesh facilities and leaders there.

The next target was the big one: Fallujah, arguably the nastiest place in Iraq, whose stubborn but losing fight with the U.S. Marines years earlier had caused major damage to the city. It was the first large city taken over by Daesh, back in 2013. Iraqi forces, including many PMFs, had conducted a lot of mostly winning battles against Daesh in the Fallujah District's Qarma and Ameriyat Al-Fallujah subdistricts without fully controlling them. Once Iraq's best troops showed up in force, however, they quickly took control of these areas and then moved on Fallujah city. While experts predicted a long drawn-out battle, our *Daesh Daily* reports indicated that the city residents had by now turned sharply against Daesh and that the actual number of Daesh fighters in the city was not that high. Led again by its Counter Terrorism troops, Iraq methodically rolled through Fallujah from the south, capturing the entire city within days.

Mosul was an even bigger target and far more complicated. The city was one of five Mosul subdistricts, the southernmost being rural Qayara, site of a major oil complex and an old military airfield the United States had used before. Iraq set up its Ninewa Operations Command in Makhmur, east of Qayara city across the Tigris, in an area controlled by the *peshmerga*, and started moving troops to the area and seizing control of Makhmur's villages. Iraq then sent troops up the main road through northwest Salahuddin, past the city of Shirqat, still awaiting its own liberation, to Qayara. It captured the airbase and the oilfield, then one village at a time, gradually dislodging Daesh from its territory in Qayara. Villages north across the border in Hamdaniya District were taken over by the *peshmerga*. The government offensive soon moved back to Shirqat, quickly dislodging Daesh from the city. Meanwhile, a detailed plan was being devised among Iraq, the *peshmerga*, and the United States, for recapturing Mosul itself. Then the real problems started.

Defeating Corruption

Friday, August 7, 2015. Something amazing happened. A massive demonstration occurred in Baghdad, as did demonstrations in other cities. Demonstrators articulated a broad anti-corruption platform, demanding among other things that the independence of the Commission of Integrity (COI) and the judiciary be restored and that the excessive salaries and benefits, and bodyguards, of elected officials be reduced. As with the 2011 demonstrations, these protests made the political leadership nervous.

Sunday, August 9. Just two days later, something even more amazing happened. Al-Abadi sided with the demonstrators. He issued a far-reaching anti-corruption reform program and demanded that the COR pass legislation to enact it. *Two days* after that, it did so almost unanimously, even though COR members themselves had something to lose from it.

Al-Abadi's reforms eliminated the three deputy prime minister positions and even the three vice president positions, one held by Al-Maliki. He eliminated party and sectarian quotas for appointments to high-level positions below the ministers, down to the director general level, which attacked one of the major sources of ministry dysfunction and potentially created an opening for a meaningful civil service appointed on merit (a Model Ministry principle). He eliminated most of the bodyguards for high officials, whose numbers had reached an absurd level, enabling their reassignment back to military and police duties, and he eliminated other special privileges. The Council of Representatives accepted a major salary reduction. Al-Abadi demanded restoration of the anti-corruption agencies' independence and cleared the way for investigating and expediting all present and previously filed corruption cases. A few days later he moved to consolidate the number of ministries from thirty-three to twenty-two, eliminating four altogether. He even claimed the power to fire provincial governors and council chairmen (perhaps an unconstitutional reach).

Even before the demonstrations, Al-Abadi held the solution for the COI and other anti-corruption agencies in his own hands. He could restore their independence by reversing Al-Maliki's decisions; encourage them to exercise their full authority; bar political appointments to these agencies; prohibit political interference in their work; protect investigators, judges, and courtrooms; and let the courts sentence the corrupt. His reform measures seemed to promise all of those things and demonstrated the top-level political will that was previously lacking. The remaining question was how much of this reform he would actually be allowed to implement.

All of this proved three points important to my story.

First, the official reactions to the demonstrations showed more clearly than ever that public opinion matters in Iraq. People couldn't get change from the elections and took to the streets. The politicians were again forced to accommodate public opinion.

Second, the demonstrators' demands showed again that people do connect the corruption to their own lives. The salient issue to many protesters was the continuing lack of adequate electricity in most of Iraq as summer temperatures soared above 120 degrees F (50 degrees C). After ten years of post-Saddam governments, patience with failure had largely run out.

Third, the successful demonstrations, like the elections, showed that voters are ahead of the politicians and that Iraq really is a democracy, despite all its dysfunctions.

Abadi's public support was that much greater because the most powerful man in Iraq had his back. Grand Ayatollah Sistani had strongly supported the demonstrations, frustrated with the performance of the political class he helped to elect ten years earlier, as he again demonstrated his democratic Shia concept of Islamic governance.

As I thought about all this, I had a flashback to my Anti-Corruption manager role, which in my own mind I have not quite abandoned. It was especially encouraging that the demonstrations were led largely by civil society organizations, probably including some of mine from ICSP. It was encouraging too that the demonstrations had no apparent sectarian motive.

So Al-Abadi actually *did* face down a lot of people to solve the corruption problem, and he took on all of them at once. However, while most parliament members seemed to go along, Al-Abadi's more important support came from the people in the streets. This made him more powerful but also more vulnerable. Most of the demonstrators would not keep coming every Friday, though hundreds did, and implementing the reforms would necessarily take time, testing their patience. Politicians targeted by investigations or who had lost positions, money, or perks from the reforms would still be around after the demonstrators were gone, and eliminating so many patronage positions would eliminate economic opportunities for a lot of party hacks. The resistance built gradually and included militia organizations.

In February 2016, however, Al-Abadi steered into the storm, proposing to replace some politically appointed ministers with nonpolitical technocrats in an effort to get cabinet members who would work together and improve government performance. This got strong support in the streets but threatened the vested interests of political parties, each benefiting from the party quota system under which cabinets are constructed. When Al-Abadi submitted his nominations on March 31, 2016, in the teeth of heavy political resistance, he had also further reduced the number of ministries from twenty-two to sixteen.

From there the whole process got bogged down by legislative scheming, punctuated by massive demonstrations staged by Moqtada Al-Sadr that were simultaneously pro-reform and anti-Abadi, one of which invaded the parliament chambers. Al-Abadi sidetracked the initiative after getting a few nominees through, apparently to avoid making the political crisis worse. The surly Council of Representatives later voted the successful minister of defense out of office (in the middle of a war), and the minister of finance too, and earlier a large bloc had tried unsuccessfully to dump the COR Speaker, Salim Al-Jubouri.

So even in the middle of a war, many COR members were unwilling to stop playing political games or to give up their share of the political spoils system. The corruption issue had finally been confronted, however. A prime minister had stood up to the corrupt. A political class that had presided over the loss of much of the country and a major financial crisis, while milking the system for its own benefit, seemed more unpopular than ever.

The Looming Economic Disaster

Contributing to the anti-corruption crusade was a financial crisis. With oil at peak prices, Iraq's revenues had soared. Members of the political class turned this gain to their own benefit, while their undignified scramble for public resources paralyzed government services. Then world oil prices went into the tank, so to speak, causing a disastrous drop in revenues and a huge budget deficit. You can understand the gravity from just a few facts. Well over 90 percent of Iraq's revenues come from oil and gas, higher than any other oil-producing country. Calculate the percentage drop that occurred in the price you pay for gas at the pump. Apply the same percentage to Iraq's budget. It's a huge crisis as long as oil prices stay low—and an economics version of having too many eggs in one basket.

Iraq already had a major unemployment problem, exacerbated by all the new workers resulting from its fast-increasing population. The war and the resulting population displacement accelerated the problem. Most working-age Iraqis and Kurds are employed by the government or state-owned enterprises. Now there was no money to keep buying off more and more people with government jobs. The energy sector could not keep absorbing workers because it was earning far less revenue. Once the Daesh crisis ended, most of the militia jobs would go away. The private sector is underdeveloped, undermined by discriminatory government practices, and hamstrung by antibusiness government regulations. Agriculture has declined precipitously, from climatic causes and government mismanagement, and most food is now imported.[8]

Even if Daesh disappears and the anti-corruption reforms soar, the downward economic slide may mean rising poverty, increasing public frustration, and more big demonstrations. Al-Abadi was soon seeking and receiving temporary help from the United States and other foreign governments and from the International Monetary Fund.

To all of that add all the people displaced by the war. Even before its Mosul liberation campaign added to the burden, Iraq already had a UN-estimated 3.2 million displaced people. A large percentage of them were living in tent camps. As all those Daesh IEDs and booby traps back in their war-torn neighborhoods had to be defused one at a time, they returned only gradually to their homes. Their cities and neighborhoods were often scenes of destruction, created by the fighting and bombing. The cost of rehab will be many billions of dollars that Iraq doesn't have. The government's reputation will be on the line, however, as the displaced are largely from places where antigovernment sentiment helped cause the Daesh crisis in the first place—the places where reconciliation between the government and Sunni Arabs most needs to work.

Showdown in Mosul

In February 2016 Iraqi troops started arriving in Ninewa for the Ninewa liberation campaign. Coalition bombing increased to several airstrikes almost every day, especially in the Mosul area. The United States increased its military presence, dispatching Special Forces units and a U.S. Marines artillery contingent, with more to come, and other Coalition countries added small numbers of troops, mostly for training and to support the airstrike operation. By then the UN was estimating that 19,000 Iraqis had been killed in the past two years.[9]

In Mosul, life was depressing and dangerous, marked by increasing daily executions, often public and often by cruel and grotesque methods, intended to keep the population in line. Daesh proudly filmed and publicized these events. Many people avoided going outside as much as possible, to avoid Daesh's cultural enforcers in the streets. Residents also suffered severe disruptions of economic life; soaring food prices; and deteriorating electric, water, hospital, internet, and cell phone service. As the pressure on Daesh grew, its behavior became even more horrifying, but incidents of anti-Daesh resistance groups assassinating Daesh fighters and officials through various tactics became an almost daily occurrence.

The long delay in the Mosul campaign led to complications, however. Former governor Atheel Nujaifi, who was in office when Daesh took over and in the aftermath was voted out of office by the Iraqi parliament, reemerged as leader of a shadowy entity called the National Mobilization Forces (NMF), which was unconnected to Iraqi forces and unwanted. Nujaifi openly promoted a separatist agenda for Ninewa.

Nujaifi's scheme was supported by KRG president Masoud Barzani, whose own agenda included acquiring for Kurdistan the northern Ninewa areas normally populated by religious minorities, as part of an independent Kurdistan. Barzani made early public claims on Iraqi territory controlled by the *peshmerga* and announced his intention to hold an independence referendum within the year.

Barzani's haste reflected the major political crisis in Kurdistan over his leadership. His term as president had run out, as had an extension voted by the KRG parliament, and he was term limited. But he refused to leave office. The Gorran opposition party, now part of the government, was leading calls for him to step down, supported by the PUK, then was accused of leading a demonstration in Suleimaniya that turned violent. Barzani responded by using KDP security personnel to physically block Gorran's ministers, including the *peshmerga* minister, from returning to their jobs in Erbil, basically a military coup against Gorran. This illegal power play was so outrageous that the PUK reunited with Gorran in a new political alliance.

The Mosul scheme also involved Turkey's increasingly autocratic president, Recep Tayyip Erdogan. Erdogan sent Turkish troops to Bashiqa, just east of Mosul, to supposedly protect a hundred or so Turkish military trainers working with the NMF, then refused to take them out, despite months of angry protests by Iraqi leaders and U.S. and international pressure. This plot was a direct threat to Iraq's territorial integrity.

Later Erdogan, reacting wildly to a July 15 coup attempt against him and obsessed with the Kurdish PKK militia, upped the ante by stating that Turkey would also participate in the Mosul liberation, possibly by invading Mosul itself, which had been part of Turkey until the 1920s. By this time his leadership had become so erratic and so confrontational that no one could assume he was bluffing. The intense U.S. diplomacy toward a coordinated approach to the Mosul liberation campaign, involving even Vice President Joe Biden, seemed to finally get Barzani on board but not the Turks.

Unfortunately, this huge crisis that *Daesh Daily* was documenting every day went largely unreported in the U.S. media. It was mid-October before Washington's leading newspaper caught up with the story. Once again, the view from the ground up proved more reliable.

It was apparent from our daily reports from Mosul that the population there was anxious for its liberation by government troops. Yet Mosul had emerged again as Iraq's most challenging place: a Baathist stronghold, bastion of the Saddam military establishment, heavily Sunni and antigovernment, and too far away geographically to control; complicated by Kurds occupying areas around it and scheming to keep the Iraqi government out; and now threatened by Turkey.

In the face of this crisis, on October 16, 2016, a determined prime minister ordered the start of the Mosul liberation campaign.

On the same day, October 16, 2016, the struggle against Daesh in Syria reached Dabiq, in reality just a small rural town in northwestern Syria, six miles (ten kilometers) from the Turkish border. It wasn't quite the epic battle foreseen by the prophecy or Daesh propaganda. A small group of opposition fighters supported by Turkey advanced into the town. The last Daesh defenders ran away.

The liberation campaign soon dislodged ISIS from its territory in Hamdaniya District and the neighboring Mosul subdistrict of Bashiqa east of the city and the four Mosul subdistricts to its south. Retaking the east side of Mosul city, east and north of the Tigris River, became a major challenge, even for Iraq's elite Counter Terrorism Service, its troops met by a wave of Daesh suicide vehicle bombs. Iraq gradually achieved a complete victory, however, and moved on to west Mosul, just as the Trump administration took power in Washington, promising the Iraqi government continued U.S. support. PMF troops, kept out of Mosul to avoid sectarian reactions, took control of southern Tal Afar District immediately west of Mosul. The military success of the liberation campaign seemed assured. All indications were that the people of Mosul and Ninewa in general were happy to get rid of ISIS.

After Ninewa, Iraq needed to recover only northwest Anbar and the Hawija District and adjoining areas in Kirkuk to take away Daesh's remaining territory in Iraq.

All the maneuvering over Mosul showed that the endgame in Iraq was already on, well before Daesh could be defeated, and that victory over Daesh would not end the threats to Iraq's territorial integrity.

A Reconciliation Strategy

The Three Narratives

Why don't the Shia, Sunni Arabs, and Kurds get along better? The answer comes largely from what I call "The Three Narratives." Each community has its own distinct narrative. All three, however, have the same first line: "We are the victims."

The problem is that in each victimization narrative one or both of the other two communities are the perpetrators. Shia resentment toward Sunnis goes back to the year 680 and reflects the Sunnis' historic political dominance in Iraq—but especially the oppression and major losses of Shia lives under Saddam. According to one version, "Our legends tell of one long succession of wrongs committed against us, and the frenzied devotion to the Imams [is] our sole source of emotional respite from what we view as centuries of pain and oppression. We are unabashedly obsessed with this stylized history of oppression and our self-reinforced culture of victimization; our mistreatment by so many is for us a point of pride and not shame."[10]

Many Sunni Arabs felt dispossessed by the U.S.-led invasion that resulted in the Shia-majority government, and a lot of anti-Americanism came with that. They blamed Shia Arabs for their disempowerment and their alleged oppression by the Al-Maliki government. A lot of Sunni Arabs actually do think their treatment by the Shia-majority government has been worse than Saddam's treatment of the Shia. Some of those alienated Sunnis feel so aggrieved that they have tried since 2003 to overthrow the government, killing tens of thousands of Shia (and many Sunnis) in stubborn pursuit of their goal.

The Kurds still feel victimized by the earlier decades of mistreatment from Sunni Arab regimes and especially from Saddam and his deadly Anfal campaign. Many thousands of Kurds have died in conflicts with the Iraqi government. Many Kurds also felt victimized by Al-Maliki.

Each narrative describes its people as fighting for their survival. According to one observer, "In Iraq some community narratives have been deliberately constructed in such a way as to demean (and even dehumanize) large sections of the population, all with a view to absolving a particular community or individual of culpability."[11]

Add to this the previously discussed instinct to control as well as the consequent unwillingness to compromise, which in turn paralyzes the ability to negotiate, and you have the decidedly steep terrain on which any future reconciliation efforts must travel.

The endgame in Iraq will not be about whether and how Daesh is defeated, as you might think from the media coverage and official statements. The endgame is mostly about reconciliation.

Reconciliation and Justice

Reconciliation requires justice. Justice is owed to hundreds of thousands of Iraqis. Thousands have committed crimes against them. How will the living victims get justice? How will the families of victims killed get justice?

Christians, Yazidis, and other displaced Iraqis who go home will have to face Arab neighbors who murdered their family members or neighbors, forced them to flee, and/or looted their homes (though many refused to do that), including people still occupying their homes. Who will protect them this time? Who will arrest the criminals? Who will ensure they recover their property? Will they be compensated for their losses?

Reconciliation requires perpetrators to acknowledge fault and victims to forgive. Much of the Daesh campaign was carried out by local Sunnis targeting non-Sunni neighbors. Ending up on the losing side will make them deserving targets of those they victimized. Some who committed no crimes but supported the Daesh members who did will also face people wanting revenge. Many who threw in with Daesh and lost will be even more resentful of the government, even an inclusive government. The Baathists who joined in the takeover will again feel the resentment of defeat (and didn't give up after their previous defeats), and the many who played a significant role will be subject to arrest and prosecution and, for some, execution. Even innocent Sunnis in mixed ethnic or religious areas will face skepticism and hostility.

Reconciliation has to work both ways. A lot of innocent Sunnis were impacted by the struggle against Daesh. Some were victims of retaliation by Shia militiamen or *peshmerga*, and some were forcibly displaced and/or had their homes destroyed. They also are entitled to justice.

If political reconciliation finally emerges from this national ordeal, it will be an achievement rightly praised and celebrated. In places most affected by the Islamic State, however, the social fabric will likely deteriorate, not improve; reconciliation at ground level will be more difficult, not less. Dealing with the real endgame is therefore a daunting and politically perilous challenge that needs a plan and a strategy just as complex as the strategy to defeat Daesh.

The legal challenges of the post-ISIS period will be enormous. There are multiple policy options that are not mutually exclusive. The most obvious is *investigation and prosecution* of as many perpetrators as possible. For that to work the court system needs more prosecutors, greater administrative capacity, secure courthouses, more personal security for judges, and the absence of political interference.

Recognizing that the courts could be overwhelmed by the volume of cases, Iraq could declare a *general amnesty* for some crimes, though not major crimes such as murder and rape. It could also accept adjudication of some cases through *tribal law* when both parties agree to it in advance. Use of tribal law could help especially to *limit revenge crimes*, a major element in Iraq's culture of violence. In post-ISIS Iraq the government's relationships with tribal leaders may be critical.

The government could pay *compensation* to Christians and others who had homes and/or property stolen (and even sold) after they left, which need not preclude prosecution. It could also make the return of property, or restitution for damaged or stolen property, a condition for amnesty.

Justice requires that punishments come from the justice system. The government needs to stop any retaliatory violence in former Daesh-held areas by army soldiers, Shia militia units, or any other unauthorized persons—and punish the perpetrators.

Various combinations of approaches could be implemented, but failure to develop a comprehensive plan could lead to chaos.

Reconciliation with Religious Minorities

Aside from reestablishing justice among neighbors, the Iraqi government needs to rebuild its own relationship with its religious minorities.

Implement "homeland" provinces for Christians and Turkmen. This legislation was proposed in January 2014 to create separate governorates for the three Nineveh Plain districts (together) and for Tal Afar District in Ninewa and Tooz District in Salahuddin. Implementing that decision with any necessary revisions for recent developments should be an immediate priority once Daesh has been removed. The district governments are already in place officially, though they were forced out by Daesh. As governorates, they should come under the Provincial Powers Law, allowing more latitude for those in office to make their own decisions. Iraq needs to provide the start-up money to move the process forward and fund each province on the same basis as existing provinces. This initiative will also be a great opportunity for Western countries, international organizations, and international NGOs to provide early support, recognizing that Iraq is in a financial crisis. Some of the Christian and other minority cities and towns, and many churches, have suffered major destruction and will need significant reconstruction in order to restore normal life for their citizens.

One reason for the haste is the large number of refugees who need to go home, especially those who fled from the Nineveh Plain, but who need protection, livable conditions and some semblance of order. Some will be anxious to return as soon as home is again in a relatively safe place. Many will never return; some are already in Europe. Another reason for fast implementation is to encourage those who are undecided, or leaning toward emigration, to go home and help rebuild their churches and communities. Previously emigrated residents should be invited to return. Few will come at first, but many more may come later as life improves. Assyrian Catholics outside Iraq are sharply divided on the separate province issue. Some urge the Christians still in Iraq to stay and rebuild; others believe Christians no longer have a future there. For Iraq, which has so badly failed its religious minorities, the stay-and-rebuild policy is the only morally defensible option. Financial support from U.S. and European Christians could make a big difference in restoring churches and communities.

An election process needs to be established by the Independent High Electoral Commission, to include a revised voter roll reflecting who has actually returned. While these new provinces were defined with Christians and Turkmen in mind, many smaller minorities and

Sunni Arabs have homes in those districts. Political control should depend on elections, not ethnic or religious preference.

USAID or other U.S. technical assistance would be valuable, and U.S. political support may be necessary, partly as a counterweight to "outside" players trying to interfere. This initiative cannot be allowed to get caught up in Ninewa politics or Kurdish expansionism. Political status decisions can be made later.

Establish a special program for Yazidi women. The Yazidis have been collectively decimated and traumatized by Daesh and deserve whatever help can be offered to ensure their protection and recovery. International recognition of this horror as a genocide would have at least symbolic importance. Special help is needed, however, for Yazidi women, over three thousand of whom were captured and in most cases subjected to the most degrading personal abuses. They face a difficult readjustment to society in conservative Iraq.

Document ISIS abuses and atrocities. For those forced to flee or forced to live under Daesh, this traumatic experience will not soon go away. The justice system needs especially to work for them. Many had family members murdered, kidnapped, raped, or abused in other awful ways. Numerous Daesh mass graves have already been found, with more to come, and will yield evidence for some of the murders. There are people specialized in this kind of investigation. Documenting these crimes, starting as soon as Daesh is removed, would facilitate legal cases against some of the guilty and begin a government reconciliation process with the victims.

Restore or reconstruct historic sites. The onslaught against Iraq's archaeological sites reached a new low in March 2015, when ISIS destroyed and looted a three-thousand-year-old site in the ancient Mesopotamian capital of Nimrud, southeast of Mosul, a UNESCO-designated World Heritage Site. Many of the mosques, churches, other minority religious sites, and other historical sites destroyed can never be restored; even partially restoring the others would take a meticulous, multiyear effort. Still, restoring some of the nation's lost heritage would restore some people's lost faith in their government.

Reconciliation with Sunni Arabs

Empower provincial governments. All the Sunni hostility toward the authority of the central government is unnecessary. The Iraq constitution provides for a federal system that limits central government powers. The Provincial Powers Law passed in 2008 and amended in 2010 and 2013 was meant to implement that provision. Full implementation would put a significant proportion of government programs operating in Sunni-majority provinces under their own control, undermine the dishonest argument that they live under a Shia dictatorship, and leave no excuses for supporting Daesh or any other antigovernment group.

So what are they fighting about? Al-Maliki disliked the law and obstructed its implementation. He is no longer in charge, however. Implementation was required to begin by 2015, and it did. It needs more support from Baghdad, however. Management and budget systems must be strengthened to make it all work. The national government needs to transfer the money on time so each province can plan, fund, and deliver many services now managed from Baghdad. A new USAID technical assistance project was on the way.

End the de-Baathification policy. De-Baathification was unavoidable and necessary at one time but is well past the point of diminishing returns and endangers internal security. The government and Shia citizens need to accept that most Sunnis consider its continuation, albeit under different laws, a sectarian miscarriage of justice. Yes, there are still many guilty Baathists who have avoided punishment—some of the worst being Shia. Just accept that some guilty people will escape justice and that a few may even hold elective office. Forgiveness for the past will do more for Iraq than holding out for a 100 percent accountability level that can never be achieved.

Promote patriotism over sectarianism. The war effort, and especially the military success against Daesh, has brought a palpable boost in Iraqi patriotism and a greater sense of unity between Shia and Sunnis. Those leading the reform effort in the streets are noticeably doing so from nonsectarian motives. Al-Abadi's term has been notable for its outreach to Sunni Arabs and Kurds. Beyond the sectarian loyalties central to much of the expert analysis about Iraq is a strong sense of Iraqi identity that we have largely forgotten. Political leaders who appeal first and foremost to Iraqis' patriotism and national pride would help Iraq to transcend some of its sectarianism and to undermine the self-defeating logic of "The Three Narratives."

Rebalance foreign and defense policy. Military reliance on Iran, especially in the early days of the anti-Daesh struggle, raised old fears that Iraq was coming under Iranian control. These fears subsided as Al-Abadi and the Iraqi military gained increasing support from the United States and the international Coalition. Even though often exaggerated, however, the argument that Iraq is in Iran's pocket has political consequences.

Iraq should continue to value Iran's support while loosening its embrace. It should strengthen its ties to the elected Iranian government and take no further orders from elements of the government not accountable to the elected government. It should strengthen its diplomatic initiatives with Sunni Arab states, despite all their previous disrespect and interference, and treat all its neighbors equally. This is essential to reconciliation with Sunnis *in Iraq.*

The line dividing most of the Shia Middle East from most of the Sunni Middle East goes right through Baghdad. This underlines Iraq's regional importance and the absolute importance of staying out of the conflict. To earn its place in the legacy of the Arab Spring, Iraq must continue emulating Sistani the democrat, not Khamenei the theocrat. By creating its own balanced relationship between Shia and Sunni, notwithstanding its Shia majority, Iraq would become a model in the Middle East on the one issue that matters most, and it would establish a principled role that all Iraqi citizens of goodwill can support, regardless of sect.

The disastrous confusion in Syria makes this goal harder but no less important. The predominantly Shia leadership of Iraq is understandably pro-Assad. Iraqi Shia militiamen have been allowed to go fight in Syria. But Iraq's real national interest in Syria is the protection of the minority Alawite population, not continuation of a Baathist dictatorship. It can't afford to let events in Syria prevent reconciliation with Sunni countries.

The "Last Sermon of the Prophet Mohammed" commands his followers, "Learn that every Muslim is a brother to every Muslim and that the Muslims constitute one brotherhood."[12] It would transform Iraq's politics if its Shia and Sunni political leaders took that command to heart.

Preserving Law and Order

The most basic obligation of government is to protect its own citizens. This obligation is precisely where Iraq has most conspicuously failed. A state of general lawlessness has prevailed since 2003; Daesh just made it worse.

Iraq's violence has had a numbing effect over the years. Long ago it became so routine that people see it as part of everyday life. Their silence should not be confused with acceptance, however. The failure of government to protect its people is a huge issue. Those mass murder incidents and all the IED and other assassination incidents in Baghdad, and elsewhere, have a political cost.

Most of the Daesh-induced violence has occurred since the last national election in 2014. Most of the politicians who failed to stop it are still in office. Winning Mosul back may win some popularity for some political leaders, including Al-Abadi, but with new elections impending for 2018, this may not be a good time for most incumbents. Moreover, some of the solutions for the law and order problem will be controversial.

The many elements of the solution include reducing militia influence, a politically neutral military, and better police work.

Limit militia influence. Continuing to strengthen the military forces will also serve the critical goal of reducing the influence of powerful and politically motivated Shia militias. Despite Iraq's recent successes, there is still a long way to go.

With ISIS defeated, the PMFs will deserve enormous credit. Certain major Shia militias within the PMFs are already obstacles to winning the endgame, however, because they have unnecessarily antagonized Sunni citizens, already hostile to them, with retaliation attacks and other abuses against innocent people, conceding that such incidents have been greatly reduced. The connection of these militias to Iran is in itself a huge issue, which is also an issue against the government. These leaders are so openly anti-American that they even opposed Coalition airstrikes. When Al-Abadi shifted from heavy reliance on the militias to greater reliance on airpower and training help from the United States and the West, it was a turning point in the war, but it frustrated these militia leaders by reducing their political power.

Those militias, not the PMFs in general, are sectarian by definition and compromise the government's credibility. The risk is that they could dictate to the government, control police and security appointments, be a conduit for excessive Iranian influence, and/or undermine government reconciliation policies. One absolute certainty is that they antagonize Sunni citizens.

Phasing out PMF units, of all kinds, would create more unemployment, however. In late 2016, the government decided to resolve the problem by absorbing all PMFs into the government military forces after the liberation campaign, under government control. How well this compromise formula finesses the political complications and the constraints of the financial crisis remains to be seen.

Depoliticize the military. A major reason for the ISIS mess is that the military leadership became politicized and more sectarian. Al-Maliki was rightly blamed.

To help avoid a similar leadership collapse in the future, Iraq should create by law a military command structure not subject to political deals. The chief of staff would be nominated by the prime minister for COR confirmation. All other high-level officers would be appointed on a strict merit system, while maintaining sectarian and ethnic balance. This system would help ensure that military decisions other than major policies are made by military professionals at all levels, including recruitment, promotions, military assignments, training, and military operations.

I have always been highly skeptical of the much-touted plan to create a decentralized national guard that would give provinces more power in military matters. That arrangement would make it too easy for provinces to secede, for the next Daesh to take over provinces by getting control of the guard troops, or for provinces to otherwise defy the central government.

Upgrade and decentralize police services. Iraq needs police who are more qualified, more reliable in a crisis, less sectarian, and loyal to the public rather than militias. A national police training academy could ensure training that is consistent nationwide, with standards based on international best practices.

Most police work is already under provincial police chiefs, but law enforcement authority should be further decentralized, consistent with the Provincial Powers Law. This change should reduce incidents of sectarian bias by the Ministry of Interior and its police.

It is important to add that the military units of the Iraqi Federal Police have performed outstandingly in the struggle against Daesh and to that extent changed the image of the IFP. The focus of this recommendation is the quality of police services to citizens.

It follows that the ministry's police should reflect the population as a whole, be selected strictly on merit, and be deployed to provinces only when there is a genuine emergency or when provincial police are provably violating constitutional rights.

Beyond all that, the police need the capabilities and confidence to assert their authority on the streets and to ensure that this role can no longer be usurped by armed militias.

Fight terrorism with education. Extremist groups such as Daesh gain recruits and supporters largely by taking advantage of their inadequate education. Many are susceptible to extremist propaganda because they don't know any better. The Iraqi government should make it an urgent priority for students who lost two or more years of education because of Daesh to return to school. Keeping kids in school and lowering Iraq's illiteracy rate will produce a more stable society.

The Endgame and American Policy

Implementation of the nuclear agreement between the world's major powers and Iran should help Iraq in multiple ways and enable a revised U.S. policy toward the regional conflict between Iran and the Sunni regimes led by Saudi Arabia. This conflict has destabilized the Middle East and undermined American security.

The United States should embrace a policy of aggressive neutrality—refusing to take sides in what is a recently developed power struggle, not a historical religious conflict, as many believe. We should, through our diplomatic support, help Iraq stay out of the conflict.

It is also time to recognize that Saudi efforts to expand their extreme, anti-Shia, anti-Christian Wahhabi version of Sunni Islam, funded by a lot of Saudi money, are as big a threat to Middle East stability as Iran's continuing efforts to extend Ayatollah Khomeini's revolution. A lot of that money has been spent to fund mosques, schools, and other institutions that implant this Wahhabi ideology in the United States and Europe. It is disturbing that we don't voice public objections to a government-sponsored ideology that tells Sunnis to kill the Shia and the Christians. ISIS in Iraq adopted and blatantly applied this ideology to justify all its mass-murder attacks against the Shia.

The United States should also take a strong position against Iranian provocations and enforce the nuclear agreement. However, we need to sustain our improved relations with Iran's elected leadership, which most Iranians support, even if the hostility of "Supreme Leader" Ali Khamenei and the nonelected leadership continues, in order to maintain a balanced policy and to give diplomacy a chance. In that context, the Trump administration's January 2017 visa ban affecting people from Iran, Iraq, and five other Muslim countries (but not Saudi Arabia, which spawned most of the 9/11 hijackers) was not helpful.

I see the following as the key requirements for U.S. policy toward Iraq under the new administration:

Help ensure that Iraq gets rid of Daesh entirely, *and do it faster*. Taking all of its "caliphate" territory in Iraq will undermine its entire media propaganda and recruitment strategy and its credibility with other Muslims.

Continue military training and other military support, with Coalition help, to further increase Iraq's combat capabilities but also to develop a long-term partnership with the Iraqi military. ISIS will be defeated in Iraq, but its Iraqi members and supporters will still be there, reduced in number but still determined and ready to be the next insurgency. This means that ISIS or something like it could return, just as ISIS succeeded Al-Qaeda in Iraq and Al-Qaeda succeeded the Baathists. Iraq needs continuing support to break the cycle.

Sustain the recently reinvigorated U.S. political engagement with Iraq so as to maintain the vital U.S. diplomatic presence on the ground and avoid repeating the disastrous political disengagement that followed the withdrawal of U.S. troops in 2011. To pursue a nonsectarian foreign policy amid the sectarian conflict dominating the Middle East, Iraq needs a powerful friend it can rely on.

Support the anti-corruption reforms initiated by Prime Minister Al-Abadi and widely supported by Iraqi citizens, recognizing that the reforms face inevitable pushback by those who benefited at the public's expense from the old and corrupt ways of doing government business and those still pushing sectarian and separatist agendas.

Resume USAID and other civilian support to strengthen democracy and civil society, build government capacity at all levels through advanced training and technical assistance, and move Iraq closer to the standards of the Model Ministry. That support needs to include Kurdistan.

Help Iraq to rebuild the places that have been destroyed, largely by our bombing. Every liberated city needs a reconstruction plan—and a lot of money. Hundreds of thousands of Iraqi citizens still need to go home.

Encourage engagement of American and European Christians with the proposed new provinces in Iraq. That support could make the crucial difference.

Substantially increase the number of Iraqis who study for and receive U.S. graduate degrees and who apply that knowledge back in Iraq. This will also strengthen long-term Iraqi ties to the United States. By the same logic, encourage the participation of some of our new Iraqi Americans in policies and programs in Iraq that don't compromise their personal security.

Finally, continue to support a united Iraq, and its current borders, until a *mutual* agreement is reached between Iraq and the KRG on political status and disputed territories. However one evaluates Obama's Iraq policy, this stance has been one of its best and most necessary elements, notwithstanding occasional critics who have bought into the Kurdish narrative. Failure to maintain this policy could render the Iraq-KRG relationship uncontrollable and undermine our *entire* Iraq policy. This is a *nonpartisan* opinion.

The Iraqi and Syrian fronts in the war against Daesh have increasingly converged, so some reference to our Syria policy is in order. Syria is even more confusing than Iraq, and I won't try to analyze all the complexities. In general I am among those who believe we could have done more to limit the enormous death toll, the massive flood of refugees that flowed into neighboring countries and even threatened to overwhelm Europe, and the sheer misery of Syria's civil war for those still in its path.

I believe the U.S. strategy has been to take Daesh out of the Syria picture first, thus reducing the number of political and military complications and leaving a situation that is more manageable and negotiable. Taking away all of its territory in Iraq, including its Iraqi capital of Mosul, helps on the Syria side too, but truly defeating Daesh also requires taking away all of its Syria territory, including its official capital of Raqqa. This will deal Daesh a decisive blow and will also reduce its threat worldwide. What to do about the rest of the Syria mess is a different subject for other books.

Winning the endgame is essential to getting Iraq back on the democratic path that USAID and the civilian coalition set for it after 2003. Reconciliation is hard in Iraq but is essential to its future.

However, Iraq after Daesh will not be the same country our military, USAID, and international development organizations helped to rebuild and democratize. We are seeing the end of Iraq as we knew it. A bridge has been crossed. Neither the Kurds nor the Sunni Arabs nor the Shia want to resume an arrangement they all dislike. This is not necessarily bad news.

With that thought in mind, reconciliation between Iraq and the Kurds is the ultimate challenge. Beware, all ye who enter here (by reading the next chapter). It's complicated!

21

Drawing Lines in the Sand

The Kurdish Horizon

The United States has put heavy pressure on Iraq's fractious leaders to stay united and work together. During the struggle against Daesh, the Obama administration consistently maintained this policy, despite pressure from the Kurds and its sympathizers in Congress and the media. This was the right policy, and it held up at first, but well before Daesh would be gone, President Masoud Barzani was pushing for both independence and for taking over parts of Iraq. Meanwhile, it went almost without notice in the United States, but not in Kurdistan, that the Kurds had almost no border left with Iraq. Their territory mostly bordered the Islamic State.

Even in mid-2014, amid the Daesh takeover, I was certain that once that threat subsided, the Kurds would insist on independence, despite years of expert predictions that it won't happen. With the war successfully concluded, Kurdish public opinion would be just too strong for the Kurdish Regional Government political leadership to resist. Subsequent events have complicated this analysis but not changed it.

Long before the army abandoned it in June 2014, Kirkuk Province was at the heart of the shaky relationship between the Arabs and the Kurds. When army troops in Kirkuk ran away from Daesh, the Kurds immediately seized control of the city and adjoining areas not taken by Daesh. A similar scenario unfolded in other disputed areas abandoned by the army. The *peshmerga* couldn't hold northern Ninewa either, in the end, but showed the courage to fight and take casualties and recovered some ground. The KRG also welcomed the internally displaced persons (IDPs) from these areas. This gave the KRG a public relations opportunity.

The huge implications were that the departure of Daesh would heighten demands for independence and that an independent Kurdistan could be much larger than the current Kurdistan region, at Iraq's expense. Shia militias moved into other parts of Kirkuk not occupied by ISIS, however, discouraging Kurdish expansion into non-Kurdish areas.

So Iraq was a mess, but the Kurds were hopeful, their long-standing dream seemingly just over the horizon.

Kirkuk and Its Multiple Complications

The central dispute between Baghdad and Erbil is over the political status of Kirkuk Province, especially the city of Kirkuk. There are also disputed territories in other provinces, covering a wide area. The Kurds want those in Kurdistan too. Most Arabs in Kirkuk and other northern provinces have been opposed, likewise the large and important Turkmen minority, as are most Arab Iraqis and the Iraqi government.

Kirkuk's provincial capital and dominant city of the same name is about 50 miles south of Erbil, 60 miles west of Suleimaniya, and 150 miles north of Baghdad. It sits on part of a huge oil reservoir. Historically, it was majority Turkmen, a mix of Sunnis and Shia, who remain a major presence in the city and a majority or important minority in other places. The Kurds, however, later became far more numerous in the city and have their own historical claims. There is also a small, long-standing Christian minority. All of this makes Kirkuk Iraq's most ethnically diverse city and one of its largest, at 900,000 people or more, over half of the province population.

Kirkuk Province borders on two of the three Kurdish provinces—Suleimaniya and Erbil—and the Arab province of Salahuddin. It was largely Kurdish until Saddam changed boundary lines to move parts of it into adjoining provinces; starting in the 1970s, he forced 200,000–300,000 Kurds out of their homes and land, and many thousands of Turkmen too, and paid tens of thousands of Arabs in other provinces to come occupy their homes and farms. It was a military strategy intended to reduce the Kurdish presence at this strategic location. These hostile moves decisively changed Kirkuk's population balance from a Kurdish near-majority to an Arab near-majority. Many other Kirkuk villages were destroyed and many villagers killed in Saddam's Anfal campaign.

Kirkuk is therefore a Kurdish cause. As soon as Saddam's troops in Kirkuk withdrew after the 2003 invasion, thousands of displaced residents and other Kurds poured in—along with PUK *peshmerga* and looters—and many Arabs were pressured directly and indirectly to leave. Saddam's Arabization policy was soon replaced by a much larger KRG Kurdification policy, under which seemingly all displaced Kurds returned to reclaim their former homes from Arabs living in them, creating chaos and a massive mess of claims and counterclaims. Most of the Arabs didn't want to leave after so many years, but many of them became displaced within Kirkuk or in adjoining provinces. Many remained alienated, and some later joined the ISIS campaign.

The KDP and PUK took advantage of the post-Saddam power vacuum to grab predominant control of Kirkuk, taking over a major share of higher-level positions in the government and police, moving in their intelligence services (*asayesh*), and using *peshmerga* to control the streets. These actions encountered predictable resistance. Arabs and Turkmen disliked the Kurds' hardball tactics and did not want to be second-class citizens in an expanded Kurdistan.

Article 140 of the constitution required "a referendum in Kirkuk and other disputed territories" by December 31, 2007, to decide the status issue, to be *preceded* by implementing all of several provisions in the Transitional Administrative Law (Article 58), including restitution of homes and property to previously displaced residents, or compensation if that were impossible; compensation through land or money to Arabs displaced; and a "fair and transparent" census. It also required measures to remedy Saddam's "unjust changes" in provincial boundaries, though not specifying restoration of the same boundaries. The Kurds would like to restore all the old boundaries, going back fifty years and a lot of population changes, which would almost ensure they would win any province-level Kirkuk referendum—one reason this change won't happen.

The referendum was repeatedly postponed—because the stakes were huge, the issues were complex, there was no mutually acceptable solution, and there was no way to reliably determine who the eligible voters were. The 1997 Kirkuk census results reflected Saddam's displacement of Kurds and Turkmen and a huge influx of Arabs that made them the majority. In 2003, however, a lot of Kurds were coming back. A large but indeterminable percentage were not previously displaced families and their children, however, but part of a poorly disguised Kurdish strategy that encouraged other Kurds—an unknowable number but probably over 100,000—to go to Kirkuk and register to vote so as to secure a majority prior to the 2007 referendum that didn't happen.[1] Some went back home, but many others just squeezed into Kirkuk, many by occupying public buildings in the city.

Less often mentioned is that a large percentage of the displaced families had little personal reason to return. They had found better lives in Kurdistan and had no financial or educational incentive to move back, even if they did register, especially as agricultural conditions had deteriorated and there was almost no industry beyond the oil industry to provide jobs.[2]

The Kurds seemed to envision a single majority-wins referendum in Kirkuk, though Article 140 didn't require that. This was one reason the Kurdish agenda generated hostility to Article 140 among non-Kurds, making it politically impossible for successive Iraqi governments to resolve the issue. A comprehensive 2009 UN report with impartial recommendations got no support from either side. The temporary but not necessarily short-term response to the impasse was to keep kicking the can down the road.

A Property Claims Commission was eventually set up with cumbersome procedures and a thankless job. It received 178,000 claims by the end of 2011, rejecting most, by which time at least 28,000 Arabs had returned to their original provinces,[3] many fleeing immediately after Saddam's exit or as soon as they saw the Kurdish flood coming. Anecdotal evidence suggests the actual number of Arabs displaced was higher. Compensation of $15,000 and a plot of land in their original home areas was announced in 2007,[4] but the complications in actual cases and the hopelessly slow process left most with neither restitution nor compensation for years, though some claimants and Arab occupants worked out mutual arrangements.[5] In 2014 compensation payments were accepted by several thousand mostly Shia Arabs, but others refused to move.

Kirkuk has not held a Provincial Council (PC) election since the first one in 2005, as there was no way to determine which would-be voters claiming Kirkuk residence actually lived there. Efforts by parliament to hold a Kirkuk provincial election in 2009 failed. So, its

2005 electees stayed in office—twenty-six of the forty-one being Kurds, an unbalanced result reflecting the Sunni election boycott that year, but prompting a long boycott of PC meetings by Arabs and Turkmen. Meanwhile, Iraq's sectarian and other violence brought a wave of displaced Arabs. Kirkuk's 2010 national election results indicated that Arabs and Turkmen combined were only slightly less numerous than the Kurds.

The complications of the political status issue go far beyond Kirkuk. Territory at stake includes a string of areas along a northwest-to-southeast corridor through four provinces, including six of Ninewa's nine districts, plus districts in Salahuddin, Diyala, and even Wasit. The Kurds want all of *them* too. Like parts of Kirkuk, a few were moved from Kurdish to Arab-majority provinces by Saddam; others (especially in Ninewa) have large numbers of Kurds, Christians, Yazidis, or other minorities.[6] *Peshmerga* and civilians moved aggressively into Ninewa and northern Diyala too after Saddam fell. *Peshmerga* continued to patrol those areas, ostensibly to protect Kurdish residents but also setting precedents for control of places outside the Kurdish region and the Green Line and antagonizing non-Kurdish residents and the Iraqi government.

As long as control of Kirkuk and other border areas remained disputed, other Iraq-KRG crises could not be resolved. This meant a constant search for temporary fixes, a lot of arguments going nowhere, and a constant air of crisis. On both sides there was a feeling that "time is on our side." In 2014 the Kurds turned out to be right. By 2016, however, the struggle against Daesh as well as other developments made the situation more uncertain.

To all the political status complications, add this one: Who will control the oil?

Kirkuk has one of the world's largest oil reservoirs. Iraq's oil comes almost entirely from the North (including Kurdistan) and the South (especially); Central and western Iraq have little oil. The good news is that Iraq has kept discovering more oil and gas, in the North and the South, using foreign companies under contract with Baghdad or Erbil. Many recently discovered fields are *within* Iraqi Kurdistan. When I left Erbil, it had a few drilling rigs, and a few people from the oil business were hanging out at the Hawler Plaza. Five years later an oil boom had the Kurds projecting a huge production increase within the decade.

The constitution assigns the KRG 17 percent of the Iraq budget based on its population, minus its share of government costs, and says (in Article 112) that the Government of Iraq and the KRG will develop oil and gas policies "together." All KRG oil and gas revenue was sent to Baghdad, and the KRG got its 17 percent share back. However, the KRG exploited Article 112's vague wording and Iraq's failure to pass a hydrocarbons law by launching an independent oil and gas policy, making its own deals with international oil firms, even big ones, including one with Exxon Mobil extending into disputed areas *outside* the KRG—confrontational but not prohibited by Article 112. The KRG offered more generous contract terms than Iraq's Ministry of Oil and fewer obstacles to doing business with government. These moves, unsurprisingly, caused huge issues with Baghdad, which refused to pay Erbil's higher contract costs. Undeterred, the KRG signed constitutionally dubious bilateral agreements with Turkey on its own, including oil and gas pipelines separate from Iraq's.[7]

Independence is the bottom-line issue. This issue is also complicated. The Kurds are part of Iraq because others put them there. They are not Arabs and don't identify with Iraq. I know from many conversations in Kurdistan that almost no Kurds care about Iraq. What they really want is *not* to be part of it. I heard this even from moderate, open-minded Kurds. Independence has always been the real game, and Baghdad knows it.

The Kurds have operated almost entirely like a separate country, with little regard for the Iraq constitution their leaders helped write. The KRG set precedents that created increasing degrees of separation, symbolized by the practice of flying the Kurdistan flag but not the Iraq flag on public buildings (finally changed in 2014). All this pressure weakened the central government. Iraq was increasingly frustrated by the transparent disrespect but, given its myriad other crises, could not do much about it.

The Daesh crisis was a common threat that produced some coordination in the war effort, but much of it had to be brokered by the United States. A joint command coordinated operations near common borders, and especially the combined operations for the Mosul liberation campaign in late 2016. In general, however, the KRG ran its own military campaign. It limited its role to territory in or near disputed areas it wants to annex. There has been occasional conflict between *peshmerga* and Shia militiamen over control of border towns in disputed areas that both had helped liberate.

The Daesh crisis aside, Kurds don't have much connection to Iraq anymore, though the recently arrived Sunni Arabs escaping the sectarian violence and the Christian and other IDPs are exceptions. There have been no Iraqi government officials in Kurdistan since Saddam pulled his out in 1991. Kurdish children had to be educated in Arabic in the past, but, while Arabic is still often heard, Kurdish has been the language of instruction since 1971. There is little connection at the cultural level, as universities, media, and books are not Iraq oriented. There are so many Kurds living in Western Europe, especially Germany, that Kurds' external interactions are more with people in other countries than with Arab Iraqis.[8]

So Kurds no longer talked much about Iraq until Daesh arrived. Most don't express opposition to it, but they have nothing invested in it. The KDP and PUK have generally worked as an alliance in the Iraqi government, and some Kurds hold high posts, but mostly to protect Kurdish interests.

Less publicized than the KRG's maneuvering for independence and territorial expansion is the antagonism felt not only by official Baghdad but also by many other Iraqis, a large percentage of whom would be happy to see the Kurds go.

Alas, it's even more complicated than that. I know you're frustrated with all these complications, but I warned you, so hang in there. The Kurds don't have their own country because the idea lacks international support. *Kurdistan* is a convenient term for Iraq's three Kurdish provinces, but the full Kurdish area is far larger. Over 5 million Kurds live in Iraq, but roughly 30 million live in eight contiguous countries in and near the Middle East, over half in Turkey and most of the rest in Iraq, Iran, and Syria. I saw hopeful wall maps in Erbil that *combine* the Kurdish areas of all four countries into one potential nation.

Understandably, those three neighbor countries have been hostile to having Iraqi Kurdistan become a nation their ethnic Kurds would then want to join. Powerful Turkey, with three times as many Kurds as Iraqi Kurdistan, would have millions of people and a huge amount of territory to lose. So, establishing Greater Kurdistan is more than a long shot. Well before Daesh arrived, however, I sensed from my own observations that independence for Iraqi Kurdistan was actually not a long shot, even within a fairly short time frame.

A related complication is an organization of Turkish Kurds called the Kurdistan Workers Party (PKK, from the Turkish spelling). The PKK is arguably part of a Kurdish quest for statehood and was the primary opponent of Turkey's longtime discrimination against its Kurdish minority. It is also a U.S. and internationally designated terrorist organization that mostly kills innocent people. PKK fighters have operated *from Iraqi Kurdistan*, in the remote and nearly impenetrable Qandil Mountains, overlapping the Iraq-Iran border and close to Turkey, and from several military camps spread out along the KRG's sparsely populated northern border, from which the PKK launches occasional attacks into Turkey. KRG parties avoided taking a clear stand against them, recognizing that their cause resonates with many Kurds, but this hardened Turkish attitudes.

In 2009 President Barzani finally put relations with Turkey first and adopted an official anti-PKK stance, offering open political support in Turkey to Prime Minister Recep Tayyip Erdogan. That initiative didn't remove the PKK's safe havens, however. Turkey has often bombed these camps, putting innocent villagers at risk, and at times has pursued the PKK across the border, as during my Zakho visit, and again in 2015, 2016, and 2017, skipping the normal diplomatic courtesy of asking permission.

The PKK broke what was then its latest cease-fire in late 2012 and killed several hundred people, despite major recent concessions by Turkey to its Kurdish minority. It declared another cease-fire in early 2013, withdrawing its personnel into Iraq, and issued a similar announcement in early 2015, only to break it again in mid-2015—so stay tuned. Over thirty years, starting in 1984, the PKK's on-again, off-again rebellion has killed 40,000 people.[9] The PKK is popular with Kurds in Turkey, however, and has allies in Syria and Iran, all trying to make that map of Greater Kurdistan come true.

As the Syria rebellion removed government control from northeastern Syria, where Kurds are the largest population group, the PKK-linked Democratic Union Party (PYD), through its militia, the People's Protection Units (YPG), seized much of the area from Daesh, working with the U.S. military. But it then started creating a Kurdish administration, consulting no one. The administrative takeover antagonized Christians and other non-Kurds in the area and turned the Turks decisively against the PYD, which it considers part of the PKK, Barzani likewise opposed them, though the Russians supported them to spite the Turks. Talk about complicated.

A related complication is Turkey's long-standing hostility to Kurds as people. Its Kurdish population in southeastern Turkey endured constant Turkish discrimination and intimidation—even to the extent of not allowing them to identify as Kurdish or study the Kurdish language—a policy that was relaxed in recent years. Iraqi Kurds entering Turkey often endure insults and other demeaning treatment.

By contrast, the Turks have positioned themselves as the friends and protectors of the ethnically related (but not Turkish) Turkmen, living primarily in Kirkuk but also numerous in Salahuddin, Diyala, and Ninewa. Turkmen consider Kirkuk their ancestral city. The message from the Turkish capital, Ankara, has had both the intent and the impact of being slightly intimidating.

Turkish hostility was softened, however, by the rapidly expanding commercial benefits generated in the KRG for Turkey and Turkish companies. In 2010, less than two years after I left Erbil, 15,000 Turks were working in the Kurdistan region, seven hundred Turkish companies were operating there, and trade with Turkey had doubled in just those two years.[10]

Turkey's attitude was further shifted by the KRG's energy boom, as it quickly became an ideal source of oil and gas. This motivated Turkey's energy agreements with the KRG, including a pipeline from fields southeast of Erbil to the Turkish border, feeding into the existing Iraq-Turkey pipeline to Ceyhan, on the Mediterranean. That deal added another layer of frustration in Baghdad and opposition from Washington, but the KRG and Turkey then made agreements for another oil pipeline and a gas pipeline.[11]

Still, Turkey also needs good economic and political relations with Iraq. It has invested a lot of money in Basra, Iraq's leading oil port, and needs oil and gas from southern Iraq too.[12] It has until now considered its interests best served by a united Iraq. By 2015, however, firmly allied with Barzani and pursuing a personalized and counterproductive Syria policy, Erdogan, now Turkey's president, stationed Turkish troops in Bashiqa, east of Mosul, then refused persistent Iraqi demands to remove them. His actions angered the Iraqi leadership and brought bilateral relations to a new low. The erratic Erdogan doubled down by insisting on interfering in Iraq's Mosul liberation campaign.

Oil and gas revenue is now directly relevant to independence. The Government of Iraq and the KRG had pooled their earnings, and the KRG got its population-based 17 percent of *all* budget revenue back. That meant it was supported (like the rest of Iraq) by the higher revenues from the South. Annual KRG energy earnings, however, were projected to soon equal and then exceed the amount sent from Baghdad each year. Once earnings exceed 17 percent of Iraq's overall revenue, the KRG would be a net contributor to Iraq's budget, eliminating Baghdad's financial trump card.[13] So, even without Kirkuk's oil, the Kurds seemed to be positioned to financially afford independence within a few years—assuming the war or oil prices or changing oil production volumes in the South or in KRG-controlled areas didn't change the calculation. In fact, the costs of the anti-Daesh struggle, the economic crisis caused by the depressed oil prices, and disappointing results from oil drilling in many Kurdistan oilfields all contributed to scrambling these assumptions.

Iraq responded to the KRG-Turkey deals by blocking the sale of Kurdish oil, with support from the United States and other countries. The Kurds then stopped sending their oil revenue to Baghdad. In March 2014 Al-Maliki counter-retaliated by holding up *all* of the KRG's money, creating a huge financial crisis for the Kurds. KRG employees went without salary payments for several months, while KRG politicians blamed it all on Baghdad.

In December 2014, with both sides suffering financially from the impasse, the KRG and Al-Abadi reached a temporary agreement. The Kurds would provide 550,000 barrels of oil a day, including 300,000 from the Kirkuk fields seized by the Kurds. The KRG could sell for itself any additional oil it produced, but all oil would be sold through Iraq's oil marketing agency. Several months later, however, the Kurds were providing the oil but not getting their money from cash-strapped Iraq and resumed selling their own oil. The KRG remained behind in its monthly salary payments to government employees and even cut government salaries, leading to harmful strikes. There was another agreement in late 2016 under which Iraq and the KRG started jointly exporting Kirkuk oil based on a revenue-sharing deal.

Until Daesh exposed Baghdad's military house of cards, Kirkuk and related political status issues had a fair chance of causing a civil war, and they still could. The two sides were "drawing lines in the sand." Western media mostly missed or downplayed this story, but the outcome of our struggle for Iraq depends largely on whether and how this incredibly complicated issue gets resolved.

Creating a New Relationship with the Kurds

Facilitating a negotiated settlement between Baghdad and Erbil to resolve all these issues is almost necessarily an American job. The United States is the indispensable third party—the only plausible mediator. No Sunni or Shia country is acceptable to both sides.

Through all the turbulent developments of recent years, the United States under both Republican and Democratic administrations has adhered to a one-Iraq policy, mindful of the sacrifices American soldiers made to preserve Iraq and recognizing its political fragility. It has shown no support for independence, despite repeated entreaties from Kurdish leaders. The arrival of ISIS made national unity even more imperative. The United States must maintain this policy, at least until ISIS goes, and it must be totally clear that we will not recognize any referendum or declaration of independence that is not linked to a comprehensive agreement with Iraq.

To succeed in this critical mediating role, however, I believe *the United States needs to reorient its own thinking about the future of Iraq.*

The Kurds have stayed reluctantly in Iraq, only to see it collapse under fire. They cooperated to defeat Daesh but will insist on independence once the crisis ends. In fact, Barzani started posturing about independence well in advance, claiming Sinjar—much of it just retaken from Daesh by the *peshmerga*—as Kurdish territory, and it's not even contiguous with Kurdistan, and proposing that a quick referendum be held on Kurdish independence.

Barzani's maneuvers aside, based on the expressed opinions of Kurds in Iraq and the United States, the intensity of Kurdish feelings should not be underestimated, especially after it has lost many of its soldiers. Trying to stuff this long-standing dream back into the bottle will make the situation worse. The challenge is to accept this new reality, not to reconstruct the past.

A wiser policy would be to *facilitate a long-term partnership between Iraq and an independent Kurdistan.* They will be stronger as friendly neighbors working together than as clashing jurisdictions in the same country.

The goal should be an agreement that resolves all issues, enabling the friendliest possible future relationship. If independence is ruled out, I believe there is almost no chance of resolving these issues, which would continue to destabilize the country. *The United States must make clear at the outset that its support for independence depends on the krg first reaching agreement with Iraq.*

An ideal starting point would be a formal public offer from Baghdad, conveyed by the prime minister, to support Kurdish independence, conditional on prior resolution of all issues. This step is not an absolute requirement, but it would initiate negotiations from a mutual position of friendship. Because it would be addressed to all KRG political leaders, and the Kurdish people, not just Barzani, it would bring all the Kurdish parties into the negotiations and hopefully avoid complications from the KRG's internal political crisis. It's not obvious that an Iraqi prime minister would take the political risk involved in such a decision, but doing nothing could incur larger risks.

In settling the political status of all disputed areas, final decisions should be based on separate referenda held in each affected area; should not be limited by current district and subdistrict boundaries; and should be adapted to ethnic, religious, demographic, and other factors, so as to ensure a democratic solution for all those affected. A winner-take-all referendum is not a democratic solution, and that includes a governorate-wide Kirkuk referendum.

Reaching a negotiated settlement first, as I am proposing, would allow referenda to be ratifications of compromises already reached, based on known voter preferences in specific jurisdictions, confirmed by consultation with local residents. This approach might lead to revising some current boundary lines to better reflect citizens' preferences. Political status decisions should be made not by clashing political forces but by voters, under an independently managed process.

The negotiations and referenda would likely move some currently disputed areas into Kurdistan. *Iraq needs to accept that.* But the fact that a given area has a significant Kurdish or other non-Arab population is not in itself a basis for honoring territorial claims on every such area, dismantling wide areas of Iraq, and forcing people to live in Kurdistan against their will. Politically, Iraqi leaders could not afford to make such concessions anyway. *If the Kurds want independence, they need to accept that.*

Results of elections since 2005 show strong support for Kurdish parties in some parts of Ninewa's disputed territories but not others. The same is true for Diyala. Kurdish political parties have dominated among Kurdish voters in Kirkuk but have had little support from Arabs and Turkmen, and there are very few Kurds in major parts of Kirkuk Province. Those election results are probably indicative of voter preferences about political status,[14] conceding that the Daesh experience could have changed some minds, as could the referendum process itself.

Two populations that lost heavily from Daesh's abuses and the failure of both the Iraqi military and the *peshmerga* to protect them are the Turkmen and the Christians. Many Shia Turkmen were among the thousands executed. Baghdad and Erbil could both set a great precedent, whatever their ultimate boundary line, by agreeing to honor and quickly implement the previous government decisions creating separate provinces for the Turkmen in Tooz and Tal Afar and for the Christians, Shabaks, and other religious minorities in the Nineveh Plain, with the understanding that their final boundaries would be set by the political status process.

Implementing the Nineveh Plain province would create a kind of Assyrian Christian homeland in the Middle East but be open to all. It would attract political and cultural support from the West, including Iraq's large Christian diaspora, and would generate more public support in the United States for helping Iraq. Many Christian IDPs still won't return, but the separate province would increase the number who do and reduce the IDP burden on the KRG, and its success would gradually draw other Iraqi Christians, displaced Syrian Christians, and some returnees from the West.

The autonomous province for Turkmen living in the Tooz District in Salahuddin could be expanded to adjoining Turkmen areas in Kirkuk Province. Whatever its boundaries, this province would also get outside political and cultural support, from Turkey at least, as would the Turkmen autonomous province in Tal Afar, which might also—and this is a key point—facilitate Turkish acceptance of KRG independence.

Many Arabs and Turkmen in Kirkuk are Shia, supported by Shia political parties, and some have been rescued from Daesh by Shia militias. This gives Shia a reason to support the Turkmen in their new province and might also facilitate Iran's acceptance of KRG independence.

Unfortunately, rearranging the map of Kirkuk and surrounding provinces won't solve a really fundamental issue over control of oil. Putting Kirkuk's Kurdish areas in Kurdistan, even if the rest stayed in Iraq, would also put most of its oil in Kurdistan, as Kirkuk's two largest fields are in those areas. As long as the revenue is shared regardless of whose oil contracts are producing it, this problem can be overcome. The prospect of Kurdish independence creates huge uncertainty, however. An independent Kurdistan would be oil rich if it controlled all the Kirkuk oil. Iraq would be a lot poorer. The livelihood of all Iraqis is tied to the oil and gas sector, and dividing budget revenues based on province populations is a settled policy. *To maintain each province's population-based share of oil and gas revenues, any political status agreement that moves some or all of Kirkuk to Kurdistan has to leave some or all of its oil outside of exclusive KRG control.*

The ideal solution is to resume joint energy management, under a joint organizational structure with largely independent authority, led by experts rather than politicians, and to continue allocating revenues by population. Iraq's membership in the Extractive Industries Transparency Initiative (EITI) could be retained as a joint membership. A joint pipeline authority would help avoid future issues over competing pipelines.

Joint management would still have to overcome policy differences on oil discovery and production. Conceding Baghdad's frustrations over the KRG's go-it-alone policy, giving better deals to oil companies would likely pay off for all of Iraq in faster development and higher revenue. Major investment is needed in southern Iraq too. Improving people's living standards is more important than addressing past grievances, however justified they seem.

If world oil prices are favorable, economic viability won't be a major problem for independent Kurdistan, conceding that its economic development is hindered by old policies and crony capitalism. It will be a significant oil and gas–producing nation, with a ready next-door market in Turkey and the further advantage of its already lively commercial economy. Before Daesh arrived, it was emerging as a tourist area too; maybe even Iraqi Jews in Israel could return for a visit. Its citizens will be better off economically than Iraqis and most other Arabs. The nosedive in world oil prices that began in 2014 made the Kurdish government financially desperate. However, economic cycles also turn upward; the defeat of Daesh and the return of Ninewa IDPs now in Kurdistan will relieve a huge financial burden; a settlement with Iraq would provide economic stability; and independence would make Kurdistan eligible for the same international and foreign assistance as Iraq and other countries.

Iraq has the fifth largest oil reserves in the world, but over 95 percent of government export revenues come from oil and gas, far higher than in the four countries with larger reserves, making it extremely energy dependent. From 2001 to 2013 its production rose only about 12.5 percent, but the world price rose more than 350 percent, which is why the economy was improving and revenues soaring, despite Iraq's many problems. Then came the precipitous fall, which Al-Abadi called "disastrous."[15]

The agreement between Iraq and the KRG should also cover many practical subjects that may be less controversial but also require adjustments and compromises. Law-abiding citizens of both countries should, for example, have the right to move freely from one to the other and to live in either country, with applicable security regulations formalized in advance. The two countries should constitute a permanent free-trade zone, and goods should move tariff free between them. This is also essential to preserve existing boundary-crossing commercial and trade patterns. Of immediate importance would be a mutual security policy under a joint military command.

U.S. support for Kurdish independence should also be conditioned on comprehensive political reforms. Even one of the KRG's leaders has called the Kurdish system a "quasi-democracy." The Soviet-style party-dominated system is inherently corrupt. As managed by its politicians, it's even more corrupt. The five-party coalition resulting from the 2013 KRG elections was a hopeful development, but that arrangement blew up when the KDP forced Gorran's KRG ministers and the parliament speaker out of the government by using KDP security police to prevent them from returning to work in Erbil. The other three coalition parties mostly supported Gorran's right to continue. That left a huge KRG political crisis that continued on.

A major factor in that crisis was that Barzani's presidential term had ended, as had an extension voted by the KRG parliament, and as of August 2015 he was no longer legally the president—but insisted on continuing to act as the president, despite Gorran's objections. His rush toward an independence referendum could be explained by his desire to finally win his father's struggle for independence before he has to step down. Barzani simply ignored objections to his unconstitutional actions against Gorran, and his lack of legal authority, and continued his personal decision making. However, Gorran and the PUK soon formed a political alliance against him, in effect putting the old PUK partners back together.

The constitution of an independent Kurdistan should be founded on internationally recognized principles of democracy, freedom, and human rights and establish a *totally* unified government. That should include a unified *peshmerga* command and an end to political party militias and political "hit" jobs by party thugs. Government decisions should be made by parliament members, ministers, and a prime minister selected by parliament (or a popularly elected and term-limited president, but not both); elected provincial council members and directly elected, term-limited governors; and directly elected municipal council members and presidents. All should be elected at legally fixed intervals not subject to political manipulation. The new system should eliminate all appointments and other government decisions by political parties; ensure that the judiciary, universities, anti-corruption agencies, and the business permitting system are independent; ensure that all budgets and government operations are transparent to the public; and require modern management practices (perhaps starting with the Model Ministry principles). Resistance from favored insiders is entirely predictable and must be overridden. All Kurdish readers should read this paragraph again. How you feel about it is a test of whether you really love Kurdistan.

To encourage acceptance by its much larger neighbors, Kurdistan should renounce in advance any intention to annex or otherwise merge with Kurdish areas in Turkey, Syria, and/or Iran or make further territorial claims against Iraq. Consistent with that policy, Kurdistan should also commit to eliminating PKK safe havens from its territory. Tell them to leave—and back it up. To be a real nation, you have to act like one. The message to the PKK is that it needs to stop killing people, immediately, and work through the political process as it previously promised to do.

Not as a requirement but potentially important, a U.S.-friendly Kurdish state could offer the United States an opportunity to establish a long-term military presence that would help deter future outside threats to Kurdish (and Iraqi) security and increase the U.S. security presence in the region. This idea got lost in 2011 when Iraqi politicians failed to extend the U.S. military presence. Or maybe Iraq would like to change that decision based on the Daesh experience?

I know what you're thinking—some version of, "This situation is unbelievably complicated." Indeed it is, and I gave you the "simplified" version. I have learned, like everyone else, that everything is complicated in the Middle East.

I concede from the lessons of Iraq that a negotiated settlement along these lines would be extremely difficult, especially given the instinct to control and the winner-take-all mentality that work against any compromise in Iraq. Pursuing an agreement along these lines is a more realistic strategy, however, than insisting indefinitely on national unity at all costs.

Moreover, the United States holds a powerful position in this scenario. Kurdish independence can be declared unilaterally, but its boundaries would be unsettled, and no such declaration would be meaningful without international recognition, which likely starts with American acceptance.

Iraq's agreement to give up part of its country would be a compromise that few countries have made willingly, but doing so would overcome its most divisive issues. The compromises required of the Kurds involve major tradeoffs, but most Kurds would agree that achieving independence would justify them. A formal mutual agreement that incorporates those compromises would enable an Iraqi political miracle: a *win-win solution* for both Iraq and the Kurds.

22

The American from Iraq

The Meaning of Public Service

I feel a special affinity for people in any country who reflect the real meaning of *public servant*. USAID and other overseas projects tend to have high stakes and high work standards, and it takes commitment just to be there if there is a risk of getting killed. To those of us willing to work in dangerous places, the risks help to define who we are. Yes, we do realize that other people think we're crazy.

A public servant puts the public interest ahead of his or her own. Being a government employee does not in itself make you a public servant but does give you the opportunity. Having no official position does not preclude being a public servant; some of the best are volunteers. In my definition, being a public servant is about working with a purpose, about caring, about not counting the hours, about fighting off the weariness and inevitable frustrations, and sometimes about taking risks.

In Iraq, however, many consider government jobs as entitlements. The low pay and typically poor management reinforce the lack of a service orientation. At all levels Iraq must rely on the minority who care to partially offset the majority who don't. Most Iraqis who worked for me were in that minority—and showed dedication even under threatening conditions. Their good salaries don't explain it all. Some of our civil society organization (CSO) members earned money from grant projects, but not a steady income, and many were volunteers. I know from experience that some government employees care deeply about their work, and many of them work heroically under great pressure.

Similarly, elected officials and political appointees who care are outnumbered in many places by those doing it to help themselves. From that starting point, it's easy to become corrupt and to corrupt others and for parliament members to accept huge salaries and benefits that most government employees can't even imagine and most

Iraqi citizens can only resent. Hopefully, the citizen-initiated anti-corruption drive started in 2015 and the next round of elections will change this picture before it's too late.

To work in a place like Iraq, it helps to bring some idealism, hopefully with an ability to apply it with realism and a results focus. The downside of bringing your ideals with you is that you crash harder if tragedies happen or if your mission is undermined by events or other people.

In Praise of True Warriors

My story is about the civilian side of the struggle for Iraq. Much of it intersected with major military developments, however. The military side of the struggle has been told in countless books, some by very brave people, and needs no help from me. Nevertheless, I feel an obligation to acknowledge with gratitude the men and women of the American, British, and other armed services who took the military risks, often under truly dangerous conditions, that made our progress on civilian programs possible.

That military success was purchased by the sacrifices of many thousands of fallen and living heroes. Many U.S. service members did three or four deployments in Iraq, multiplying their risks. There were about 4,800 Coalition military deaths—about 4,500 Americans, most of the rest British. Add to those tragedies the thousands of wounded warriors who brought their sacrifices home, to be borne by them and their families for the rest of the veterans' lives, even after most people have forgotten. I promise I won't.

The American military's greatest Iraq achievement turned out to be not its impressive and swiftly victorious invasion with its British allies but the "surge" strategy of 2006–8 that pacified the Baghdad area and defeated Al-Qaeda in Iraq in coordination with tribal leaders. Bush's daring decision was based on a change of strategy devised by Gen. David Petraeus and implemented by Petraeus and Gen. Raymond Odierno, aided by some of the smartest people who ever put on military uniforms.[1]

Success is not only about battles won but about people saved. Many years after Saddam's exit, Iraq was still digging up mass graves, adding to the ghastly toll in lives destroyed by his regime. It's a reminder of the horrors our soldiers stopped. Many thousands of those still alive in Iraq would otherwise have been added to that toll.

I had a family connection to the military side of the story. My son-in-law, Arthur Barnes, a Jamaican immigrant when he joined the U.S. Army in 1998, served in Iraq in 2007–8, overlapping my tour in Erbil. He served at the Special Operations Command on the large U.S. base in Balad, north of Baghdad. Like thousands of others who returned with troubling memories, he continues in civilian life to feel the burden of a difficult experience.

In my story many of the remarkable soldiers were British. There were several visits to Camp Abu Naji, two of them involuntary, as I reported, but I also had the pleasure of working with the British Civil-Military Affairs team in Amarah. The experience generated a lot of respect and admiration for the British military and for civil affairs officers.

It's tough being a soldier at war, and at times the Brits in southern Iraq were definitely at war and needing all their skill, smarts, training, and toughness to win and survive. Their heroism got little public acknowledgment from the Iraqis served by it, and not enough attention in British or American newspapers, but they deserve the gratitude of citizens in all three countries.

Much has been made of Great Britain's strong partnership with the United States in Iraq, which many Brits never liked. Whatever one's opinion about Tony Blair or going to war with Saddam, however, Iraq was the latest demonstration in the conflicts of recent times that Great Britain has been America's best friend in the world, through administrations both Republican and Democrat, Tory and Labour. This relationship is too often buried in the political "smart talk" of the day, but some patriotic citizens on both sides of the pond do notice and appreciate it. I bring this up to explain why I, an Irish American, love the British.

Among the amazing people in American uniform were the doctors and other medical staff of the Green Zone military hospital. On the few occasions when I needed their help, the range of expertise shown by military medical personnel was astonishing. It didn't seem to matter that I was a civilian monitoring a thyroid cancer condition and not a soldier with typical wartime injuries or illnesses.

I make a point of recognizing security personnel—warriors of a different kind but sharing similar risks. Many were former military or police. The military lacked enough personnel to protect civilian contractors too, so a huge number of brave guys (and a few ladies) from private security companies provided the margin of safety that enabled the civilian coalition to do its work, protecting us where we lived and on the road. Everyone has read and heard stories about fatal and controversial incidents involving the Blackwater firm. The ground-level view is more balanced. Most PSDs have given dedicated service. They and their clients sometimes come under fire, and a surprisingly high number did not return from their last assignment.

And so my appreciation to Jim, Mark, Big Mark, Jock, and Dennis; and to Eddie, Philip, and Siegfried, Pottie and Hamish, and all of Marius's intrepid crew—and our diligent friends from Nepal—for taking the risks to be part of our mission.

To all the men and women in uniform who served in Iraq and made it possible for all of us in the civilian coalition to serve too and make a difference, I offer a heartfelt toast in praise of true warriors.

The Price of Dedication

Almost forgotten in our instinctive concern about military casualties are all the civilian contract personnel in Iraq who have also died by violence. No one really knows how many because it was no U.S. agency's job to collect the casualty information in one place. Most were apparently security men, some of whom died protecting people like me. Others *were* people like me, working on projects for USAID or other agencies.

During the bad days of sectarian violence, a briefing paper noted that on average nine civilian contract employees were dying every week, most non-American. In July 2012 the Special Inspector General for Iraq Reconstruction (SIGIR) reported that 719 or more civilian contract employees, expats and Iraqis, had been killed on U.S. projects through August 2010, including military personnel working civilian-type projects, but SIGIR admitted the real number was higher.[2] A Brown University study in 2013 put the real number at over 3,400.[3] For comparison, remember that total military deaths were around 4,800.

Death has also come to many Iraqis who worked for U.S. or other foreign contractors or for the U.S. or British military. By the time I left Baghdad, the big engineering company Bechtel had lost fifty-two employees. That's one company! USAID counted ninety-five Iraqi civilians killed on its projects but admitted the real number was far higher.[4] Its number doesn't include deaths of nonemployees who were active program participants; we had several at ICSP alone. Every death of an Iraqi employee was a tragedy, just as tragic as the death of any Coalition soldier or civilian. They were as much a part of the war and civilian projects as our own people, taking the same risks during the workday and the added risk of getting home and back with no security.

Having been touched by several of these tragedies, I feel this very deeply. Five of my Amarah staff members died, three of them assassinated for their public service. Another had a car bomb go off in front of his house. Several of my ICSP staff endured horrible personal or family experiences, including having family members murdered. Two Baghdad Center advisory board members were assassinated. A key Basra employee was almost assassinated in his own home. Haider's female office mate was later murdered in a horrible family violence incident. My Kurdish interpreter was almost assassinated in Kirkuk. There are surely other sad and shocking stories about former associates that I don't know about. At least three CSO leaders who worked with my ICSP program died by violence, and who knows how many other ICSP civil society organization members died trying to help their country. Few people in the West have any frame of reference for this level of civilian casualties among people they know.

Public service has come at an especially high price for Iraq's government employees, uniformed and civilian. In every *Daesh Daily* report, that toll rises. In few places on Earth have so many people wanted to kill those trying to help them.

Thousands of Iraq's intellectuals, physicians, and other professionals had to abandon their careers and flee the country, or escape to Kurdistan, after hundreds of their colleagues were murdered. One distinguished university professor and author forced out by the Mehdi Army spent many years in Syria, getting no help from Canada, where he had once lived. In 2013, as I was working with an international nonprofit in New York to arrange a grant for him to work in another Middle East country, the Syrian civil war became so dangerous in his neighborhood that he was forced to return to Iraq.

In late January 2013 the civil society field lost one of its ardent advocates when Michael Miller, founder and president of America's Development Foundation, died at age seventy-one. When I saw him a year or so earlier to ask questions for the book, he was in good health and great spirits at his new home in Maryland and looking forward to playing golf, so attending his funeral Mass in Georgetown was an unexpected and jarring experience.

Thousands of dedicated Iraqis joined USAID and other projects to help their country. Many who died left lasting memories. Losing Kifaya, Haider, and Nazaar left me an obligation to remember them and tell their story. I can't think about the struggle for women's rights without thinking about Kifaya, who symbolized it; or about the desperate need to transform Iraqi politics without thinking about Haider, who might have made a difference; or about the continuing risks to independent journalists without thinking about Nazaar.

Working in Iraq did not make me cynical, however, about Iraq or international development. We owe it to martyrs such as Kifaya Hussein, Haider Al-Maliki, and Nazaar Abdul Wahid—and the many others who have made personal sacrifices and taken serious risks—to ensure that the mission of the civilian coalition in Iraq succeeds in the end in bringing meaningful democracy and a better life to the people of Iraq.

Helping Those Who Took the Risk

My Iraq story did not end in Iraq. It won't end with this book either. Part of the personal price of my own dedication is the felt need to continue caring about my Iraqi friends. It would qualify as a part-time job if anyone paid me for the time invested.

Because of my three staff members who were killed, and others who survived close calls or remain at risk, I am extremely sensitive about helping those who need to leave Iraq for their own safety. Over time several people who worked for me have sought my help, and other Iraqis were referred or self-referred to me. A few of these cases, with people at serious risk, have been extremely tense.

Thousands of Iraqis have found themselves endangered by their loyalty to the Americans or the British, receiving threats against their lives or other family members. It makes sense that they would seek help from people like me, whom they worked for. You might assume there is an expedited way to get them to safety in the United States, but there isn't. The primary obstacle is the U.S. government.

I don't encourage emigration by those not threatened, for three reasons. First, the U.S. immigration application process for Iraqis is hard and uncertain. Second, it's difficult for Iraqi refugees to establish careers in the United States commensurate with their education and experience; in fact, it's difficult to get menial jobs, even for the high percentage of Iraqi refugees who are college educated. Third, we trained these people to play a larger role in Iraq, not to follow us home. It's a lost investment when they leave. When asked directly, "Should I stay or go?" my answer is that if you are in danger, leave as fast as possible; if not, stay in Iraq.

I have said to many Iraqi refugees that being a refugee stinks—it's one of the worst experiences in life. You have no legal status, usually little or no money, little or no right to work and earn money, no friends, and worst of all, you don't know when or if you will finally get placed in a new country. Refugees become official through acceptance by the UN High Commissioner for Refugees (UNHCR); you must already be outside your own country in order to qualify. Securing that status only makes you eligible for placement in another country, probably not soon and not necessarily in the country you prefer.

To come to America, you apply to the State Department. If you pass its scrutiny, your case is in the hands of the Department of Homeland Security, specifically employees who do the security checks. From there the process is frustrating, unexplainable, and seemingly endless. The delay is primarily from waiting for the security background check, which follows a never-timely security interview. The lengthy wait puts the refugee's life on hold for several months and often well over a year, or more, and not because the background checks themselves are all that time-consuming. Despite trying to help applicants in numerous cases, I have never found out who was actually doing these security checks. The system is designed perfectly to avoid accountability.

One could logically assume that Iraqis in danger of being murdered for helping us would get some kind of fast-track treatment. To many security people, however, every Iraqi male is a potential terrorist. No matter how desperate his case, the bottom-line fear in the security establishment is the potentially career-threatening case of the one terrorist who gets through their screening.

My education started with Haider's sister and brother, Ta'meem and Ali, themselves threatened in the immediate aftermath of his assassination. In spite of Molly Phee's advocacy within the State Department, help from the Baghdad embassy's refugee coordinator, and the concern of many others, it still took a year to get them out of their home isolation in Amarah to Jordan and five months more of languishing in Jordan before they finally reached the United States. The full story is a soap opera with seemingly endless frustrations.

Our Amarah interpreter Joe Hannoon, who fled Iraq after receiving threats, languished for several years in Syria with his wife and had two children before we finally got them out of Syria. The State Department seemed to have provisionally accepted him early on, but the process dragged on because of the unbelievable obstacles thrown up by immigration procedures and diplomatic complications. As a final indignity, Joe and his wife had to wait a few more months for a follow-up security interview after the second baby was born (just in case the baby was a terrorist).

In certain cases I have been able to intervene with one office or another to help applicants get admitted. For the most part, however, people trying to help are as powerless as the applicants. I've spent a lot of time exchanging communications with applicants during the long delays, sometimes to discuss and explain the latest government communications, if any, but often just to keep their spirits up.

The standard route for refugees to the United States is the U.S. Refugee Admissions Program (USRAP). Aside from providing a lot of personal and family data, you have to show specifically why you are threatened in your country. It needs to be factual and verifiable, not just a story. The USRAP people in my limited experience were responsive, though not exactly fast, but they didn't control the rest of the timeline. As a result, the number of endangered Iraqis kept rising.

The enormous backlog prompted Congress to authorize Special

Immigrant Visas (SIVS) for endangered Iraqis who had worked for the Coalition in any capacity for a year or more. This measure eased the process for thousands, but many valued and endangered Iraqi employees have been blocked by the opaque security process. We have through this process admitted many who were not in imminent danger while excluding some who were.

If you can hold out through all the delays and are not victimized by an unfair rejection, you will have the joy of arriving exhausted at one of America's airports to begin a new life. For most Iraqis the joy is soon undermined by the ordeal that follows. The erroneous but widespread belief that America is the land of milk and honey quickly disappears. Whatever status you had in Iraq is gone. Your certification as a physician or other professional likely won't be recognized. Your degree is from a university no one here has heard of. Any limitations in your English will make it harder to impress employers. Most of you who do make it to the United States are starting again at the bottom.

To get you started, the State Department will assign you to its nonprofit contractor in your geographic area. It will find you an apartment and pay the rent for a month or so and help you sign up for a Social Security card, Medicaid, and Food Stamps, but you need a job fast to avoid going under. That pressure is hard on almost any immigrant. If that meager help isn't enough, you end up exhausting any savings brought from Iraq and going on welfare with your battered pride.

A true story: I once briefly helped a former Baghdad businessman with a wife and four kids, living in Virginia. He had a hand chopped off on Saddam's orders in the 1990s, came to the United States after 2003 for surgery in Texas to attach an artificial hand, was invited to the White House, and owned treasured photos of himself with President George W. Bush and Secretary of State Colin Powell. After returning to Iraq, however, the Mehdi Army destroyed his house and he was forced to leave the country. He was frustrated by the time I met him, as it had gradually become clear that neither his presidential recognition nor his disability gave him higher status than any other Iraqi in America.

The most prominent advocate for endangered Iraqi refugees is Kirk Johnson, who did his own USAID civilian tour of Iraq as an Arabic-speaking young man, highlighted by positions at the embassy and in beautiful downtown Fallujah. Johnson started a list, the core of his List Project founded in 2007, and if you are endangered in Iraq for working for the U.S. government or civilian organizations and need to leave, he will put you on his list if he knows. He will also find you a pro bono immigration lawyer to help you deal with the intimidating application process and the seemingly immovable bureaucracy. Kirk has experienced the same frustrations I have but much more often. His own book chronicles his near-constant frustration dealing with the U.S. government on behalf of endangered Iraqis.[5]

When he gave his first list to State Department officials, they ignored him, and other government officials, even at USAID, turned out to care more about the possible bad publicity than the lives at risk. He assumed they would want to help once they understood the problem, but government policy makers feared that admitting a lot of threatened Iraqis would undermine the war effort and the ongoing effort to spin it in a positive direction. Still, Secretary of State Condi Rice promised publicly to let in 7,000 Iraqis within the 2007 fiscal year.[6]

Kirk's ability to generate publicity for his cause through his op-ed articles and supportive coverage from George Packer of the *New Yorker* and other media figures forced official Washington to deal with the issue while prompting pleas from many more endangered Iraqis to get on his list. Senator Ted Kennedy of Massachusetts, who had opposed the Iraq invasion, became his strongest ally in Congress. Kennedy led a bipartisan effort to expand the Special Immigrant Visa program to admit up to 5,000 Iraqis annually and allow them to apply in Iraq instead of having to go first to Jordan or Syria or another country so as to become UN-designated refugees.[7] It would turn out, however, that Rice's 7,000-person target and the SIV legislation's 5,000 were both wildly optimistic, undermined by inherent complexities and the usual bureaucratic snags and by incompetence and indifference at multiple (including high) government levels. Meanwhile, Iraqis who helped us were being assassinated.

I have been helped at times by a few of the same Washington lawyers as the List Project, especially Chris Nugent, initially at the Holland and Knight law firm and later in his own firm. Kirk credits Chris with single-handedly helping scores of Iraqis on his list to safety in the United States.[8] In my own experience Chris worked constantly and with little sleep on a seven-day schedule, handled one phone call after another, answered emails well after midnight, and operated at a frantic pace in an impossible race against time. On the few occasions when I met him in his office, I felt concerned about his health. Sadly, he was diagnosed with multiple sclerosis shortly afterward, in 2011, forcing him to discontinue his legal practice at a fairly young age. Threatened Iraqis lost an amazingly dedicated ally.

Chris Nugent and other dedicated pro bono lawyers have worked against the bureaucratic odds. The change of administrations after 2008 apparently made little difference. Even a great lawyer is often not enough. I helped Chris with a lengthy appeal in one case that succeeded, enabling an endangered Christian in Baghdad to get to Chicago. But our appeal for a man and his wife in Baghdad was willfully mishandled by the office responsible for their case, and their application was rejected. The United States managed to admit the couple's son, daughter, and grandchildren while stranding the parents in Iraq. The insensitivity of some federal employees is astonishing, and the lack of transparency or accountability is unforgivable. The will of Congress has been defied, and Homeland Security's own internal rules have been routinely ignored. This is why the immigration system has failed so many Iraqis who helped us and left some of them dead.

The most frustrating and frightening case for me involves a highly capable, dedicated former staff member in South-Central Iraq who had no desire to leave Iraq but was threatened four times, by both the Mehdi Army *and* Sunni extremists. After the usual long delays, he received his SIV to come to the United States—only to have it denied a day or two later. The denial came with the usual no-explanation form letter. No one tried to explain how he got rejected after he had already been approved. To get the visa, he had to have passed all the security screenings. My determined letter to the U.S. embassy refugee coordinator in Baghdad got me nowhere. When U.S. senator Ben Cardin of Maryland wrote to her to back up my argument, she sent him an answer that actually dismissed all the death threats on the grounds that Iraqis lie about these things all the time! Indeed, I and others know the explanation for the denial, but it is embarrassing to the government and so will not be admitted. The applicant is the victim and may still be at risk.

This really great employee has spent the last fourteen years working loyally for U.S. organizations, in increasingly important management roles. He was one of the greatest employees I ever had. His continuing predicament hangs over me constantly because of what happened to Haider.

Kirk Johnson provided a detailed and documented case study of how the State Department handled one case that was an imminent emergency. Starting in June 2011, an increasingly desperate former U.S. Army employee in Kirkuk wrote repeatedly to State seeking refuge in the United States because of terrorist threats against him. State kept responding with brief form letters asking for more information, even when they already had the information. They were still playing games with his application 338 days after he first submitted it—the day he was beheaded. When his brother notified the State Department, they requested a death certificate for verification. When his brother wrote again to say he and his murdered brother's wife and child had received a death threat, enclosing the threat letter, the State Department started again with requests for more information and did not expedite the case.[9] The List Project efforts finally got the widow and son out of Iraq, but the United States refused to admit the brother, despite repeated appeals. If this story does not make you angry at the U.S. government, nothing will.

As of October 2014, new SIV applications were no longer accepted, there was a huge backlog of previous applicants awaiting SIV interviews, and some of those endangered and still waiting now lived in areas captured by ISIS. In March 2015 the Iraqi Refugee Assistance Project, organized around many of the nation's law schools, announced it was suing the U.S. government on behalf of nine SIV applicants.

In January 2017, when the one-week-old Trump administration issued a blanket temporary ban on refugee admissions from seven countries including Iraq, loyal Iraqis who had risked their lives to work with us were among those put at further risk by the executive order.

Finally on this frustrating subject, there are at least two things you, my readers, can do for Iraqis in America.

First, offer your friendship to any Iraqi you meet. Don't be put off if they look different, don't smile, or seem nervous about interacting with others. They all have a story, often sad, about why they came to America. Care enough to ask.

Second, if you have authority or influence on hiring decisions, you can make a huge difference. Most Iraqis new to the United States need two key breaks: the first job, just to survive financially; and the first professional job commensurate with their education and experience. Many who don't get this help are forced into poverty. A lot of well-educated, well-qualified, English-speaking Iraqis are walking around with résumés you would be impressed to read.

Helping those who helped us has its occasional happy moments too. I was proud to attend American citizenship ceremonies for Ta'meem and Ali in early 2013. Others would follow.

Democracy Is About You!

For the vast majority of Iraqis still living in their country, the struggle for Iraq continues. The internal security crisis that started in 2014 made it even more difficult. Some Americans want to pronounce our efforts to create a democracy a failure, but it's too soon to make such a judgment.

Democracies must be built over time. Unfortunately for Iraq, its democracy came suddenly. The great majority of Iraqis were happy it came, but they were not prepared. They were victimized by the self-serving and the corrupt, and tens of thousands of new victims have joined those lost in Saddam's terror. To build and maintain a truly democratic Iraq, not only ISIS but a lot of other scoundrels have to go. Many Iraqis I know want to be part of the democratic solution. My confidence is with them and Iraqis like them.

One of my strongest opinions about democracy is that voters are accountable too. Voting decisions, like all decisions, have consequences. When elections have bad consequences, don't just blame the politicians who got elected. Blame the people who voted for them or who failed to vote.

In a democracy, public opinion matters. It hasn't yet mattered enough in Iraq, but at times it has made a difference. The sudden adoption of sweeping anti-corruption reforms in mid-2015 followed major street demonstrations.

Democracies can also be measured by the number of people participating between elections. Dictatorships lack citizen involvement, Saddam's included. New democracies must overcome that legacy and make citizens part of the solution. This is why the number of civil society organizations and CSO members is so important. Joining a CSO or volunteering in some other way takes a commitment of time but helps make a difference where you live. Thousands of Iraqis have made that commitment. A very high number have also been election candidates, many probably CSO members. Civil society in many countries has often taken the lead on public policy issues and persuaded the government to follow.

The occupation of large areas of Iraq by ISIS challenged all of our hopes for Iraqi democracy. Iraq's political system has not been changed, however, nor has its government been overthrown. A lot of volunteers stepped up, risking their lives and sometimes losing them to make sure those things don't happen. Beyond today's military imperatives, the loyalty and talents of many more citizens will be needed.

THE VOICE OF HAIDER

Democracy is about *you*! It is about your freedom. It is about your rights. It is also about your responsibilities. . . .

Your country needs you to participate. Your opinion matters whether you are highly educated or uneducated. The future of Iraq will be decided by elections, by you and me. When elections come, make sure you vote for the candidates that *you* want. . . .

Whatever your experiences in life, good and bad, the joy of freedom from living in a democracy will never leave you.

Ultimately, Iraq's democracy belongs to its people, not to the politicians. No matter what any political leader or party says, in any country, in the end democracy really *is* about you.

Giving Iraq a Chance

I can almost hear American and British readers asking, "So, where the hell does this leave us?" It's more than a fair question after several thousand lives lost and maybe $2–3 trillion spent, a cost that is still rising.

Having read my story this far, you are probably one of those who cares about Iraq and what happens there. For many Americans, however, the diminished news coverage prompted by the final U.S. troop withdrawal in 2011 moved Iraq out of their attention span—until the disastrous events of 2014 moved it back in. For others it's a case of repressing bad memories. But we still need to care about Iraq, out of concern for its people and because we have important national interests there.

Iraq is still important. First, Iraq still needs our continued friendship and support, which includes military support but also political support. We still have major influence there and are in the best position to mediate when opposing sides aren't communicating well with each other.

Second, we must not sell out those whose sacrifices made it possible to get this far—an enormous number of Iraqis as well as Americans, Brits, and others.

Third, even conceding its huge faults and ongoing crises, Iraq's democracy puts it on the leading edge in the Middle East. Making democracy work there will improve its chances in other Middle East countries.[10] Failure would have the opposite effect.

Finally, Iraq is on the Sunni-Shia dividing line. Many of its Shia citizens are neighbors of Iran to the east; many Sunni citizens are neighbors of Saudi Arabia to the south—both with sectarian governments that are hostile to each other.[11] Reducing sectarian conflict in Iraq will have a positive impact throughout the Middle East. Failure would have the opposite effect.

Our work in Iraq is unfinished. ISIS must be totally defeated and removed and its Iraqi collaborators brought to justice. Political reconciliation must be achieved and a lot of mistrust finally overcome. The long-term relationship between Iraq and the Kurds must be negotiated. In all three areas the United States has a critical role to play.

The United States also needs a long-range strategy to strengthen democracy in Iraq. This means providing technical assistance to support the ongoing decentralization of government powers, supporting implementation of the new ministry reforms, broadening access to the U.S. higher education system, and resuming democracy and civil society programs. It's disappointing that the Obama administration sharply reduced democracy assistance, especially in the Middle East.[12]

Concerned citizens can help. First, take the long view. The post-Saddam government system is still new. In the years covered by this story, Iraq has seen a lot of changes, some of them negative, some positive. The next ten years will see a lot more changes.

Second, believe in the Iraqi people. Don't judge the worthiness of the country based on the corrupt politicians or the terrorists. Apply your religious tolerance to moderate Muslims, who are the vast majority, in Iraq as in America, and affirm the compatibility of Islam and democracy.

Third, stay engaged with developments in Iraq but don't fixate on the media's issues. Iraq is not, for example, an Iranian satellite. Iran gained more influence in Iraq after 2011 because the United States withdrew its remaining troops and reduced its diplomatic engagement, leaving a vacuum. Its influence faded as U.S. and Coalition assistance against Daesh increased. Moreover, Iraqi voters have made it clear, in elections and public opinion surveys, that they don't want a political system like Iran's or to have their government too close to Iran. This opinion has been expressed by Shia (strongly) as well as Sunni Arabs and Kurds (even more strongly).[13]

The recommendation to stay engaged applies also to Iraqis now in the United States and moving into citizenship. To these people I say that the number of Iraqis in America is now large enough to have a public impact if you get organized and find a collective voice. I encourage you to join organizations of Iraqi Americans, including Kurdish Americans, who are committed to helping in Iraq.

Finally, think internationally. We can't just live in our own world anymore. Support international development around the world and other foreign assistance that helps people. It's in our national interest, and it's about caring for others by applying our moral principles to help change lives. Millions of people are alive today, or living better lives, as a result of assistance from developed countries, the UN and other international agencies, and nonprofit organizations, some of them perhaps supported by your donations.

It's easy to be cynical about policy decisions on Iraq and to dwell on the mistakes. There is much to be cynical about, and there have been too many mistakes. We have no excuse not to learn from them.

A fair account of the struggle for Iraq requires some balance, however, between the good and the bad, the successful and the unsuccessful, the heroic and the self-serving. That is especially a message to those who opposed invading Iraq in the first place and continued to demand immediate withdrawal. There will always be fair issues over the decision to go to war with Saddam's Iraq and especially over how we managed the aftermath. That doesn't justify rooting for the policy to fail so as to validate one's opinion. The policy questions are about what to do now. To quote one scholar, "Too many Americans appear willing to sacrifice Iraq's future upon the altar of their own antagonism toward George W. Bush."[14]

A State Department official produced an unauthorized but witty and engaging account of his time in Iraq, saying that virtually none of the projects to which he was assigned were productive and a lot of taxpayers' money was wasted.[15] This played well with people who were already skeptical, but some who worked in Iraq felt that it did not fairly represent their experiences.[16] By telling my own story, explaining Iraq from the ground up, I have hopefully given you a balanced perspective often missing.

Shared Dreams, Shared Tears

Iraqis who worked for me and shared my commitment to help their country will always be my friends and have a place in my heart. I won't forget their contributions or their sacrifices. Accomplishments in Iraq have come at a high price in lives ended and lives imperiled. Many of my team members from my three tours in Iraq no longer live there, for most because they were no longer safe there. A lot of dreams have died in Iraq, many buried with the deceased.

In June 2008 I organized a memorial program for Haider Al-Maliki at Georgetown University, on the second anniversary of his death, with help from Freedom House, which had once honored him. It was a gesture of sympathy and solidarity from Americans who had met Haider or heard his story. Seeing the presentation of beautiful photos arranged by his two friends living in Belgium was especially touching and to me an emotional experience.

Haider is ever on my mind. As I write this, he would be thirty-seven, perhaps too young to hold a high position but old enough to be in parliament or another significant position and make a difference, perhaps moving to the forefront of that next generation of leaders whom Iraq sorely needs.

Iraqi staff who stayed in Iraq have mostly done well professionally, two with the United Nations in Iraq and several others for international development organizations, at least two of whom became project managers. Others returned to their previous profession; a few have since retired. Spouses and a lot of new children have been added to families. I helped one romance along, contributing the dowry for the intended's father. It's now a family of five.

Some of those with dreams of helping Iraq in 2003 were Iraqis living abroad, many comfortably, who returned to Iraq to help rebuild their native country. Many made a difference, in the government or in some other capacity. Most were not protected by security men, and once Iraq's violence made life there unsafe, some died for their dedication.

In 2013 Jawaad lost both his parents to medical causes. His father was a quiet symbol of the new Iraq we tried to create—forward thinking, open-minded, Islamic but democratic—and instructed his children accordingly. His passing was a reminder of all the Iraqis we don't hear about, whose contributions are quietly positive and who represent the silent majority of Iraqis who deserve our continued support.

I Love You Too

After everything I went through in this adventure of a lifetime, I realized at some point that I am at heart the American from Iraq. I was just one person who joined the struggle, and difficult circumstances prevented me from doing enough. So, I did not change Iraq despite some accomplishments, but Iraq changed me.

Even though I am not there, I still pay close attention to Iraq news, especially through *Daesh Daily*, and still devote time to Iraqi friends, in America and Iraq. Writing the book added greatly to my knowledge of the country. The deeper one's knowledge, the more compelling is the enormity of the people's struggle as well as their losses and sacrifices. I can't say I love all the Iraqis; too many are unlovable because of their crimes. I feel an emotional commitment, however, to the millions who still hope for a better life. I hope I still have time to make a difference. I hope the book helps too.

Iraqis who worked with me during my three civilian tours in their country live in Maryland, Virginia, Tennessee, and North Carolina; New York and New Jersey; Michigan and Illinois; Oregon and California. Then there are the refugees who went to England, Ireland, and Sweden. For most the adjustment was not easy and financial security has been elusive.

I take a personal interest in my Iraqi friends in America, but I take no joy in their being here. Iraq needs them more. Iraq's refugees represent one of the largest brain drains in recent history. Yet just as good times don't last indefinitely, neither do bad times. Some Iraqi refugees in Syria and Jordan have gone back. Many more will go if Iraq can finally deal decisively with the violence and its political causes. Many Iraqis now in the United States have SIVs that allow them to do some work in Iraq, and a growing number will be American citizens with passports.

One major personal satisfaction from my Iraq experience has been the positive relationships that came from it. My concern for Iraq has been recognized and appreciated by many Iraqis. It means a lot to be important to others, conceding that it adds to one's obligations, and I made many friends who have enriched my life. The internet is a particular blessing for those of us who communicate across borders and oceans.

One afternoon in Baghdad in 2006, I got a call from one of my Amarah staff members who had liked me the most. His conversation transitioned to a series of heartfelt compliments about how much I had cared and how well I had treated him and others on the Democracy Team. I needed to finish something important but was touched by his words and wanted to respond with something meaningful. My instinctive answer expressed my deep feelings toward Iraqis like him who shared the burden of my commitment to Iraq: "I love you too."

Acknowledgments

This book has been a major project over several years. It would not have happened without the support of many people.

I completed my project in southern Iraq without even thinking about writing a book. One day a medical doctor friend, Elmer Carreno, put the idea in my head. After several months on my second project, in Baghdad, I realized Elmer was right—I was accumulating a lot of knowledge and experience that needed to be shared.

I started writing after returning from Baghdad, but my third Iraq project, in Kurdistan, intervened. Major developments then followed in Iraq that had to be covered to complete my story properly, thus lengthening the timeline of the material and the book project.

Along the way, however, I got a lot of help from my friends. Lois Gorman, a Greenbelt, Maryland, friend who avidly follows Iraq events, read and commented on the original draft of part 1, and Joe Flick, Ed Putens, Gene Milgram, and former Amarah team leader Denny Lane all read parts of it. Former Baghdad colleague Dan Killian gave some early advice on writing. Jared Hayes, a former Baghdad program manager for RTI International, took a positive interest and provided missing information.

After I finished part 2, Tom McClure, a Kentucky native and the America's Development Foundation man in Cairo for years, read all the chapters and was especially insightful about how different types of readers might react to each one. Tom was also a connection to author and editor Susan Giffin in Michigan, who provided helpful feedback. Iraqi American journalist Atheer Kakan applied his knowledge of Baghdad and Iraqi elections to chapters 5 and 6. A few people from my story agreed to talk with me, including Radhi Al-Radhi, former head of Iraq's Commission on Integrity.

Several former staff members from the Iraq Civil Society Program (ICSP) answered questions on specific topics, including developments after I left Amarah, Baghdad, and Erbil. (You probably wondered where I got all that information.) Having used substitute names or just first names in the book, I can only acknowledge them collectively here. I can mention my former Anti-Corruption coordinator in Erbil, Abdulla Barzangy, now an American citizen and international development specialist, who was a valuable source of information and insights.

Also helpful were ADF's president, Michael Miller, and its program manager, Karen Diop; Marius Van der Riet, president of Reed Security in Virginia; and a great Iraqi staff member from Baghdad who was forced to leave Iraq, Zainab Salman, an expert on women's rights.

Former Erbil colleague Ann Mirani commented on the Kurdistan chapters. Special thanks are owed to my longtime city management friend Roylene Roberts, now in Texas, who volunteered to read the entire completed manuscript and as usual insisted I make some changes.

No matter how much an American learns about Iraq, there is a deeper level that Iraqi scholars understand better. On many subjects my authoritative source has been Ali Sada, Iraqi American founder of the Iraqi Research Foundation for Analysis and Development (IRFAD). He later retaliated for all the chapters he read by insisting that I become coeditor of the *Daesh Daily* newsletter. His commitment to Iraq is still powerful, and his depth of knowledge is amazing.

Writing it doesn't help if you can't publish it. Learning *how* to write and sell a book is daunting, as every writer learns, so I am thankful to talented editor-advisor Ally (Peltier) Machate of Ambitious Enterprises in Maryland, who also identified a possible agent. Special thanks are owed to that agent, Kevin Moran in New York City, whose friendship and long experience in the publishing game were really helpful to a new author. Professional editor Katherine Pickett helped put my completed submission together.

I am grateful to the University of Nebraska Press for believing in the book and agreeing to publish it through Potomac Books and especially to acquisitions editor Tom Swanson for making it all happen. Thanks also to his assistant, Emily Wendell, for all her efforts on the book. Thanks in abundance to the book's project editor, Sara Springsteen, for steering me through the editing process and to the copyeditor for her diligent and challenging work. Thanks also to the production and design professionals for making it all look good and to publicity manager Rosemary Vestal and the marketing team for bringing it to your attention. Finally, a special thanks to you, my readers, for taking an interest in my story and caring about the people of Iraq.

Both professional and aspiring writers are part of a community, and the support from other writers, including the Maryland Writers Association and its associated Montgomery County organization, including many helpful seminars, is appreciated, as are members of my local Greenbelt Writers Group.

Also contributing were my family and several friends in Maryland and Massachusetts who showed sustained interest and moral support during this long project, the most frequent comment being "When is this book going to get finished?"

I thank the International City/County Management Association (ICMA), RTI International, America's Development Foundation (now gone, with Michael Miller's passing), and Rich Michael and Carole O'Leary of Michael-Moran Associates—and of course USAID—for their confidence that I could help Iraq.

I thank all my expat colleagues from Amarah, Baghdad, and Erbil who shared in the civilian mission to help the Iraqi people. Writing a book that necessarily focuses on personal experience and perspectives necessarily gives greater prominence to one's own story, but the much greater impact and importance of the team's work deserve respect and appreciation.

A general appreciation is owed to all my international development counterparts, past and present, for their underpublicized efforts to help others, in the Middle East and in many other places in this challenging world. I learned that very few of us write books about our experience. I thought someone should. This one is for you.

Finally but most important, a personal appreciation to all my Iraqi staff—the many still in Iraq and those compelled to leave. Thank you for being my friend, sharing my efforts to help Iraq, and helping to make me feel like part of it. Most of you took serious risks and accomplished a lot in spite of those risks. Whether or not you are mentioned in the book, you are appreciated and remembered always.

To three Iraqi staff who lost their lives in service to their country, I owe the most profound and grateful acknowledgment.

Notes

1. An American Advisor

1. Most large Iraqi cities, including Amarah, are on one of two famous rivers, the Euphrates or the Tigris, called Forat and Dijle by Iraqis.

2. One explanation behind the elder Bush's decision not to intervene is that Saudi Arabia persuaded him that if Saddam were overthrown, Iran would get control of Iraq. Nasr, *Shia Revival*, 188.

3. Post-Saddam restoration efforts brought water and people back to some of the land, but dams built upstream by Iran, Turkey, and Syria reduced water levels and canceled out much of that progress.

4. Allawi, *Occupation of Iraq*, 49–50. This is an excellent, detailed account of government in Iraq after the Coalition invasion.

5. Shadid, *Night Draws Near*, 131–34, 137–38, 143–47, 153–57. Shadid was in Baghdad during and after the invasion.

6. Shadid, *Night Draws Near*, 262–69, 277–85.

7. Stewart gives his own account of his time in Amarah and later in Nasariya in a fascinating book called *The Prince of the Marshes*.

8. The term *Abu* means "father of," so Kareem is the father of Hatim. Many Arabs become better known by their alternate name.

9. The final list of committees: Public Safety; Public Services; Health and Environment; Education, Youth, and Sport; Agriculture, Irrigation, and Livestock; Industry and Oil; Public, Social, and Cultural Affairs; Finance, Trade, and Tourism; Human Rights and Immigration; and Rules and Administration.

10. Stewart, *Prince of the Marshes*, esp. 259–60, 266–69.

11. Stewart, *Prince of the Marshes*, 271–74.

12. This and preceding paragraph based on Stewart, *Prince of the Marshes*, 274–80.

13. Synnott, *Bad Days in Basra*, 42.

14. The follies and eccentricities of the CPA were well chronicled in various books, most notably in *Imperial Life in the Emerald City* by *Washington Post* reporter Rajiv Chandrasekaran.

15. Agresto, *Mugged by Reality*, 26, 31.

16. Diamond, *Squandered Victory*, 129–30.

2. The Campaign for Democracy

1. Diamond, *Squandered Victory*, 71–72.

2. Diamond, *Squandered Victory*, 140–45. Chapter 6 is a detailed behind-the-scenes description of the writing of the TAL, reflecting all the complex issues and hard choices involved.

3. Allawi, *Occupation of Iraq*, 222–23; Diamond, *Squandered Victory*, 171–78.

4. Diamond, *Squandered Victory*, 183–87, 201–3.

5. Stephenson, *Losing the Golden Hour*, 29–36, 141–42. Stephenson was USAID mission director in Baghdad during my time in Amarah.

6. Stewart, "My Extreme MBA," 6.

7. Diamond, *Squandered Victory*, 298–99.

3. The Culture of Violence

1. Cole, "Marsh Arab Rebellion," 8. This is an excellent analysis of the problems surrounding the Marsh Arabs during the early post-invasion period.

2. Diamond, *Squandered Victory*, 122.

3. See, for example, Stewart, *Prince of the Marshes*, 214–24.

4. Etherington, *Revolt on the Tigris*, 63, 84–85.

5. Kevin Begos, "Plan for Democracy Comes under Siege," *Winston-Salem Journal*, December 20, 2004.

6. Elizabeth Rubin, "Fern Holland's War," *New York Times*, September 19, 2004.

7. Allawi, *Occupation of Iraq*, 57–61.

8. Shadid, *Night Draws Near*, 229–30.

9. Knights and Williams, *Calm before the Storm*, 13.

10. Diamond, *Squandered Victory*, 214–15.

11. Diamond, *Squandered Victory*, 228–30.

12. Diamond, *Squandered Victory*, 225.

13. Shadid, *Night Draws Near*, 439–42.

14. In 2007 Martha Raddatz, then senior national security correspondent for ABC News, wrote a compelling book about this incident and the impact on the soldiers' families, *The Long Road Home: A Story of War and Family*.

15. Etherington, *Revolt on the Tigris*, 187, 196–97.

16. Etherington, *Revolt on the Tigris*, 168, 171–74.

17. Etherington, *Revolt on the Tigris*, 177–83.

18. Etherington, *Revolt on the Tigris*, 190–92.

19. Holmes, *Dusty Warriors*, 120. This book gives a detailed military account of what happened in Amarah and Basra during the Sadrist uprising.

20. Knights and Williams, *Calm before the Storm*, 19–20.

21. Stewart, *Prince of the Marshes*, 347–72.

22. Holmes, *Dusty Warriors*, 185–202, 208–21.

23. Holmes, *Dusty Warriors*, 226–37, 242.

24. Holmes, *Dusty Warriors*, 242–46.

25. Stewart, *Prince of the Marshes*, 382–83.

26. Holmes, *Dusty Warriors*, 251; and Stewart, *Prince of the Marshes*, 382.

27. Holmes, *Dusty Warriors*, 252–56.

28. Holmes, *Dusty Warriors*, 257.

4. Bottoming Out

1. Kevin Begos, "The Price of Democracy: A Woman Trapped in a Clash of Visions," *Winston-Salem Journal*, December 21, 2004.

2. James Sterngold, "Stanford Expert Says Iraq Spinning Out of Control," *San Francisco Chronicle*, April 25, 2004.

3. Diamond, *Squandered Victory*, 208-9.

4. Stewart, *Prince of the Marshes*, 383.

5. Stewart, *Prince of the Marshes*, 383-84.

6. Synnott, *Bad Days in Basra*, x, 66, 163, 25-29, 239-40, 247.

7. Allawi, *Occupation of Iraq*, 130-31.

8. Synnott, *Bad Days in Basra*, 171-72.

9. Bowen, *Hard Lessons*, 323-28. The author was the Special Inspector General for Iraq Reconstruction (SIGIR).

10. Diamond, *Squandered Victory*, 210.

11. Diamond, *Squandered Victory*, 258-59; Allawi, *Occupation of Iraq*, 284-85.

12. See, for example, Lawrence, *Invisible Nation*, 241-42.

13. Bremer, *My Year in Iraq*, 358-60, 364-66, 368-70.

14. Diamond, *Squandered Victory*, 259-62; Bremer, *My Year in Iraq*, 366, 372-77.

15. Diamond, *Squandered Victory*, 260-62; Bremer, *My Year in Iraq*, 371-72.

16. Holmes, *Dusty Warriors*, 275-83.

17. Holmes, *Dusty Warriors*, 286-301.

18. Holmes, *Dusty Warriors*, 305-6, 323-26. Those who served have the honor of being the subjects of Holmes's book, a rolling commentary on the experience as the individual soldiers saw it, from the ground up.

19. Stewart, *Prince of the Marshes*, 391-92.

20. I use the term *Sunni Arabs* rather than just *Sunnis* because most Kurds are also Sunnis.

21. Allawi, *Occupation of Iraq*, 335. For in-depth analysis of the impact of religion on the election, see 384-87.

22. Knights and Williams, *Calm before the Storm*, 23.

23. Karl Vick and Robin Wright, "Coaching Iraq's New Candidates, Discreetly," *Washington Post*, January 26, 2005.

24. It was revealed later that Bush instructed the CIA in 2004 to provide secret financial support to moderate parties, to offset the heavy Iranian support to Iran-friendly Islamic parties. However, House minority leader Nancy Pelosi heard about the plan and made a huge issue of it to Condoleezza Rice. The president backed off. The USAID Mission also opposed the idea.

25. Stewart, "Losing the South."

26. Allawi, *Occupation of Iraq*, 406.

27. Zalmay Khalilzad, "Politics Breaks Out in Iraq," *Washington Post*, September 4, 2005.

5. "Welcome Back to Your Country"

1. Stephenson, *Losing the Golden Hour*, 13.

2. Jackie Spinner, "Easy Sailing along Once-Perilous Road to Baghdad Airport," *Washington Post*, November 4, 2005.

3. Bowen, *Hard Lessons*, 179.

4. RTI published a helpful "Lessons Learned Brief," *Creating Representative Councils in Baghdad* (brief no. 6), in May 2005, which details RTI's process and the problems encountered.

5. Rajiv Chandrasekaran, "Death Stalks an Experiment in Democracy," *Washington Post*, June 22, 2004.

6. Renae Merle and Griff Witte, "Security Costs Slow Iraq Reconstruction," *Washington Post*, July 29, 2005.

7. Kirk Semple, "As Iraqi Lights Flicker, 'Generator Man' Feels Heat," *New York Times*, Baghdad Journal, September 25, 2006.

6. Islam and Democracy

1. Visser, *Sistani, the United States and Politics in Iraq*, 9–13. This is an excellent, precisely documented summary of Sistani's writing on political subjects.

2. For a detailed analysis of Sistani's governance model and his impact, see Nasr, *Shia Revival*, 171–78.

3. Visser, *Sistani, the United States and Politics in Iraq*, 19–20.

4. Shadid, *Night Draws Near*, 360–62; Allawi, *Occupation of Iraq*, 245–48.

5. For a detailed analysis, see Fink and Leibowitz, "Muslim Scholars Association."

6. Moqtada is not the grandson of Mohammed Baqir Al-Sadr, though Mohammed was his father's cousin.

7. Islamic Dawa puts the execution death toll at 200,000. A former resident of Karbala conveyed the horrifying scale of these executions when he told me that everyone he knew there during his youth, including everyone he knew in his high school of 1,600 students, had lost one or more family members.

8. For a fascinating analysis of the theological politics behind the competing concepts of Khomeini and the Najaf *hawza*, see Nasr, *Shia Revival*, 124–26. Khomeini's own theory was developed at Najaf and was opposed by Grand Ayatollah Al-Khoei. Nasr credits Al-Khoei with enabling the democratic governance model in Iraq.

9. Stewart, *Prince of the Marshes*, 237.

10. Allawi, *Occupation of Iraq*, 111.

11. The spelling *Abdul* or *Abdel* is an accommodation to Western readers. The more exact spelling is *Abd* (given name) followed by *ul* (or *al* or *el*) and the rest of the family name, in this case Abd Al-Aziz Al-Hakim.

12. Visser, *Iran's Role in Post-Occupation Iraq*, 11.

13. Cordesman, *Impact of the Iraqi Election*, 6.

14. For an inside explanation of why Al-Maliki got the job, see Filkins, "Letter from Iraq," 6–7.

15. Bowen, *Hard Lessons*, 250–51.

7. The Struggle to Reduce Corruption

1. Allawi, *Occupation of Iraq*, 351–52.

2. Allawi, *Occupation of Iraq*, 361–68.

3. Walter Pincus, "Corruption Cited in Iraq's Oil Industry," *Washington Post*, July 17, 2006; James Glanz and Robert F. Worth, "Attacks on Iraq Oil Industry Aid Vast Smuggling Scheme," *New York Times*, June 4, 2006.

4. For an excellent summary of the sources and consequences of Iraq's disastrous economics, see Munson, *Iraq in Transition*, 37–40.

5. Etherington, *Revolt on the Tigris*, 157.

8. The Anti-Corruption Struggle

1. Office of the Special Inspector General for Iraq Reconstruction, *Joint Survey*, 19.

2. Office of the Special Inspector General for Iraq Reconstruction, *Joint Survey*; U.S. Department of State, Office of Inspector General, *Survey of Anticorruption Programs*, 5–28.

3. U.S. Department of State, *Survey of Anticorruption Programs*, 1–2, 4, 13.

4. U.S. Department of State, *Survey of Anticorruption Programs*, 14–15; emphasis added.

5. U.S. Department of State, *Survey of Anticorruption Programs*, 4, 17–18.

9. The Struggle for Human Rights

1. Bowen, *Hard Lessons*, 274.

2. Jessica Stern, "Myths About Who Becomes a Terrorist," *Washington Post*, January 10, 2010.

3. Shadid, *Night Draws Near*, 1–9.

4. Estimates of civilian deaths differ widely, depending on the source, and are therefore controversial. Civilians killed by warfare added to the total killed by sectarian violence.

5. Dan Murphy, "Iraq's Neighborhood Councils Are Vanishing," *Christian Science Monitor*, February 25, 2005.

6. Bowen, *Hard Lessons*, 247–48.

7. Munson, *Iraq in Transition*, 68–69.

8. Nancy A. Youssef, "Shiite Leaders Distance Themselves from Iraqi Government," McClatchy Newspapers, August 1, 2006, cited in Allawi, *Occupation of Iraq*, 452.

9. Coleman, "Women, Islam, and the New Iraq," 25–26.

10. Dowries are often in two parts: one portion paid before the marriage, the second after a divorce. The second is often much larger—a kind of "poison pill" to discourage divorce.

11. Why Islam, *Status of Women in Islam*, 1–2.

12. Why Islam, *Status of Women in Islam*, 5.

13. Anthony Shadid, "Picnic Is No Party in the New Basra," *Washington Post*, March 29, 2005; Knights and Williams, *Calm before the Storm*, 27.

14. Holmes, *Dusty Warriors*, 319.

15. Coleman, "Women, Islam, and the New Iraq," 25.

10. Civil Society Organizations

1. Malo, "Future of Civil Society in Iraq," 1, 3.

11. The Personal Meaning of Terrorism

1. Keiger, "The Number," 30–34. The study, conducted by Gilbert Burnham and Leslie F. Roberts, was published in October 2006 by the British medical journal the *Lancet*.

2. Leila Fadel, "U.S. Reports 77,000 Iraqi Fatalities from 2004 to August 2008," *Washington Post*, October 15, 2010. The article cites a U.S. military estimate.

3. Glenn Kessler, "U.S. Cites 91 Percent Rise in Terrorist Acts in Iraq," *Washington Post*, May 5, 2007. Data were based on figures from the National Counterterrorism Center.

4. Al-Khalidi and Tanner, *Sectarian Violence*, 2–3. Among those who didn't move, many slept in different places, shopped in different markets, used different routes or modes of transport, or stayed home from work or school (28–29).

5. As of September 2007, total refugees and IDPs would peak at about 4.5 million, over 15 percent of the Iraq population. Munson, *Iraq in Transition*, 205.

6. Anthony Shadid, "One Man, One Nation, Defined by Resilience," *Washington Post*, March 20, 2005.

7. Allawi, *Occupation of Iraq*, 376–77.

8. Gian P. Gentile, "In the Middle of a Civil War," *Washington Post*, August 7, 2007.

9. Knight, "In the Face of Death," 34–37.

10. Al-Khalidi and Tanner, *Sectarian Violence*, 16–17.

11. Knights and Williams, *Calm before the Storm*, 31

12. David Ignatius, "Buying the Vote," *Washington Post*, February 25, 2010.

13. International Crisis Group, *Where Is Iraq Heading*, 10–16. This is an excellent detailed account of major developments and issues in Basra at that time.

14. Cole, "Marsh Arab Rebellion," 15.

15. Knights and Williams, *Calm before the Storm*, 27, 29.

16. To its credit the *Christian Science Monitor* wrote a tribute to Allan Enwiya: "Remembering Allan: A Tribute to Jill Carroll's Interpreter," March 6, 2006.

13. Sinking Your Own Ship

1. Munson, *Iraq in Transition*, 162.

2. Andi's journalist boyfriend, Michael Hastings, wrote a book about the tragedy: *I Lost My Love in Baghdad* (New York: Scribner, 2008). Hastings lost his own life in a car crash in Los Angeles in 2013, at age thirty-three.

3. United States Agency for International Development (USAID), *Building on Transition*, i.

4. USAID, *Building on Transition*, 14–15, 35, 40.

5. USAID, *Building on Transition*, iv–v.

6. USAID, *Building on Transition*, v.

7. USAID, *Building on Transition*, v.

8. USAID, *Building on Transition*, 45.

9. USAID, *Building on Transition*, v–vi.

10. USAID, *Building on Transition*, ii, 16.

11. USAID, *Building on Transition*, 18.

12. USAID, *Building on Transition*, 19, 21, 48–49.

13. USAID, *Building on Transition*, 41–47.

14. America's Development Foundation, *Final Report*, 2.

15. America's Development Foundation, *Final Report*, 4, 17–18.

16. America's Development Foundation, *Final Report*, 16.

17. America's Development Foundation, *Final Report*, 2–3.

18. America's Development Foundation, *Final Report*, 7.

19. America's Development Foundation, *Final Report*, 6.

14. The Instinct to Control

1. Testimony of Judge Radhi Hamza Al-Radhi, Senate Committee on Appropriations, March 11, 2008, 5.

2. International Crisis Group, *Failing Oversight*, 9, based on COI annual reports.

3. International Crisis Group, *Failing Oversight*, 4–10; Corn, "Secret Report," 3. Corn's article is a valuable summary of the dire situation faced by CPI at that time.

4. Office of the Special Inspector General for Iraq Reconstruction, *Anticorruption Efforts in Iraq*, 8–9.

5. Anne Flaherty, "Ex-State Officials Allege Corruption Cover-Up," Associated Press, May 12, 2008.

6. U.S. Department of Justice, *Fact Sheet*.

7. Bowen, *Hard Lessons*, 212–13.

8. "Integrity Commission Report on Iraqi Corruption," McClatchy Newspapers, September 22, 2009.

9. International Crisis Group, *Failing Oversight*, 3, 13.

10. Bowen, *Hard Lessons*, 213.

11. International Crisis Group, *Failing Oversight*, 24.

12. Allawi, *Occupation of Iraq*, 486.

13. Michael S. Schmidt and Jack Healy, "Maliki's Broadened Powers Seen as a Threat in Iraq," *New York Times*, March 5, 2011.

14. International Crisis Group, *Failing Oversight*, 5, 23–25.

15. Bowen, *Hard Lessons*, 291.

16. Adam Schreck, "Iraqi Demonstrators Rail against Lawmakers' Pension Benefits," *Washington Post*, September 1, 2013.

17. International Crisis Group, *Failing Oversight*, 20–22.

18. International Crisis Group, *Failing Oversight*, 8.

19. International Crisis Group, *Failing Oversight*, 7.

20. Surowiecki, "Payola Game," 54.

21. International Federation of Journalists, press release, December 31, 2006.

22. Ricchiardi, *Iraq's News Media after Saddam*, 21. This is an excellent study on the evolving status of journalism in Iraq.

23. Ricchiardi, *Iraq's News Media after Saddam*, 5–6, 12, 27. A good short summary of the state of post-Saddam journalism in Iraq is Gambill, "Iraqi Media."

24. Ricchiardi, *Iraq's News Media after Saddam*, 33–34

25. Ricchiardi, *Iraq's News Media after Saddam*, 35.

15. USAID and Lessons Learned in Iraq

1. Carothers, *Revitalizing Democracy Assistance*, 1, 19, 22–24, 33. Carothers's analysis has many other valuable observations and conclusions.

2. Carothers, *Revitalizing Democracy Assistance*, 24.

3. Easterly, "Planners versus Searchers in Foreign Aid," 1–35. See also Sen, "Man without a Plan," 1–6.

4. USAID, *Building on Transition*, 40.

5. Synnott, *Bad Days in Basra*, 256–57.

6. USAID, *Audit of USAID/Iraq's Local Governance Activities*, July 31, 2007, 1, 5, cited in Bowen, *Hard Lessons*, 255.

7. USAID, *Building on Transition*, 35.

8. Van Buren, *We Meant Well*, 59; Bowen, *Hard Lessons*, 292, 329, 333–34. For a complete summary of "First Principles for Contingency Relief and Reconstruction Operations," see Bowen, *Hard Lessons*, 331–42; for a similar British view, see Synnott, *Bad Days in Basra*, 257.

9. Van Buren, *We Meant Well*.

10. Bowen, *Hard Lessons*, vii.

11. Bowen, *Hard Lessons*, 238.

16. The Kurds

1. Lawrence, *Invisible Nation*, 98.

2. Hamoudi, *Howling in Mesopotamia*, 255–57.

3. Lawrence, *Invisible Nation*, 237–38.

4. Hamoudi, *Howling in Mesopotamia*, 247.

5. For a highly negative but impressively thorough analysis of the KRG's party-dominated political system and the resulting corruption, see Kamal Said Qadir, "Iraqi Kurdistan's Downward Spiral," 19–26.

6. Meiselas, *Kurdistan in the Shadow of History*, 242. This is an imposing and iconic book, full of historical photographs and documents and meticulously researched.

7. Lawrence, *Invisible Nation*, 26–29. Lawrence reports that Masoud Barzani refused to meet with Kissinger even decades later.

8. Lawrence, *Invisible Nation*, 30.

9. Lawrence, *Invisible Nation*, 31–33, 228–30; Allawi, *Occupation of Iraq*, 141.

10. Lawrence, *Invisible Nation*, 40–41; Meiselas, *Kurdistan in the Shadow of History*, 312.

11. Wing, "Iraq's Anfal Campaign," 6. This blog is in general a valuable resource.

12. Meiselas, *Kurdistan in the Shadow of History*, 324, 329; and Lawrence, *Invisible Nation*, 58–60.

13. Lawrence, *Invisible Nation*, 78–86.

14. Lawrence, *Invisible Nation*, 84–85.

15. Munson, *Iraq in Transition*, 144–45.

16. Lawrence, *Invisible Nation*, 114–18, 138–40, 145–47, 168, 172–79.

17. A secondary reason for the minister avoiding site visits was that local people often take advantage of visits by prominent people to make unrelated personal assistance requests, and there is a cultural expectation that such requests will be honored. She would otherwise lose face. The solution was not to go.

18. Natali, *Kurdish Quasi-State*, 89, 91.

17. A Ministry from the Ground Up

1. Iraq has not held a recent census, and published population estimates are often conflicting, sometimes exaggerated, and generally unreliable. Since my time in Erbil, some cities have grown enormously. Estimates here are for 2008, when I made the site visits. Most of them came from municipal officials or were adapted from 2010

data of the Kurdistan Regional Statistical Office. In other words, don't use these numbers for any research purpose.

2. *Ninewa* and *Nineveh* are the same word; *Nineveh* is closer to the spelling in the Bible and reflects Christian preference.

18. Reforming a Ministry

1. Natali, *Kurdish Quasi-State*, 112.

2. "Ministry of Municipalities Is to Be More Decentralized as New Minister Takes Office," *Kurdish Globe*, May 14, 2012.

3. Minister Dilshad Shahab, interview by the Report Company, September 19, 2013.

19. Picking Up the Pieces

1. Dawisha, *Post Occupation Iraq*, 6. This is one of the best analyses ever about politics in Iraq.

2. For a detailed political analysis of the 2009 election, see Munson, *Iraq in Transition*, 229–35; and International Crisis Group, *Iraq's Uncertain Future*, 2–7.

3. Munson, *Iraq in Transition*, 230.

4. Munson, *Iraq in Transition*, 225–27.

5. For a thorough study of the judiciary's role in the 2010 election, see Trumbull and Moran, "Elections and Government Formation in Iraq," 331–88.

6. Al-Ali, *Struggle for Iraq's Future*, 124.

7. Filkins, "What We Left Behind," 15–16. Filkins alleges that one pro-Iran consideration was removing all U.S. troops from Iraq by the end of 2011.

8. Gunter, "Economic Opportunities in Iraqi Kurdistan," 3.

9. Katzman, *Iraq: Politics, Governance, and Human Rights*, 14.

10. Iraq polling places were again set up in the United States, with nine locations in seven states. One of my former Iraqi coordinators was hired to manage one of them, which became a tough assignment. There, and in other U.S. polling places, people were really energized by this election, including many who hadn't lived in Iraq for years, and some of Iraq's political animosities carried over to Iraqis voting in the United States. Many who came to vote were disqualified—mostly due to expired, non-original (copied), or absent Iraqi ID—prompting many complaints.

11. International Crisis Group, *Make or Break*, 22.

12. The Assyrian International News Agency (AINA) made noteworthy efforts to document the increasingly bad conditions for Christians in Iraq. Cited data came largely from AINA press releases.

13. The website for the Iraqi Kurdistan Christianity Project, a project of the Middle Eastern Religious Freedom Program, is http://www.mena-rf.org.

14. Perito, *Iraq Federal Police*, 9–11. The IFP later had a major role in the war against ISIS.

15. Annie Gowen, "Report: 12,000 Iraqi Civilians Killed in Suicide Attacks since '03," *Washington Post*, September 4, 2011.

16. Michael S. Schmidt, "Mass Grave in Iraqi Town Held Bodies of 30 Cabbies," *New York Times*, September 12, 2011.

17. Eakin, "Syria: Which Way to Kurdistan?," 2.

18. People inside the Property Directorate, e.g., gave ISIS the addresses of Christians. The *Assyrian International News Agency* reported on May 25, 2014, before the

Mosul takeover, that since early 2013 ISIS had forced hundreds of Christians to leave Mosul and had assassinated and even beheaded real estate brokers who sold homes for Christians who were leaving.

19. Sherlock, "Inside the Leadership of Islamic State"; and Al-Hashimi, "Revealed." Supporting his declaration that the Islamic State is a caliphate, Al-Baghdadi took the name of the first Muslim caliph, so is called Abu Bakr Al-Baghdadi. In fact, he had no connection to the Prophet's bloodline, as he claimed, and came from Samarra, not Baghdad.

20. An official KRG source reported that "on August 15 the entire male population of the village of Kocho, 80 Yazidi men, were slaughtered, with hundreds of women kidnapped, enslaved, and sold for as little as $15." Kurdistan Regional Government, "Updates on the Kurdistan Region," 3.

21. The awful details of the Yazidi disaster were reported in Amnesty International, *Ethnic Cleansing on a Historic Scale*, 7–19.

22. Assyrian International News Agency, "Assyrian Describes ISIS Takeover of His City in North Iraq," October 25, 2014, 1.

23. Erin Cunningham, "Old Tensions Feeding Battles in Iraq," *Washington Post*, August 30, 2014.

24. Abigail Hauslohner, "With the Rise of the Islamic State, the Destruction of Trust," *Washington Post*, October 1, 2014. This is an excellent summary of the sectarian and ethnic cleansing effect of the ISIS campaign.

25. An impressive, stunning analysis of ISIS ideology and its implications is provided in a lengthy article by Graeme Wood, "What ISIS Really Wants," *Atlantic*, March 2015.

26. Kurdistan Regional Government, "Updates on the Kurdistan Region," 2.

20. Winning the Endgame in Iraq

1. Filkins, "What We Left Behind," 18–19.

2. One analysis of the army's corruption and collapse is in Cockburn, "Battle for Baghdad," 6. More revelations soon followed.

3. Aki Peritz, "Where Are Iraq's 'Monuments Men'?" *Washington Post*, August 24, 2014; Loveday Morris, "Islamic State's Pillaging of Antiquities Now Systematic," *Washington Post*, June 9, 2015.

4. In 2015 Iraq started holding salary payments owed to government staff in ISIS-controlled areas so as to stop subsidizing ISIS; it was unclear how the affected employees would get by while waiting.

5. Loveday Morris, "50,000 'Ghost Soldiers' Found in Iraq's Army," *Washington Post*, December 1, 2014; Morris, "Mosul's Fall Blamed on Poor Leadership," *Washington Post*, August 28, 2015.

6. If you want to check it out, go to www.daeshdaily.com. All back issues are available on the website.

7. Liz Sly, "Islamic State Appears to Fray," *Washington Post*, March 9, 2015.

8. A highly critical analysis of Iraq's economic problems is in Al-Ali, *Struggle for Iraq's Future*, chap. 6, 161–80. For the author's analysis of the government's failed agriculture policy, see 221–37.

9. Ishaan Tharoor, "Islamic State Is Holding About 3,500 Iraqis as 'Slaves,' UN Report Says," *Washington Post*, January 20, 2016.

10. Hamoudi, *Howling in Mesopotamia*, 26.

11. Al-Ali, *Struggle for Iraq's Future*, 63.

12. Imam Abdullah Antepli, "The Last Sermon of the Prophet Muhammad," *Huffington Post*, February 3, 2012, http://www.huffingtonpost.com/imam-abdullah-antepli/the-last-sermon-of-prophe_b_1252185.html.

21. Drawing Lines in the Sand

1. Total registered voters went from 500,000 in January 2005 to 900,000 in 2009. Kane, *Iraq's Disputed Territories*, 24.

2. Bartu, "Wrestling with the Integrity of a Nation," 1334-35.

3. Katzman, *Iraq: Politics, Governance, and Human Rights*, 18.

4. Karin Brulliard, "Iraq Prepares to Resettle Arabs Sent to Kirkuk by Hussein Edict," *Washington Post*, April 1, 2007.

5. For more on the claims process, see Knights and Ali, *Kirkuk in Transition*, 14-15.

6. For a detailed and excellent categorization and summary description of all the disputed territories, see Anderson, *Politics and Security of the Disputed Territories*, 22-28.

7. Article 110 specifies the nine "exclusive authorities" of the federal government. First is: "Formulating foreign policy and diplomatic representation; negotiating, signing, and ratifying international treaties and agreements; negotiating, signing, and ratifying debt policies; and formulating foreign sovereign economic and trade policy."

8. Meiselas, *Kurdistan in the Shadow of History*, 374, 379.

9. Vick, "Turkey's Triumphs," 28-29.

10. Anthony Shadid, "Resurgent Turkey Flexes Its Muscles around Iraq," *New York Times*, January 4, 2011.

11. For more on the Turkey-KRG energy relationship and its implications, see Ottaway and Ottaway, "How the Kurds Got Their Way," 141-44.

12. Shadid, "Resurgent Turkey," 5-6.

13. Ottaway, "Iraq's Kurdistan Takes a Giant Step," 1.

14. Kane, *Iraq's Disputed Territories*, 17-21, 25-37. This valuable study analyzes likely referendum outcomes in disputed territories using past election results.

15. Al-Ali, *Struggle for Iraq's Future*, 162, 167; Katzman, *Iraq: Politics, Governance, and Human Rights*, 24.

22. The American from Iraq

1. For the full story behind the strategy, see Ricks, *The Gamble*. For a further military analysis, see Kagan, *The Surge*.

2. Office of the Special Inspector General for Iraq Reconstruction, *Human Toll*, 3.

3. Brown University, Costs of War project, "Iraq War," 3.

4. Office of the Special Inspector General for Iraq Reconstruction, *Human Toll*, 10.

5. Johnson, *To Be a Friend Is Fatal*.

6. Johnson, *To Be a Friend Is Fatal*, 179-86.

7. Johnson, *To Be a Friend Is Fatal*, 189-95.

8. Johnson, *To Be a Friend Is Fatal*, 255.

9. Johnson, *To Be a Friend Is Fatal*, 283-96.

10. For an excellent analysis of democracy and the Middle East, see Diamond, "Why There Are No Arab Democracies," 93-104.

11. For a summary of how this deep conflict developed, see Nasr, *Shia Revival*, 147–58.

12. Thomas Carothers, "Shortchanging Democracy," *Washington Post*, February 23, 2014.

13. Pollock and Ali, "Iran Gets Negative Reviews in Iraq," 1.

14. Michael Rubin, "Don't Forget about Iraq," 2.

15. Referring to Van Buren, *We Meant Well*, cited in chap. 15.

16. Donnelly, "We Did Mean Well," 1–11.

Glossary

Abu Naji   Iraqi military camp near Amarah; the British base of operation in Maysan Province until late 2006, when Iraq resumed security responsibility there.

Al Arabiya   Saudi-owned, UAE-based television news channel widely watched in Iraq.

Al Jazeera   Qatar government–owned satellite television network whose news channel is widely watched in Iraq.

Al-Qaeda in Iraq   Terrorist organization affiliated with but not part of the international Al-Qaeda organization. It played the leading role in Iraq's sectarian violence and was later succeeded by ISIS.

anti-corruption   (1) A subfield of public management focused on reducing corrupt behavior by public officials, often through public awareness raising, advocacy, government corrective actions, and/or law enforcement; (2) when capitalized, one of six component programs of ICSP.

Assyrians   A Christian, heavily Catholic minority living largely in northern Iraq and northeastern Syria, with historical roots back to the pre-Islamic period. Successive persecutions, the United Nations (UN) sanctions in the 1990s, and post-2003 anti-Christian violence caused large out-migrations to Europe, North America, and Australia, sharply reducing their numbers in Iraq.

ayatollah   A high-level religious teacher in Shia Islam, with authority to interpret religious and other knowledge to adherents. A small number attain the status of grand ayatollah.

Baath Party   The secular, pan-Arab, and socialist political party that seized power in Iraq in 1968. It was led from 1979 to 2003 by Saddam Hussein, was deposed by the U.S.-led Coalition in 2003, and then abolished.

Badr Organization   A major pro-Iran militia organization established in 2003 as the post-Saddam successor to the Badr Corps, which had succeeded the Badr Brigades. Badr was trained and led by Iranians in Iran, became the military wing of SCIRI in 1982, and fought on Iran's side in the Iran-Iraq War. It became a separate political entity in 2012. Its militia became an important PMF component against ISIS.

capacity building   The process of increasing an organization's internal capabilities through training and technical assistance. This is a typical focus of USAID projects that support government agencies and civil society organizations.

Central Region   As defined by the USAID Local Governance Program, the governorates of Anbar, Baghdad, Diyala, and Salahuddin.

chief of party   The contractor's project manager on a USAID international development project.

Christians   In Iraq a small and shrinking minority, mostly ethnic Assyrians who belong to the Chaldean Catholic tradition. There are other similar Christian denominations as well as Armenian Orthodox Christians.

Civic Dialogue Program   Within the initial Local Governance Program, the umbrella program for promoting democratic values and processes in Iraq, which included the Democracy Dialogue Activity.

civic education   (1) By definition, educational and other programs that improve the capacity and confidence of citizens to participate in and affect a democratic political system; (2) when capitalized, one of six component programs of ICSP.

civil society   The sum total of voluntary organizational and citizen participation in a nation's political process, highly variable from country to country and within the same country over time, depending on differences in political culture and extent of democratization and especially the extent of freedom from political interference.

civil society organization   Generally, a nonprofit organization independent of the government whose activities contribute to society at some level.

Civil Society Resource Center   One of four ICSP regional offices—in Baghdad, Hilla, Basra, and Erbil.

coalition   (1) An alliance of multiple governments sharing a common regional or international purpose (e.g., the Coalition Provisional Authority in Iraq); (2) an association of multiple organizations working for a common public purpose. In Iraq an alliance of civil society organizations working to influence public policy decisions.

Coalition Provisional Authority (CPA)   The temporary U.S.-led entity that governed Iraq between the overthrow of Saddam in 2003 and the restoration of Iraqi sovereignty in 2004.

Commission on Public Integrity   Iraq's primary anti-corruption agency, later renamed the Commission of Integrity. Established under the CPA as an independent agency, it endured major interference from Prime Minister Al-Maliki, then regained some of its independence under Prime Minister Al-Abadi in response to public pressure.

Council of Representatives   The national legislature of Iraq, often called the "parliament."

Daesh   The common and pejorative Arab term for ISIS. It comes from the pronunciation of the acronym for ISIS in Arabic, Al-Dawla al-Islamiya fi al-Iraq wa al-Sham, and is pronounced "Dahsh" in English.

de-Baathification   The policy of purging and excluding high-level Baathists from public life, adopted under the CPA and then continued. This was a Shia cause, but its excesses raised sectarian tensions and undermined national security.

Democracy Dialogue Activity   The major component of the Local Government Program's Civic Dialogue Program. It organized and conducted community meetings about democracy with multiple segments of the population throughout most of Iraq.

Democracy Team   The author's Iraqi staff for the democracy program in Maysan Province.

Department for International Development   The British government counterpart of the U.S. Agency for International Development, but unlike USAID, it is a separate agency rather than part of a larger department.

deputy chief of party   The deputy project manager on a USAID project.

diaspora   A homogeneous major population living in one or more countries other than its country of origin, often due to threatening or harsh conditions in the home country (e.g., all the Iraqis displaced by sectarian violence).

director general   In Iraq, including Kurdistan, the manager of a headquarters-level program or administrative office in a ministry or head of its governorate-level ministry office; usually a politically appointed policy-level official.

disputed territories   Extensive parts of Iraq claimed by the KRG, including Sinjar, Tal Afar, Tel Keif, Shikhan, Hamdaniya, and Makhmur Districts in Ninewa; all of Kirkuk Province; Tooz District in Salahuddin; Kifri, Khanaqin, and Balad Ruz Districts in Diyala; and Badra District in Wasit.

district   One of several political subdivisions of a governorate, usually composed of multiple subdistricts.

expat   Informal name for an "expatriate"—someone residing in a country other than his or her own, either permanently or temporarily, as with international development professionals working abroad.

Friday prayers   The mosque religious service on the Muslim Sabbath, led by an imam or other cleric and sometimes including political rhetoric.

Gorran   A recently formed but now major political party in the KRG, with a platform focusing especially on government corruption.

governorate   Iraqi term for a province.

governorate coordinator   Under the CPA, the top appointed official in a governorate, in effect the temporary governor.

grand ayatollah   An ayatollah of preeminent status, based on his knowledge of Islamic law and the Shia faith and on the number of believers who declare themselves followers of his leadership. Among Iraq's grand ayatollahs, the four leaders of the Najaf seminary (*hawza*), from four different countries, have the highest status, especially Ali Sistani.

Green Line   The official but imprecise demarcation line for the territory controlled by the Kurdistan Regional Government. The line, established in 1991, does not conform exactly to the boundaries of Kurdistan's three governorates, leaving some Iraq territory with predominantly Kurdish populations north of the line and some territory of Kurdish governorates south of the line. The unclear boundaries have contributed to the disputed territories issue between Iraq and the KRG.

Green Zone   The informal but common name for a security-protected area of central Baghdad that includes the parliament, major ministries and other agencies, and embassies; also called the International Zone, or IZ. The term came from its relative safety (Green = Go) versus the rest of Baghdad (Red Zone).

hawza   A seminary and religious studies center for training Shia clergy, headed by preeminent scholars called "grand ayatollahs." The *hawza* in Najaf, Iraq, led by Ali Sistani, is the most prestigious one and is highly influential.

hijab   In Iraq and other Muslim countries a customary piece of women's clothing worn in public that covers the head, neck, and chest. It is intended to symbolize modesty and religious observance but is resisted by some, mostly younger women as a symbol of gender inequality.

imam   By definition, one who leads. A Muslim cleric with leadership responsibilities, typically as a prayer leader and/or religious counselor, often as manager of a mosque. A role defined differently by Shia and Sunnis and more exalted by the Shia.

improvised explosive device (IED)   A bomb, constructed from an explosive and a detonating device, used by ISIS and earlier Iraq terrorists as an antipersonnel weapon, or as a roadside bomb targeting vehicles with military or civilian personnel; or placed in crowded places so as to cause mass casualties; or driven by vehicle into military defense lines or crowded civilian areas; or carried in an explosives vest by suicide bombers.

Independent High Electoral Commission   The independent agency responsible for supervising elections in all parts of Iraq.

inspector general (IG)   In each U.S. government department the official responsible for politically independent audits, evaluations, and investigations. The same system was established in Iraq as one of four components of its anti-corruption system.

internally displaced person   Someone compelled to leave his or her geographical location by war, violence, oppression, fear of persecution, or extreme deprivation and who moves to another location within his or her own country.

International City/County Management Association (ICMA)   The membership organization for the municipal management profession. Nine ICMA members joined the original Local Governance Program, including the author, and many more served later on projects in Iraq.

Iraq Civil Society Program (ICSP)   The USAID project implemented by America's Development Foundation, with six programs: Anti-Corruption, Civic Education, Civil Society Capacity Building, Human Rights, Independent Media, and Women's Rights.

Iraqi Governing Council   The organization of Iraqi political leaders appointed by the CPA to share decision-making authority with CPA administrator Paul Bremer. It was dissolved with the return to self-government in June 2004.

Iraqi National Alliance   A coalition of Shia political parties and factions; a successor to the original United Iraqi Alliance formed in 2005 that later broke up.

Islamic Dawa   A major Shia political party that produced all three of Iraq's elected prime ministers as of 2016—Al-Jaafari, Al-Maliki, and Al-Abadi.

Islamic State   The "caliphate" declared and managed by ISIS.

Islamic State of Iraq and Syria (ISIS)   The terrorist organization that seized Syrian and Iraqi territory in 2014 and declared the establishment of the Islamic caliphate and that aspires to unite all Muslims under its leadership to conquer the West.

Islamic Supreme Council of Iraq   The renamed Shia party formerly called the Supreme Council for the Islamic Revolution in Iraq.

jihadis   A Western term used to describe Sunni Muslim extremists (e.g., ISIS fighters) who join military campaigns against people they consider infidels.

Kurdistan   The autonomous region of Iraq governed by the Kurdish Regional Government, including the governorates of Dahuk, Erbil, and Suleimaniya. Often called Iraqi Kurdistan to distinguish it from nonautonomous Kurdish areas in Turkey, Syria, and Iran.

Kurdistan Democratic Party (KDP)   The dominant political party in Erbil and Dahuk, led by Masoud Barzani, a son of its founder.

Kurdistan Regional Government (KRG)   The government of the Kurdistan region of Iraq, which was accorded regional autonomy under the current Iraq constitution.

Kurdistan Workers Party (Turkey)   An internationally designated terrorist organization seeking to establish a Kurdish nation-state that combines Kurdish areas of Turkey, Iraq, Iran, and Syria. Best known by its Turkish initials, PKK.

Local Governance Program   The major USAID project, started in 2003, to help Iraqis build and develop provincial and local governments and a democratic process.

mayor   A district manager, appointed by the governor or elected by the district council to coordinate government services (and not a municipal official).

Mehdi Army   The Shia militia created in 2003 by Moqtada Al-Sadr that staged two military uprisings in the CPA period and played a major destructive role during the sectarian violence. Officially demobilized by Al-Sadr in 2008.

Michael-Moran Associates   A small Maryland consulting firm active in Kurdistan that organized the advisor team (including the author) for the Ministry of Municipalities.

Ministry of Municipalities   The KRG ministry responsible for coordinating and funding municipal governments and municipal public services, now the Ministry of Municipalities and Tourism. There is a similar ministry in Iraq's national government.

Monitoring and Evaluation   The specialization within international development responsible for monitoring, evaluating, and improving project effectiveness.

mosque   A formal place of worship for Muslims, typically managed by an imam.

National Assembly   The Iraqi parliament under the Transitional Government, elected in January 2005 and tasked primarily with writing a new constitution. It was replaced by the Council of Representatives after the December 2005 election.

nongovernmental organization   A nonprofit entity independent of government, generally with a public service mission, operating at a local, provincial/regional, national, or international level, using paid staff or volunteers or both.

parliament   A national legislature; the informal name of Iraq's Council of Representatives.

Patriotic Union of Kurdistan (PUK)   Historically, the dominant political party in Suleimaniya, cofounded and until recently led by Jalal Talabani, former president of Iraq.

personal security detail   A unit of security personnel responsible for protecting people during road travel, typically in multivehicle armed convoys, and where they live.

peshmerga   The armed forces of the KRG. Previously, two separate militias controlled by its two dominant political parties, the KDP and PUK, and still not fully unified.

Pink Palace   The informal name for the governorate building in Amarah, Maysan, so named for its color.

Popular Mobilization Forces (PMF)   The militia component of Iraqi forces fighting ISIS, coordinated through a commission but composed of disparate elements, including pro-Iran and other Shia militias, citizen volunteers, and Sunni and Shia tribal forces.

prime minister   The executive leader of a parliamentary type of government, as in Iraq, generally elected by and responsible to the national legislature.

provincial council   Informal but commonly used name for a governorate council, often used because it is less awkward to say and write.

public service announcement   A television or radio advertisement produced by a government agency or nonprofit organization, for public awareness or advocacy purposes, and broadcast free of charge.

Red Zone   An informal term for all of Baghdad other than the Green Zone; by inference all the neighborhoods not security protected, therefore unsafe for expat civilians (Red = Stop).

refugee   A person who flees his or her country due to war, violence, oppression, fear of persecution, or extreme deprivation and seeks residency in a new country. People become official refugees by registering with the UNHCR while living in a country other than their own.

religious minorities   In Iraq, citizens in non-Muslim religious denominations, mostly Christians, Yazidis, Shabaks, and Kakais. However, Shia Turkmen were a Muslim minority targeted by ISIS because they were Shia.

RTI International   A major U.S. NGO headquartered in North Carolina that manages a wide range of projects in other countries (e.g., the Local Governance Program in Iraq). Previously named Research Triangle Institute, thus the abbreviation.

Sadrists   Active followers of Moqtada Al-Sadr and his political organization and/or members and supporters of his Mehdi Army or later militia organizations.

sectarian   In Iraq, (1) having personal and/or political motives that favor Sunnis over Shia or vice versa; and/or (2) the impact of public policies and government decisions based on such motives.

sharia   The body of Islamic law developed by religious scholars after the death of the Prophet Mohammed, including interpretations of the Koran and recorded teachings and practices of the Prophet called the Sunna.

sheikh   The usually hereditary leader of a tribe or subtribe. Also an honorary title afforded to Islamic religious leaders.

South-Central Region   As defined by the Local Governance Program, the governorates of Wasit, Qadisiya, Babil, Najaf, and Karbala.

South Region   As defined by the Local Governance Program, the governorates of Basra, Maysan, Dhi Qar, and Muthanna.

Special Immigrant Visa   A congressionally enacted temporary visa category allowing endangered Iraqis who worked for Coalition organizations for a year or more to apply for admission to the United States without leaving Iraq to qualify for refugee status.

Special Inspector General for Iraq Reconstruction   A U.S. federal office created to oversee Iraq reconstruction programs and operations, existing from 2004 to 2013. Periodic published reports by Special IG Stuart Bowen evaluated the results gained for the money spent and documented all the problems experienced.

State of Law   A political coalition initially organized around then prime minister Nouri Al-Maliki, including his Islamic Dawa Party and other groups.

subdistrict   A political subdivision of a district, in all Iraq governorates.

Sunni Arabs   Iraqis of Arab ethnicity who identify with the Sunni sect. The term was adopted for clarity, as most Kurds are also Sunnis.

Supreme Council for the Islamic Revolution in Iraq (SCIRI)   A pre-2003 Islamic political organization established in Iran that became a major political party in post-Saddam Iraq and played a leading role in the multiparty Shia political coalition. Later renamed the Islamic Supreme Council of Iraq.

theocracy   A nation governed predominantly under religious leadership claiming divine authority, of which Iran is an example, though it also has democratic elements.

Training of Trainers   A program for training people to train others.

Transitional Administrative Law   The temporary and controversial constitution enacted under the CPA, replaced by the permanent constitution adopted by voters in October 2005.

Transparency International   The world's leading anti-corruption advocacy organization. Its annual Corruption Perceptions Index rates all nations from least to most corrupt—an evaluation that has annually placed Iraq near the bottom.

tribe   A tradition-based sociopolitical organization consisting of families and communities with a common paternal lineage, typically living in the same general area, under a usually hereditary leader called a "sheikh," and focused on mutual protection and shared tribal interests. Most Iraqis and Kurds have a tribal name—the last part of their name—with most Arab tribal names starting with *Al-*. Some use their tribal name as their surname.

Turkmen   Iraq's third largest ethnic group after Arabs and Kurds; a mix of Sunni and Shia residing primarily in Kirkuk, the adjoining Tooz District of Salahuddin, Mosul and Tal Afar in northern Ninewa, Erbil, and Baghdad.

United Iraqi Alliance   The original post-Saddam coalition of Shia political parties, assembled largely on the initiative of Grand Ayatollah Sistani, to contest national elections. Its cohesion declined after the 2005 elections, and it eventually broke up, replaced by the Iraqi National Alliance.

United Nations Assistance Mission for Iraq   The special UN office started in 2003 to help post-Saddam Iraq, including the promotion of human rights and the rule of law; it continues to play an important role.

United Nations High Commissioner for Refugees (UNHCR)   The United Nations organization responsible for designating people as refugees and facilitating their resettlement in new countries willing to accept them.

United States Agency for International Development (USAID)   The agency within the Department of State that initiates, funds, and manages projects in foreign countries and is the primary U.S. foreign assistance organization, often working through private international development companies and nonprofits.

United States Refugee Admissions Program   The primary U.S. government

program, working primarily through the State Department, for processing applications from refugees for resettlement in the United States.

World Bank   A major international organization that makes investment loans
in less-developed nations for government projects intended to alleviate poverty.

Yazidis   A Kurdish-speaking religious minority prominent in northern Ninewa
and Dahuk, especially Ninewa's Sinjar District, that observes an ancient monotheistic faith that synthesizes different religious traditions. The Yazidis in Sinjar took the brunt of ISIS attacks in northern Ninewa, suffering massacres and
mass abductions, followed by horrible abuses of women.

Bibliography

Agresto, John. *Mugged by Reality: The Liberation of Iraq and the Failure of Good Intentions*. New York: Encounter Books, 2007.

Al-Ali, Zaid. *The Struggle for Iraq's Future: How Corruption, Incompetence and Sectarianism Have Undermined Democracy*. New Haven: Yale University Press, 2013.

Al-Hashimi, Hisham. "Revealed: The Islamic State 'Cabinet,' from Finance Minister to Suicide Bomb Deployer." *Telegraph*, July 9, 2014. http://www.telegraph.co.uk /news/worldnews/middleeast/iraq/10956193/Revealed-the-Islamic-State -cabinet-from-finance-minister-to-suicide-bomb-deployer.html.

Al-Khalidi, Ashraf, and Victor Tanner. *Sectarian Violence: Radical Groups Drive Internal Displacement in Iraq*. Report. Brookings Institution, University of Bern, October 2006, https://www.brookings.edu/wp-content/uploads/2016/06/1018iraq _al-khalidi.pdf.

Allawi, Ali A. *The Occupation of Iraq: Winning the War, Losing the Peace*. New Haven: Yale University Press, 2007.

America's Development Foundation. *Final Report: USAID Iraq Civil Society and Independent Media Program (ICSP)*. September 1, 2007, http://pdf.usaid.gov/pdf _docs/Pdacl917.pdf.

Amnesty International. *Ethnic Cleansing on a Historic Scale: Islamic State's Systematic Targeting of Minorities in Northern Iraq*. London, September 2014.

Anderson, Liam. *The Politics and Security of the Disputed Territories*. Academia.edu, 2011, http://www.academia.edu/1542286/the_Disputed_Territories_of_Northern_Iraq.

Bartu, Peter. "Wrestling with the Integrity of a Nation: The Disputed Internal Boundaries in Iraq." *International Affairs* 86, no. 6 (2010).

Bowen, Stuart W., Jr. *Hard Lessons: The Iraq Reconstruction Experience*. Washington DC: U.S. Government Printing Office, 2009.

Bremer, L. Paul, III, with Malcolm McConnell. *My Year in Iraq: The Struggle to Build a Future of Hope*. New York: Threshold Editions, 2006.

Brown University, Costs of War project. "Iraq War: 190,000 Lives, $2.2 Trillion." March 14, 2013, https://news.brown.edu/articles/2013/03/warcosts.

Carothers, Thomas. *Revitalizing Democracy Assistance: The Challenge of USAID*. Report. Carnegie Endowment for International Peace, Washington DC, October 27, 2009, http://carnegieendowment.org/2009/10/27/revitalizing-democracy -assistance-challenge-of-usaid-pub-24047.

Chandrasekaran, Rajiv. *Imperial Life in the Emerald City: Inside Iraq's Green Zone*. New York: Knopf, 2006.

Cockburn, Patrick. "Battle for Baghdad." *London Review of Books*, July 17, 2014.

Cole, Juan. "Marsh Arab Rebellion: Grievance, Mafias and Militias in Iraq." Fourth Wadie Jwaideh Memorial Lecture. Indiana University, 2008.

Coleman, Isobel. "Women, Islam, and the New Iraq." *Foreign Affairs* 85, no. 1 (January–February 2006).

Cordesman, Anthony H. *The Impact of the Iraqi Election: A Working Analysis*. Washington DC: Center for Strategic and International Studies, December 2005.

Corn, David. "Secret Report: Corruption Is 'Norm' within Iraqi Government." *Nation*, August 30, 2007.

Dawisha, Adeed. *Post Occupation Iraq: The Brittleness of Political Institutions*. Occasional Paper Series. Middle East Program, Woodrow Wilson International Center for Scholars, Spring 2012.

Diamond, Larry. *Squandered Victory: The American Occupation and the Bungled Effort to Bring Democracy to Iraq*. New York: Times Books, Holt, 2005.

———. "Why There Are No Arab Democracies." *Journal of Democracy* 21, no. 1 (January 2010).

Donnelly, Stephen. "We Did Mean Well." *Foreign Policy*, October 5, 2011.

Eakin, Hugh. "Syria: Which Way to Kurdistan?" *New York Review of Books*, August 28, 2013, reprinted from *NYR Daily*, http://www.nybooks.com/daily/2013/08/28/syria-which-way-kurdistan/.

Easterly, William. "Planners versus Searchers in Foreign Aid." *Asian Development Review* 23, no. 2 (January 2006).

Etherington, Mark. *Revolt on the Tigris: The Al-Sadr Uprising and the Governing of Iraq*. Ithaca NY: Cornell University Press, 2005.

Filkins, Dexter. "Letter from Iraq: What We Left Behind." *New Yorker*, April 28, 2014.

Fink, Daniel, and Steven Leibowitz. "The Muslim Scholars Association: A Key Actor in Iraq." *Research Notes*, no. 12. Washington Institute for Near East Policy, December 2006.

Gambill, Gary. "The Iraqi Media." *Global Journalist*, May 14, 2009.

Gunter, Michael M. "Economic Opportunities in Iraqi Kurdistan." *Middle East Policy* 18, no. 2 (Summer 2011).

Hamoudi, Haider Ala. *Howling in Mesopotamia: An Iraqi-American Memoir*. New York: Beaufort Books, 2008.

Holmes, Richard. *Dusty Warriors: Modern Soldiers at War*. London: Harper Press, 2006.

International Crisis Group. "Failing Oversight: Iraq's Unchecked Government." *Middle East Report*, no. 113 (September 26, 2011).

———. "Iraq's Uncertain Future: Elections and Beyond." *Middle East Report*, no. 94 (February 25, 2010).

———. "Make or Break: Iraq's Sunnis and the State." *Middle East Report*, no. 144 (August 4, 2013).

———. "Where Is Iraq Heading? Lessons from Basra." *Middle East Report*, no. 67 (June 25, 2007).

Johnson, Kirk W. *To Be a Friend Is Fatal: The Fight to Save the Iraqis America Left Behind*. New York: Scribner, 2013.

Kane, Sean. *Iraq's Disputed Territories: A View of the Political Horizon and Implications for U.S. Policy*. Washington DC: United States Institute of Peace, 2011.

Katzman, Kenneth. *Iraq: Politics, Governance, and Human Rights*. Report. Congressional Research Service, December 17, 2013.

Keiger, Dale. "The Number." *Johns Hopkins Magazine*, February 2007.

Knight, Sam. "In the Face of Death." *Newsweek*, September 24, 2007.

Knights, Michael, and Ahmed Ali. "Kirkuk in Transition: Confidence Building in Northern Iraq." *Policy Focus*, no. 102. Washington Institute for Near East Policy, April 2010.

Knights, Michael, and Ed Williams. "The Calm before the Storm: The British Experience in Southern Iraq." *Policy Focus*, no. 66. Washington Institute for Near East Policy, February 2007.

Kurdistan Regional Government–Iraq, Representation in the United States. "Updates on the Kurdistan Region." August 22, 2014.

Lawrence, Quil. *Invisible Nation: How the Kurds' Quest for Statehood Is Shaping Iraq and the Middle East*. New York: Walker & Co., 2008.

Malo, Hoshyar. "The Future of Civil Society in Iraq: A Comparison of Draft Civil Society Laws Submitted to the Iraqi Council of Representatives." *International Journal of Not-for-Profit Law* 10, no. 4 (August 2008).

Meiselas, Susan. *Kurdistan in the Shadow of History*, 2nd ed. Chicago: University of Chicago Press, 1997.

Munson, Peter J. *Iraq in Transition: The Legacy of Dictatorship and the Prospects for Democracy*. Dulles VA: Potomac Books, 2009.

Nasr, Vali. *The Shia Revival: How Conflicts within Islam Will Shape the Future*. New York: Norton, 2006.

Natali, Denise. *The Kurdish Quasi-State: Development and Dependency in Post–Gulf War Iraq*. Syracuse NY: Syracuse University Press, 2010.

Office of the Special Inspector General for Iraq Reconstruction. *Anticorruption Efforts in Iraq: U.S. and Iraq Take Actions but Much Remains to Be Done*. SIGIR 08-023. Washington DC, July 29, 2008.

———. *The Human Toll of Reconstruction on Stabilization Operations during Operation Iraqi Freedom*. SIGIR Special Report No. 2. Washington DC, July 27, 2012.

———. *Joint Survey of the U.S. Embassy-Iraq's Anticorruption Program*. SIGIR-06-021. Arlington VA, July 28, 2006.

Ottaway, David B. "Iraq's Kurdistan Takes a Giant Step toward Independence." *Viewpoints*, no. 46. Middle East Program, Woodrow Wilson International Center for Scholars, December 2013.

Ottaway, Marina, and David Ottaway. "How the Kurds Got Their Way: Economic Cooperation and the Middle East's New Borders." *Foreign Affairs* 93, no. 3 (May–June 2014).

Perito, Robert M. *The Iraq Federal Police: U.S. Police Building under Fire*. Special Report 291. United States Institute of Peace, 2011.

Pollock, David, and Ahmed Ali. "Iran Gets Negative Reviews in Iraq, Even from Shiites." *Policywatch* 1653. Washington Institute for Near East Policy, May 4, 2010.

Qadir, Kamal Said. "Iraqi Kurdistan's Downward Spiral." *Middle East Quarterly* 14, no. 3 (Summer 2007).

Raddatz, Martha. *The Long Road Home: A Story of War and Family*. New York: G. P. Putnam's Sons, 2007.

Ricchiardi, Sherry. *Iraq's News Media After Saddam: Liberation, Repression, and Future Prospects.* Washington DC: Center for International Media Assistance, National Endowment for Democracy, 2011.

Ricks, Thomas E. *The Gamble: General David Petraeus and the American Military Adventure in Iraq, 2006–2008.* New York: Penguin, 2009.

Rubin, Michael. "Don't Forget about Iraq." *Global Public Square* (blog), CNN.com, October 31, 2012, http://globalpublicsquare.blogs.cnn.com/2012/10/31/dont -forget-about-iraq/.

Sen, Amartya. "The Man without a Plan." *Foreign Affairs* 85, no. 2 (March–April 2006).

Shadid, Anthony. *Night Draws Near: Iraq's People in the Shadow of America's War.* New York: Picador, Holt, 2006.

Sherlock, Ruth. "Inside the Leadership of Islamic State: How the New 'Caliphate' Is Run." *Telegraph*, July 9, 2014. http://www.telegraph.co.uk/news/worldnews /middleeast/iraq/10956280/Inside-the-leadership-of-Islamic-State-how-the -new-caliphate-is-run.html.

Stephenson, James. *Losing the Golden Hour: An Insider's View of Iraq's Reconstruction.* Dulles VA: Potomac Books, 2007.

Stewart, Rory. "Losing the South." *Prospect Magazine*, no. 116 (November 2005).

———. "My Extreme MBA." *Harvard Business Review* 85, no. 10 (October 2007).

———. *The Prince of the Marshes: And Other Hazards of a Year in Iraq.* New York: Harcourt, 2006.

Surowiecki, James. "The Payola Game." *New Yorker*, April 24, 2006.

Synnott, Hilary. *Bad Days in Basra: My Turbulent Time as Britain's Man in Southern Iraq.* London: I. B. Tauris, 2008.

Trumbull, Charles P., IV, and Julie B. Moran. "Elections and Government Formation in Iraq: An Analysis of the Judiciary's Role." *Vanderbilt Journal of Transnational Law* 44, no. 2 (June 27, 2012).

United States Agency for International Development. *Building on Transition: Iraq Civil Society Program (ICSP) Final Evaluation.* Final Report. Study conducted by International Business & Technical Consultants, Inc., May 24, 2007.

U.S. Department of Justice. *Fact Sheet: Department of Justice Efforts in Iraq.* February 13, 2008.

U.S. Department of State, Office of Inspector General. *Survey of Anticorruption Programs, Embassy Baghdad, Iraq.* ISP-IQO-06-50. Washington DC, August 2006.

Van Buren, Peter. *We Meant Well: How I Helped Lose the Battle for the Hearts and Minds of the Iraqi People.* New York: Metropolitan Books, 2011.

Vick, Karl. "Turkey's Triumphs." *Time*, April 8, 2013.

Visser, Reidar. *Iran's Role in Post-Occupation Iraq: Enemy, Good Neighbor, or Overlord.* New York: Century Foundation, 2009.

———. *Sistani, the United States and Politics in Iraq: From Quietism to Machiavellianism?* Working Paper 700. Norwegian Institute of International Affairs, 2006.

Why Islam. *Status of Women in Islam.* Piscataway NJ: Why Islam, n.d.

Wing, Joel. "Iraq's Anfal Campaign and the Destruction of the Kurdish Opposition." *Musings on Iraq* (blog), September 5, 2011, http://musingsoniraq.blogspot .com/2011/09/iraqs-anfal-campaign-and-destruction-of_05.html.

Wood, Graeme. "What ISIS Really Wants." *Atlantic*, March 2015.

Index

Anti-Corruption program (*continued*)
189–95, 298–304; and complaints procedure proposed to CPI, 192–93; and Condoleezza Rice, 199, 301; consultants in, 179–80; and definition of *corrective action*, 188; and Extractive Industries Transparency Initiative, 306; and final report of ADF on ICSP, 294–97; and General Legal Center, 183, 246–47; grant projects of, 181–82; and INL initiative, 198–203; in joint survey, 194–95; and Kurdistan Anti-Corruption Legislative Coalition, 200–201; and Kurdistan anti-corruption resistance, 186–87, 192; and legislation, 308; and National Anti-Corruption Awareness Raising Campaign, 179–80; and National Anti-Corruption Legislative Coalition, 196–98, 200; national election (2010) and, 305; and training of corruption fighters, 201–3; and Transparency International, 171, 177, 178, 201, 309–10. *See also* anti-corruption, field of; anti-corruption system in Iraq; corruption in Iraq
anti-corruption system in Iraq: and anti-corruption reforms, 422–25; and Board of Supreme Audit, 194, 303; and Central Criminal Court of Iraq, 194, 195, 304, 307; and Extractive Industries Transparency Initiative, 306; and institution building, 193–94; interference in, by Nouri Al-Maliki, 195, 299–304, 305, 306–7; in joint survey, 194–95; and legislation, 308; and Office of Inspector General, 193–94, 303; and threats against CPI commissioner, 298. *See also* anti-corruption, field of; Anti-Corruption program (ICSP); Commission on Public Integrity (CPI); corruption in Iraq
Arnheim, Ethan, 138
assassination(s), 161, 251–53, 298; of Abu Rashid, 34–35; of academics, 245; of Andrea Parhamovich, 281–82; of Atwar Bahjat, 311; of BSA staff, 303; of CPI staff, 299; of Democracy Team members, 310; of Fern Holland, 79; of Haider Al-Maliki, 261–68; of IGs, 303; of Imam Abdul Majid Al-Khoei, 80–81; of Kawa Garmiany, 403; of Kifaya Hussein, 100–104; of Majeed Shekho, 282; of Mohammed Baqir Al-

Hakim, 163; of Mohammed Baqir Al-Sadr, 161; of Mohammed Mohammed Sadeq Al-Sadr, 79–80; of Nazaar Abdul Wahid, 310–11; of Robert Zangas, 79; of Salah Al-Awsi, 314; of Salwa Oumashi, 79. *See also* deaths of Iraqi civilians; terrorism
Aswat Al-Iraq (Voices of Iraq), 313–14
Awene, 369
Awsi, Salah Al-, 232–33, 314
Aziz, Tariq, 161, 211

Baathists, 20–21, 37, 412, 434
Badr Corps, 162–63
Baghdad: cuisine in, 135–36; demonstrations in, 422–24; elections in, 155–56; electricity in, 153–54; government councils system in, 152–53; Red Zone in, 147–48, 256–60; transportation risks in, 148–50; U.S. reconstruction money for, 153; water in, 153–54. *See also* Green Zone
Bahjat, Atwar, 311
Barwari, Nasreen, 41
Barzangy, Abdulla, 284
Barzani, Masoud, 353, 442; Erdogan Nujaifi and, 427; as KRG president, 186, 349; opposition of, to PKK, 449–50; tenure expiration of, 457
Barzani, Mulla Mustafa, 350–51
Barzani, Nechirvan, 343, 355, 397
Basra, 14, 16, 117, 251–54
Bastora (KRG municipality), 360
Benedict, Peter, 24, 41, 92, 121
Blackwater Agency, 82
Blackwill, Robert, 116
Board of Supreme Audit (BSA), 194, 303
Bowen, Stuart, 301, 331–32
Brahimi, Lakhdar, 53, 68, 114–16
Bremer, L. Paul: AID and, 113; and anti-corruption institution building, 193–94; contradictory policies of, 67–68; as CPA administrator, 26; and CPA support, 45, 112; and CPI initiative, 189; as decision maker, 39, 40, 83; departure of, 116; and Iraqi Governing Council, 40; on Iraqi Media Network, 144; on prime minister selection, 115; privatization efforts and, 37; and sharia law veto, 222
British Civil-Military Affairs team, 26, 37, 38–39, 264, 462

Council of Representatives (*continued*)
representation election method, 164–66;
Salim Al-Jubouri as elected speaker for, 413
CPA. *See* Coalition Provisional Authority (CPA)
CPA-Maysan, 17; and funding of LGP Community Development program, 60; and
local council refreshment process, 68–71;
and NGO coordination meetings, 17–18;
and provincial council appointments, 28–
31; and Public Safety Committee, 34–35; on
Riyadh Mahood, 67; utilities support projects of, 66
CPI. *See* Commission on Public Integrity (CPI)
Crane, Ed, 344, 345, 358, 362
Cravens, Lamar, 92
CSOS. *See* civil society organizations (CSOS)
CSRCS. *See* Civil Society Resource Centers
(CSRCS)
culture of violence: and CPI, 298–301; and
criminal corruption and politics, 298–
301; and death squads, 77, 207–10, 214;
and independent journalism, 310–13; and
indictment of Riyadh Mahood, 88; and
lack of trust, 78; and Mehdi Army, 81–82;
and militia as police, 77; and Ministry of
Interior, 191, 194, 214–15, 403; Moqtada
Al-Sadr and, 79–83; and RTI Local Governance Program, 213–14; and rumors, lies,
and threats, 73–75; Saddam Hussein and,
18–22, 77; and Sadrist uprising, 83–85, 87–
89, 116–17; and sectarian violence, 206–11;
and torture, 206; and UNAMI, 212–13. *See
also* assassination(s); kidnappings
Custer Battles, 25

Daesh: ideology and propaganda of, 417–18;
military attacks and executions by, 405–11;
military losses of, 418–22, 428; as popular
term for ISIS, 405; symbolic defeat of, at
Dabiq, 428. *See also* ISIS
Daesh Daily, 416–18
Dahuk (KRG municipality), 362
Dahuk Province, municipal site visits in, 362,
363–67
Darroch, Fiona, 179
Dashti, 138–39, 178, 185, 190, 219, 248–49,
252, 343
Davis, Craig, 134, 137, 179, 188, 220, 248, 290;
and anti-corruption grant, 199–200; on

death of Haider Al-Maliki, 262; resignation
of, 274; on Transparency International, 201
deaths of Iraqi civilians, 204–12, 242–47. *See
also* assassination(s)
death squads, 207–10, 214
de-Baathification policy, 113, 206, 245, 252–
53, 398, 434
decentralization, 40–42
Degala (KRG municipality), 361
de Mello, Sergio, 212
democracy: campaign for, 45–72, 85, 107–9;
and civil society, 142–43; and community
development, 60–62, 109; and elections,
121–27, 155–56, 164–66, 168–70, 391–98;
and equality and justice, 62–65; and the
Grand Ayatollah, 51–53, 158–60; Hammurabi Code of Laws and, 64–65; and instinct
to control, 317–18; and Islam, 48–51, 126–
27; and refreshing of local councils in
Maysan, 68–71; and voter accountability,
472–73; and women's rights, 62–64, 220–27
Democracy Dialogue Activity (DDA), 45–60,
89, 94–95, 105, 107–9
Democracy Kits, 56
Democracy Survey, 53–55, 97–99; on Islam in
politics, 159; on women's rights, 54, 62
Democracy Team, 45–60; assassinations of
staff of, 310; campaign manager of, 45–51;
Democracy Survey by, 45, 53–55, 97–99;
Haider Al-Maliki and, 56–59; media team
of, 56–59; presentation strategy of, 55–56;
public service announcements of, 57–59;
and reconciling Islam and democracy, 48–
51; and salaries, 47; school outreach by,
47–48, 89; success of, 59–60, 96–99
DeVries, Deanne, 59
Diamond, Larry, 52, 53, 68, 107
displaced persons, 243–44, 411
Doane, John, 17
Dokan (KRG municipality), 368–69
Donahue, Katie, 44, 106–7, 199
Drugs and Thugs, 198–203. *See also* Bureau of
International Narcotics and Law Enforcement Affairs (INL)

Easterly, William, 320
economic disaster and displaced persons,
425–26
economics, 35–39

EITI. *See* Extractive Industries Transparency Initiative (EITI)

elections: Iraq (Jan. 2005), 121–25; Iraq (Oct. 2005), 126–27; Iraq (Dec. 2005), 155–56, 164–66, 168–70; Iraq (2009), 391, 393–94; Iraq (2010), 391, 394–95; Iraq (2013), 391, 395–97; Iraq (2014), 391, 397–98; KRG (2009), 385–86, 393–94; KRG (2013), 397

electricity, struggle for, 65–67, 153–54, 423

emigration of endangered Iraqis: difficulties with, 466–68; how readers can help, 471–72; and List Project, 468–71; and Refugee Admissions Program, 467–68; and Special Immigrant Visas, 467–68, 469

Erbil (KRG municipality), 341–43, 345–47, 361

Erbil #6 (KRG municipality), 361, 380

Erbil Province, municipal site visits in, 359–63

Etherington, Mark, 78

Extractive Industries Transparency Initiative (EITI), 306, 455

Fadhila (Islamic Virtue) Party, 163, 253–54, 393, 394

Fallujah, 82, 421

Fayda, 366

female genital mutilation, 226

Fi'el, Ismael (Abu Maythem), 35, 255

financial disclosure law, 302

Firas, 250

Freedom House, 119–20, 313, 476

Froukh, Loay, 344

Garmiany, Kawa, 403

Geetan, Sa'ad, 31

General Legal Center, 183, 246–47

Ghassak, 139, 248

Gladstone, Jim, 25, 36

Goran, Luqman, 344–45, 359, 361, 363, 367–68, 373–74, 382–83

Gorran, 356, 391–97, 402

Green Line, 340, 364, 366–67

Green Zone, 39–40, 147, 150, 190–91, 250–51

Hadad, Wirya, 344–45, 370

Haider. *See* Maliki, Haider Al-

Hakim, Abd Al-Aziz Al-, 163, 393

Hakim, Mohammed Baqir Al-, 162–63

Halabja (KRG municipality), 370–71, 373–74

Hammurabi Code of Laws, 64–65

Hammurabi Humanitarian Association, 228

Hannoon, Yousif, 74–75, 467

Harazi, Ahmed Al-, 16, 42, 47, 93, 100–101, 103, 108, 121

Harris, Robbie, 46

Hart Security, 84

Hashimi, Tariq Al-, 399

Hassen, Amanj, 345, 347, 359, 365, 368, 464

Hayes, Jared, 94, 106

Haynes, Victoria, 86

Hedges, Minda, 94

Hersman, Frank, 24, 63, 64, 69–70, 121

historic sites, recommendation on restoration of, 433

Hmood, Ali, 30–31, 37, 63

Holland, Fern, 79

honor killings, 225–26

Hornbuckle, Wyn, 109–10

Huang, Yuen, 16, 85, 92, 120

human rights: and Al-Qaeda in Iraq, 214; and antigovernment insurgents, 213; and assassination of Baghdad officials, 213–14; and car bombs, 204–5; and civil law system in Iraq, 215–16; and constitution Article 14, 221; and constitution Article 39, 221–22; CSOs and, 228–41; and culture of violence, 212–16; and death squads, 207–10; and female genital mutilation, 226; and honor killings, 224–26; and jihadist insurgents, 211; and lawlessness, 210–11; and Mehdi Army, 210; and Ministry of Interior, 214, 218–19, 403; and rule of law, 215; and sectarian violence, 206, 207–10; and street violence against women, 224–26; struggle for, 204–27; and treatment of prisoners, 214–16; and UNAMI, 212–13; and UN report on civilians killed, 212; and women's rights and Islamic law, 220–24. *See also* kidnappings

Human Rights program (ICSP), 204; antiviolence outreach initiative of, 219–20, 276, 291; civil society success stories of, 217–19; as a cross-cutting theme, 216–17, 275–76; and Ministry of Human Rights, 218–19; suspension of, 265–76; training modules of, 216–17; and Women's Advocacy program (ICSP), 220–22

Hussein, Kifaya. *See* Kifaya Hussein

Hussein, Saddam, 2, 13, 154; and Anfal campaign, 19, 352–53; and Baathist favoritism,

Hussein, Saddam (*continued*)
21; BSA and, 194; capture of, 22–24; chemical attack at Halabja by, 370; Christians and, 211, 400, 401; corruption and, 171–72; counterattack of, against Kurds, 353; execution of, 279–81; execution of Dawa Party leaders by, 21; execution of Qushtapa prisoners by, 352; and Iran-Iraq War, 18–19; in Kurdish civil war, 354; Kurds and, 342–46, 351–55, 443–44; and Kuwait invasion, 19–20; legacy of, 18–22; military adventurism of, 18–20; no-fly zone against, 186; and prisoner amnesty, 210; and terrorism against Shia, 21–22; UN economic sanctions against, 20–21; U.S. support of, 352; women and, 224
Husson, Thierry, 44, 120
Hutton, Mark, 25, 347

IBTCI. *See* International Business & Technical Consultants, Inc. (IBTCI)
ICMA. *See* International City/County Management Association (ICMA)
ICNL. *See* International Center for Not-for-Profit Law (ICNL)
ICSP (Iraq Civil Society Program), 136–42; ADF final report on, 294–97; and independent media sector, 138, 143–45, 277, 292, 294; and living arrangements, 133–36; new leadership of, 274–75; project evaluation of, 286–90, 328–29; project termination of, 290–93; sectors and team members of, 136–40; and security, 145–51; and sustainability planning, 238–40, 293–94; threats against staff of, 246–51, 261–68; violence against employees of, 246–47
IGC. *See* Iraqi Governing Council (IGC)
Independent Electoral Commission of Iraq, 155, 306, 392
INL. *See* Bureau of International Narcotics and Law Enforcement Affairs (INL)
International Business & Technical Consultants, Inc. (IBTCI), 286–90
International Center for Not-for-Profit Law (ICNL), 234, 315–17
International City/County Management Association (ICMA), 13, 105
International Research & Exchanges Board (IREX): and independent media support,

138, 143–45, 292, 294, 312–14; *Media Sustainability Index—Middle East and North Africa*, 312; and National Iraqi News Agency, 143, 313–14; separation of, from ICSP, 277, 314
Iran and Iraqi politics, 18, 161–64, 352
Iran-Iraq War, 18–19, 161, 352
Iraq: Christmas in, 166–68; civil law system of, 215–16; and Coalition invasion in Kurdistan (2003), 354–55; communicating in, 27; importance of, 473–76; internally displaced persons in, 243–44; preserving law and order in, 436–38; reconciliation strategy in, 428–35; struggle for balance in, 475–76; Supreme Court of, 330; the Three Narratives of, 429–30; U.S. policy and recommendations for, 438–41; voters and elections in, 391–98
Iraqi Accord Front, 160, 165
Iraqi Federal Police (IFP), 404, 419, 438. *See also* police
Iraqi Governing Council (IGC), 52–53, 114–16
Iraqi Media Network, 143–45, 312–14
Iraqi National Dialogue Front, 160, 165
Iraqi Research Foundation for Analysis and Development (IRFAD), 415, 416–18
Iraq Reconstruction Management Office (IRMO), 173, 175
IRFAD. *See* Iraqi Research Foundation for Analysis and Development (IRFAD)
IRMO. *See* Iraq Reconstruction Management Office (IRMO)
ISIS, 403–11, 414–22, 426–28; cruelty of, toward females, 414; documentation of abuses and atrocities of, 433; and legal challenges, 431; Nouri Al-Maliki and, 298, 412–13; religious minorities and, 414; Sunnis and, 413–14. *See also* Daesh
Islam and democracy, reconciling, 48–51, 126–27
Islamic Dawa: early history of, 21, 161–62; and Haider Al-Abadi, 413; and Ibrahim Al-Jaafari, 123; and Nouri Al-Maliki, 169; opposition of, to prime minister selection, 115–16; in United Iraqi Alliance, 122–24, 164
Istrabadi, Feisal, 52

Jaafari, Ibrahim, Al-, 115, 116, 123, 168–69, 394
Jabiry, Kadhim Ibrahim al-, 29, 31

Local Governance Program (*continued*)
award of, 13; and Democracy Survey, 53–
55, 97–99; lost opportunities of, 109–11;
and Maysan Provincial Council, 18–34, 39–
42; and RTI-Kuwait, 89–96; and rule of law
program, 64–65; and women's rights program, 62–64, 110; and *You and Democracy*
booklet, 48–51

MacIntyre, Hamish, 146, 258
Madhi, Adel Abd Al-, 116, 169
Mahood, Kareem (Abu Hatim), 28, 34–35, 70,
78, 87–88, 163
Mahood, Riyadh, 35–36, 63–64, 67; alliance
of, with Sadrists, 111; and Amarah conference on women, 63; on corruption, 299–
301; and CPA-funded jobs program, 35–36;
and CPA-Maysan, 35, 67; election of, as
governor, 29–30; indictment of, 86, 88;
limited authority of, 35, 36
Maliki, Haider Al-, 58–59; assassination
of, 261–68; as caucus refreshment assistant, 69; and Caux, Switzerland, program,
259–60; as Civic Education coordinator,
140–42, 236; Freedom House selection
of, 119–20; memorial program for, Switzerland, 268–72; memorial program for,
Washington DC, 476; as PSA spokesman,
58–59, 109; as symbol of change and martyr, 465; U.S. visit of, 119–20
Maliki, Nouri Al-: IG appointments of, 303;
interference with Commission on Integrity by, 299–301, 302; and Iraq elections
(2009), 393; and Iraq elections (2010),
394–95; and Iraq elections (2013), 395–
96; and Iraq elections (2014), 397–98; lack
of commitment to anti-corruption from,
195, 305; as minister of defense, 298, 413;
pledge of, to step down as prime minister, 308; and prime minister election, 169;
replacement of, as prime minister, 413;
sending of army to Basra by, 393; and State
of Law coalition, 393
Maliki, Ta'meem, Al-, 57, 96; on death of
Haider Al-Maliki, 262, 264; emigration
complications for, 467; happy ending for,
472; threat against, 117–19
Masoom, Fuad, 413
Maysan Provincial Council (PC), 24, 28–34;

chairman election of, 30; committee system of, 32–33; corrupt decision of, 110–
11; governor election of, 29–31; legislative
framework of, 31–33; legislative staff of,
33; members and leaders of, 28–31; and PC
authority issue, 34; and Public Safety Committee, 35; and Rules and Procedures Committee, 31–32; and salary payment issue, 34
MCC. *See* Millennium Challenge Corporation (MCC)
McClure, Tom, 201
media, 143–45; Al-Iraqiya, 57–59; *Al-Sabah*,
144; and Asos Hardi, 369, 402–3; Aswat Al-
Iraq (Voices of Iraq), 313–14; *Daesh Daily*,
416–18, 427–28; government attacks on,
312–13, 369, 403; journalists, dangers to,
310–12; Kurdistan independent, 369, 402–
3; and Media Sustainability Index, 312;
and murder of Atwar Bahjat, 311; and murder of Kawa Garmiany, 403; and murder
of Nazaar Abdul Wahid, 310, 312; National
Iraqi News Agency, 143, 313–14
Mehdi Army: in Amarah power struggle, 34;
and Amarah uprising, 83–85; and Basra
attacks, 117, 224–25, 252; as competitor of
Badr Organization, 163; death squads of,
207, 210, 212; demobilization of, 404; infiltration of police by, 76–77; and Maysan
attacks, 87, 116–17; and Ministry of Interior
abuses, 214; Moqtada Al-Sadr's leadership
of, 81; and Najaf attacks, 117; as religious
movement, 81–82; and sectarian cleansing
in Baghdad, 245–46, 249
Mergasor (KRG municipality), 363–65
Michael, Richard, 341
Michael-Moran Associates (MMA), 341–45, 385
Mikulski, Barbara, 199
Millennium Challenge Corporation (MCC),
177, 324–25
Miller, Michael, 131, 201, 284, 290–91, 465
Ministry of Interior, 191, 194, 214, 218–19, 403
Ministry of Municipalities (MOM), 341–42,
356–58; and automation, lack of, 380, 385;
and basic requirements, 356–58, 380–81;
and consultant project, 341–42, 343–45;
and digitized mapping system, 384–85;
and Directorate of Municipalities, 342,
344, 357; and finance and administration issues, 348, 349, 380, 385; and Gov-

ernment Information Systems program, 345; and Green Line impact, 345, 366–67; and Halabja Anfal massacre, anniversary of, 370–71; and human resources issues, 357; media and public relations strategy of, 356–57; and Model Ministry, 386–88; and municipal common problems, 379–80; and municipal elections issue, 383–84; and municipal site visits, Dahuk, 362, 365–67; and municipal site visits, Erbil, 359–63; and municipal site visits, Suleimaniya, 367–74; Nazaneen Muhammad Wusu as minister of, 342, 344, 353, 356–57, 358, 359, 373, 374, 380, 381–83; report and recommendations on, 376–81; and space management improvement, 381; and training issues, 357–58

Ministry of State for Civil Society, 169, 233, 236, 317

Mirani, Ann, 344, 382, 384

the Model Ministry, 386–88

Mohammed, Ragheb, 134

Mohammed N., 236, 248, 283

MOM. *See* Ministry of Municipalities (MOM)

Monument of Halabja Martyrs, 371

Morris, Charlotte, 264

Mosul, 282, 367, 406–8, 421–22, 426–28

Mustafa, Nawshirwan, 356, 370, 383–84, 396

National Anti-Corruption Awareness Raising Campaign, 179–80

National Anti-Corruption Legislative Coalition, 196–98, 200, 276, 304–6, 317

National Assembly election (2005), 121–24

National Democratic Institute, 124, 134, 149, 281–82

National Integrity System, 193–95

National Iraqi News Agency (NINA), 143, 313–14

National Legislative Observatory, 196, 291

NGOs (nongovernmental organizations), 17–18; and CSO enabling law, 231–38, 314–15; and International Center for Not-for-Profit Law, 234, 315–16; KRG enabling law for, 317; and Kurdish Human Rights Watch, 238; in Maysan, 17–18; and NGO Coordination Committee in Iraq, 314; and NGOs Department, Council of Ministers, 315, 316–17; and refugee support in Maysan, 21–

22; and UN Office for Project Services, 314; for women, 62–63

NINA. *See* National Iraqi News Agency (NINA)

Ninewa liberation campaign, 426–27

Noser, Andy, 42

Noyes, Michael, 215

Nugent, Chris, 469–70

OAT. *See* Organizational Assessment Tool (OAT)

Obama administration: and airstrikes to stop ISIS, 408–9; Daesh struggle against, 442; Iraq policy of, 2, 440–41, 474; reaction of, to ISIS attacks, 410–11; on removal of Nouri Al-Maliki, 413; on USAID and national security, 321; and U.S. troop withdrawal, 404–5

oil: expanded KRG production of, 450–51; Iraq-KRG issues over control of, 446–47, 450–52, 455–56; in Kuwait, 89–90; reservoir of, under Kirkuk, 443; smuggling racket of, and mismanagement of fuel supplies, 172; smuggling racket of, under Basra governor, 253; in southern Iraq, 89–90

Okaili, Rahim Al-, 302

O'Leary, Carole, 341, 348

Omar, 228, 230

Organizational Assessment Tool (OAT), 238–39, 295, 329

Oumashi, Salwa, 79

Pachachi, Adnan, 52, 115–16

Parhamovich, Andrea, 281–82

Patriotic Union of Kurdistan (PUK), 123, 186, 192, 343, 348–50, 352, 353–54, 356, 383–84, 397, 457

personal security details (PSDs), 15, 25–26, 145–47, 148–51, 347

peshmerga, 349, 355–56

peshmerga militia, 353–54, 409–10, 418, 419, 421–22

Phee, Molly, 24, 27, 49, 87, 88; and Amarah women's center, 63–64, 91; on death of Haider Al-Maliki, 262–63; on death of Kifaya Hussein, 102; and indictment of Riyadh Mahood, 88; as Maysan GC, 26, 40; in Maysan PC, 29, 34, 67

Pink Palace, 26–27, 29, 33, 35, 36

PKK. *See* Kurdistan Workers Party (PKK)

Shia, 23; and Grand Ayatollah Ali Sistani, 158–60; political parties of, 161–64;
and Samarra shrine bombing, 206, 311;
and Sunni, history of, 156–58; terrorism
against, by Saddam Hussein, 21–22
Siany, Zito, 187, 192
Sijad, 56
Singh, Gurbux, 94–95, 105, 106
Sistani, Grand Ayatollah Ali, 51–53, 81,
393, 423; ceasefires brokered by, 117; and
democracy, 51–52; role of, in Iraq elec-
tions (2005), 121–22, 158–60, 394; and Shia,
158–60
Smith, Tommie, 37
Soran (KRG municipality), 362–63
Special Inspector General for Iraq Reconstruction (SIGIR), 113, 331–32
Stewart, Rory, 26, 67, 78, 83, 87, 125–26, 263
Styp-Rekowski, Adam, 316
Suleimaniya (KRG municipality), 369–70
Suleimaniya Province, 367–74
Sullivan, Tressan, 24–25, 60–62, 109
Sunni Arabs, 21, 23; and Association of Muslim Scholars, 160–61; constitution opposition of, 126; election boycott of (Jan. 2005),
122; hostility of, toward government, 412,
415; ISIS and, 413–14; and lack of leadership, 160; political parties of, 160; reconciliation with, 434–36
Supreme Council for the Islamic Revolution
in Iraq (SCIRI), 28, 34, 77, 152, 162–63
sustainability: of CSOs, 238–41; and ICSP
project evaluation, 286–90; lost struggle
for, 286–90; progress reports and, 240–41;
recommendations to USAID on, 327–28

Takia (KRG municipality), 372
TAL (Transitional Administrative Law), 51–
52, 55, 108, 125–26, 159–60, 221–22, 444
Talabani, Jalal: as president of Iraq, 123,
186, 397; as PUK founder, 123, 352; as PUK
secretary-general, 349
Talib, Miami, 139
Taylor, Jock, 25
terrorism, 39–40, 242–60; and deaths of Iraqi
civilians, 242–47; and de-Baathification
policy, 252–53, 434; and displaced persons
and refugees, 243–44; education to fight,
438; of ICSP employees, 246–47; of Iraqi

interpreters, 256; of Iraq medical system,
245; oil smuggling and, 172, 253; sectarian
cleansing and, 245–46; of universities, 245.
See also assassination(s)
the Three Narratives, 429–30
TI. *See* Transparency International (TI)
Timimi, Hassan Al-, 31
TOT (Training of Trainers), 200, 219–20,
278–79, 282, 285
training corruption fighters, 201–3
transitional government, UN selection of
ministers for, 53
transparency, definition of, 177
Transparency International (TI), 171, 177,
178, 201, 309–10. *See also* anti-corruption,
field of
transportation, high-profile vs. low-profile,
148–50
tribal law, 75–76
Trump administration, 439, 452–59, 471
Turkmen, 432, 443–44, 450, 454–55

UIA. *See* United Iraqi Alliance (UIA)
UNAMI. *See* UN Assistance Mission for Iraq
(UNAMI)
UN Assistance Mission for Iraq (UNAMI),
212–13, 237
United Iraqi Alliance (UIA), 122–23, 155–56,
164–65, 169–70, 394
United Nations, 53, 114–16, 122, 212–13, 316
USAID (United States Agency for International Development), 13; anti-corruption
leadership role of, 176–77; anti-corruption
strategy of, 330–31; Bush (George W.)
administration and, 321; and Community
Action Group funding, 329; Congress's
relationship with, 337; critics of, 319–21;
downsizing of, 321; funding of, 336–37;
future of, 335–37; improvements for, 321–27;
and international development, 333–35; and
Local Governance Program, 40; and Millennium Challenge Corporation, 324–25;
Obama administration and, 321; and recommendation for contracts, 326–27; and
recommendation for CSOs, 328–29; and
recommendation for empowering lawyers,
329–30; and recommendation for flexibility
and adaptability, 321–22; and recommendation for interagency coordination, 331; and